KAPLAN PUBLISHING

GH00734523

THIS EXAM KIT COMES WITH
FREE ONLINE ACCESS
TO EXTRA RESOURCES AIMED AT HELPING YOU PASS YOUR EXAMS

IN ADDITION TO THE OFFICIAL QUESTIONS AND ANSWERS IN THIS BOOK, GO ONLINE AND EN-gage WITH:

- An iPaper version of the Exam Kit
- Articles including Key Examinable Areas
- Material updates
- Latest Official ACCA exam questions
- Extra question assistance using the Signpost icon
- Timed Questions with an online tutor debrief using the Clock icon

And you can access all of these extra resources anytime, anywhere using your EN-gage account.

How to access your online resources

If you are a Kaplan Financial tuition, full-time or distance learning student

You will already have an EN-gage account and these extra resources will be available to you online. You do not need to register again, as this process was completed when you enrolled. If having problems accessing online materials, please ask your course administrator.

If you purchased through Kaplan Flexible Learning or via the Kaplan Publishing website

You will automatically receive an e-mail invitation to EN-gage online. Please register your details using this e-mail to gain access to your content. If you do not receive the e-mail or book content, please contact our Technical Support team at engage@twinsystems.com.

If you are already a registered EN-gage user

Go to www.EN-gage.co.uk and log in. Select the 'add a book' feature and enter the ISBN number of this book and the unique pass key at the bottom of this card. Then click 'finished' or 'add another book'. You may add as many books as you have purchased from this screen.

If you are a new EN-gage user

Register at www.EN-gage.co.uk and click on the link contained in the e-mail we sent you to activate your account. Then select the 'add a book' feature, enter the ISBN number of this book and the unique pass key at the bottom of this card. Then click 'finished' or 'add another book'.

Your Code and Information

This code can only be used once for the registration of one book online. This registration will expire when the final sittings for the examinations covered by this book have taken place. Please allow one hour from the time you submitted your book details for us to process your request.

ONbB-9mEv-tQN4-FvPr

Please be aware that this code is case-sensitive and you will need to include the dashes within the passcode, but not when entering the ISBN. For further technical support, please visit www.EN-gage.co.uk

For technical support, please visit www.EN-gage.co.uk

Paper P3

Business Analysis

EXAM KIT

KAPLAN

PUBLISHING

British Library Cataloguing-in-Publication Data

A catalogue record for this book is available from the British Library.

Published by:

Kaplan Publishing UK

Unit 2 The Business Centre

Molly Millar's Lane

Wokingham

Berkshire

RG41 2QZ

ISBN: 978-0-85732-000-1

© Kaplan Financial Limited, 2010.

Printed in the UK by CPI William Clowes, Beccles, NR34 7TL.

Acknowledgements

The past ACCA examination questions are the copyright of the Association of Chartered Certified Accountants. The original answers to the questions from June 1994 onwards were produced by the examiners themselves and have been adapted by Kaplan Publishing.

We are grateful to the Chartered Institute of Management Accountants and the Institute of Chartered Accountants in England and Wales for permission to reproduce past examination questions. The answers have been prepared by Kaplan Publishing.

CONTENTS

Section

Key features in this edition

In addition to providing a wide ranging bank of real past exam questions, we have also included in this edition:

- An analysis of all of the recent new syllabus examination papers.

- Paper specific information and advice on exam technique.

- Our recommended approach to make your revision for this particular subject as effective as possible.

  This includes step by step guidance on how best to use our Kaplan material (Complete text, pocket notes and exam kit) at this stage in your studies.

- Enhanced tutorial answers packed with specific key answer tips, technical tutorial notes and exam technique tips from our experienced tutors.

- Complementary online resources including full tutor debriefs and question assistance to point you in the right direction when you get stuck.

December 2010 – Real examination questions with enhanced tutorial answers

The real December 2010 exam questions with enhanced "walk through answers" and full "tutor debriefs" is available on Kaplan EN-gage at:

www.EN-gage.co.uk

You will find a wealth of other resources to help you with your studies on the following sites:

www.EN-gage.co.uk

www.**acca**global.com/students/

INDEX TO QUESTIONS AND ANSWERS

INTRODUCTION

The style of the P3 paper has rarely changed over the last ten or fifteen years. It mainly starts with a strategic case study (see the scenario based questions) and strategic implementation has formed the majority of the option questions. This style has not changed under the current examiner. However there has been a slight change in the way that the syllabus has been examined – strategic implementation has begun to feature as one part of the scenario question, whilst strategic analysis (such as the value chain) has begun to appear in the option questions. The exam kit tries to reflect this by having all three strategic planning areas (analysis, choice and action/implementation) reflected in both the scenario based questions section and the option question section.

Note that the majority of the questions within the kit are past ACCA exam questions – though, since the change of the examiner in 2007 and the change in syllabus this year, some new topics have been introduced to the syllabus and there are fewer past exam questions in these areas.

KEY TO THE INDEX

PAPER ENHANCEMENTS

We have added the following enhancements to the answers in this exam kit:

Key answer tips

Most answers include key answer tips to help your understanding of each question.

Tutorial note

Most answers include more tutorial notes to explain some of the technical points in detail.

Top tutor tips

For selected questions, we "walk through the answer" giving guidance on how to approach the questions with helpful 'tips from a top tutor', together with technical tutor notes.

These answers are indicated with the "footsteps" icon in the index.

ONLINE ENHANCEMENTS

 Timed question with Online tutor debrief

For selected questions, we recommend that they are to be completed in full exam conditions (i.e. properly timed in a closed book environment).

In addition to the examiner's technical answer, enhanced with key answer tips and tutorial notes in this exam kit, online you can find an answer debrief by a top tutor that:

- works through the question in full

- points out how to approach the question

- how to ensure that the easy marks are obtained as quickly as possible, and

- emphasises how to tackle exam questions and exam technique.

These questions are indicated with the "clock" icon in the index.

 Online question assistance

Have you ever looked at a question and not known where to start, or got stuck part way through?

For selected questions, we have produced "Online question assistance" offering different levels of guidance, such as:

- ensuring that you understand the question requirements fully, highlighting key terms and the meaning of the verbs used

- how to read the question proactively, with knowledge of the requirements, to identify the topic areas covered

- assessing the detail content of the question body, pointing out key information and explaining why it is important

- help in devising a plan of attack

With this assistance, you should then be able to attempt your answer confident that you know what is expected of you.

These questions are indicated with the "signpost" icon in the index.

Online question enhancements and answer debriefs will be available from spring 2010 on Kaplan EN-gage at:

www.EN-gage.co.uk

PRACTICE QUESTIONS

$4 \leftrightarrow 3.$

STRATEGIC ANALYSIS

INFORMATION TECHNOLOGY

KAPLAN PUBLISHING

STRATEGY AND PEOPLE

MANAGING STRATEGIC CHANGE

SCENARIO-BASED QUESTIONS

ANALYSIS OF PAST PAPERS

The table below summarises the key topics that have been tested in the new syllabus examinations to date.

Note that the references are to the number of the question in this edition of the exam kit, but the Pilot Paper is produced in its original form at the end of the kit and therefore these questions have retained their original numbering in the paper itself.

	Pilot 11	Dec 07	Jun 08	Dec 08	Jun 09	Dec 09	Jun 10
Strategic planning				Q1			
PESTEL	Q1			Q1			
5 FORCES	Q1		Q1			Q1	
Strengths/weaknesses		Q1			Q2		Q1
Value chain	Q4	Q3				Q2	
SWOT					Q1		
Stakeholders						Q1	
Strategy evaluation		Q1	Q1	Q1	Q1		
Strategic choice		Q1					
Methods of strategic development				Q2	Q2	Q1	Q1
Organisational structure							
Business process change			Q2		Q1	Q3	Q3
Project management	Q1	Q2		Q3			Q1
Information technology	Q2	Q3		Q3	Q3		Q1
Marketing			Q3				
Financing/ cost accounting	Q3						
Strategy and people					Q4		Q4
Change management			Q4				

APPROACH TO EXAMINING THE SYLLABUS

For the June 2009 exams onwards, the ACCA have changed the specification of how different parts of the syllabus will be examined.

Section A contains one multi-part question based on a case study scenario. The question is worth 50 marks and will be based on capabilities defined in sections A, B, C, D, E, F, G and I of the syllabus, supported by capabilities defined in section H. The case study scenario will always include quantitative information, which might be financial data. (Note that previously the Section A question was firmly based on sections A, B and C only)

Section B will contain three discrete questions, each worth 25 marks. The candidate must answer two questions in this section. Capabilities defined in section H of the syllabus may be used to support questions in this section.

EXAM TECHNIQUE

- Use the allocated **15 minutes reading and planning time** at the beginning of the exam:
  - read the questions and examination requirements carefully, and
  - begin planning your answers.

  See the Paper Specific Information for advice on how to use this time for this paper.

- **Divide the time** you spend on questions in proportion to the marks on offer:
  - there are 1.8 minutes available per mark in the examination
  - within that, try to allow time for reading the long scenarios, and at the end of each question to review your answer and address any obvious issues

  Whatever happens, always keep your eye on the clock and **do not over run on any part of any question!**

- Spend the last **five minutes** of the examination:
  - reading through your answers, and
  - **making any additions or corrections**.

- If you **get completely stuck** with a question:
  - leave space in your answer book, and
  - **return to it later.**

- Stick to the question and **tailor your answer** to what you are asked.
  - pay particular attention to the verbs in the question.

- If you do not understand what a question is asking, **state your assumptions**.

  Even if you do not answer in precisely the way the examiner hoped, you should be given some credit, if your assumptions are reasonable.

- You should do everything you can to make things easy for the marker.

  The marker will find it easier to identify the points you have made if your **answers are legible**.

- **Written questions**:

  Your answer should have:
  - a clear structure
  - a brief introduction, a main section and a conclusion.

  Be concise.

  It is better to write a little about a lot of different points than a great deal about one or two points.

- **Reports, memos and other documents**:

  Some questions ask you to present your answer in the form of a report, a memo, a letter or other document.

  Make sure that you use the correct format – there could be easy marks to gain here.

PAPER SPECIFIC INFORMATION

THE EXAM

FORMAT OF THE EXAM

	Number of marks
1 compulsory questions	50
A choice of 2 from 3 option questions worth 25 marks each	50

Total time allowed: 3 hours plus 15 minutes reading and planning time.

Note that:

- All syllabus areas will be examined.

- The exam may contain one question from each syllabus area. However, some exam questions have examined more than one syllabus area in the same question.

- Questions will be based around a long scenario. It is important to refer back to this scenario when answering the question.

PASS MARK

The pass mark for all ACCA Qualification examination papers is 50%.

READING AND PLANNING TIME

Remember that all three hour paper based examinations have an additional 15 minutes reading and planning time.

ACCA GUIDANCE

ACCA guidance on the use of this time is as follows:

This additional time is allowed at the beginning of the examination to allow candidates to read the questions and to begin planning their answers before they start to write in their answer books.

This time should be used to ensure that all the information and, in particular, the exam requirements are properly read and understood.

During this time, candidates may only annotate their question paper. They may not write anything in their answer booklets until told to do so by the invigilator.

KAPLAN GUIDANCE

As all questions are compulsory, there are no decisions to be made about choice of questions, other than in which order you would like to tackle them.

Therefore, in relation to P3, we recommend that you take the following approach with your reading and planning time:

- **Skim through the whole paper**, assessing the level of difficulty of each question.

- **Write down** on the question paper next to the mark allocation **the amount of time you should spend on each part.** Do this for each part of every question.

- **Decide the order** in which you think you will attempt each question:

  This is a personal choice and you have time on the revision phase to try out different approaches, for example, if you sit mock exams.

  A common approach is to tackle the question you think is the easiest and you are most comfortable with first.

  Psychologists believe that you usually perform at your best on the second and third question you attempt, once you have settled into the exam, so not tackling the most difficult question first may be advisable.

  It is usual however that students tackle their least favourite topic and/or the most difficult question in their opinion last.

  Whatever you approach, you must make sure that you leave enough time to attempt all questions fully and be very strict with yourself in timing each question.

- **For each question** in turn, read the requirements and then the detail of the question carefully.

  Always read the requirement first as this enables you to **focus on the detail of the question with the specific task in mind**.

  Models:

  Most questions will require you to use a model from the syllabus as the structure for your answer. You therefore need to be clear as to which model(s) are required in each question. If you cannot determine which model to use it may be better for you to choose an alternative question.

  For written questions:

  Take notice of the format required (e.g. letter, memo, notes) and identify the recipient of the answer. You need to do this to judge the level of financial sophistication required in your answer and whether the use of a formal reply or informal bullet points would be satisfactory.

  Plan your beginning, middle and end and the key areas to be addressed and your use of titles and sub-titles to enhance your answer.

  For all questions:

  Spot the easy marks to be gained in a question and parts which can be performed independently of the rest of the question. For example, a definition of a model such as the CMMI.

  Make sure that you do these parts first when you tackle the question.

Don't go overboard in terms of **planning time** on any one question – you need a good measure of the whole paper and a plan for all of the questions at the end of the 15 minutes.

By covering all questions you can often help yourself as you may find that facts in one question may remind you of things you should put into your answer relating to a different question.

- With your plan of attack in mind, **start answering your chosen question** with your plan to hand, as soon as you are allowed to start.

 Always keep your eye on the clock and do not over run on any part of any question!

DETAILED SYLLABUS

The detailed syllabus and study guide written by the ACCA can be found at:

www.**acca**global.com/students/

KAPLAN'S RECOMMENDED REVISION APPROACH

QUESTION PRACTICE IS THE KEY TO SUCCESS

Success in professional examinations relies upon you acquiring a firm grasp of the required knowledge at the tuition phase. In order to be able to do the questions, knowledge is essential.

However, the difference between success and failure often hinges on your exam technique on the day and making the most of the revision phase of your studies.

The **Kaplan complete text** is the starting point, designed to provide the underpinning knowledge to tackle all questions. However, in the revision phase, pouring over text books is not the answer.

Kaplan Online fixed tests help you consolidate your knowledge and understanding and are a useful tool to check whether you can remember key topic areas.

Kaplan pocket notes are designed to help you quickly revise a topic area, however you then need to practice questions. There is a need to progress to full exam standard questions as soon as possible, and to tie your exam technique and technical knowledge together.

The importance of question practice cannot be over-emphasised.

The recommended approach below is designed by expert tutors in the field, in conjunction with their knowledge of the examiner and their recent real exams.

The approach taken for the fundamental papers is to revise by topic area. However, with the professional stage papers, a multi topic approach is required to answer the scenario based questions.

You need to practice as many questions as possible in the time you have left.

OUR AIM

Our aim is to get you to the stage where you can attempt exam standard questions confidently, to time, in a closed book environment, with no supplementary help (i.e. to simulate the real examination experience).

Practising your exam technique on real past examination questions, in timed conditions, is also vitally important for you to assess your progress and identify areas of weakness that may need more attention in the final run up to the examination.

In order to achieve this we recognise that initially you may feel the need to practice some questions with open book help and exceed the required time.

The approach below shows you which questions you should use to build up to coping with exam standard question practice, and references to the sources of information available should you need to revisit a topic area in more detail.

Remember that in the real examination, all you have to do is:

- attempt all questions required by the exam

- only spend the allotted time on each question, and

- get them at least 50% right!

Try and practice this approach on every question you attempt from now to the real exam.

EXAMINER COMMENTS

We have included the examiners comments to the specific new syllabus examination questions in this kit for you to see the main pitfalls that students fall into with regard to technical content.

However, too many times in the general section of the report, the examiner comments that students had failed due to:

- "not answering the question"

- "a poor understanding of why something is done, not just how it is done"

- "simply writing out numbers from the question. Candidates must understand what the numbers tell them about business performance"

- "a lack of common business sense" and

- "ignoring clues in the question".

Good exam technique is vital.

THE KAPLAN PAPER P3 REVISION PLAN

Stage 1: Assess areas of strengths and weaknesses

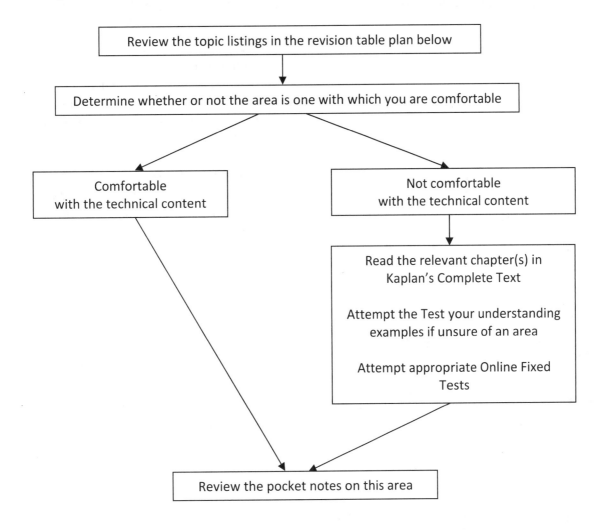

Stage 2: Practice questions

Follow the order of revision of topics as recommended in the revision table plan below and attempt the questions in the order suggested.

Try to avoid referring to text books and notes and the model answer until you have completed your attempt.

Try to answer the question in the allotted time.

Review your attempt with the model answer and assess how much of the answer you achieved in the allocated exam time.

Fill in the self-assessment box below and decide on your best course of action.

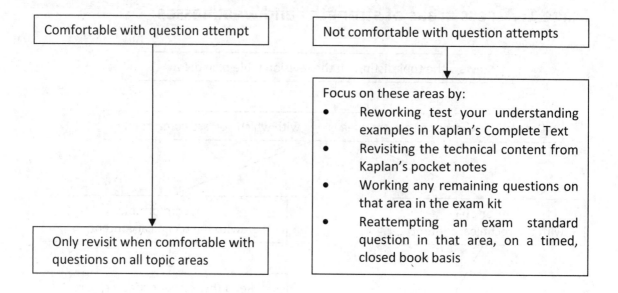

Note that:

 The "footsteps questions" give guidance on exam techniques and how you should have approached the question.

 The "clock questions" have an online debrief where a tutor talks you through the exam technique and approach to that question and works the question in full.

Stage 3: Final pre-exam revision

We recommend that you **attempt at least one three hour mock examination** containing a set of previously unseen exam standard questions.

It is important that you get a feel for the breadth of coverage of a real exam without advanced knowledge of the topic areas covered – just as you will expect to see on the real exam day.

Ideally this mock should be sat in timed, closed book, real exam conditions and could be:

- a mock examination offered by your tuition provider, and/or

- the pilot paper in the back of this exam kit, and/or

- the last real examination paper (available shortly afterwards on Kaplan EN-gage with "enhanced walk through answers" and a full "tutor debrief").

THE DETAILED REVISION PLAN

Topic	Complete Text Chapter	Pocket note Chapter	Questions to attempt	Tutor guidance	Date attempted	Self assessment
Strategic position						
- strategic planning	1	1		This chapter pulls all the other chapters together. It means that strategic planning could be combined with a question on almost any other topic. It is important that you understand the two key models: J,S & W, and the strategy lenses.		
- external analysis	2	2	78	Key models are the PESTEL and 5 Forces. Q78 will test the PESTEL. You may want to leave part (c) for now if you haven't yet revised project appraisal. But you should attempt the other parts of the question to time (you would be left with around 60 minutes).		
- internal analysis	3	3	9, 63	A key skill in this chapter will be the ability to perform good quantitative analysis. These questions will ensure you can do this well.		
- objectives	4	4	8, 56	The key model in this chapter is Mendelow's matrix. In any question on stakeholders you should aim to apply this model to the scenario. For governance and ethics you should focus on the strategic aspects rather than the operational rules.		

Topic	Complete Text Chapter	Pocket note Chapter	Questions to attempt	Tutor guidance	Date attempted	Self assessment
Strategic choice						
- competitive strategies and strategy evaluation	5 – 6	5 – 6	63, 74	Competitive strategies will have already been tested in Q63. Strategy evaluation appears in almost every compulsory question and it is vital that you can apply the J,S &W technique.		
- strategic development	7	7	15, 16	It is important in these types of question that you do not just regurgitate the lists that are presented in the pocket notes. You need to apply the lists to the scenario and ensure you focus on the actual requirement in the scenario.		
Strategy in action						
- Organisational structure	8	8	19	There are no recent exam questions on this area. But Q19 should test your application of the pocket note material to a question scenario. The key in this question is to spot the most appropriate type of structure.		
- Business process change	9	9	22, 72	Harmon's models are the key models in this chapter. The first model helps decide which processes should be redesigned, the second model helps explain how the redesign should happen. Q22 is a good test of the first model, whilst the second model has already been covered in Q74.		

Topic	Complete Text Chapter	Pocket note Chapter	Questions to attempt	Tutor guidance	Date attempted	Self assessment
- Information technology	10	10	27	The examiner is likely to focus on supply chain management – an area covered well in Q27.		
- Marketing	11	11	32, 35	This area is deceptively tough. The knowledge seems straightforward and common sense, and a lot of it is carried forward from paper F1. But you will only score in this area of the syllabus if you use the appropriate models and make your answers as relevant and specific to the scenario as possible. Pricing has been extended in the syllabus from 2011, so there are no past exam questions on that area. But Q35 will be a good test of your knowledge on this area.		
- Project management	12 & 13	12 & 13	36, 73, 78	Covering two chapters, this is a very important and significant part of the syllabus. Q78 (c) will test the numerical aspects, whilst the other questions will test different elements of the project management process. It is strongly advised that you attempt all three questions.		

Topic	Complete Text Chapter	Pocket note Chapter	Questions to attempt	Tutor guidance	Date attempted	Self assessment
- Financing	14	14	49, 54	This chapter focuses primarily on cost accounting techniques. You should focus on areas of weakness rather than doing questions on topics that you are comfortable with. Q54 is the most exam focused question in this section.		
- Strategy and people	15	15	57, 58	You may benefit in this area if you can remember some of your brought forward knowledge from paper F1 on leadership and motivation (though you will not lose out in any way if you cannot remember this material). These questions will show you how to apply the chapter to real world scenarios.		

KAPLAN PUBLISHING

Topic	Complete Text Chapter	Pocket note Chapter	Questions to attempt	Tutor guidance	Date attempted	Self assessment
– Managing strategic change	16	16	61	This is another chapter that can be linked to almost any other chapter. For example, launching new strategies, changing organisational structure, redesigning processes etc. will all require good change management. There are a lot of models in the chapter but the examiner is keen for you to have quite a broad syllabus knowledge so it is important that you are familiar with them all. Q61 will test how well you have done this.		

Note that not all of the questions are referred to in the programme above. We have recommended a large number of exam standard questions and successful completion of these should reassure you that you have a good grounding of all of the key topics and are well prepared for the exam.

The remaining questions are available in the kit for extra practice for those who require more question on some areas.

Section 1

PRACTICE QUESTIONS

STRATEGIC ANALYSIS

1 CTC TELECOMMUNICATION

CTC, a telecommunications company, has recently been privatised by the government of C after legislation was passed which removed the state monopoly and opened up the communications market to competition from both national and overseas companies – a process known as deregulation.

Prior to the deregulation, CTC was the sole, protected, supplier of telecommunications and was required to provide 'the best telecommunications service the nation can afford'. At that time the government dictated the performance levels required for CTC, and the level of resources it would be able to bring to bear to meet its objectives.

The shares were floated on the C Stock Exchange with 80% being made available to the population of C and up to 20% being made available to foreign nationals. The government of C retained a 'golden share' to prevent the acquisition of CTC by any foreign company. However, the privatisation meant that many of the traditional ways in which the industry had operated would need to change under the new regulations. Apart from the money received from the flotation, the government privatised CTC in recognition of both the changing global environment for telecommunications companies, and the overseas expansion opportunities that might exist for a privatised company. The government recognises that foreign companies will enter the home market but feels that this increased competition is likely to make CTC more effective in the global market.

You have recently been appointed as the management accountant for CTC and have a background in the commercial sector. The Board of Directors is unchanged from CTC's pre-flotation days.

Required:

(a) **Explain to the Board of Directors why the objectives of CTC will need to change as a result of the privatisation of CTC and the deregulation of the market.   (10 marks)**

(b) **Produce two examples of suitable strategic objectives for CTC, following its privatisation and the deregulation of the market, and explain why each would be an appropriate long term objective.   (4 marks)**

(c) **Advise the Board of Directors on the stages of an appropriate strategic planning process for CTC in the light of the privatisation and deregulation.   (11 marks)**

(Total: 25 marks)

2   3C PHARMACEUTICALS

3C is a medium-sized pharmaceutical company. It is based in Asia, but distributes and sells its products world-wide.

In common with other pharmaceutical companies, 3C has a large number of products in its portfolio, though most of these are still being developed. The success rate of new drugs is very low, as most fail to complete clinical trials or are believed to be uneconomic to launch. However, the rewards to be gained from a successful new drug are so great that it is only necessary to have a few successful drugs on the market to be very profitable.

At present 3C has 240 drugs at various stages of development, being tested or undergoing clinical trials prior to a decision being made whether to launch the drug. 3C has only three products that are actually 'on the market':

- Epsilon is a drug used in the treatment of heart disease. It has been available for eight months and has achieved significant success. Sales of this drug are not expected to increase from their current level.

- Alpha is a painkiller. It was launched more than ten years ago, and has become one of the leading drugs in its class. In a few months the patent on this drug will expire, and other manufacturers will be allowed to produce generic copies of it. Alpha is expected to survive a further twelve months after it loses its patent, and will then be withdrawn.

- Beta is used in the hospital treatment of serious infections. It is a very specialised drug, and cannot be obtained from a doctor or pharmacist for use outside the hospital environment. It was launched only three months ago, and has yet to generate a significant sales volume.

The directors of 3C meet every month to review the product portfolio and to discuss possible investment opportunities. At their next meeting, they are to be asked to consider three investments. Due to a limited investment budget, the three investments are mutually exclusive. The options are as follows:

- The directors can invest in a new version of Alpha, Alpha2, which offers improved performance. This will allow 3C to apply for a new patent for Alpha2, and maintain the level of sales achieved by Alpha for an additional five years. Alpha2 has successfully completed all its clinical trials, and can be launched immediately.

- The directors can invest in a major marketing campaign to promote the use of Beta to specialist hospital staff. While this investment should lead to a significant growth in the sales of Beta, 3C is aware that one of its competitors is actively promoting a rival product with similar performance to that of Beta.

- The directors can invest in the final stage of clinical trials for Gamma. This is a 'breakthrough' drug, as it has no near rivals on the market. Gamma is used in the treatment of HIV, and offers significantly better success rates than any treatment currently available. The team of 3C specialists managing the development of Gamma is confident it can successfully complete clinical trials within six months. The team also believes that Gamma should be sold at the lowest price possible, to maximise the benefits of Gamma to society. However, the marketing department of 3C believes that it would be possible to earn very large profits from Gamma, due to its success rate and breakthrough status.

Required:

(a) Briefly explain how the product life cycle model can be used to analyse the current product portfolio of 3C (that is, BEFORE the planned investment). **(8 marks)**

(b) Evaluate the potential impact of each of the three investment options on the product portfolio of 3C, referring to your answer to part (a) above. **(9 marks)**

(c) Discuss the social responsibility implications of each of the three investment options, for the directors of 3C. **(8 marks)**

(Total: 25 marks)

3 EEE FLAVOURINGS

EEE is an established chemical company extracting flavours and oils from plant materials and supplying them to the flavours and fragrances industries. The shareholders include institutional investors (20%), employees and pensioners of the company (20%) and the descendants of the family (30%) who founded the business approximately 100 years ago. The remainder of the shares are in public ownership. The company is reasonably successful but, recently, there has been pressure on margins and its future is not guaranteed.

The majority of the Board of Directors are members of the founding family who have always taken an active part in the management of the business.

When the company was originally started, the surrounding area was mainly used as agricultural land but, over time, a residential area has developed around the factory. Although many of the workers in the factory live locally, some of the housing is quite expensive and has attracted affluent residents from the local city.

The chemical engineers at EEE have recently developed, and patented, a new process which would allow EEE to extract onion oil and garlic oil at far better yields than those obtained by existing processes. The market for these oils is very profitable and presents a significant opportunity for EEE to gain a real competitive advantage in its industry.

Unfortunately, as with all extraction processes, there will be some leakage and, although perfectly safe and compliant with all safety legislation, the smell of the oils offends some of the more affluent residents who have complained to local government officers.

There is very little other industry in the area and EEE is a large contributor to the local economy. One of the trade union representatives working in EEE is also an elected council member serving in the local government.

Required:

As management accountant you have been asked to:

(a) Advise the Board of Directors of the advantages to EEE of conducting a stakeholder analysis in the context of the proposed investment decision; **(5 marks)**

(b) Analyse the principal stakeholders in EEE in the context of the proposed investment in the new process; **(15 marks)**

(c) Recommend an acceptable course of action to the Board of Directors in the light of the stakeholder analysis conducted in (b). **(5 marks)**

(Total: 25 marks)

4 SWIFT

Ambion is the third largest industrial country in the world. It is densely populated with a high standard of living. Joe Swift Transport (known as Swift) is the largest logistics company in Ambion, owning 1500 trucks. It is a private limited company with all shares held by the Swift family. It has significant haulage and storage contracts with retail and supermarket chains in Ambion. The logistics market-place is mature and extremely competitive and Swift has become market leader through a combination of economies of scale, cost efficiencies, innovative IT solutions and clever branding. However, the profitability of the sector is under increased pressure from a recently elected government that is committed to heavily taxing fuel and reducing expenditure on roads in favour of alternative forms of transport. It has also announced a number of taxes on vehicles which have high carbon emission levels as well as reducing the maximum working hours and increasing the national minimum wage for employees. The company is perceived as a good performer in its sector. The 20X9 financial results reported a Return on Capital Employed of 18%, a gross profit margin of 17% and a net profit margin of 9.15%. The accounts also showed a current liquidity ratio of 1.55 and an acid test ratio of 1.15. The gearing ratio is currently 60% with an interest cover ratio of 8.

10 years ago the northern political bloc split up and nine new independent states were formed. One of these states was Ecuria. The people of Ecuria (known as Ecurians) traditionally have a strong work ethic and a passion for precision and promptness. Since the formation of the state, their hard work has been rewarded by strong economic growth, a higher standard of living and an increased demand for goods which were once perceived as unobtainable luxuries. Since the formation of the state, the government of Ecuria has pursued a policy of privatisation. It has also invested heavily in infrastructure, particularly the road transport system, required to support the increased economic activity in the country.

The state haulage operator (EVM) was sold off to two Ecurian investors who raised the finance to buy it from a foreign bank. The capital markets in Ecuria are still immature and the government has not wished to interfere with or bolster them. EVM now has 700 modern trucks and holds all the major logistics contracts in the country. It is praised for its prompt delivery of goods. Problems in raising finance have made it difficult for significant competitors to emerge. Most are family firms, each of which operates about 20 trucks making local deliveries within one of Ecuria's 20 regions.

These two investors now wish to realise their investment in EVM and have announced that it is for sale. In principle, Swift are keen to buy the company and are currently evaluating its possible acquisition. Swift's management perceive that their capabilities in logistics will greatly enhance the profitability of EVM. The financial results for EVM are shown in Figure 1. Swift has acquired a number of smaller Ambion companies in the last decade, but has no experience of acquiring foreign companies, or indeed, working in Ecuria.

Joe Swift is also contemplating a more radical change. He is becoming progressively disillusioned with Ambion. In a recent interview he said that 'trading here is becoming impossible. The government is more interested in over regulating enterprise than stimulating growth'. He is considering moving large parts of his logistics operation to another country and Ecuria is one of the possibilities he is considering.

Figure 1 – Extract from financial results: EVM 20X9

Extract from the statement of financial position

	$million
Assets	
Non-current assets	
Intangible assets	2,000
Property, plant, equipment	6,100
	8,100
Current assets	
Inventories	100
Trade receivables	900
Cash and cash equivalents	200
	1,200
Total assets	9,300
Equity and liabilities	
Equity	
Share capital	5,700
Retained earnings	50
Total equity	5,750
Non-current liabilities	
Long-term borrowings	2,500
Current liabilities	
Trade payables	1,000
Current tax payable	50
	1,050
Total liabilities	3,550
Total equity and liabilities	9,300

Extract from the statement of comprehensive income

	$million
Revenue	20,000
Cost of sales	(16,000)
Gross profit	4,000
Administrative expenses	(2,500)
Finance cost	(300)
Profit before tax	1,200
Income tax expense	(50)
Profit for the year	1,150

S   A.   F.

Required: SWOT (8')   (6')

(a) **Assess, using both financial and non-financial measures, the attractiveness, from Swift's perspective, of EVM as an acquisition target.** **(15 marks)**

(b) Porter's Diamond can be used to explore the competitive advantage of nations and could be a useful model for Joe Swift to use in his analysis of countries that he might move his company to.

Examine using Porter's Diamond (or an appropriate alternative model/framework) the factors which could influence Swift's decision to move a large part of its logistics business to Ecuria. **(10 marks)**

                                                  (Total: 25 marks)

- Factor conditions
- Demand Conditions
- Related & Supporting Industries
- Firm strategy & rivalry

5   BOWLAND

Bowland Carpets Ltd is a major producer of carpets within the UK. The company was taken over by its present parent company, Universal Carpet Inc., in 20X3. Universal Carpet is a giant, vertically integrated carpet manufacturing and retailing business, based within the USA but with interests all over the world.

Bowland Carpets operates within the UK in various market segments, including the high value contract and industrial carpeting area – hotels and office blocks, etc. – and in the domestic (household) market. Within the latter the choice is reasonably wide, ranging from luxury carpets down to the cheaper products. Industrial and contract carpets contribute 25% of Bowland Carpets' total annual turnover which is currently $80 million. Up until 15 years ago the turnover of the company was growing at 8% per annum, but since 20X2 sales revenue has dropped by 5% per annum in real terms.

Bowland Carpets has traditionally been known as a producer of high quality carpets, but at competitive prices. It has a powerful brand name, and it has been able to protect this by producing the cheaper, lower quality products under a secondary brand name. It has also maintained a good relationship with the many carpet distributors throughout the UK, particularly the mainstream retail organisations.

The recent decline in carpet sales revenue, partly recession induced, has worried the US parent company. It has recognised that the increasing concentration within the European carpet manufacturing sector has led to aggressive competition within a low growth industry. It does not believe that overseas sales growth by Bowland Carpets is an attractive proposition as this would compete with other Universal Carpet companies. It does, however, consider that vertical integration into retailing (as already practised within the USA) is a serious option. This would give the UK company increased control over its sales and reduce its exposure to competition. The president of the parent company has asked Jeremy Smiles, managing director of Bowland Carpets, to address this issue and provide guidance to the US board of directors. Funding does not appear to be a major issue at this time as the parent company has large cash reserves on its balance sheet.

Required:

Acting in the capacity of Jeremy Smiles you are required to outline the various issues which might be of significance for the management of the parent company. Your answer should cover the following:

(a) **To what extent do the distinctive competences of Bowland Carpets conform with the key success factors required for the proposed strategy change?** **(10 marks)**

(b) **In an external environmental analysis concerning the proposed strategy shift what are likely to be the key external influences which could impact upon the Bowland Carpets decision?** **(15 marks)**

(Total: 25 marks)

6 MCGEORGE HOLDINGS PLC

McGeorge Holdings plc is a large, international consumer goods company specialising in household cleaning products and toiletries. It has many manufacturing and sales facilities throughout the world. Over several years it has offered an increasingly wide range of products appealing to differing market segments based on both socio-demographic and geographic criteria. However this product spread has not only resulted in increased sales volume but production, marketing and distribution costs have also increased disproportionately. McGeorge's costs are now about 20% higher than those of its nearest competitors. In such a competitive market it is difficult to pass on these extra costs to the customer.

In order to regain a competitive position Adrian Reed, the Managing Director of McGeorge Holdings, has been advised to reduce the range of products and the product lines. Advisors have suggested that a cut back in the product mix by about 20% could increase profits by at least 40%. Reed is keen to implement such a product divestment strategy but he fears that this cutting back could alienate customers. He needs to know which products need to be removed and which products are important to the survival of the company. He is unhappy about the overall performance of his company's activities. Benchmarking has been recommended as a method of assessing how his company's performance compares with that of his competitors.

Required:

(a) **Using appropriate analytical models discuss how Adrian Reed might select the products to be removed from the portfolio as part of his product divestment strategy.** **(13 marks)**

(b) **Examine how benchmarking can be carried out and discuss its limitations.** **(12 marks)**

(Total: 25 marks)

7 SALT AND SOAP

David Kirk is the recently appointed Sales and Marketing Director of the Salt and Soap Company, a medium-sized business supplying salt and soap products to the major supermarket chains operating in the UK. Salt was bought in bulk and then repackaged into convenient packet sizes using the supermarket's own brand. On the soap side, the company manufactured a range of cleaning materials, including soda crystals and soap flakes, with, again, the majority of its sales revenue coming from supplying the supermarkets with their own label products. The use of soda and soap as 'natural' cleaning materials was now an insignificant part of the UK market for detergents and cleansers dominated by global manufacturers with powerful brand names.

The company's reliance on the supermarket majors was now causing some problems. The power of the supermarkets was such that 70% of the company's products were now for own label brands. The supermarkets were looking to drive costs down and impose price cuts on suppliers such as Salt and Soap. There was little opportunity to add to the product range supplied and one of their major supermarket customers was looking to reduce its cleaning product range by 15%. On the positive side, Salt and Soap now had a virtual monopoly of 'natural' cleaning products: soap flakes and soda crystals. These cleansing products were environmentally friendly, as they did not cause disposal and other problems associated with household detergents. Soda based products could also be used as safe disinfecting agents in 'commercial catering', where hygiene was of paramount importance, and also in gardens to clean concrete slabs, ponds and ornaments. David was aware that household users were buying these products from hardware stores and garden centres and that he could access these new markets and uses through specialist wholesalers and thus reduce Salt and Soda's heavy dependence on own label supermarket customers.

Required:

(a) **Provide David with a brief report using appropriate analytical tools assessing Salt and Soap's current position and showing the relevance of marketing to the company.** (15 marks)

(b) **What are the advantages of Salt and Soap becoming a 'niche player' in the new markets it is looking to develop?** (10 marks)

(Total: 25 marks)

8 INDEPENDENT LIVING

Introduction

IL (Independent Living) is a charity that provides living aids to help elderly and disabled people live independently in their own home. These aids include walkers, wheelchairs, walking frames, crutches, mobility scooters, bath lifts and bathroom and bedroom accessories.

IL aims to employ people who would find it difficult or impossible to work in a conventional office or factory. IL's charitable aim is to provide the opportunity for severely disabled people to 'work with dignity and achieve financial independence'. IL currently employs 200 severely disabled people and 25 able bodied people at its premises on an old disused airfield site. The former aircraft hangars have been turned into either production or storage facilities, all of which have been adapted for severely disabled people.

Smaller items (such as walking frames and crutches) are manufactured here. These are relatively unsophisticated products, manufactured from scrap metal bought from local scrap metal dealers and stored on-site. These products require no testing or training to use and they are packaged and stored after manufacture. IL uses its own lorry to make collections of scrap metal but the lorry is old, unreliable and will soon need replacing.

Larger and more complex items (such as mobility scooters and bath lifts) are bought in bulk from suppliers and stored in the hangars. Delivery of these items to IL is organised by their manufacturers. These products are stored until they are ordered.

When an order is received for such products, the product is unpacked and tested. An IL transfer logo is then applied and the product is re-packaged in the original packing material with an IL label attached. It is then dispatched to the customer. Some inventory is never ordered and last year IL had to write-off a significant amount of obsolete inventory.

All goods are sold at cost plus a margin to cover wages and administrative costs. Prices charged are the same whether goods are ordered over the web or by telephone. Customers can also make a further voluntary donation to help support IL if they wish to. About 30% of customers do make such a donation.

Ordering and marketing

IL markets its products by placing single-sided promotional leaflets in hospitals, doctors' surgeries and local social welfare departments. This leaflet provides information about IL and gives a direct phone number and a web address. Customers may purchase products by ringing IL directly or by ordering over their website. The website provides product information and photos of the products which are supplied by IL. It also has a secure payment facility. However, customers who ring IL directly have to discuss product requirements and potential purchases with sales staff over the phone. Each sales discussion takes, on average, ten minutes and only one in two contacts results in a sale. 20% of sales are through their website (up from 15% last year), but many of their customers are unfamiliar with the Internet and do not have access to it. Goods are delivered to customers by a national courier service. Service and support for the bought-in products (mobility scooters, bath lifts) are supplied by the original manufacturer.

Commercial competitors

IL is finding it increasingly difficult to compete with commercial firms offering independent living aids. Last year, the charity made a deficit of $160,000, and it had to sell some of its airfield land to cover this. Many of the commercial firms it is competing with have sophisticated sales and marketing operations and then arrange delivery to customers directly from manufacturers based in low labour cost countries.

Required:

IL fears for its future and has decided to review its value chain to see how it can achieve competitive advantage.

(a)   **Analyse the primary activities of the value chain for the product range at IL.**

(10 marks)

(b)   **Evaluate what changes IL might consider to the primary activities in the value chain to improve their competitiveness, whilst continuing to meet their charitable objectives.** (15 marks)

(Total: 25 marks)

9 ONE ENERGY PLC *Walk in the footsteps of a top tutor*

OneEnergy plc supplies over half of the electricity and gas in the country. It is an expanding, aggressive company which has recently acquired two smaller, but significant, competitors.

Just over a year ago, OneEnergy purchased the RitePay payroll software package from RiteSoftware. The recently appointed Human Resources (HR) director of OneEnergy recommended the package because he had used it successfully at his previous employer – a major charity. His unreserved recommendation was welcomed by the board because the company was currently running three incompatible payroll systems. The purchase of the RitePay payroll system appeared to offer the opportunity to quickly consolidate the three separate payroll systems into one improved solution. The board decided to purchase the software without evaluating alternative solutions. It was felt that payroll rules and processes were relatively standard and so there was no need to look further than a package recommended by the HR director. The software was purchased and a project initiated for converting the data from the current systems and for training users in the features and functions of the new software.

However, it soon became apparent that there were problems with the suitability of the RitePay software package. Firstly, OneEnergy had a wide variety of reward and pay schemes to reflect previous employment in the acquired companies and to accommodate a wide range of different skills and grades. Not all of these variations could be handled by the package. Consequently, amendments had to be commissioned from the software house. This led to unplanned costs and also to delays in implementation. Secondly, it also became clear that the software was not as user-friendly as the previous systems. Users had problems understanding some of the terminology and structure of the software. 'It just does not work like we do', commented one frustrated user. Consequently users made more errors than expected and training costs exceeded their budget.

Three months ago, another set of amendments was requested from RiteSoftware to allow one of the acquired companies in OneEnergy to pay bonuses to lorry drivers in a certain way. Despite repeated requests, the amendments were not received. Two weeks ago, it was announced that RiteSoftware had filed for bankruptcy and all software support was suspended. Just before this was announced the HR director of OneEnergy left the company to take up a similar post in the public sector.

OneEnergy has engaged W&P consultants to advise them on the RitePay project. An interim report from W&P suggests that OneEnergy should abandon the RitePay package. 'It is clear to us that RitePay never had the functionality required to fulfil the variety of requirements inevitable in a company the size of OneEnergy.' They also commented that this could have been avoided if the project had followed the competitive procurement policy defined in company operating procedures.

W&P also reports that:

- The procurement department at OneEnergy had requested two years of accounts from RiteSoftware. These were provided (see Figure 1) but not interpreted or used in the selection process in any way. W&P concluded 'that there were clear signs that the company was in difficulty and this should have led to further investigation'.

- They discovered that the former HR director of OneEnergy was the brother of the managing director of RiteSoftware.

Figure 1: RiteSoftware Accounts

Extract from the statement of financial position	$000	
Assets		
Non-current assets	*20X8*	*20X7*
Property, plant and equipment	30	25
Goodwill	215	133
	245	158
Current assets		
Inventories	3	2
Trade receivables	205	185
	208	187
Total assets	453	345
Liabilities		
Current liabilities		
Trade payables	257	178
Current tax payable	1	2
Bank overdraft	10	25
	268	205
Non-current liabilities		
Long-term borrowings	80	35
Total liabilities	348	240
Equity		
Share capital	105	105
Total equity and liabilities	453	345

Extract from the statement of comprehensive income	$000	
Revenue	2,650	2,350
Cost of sales	(2,600)	(2,300)
Gross profit	50	50
Other costs	(30)	(20)
Finance costs	(10)	(4)
Profit before tax	10	26
Income tax expense	(1)	(2)
Profit for the year	9	24
Extract from the annual report		
Number of staff	90	70

Required:

(a)   W&P concluded in their report 'that there were clear signs that the company (RiteSoftware) was in difficulty and this should have led to further investigation'.

Assess, using the financial information available, the validity of W&P's conclusion.

(13 marks)

what did they do ?

(b)   Examine <u>FOUR ways</u> in which OneEnergy failed to follow a proper evaluation procedure in the selection of the RitePay software package. Include in your examination a discussion of the implication of each failing.   **(12 marks)**

(Total: 25 marks)

10   4QX

4QX is a large exclusive hotel set in an area of outstanding natural beauty. The hotel is a little remote due to the relatively poor transport network. It is located ten miles away from the region's main centre Old Town (the castle ruins of which attract a few tourists during holiday periods). The hotel has attained a high national star rating and specialises in offering executive conference facilities. Unsurprisingly therefore, it caters mainly for corporate guests.

It is a requirement of the hotel rating system that 4QX has, amongst other things, sports and leisure facilities of an approved standard. In order to attain this standard it has, within the last two years, installed a sports and fitness centre ('the centre'), employing fully qualified staff to give instruction and assistance. (Facilities include a small indoor heated swimming pool, an extensively equipped gymnasium, a spa bath and a steam room.) Due to legislation, children under the age of 16 staying in the hotel cannot use the pool without adult supervision or the gymnasium without the supervision of a suitably qualified member of staff. The centre is costly to maintain and underused.

The hotel's manager is currently drawing up a business plan for the hotel and is reviewing all areas of operation. In discussions with sport and fitness centre staff, a proposal has emerged to offer the facility to carefully selected non-guests at certain times of the day in order to bring in some revenue. This could be in the form of annual membership fees (the manager's preferred idea) or a 'pay-as-you-go' charge. The discussions with staff confirm a number of facts:

The local economy is extremely healthy. The local population is relatively affluent with high levels of disposable income.

Professional groups are used to paying annual membership fees for the local theatre, a nearby golf club (the manager is also a member and has contacts there), and substantial fees for their children's activities (e.g. dance academies and junior football teams, etc).

Old Town has a public swimming pool that is dated but almost of Olympic standard. It is used mainly by school children in the day and by a swimming club in the evenings. Taking advantage of government tax incentives to help keep the population fit and healthy, a privately operated, female only, health and beauty facility has recently opened in Old Town. Beyond these facilities, little else in the way of sports and fitness provision exists in the region.

The manager explains that:

- the hotel is unlikely to upgrade the centre's facilities any further in the short term, despite the fact that new, more sophisticated fitness equipment is coming onto the market all the time
- any promotional budget to attract members would be limited
- an estimate of additional revenue potential is needed to complete the business plan.

Required:

(a) Explain the importance of the centre understanding its external (or macro) environment and identify the most significant influences in that external environment that are relevant to the centre. **(10 marks)**

(b) Explain how the centre should undertake market segmentation and describe the most likely segmentation variables that will be identified by such a process.

(10 marks)

(c) Explain how the centre's income potential can be estimated. **(10 marks)**

(Total: 30 marks)

STRATEGIC CHOICE

11   DDD CHEMICALS

DDD is a relatively small, specialist manufacturer of chemicals that are used in the pharmaceutical industry. It does not manufacture any pharmaceutical products itself since these are made by different processes and under different conditions. DDD obtains its raw materials, which are quite simple, from large chemical companies, and modifies them by a number of patented processes before selling them on to a few pharmaceutical companies. DDD makes significantly higher margins than its suppliers, which manufacture in bulk. Several patents are due to expire in the next three years. The large pharmaceutical companies, which are DDD's customers, are suffering reduced profits as governments reduce the price they are prepared to pay for drugs. As a result, the pharmaceutical companies are pressuring DDD to reduce its prices. The majority of the shares are owned by members of the family which started the business some years ago and who still take an active part both as managers of the business and as development chemists. There is a share option scheme for the employees and this is well supported.

Required:

(a) Advise the Board of Directors of the possible threats related to the patent expiries;

(10 marks)

(b) Evaluate suitable courses of action that DDD might take to maintain its profits in the face of the threats identified in (a); **(12 marks)**

(c) From your analysis recommend, with a brief justification, the most appropriate course of action for DDD. **(3 marks)**

(Total: 25 marks)

12   JURANIA

Introduction

The 222 Organisation (222) is a large information systems consultancy, based in the southern African country of Jurania. 222 was founded in 1987 and has become very successful, both within Jurania and in neighbouring countries, due to growth in the economies of those countries and the highly developed technology sector of the Juranian economy. 222 advises organisations on the development of Intranet and knowledge-sharing systems, and has many clients among the top 100 companies in Jurania.

222 employs over 500 staff in its very impressive modern office building on a business park near the capital city of Jurania. Also based on the business park are several IT hardware and software companies, and the country's largest internet service provider (ISP), JuraWeb. Many of 222's staff were trained at Jurania's university, which has an excellent reputation. Whenever 222 advertises for additional staff, it receives a large number of applications from suitably qualified applicants.

The internet strategy

Recognising that the growth of 222 is limited by the size of the local market for its services, the directors of 222 are considering the further development of its rather basic website. At present, the 222.com website only contains a description of the organisation and contact details. The site was designed by employees of 222 and is hosted by JuraWeb. The directors hope that a better website will allow the organisation to develop new business in other parts of Africa, but have no desire to become a global business at this stage.

The directors are considering using the services of a local specialist web design company to develop a sophisticated website with case studies of previous 222 contracts, and detailed descriptions of staff and services. The directors also believe that 222 should be hosting the website itself, and are considering the purchase of a powerful web server. They also want to upgrade the telecommunications infrastructure of the organisation by investing in a new fibre-optic broadband service, which is available from a recently formed company that has just opened its office on the business park.

Required:

(a)   Evaluate whether the 222 Organisation might gain a competitive advantage as a result of being based in Jurania.   **(13 marks)**

(b)   Evaluate the risks to 222 if it decides to pursue its internet strategy as the directors have suggested.   **(12 marks)**

(Total: 25 marks)

13   ELITE FABRICS

Elite Fabrics (EF) is a medium-sized manufacturer of clothing fabrics. Historically, EF has built up a strong reputation as a quality fabric manufacturer with appealing designs and has concentrated mainly on the women's market, producing fabrics to be made up into dresses and suits. The designs of the fabrics are mainly of a traditional nature but the fabrics, almost all woven from synthetic yarns, include all the novel features which the large yarn producers are developing. Three years ago EF decided that more profit and improved control could be obtained by diversifying through forward integration into designing and manufacturing the end products (i.e. clothes) in-house rather than by selling its fabrics directly to clothing manufacturing companies.

EF's intention had been to complement its fabric design skills with the skills of both dress design and production. This had been achieved by buying a small, but well-known, dress design and manufacturing company, specialising in traditional products, targeted mainly at the middle-aged and middle-income markets. This acquisition appears to have been successful, with combined sales revenue during the first two years increasing to $100 million (+34%) with a pre-tax profit of $14 million (+42%). This increased turnover and profit could be attributed to two main factors: firstly the added value generated by designing and manufacturing end-products and secondly, the increased demand for fabrics as EF was more able to influence their end-users more directly.

In the last financial year, however, EF had experienced a slowdown in its level of growth and profitability. EF's penetration of its chosen retail segment – the independent stores specialising in sales to the middle-class market – may well have reached saturation point. The business had also attempted to continue expansion by targeting the large multiple stores which currently dominate the retail fashion sector. Unfortunately the buying power of such stores has forced EF to accept significantly lower, and potentially unacceptable, profit margins. The management team at EF believes that the solution is to integrate even further forward by moving into retailing itself. EF is now considering the purchase of a chain of small, but geographically dispersed, retail fashion stores. At the selling price of $35 million, EF would have to borrow substantially to finance the acquisition.

Required:

(a)   **Consider how the EF strategy of integrating forward into dress manufacturing has affected its ability to compete. Use an accepted model as a framework for analysis.**

(15 marks)

(b)   **EF's potential expansion into retailing presents both advantages and disadvantages to the company. Evaluate the consequences of such a move for the business and assess the change in competences which would be required by the newly expanded business.** **(10 marks)**

(Total: 25 marks)

14   GREENFIELD NURSERIES

Mark Roberts is the owner of Greenfield Nurseries, a company specialising in growing plants for sale to garden centres and to specialist garden designers. With the growth in home ownership and an increase in leisure time this sector of the economy has seemed recession-proof. The company has grown over the past ten years and with 30 employees and several glasshouses it has a turnover of almost $1 million. The company is located on one relatively large site near to a rapidly expanding urban area. There is currently within the site no physical room for expansion. If the company is to increase its profits as a garden nursery it must either acquire additional land for growing plants or it must direct more of its sales to the ultimate user (the general public) away from sales to other intermediaries (the garden centres) and so obtain higher margins.

Mark is annoyed when he sees garden centres putting large margins on his products for re-sale. Why are these profits not coming to Greenfield Nurseries he wonders? He is now contemplating re-focusing his activities on selling plants and not producing them. It has been suggested that he turns his growing areas into a garden centre. He also should buy from other specialist nurseries, transforming his glass house space into selling areas. There is a large market nearby, with several new housing developments, all generating a huge demand for horticultural products. Mark has read that the further one moves downstream in the business chain – into dealing directly with the consumer – the greater is the profit margin. He is very tempted by this strategy, but he is not fully convinced of the wisdom of such a move.

Required:

(a) Examine the arguments that may be used to support or reject such a 'buy instead of grow' strategy for Greenfield Nurseries. **(15 marks)**

(b) 'Outsourcing' has become a popular strategy for many companies in attempting to reduce their commitment to non-core activities. Identify the main management problems such a policy might generate. **(10 marks)**

(Total: 25 marks)

15 ENVIRONMENT MANAGEMENT SOCIETY

The Environment Management Society (EMS) was established in 1999 by environment practitioners who felt that environmental management and audit should have its own qualification. EMS has its own Board who report to a Council of eight members. Policy is made by the Board and ratified by Council. EMS is registered as a private limited entity.

EMS employs staff to administer its qualification and to provide services to its members. The qualification began as one certificate, developed by the original founding members of the Society. It has since been developed, by members and officers of the EMS, into a four certificate scheme leading to a Diploma. EMS employs a full-time chief examiner who is responsible for setting the certificate examinations which take place monthly in training centres throughout the country. No examinations are currently held in other countries.

[handwritten note: not listed. Access to funds hard.]

If candidates pass all four papers they can undertake an oral Diploma examination. If they pass this oral they are eligible to become members. All examinations are open-book one hour examinations, preceded by 15 minutes reading time. At a recent meeting, EMS Council rejected the concept of computer-based assessment. They felt that competence in this area was best assessed by written examination answers.

Candidate numbers for the qualification have fallen dramatically in the last two years. The Board of EMS has concluded that this drop reflects the maturing marketplace in the country. Many people who were practitioners in environmental management and audit when the qualification was introduced have now gained their Diploma. The stream of new candidates and hence members is relatively small.

[handwritten note: Disadvantage of organic growth.]

Consequently, the EMS Board has suggested that they should now look to attract international candidates and it has targeted countries where environmental management and audit is becoming more important. It is now formulating a strategy to launch the qualification in India, China and Russia. *[handwritten note: BRICS]*

However, any strategy has to recognise that both the EMS Board and the Council are very cautious and notably risk-averse. EMS is only confident about its technical capability within a restricted definition of environmental management and audit. Attempts to look at complementary qualification areas (such as soil and water conservation) have been swiftly rejected by Council as being non-core areas and therefore outside the scope of their expertise.

[handwritten notes: disadvantage of acquisition. / advantage - Organic. / negative of organic growth. new product development. (risky).]

Required:

Internal development, acquisitions and strategic alliances are three development methods by which an organisation's strategic direction can be pursued.

Organic growth?

(a) Explain the principles of internal development and discuss how appropriate this development method is to EMS. (8 marks)

1' each

(b) Explain the principles of acquisitions and discuss how appropriate this development method is to EMS. *2-3 advantages / disadvantages.* (8 marks)

(c) Explain the principles of strategic alliances and discuss how appropriate this development method is to EMS. (9 marks)

(Total: 25 marks)

16 MMI 👣 *Walk in the footsteps of a top tutor*

Chap 7. Review.

In 20X2 the board of MMI met to discuss the strategic direction of the company. Established in 1952, MMI specialised in mineral quarrying and opencast mining and in 20X2 it owned fifteen quarries and mines throughout the country. However, three of these quarries were closed and two others were nearing exhaustion. Increased costs and falling reserves meant that there was little chance of finding new sites in the country which were economically viable. Furthermore, there was significant security costs associated with keeping the closed quarries safe and secure.

Consequently the Chief Executive Officer (CEO) of MMI suggested that the company should pursue a corporate-level strategy of diversification, building up a portfolio of acquisitions that would 'maintain returns to shareholders over the next fifty years'. In October 20X2 MMI, using cash generated from their quarrying operations, acquired First Leisure, a company that owned five leisure parks throughout the country. These leisure parks provided a range of accommodation where guests could stay while they enjoyed sports and leisure activities. The parks were all in relatively isolated country areas and provided a safe, car-free environment for guests.

The acquisition was initially criticised by certain financial analysts who questioned what a quarrying company could possibly contribute to a profitable leisure group. For two years MMI left First Leisure managers alone, letting them get on with running the company. However, in 20X4 a First Leisure manager commented on the difficulty of developing new leisure parks due to increasingly restrictive government planning legislation. This gave the CEO of MMI an inspired idea and over the next three years the five quarries which were either closed or near exhaustion were transferred to First Leisure and developed as new leisure parks. Because these were developments of 'brown field' sites they were exempted from the government's planning legislation. The development of these new parks has helped First Leisure to expand considerably (see table 1). The company is still run by the managers who were in place when MMI acquired the company in 20X2 and MMI plays very little role in the day-to-day running of the company.

pure development & Developer.

In 20X4 MMI acquired two of its smaller mining and quarrying competitors, bringing a further five mines or quarries into the group. MMI introduced its own managers into these companies resulting in a spectacular rise in revenues and profits that caused the CEO of MMI to claim that corporate management capabilities were now an important asset of MMI.

In 20X6 MMI acquired Boatland, a specialist boat maker constructing river and canal boats. The primary rationale behind the acquisition was the potential synergies with First Leisure. First Leisure had experienced difficulties in obtaining and maintaining boats for its leisure parks and it was expected that Boatland would take on construction and maintenance of these boats. Cost savings for First Leisure were also expected and it was felt that income from the First Leisure contract would also allow Boatland to expand its production of boats for other customers. MMI perceived that Boatland was underperforming and it replaced the current management team with its own managers. However, by 20X8 Boatland was reporting poorer results (see table 1). The work force had been used to producing expensive, high quality boats to discerning customers who looked after their valued boats. In contrast, the boats required by First Leisure were for the casual use of holiday makers who often ill-treated them and certainly had no long-term investment in their ownership. Managers at First Leisure complained that the new boats were 'too delicate' for their intended purpose and unreliability had led to high maintenance costs. This increase in maintenance also put Boatland under strain and its other customers complained about poor quality workmanship and delays in completing work. These delays were compounded by managers at Boatland declaring First Leisure as a preferred customer, requiring that work for First Leisure should take precedence over that for established customers. Since the company was acquired almost half of the skilled boat builders employed by the company have left to take up jobs elsewhere in the industry.

Three months ago, InfoTech – an information technology solutions company approached MMI with a proposal for MMI to acquire them. The failure of certain contracts has led to falling revenues and profits and the company needs new investment. The Managing Director (MD) of InfoTech has proposed that MMI should acquire InfoTech for a nominal sum and then substantially invest in the company so that it can regain its previous profitability and revenue levels. However, after its experience with Boatland, the CEO of MMI is cautious about any further diversification of the group.

Table1: Financial and market data for selected companies (all figures in $millions)

MMI Quarrying and Mining	20X8	20X6	20X4	20X2
Revenue	1,680	1,675	1,250	1,275
Gross Profit	305	295	205	220
Net Profit	110	105	40	45
*Estimated Market Revenue	6,015	6,050	6,200	6,300
First Leisure	**20X8**	**20X6**	**20X4**	**20X2**
Revenue	200	160	110	100
Gross Profit	42	34	23	21
Net Profit	21	17	10	9
*Estimated Market Revenue	950	850	770	750
Boatland	**20X8**	**20X6**	**20X4**	**20X2**
Revenue	2.10	2.40	2.40	2.30
Gross Profit	0.30	0.50	0.50	0.60
Net Profit	0.09	0.25	0.30	0.30
*Estimated Market Revenue	201	201	199	198
InfoTech	**20X8**	**20X6**	**20X4**	**20X2**
Revenue	21	24	26	25
Gross Profit	0.9	3	4	4
Net Profit	−0.2	2	3	3
*Estimated Market Revenue	560	540	475	450

(handwritten note beside First Leisure Net Profit row: "Net Profit Margin = 9%")

*The estimated size of the market (estimated market revenue) is taken from Slott's Economic Yearbooks, 20X2–20X8.

Synergy. Portfolio. Developer

Required:

parent.

(a) In the context of MMI's <u>corporate-level strategy</u>, explain the (rationale) for MMI acquiring First Leisure and Boatland and assess the subsequent performance of the two companies. **(15 marks)**

(b) Assess the extent to which the proposed acquisition of InfoTech represents an appropriate addition to the MMI portfolio. **(10 marks)**

(Total: 25 marks)

17   RAMON SILVA

Ramon Silva is a Spanish property developer, who has made a considerable fortune from the increasing numbers of Europeans looking to buy new homes and apartments in the coastal regions of Spain. His frequent contact with property buyers has made him aware of their need for low cost hotel accommodation during the lengthy period between finding a property to buy and when they actually move into their new home. These would-be property owners are looking for inexpensive hotels in the same locations as tourists looking for cheap holiday accommodation.

Closer investigation of the market for inexpensive or budget hotel accommodation has convinced Ramon of the opportunity to offer something really different to his potential customers. He has the advantage of having no preconceived idea of what his chain of hotels might look like. The overall picture for the budget hotel industry is not encouraging with the industry suffering from low growth and consequent overcapacity. There are two distinct market segments in the budget hotel industry; firstly, no-star and one-star hotels, whose average price per room is between 30 and 45 euros. Customers are simply attracted by the low price. The second segment is the service provided by two-star hotels with an average price of 100 euros a night. These more expensive hotels attract customers by offering a better sleeping environment than the no-star and one-star hotels. Customers therefore have to choose between low prices and getting a poor night's sleep owing to noise and inferior beds or paying more for an untroubled night's sleep. Ramon quickly deduced that a hotel chain that can offer a better price/quality combination could be a winner.

The two-star hotels typically offer a full range of services including restaurants, bars and lounges, all of which are costly to operate. The low price budget hotels offer simple overnight accommodation with cheaply furnished rooms and staffed by part-time receptionists. Ramon is convinced that considerable cost savings are available through better room design, construction and furniture and a more effective use of hotel staff. He feels that through offering hotel franchises under the 'La Familia Amable' ('The Friendly Family') group name, he could recruit husband and wife teams to own and operate them. The couples, with suitable training, could offer most of the services provided in a two-star hotel, and create a friendly, family atmosphere – hence the company name. He is sure he can offer the customer two-star hotel value at budget prices. He is confident that the value-for-money option he offers would need little marketing promotion to launch it and achieve rapid growth.

Required:

(a) Provide Ramon with a brief report, using strategic models where appropriate, showing where his proposed hotel service can add value to the customer experience.

(15 marks)

(b)   What are the advantages and disadvantages of using franchising to develop La Familia Amable budget hotel chain?   **(10 marks)**

(Total: 25 marks)

18   CLYDE WILLIAMS

Clyde Williams is facing a dilemma. He has successfully built up a small family-owned company, Concrete Solutions Ltd, manufacturing a range of concrete based products used in making roads, pavements and walkways. The production technology is very low tech and uses simple wooden moulds into which the concrete is poured. As a consequence he is able to use low skilled and low cost labour, which would find it difficult to find alternative employment in a region with high unemployment levels. The company has employed many of its workforce since its creation in 1996. The company's products are heavy, bulky and costly to transport. This means its market is limited to a 30-mile area around the small rural town where the manufacturing facility is located. Its customers are a mix of private sector building firms and public sector local councils responsible for maintaining roads and pavements. By its nature much of the demand is seasonal and very price sensitive.

A large international civil engineering company has recently approached Clyde with an opportunity to become a supplier of concrete blocks used in a sophisticated system for preventing coast and riverbank erosion. The process involves interlocking blocks being placed on a durable textile base. Recent trends in global warming and pressure in many countries to build in areas liable to flooding have created a growing international market for the patented erosion prevention system. Clyde has the opportunity to become the sole UK supplier of the blocks and to be one of a small number of suppliers able to export the blocks to Europe. To do it he will need to invest a significant amount in CAM (computer aided manufacturing) technology with a linked investment in the workforce skills needed to operate the new technology. The net result will be a small increase in the size of the labour force but redundancy for a significant number of its existing workers either unwilling or unable to adapt to the demands of the new technology. Successful entry into this new market will reduce his reliance on the seasonal low margin concrete products he currently produces and significantly improve profitability.

One further complication exists. Concrete Solutions is located in a quiet residential area of its home town. Clyde is under constant pressure from the local residents and their council representatives to reduce the amount of noise and dust created in the production process. Any move into making the new blocks will increase the pollution problems the residents face. There is a possibility of moving the whole manufacturing process to a site on a new industrial estate being built by the council in a rival town. However, closure of the existing site would lead to a loss of jobs in the current location. Clyde has asked for your help in resolving his dilemma.

Required:

(a)   Using models where appropriate, advise Clyde on whether he should choose to take advantage of the opportunity offered by the international company.   **(15 marks)**

(b)   Assess the extent to which social responsibility issues could and should affect his decision to move into the new product area.   **(10 marks)**

(Total: 25 marks)

ORGANISATIONAL STRUCTURE

19 ALG TECHNOLOGY

John Hudson is the Managing Director of ALG Technology, a medium-sized high tech company operating in several geographic markets. The company provides software and instrumentation, mainly for military projects but it also does have civilian interests. It currently has four key projects – (1) a command, communication and control system for the army's gunnery regiments, (2) avionics for the fighter aircraft within the airforce, (3) an air traffic control system for a regional airport and (4) radar installations for harbour authorities in the Middle East. All these projects were expected to have a life expectancy of at least five years before completion. However, Hudson was worried because each of these projects was increasingly falling behind schedule and the contracts which he had negotiated had late delivery penalties.

Hudson is convinced that a significant cause of the problem is the way that the company is organised. It has been shown that a competitive advantage can be obtained by the way a firm organises and performs its activities. Hudson's organisation is currently structured on a functional basis, which does not seem to work well with complex technologies when operating in dynamic markets. The functional structure appears to result in a lack of integration of key activities, reduced loyalties and an absence of team work. Hudson has contemplated moving towards a divisionalised structure, either by product or by market so as to provide some element of focus, but his experience has suggested that such a structure might create internal rivalries and competition which could adversely affect the performance of the company. Furthermore, there is a risk that such a structure may lead to an over-emphasis on either the technology or the market conditions. He is seeking a structure which encourages both integration and efficiency. Any tendency towards decentralisation, whilst encouraging initiative and generating motivation may result in a failure to pursue a cohesive strategy, whereas a move towards centralisation could reduce flexibility and responsiveness.

The company is already relatively lean and so any move towards delayering, resulting in a flatter organisation is likely to be resisted. Furthermore the nature of the market – the need for high technical specifications and confidentiality – is likely to preclude outsourcing as a means of achieving both efficiency and rapidity of response.

Required:

(a) **Provide an alternative organisational structure for ALG Technology, discussing both the benefits and problems which such a structure might bring.**   **(13 marks)**

(b) **Evaluate the main factors which can influence organisational design relating these, where possible, to ALG Technology.**   **(12 marks)**

(Total: 25 marks)

20 RAMESES INTERNATIONAL

Jeanette Singh is the Strategic Policy Director of Rameses International, a large marketing company specialising in buying a variety of manufactured products from Western Europe and the USA for re-sale in Africa and in the Middle East. It was acting in the capacity of a large export house. In recent years the company had met strong opposition from other companies who were providing a similar sales service, in particular from the strong manufacturing companies who resented companies such as Rameses re-selling their products and obtaining profits which they considered to be rightly theirs.

Rameses International had initiated a number of strategies over the last year in order to minimise their problems. These strategies have varied from seeking a wider range of products to re-sell from a broader supply-base (more suppliers), attempting to have closer collaborative agreements with major suppliers to minimise any potential conflict, and attempting to operate in more markets. None of these strategies has worked.

Jeanette has been asked by the Board of Rameses to investigate the reasons for the failure of these strategies.

Required:

(a)   Acting in the role of Jeanette Singh prepare a brief report to the Board, identifying major reasons why selected strategies might not be successful.   **(15 marks)**

(b)   Identify the issues that have to be considered before a strategy can be successfully implemented.   **(10 marks)**

(Total: 25 marks)

21   ICC ORGANISATION

International Computer Corporation (ICC) has two major world-wide customer functions. The sales and marketing (S&M) function which sells the product and the sales engineering support (SES) function which installs the product and provides customer technical support and maintenance. Within each country functional management (S&M, SES and other functions such as Finance) report to the country Vice President (Operations) and also to the functional Vice President located at the Head Office in the USA. For example, the ICC country Finance Manager for Germany reports and provides support to the German Vice President (Operations) but also has a line responsibility to the Vice President (Finance) located at head office in the USA.

Within each country however S&M and SES are organised as independent divisions. The S&M division organises its sales teams on the basis of product groups, for example, printers or network hardware. S&M product specialisation is seen as essential if sales staff are to develop the level of product technical expertise deemed necessary to sell advanced technologies to computing professionals. The SES division on the other hand organises on the basis of customers not products. The intention being that the customer has only one SES contact for any hardware or software problem and the SES teams are equipped to deal with any aspect of technical support. SES activity is seen as a means of assisting product sales as potential sales leads are picked up by SES staff and passed on to the S&M sales teams. Recently there have been a growing number of country based problems in co-ordination between S&M and SES. One result has been a number of instances of sales leads not being passed by SES to S&M. Another has been instances of hardware being sold by S&M which later proved unsuitable in performance terms. This created significant workload problems for SES engineers in re-configuring to a specification which met the customers' performance criteria.

Required:

(a)   The 'international to country' functional management at ICC provides an example of the matrix form of organisational structure.

Briefly explain why you feel that ICC has chosen to manage its international operations in this way.   **(8 marks)**

(b) **Suggest how the adoption of a country-based matrix structure combining S&M and SES could assist in resolving the apparent co-ordination problems between the two divisions.** **(9 marks)**

(c) **The matrix organisational form has been described as 'no place for a middle manager seeking security and stability'.**

Examine the issues which organisation design must address if the matrix form is to function effectively. **(8 marks)**

(Total: 25 marks)

BUSINESS PROCESS CHANGE

22 **COUNTRY CAR CLUB**

Introduction

The Country Car Club (3C) was established fifty years ago to offer breakdown assistance to motorists. In return for an annual membership fee, members of 3C are able to phone for immediate assistance if their vehicle breaks down anywhere in the country. Assistance is provided by 'service patrol engineers' who are located throughout the country and who are specialists in vehicle repair and maintenance. If they cannot fix the problem immediately then the vehicle (and its occupants) are transported by a 3C recovery vehicle back to the member's home address free of charge.

Over the last fifteen years 3C has rapidly expanded its services. It now offers vehicle insurance, vehicle history checks (to check for previous accident damage or theft) as well as offering a comprehensive advice centre where trained staff answer a wide range of vehicle-related queries. It also provides route maps, endorses hotels by giving them a 3C starred rating and lobbies the government on issues such as taxation, vehicle emissions and toll road charging. All of these services are provided by permanent 3C employees and all growth has been organic culminating in a listing on the country's stock exchange three years ago.

However, since its stock market listing, the company has posted disappointing results and a falling share price has spurred managers to review internal processes and functions. A Business Architecture Committee (BAC) made up of senior managers has been charged with reviewing the scope of the company's business activities. It has been asked to examine the importance of certain activities and to make recommendations on the sourcing of these activities (in-house or outsourced). The BAC has also been asked to identify technological implications or opportunities for the activities that they recommend should remain in-house.

First review

The BAC's first review included an assessment of the supply and maintenance of 3C's company vehicles. 3C has traditionally purchased its own fleet of vehicles and maintained them in a central garage. When a vehicle needed servicing or maintenance it was returned to this central garage. Last year, 3C had seven hundred vehicles (breakdown recovery vehicles, service patrol engineer vans, company cars for senior staff etc) all maintained by thirty staff permanently employed in this garage. A further three permanent employees were employed at the garage site with responsibility for the purchasing and disposal of vehicles. The garage was in a residential area of a major town, with major parking problems and no room for expansion.

The BAC concluded that the garage was of low strategic importance to the company and, although most of the processes it involved were straightforward, its remoteness from the home base of some vehicles made undertaking such processes unnecessarily complicated. Consequently, it recommended outsourcing vehicle acquisition, disposal and maintenance to a specialist company. Two months ago 3C's existing vehicle fleet was acquired by AutoDirect, a company with service and repair centres nationwide, which currently supplies 45,000 vehicles to companies throughout the country. It now leases vehicles back to 3C for a monthly payment. In the next ten years (the duration of the contract) all vehicles will be leased from AutoDirect on a full maintenance basis that includes the replacement of tyres and exhausts. 3C's garage is now surplus to requirements and all the employees that worked there have been made redundant, except for one employee who has been retained to manage the relationship with AutoDirect.

Second review

The BAC has now been asked to look at the following activities and their supporting processes. All of these are currently performed in-house by permanent 3C employees.

- *Attendance of repair staff at breakdowns* – currently undertaken by permanent 'service patrol engineers' employed at locations throughout the country from where they attend local breakdowns.

- *Membership renewal* – members must renew every year. Currently renewals are sent out by staff using a bespoke computer system. Receipts are processed when members confirm that they will be renewing for a further year.

- *Vehicle insurance services* providing accident insurance which every motorist legally requires.

- *Membership queries* handled by a call-centre. Members can use the service for a wide range of vehicle-related problems and issues.

- *Vehicle history checks*. These are primarily used to provide 'peace of mind' to a potential purchaser of a vehicle. The vehicle is checked to see if it has ever been in an accident or if it has been stolen. The check also makes sure that the car is not currently part of a loan agreement.

Required:

(a)   The Business Architecture Committee (BAC) has been asked to make recommendations on the sourcing of activities (in-house or outsourced). The BAC has also been asked to identify technological implications or opportunities for the activities that they recommend should remain in-house.

   Suggest and justify recommendations to the BAC for each of the following major process areas:

   (i)   Attendance of repair staff at breakdowns;

   (ii)   Membership renewal;

   (iii)   Vehicle insurance services;

   (iv)   Membership queries; and

   (v)   Vehicle history checks.   (15 marks)

(b)   Analyse the advantages that 3C will gain from the decision to outsource the purchase and maintenance of their own vehicles.   (10 marks)

(Total: 25 marks)

23   GGE

At a recent board meeting at GGE, there was a lengthy discussion about the problems the company has been experiencing. In the past 12 months, competitors have introduced some new products into the market, which are technically superior to GGE's products, and competitors appear to be capturing a much bigger share of the market.

The quality of service to customers has been a problem. Sales orders seem to take a long time to process, and there have been problems with production scheduling. The despatch department and the production department do not liaise as closely as they should, in spite of long and frequent meetings between the departments to discuss production and despatching difficulties.

The finance director has suggested that the company should consider introducing a continuous improvement programme. The production director believes that the company's problems are serious, and a continuous improvement programme would be of little value. He is in favour of hiring a firm of management consultants with a view to designing a business process re-engineering project.

The managing director recognises the competitive threat from rival companies, and he is concerned that GGE has not responded to technological change as fast as it should.

Required:

(a)   **Describe the main features of business process re-engineering (BPR).**   **(4 marks)**

(b)   **Compare a continuous improvement or kaizen approach to process improvement with a BPR approach, and suggest the circumstances in which a BPR approach might be more appropriate.**   **(12 marks)**

(c)   **Describe the use of Harmon's process-strategy matrix.**   **(9 marks)**

(Total: 25 marks)

24   PATTERSON'S ELECTRICAL SUPPLIERS

Patterson's Electrical Suppliers own a chain of retail outlets throughout the city and surrounding area. In recent years they have expanded these outlets from their one original store to the current seven stores. The head office is based on the original site. The business originated as a cash and carry company supplying the public with all types of electrical appliances, varying from light bulbs to fridge freezers. Electrical goods supply is a very competitive business; Patterson's have to compete with all the national suppliers that tend to dominate the market. In order to compete successfully they have adopted a business strategy of fast turnover and low profit margins coupled with a high customer service level.

Each store holds approximately nine thousand item lines; the majority of the smaller items are on display in the sales area, a selection of the larger appliances are also on display, and this is complemented by a variety of brochures that carry information about the whole range of products. Experienced sales personnel are available to assist customers in their selection of appropriate goods. Following selection and payment of goods, customers tend to 'carry' the smaller items from the store; larger items are delivered within forty-eight hours. Each store has its own warehouse that is replenished when necessary from the company's main storage depot; the main storage depot's inventory control system is managed by head office.

Every store has its own computer system to control the day-to-day business; all of these are linked to the head office system. Information Technology and Information Systems (IT/IS) development strategy has gone hand-in-hand with the Business strategy this has enabled the dramatic expansion of the business. The IT centre is based in the head office and offers support to all of the satellite stores.

The Chairman and the Board of Directors recently employed the services of a business management consultant; the major aim of the exercise was to aid the development of a business strategy for the medium to long term. At a recent meeting of the Board, the directors discussed the consultant's report. One of the recommendations stated 'Pattersons have previously been successful in automation and rationalisation of its business processes, maybe it's time for the business to consider reengineering in its future long term business strategy'. This statement resulted in a heated discussion and disagreement, so much so that it was eventually decided to commission an internal study that would report back to the board at a later date.

A further recommendation involved the development of an integrated inventory distribution system, currently when goods reach their re-order level in the individual stores and the main storage depot cannot supply the goods, they are purchased from suppliers even though other stores have more than adequate levels of the goods. It was decided to conduct a feasibility study, including a cost benefit analysis before the proposed project would be given support.

Overall the consultant's report was encouraging, generally indicating a healthy business position from a management perspective. One point of concern was the recent implementation of a companywide computerised shift scheduling system, for the shop workers, warehouse personnel and support staff. This system basically involves the scheduling of shift patterns and hours worked by the individuals. Previously individuals negotiated their working shifts with middle management within the bounds of certain parameters, number of shifts per week, maximum number of hours etc. There is resistance to the imposition of the system, thus the system is still not fully utilised, to work successfully the system requires a great deal of manual intervention and updating. Generally the system is viewed as a failure by both middle management and the staff affected.

Currently Patterson's' computer-based systems applications portfolio predominantly consists of in-house business systems. They are considering expanding this portfolio to include the 'new' Web based technologies and systems.

Required:

(a) A statement in the scenario 'Information Technology and Information Systems (IT/IS) development strategy, has gone hand-in-hand with the Business strategy this has enabled the dramatic expansion of the business'. Discuss the implications and importance of this statement in respect of Pattersons. **(5 marks)**

(b) Explain in terms of business processes what is meant by the terms: Automation, Rationalisation and Re-engineering (give examples where appropriate in relation to the case-study). **(10 marks)**

(c) Discuss the reasons for the apparent high levels of failure in the implementation of information systems. Where appropriate, make reference to the computerised shift scheduling system recently installed into Pattersons. **(10 marks)**

(Total: 25 marks)

25 4D TEACHING HOSPITAL

4D is a large teaching hospital. While it offers a full range of hospital services to its local community, it also has a large staff of professors and lecturers who teach and train all kinds of medical students. 4D has a very good reputation for clinical excellence.

One of the areas in which 4D is very highly regarded is the training of surgeons. Three of the nine operating theatres in the hospital can be observed from a gallery, though only a limited number of students can watch any operation due to space constraints. This allows the students to watch an experienced surgeon carry out a procedure and then ask questions of their lecturer or the surgeon. Later in their training, students can use the same facilities to carry out operations while being observed by experienced staff and fellow students.

The IT department of 4D has just developed a new Information System for use in operating theatres. This system (OTIS – the Operating Theatre Information System) uses web technology to allow students anywhere in the world to videoconference with a lecturer during an operation. The students can observe the operation and the surgical team, and discuss the procedure with the surgeon and their lecturer. The system also works 'in reverse' so a surgeon at 4D can watch a student perform an operation elsewhere in the world, and provide guidance and support. The OTIS system is currently being tested, prior to introduction.

Required:

(a) (i)   Distinguish between **Business Process Re-engineering (BPR) and Process Innovation (PI)**, and explain the role of information technology in each of these techniques.   **(6 marks)**

      (ii) Discuss whether, in your opinion, the **Operating Theatre Information System (OTIS)** implementation is an example of BPR or PI.   **(4 marks)**

(b) Evaluate **THREE** benefits to 4D and **TWO** benefits to society, of the **Operating Theatre Information System (OTIS)**.   **(15 marks)**

                                                                                    (Total: 25 marks)

26 CADCO INC

Cadco Inc has a chain of twenty supermarkets. When stock items reach their re-order level in a supermarket the in-store computerised inventory system informs the stock clerk. The clerk then raises a request daily to the Cadco central warehouse for replenishment of stocks via fax or e-mail. If the local warehouse has available stock it is forwarded to the supermarket within twenty-four hours of receiving the request. If the local warehouse cannot replenish the stock from its inventory holding then it raises a purchase order to one of its suppliers. The supplier delivers the stock to the warehouse and the warehouse then delivers the required stock to the supermarkets within the area. The Cadco area warehouse staff conduct all business communication with suppliers.

Cadco recently contracted an IT consultant to analyse and make recommendations concerning their current supply chain briefly described above. Following the initial investigation the consultant reported.

'To enable an established traditional company like Cadco to develop a Virtual Supply Chain system it may be necessary to employ a Business Process Re-engineering (BPR) approach.'

Required:

(a) With reference to the above scenario, describe what is meant by a Business Process Re-engineering approach. **(10 marks)**

(b) Discuss the notion of a supply chain, identifying the major activities and supporting information systems that are required to develop a virtual supply chain. **(15 marks)**

(Total: 25 marks)

INFORMATION TECHNOLOGY

27 PERFECT SHOPPER *Walk in the footsteps of a top tutor*

Local neighbourhood shops are finding it increasingly difficult to compete with supermarkets. However, three years ago, the Perfect Shopper franchise group was launched that allowed these neighbourhood shops to join the group and achieve cost savings on tinned and packaged goods, particularly groceries. Perfect Shopper purchases branded goods in bulk from established food suppliers and stores them in large purpose-built warehouses, each designed to serve a geographical region. When Perfect Shopper was established it decided that deliveries to these warehouses should be made by the food suppliers or by haulage contractors working on behalf of these suppliers. Perfect Shopper places orders with these suppliers and the supplier arranges the delivery to the warehouse. These arrangements are still in place. Perfect Shopper has no branded goods of its own.

Facilities are available in each warehouse to re-package goods into smaller units, more suitable for the requirements of the neighbourhood shop. These smaller units, typically containing 50–100 tins or packs, are usually small trays, sealed with strong transparent polythene. Perfect Shopper delivers these to its neighbourhood shops using specialist haulage contractors local to the regional warehouse. Perfect Shopper has negotiated significant discounts with suppliers, part of which it passes on to its franchisees. A recent survey in a national grocery magazine showed that franchisees saved an average of 10% on the prices they would have paid if they had purchased the products directly from the manufacturer or from an intermediary – such as cash and carry wholesalers.

As well as offering savings due to bulk buying, Perfect Shopper also provides, as part of its franchise:

(i) Personalised promotional material. This usually covers specific promotions and is distributed locally, either using specialist leaflet distributors or loosely inserted into local free papers or magazines.

(ii) Specialised signage for the shops to suggest the image of a national chain. The signs include the Perfect Shopper slogan 'the nation's local'.

(iii) Specialist in-store display units for certain goods, again branded with the Perfect Shopper logo.

Perfect Shopper does not provide all of the goods required by a neighbourhood shop. Consequently, it is not an exclusive franchise. Franchisees agree to purchase specific products through Perfect Shopper, but other goods, such as vegetables, fruit, stationery and newspapers they source from elsewhere. Deliveries are made every two weeks to franchisees using a standing order for products agreed between the franchisee and their Perfect Shopper sales representative at a meeting they hold every three months. Variations to this order can be made by telephone, but only if the order is increased. Downward variations are not allowed. Franchisees cannot reduce their standing order requirements until the next meeting with their representative.

Perfect Shopper was initially very successful, but its success has been questioned by a recent independent report that showed increasing discontent amongst franchisees. The following issues were documented.

(i)   The need to continually review prices to compete with supermarkets.

(ii)   Low brand recognition of Perfect Shopper.

(iii)   Inflexible ordering and delivery system based around forecasts and restricted ability to vary orders (see above).

As a result of this survey, Perfect Shopper has decided to review its business model. Part of this review is to re-examine the supply chain, to see if there are opportunities for addressing some of its problems.

Required:

(a)   **Describe the primary activities of the value chain of Perfect Shopper.**   **(5 marks)**

(b)   **Explain how Perfect Shopper might re-structure its upstream supply chain to address the problems identified in the scenario.**   **(10 marks)**

(c)   **Explain how Perfect Shopper might re-structure its downstream supply chain to address the problems identified in the scenario.**   **(10 marks)**

(Total: 25 marks)

28   5E INTRANET UPGRADE

5E is a management consultancy practice. It is a limited liability partnership with eight equal partners. Over the past ten years, 5E has invested heavily in the development of knowledge management. It now has a very large knowledgebase, with over half a million documents that have been produced by 5E staff. These range from internal memos, emails and research reports to major client project reports and articles that have been published in professional journals. The knowledgebase is stored on, and accessed through, 5E's intranet. The intranet is currently managed by X, a facilities management company which owns all the necessary hardware and software. PCs and laptops are all owned by 5E and maintained by X.

5E also has a website containing contact details for all of 5E's offices, and detailed descriptions of the products and services offered to clients. It also has mini case studies of successful 5E consultancy projects. These case studies have each been approved by the relevant client, as some of the content could have been perceived as commercially sensitive. The website is hosted by an Internet Service Provider (ISP). The same ISP also handles all incoming and outgoing email traffic on behalf of 5E.

Ms Y, the Chief Knowledge Officer (CKO) of 5E, has proposed a major upgrade to the Intranet. This would involve a significant investment, and the major aspects of the planned upgrade are as follows:

*   to bring web hosting and the management of the intranet in-house

*   to redesign the website so it gives clients of 5E password-protected access to the knowledgebase.

Required:

(a) Recommend the information technology hardware and software that would be required by 5E in order to complete the intranet upgrade project. **(10 marks)**

(b) Using Mendelow's stakeholder mapping model, identify FIVE major stakeholders of the intranet project. Explain the classification you have given, within the model, to each stakeholder. **(15 marks)**

(Total: 25 marks)

29 PROTECH-PUBLIC

Ergo city authority administers environmental, social care, housing and cultural services to the city of Ergo. The city itself has many social problems and a recent report from the local government auditor criticised the Chief Executive Officer (CEO) for not spending enough time and money addressing the pressing housing problems of the city.

Since 1970 the authority has had its own internal Information Technology (IT) department. However, there has been increasing criticism of the cost and performance of this department. The CEO has commented that 'we seem to expand the department to cope with special demands (such as the millennium bug) but the department never seems to shrink back to its original size when the need has passed'. Some employees are lost through natural wastage, but there have never been any redundancies in IT and the labour laws of the nation, and strong trade unions within the authority, make it difficult to make staff redundant.

In the last few years there has been an on-going dispute between managers in the IT department and managers in the finance function. The dispute started due to claims about the falsification of expenses but has since escalated into a personal battle between the director of IT and the finance director. The CEO has had to intervene personally in this dispute and has spent many hours trying to reconcile the two sides. However, issues still remain and there is still tension between the managers of the two departments.

A recent internal human resources (HR) survey of the IT department found that, despite acknowledging that they received above average pay, employees were not very satisfied. The main complaints were about poor management, the ingratitude of user departments, ('we are always being told that we are overheads, and are not core to the business of the authority') and the absence of promotion opportunities within the department. The ingratitude of users is despite the IT department running a relatively flexible approach to fulfilling users' needs. There is no cross-charging for IT services provided and changes to user requirements are accommodated right up to the release of the software. The director of IT is also critical of the staffing constraints imposed on him. He has recently tried to recruit specialists in web services and 'cloud computing' without any success. He also says that 'there are probably other technologies that I have not even heard of that we should be exploring and exploiting'.

The CEO has been approached by a large established IT service company, ProTech, to form a new company ProTech-Public that combines the public sector IT expertise of the authority with the commercial and IT knowledge of ProTech. The joint company will be a private limited company, owned 51% by ProTech and 49% by the city authority. All existing employees in the IT department and the IT technology of the city authority will be transferred to ProTech who will then enter into a 10 year outsourcing arrangement with the city authority. The CEO is very keen on the idea and he sees many other authorities following this route.

The only exception to this transfer of resources concerns the business analysts who are currently in the IT department. They will be retained by the authority and located in a new business analysis department reporting directly to the CEO.

The CEO has suggested that the business analysts have the brief to 'deliver solutions that demonstrably offer benefits to the authority and to the people of the city, using information technology where appropriate'. They need to be 'outward looking and not constrained by current processes and technology'. They will also be responsible for liaising between users and the newly outsourced IT company and, for the first time, defining business cases with users.

In principle, the creation of the new company and the outsourcing deal has been agreed. One of the conditions of the contract, inserted by the finance director, is that the new company achieves CMMI level 5 within three years. The current IT department has been recently assessed as CMMI level 2. ProTech has recently been assessed at CMMI level 3.

Required:

(a)   **Evaluate the potential benefits to the city authority and its IT employees, of outsourcing IT to ProTech-Public.**   **(12 marks)**

(b)   **The role of the business analyst is currently being re-designed.**

        Analyse what new or enhanced competencies the business analysts will require to undertake their proposed new role in the city authority.   **(7 marks)**

(c)   **This question element is no longer examinable.**   **(6 marks)**

                                                                    (Total: 25 marks)

30   GOOD SPORTS

Good Sports Limited is an independent sports goods retailer owned and operated by two partners, Alan and Bob. The sports retailing business in the UK has undergone a major change over the past ten years. First of all the supply side has been transformed by the emergence of a few global manufacturers of the core sports products, such as training shoes and football shirts. This consolidation has made them increasingly unwilling to provide good service to the independent sportswear retailers too small to buy in sufficiently large quantities. These independent retailers can stock popular global brands, but have to order using the Internet and have no opportunity to meet the manufacturer's sales representatives. Secondly, UK's sportswear retailing has undergone significant structural change with the rapid growth of a small number of national retail chains with the buying power to offset the power of the global manufacturers. These retail chains stock a limited range of high volume branded products and charge low prices the independent retailer cannot hope to match.

Good Sports has survived by becoming a specialist niche retailer catering for less popular sports such as cricket and hockey. They are able to offer the specialist advice and stock the goods that their customers want. Increasingly since 2000 Good Sports has become aware of the growing impact of e-business in general, and e-retailing in particular. They employed a specialist website designer and created an online purchasing facility for their customers. The results were less than impressive, with the Internet search engines not picking up the company website. The seasonal nature of Good Sports' business, together with the variations in sizes and colours needed to meet an individual customer's needs, meant that the sales volumes were insufficient to justify the costs of running the site.

Bob, however, is convinced that developing an e-business strategy suited to the needs of the independent sports retailer such as Good Sports will be key to business survival. He has been encouraged by the growing interest of customers in other countries to the service and product range they offer. He is also aware of the need to integrate an e-business strategy with their current marketing, which to date has been limited to the sponsorship of local sports teams and advertisements taken in specialist sports magazines. Above all, he wants to avoid head-on competition with the national retailers and their emphasis on popular branded sportswear sold at retail prices that are below the cost price at which Good Sports can buy the goods.

Required:

(a) **Provide the partners with a short report on the advantages and disadvantages to Good Sports of developing an e-business strategy and the processes most likely to be affected by such a strategy.** **(15 marks)**

(b) **Good Sports Limited has successfully followed a niche strategy to date. Assess the extent to which an appropriate e-business strategy could help support such a niche strategy.**

(10 marks)

(Total: 25 marks)

31 NEW SYSTEM

A component supply company is planning a major new IT system for order processing, inventory control and order despatch operations as their existing system is unreliable and prone to error, so that, too often, the wrong products are dispatched or promised products are discovered not, in fact, to be in inventories. One of the main reasons for introducing the new system is that customers for the company's products (all businesses) demand reliable delivery dates for the items they order, and several rival companies have been gaining market share because they have been able to develop better order delivery systems. The company's new system will be used for taking customer orders and informing customers about the availability of the items, and will provide the customer with a 'guaranteed' delivery date. Senior management would prefer to develop a bespoke system, although an off-the-shelf software package is available that could be used instead. The IT manager recognises the need for the new system to be introduced quickly, and has suggested that the systems development, if done in-house, would make use of prototyping.

Required:

(a) **Explain the main advantages and disadvantages of buying off-the-shelf software rather than developing a bespoke information system.** **(7 marks)**

(b) **Explain how prototyping would speed up system implementation and improve the quality of the final system.** **(3 marks)**

(c) **The new computer system is intended to improve operating processes within the company. Using the Harmon Process Strategy Matrix as a framework, explain the importance of operations strategy for the company.** **(6 marks)**

(d) **Suggest how the new IT system might be seen as an element of the marketing mix by the company's marketing management.** **(5 marks)**

(e) **Suggest how staff should be trained in operating the new system.** **(4 marks)**

(Total: 25 marks)

MARKETING

32   AEC *Walk in the footsteps of a top tutor*

Introduction

The Accounting Education Consortium (AEC) offers professional accountancy education and training courses. It currently runs classroom-based training courses preparing candidates for professional examinations in eight worldwide centres. Three of these centres are also used for delivering continuing professional development (CPD) courses to qualified accountants. However, only about 30% of the advertised CPD courses and seminars actually run. The rest are cancelled through not having enough participants to make them economically viable.

AEC has developed a comprehensive set of course manuals to support the preparation of its candidates for professional examinations. There is a course manual for every examination paper in the professional examination scheme. As well as being used on its classroom-based courses, these course manuals are also available for purchase over the Internet. The complete set of manuals for a professional examinations scheme costs $180.00 and the web site has a secure payment facility which allows this to be paid by credit card. Once purchased, the manuals may be downloaded or they may be sent on a CD to the home address of the purchaser. It is only possible to purchase the complete set of manuals for the scheme, not individual manuals for particular examinations. To help the student decide if he or she wishes to buy the complete manual set, the web site has extracts from a sample course manual. This sample may be accessed, viewed and printed once a student has registered their email address, name and address on the web site.

AEC has recently won a contract to supply professional accountancy training to a global accounting company. All students working for this company will now be trained by AEC at one of its worldwide centres.

Web site

The AEC web site has the following functionality:

Who we are: A short description of the company and its products and services.

Professional education courses: Course dates, locations and standard fees for professional examination courses. This schedule of courses is printable.

Continuing professional development: Course dates, locations and standard fees for CPD courses and seminars. This schedule is also printable.

CPD catalogue: Detailed course and seminar descriptions for CPD courses and seminars.

Downloadable study material: Extracts from a sample course manual. Visitors to the site wishing to access this material must register their email address, name and address. 5,500 people registered last year to download study material.

Purchase study material: Secure purchase of a complete manual set for the professional scheme. Payment is by credit card. On completion of successful payment, the visitor is able to download the manuals or to request them to be shipped to a certain address on a CD. At present, 10% of the people who view downloadable study material proceed to purchase.

Who to contact: Who to contact for booking professional training courses or CPD courses and seminars. It provides the name, email address, fax number, telephone number and address of a contact at each of the eight worldwide centres.

Marketing strategy

The marketing manager of AEC has traditionally used magazines, newspapers and direct mail to promote its courses and products. Direct mail is primarily used for sending printed course catalogues to potential customers for CPD courses and seminars. However, she is now keen to develop the potential of the Internet and to increase investment in this medium at the expense of the traditional marketing media. Table 1 shows the percentage allocation of her budget for 20X8, compared with 20X7. The actual budget has only been increased by 3% in 20X8.

Table 1

Percentage allocation of marketing budget (20X7–20X8)

	20X8	20X7
Advertising	30%	40%
Direct mail	10%	30%
Sponsorship	10%	10%
Internet	50%	20%

Required:

(a) **Explain, in the context of AEC, how the marketing characteristics of electronic media (such as the Internet) differ from those of traditional marketing media such as advertising and direct mail.** **(10 marks)**

(b) **Evaluate how the marketing manager might use electronic marketing (including the Internet) to vary the marketing mix at AEC.** **(15 marks)**

(Total: 25 marks)

33 THE FANCY PACKAGING COMPANY

Eddie Lomax is the Marketing Director of The Fancy Packaging Company, a wholly owned subsidiary of the Acme Paper Company plc. Acme is a major industrially integrated European corporation comprising timber interests, pulp and paper production, as well as down-stream consumer-focused activities such as publishing and paper products (paper plates, computer paper and note paper). Fancy Packaging was set up in the 1960s when conglomerates and operations in many different industries was popular. The subsidiary concentrates on the European market and produces packaging material, either paper or cardboard, focusing on the fast moving consumer goods sectors. The nature of this packaging is more decorative than protective.

The Fancy Packaging Company is now operating in a much more hostile environment. First, there is increasing competition from other European suppliers, particularly those from the old Soviet bloc who currently have a lower cost base. Second, the demand for this decorative type of packaging is falling. There are a number of reasons for this but two stand out. There is an increasing trend to strip out frivolous packaging which adds little value. There is a growing fashion among some consumers to avoid conspicuous wastage and the dissipation of the world's scarce natural resources. This trend has developed as a result of the growing adverse public reaction to the increases in environmental pollution. Issues such as global warming have had a knock-on effect in alerting consumers to the dangers of resource wastage. A second reason for the decline in the demand for packaging is the increasing price competition within the fast moving consumer goods industries. Manufacturers are now looking for ways to reduce costs and not just differentiate their products. Packaging appears to be one of the areas where cost savings may be found.

Eddie Lomax believes that the potential for growth in Europe is not only limited but that the current level of sales revenue is now threatened. He is convinced that the company must look to other non-European countries for survival. However, the company has no experience in sales outside Europe and so he has approached a marketing research consultancy for guidance.

Required:

(a)   Prepare a brief report to Eddie Lomax stating the key areas of information that would be of importance prior to deciding which overseas markets should be focused upon. **(15 marks)**

(b)   Recommend a methodology for obtaining the required information by a company (Acme) which has, up to now, had little experience in marketing research. **(10 marks)**

(Total: 25 marks)

34   RESTFUL HOTELS

Restful Hotels operates a chain of four-star hotels in several countries. Some of the hotels are situated in city centres, but others are in holiday resort centres and on holiday islands. The company's management has been very successful in controlling its operating costs, and the company is profitable. The company is opening new hotels currently at the rate of about three each year.

However, the management are concerned that total sales revenue is growing slowly, and sales income at the new hotels is particularly disappointing. The room occupancy rate is below budget, and there are vacant rooms in most hotels at most times of the year. The quality of service to guests does not appear to have deteriorated, and customers appear to be satisfied with the service they receive.

Two suggestions have been made to increase the rate of revenue growth. One is to use pricing as a marketing tool to attract more customers. The other is to try to attract more customers by focusing on an additional segment of the market.

Required:

(a)   Suggest how the company might use pricing as an element in its marketing mix, as a means of increasing total sales revenue. **(8 marks)**

(b)   Suggest how market segmentation, and focusing on new segments of the market, might possibly help to increase total sales. **(6 marks)**

(c)   Suggest why the company has to be careful in using pricing as an element of its marketing strategy. **(6 marks)**

(Total: 20 marks)

35   REPLEX

Replex is launching a new product to the market next year and is currently considering its pricing strategy for this new product. The product will be unlike any other product that is currently available and will considerably improve the efficiency with which garages can service motor vehicles. This unique position in the market place is expected to remain for only six months before one of the company's competitors develops a similar product.

The prototype required a substantial amount of time to develop and as a result the company is keen to recover its considerable research and development costs as soon as possible. The company has now developed its manufacturing process for this product and as a result the time taken to produce each unit is much less than was required for the first few units. This time reduction is expected to continue for a short period of time once mass production has started, but from then a constant time requirement per unit is anticipated.

Required:

(a)   Explain the alternative pricing strategies that may be adopted when launching a new product.   **(6 marks)**

(b)   Recommend a pricing strategy to the company for its new product and explain how the adoption of your chosen strategy would affect the sales revenue, costs and profits of this product over its life cycle.   **(9 marks)**

(Total: 15 marks)

PROJECT MANAGEMENT

36   ASW   *Walk in the footsteps of a top tutor*

ASW is a software house which specialises in producing software packages for insurance companies. ASW has a basic software package for the insurance industry that can be used immediately out of the box. However, most customers wish ASW to tailor the package to reflect their own products and requirements. In a typical ASW project, ASW's business analysts define the gap between the customer's requirements and the basic package. These business analysts then specify the complete software requirement in a system specification. This specification is used by its programmers to produce a customised version of the software. It is also used by the system testers at ASW to perform their system tests before releasing it to the customer for acceptance testing.

One of ASW's new customers is CaetInsure. Initially CaetInsure sent ASW a set of requirements for their proposed new system. Business analysts from ASW then worked with CaetInsure staff to produce a full system specification for CaetInsure's specific requirements. ASW do not begin any development until this system specification is signed off. After some delay (see below), the system specification was eventually signed off by CaetInsure.

Since sign-off, ASW developers have been working on tailoring the product to obtain an appropriate software solution. The project is currently at week 16 and the software is ready for system testing. The remaining activities in the project are shown in figure 1. This simple plan has been put together by the project manager. It also shows who has responsibility for undertaking the activities shown on the plan.

The problem that the project manager faces is that the plan now suggests that implementation (parallel running) cannot take place until part way through week 28. The original plan was for implementation in week 23. Three weeks of the delay were due to problems in signing off the system specification. Key CaetInsure employees were unavailable to make decisions about requirements, particularly in the re-insurance part of the system. Too many requirements in this module were either unclear or kept changing as users sought clarification from their managers. There have also been two further weeks of slippage since the sign-off of the system specification.

The CaetInsure contract had been won in the face of stiff competition. As part of securing the deal, the ASW sales account manager responsible for the CaetInsure contract agreed that penalty clauses could be inserted into the contract. The financial penalty for late delivery of the software increases with every week's delay. CaetInsure had insisted on these clauses as they have tied the delivery of the software in with the launch of a new product. Although the delay in signing off the system specification was due to CaetInsure, the penalty clauses still remain in the contract. When the delay was discussed with the customer and ASW's project manager, the sales account manager assured CaetInsure that the 'time could be made up in programming'.

The initial planned delivery date (week 23) is now only seven weeks away. The project manager is now under intense pressure to come up with solutions which address the project slippage.

Required:

(a)   **This requirement is no longer examinable.**

(b)   **Evaluate the alternative strategies available to ASW's project manager to address the slippage problem in the CaetInsure project.**   **(10 marks)**

(c)   **As a result of your evaluation, recommend and justify your preferred solution to the slippage problem in the CaetInsure project.**   **(6 marks)**

(Total: 16 marks)

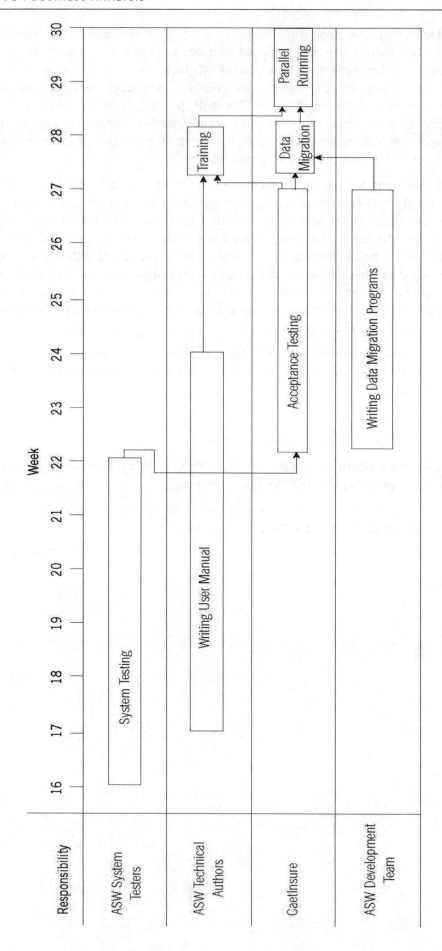

Figure 1: Project Plan – ASW: CaetInsure Contract

37   QUARAX

Quarax is a small manufacturer of replacement machine components for machinery used in the mining and oil exploration industries. It is based in an African country, Zedland. It was formed in 1952, as a partnership between two engineers, and incorporated in 1977. Quarax now employs 120 staff, and has an annual turnover equivalent to one million US dollars. Quarax is proud to offer the very highest levels of customer service. Much of the machinery used by Quarax's customers is quite old and, as a result, components are no longer available from the original equipment manufacturers (OEMs), most of which are large multinational companies. Quarax mostly supplies parts directly to the end-users but also receives a small but significant proportion of its business from OEMs, who then supply the components to their customers.

The current business model

Quarax has always run its business in a very traditional way. The sales manager receives most orders by telephone or fax. The order specifies the OEM part number that the component is to replace. If Quarax has previously supplied that component, the sales manager checks the price list and tells the customer the price. Quarax holds very low levels of finished goods inventory, and then only of the most commonly ordered components.

Where Quarax needs to make a component for the first time, an Quarax 'estimator' (a qualified engineer, responsible for producing an estimate of the material and labour involved in manufacturing the item) obtains the original drawings of the component, either from Quarax's extensive archives or from the OEM. The estimator then produces detailed engineering drawings, a list of materials and parts required, and an estimate of the labour hours likely to be used at each stage of the manufacturing process. The estimate is passed to a costing clerk in the accounts department who calculates the likely product cost (labour, materials and overheads), adds a 'mark-up' of 50%, and advises the sales manager of the price. If the customer accepts the price, an order is passed to the production department, which schedules and completes the work. If the actual cost of production is significantly different from that estimated, the price list is amended to reflect the actual manufacturing cost.

Very occasionally, a customer sends (or brings in) an old component, which cannot be traced back to an OEM. The sales manager gives the component to an estimator, who dismantles the component and produces the necessary engineering drawings and estimate. This process is called 'reverse engineering', and is common in the component manufacturing industry. Reverse engineering currently accounts for about 5% of Quarax's business.

When an order is fulfilled, the component is delivered to the customer, together with an invoice. Most customers pay within 30 days, by cash or cheque. Quarax does not have a problem with bad debts. An increasing proportion of Quarax's business is now transacted in US dollars, as African currencies tend to be unstable.

Quarax prides itself on the personal service it provides. The close contact it has with its customers means that Quarax receives a significant amount of repeat business. Quarax has never advertised its services, but grew significantly until 2007 as a result of 'word of mouth' recommendations by satisfied customers. Quarax, however, has not experienced growth for the last two years, although turnover and profit have remained stable.

Quarax uses only very basic Information Systems (IS), and reports its performance using a simple comparison between budget and actual, which is produced using a spreadsheet package. Quarax's accounting system is not automated, and transactions are recorded in traditional ledgers.

E-commerce

The sales manager of Quarax has noticed that customers are increasingly mentioning that they would like to be able to order online. He knows that there has been a significant growth in business-to-business (B2B) e-commerce in recent years. The sales manager has recognised that in order to grow and to make a move into e-commerce possible, Quarax's accounting system will have to be updated to a computerised one.

Having spoken to a number of potential suppliers, the sales manager has now received a proposal from SSS, a local company, to supply tailored 'off-the-shelf' systems for both accounting and e-commerce. SSS has provided a detailed breakdown of its proposal, to be known as Project E, which is summarised below.

The sales manager believes that, following implementation of the new systems (likely to be 12 months from contract agreement) e-commerce should lead to an increase in the company's turnover of 10% in its first year of operation. Thereafter, the turnover resulting from e-commerce should grow at a rate of 10% each year for the foreseeable future.

The sales manager also thinks that any increase in indirect costs as a result of this higher volume of business will be fully offset by a reduction in administration workload as a result of the new computerised accounting system. The gross margin earned from e-commerce business can therefore be used as the effective cash inflow for evaluation purposes. The current turnover of Quarax is, as stated earlier, $1 million a year. The mark-up on products sold by e-commerce will be the same as at present (that is, 50%).

However, the sales manager thinks that a cautious approach should be taken to the evaluation of the proposal, and that any benefits after 5 years from implementation should be ignored. Quarax has a weighted average cost of capital (WACC) of 15%.

The following information has been provided by SSS, the preferred systems supplier:

		Project E
Item	*Timing*	*Cost* US$
'Mage Gold' accounting package	On agreement of contract	14,000
Tailoring of the above	During the first 6 months	20,000
'SellitOnline' e-commerce package	On agreement of contract	11,000
Tailoring of the above	During the first 6 months	8,000
Populating the e-commerce database	During the first 6 months	5,000
Training	During months 7 – 12	10,000
Support	Split over the five years following implementation	25,000
Hardware, networking and connection	During the first 12 months	40,000
Broadband service costs	Split over the five years following implementation	20,000
TOTAL COST		**153,000**

Note: You should assume that all cash flows arise at the end of the period to which they relate, for example 'Tailoring' at the end of 6 months, and 'Training' at the end of 12 months.

Required:

(a)   **Prepare a financial evaluation of Project E.**

        Note: **You should ignore the effects of inflation and taxation.**   **(12 marks)**

(b)   **Evaluate the strategic and competitive benefits to Quarax of the proposed e-commerce system.**   **(13 marks)**

                                                                    (Total: 25 marks)

38   A CLOTHING COMPANY

A clothing company sells 40% of its goods directly to customers through its website. The marketing manager of the company (MM) has decided that this is insufficient and has put a small team together to re-design the site. MM feels that the site looks 'amateur and old-fashioned and does not project the right image'. The board of the company has given the go-ahead for the MM 'to re-design the website'. The following notes summarise the outcomes of the meetings on the website re-design. The team consists of the marketing manager (MM), a product range manager (RP),a marketing image consultant (IC) and a technical developer (TD).

Meeting 1: 9 July attended by MM, RP, IC and TD

The need for a re-designed website to increase sales volume through the website and to 'improve our market visibility' was explained by MM. IC was asked to produce a draft design.

Meeting 2: 16 August attended by MM, RP, IC and TD

IC presented a draft design. MM and RP were happy with its image but not its functionality, suggesting that it was too similar to the current site. 'We expected it to do much more' was their view.

Meeting 3: 4 September attended by MM, RP and IC

IC produced a re-drafted design. This overall design was agreed and the go-ahead was given for TD to produce a prototype of the design to show to the board.

Meeting 4: 11 September attended by RP, IC and TD

TD explained that elements of the drafted re-design were not technically feasible to implement in the programming language being used. Changes to the design were agreed at the meeting to overcome these issues and signed off by RP.

Meeting 5: 13 October attended by MM, RP, IC and TD

The prototype re-design was demonstrated by TD. MM was unhappy with the re-design as it was 'moving too far away from the original objective and lacked functionality that should be there'. TD agreed to write a technical report to explain why the original design (agreed on 4 September) could not be adhered to.

Meeting 6: 9 November attended by MM, IC and TD

It was agreed to return to the 4 September design with slight alterations to make it technically feasible. TD expressed concerns that the suggested design would not work properly with all web browsers.

At the board meeting of 9 December the board expressed concern about the time taken to produce the re-design and the finance director highlighted the rising costs (currently $25,000) of the project. They asked MM to produce a formal cost-benefit of the re-design. The board were also concerned that the scope of the project, which they had felt to be about re-design, had somehow been interpreted as including development and implementation.

On 22 December MM produced the following cost-benefit analysis of the project and confirmed that the word 'redesign' had been interpreted as including the development and implementation of the website.

	Year 1	Year 2	Year 3	Year 4	Year 5
Costs	$50,000	$10,000	$10,000	$10,000	$10,000
Benefits*	0	$15,000	$25,000	$35,000	$35,000

*These benefits are extra sales volumes created by the website's extra functionality and the company's increased visibility in the market place.

On 4 January the board gave the go ahead for the development and implementation of the website with a further budget of $25,000 and a delivery date of 1 March. TD expressed concern that he did not have enough developers to deliver the re-designed website on time.

Meeting 7: 24 February attended by MM, RP, IC and TD

A partial prototype system was demonstrated by TD. RP felt that the functionality of the re-design was too limited and that the software was not robust enough. It had crashed twice during the demonstration. He suggested that the company delay the introduction of the re-designed website until it was complete and robust. MM declared this to be impossible.

Conclusion

The re-designed website was launched on 1 March. MM declared the re-design a success that 'had come in on time and under budget'. On 2 and 3 March, numerous complaints were received from customers. The website was unreliable and did not work with a particular popular web browser. On 4 March an emergency board meeting decided to withdraw the site and reinstate the old one. On 5 March, MM resigned.

Required:

Most project management methods have an initiation or definition stage which includes the production of a document that serves as an agreement between the sponsors and deliverers of the project. This may be called a project initiation document or a project charter. Defining the business case is also an important part of the initiation or definition stage of the project.

(a) **Explain how a business case and a project initiation document would have helped prevent some of the problems that emerged during the conduct of the website re-design project.** **(15 marks)**

(b) **Analyse how effective project management could have further improved both the process and the outcomes of the website re-design project.** **(10 marks)**

(Total: 25 marks)

39   M UNIVERSITY

As part of M University's ambitious strategy for growth, investment is being made in the development of a student village.

The finance director of M University has been appointed as the project manager and is in the early stages of setting up the project. This will be a complex project involving the construction of new buildings to provide for the growth in student numbers, including living accommodation for students, teaching rooms, a state-of-the-art business and conference facility aimed at attracting corporate clients to work with the University, and sports and recreation facilities. The build will be a collaborative venture funded by the University and investments from two local businesses.

The regional authority currently owns the land that the University wants to acquire to build the student village. The authority, the members of which are directly elected by local residents, makes the decisions on whether to accept or reject planning proposals made. It was recently reported in the local paper that the local residents are unhappy about the proposal.

The development will mean that staff from two University departments will be relocated to the new site which is two miles away from the main campus. In the first open meeting held by the finance director to communicate the proposals, he was met with a hostile reaction from staff, with most of them being very unhappy about moving to the new site.

The finance director knows that this will be a complex project to manage and that project management software will be essential in making his job objectives achievable. He is also aware that the project has a number of different stakeholders that he must consider.

Required:

(a)   **Discuss how project management software might help the finance director and his team successfully carry out the project.**   **(15 marks)**

(b)   **Using examples, explain why the finance director should consider the interests of the different stakeholders in the student village project.**   **(10 marks)**

(Total: 25 marks)

40   ASHFELT

Ashfelt is a major construction company that has just won a major contract for a large road-widening scheme through an area of countryside that has been officially designated as an 'area of outstanding natural beauty'. The work will be carried out to some extent by direct employees of Ashfelt, but most of the work will be undertaken by sub-contractors.

The scheme has already attracted a considerable amount of publicity and the Preserve the Countryside Movement, a large national pressure group, has already announced its intention to organise demonstrations and protests against the construction work. More extreme and radical protest groups have threatened disruptive action.

The project is being financed by the transport department of the central government, and the managers of Ashfelt who are responsible for the project have already spoken to the police authorities about the preservation of public order. A security firm will be employed to provide physical protection to employees and assets. Ashfelt is also aware, however, that some local government authorities of areas through which the road passes oppose the plans of the central government transport department for the road widening. These local authorities believe that the damage to the environment will be unacceptably heavy.

A traffic survey conducted for the central government has suggested that, during the time that the road widening is taking place, there will be severe disruption to normal road traffic and severe delays for drivers on their journeys will be inevitable. Ashfelt relies on a large number of sub-contractors to do work on the project.

Required:

(a) **Identify the stakeholders in this project, how their relative strengths might be assessed and how an understanding of the project stakeholders and their concerns can assist with project management.** **(15 marks)**

(b) **Describe the broad issues that the management of Ashfelt should consider when undertaking a feasibility study for this road-widening scheme.** **(10 marks)**

(Total: 25 marks)

41 CFS

Graham Smith is Operations Director of Catering Food Services (CFS) a $1.5 billion UK based distributor of foods to professional catering organisations. It has 30 trading units spread across the country from which it can supply a complete range of fresh, chilled and frozen food products. Its customers range from major fast food chains, catering services for the armed forces down to individual restaurants and cafes. Wholesale food distribution is very much a price-driven service, in which it is very difficult to differentiate CFS's service from its competitors.

Graham is very aware of the Government's growing interest in promoting good corporate environmental practices and encouraging companies to achieve the international quality standard for environmentally responsible operations. CFS operates a fleet of 1,000 lorries and each lorry produces the equivalent of its own weight in pollutants over the course of a year without the installation of expensive pollution control systems. Graham is also aware that his larger customers are looking to their distributors to become more environmentally responsible and the 'greening' of their supply chain is becoming a real issue. Unfortunately his concern with developing a company-wide environmental management strategy is not shared by his fellow managers responsible for the key distribution functions including purchasing, logistics, warehousing and transportation. They argued that time spent on corporate responsibility issues was time wasted and simply added to costs.

Graham has decided to propose the appointment of a project manager to develop and implement a company environmental strategy including the achievement of the international quality standard. The person appointed must have the necessary project management skills to see the project through to successful conclusion. You have been appointed project manager for CFS's 'environmentally aware' project.

Required:

(a) **What are the key project management skills that are necessary in achieving company-wide commitment in CFS to achieve the desired environmental strategy?** **(15 marks)**

(b) **How could pursuing a corporate environmental strategy both add to CFS's competitive advantage and be socially responsible?** **(10 marks)**

(Total: 25 marks)

42   JJG PLC

The Board of JJG plc are considering the implementation of three new computer systems.

Salary system

This will replace the existing three salaries systems with one global system. The change has been prompted partly by the lack of available record space within the existing systems, and partly by new legislation making parts of the old systems legally incorrect. The new system will be purchased 'off-the-shelf' from a specialist supplier of payroll systems and will be implemented at the end of the fiscal year.

Inventory records

Inventory records are currently maintained using third party software. The system has been in the organisation for a number of years and uses DOS as the main operating system. Although the functionality of this package is adequate for existing requirements, the software will not be compatible with the new Windows interface being introduced next year. The development and implementation of the system must be completed within 24 weeks, as the old operating system will be discontinued at this date, detailed GANTT and network charts indicate that this is an achievable target. New online inventory control equipment will be integrated into the overall operating system.

Extranet links

The directors have recognised the need to provide some form of online access to the company database, partly because of falling orders in established trading systems, and partly due to competitors providing similar systems. A recent survey of customers indicated that additional online support to help repair and maintain JJG's products would be useful. A project manager has been appointed to investigate this requirement, with the brief to start a systems analysis and prepare detailed plans. An initial budget has been allocated to the project, although there are no deadlines for a feasibility report or appropriate budget monitoring systems in place.

Required:

(a)   **Explain the main factors that affect the overall risk of failure of IT projects within organisations.** **(10 marks)**

(b)   **Evaluate, stating your reasons, the degree of risk of failure of each of these system projects.** **(15 marks)**

(Total: 25 marks)

43   LDB

Four years ago Lowlands Bank acquired Doe Bank, one of its smaller rivals. Both had relatively large local branch bank networks and the newly merged bank (now called LDB) found that it now had duplicated branches in many towns. One year after the takeover was finalised, LDB set up a project to review the branch bank network and carry out a rationalisation that aimed to cut the number of branches by at least 20% and branch employment costs by at least 10%. It was agreed that the project should be completed in two years. There were to be no compulsory staff redundancies. All branch employment savings would have to be realised through voluntary redundancy and natural wastage.

LDB appointed its operations director, Len Peters as the sponsor of the project. The designated project manager was Glenys Hopkins, an experienced project manager who had worked for Lowlands Bank for over fifteen years. The project team consisted of six employees who formerly worked for Lowlands Bank and six employees who formerly worked for Doe Bank. They were seconded full-time to the project.

Project issues and conclusion

During the project there were two major issues. The first concerned the precise terms of the voluntary redundancy arrangements. The terms of the offer were quickly specified by Len Peters. The second issue arose one year into the project and it concerned the amount of time it took to dispose of unwanted branches. The original project estimates had underestimated how long it would take to sell property the bank owned or to re-assign or terminate the leases for branches it rented. The project board overseeing the project agreed to the project manager's submission that the estimates had been too optimistic and they extended the project deadline for a further six months.

The project team completed the required changes one week before the rearranged deadline. Glenys Hopkins was able to confirm that the branch network had been cut by 23%. Six months later, in a benefits realisation review, she was also able to confirm that branch employment costs had been reduced by 12%. At a post-project review the project support office of the bank confirmed that they had changed their project estimating assumptions to reflect the experience of the project team.

Potential process initiatives

LDB is now ready to undertake three process initiatives in the Information Technology area. The IT departments and systems of the two banks are still separate. The three process initiatives under consideration are:

(1)   The integration of the two bespoke payroll systems currently operated by the two banks into one consolidated payroll system. This will save the costs of updating and maintaining two separate systems.

(2)   The updating of all personal desktop computer hardware and software to reflect contemporary technologies and the subsequent maintenance of that hardware. This will allow the desktop to be standardised and bring staff efficiency savings.

(3)   The bank has recently identified the need for a private personal banking service for wealthy customers. Processes, systems and software have to be developed to support this new service. High net worth customers have been identified by the bank as an important growth area.

The bank will consider three solution options for each initiative. These are outsourcing or software package solution or bespoke development.

Required:

(a)   **The branch rationalisation was a successful project.**

      Identify and analyse the elements of good project management that helped make the branch rationalisation project successful. (12 marks)

(b)   **The bank has identified three further desirable process initiatives (see above).**

      (i)   **Explain, using Harmon's process-strategy matrix, how the complexity and strategic importance of process initiatives can be classified.** (4 marks)

      (ii) **Recommend and justify a solution option for each of the three process initiatives.** (9 marks)

(Total: 25 marks)

44 ELASH INCORPORATED

A project team has been set up to introduce an integrated production planning and management reporting system at Elash Incorporated.

The team consists of a senior consultant from the systems software design company, Zurtoc, in the role of Project Manager, six systems analysts from Zurtoc (each of whom would lead a module design team), along with the IT Manager, the Internal Audit Manager, the Management Accountant and the Production Manager of Elash Incorporated. The Project Manager is also currently working on completion of another Zurtoc project for another organisation, which he assures Elash Incorporated will be finished by Week 8 of the Zurtoc Integrated Production System (ZIPS) project. The Project Manager has stated to the steering committee: 'The analysts don't need me to tell them what to do'.

The Project Manager and the systems analysts have produced the following plan for the project.

Project phases

Systems analysis and design (including systems development)	24 weeks	(Weeks 1–24)
Module integration	12 weeks	(Weeks 25–36)
Systems testing (*see note 1*)	5 weeks	(Weeks 37–41)
File conversion	8 weeks	(Weeks 42–49)
Changeover (direct)	1 week	(Week 50)

Note: In addition, two weeks of training are built into the programme to be carried out at the same time as systems testing and file conversion (weeks 41 and 42) and this training phase is for senior managers only: all other staff will be trained once the system goes live.

As part of the project plan the following Gannt chart was created for the project:

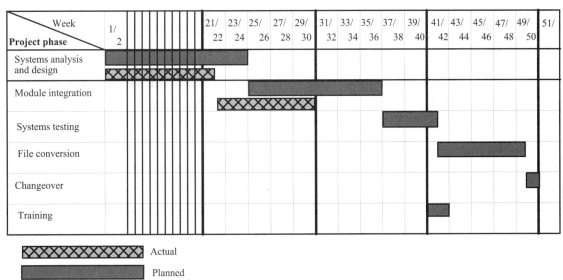

Analysis and design teams, consisting of analysts and programmers from Zurtoc, have been set up to build the individual systems modules. The analysts do not anticipate that the individual module teams will need to meet before integration begins in Week 25. Two weeks' floating contingency is built into the overall programme.

Project progression

The project commenced on schedule, and the systems analysis and design phase progressed as expected. However, there was some concern from the project team members within Elash Incorporated that there was very little co-ordination between the end-users of the existing system and the module design teams. It was also noted that the Project Manager was rarely available in the first 10 to 12 weeks, as he was busy dealing with problems on other Zurtoc jobs. In fact, he did not take over full-time responsibility for the ZIPS project until Week 16, at which point the first official project team meeting took place.

At this meeting, the IT manager of Elash Incorporated voiced his considerable concern that the module teams had not yet met to co-ordinate and discuss the design considerations prior to integration of the individual systems modules. However, the Project Manager was unconcerned: 'What's the problem? The project is on time and you have got 12 weeks built into the schedule for integration. Plenty of time.'

Module integration began early, in Week 22. Problems began to occur soon after, as it became obvious that the individual systems modules were not integrating as expected. Over the next eight weeks the module design teams continued to re-design the modules to overcome the integration problems, but most changes were not to the satisfaction of the project team members from Elash Incorporated.

The project is now in Week 30, and most of the integration phase remains incomplete. Following a crisis meeting between the project team and the steering committee, it has been decided that the IT Manager of Elash Incorporated should become the ZIPS Project Manager and that a new project plan be drawn up immediately. As the Management Accountant, you will continue to work with the project team for the remainder of the project.

Required:

(a) **Produce a Gantt chart, using the project plan data, clearly identifying the position to date together with the current forecast plan. Explain the problems with this plan and recommend changes that should be made.** **(12 marks)**

(b) **Evaluate the problems that occurred in the ZIPS project team relationships, and explain how these team relationship problems could have been reduced.** **(6 marks)**

(c) **Discuss the potential communication and team meeting problems that may occur in any complex project. Explain how communications should have been undertaken and team meetings conducted for the ZIPS project.** **(7 marks)**

(Total: 25 marks)

45 MICKEY'S KITS

Mickey's Kit Inc. designs and manufactures sports equipment and is currently positioned as the market leader in the industry. However, whilst operating in a growth market there are new competitors entering the market with innovative new product offerings which make better use of new technologies that have become available to manufacturers.

The Marketing Director, Donna Derry, is aware that to retain market leader position the company must improve its practices involved with New Product Development (NPD), and the time taken to get from the product idea to launch needs to be much quicker. She plans to take advantage of new production techniques and launch a special project aimed at copying the developments of new rivals.

The company has a functional structure with Donna Derry heading up the marketing function and the Research and Development Director, Liam Walsh, heading up the function responsible for research and product development. In addition there are separate functions for Production, Human Resources, Finance, Sales and IT.

She appointed George Peters, who has an impressive record of managing successful projects, to be project manager. However, Donna is already interfering in the management of the project and is in conflict with George. She is frustrated by the time George seems to need in the planning phase, and is irritated by his insistence on formalising the project management process. Donna is now putting pressure on George to miss out elements in the first stages of planning the project, and to get started on the new designs and product innovations.

George feels that the functional structure is impeding the company's NPD. He is proposing that the best way to manage the process is to adopt a project management approach. This will involve introducing a matrix structure and the use of cross-functional teams. However, at a recent meeting of the functional heads, Liam Walsh said that, in his experience, the potential difficulties in using a matrix structure for project management offset the benefits.

Required:

(a) **Explain the potential problems that the new project could face without good project planning.** **(15 marks)**

(b) **Describe the advantages and disadvantages for Mickey's Kits of using a matrix structure in project management work for New Product Development (NPD).** **(10 marks)**

(Total: 25 marks)

FINANCING

46 PUBLICLY FUNDED DEPARTMENT

A publicly funded department within a local administrative authority provides a health advisory service to its local community. This is not a hospital. Its function is purely advisory in respect of preventive medicine and focuses on good health promotion and prevention of accidents and illness.

In recent years, the funding for this service has been reduced in real terms, requiring greater levels of efficiency to be provided. The manager of the service has recognised the need to make economies. Despite receiving criticisms and complaints from the local administrative authority's elected representatives, the manager has reduced the level of service provision in an attempt to remain within budget. However, there has been no reduction in the staffing level which accounts for about 80% of expenditure.

Last year, an independent public audit report criticised the management of the service. The report focused on the fact that the service overspent its budget, was considered to be inefficient in its methods of delivery, and wasted resources allocated to it. The report went on to state that, according to annual performance indicator statistics, there is a decline in the numbers of people using the service. It concluded that the service was failing to operate economically, efficiently or effectively. The result of this was that the local administrative authority reduced the funding still further and gave the manager a warning that the whole service would be reviewed if there were not an improvement in this financial year. The manager has responded by making further cuts to the service, but has protected the staffing levels. It is projected that the service will remain just within its budget allocation this year.

Required:

Discuss the reasons why the service has received criticism.

Explain how the manager can improve the effectiveness and efficiency of the service while ensuring that it remains economic and within its allocated budget. **(25 marks)**

47 WOODS EDUCATIONAL INSTITUTION

(a) You are a newly appointed Finance Manager of the Woods Educational Institution that is mainly government funded, having moved from a similar post in a service company in the private sector. The objective, or mission statement, of this Institution is shown in its publicity material as: *'to achieve recognised standards of excellence in the provision of teaching and research.'*

The only financial performance measure evaluated by the government is that the Institution has to remain within cash limits. The cash allocation each year is determined by a range of non-financial measures such as the number of research publications the Institution's staff have achieved and official ratings for teaching quality.

However, almost 20% of total cash generated by the Institution is now from the provision of courses and seminars to private sector companies, using either its own or its customers' facilities. These customers are largely unconcerned about research ratings and teaching quality as they relate more to academic awards such as degrees.

The Head of the Institution aims to increase the percentage of income coming from the private sector to 50% over the next five years. She has asked you to advise on how the management team can evaluate progress towards achieving this aim as well as meeting the objective set by government for the activities it funds.

Required:

Discuss the main issues that an institution such as this has to consider when setting objectives. Advise on:

- **whether a financial objective, or objectives, could or should be determined, and**

- **whether such objective(s) should be made public.** **(9 marks)**

(b) The following is a list of financial and non-financial performance measures that were in use in your *previous company*:

FINANCIAL	NON-FINANCIAL
Value added	Customer satisfaction
Profitability	Competitive position
Return on investment	Market share

Required:

Choose *two of each* type of measure, explain their purpose and advise on how they could be used by the Educational Institution over the next five years to assess how it is meeting the Head of the Institution's aims. **(16 marks)**

(Total: 25 marks)

48   POTATO-TO-GO INC

Potato-to-go Inc ('PTG'), a quoted company, owns and operates a chain of fast food outlets in Europe selling baked potatoes with a range of healthy fillings.

Company background

Since being set up in 1983, PTG has expanded rapidly through organic growth and the acquisition of some smaller competing companies. The expansion was originally financed from retained profits but the company was floated in 1994 to enable larger sums to be raised.

51% of PTG's ordinary share capital is currently owned by the founding Edwards family (who also control the Board of Directors), 35% by large institutions, and the remaining shares by private investors.

The company's five-year record can be summarised as follows:

Years to 31 December	20X2	20X3	20X4	20X5	20X6
Turnover ($m)	370	440	450	420	400
Profit before tax ($m)	120	150	110	66	42
Number of outlets	690	740	770	790	800

Summary income statement for 20X6

	$m	$m
Turnover		400
Operating costs	350	
Interest paid	8	
		(358)
Profit before tax		42
Taxation		(14)
Profit after tax		28
Dividends		20
Retained profit		8

Summary statement of financial position (balance sheet) at 31 December 20X6

	$m
Non-current assets	180
Net current assets	60
	240
Less 10% loan stock 20X7	(80)
	160
Ordinary $1 shares	24
Reserves	136
	160

Note: PTG's P/E ratio at the end of 20X6 was 9 compared to an industry average of 10.

Current issues facing the firm

(1)   Redemption of loan stock

Internally generated funds will be insufficient to enable the loan stock to be redeemed at the end of 20X7 and no sinking fund has been set up. Further finance is thus required. The Edwards family have indicated that they are unwilling to subscribe further equity.

(2)   Overseas expansion

The directors of PTG believe that their current markets have reached saturation and that there is a potential new market in North America. An initial strategy would be to open 50 outlets early in 20X8 in New York and New England. The total investment required is estimated to be $130m.

Required:

Prepare briefing notes on the following:

(a)	**PTG's financial performance.**	**(7 marks)**
(b)	**The proposed expansion in the USA.**	**(8 marks)**
(c)	**Financing the overseas expansion.**	**(10 marks)**

(Total: 25 marks)

49   DAVID SILVESTER

David Silvester is the founder and owner of a recently formed gift packaging company, Gift Designs Ltd. David has spotted an opportunity for a new type of gift packaging. This uses a new process to make waterproof cardboard and then shapes and cuts the card in such a way to produce a container or vase for holding cut flowers. The containers can be stored flat and in bulk and then simply squeezed to create the flowerpot into which flowers and water are then put. The potential market for the product is huge. In the UK, in hospitals alone there are 200,000 bunches of flowers bought each year for patients. David's innovative product does away with the need for hospitals to provide and store glass vases. The paper vases are simple, safe and hygienic. He has also identified two other potential markets. Firstly, the market for fresh flowers supplied by florists, and secondly, the corporate gift market where clients such as car dealers present a new owner with an expensive bunch of flowers when the customer takes delivery of a new car. The vase can be printed using a customer's design and logo, and creates an opportunity for real differentiation and impact at sales conferences and other high profile PR events.

David anticipates a rapid growth in Gift Designs as its products become known and appreciated. The key question is how quickly the company should grow and the types of funding needed to support its growth and development. The initial financial demands of the business have been quite modest but David has estimated that the business needs $500k to support its development over the next two years and is uncertain as to the types of funding best suited to a new business as it looks to grow rapidly. He understands that business risk and financial risk are not the same thing and is looking for advice on how he should organise the funding of the business. He is also aware of the need to avoid reliance on friends and family for funding and to broaden the financial support for the business. Clearly the funding required would also be affected by the activities David decides to carry out himself and those activities better provided by external suppliers.

Required:

(a) Provide David with a short report on the key issues he should take into account when developing a strategy for funding Gift Designs' growth and development.

(15 marks)

(b) Using models where appropriate, what are likely to be the critical success factors (CSFs) as the business grows and develops?

(10 marks)

(Total: 25 marks)

50 X PLC

X plc manufactures specialist insulating products that are used in both residential and commercial buildings. One of the products, Product W, is made using two different raw materials and two types of labour. The company operates a standard absorption costing system and is now preparing its budgets for the next four quarters. The following information has been identified for Product W:

Sales

Selling price	$220 per unit

Sales demand

Quarter 1	2,250 units
Quarter 2	2,050 units
Quarter 3	1,650 units
Quarter 4	2,050 units
Quarter 5	1,250 units
Quarter 6	2,050 units

Costs

Materials

A	5 kgs per unit @ $4 per kg
B	3 kgs per unit @ $7 per kg

Labour

Skilled	4 hours per unit @ $15 per hour
Semi-skilled	6 hours per unit @ $9 per hour
Annual overheads	$280,000
	40% of these overheads are fixed and the remainder varies with total labour hours. Fixed overheads are absorbed on a unit basis.

Inventory holding policy	
Closing inventory of finished goods	30% of the following quarter's sales demand
Closing inventory of materials	45% of the following quarter's materials usage

The management team is concerned that X plc has recently faced increasing competition in the marketplace for Product W. As a consequence there have been issues concerning the availability and costs of the specialised materials and employees needed to manufacture Product W, and there is concern that these might cause problems in the current budget-setting process.

Required:

(a)   Prepare the following budgets for each quarter for X plc:

(i)   Production budget in units

(ii)   Raw material purchases budget in kgs and value for Material B.   **(5 marks)**

(b)   X plc has just been informed that Material A may be in short supply during the year for which it is preparing budgets. Discuss the impact this will have on budget preparation and other areas of X plc.   **(5 marks)**

(c)   X plc currently uses incremental budgeting. Explain how Zero-Based Budgeting could overcome the problems that might be faced as a result of the continued use of the current system.   **(5 marks)**

(d)   Briefly explain how linear regression analysis can be used to forecast sales and briefly discuss whether it would be a suitable method for X plc to use.   **(5 marks)**

The same company is also considering investing in one of three marketing campaigns to increase its profitability. All three marketing campaigns have a life of five years, require the same initial investment and have no residual value. The company has already evaluated the marketing campaigns taking into consideration the range of possible outcomes that could result from the investment. A summary of the calculations is shown below:

Marketing campaign	J	K	L
Expected net present value	$400,000	$800,000	$400,000
Standard deviation of net present value	$35,000	$105,000	$105,000

(e)   Explain

(i)   the meaning of the data shown above.

(ii)   how the data may be used by the company when choosing between alternative investments.   **(5 marks)**

(Total: 25 marks)

51   SATELLITE NAVIGATION SYSTEMS

Satellite Navigation Systems Limited installs complex satellite navigation systems in cars, at a very large national depot. The standard cost of an installation is shown below. The budgeted volume is 1,000 units installed each month. The operations manager is responsible for three departments, namely: purchasing, fitting and quality control. Satellite Navigation Systems Limited purchases navigation systems and other equipment from different suppliers, and most items are imported. The fitting of different systems takes differing amounts of time, but the differences are not more than 25% from the average, so a standard labour time is applied.

Standard cost of installation of one navigation system

	$	Quantity	Price ($)
Materials	400	1 unit	400
Labour	320	20 hours	16
Variable overheads	140	20 hours	7
Fixed overheads	300	20 hours	15
Total standard cost	1,160		

The Operations Department has gathered the following information over the last few months. There are significant difficulties in retaining skilled staff. Many have left for similar but better paid jobs and as a result there is a high labour turnover. Exchange rates have moved and commentators have argued this will make exports cheaper, but Satellite Navigation Systems Limited has no exports and has not benefited. Some of the fitters have complained that one large batch of systems did not have the correct adapters and would not fit certain cars, but this was not apparent until fitting was attempted. Rent, rates, insurance and computing facilities have risen in price noticeably.

The financial results for September to December are shown below.

Operating statement for Satellite Navigation Systems Limited for September to December

	September $	October $	November $	December $	4 months $
Standard cost of actual output	1,276,000	1,276,000	1,102,000	1,044,000	4,698,000
Variances materials					
Price	5,505 F	3,354 F	9,520 A	10,340 A	11,001 A
Usage	400 A	7,200 A	800 A	16,000 A	24,400 A
Labour rate	4,200 A	5,500 A	23,100 A	24,000 A	56,800 A
Efficiency	16,000 F	0	32,000 A	32,000 A	48,000 A

	September $	October $	November $	December $	4 months $
Variable overheads					
Expenditure	7,000 A	2,000 A	2,000 F	0	7,000 A
Efficiency	7,000 F	0	14,000 A	14,000 A	21,000 A
Fixed overheads					
Expenditure	5,000 A	10,000 A	20,000 A	20,000 A	55,000 A
Volume	30,000 F	30,000 F	15,000 A	30,000 A	15,000 F
Actual costs	1,234,095	1,267,346	1,214,420	1,190,340	4,906,201

A = adverse variance   F = favourable variance

Required:

Prepare a report to the operations manager of Satellite Navigation Systems Limited commenting on the performance of the company for the four months to 31 December. State probable causes for the key issues you have included in your report and state the further information that would be helpful in assessing the performance of the company.

(15 marks)

52   ARLAND BANK

Arland Bank is reviewing the bank account it offers to its business customers and the charges it makes for routine transactions (for example paying into the account, writing cheques, making electronic payments and transfers). Currently, the bank's charges to its business customers are £0.60 per routine transaction. The bank pays interest to the customer at 0.1% per year on any balance in the account.

According to the bank's records, there are currently one million business customers. Each customer makes one thousand routine transactions each year; 45% of business customers maintain an average balance of £2,000 in their account. The accounts of the other 55% of business customers are overdrawn with an average overdraft balance of £4,000. Interest on overdrawn accounts is charged at 20% per year.

In addition, the bank has a number of savings account customers which, together with the bank's business customers, result in a balance of net funds that are invested by the bank and yield an annual return by 3% per year.

The bank is concerned about a growing tendency for its competitors to provide routine transactions free of charge to their business customers. As a result the bank is considering two account options:

Account Option One

An account that charges the business customer a fixed fee of £10 per month, with no further charges for any routine transactions. Interest would be paid to the business customer at 0.5% per year on any balances in the account. The bank expects that if it adopts this charging structure, it will increase the number of business customers by 5% from its present level.

Account Option Two

An account that does not charge the customer for any routine transactions, but pays no interest on any balances in the account. The bank expects that if it adopts this charging structure, this will increase the number of business customers by 10% from its present level. The bank does not expect the profile of new business customers to be different from existing business customers in terms of the balances in their accounts or the number of routine transactions they make. Interest will continue to be charged at 20% per year on overdrawn accounts. The bank does not expect that either of these options will result in any changes to its existing staffing or other resources.

The bank also expects that if it takes no action and continues with its existing bank account that the number of business customers will fall by 20%.

Required:

Recommend which course of action the bank should take by preparing calculations to show the annual profits from:

(i)   continuing with the existing bank account

(ii)   each of the two account options described above.   **(12 marks)**

53 OFFMAT INC

Offmat Inc manufactures many different products. Each product has a Product Manager. The company's management information system produces cost reports for each of the products that are made.

An analysis of previous reports has revealed the following information for Product X:

Units produced	Average variable cost per unit	Total product-specific costs	Head office costs
	$	$000	$000
5,000	160	500	300
10,000	150	500	600
15,000	140	800	900
20,000	140	800	1,200
25,000	155	1,100	1,500
30,000	170	1,100	1,800

Required:

(a) **Explain, for each of the three costs in the above table, possible reasons for the cost/volume relationships.** **(6 marks)**

Budgeted and actual information for Product Y for the previous period was as follows:

	Budget	Actual
Output	80,000 units	76,000 units
Direct materials	480,000 kg	430,000 kg
Direct labour	200,000 hours	196,000 hours
	$	$
Direct materials	960,000	924,500
Direct labour	1,600,000	1,626,800
Fixed production overheads	640,000	590,000

The company uses standard absorption costing.

Required:

(b) **Produce a statement that reconciles the standard and actual total costs for the previous period's output and shows the variances in as much detail as possible.** **(11 marks)**

(Total: 17 marks)

54 COOLFREEZE

CoolFreeze construct refrigeration systems for supermarkets, food processing plants, warehouses and other industrial premises. It has a sales forecasting committee consisting of the company's sales manager, procurement manager, production manager and the head of administration. The committee produces annual sales forecasts for the company which they review quarterly. Historically, these forecasts have been reasonably accurate.

In the second quarter of 2009 they revised/produced their estimates for the next four quarters. The predicted unit sales volume and prices are given in figure one.

Figure one: Sales forecast 2009–2010

Year	Quarter	Predicted sales	Predicted sales price	Revenue
2009	3	81	$1000	$81,000
	4	69	$1000	$69,000
2010	1	62	$1000	$62,000
	2	83	$1000	$83,000

At the meeting that agreed this forecast the sales manager expressed some doubts about the figures. "My team are telling me that it is very tough out there. Companies are not replacing old equipment or constructing new plants. Furthermore, cheaper foreign products are becoming available – undercutting our prices by 10%". Despite these reservations, the sales manager agreed the sales forecasts produced by the committee.

Actual sales performance

The actual sales for the four projected quarters were as follows (figure two).

Figure two: Actual sales 2009–2010

Year	Quarter	Predicted sales	Actual sales
2009	3	81	82
	4	69	68
2010	1	62	61
	2	83	50

The sudden drop in quarter 2 sales caused consternation in the boardroom, particularly as it was a quarter when high demand and profits were anticipated. An analysis of the quarter 2 trading is shown in figure three.

The managing director of CoolFreeze has called you in to review the forecasting model used by the sales forecasting team. "It must be very flawed to go so badly wrong. I have the feeling that the model is not based on a well-accepted approach". He has obtained a copy of the spreadsheet used by the sales forecasting team (see figure four) to help you in your analysis.

The managing director recognises that the actual quarter 2 performance has to be analysed against the budgeted one. "I think everyone here has made mistakes – the sales manager, procurement manager, production manager, administration manager. They all have to take responsibility. We are in this together and now we must pull together to get out of this mess".

Figure three: Analysis of quarter 2 trading; budget and actual

Quarter 2 – 2010	Budget	Actual
Units	83	50
Revenue	$83,000.00	$45,000.00
Raw materials	($29,050.00)	($15,000.00)
Labour	($26,975.00)	($15,750.00)
Fixed overheads	($18,000.00)	($18,000.00)
Operating profit	$8,975.00	($3,750.00)

Figure four: Forecasting spreadsheet

A	B	C	D	E	F	G	H	I

Part 1

Year	Quarter	Units		Trend	Variation	Seasonal	Residual	Check
2006	1	56						
	2	70						
	3	74	524	65.50	-18.50	-17.35	-1.15	74.00
	4	60	538	67.25	-7.25	-4.73	-2.52	60.00
2007	1	60	554	69.25	-9.25	-11.65	-2.40	60.00
	2	80	570	71.25	-18.75	-19.02	-0.27	80.00
	3	80	582	72.75	-17.25	-17.35	-0.10	80.00
	4	70	586	73.25	-3.25	-4.73	-1.48	70.00
2008	1	62	588	73.50	-11.50	-11.65	-0.15	62.00
	2	82	588	73.50	-18.50	-19.02	-0.52	82.00
	3	80	586	73.25	-16.75	-17.35	-0.60	80.00
	4	70	586	73.25	-3.25	-4.73	-1.48	70.00
2009	1	60	590	73.75	-13.75	-11.65	-2.10	60.00
	2	84	590	73.75	-10.25	-19.02	-1.23	84.00
	3	82						
	4	68						

Part 2

	1	2	3	4	
2006		28.50	-7.25		
2007	-9.25	18.75	27.25	-3.25	
2008	-11.50	18.50	26.75	-3.25	
2009	-13.75	10.25			
Total	-34.50	27.50	22.50	-13.75	
Average	-11.50	19.17	27.50	-4.58	0.58
Adj	-10.15	10.15	20.15	-10.15	
NewAvg	-11.65	19.02	27.35	-4.73	0.00

Forecast

2009	3	73.50	-17.35	81
	4	73.50	-4.73	69
2010	1	73.65	-11.65	62
	2	74.00	-19.02	83

Required:

Write a briefing paper for the managing director that:

(a) Explains and evaluates the spreadsheet used by the sales forecasting team. **(12 marks)**

(b) Analyses the quarter 2 – 2010 performance of CoolFreeze. **(13 marks)**

(Total: 25 marks)

STRATEGY AND PEOPLE

55   JOB DESIGN

Harriet has just been appointed to take charge of part of an accounting department concerned with processing information from the operating division of a large company.

Based on her previous experience she has determined that the running costs of the department are too high, due to absenteeism, lateness, low productivity and time spent in correcting errors.

Investigation of the design of the jobs in the department reveals that each employee is trained in a task which is made as simple as possible. The equipment used is maintained by a service department. Strict discipline ensures that clerks do not carry on conversations during working hours, and tasks are performed in exactly the order and method laid down.

Harriet has decided that performance can be improved by changing the job design.

Assume that Harriet's superiors approve the changes, that correct training is provided and that resistance by the clerks to change is properly overcome.

Required:

(a)   Discuss the likely consequences for organisations and employees of designing jobs which are repetitive, routine and lacking in significant skill requirements. **(10 marks)**

(b)   Differentiate between job enrichment and job enlargement and give examples of these techniques in action.   **(4 marks)**

(c)   Comment on the benefits of job design.   **(5 marks)**

(d)   Explain four problems which may make it difficult to change the design of such jobs.   **(6 marks)**

(Total: 25 marks)

56   GRUMIT

David Omega is the finance and administration (F&A) manager of Grumit, a company manufacturing and supplying water filters to the domestic market. Grumit not only manufactures water filters but imports a wide range of filters and associated products from its overseas parent company. All products require installation and after sales service which is carried out by Grumit's trained service engineers.

The numbers employed by Grumit are:

Management and associated administrative and support staff   45

Manufacturing facility   220

Marketing, sales and distribution   75

Installation and after-sales service engineers   65

Trade unions are recognised only in the manufacturing facility – with one for skilled workers, and another for unskilled workers. There is no recognised union in any other part of Grumit, although the majority of field service engineers are thought to be members of an unrecognised union.

For a few years now the manufacturing facility at Grumit has been struggling to break even. Grumit's managing director has just returned from a visit to the parent company and informs David that the manufacturing facility is to be closed as it has not been possible to reach the required levels of quality and productivity. In addition management of the parent company believe that Grumit as a whole is over-staffed in relation to the volume of sales. Management has been given 12 months to produce significant improvements. The manufacturing facility is to be closed as soon as possible and, in future, all products will be imported from the parent company. There will be a need to restructure marketing and also for the retraining of most service engineers to equip them to deal with the new product range.

Grumit's managing director has not told any other employees of the directive from the parent company and is very anxious that the prospective changes are managed so as to minimise loss of morale and keep staff motivated. As F&A also has responsibility for personnel matters, David has been asked to provide advice on three issues: letting people know about the changes, the redundancies arising from the closure of the manufacturing plant and the plans for restructuring and retraining.

Required:

(c) **Recommend and describe a suitable human resource management approach to deal with the situation at Grumit and advise on policy and procedures in relation to the three issues of communication, redundancy and restructuring/retraining.**

(15 marks)

(b) **Examine the lessons which are available to Grumit from other organisations' experiences in the successful management of change.** **(10 marks)**

(Total: 25 marks)

57 ROCK BOTTOM *Walk in the footsteps of a top tutor*

This scenario summarises the development of a company called Rock Bottom through three phases, from its founding in 1965 to 20X8 when it ceased trading.

Phase 1 (1965–1988)

In 1965 customers usually purchased branded electrical goods, largely produced by well-established domestic companies, from general stores that stocked a wide range of household products. However, in that year, a recent university graduate, Rick Hein, established his first shop specialising solely in the sale of electrical goods. In contrast to the general stores, Rick Hein's shop predominantly sold imported Japanese products which were smaller, more reliable and more sophisticated than the products of domestic competitors. Rick Hein quickly established a chain of shops, staffed by young people who understood the capabilities of the products they were selling. He backed this up with national advertising in the press, an innovation at the time for such a specialist shop. He branded his shops as 'Rock Bottom', a name which specifically referred to his cheap prices, but also alluded to the growing importance of rock music and its influence on product sales. In 1969, 80% of sales were of music centres, turntables, amplifiers and speakers, bought by the newly affluent young. Rock Bottom began increasingly to specialise in selling audio equipment.

Hein also developed a high public profile. He dressed unconventionally and performed a number of outrageous stunts that publicised his company. He also encouraged the managers of his stores to be equally outrageous. He rewarded their individuality with high salaries, generous bonus schemes and autonomy. Many of the shops were extremely successful, making their managers (and some of their staff) relatively wealthy people.

However, by 1980 the profitability of the Rock Bottom shops began to decline significantly. Direct competitors using a similar approach had emerged, including specialist sections in the large general stores that had initially failed to react to the challenge of Rock Bottom. The buying public now expected its electrical products to be cheap and reliable. Hein himself became less flamboyant and toned down his appearance and actions to satisfy the banks who were becoming an increasingly important source of the finance required to expand and support his chain of shops.

Phase 2 (1989–20X2)

In 1988 Hein considered changing the Rock Bottom shops into a franchise, inviting managers to buy their own shops (which at this time were still profitable) and pursuing expansion though opening new shops with franchisees from outside the company. However, instead, he floated the company on the country's stock exchange. He used some of the capital raised to expand the business. However, he also sold shares to help him throw the 'party of a lifetime' and to purchase expensive goods and gifts for his family. Hein became Chairman and Chief Executive Officer (CEO) of the newly quoted company, but over the next thirteen years his relationship with his board and shareholders became increasingly difficult. Gradually new financial controls and reporting systems were put in b3place. Most of the established managers left as controls became more centralised and formal. The company's performance was solid but unspectacular. Hein complained that 'business was not fun anymore'. The company was legally required to publish directors' salaries in its annual report and the generous salary package enjoyed by the Chairman and CEO increasingly became an issue and it dominated the 20X2 Annual General Meeting (AGM). Hein was embarrassed by its publication and the discussion it led to in the national media. He felt that it was an infringement of his privacy and civil liberties.

Phase 3 (20X3–20X8)

In 20X3 Hein found the substantial private equity investment necessary to take Rock Bottom private again. He also used all of his personal fortune to help re-acquire the company from the shareholders. He celebrated 'freeing Rock Bottom from its shackles' by throwing a large celebration party. Celebrities were flown in from all over the world to attend. However, most of the new generation of store managers found Hein's style to be too loose and unfocused. He became rude and angry about their lack of entrepreneurial spirit. Furthermore, changes in products and how they were purchased meant that fewer people bought conventional audio products from specialist shops. The reliability of these products now meant that they were replaced relatively infrequently. Hein, belatedly, started to consider selling via an Internet site. Turnover and profitability plummeted. In 20X7 Hein again considered franchising the company, but he realised that this was unlikely to be successful. In early 20X8 the company ceased trading and Hein himself, now increasingly vilified and attacked by the press, filed for personal bankruptcy.

Required:

(a) Analyse the reasons for Rock Bottom's success or failure in each of the three phases identified in the scenario. Evaluate how Rick Hein's leadership style contributed to the success or failure of each phase. **(18 marks)**

(b) Rick Hein considered franchising the Rock Bottom brand at two points in its history – 1988 and 20X7.

Explain the key factors that would have made franchising Rock Bottom feasible in 1988, but would have made it 'unlikely to be successful' in 20X7. (7 marks)

(Total: 25 marks)

58 NATIONAL COLLEGE

Judy Sodhi is in her first teaching year at the National College, a private college offering short courses in accounting, auditing and management. In her first year Judy has primarily taught the Certificate in Managerial Finance. This is a three-day short course which ends in an externally set examination, marked and invigilated by staff employed by the Institute of Managerial Finance (IMF). The IMF also defines the syllabus, the length of the course and accredits colleges to run the course. There are no pre-conditions for candidates who wish to attend the course. Last year Judy ran the course 20 times with an average of nine students on each running of the course. At the end of each course every student has to complete a post-course evaluation questionnaire. Judy does not see these questionnaires and has received no feedback about her performance.

As the college is a virtual organisation using serviced training rooms, Judy rarely sees her manager Blake Jones. However, he contacted her recently to suggest that they should conduct her first appraisal and a date and time was agreed. Blake explained that 'it would be just a general chat looking at how the year had gone. We need to do one to satisfy the college and the IMF'. The time of the appraisal was set for 3.00 pm, finishing at 5.00 pm.

The appraisal did start with a general discussion. Blake outlined the plans of the organisation and his own promotion hopes. Judy was surprised to see that Blake was not following any standard list of questions or noting down any of the answers she made. She told him that one of her main problems was the numeracy level of some of the candidates. She recognised that the course had no pre-conditions, 'but it does require some basic mathematical skills that some of our candidates just do not have'.

After listening to Judy for a while Blake produced a statistical summary of the feedback questionnaires from the courses she had run in the last year. He said that the organisation expected its lecturers to attain an acceptable result in all 10 questions given in the post-course questionnaire. An acceptable result 'is that 90% of all candidates said that they were 'satisfied or very satisfied' with key aspects of the course'. Judy had achieved this on seven of the questions but specifically failed on the following performance measures;

- Percentage of candidates who felt that the course was relevant to their current job – *only 65% of your candidates felt that the course was relevant to their current job.*

- Percentage of candidates who passed the examination – *only 88.88% of your candidates passed the examination.*

- Percentage of candidates who felt that the course pace was satisfactory – *only 75% of your candidates felt that the pace of the course was satisfactory.*

After expressing her surprise that she had not been given this information before, she immediately returned to the problem of numeracy skills. 'As I told you' she said 'some of these students lack the mathematical skills to pass. That's not my fault, it is yours – you should not have let them on the course in the first place. You are just filling the places to make money'.

After a heated discussion, Blake then turned to the 'last thing on my agenda'. He explained that it was only college policy to give pay increases to lecturers who had achieved 90% in all 10 questions, so there would be no increase for Judy next year. However, he also needed to discuss her workload for next year. He produced a spreadsheet and had just begun to discuss course planning and locations in great detail when his mobile phone rang. 'I am sorry, Judy, I have to collect the children from school – I must go. I will write down your planned course assignments and e-mail them to you. I think that was a very useful discussion. Overall we are very happy with you. See you at the end-of-year party, and of course at next year's appraisal.' He left at 4.30 pm.

Required:

(a)   This requirement is no longer examinable.   **(15 marks)**

(b)   Explain the concept and purpose of competency frameworks for organisations, assessing their potential use at the National College and the Institute of Managerial Finance.   **(10 marks)**

(Total: 25 marks)

59   GLOBAL IMAGING

Global Imaging is a fast growing high tech company with some 100 employees which aims to double in size over the next three years. The company was set up as a spin out company by two research professors from a major university hospital who now act as joint managing directors. They are likely to leave the company once the growth objective is achieved.

Global Imaging's products are sophisticated imaging devices facing a growing demand from the defence and health industries. These two markets are very different in terms of customer requirements, but share a related technology. Over 90% of sales revenue is from exports and the current strategic plan anticipates a foreign manufacturing plant being set up during the existing three-year strategic plan. Current management positions are largely filled by staff who joined in the early years of the company and reflect the heavy reliance on research and development to generate the products to grow the business. Further growth will require additional staff in all parts of the business, particularly in manufacturing and sales and marketing.

Paul Simpson, HR manager at Global Imaging is annoyed. This stems from the fact that HR is the one management function not involved in the strategic planning process shaping the future growth and direction of the company. He feels trapped in a role traditionally given to HR specialists, that of simply reacting to the staffing needs brought about by strategic decisions taken by other parts of the business. He feels even more threatened by one of the joint managing directors arguing that HR issues should be the responsibility of the line managers and not a specialist HR staff function. Even worse, Paul has become aware of the increasing number of companies looking to outsource some or all of their HR activities.

Paul wants to develop a convincing case why HR should not only be retained as a core function in Global Imaging's activities, but also be directly involved in the development of the current growth strategy.

Required:

Paul has asked you to prepare a short report to present to Global Imaging's board of directors:

(a)   Write a short report for Paul Simpson on the way a Human Resource Plan could link effectively with Global Imaging's growth strategy.   **(15 marks)**

(b)   What advantages and disadvantages might result from outsourcing Global Imaging's HR function?   **(10 marks)**

(Total: 25 marks)

MANAGING STRATEGIC CHANGE

60   TC COMPANY

TC Company was, until about 20 years ago, a national telephone company that enjoyed monopoly status, but a decision to deregulate by the government means that it is now exposed to aggressive competition from new suppliers, in particular:

* Telephone services being supplied by cable TV companies; and

* Mobile phone services.

TC Company did set up a mobile phone network, but it was late into the market with relatively poor marketing skills and never achieved a profitable market share. After a few years the company sold its mobile phone undertaking to a larger mobile phone operator. More recently, the company sought additional income through the provision of broadband services. Although the company has been successful in attracting many subscribers to these services, it found that VOIP (voice over internet protocol) suppliers, such as Skype, had developed technology that would allow broadband customers to hold telephone conversations for no additional call costs. As customers increasingly choose mobiles, broadband and VOIP, TC Company's is finding it difficult to maintain its call revenues.

TC Company also, even after 20 years, still suffers from its history as a monopoly provider; its bureaucratic culture and structure means that it tends to be slower to respond to market changes than the new entrants. The high proportion of telephone engineers who belong to the telecoms trade union does not help this situation. When earlier this year, TC Company announced job cuts, the trade union members voted for industrial action that lasted for several weeks and cost the Company millions in lost revenue.

Additional, recent innovations being marketed by the company include:

* The introduction of a service that allows people on the move to access the Internet at selected public venues using a wireless enabled laptop.

* Related to the above service, technology which will allow mobile phone users to make cheap VOIP calls.

This installation of the required wireless access points does, however, require training in new skills and the engineers required to undertake this training have threatened strike action in support of a large pay increase to compensate them for using the new skills required for the job.

Required:

(a)   **Identify the internal and external triggers for change in the strategy and operations of TC Company. Discuss the difficulties that the Company is likely to experience in introducing the change programme.**   **(9 marks)**

(b)   **Evaluate the success of TC Company in managing the change process to date. By application of any model of change management, explain how TC Company might go about managing change in the future.**   **(10 marks)**

(c)   **Assuming that the need to transform TC Company was identified and championed by senior management, describe some of the political mechanisms that they might have used to deal with any reluctance of middle managers to resist change.**

(6 marks)

(Total: 25 marks)

61   PSI

Introduction

Retail pharmacies supply branded medicinal products, such as headache and cold remedies, as well as medicines prescribed by doctors. Customers expect both types of product to be immediately available and so this demands efficient purchasing and stock control in each pharmacy. The retail pharmacy industry is increasingly concentrated in a small number of nationwide pharmacy chains, although independent pharmacies continue to survive. The pharmacy chains are increasingly encouraging their customers to order medicinal products online and the doctors are being encouraged to electronically send their prescriptions to the pharmacy so that they can be prepared ready for the patient to collect.

Pharmacy Systems International (PSI)

Pharmacy Systems International (PSI) is a privately owned software company which has successfully developed and sold a specialised software package meeting the specific needs of retail pharmacies. PSI's stated objective is to be a 'highly skilled professional company providing quality software services to the retail pharmacy industry'. Over the last three years PSI has experienced gradual growth in turnover, profitability and market share (see Figure 1).

Figure 1: PSI Financial information

	20X7	20X6	20X5
Turnover ($000)	11,700	10,760	10,350
Profits ($000) (pre-tax)	975	945	875
Estimated market share	26%	24%	23%
Number of employees	120	117	115

PSI has three directors, each of whom has a significant ownership stake in the business. The chief executive is a natural entrepreneur with a past record of identifying opportunities and taking the necessary risks to exploit them. In the last three years he has curbed his natural enthusiasm for growth as PSI has consolidated its position in the market place. However, he now feels the time is right to expand the business to a size and profitability that makes PSI an attractive acquisition target and enables the directors to realise their investment in the company. He has a natural ally in the sales and marketing director and both feel that PSI needs to find new national and international markets to fuel its growth. The software development director, however, does not share the chief executive's enthusiasm for this expansion.

The chief executive has proposed that growth can best be achieved by developing a generic software package which can be used by the wider, general retail industry. His plan is for the company to take the current software package and take out any specific references to the pharmaceutical industry. This generic package could then be extended and configured for other retail sectors. The pharmaceutical package would be retained but it would be perceived and marketed as a specialised implementation of the new generic package.

This proposed change in strategic direction is strongly resisted by the software development director. He and his team of software developers are under constant pressure to meet the demands of the existing retail pharmacy customers. On-line ordering of medicinal products and electronic despatch of prescriptions are just two examples of the constant pressure PSI is under from their retail customers to continuously update its software package to enable the pharmacies to implement technical innovations that improve customer service.

[handwritten: phamacy → general.]

Ideally, the software development director would like to acquire further resources to develop a more standardised software package for their current customers. He is particularly annoyed by PSI's salesmen continually committing the company to producing a customised software solution for each customer and promising delivery dates that the software delivery team struggle to meet. Frequently, the software contains faults that require expensive and time consuming maintenance. Consequently, PSI is being increasingly criticised by customers. A recent user group conference expressed considerable dissatisfaction with the quality of the PSI package and doubted the company's ability to meet the published deadline for a new release of the software.

Required:

[handwritten: From Directors' point of view transfomational]

(a) The proposal to develop and sell a software package for the retail industry represents a major change in strategy for PSI. Analyse the nature, scope and type of this proposed strategic change for PSI. *[handwritten: Balogun & Hope Hailey]* **(10 marks)**

(b) The success of any attempt at managing change will be dependent on the context in which that change takes place. Identify and analyse, using an appropriate model, the internal contextual features that could influence the success or failure of the chief executive's proposed strategic change for PSI. **(15 marks)**

[handwritten: Triger for using Balogun & Hope Hailey.]

(Total: 25 marks)

62 STRATEGIES

Honda is a leading manufacturer of motorbikes. The company is credited with identifying and targeting an untapped market for small 50cc bikes in the US, enabling it to expand, overwhelm European competition and severely damage US bike manufacturers. By the late 60s, Honda had more than 60% of the US market. But this occurred by accident.

On entering this market, Honda had wanted to compete with the larger European and American bikes of 250ccs and over. These bikes had a defined market, and were sold through dedicated motorbike dealerships. Disaster struck when Honda's larger machines developed faults – they had not been designed for the hard wear and tear imposed by US motorcyclists. Honda had to recall them. Up until then Honda had made little effort to sell their small 50cc motorbikes – their staff rode them on errands around Los Angeles. Sports goods shops and ordinary bicycle and department stores had expressed an interest, but Honda did not want to confuse its image in its 'target' market of men who bought the larger bikes.

The faults in Honda's larger machines meant that reluctantly, Honda had to sell the small 50cc bikes just to raise money. They proved very popular with people who would never have bought motorbikes before. Eventually the company adopted this new market with enthusiasm with the slogan: 'You meet the nicest people on a Honda'. The strategy had emerged, against managers' conscious intentions, but they eventually responded to the new situation.

Required:

(a) Explain why the actual strategy pursued by a company over a three- to five-year period may diverge from the deliberate strategy that the company initiated at the outset of that period. **(13 marks)**

(b) Differentiate between the rational model of strategy making and the concept of limited or 'bounded' rationality. **(12 marks)**

(Total: 25 marks)

Section 2

SCENARIO-BASED QUESTIONS

Internal Analysis.

63 OCEANIA NATIONAL AIRLINES (ONA) *Walk in the footsteps of a top tutor*

The island of Oceania attracts thousands of tourists every year. They come to enjoy the beaches, the climate and to explore the architecture and history of this ancient island. Oceania is also an important trading nation in the region and it enjoys close economic links with neighbouring countries. Oceania has four main airports and until ten years ago had two airlines, one based in the west (OceaniaAir) and one based in the east (Transport Oceania) of the island. However, ten years ago these two airlines merged into one airline – Oceania National Airlines (ONA) with the intention of exploiting the booming growth in business and leisure travel to and from Oceania.

Market sectors

convenient flight.

Market Strength.

ONA serves two main sectors. The first sector is a network of routes to the major cities of neighbouring countries. ONA management refer to this as the regional sector. The average flight time in this sector is one and a half hours and most flights are timed to allow business people to arrive in time to attend a meeting and then to return to their homes in the evening. Twenty five major cities are served in the regional sector with, on average, three return flights per day. There is also significant leisure travel, with many families visiting relatives in the region. The second sector is what ONA management refer to as the international sector. This is a network of flights to continental capitals. The average flight time in this sector is four hours. These flights attract both business and leisure travellers. The leisure travellers are primarily holiday-makers from the continent. Twenty cities are served in this sector with, on average, one return flight per day to each city.

Image, service and employment

⌐ Brand. Loyalty.

Make-up branding

ONA is the airline of choice for most of the citizens of Oceania. A recent survey suggested that 90% of people preferred to travel ONA for regional flights and 70% preferred to travel with ONA for international flights. 85% of the respondents were proud of their airline and felt that it projected a positive image of Oceania. The company also has an excellent safety record, with no fatal accident recorded since the merging of the airlines ten years ago.

Business Charge Premium

The customer service of ONA has also been recognised by the airline industry itself. In 20X5 it was voted Regional Airline of the Year by the International Passenger Group (IPG) and one year later the IPG awarded the ONA catering department the prestigious Golden Bowl as provider of the best airline food in the world.

may also be weakness get togethe

The courtesy and motivation of its employees (mainly Oceanic residents) is recognised throughout the region. 95% of ONA employees belong to recognised trade unions. ONA is perceived as an excellent employer. It pays above industry average salaries, offers excellent benefits (such as free health care) and has a generous non-contributory pension scheme. In 20X4 ONA employed 5400 people, rising to 5600 in 20X5 and 5800 in 20X6.

weakness.

Fleet

Fleet details are given in Table 1. Nineteen of the Boeing 737s were originally in the fleet of OceaniaAir. Boeing 737s are primarily used in the international sector. Twenty-three of the Airbus A320s were originally part of the Transport Oceania fleet. Airbuses are primarily used in the regional sector. ONA also used three Embraer RJ145 jets in the regional sector.

Table 1: Fleet details

	Boeing 737	Airbus A320	Embraer RJ145
Total aircraft in service			
20X6	21	27	3
20X5	21	27	3
20X4	20	26	2
Capacity (passengers)	147	149	50
Introduced	October 1991	November 1988	January 1999
Average age	12.1 years	12.9 years	6.5 years
Utilisation (hrs per day)	8.70	7.41	7.50

Performance

Since 20X4 ONA has begun to experience significant competition from 'no frills' low-cost budget airlines, particularly in the international sector. Established continental operators now each offer, on average, three low fares flights to Oceania every day. 'No frills' low-cost budget airlines are also having some impact on the regional sector. A number of very small airlines (some with only one aircraft) have been established in some regional capitals and a few of these are offering low-cost flights to Oceania. A recent survey for ONA showed that its average international fare was double that of its low-cost competitors. Some of the key operational statistics for 20X6 are summarised in Table 2.

Table 2: Key operational statistics for ONA in 20X6

	Regional	International	Low-cost competitor average
Contribution to revenue ($m)			
Passenger	400	280	Not applicable
Cargo	35	15	Not applicable
Passenger load factor			
Standard class	73%	67%	87%
Business class	90%	74%	75%
Average annual pilot salary	$106,700	$112,500	$96,500
Source of revenue			
On-line sales	40%	60%	< 84%
Direct sales	10%	5%	12%
Commission sales	50%	35%	> 4%
Average age of aircraft	See Table 1		4.5 years
Utilisation (hrs per day)	See Table 1		9.10 *can fly more times.*

ONA have made a number of operational changes in the last few years. Their website, for example, now allows passengers to book over the internet and to either have their tickets posted to them or to pick them up at the airport prior to travelling. Special promotional fares are also available for customers who book on-line. However, the website does not currently allow passengers to check-in on-line, a facility provided by some competitors. Furthermore, as Table 2 shows, a large percentage of sales are still commission sales made through travel agents. Direct sales are those sales made over the telephone or at the airport itself.

Most leisure travellers pay standard or economy fares and travel in the standard class section of the plane. Although many business travellers also travel in standard class, some of them choose to travel business class for which they pay a price premium.

In the last three years, the financial performance of ONA has not matched its operational success. The main financial indicators have been extracted and are presented in Table 3. In a period (20X4–20X6) when world-wide passenger air travel revenue increased by 12% (and revenue from air travel to Oceania by 15%) and cargo revenue by 10%, ONA only recorded a 4.6% increase in passenger revenue.

Table 3: Extracted Financial Information (All figures in $m)

Extracted from the Statement of Financial Position (Balance Sheet)

		20X6	20X5	20X4
Non-current assets				
Property, plant and equipment		788	785	775
Other non-current assets		60	56	64
	Total	848	841	839
Current assets				
Inventories		8	7	7
Trade receivables		68	71	69
Cash and cash equivalents		289	291	299
	Total	365	369	375
Total assets		**1,213**	**1,210**	**1,214**
Total shareholders' equity		250	259	264
Non-current liabilities				
Interest bearing long-term loans		310	325	335
Employee benefit obligations		180	178	170
Other provisions		126	145	143
Total non-current liabilities		616	648	648
Current liabilities				
Trade payables		282	265	255
Current tax payable		9	12	12
Other current liabilities		56	26	35
Total current liabilities		347	303	302
Total equity and liabilities		**1,213**	**1,210**	**1,214**

Extracted from the income statement

		20X6	20X5	20X4
Revenue				
Passenger		680	675	650
Cargo		50	48	45
Other revenue		119	112	115
	Total	849	835	810
Cost of sales				
Purchases		535	525	510
Gross profit		314	310	300
Wages and salaries		215	198	187
Directors' salaries		17	16	15
Interest payable		22	21	18
	Total	254	235	220

	20X6	20X5	20X4
Net Profit before tax	60	75	80
Tax Expense	18	23	24
Net Profit after tax	42	52	56

Future strategy

The management team at ONA are keen to develop a strategy to address the airline's financial and operational weaknesses. One suggestion has been to re-position ONA itself as a 'no frills' low-cost budget airline. However, this has been angrily dismissed by the CEO as likely to lead 'to an unnecessary and bloody revolution that could cause the death of the airline itself'.

Required:

(a)   Using the information provided in the scenario, <u>evaluate the strengths and weaknesses of ONA</u> and their <u>impact on its performance</u>. Please note that opportunities and threats are NOT required in your evaluation.   **(20 marks)**

(b)   The CEO of Oceania National Airways (ONA) has already strongly rejected the re-positioning of ONA as a 'no frills' low-cost budget airline.

    (i)   Explain the key features of a 'no frills' low-cost strategy. ✓   **(4 marks)**

    (ii)   Analyse why moving to a 'no frills' low-cost strategy would be <u>inappropriate for ONA</u>.

    Note: Requirement (b) (ii) includes 3 professional marks   **(16 marks)**

(c)   Identify and evaluate other strategic options ONA could consider to address the airline's current financial and operational weaknesses.

    Note: Requirement (c) includes 2 professional marks   **(10 marks)**

          (Total: 50 marks)

64   THE NATIONAL MUSEUM   *Walk in the footsteps of a top tutor*

Introduction

The National Museum (NM) was established in 1857 to house collections of art, textiles and metal ware for the nation. It remains in its original building which is itself of architectural importance. Unfortunately, the passage of time has meant that the condition of the building has deteriorated and so it requires continual repair and maintenance. Alterations have also been made to ensure that the building complies with the <u>disability access</u> and <u>health and safety laws</u> of the country. However, these alterations have been criticised as being unsympathetic and out of character with the rest of the building. The building is in a previously affluent area of the capital city. However, what were once large middle-class family houses have now become multi-occupied apartments and the socio-economic structure of the area has radically changed. The area also suffers from an increasing crime rate. A visitor to the museum was recently assaulted whilst waiting for a bus to take her home. The assault was reported in both local and national newspapers.

funding based on collection (exp.)

Thirty years ago, the government identified museums that held significant Heritage Collections. These are collections that are deemed to be very significant to the country. Three Heritage Collections were identified at the NM, a figure that has risen to seven in the intervening years as the museum has acquired new items.

Funding and structure

The NM is currently 90% funded by direct grants from government. The rest of its income comes from a nominal admission charge and from private sponsorship of exhibitions. The direct funding from the government is based on a number of factors, but the number of Heritage Collections held by the museum is a significant funding influence. The Board of Trustees of the NM divide the museum's income between departments roughly on the basis of the previous year's budget plus an inflation percentage. The division of money between departments is heavily influenced by the Heritage Collections. Departments with Heritage Collections tend to be allocated a larger budget. The budgets for 20X8 and 20X9 are shown in Figure 1.

[handwritten margin notes: strategy as exp ✓]

Collection Sections	Number of Heritage Collections	Budget ($000s) 20X8	Budget ($000s) 20X9
Architecture	2	120.00	125.00
Art	2	135.00	140.00
Metalwork	1	37.50	39.00
Glass		23.00	24.00
Textiles	1	45.00	47.50
Ceramics		35.00	36.00
Furniture		30.00	31.50
Print & Books		35.00	36.50
Photography		15.00	15.50
Fashion		10.00	10.50
Jewellery	1	50.00	52.50
Sculpture		25.00	26.00
Administration		60.50	63.00
Total		621.00	647.00

[handwritten margin note: exp.]

The head of each collection section is an important position and enjoys many privileges, including a large office, a special section heads' dining room and a dedicated personal assistant (PA). The heads of sections which have 'Heritage Collections' also hold the title of professor from the National University.

The departmental structure of the NM (see Figure 2) is largely built around the twelve main sections of the collection. These sections are grouped into three departments, each of which has a Director. The Board of Directors is made up of the three directors of these departments, together with the Director of Administration and the Director General. The museum is a charity run by a Board of Trustees. There are currently eight trustees, two of whom have been recently appointed by the government. The other six trustees are people well-known and respected in academic fields relevant to the museum's collections.

[handwritten margin notes: experience weak; What's Changing; successful in the past]

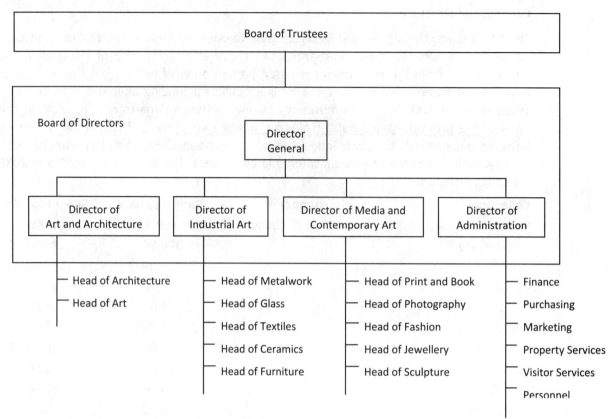

Figure 2: Current Organisational Structure

Government change

One year ago, a new national government was elected. The newly appointed Minister for Culture implemented the government's election manifesto commitment to make museums more self-funding. The minister has declared that in five year's time the museum must cover 60% of its own costs and only 40% will be directly funded by government. This change in funding will gradually be phased in over the next five years. The 40% government grant will be linked to the museum achieving specified targets for disability access, social inclusion and electronic commerce and access. The government is committed to increasing museum attendance by lower socio-economic classes and younger people so that they are more aware of their heritage. Furthermore, it also wishes to give increasing access to museum exhibits to disabled people who cannot physically visit the museum site. The government have asked all museums to produce a strategy document showing how they intend to meet these financial, accessibility and technological objectives. The government's opposition has, since the election, also agreed that the reliance of museums on government funding should be reduced.

Traditionally, the NM has provided administrative support for sections and departments, grouped together beneath a Director of Administration. The role of the Director General has been a part-time post. However, the funding changes introduced by the government and the need to produce a strategy document, has spurred the Board of Trustees to appoint a full-time Director General from the private sector. The trustees felt they needed private industry expertise to develop and implement a strategy to achieve the government's objectives. The new Director General was previously the CEO of a major chain of supermarkets.

Director General's proposal

The new Director General has produced a strategic planning document showing how the NM intends to meet the government's objectives. Proposals in this document include:

(1) Allocating budgets (from 20Y0) to sections based on visitor popularity. The most visited collections will receive the most money. The idea is to stimulate sections to come up with innovative ideas that will attract more visitors to the museum. Visitor numbers have been declining (see Figure 3) since 20X4.

Visitor Numbers (000s)	20X7	20X6	20X5	20X4
Age 17 or less	10	12	15	15
Age 18–22	5	8	12	10
Age 23–30	10	15	20	20
Age 31–45	20	20	18	25
Age 46–59	35	35	30	30
Age 60 or more	40	35	35	30
Total	120	125	130	130

Figure 3: Visitor numbers 20X4–20X7

Designing (2) Increasing entrance charges to increase income, but to make entry free to pensioners, students, children and people receiving government benefit payments.

(3) Removing the head of sections' dining room and turning this into a restaurant for visitors. An increase in income from catering is also proposed in the document.

(4) Removing the head of sections' personal assistants and introducing a support staff pool to reduce administrative costs.

(5) Increasing the display of exhibits. Only 10% of the museum's collection is open to the public. The rest is held in storage.

(6) Increasing commercial income from selling posters, postcards and other souvenirs.

The Director General has also suggested a major re-structuring of the organisation as:

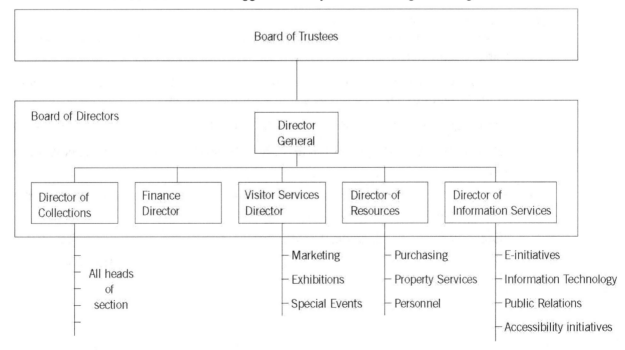

Figure 4: **Proposed Organisational Structure**

Reaction to the proposals

Employees have reacted furiously to the Director General's suggestions. The idea of linking budgets to visitor numbers has been greeted with dismay by the Director of Art and Architecture. 'This is a dreadful idea and confuses popularity with historical significance. As previous governments have realised, what is important is the value of the collection. Heritage Collections recognise this significance by putting the nation's interests before those of an undiscerning public. As far as I am concerned, if they want to see fashion, they can look in the high street shops. Unlike fashion, great art and architecture remains.' The Director of Art and Architecture and the two professors who hold the Head of Architecture and Head of Art posts have also lobbied individual members of the Board of Trustees with their concerns about the Director General's proposals.

The Director of Industrial Arts and the Director of Media and Contemporary Art have contacted powerful figures in both television and the press and as a result a number of articles and letters critical of the Director General's proposals have appeared. A recent television programme called 'Strife at the NM' also featured interviews with various heads of collections criticising the proposed changes. They were particularly critical of the lack of consultation; 'these proposals have been produced with no input from museum staff. They have been handed down from on high by an ex-grocer', said one anonymous contributor.

Eventually, the criticism of staff and their lack of cooperation prompted the Director General to ask the Board of Trustees to publicly back him. However, only the two trustees appointed by the government were prepared to do so. Consequently, the Director General resigned. This has prompted an angry response from the government which has now threatened to cut the museum's funding dramatically next year and to change the composition of the Board of Trustees so that the majority of trustees are appointed directly by the government. The Minister of Culture has asked the museum to develop and recommend a new strategy within one month.

Required:

(a) Analyse the macro-environment of the National Museum using a PESTEL analysis.
(20 marks)

(b) The failure of the Director General's strategy has been explained by one of the trustees as 'a failure to understand our organisational culture; the way we do things around here'.

Assess the underlying organisational cultural issues that would explain the failure of the Director General's strategy at the National Museum.

Note: requirement (b) includes 2 professional marks. (20 marks)

(c) Johnson, Scholes and Whittington identify three strategy lenses; design, experience and ideas. *3 ways split, strategy ideas*

Examine the different insights each of these lenses gives to understanding the process of strategy development at the National Museum.

Note: requirement (c) includes 2 professional marks. (10 marks)

(Total: 50 marks)

65 PLAYWELL LTD

(**Note**: Assume that 'now' is June 20X7.)

Alexander Simmonds is the founder and Managing Director of Playwell Ltd, a privately owned UK company specialising in making educational toys for young children and for children with special educational needs. These toys are robust and of simple construction made from high quality materials, mainly wood, acquired from a local supplier. The main selling lines are building blocks of different shapes, sizes and colours, and toy trains and carriages (with no mechanical or electrical components). These simple toys are intended to stimulate the imagination of young children and to help them develop their visual and co-ordination abilities.

Alexander started the company over 20 years ago. He had initially made toys in his garage for his own children. He soon was persuaded to expand his activities and he had a ready demand for his products from friends and neighbours. Eighteen years ago he was made redundant from his full-time job and he decided to put his redundancy money into setting up his own company. To his surprise the demand for his products grew at a faster rate than he had expected. There was an obvious gap in the market for simple and high quality toys. Young children did not appear to want the complex and high technology products which were expensively promoted on television and in magazines. The early success of the company was helped by being a low-cost operation. At the start, Alexander's sales were made on a direct basis, using no intermediaries. He promoted his products within a 50-mile radius using local newspapers; orders were shipped directly to the customers. Additionally the supplier of the materials provided Playwell with extended and low cost credit until the final payment was made to the company for the completed toys. This arrangement has continued to the present time.

For the first five years sales revenue grew from a figure of $30,000 to almost $700,000. Net profit after tax was about 12% and Alexander's policy had been to reinvest these profits into the business. Thirteen years ago he had moved out of his garage and had taken over a small factory in an industrial development area in a nearby town. Skilled labour was relatively easy to acquire. There was high unemployment in the area as a result of recent factory closures. Thirteen years ago Alexander employed nearly 30 people in a range of jobs from design, manufacturing, sales, invoicing and distribution. Labour turnover was, unsurprisingly, very low. The workers were very loyal and Alexander paid them competitive wages and provided them with above-average benefits, particularly attractive in an area where unemployment was still high. The firm continued to grow at a rate of about 20% a year between 10 and 15 years ago. Although most of the sales were still marketed directly to the customer a significant proportion of sales were now made through one retailer who had a group of 15 shops. This retailer sells products for young children, ranging from clothing, cots and prams as well as toys, and even currently, in 20X7, this retailer still relies on Playwell for a significant amount of its toy purchases. About 40% of the UK sales (excluding those to the special educational needs market) are currently made to this retailer. The target market for these shops is professional and middle-class parents who generally value quality above price.

As in any growing organisation Alexander now found himself moving away from a hands-on operation and becoming more concerned with future growth and strategy. By the end of 20X2 Alexander decided to look at another market to generate increased growth in sales revenue. Although sales revenue was now almost $1.5 million a year and there were nearly 50 employees, the company now had the capacity to double its output. Fixed costs, including labour, accounted for 60% of total costs and any future increase in sales revenue ought to generate improved profit margins. This was important if the company was to prosper and grow and provide security for the workers in an area where employment opportunities were limited. The company was then looking for sales revenue to increase by about 30% a year. However, such an increase could not be easily funded out of retained earnings. Playwell's past performance and conservative financial record was sufficiently attractive for the company's bank to be more than willing to extend its credit lines so as to provide the necessary working capital.

The new area that Playwell was interested in was the development of toys designed for the 'special education needs' market. This term is generally used to refer to the education of children who have one or more physical, mental or emotional disabilities. Toys such as shaped building blocks, sponge balls, pegboards and three-dimensional puzzles can all help children with disabilities to improve their visual perception, spatial awareness, memory and muscle control. In addition there were other products such as balance boards and beams and discs, all made from high quality wood, which can help to co-ordinate mental and muscular activities. However it was likely that the method of marketing and distribution might have to be adapted. The new market segment was much more easily identifiable and accessible.

Databases of parents of children with special educational needs were readily available and it was possible to access the parents of these children via the specialist schools which these children attended. These schools were enthusiastic about Playwell's products but they alone could not support this new range of products. In fact part of Playwell's strategy was to distribute its products to these schools at very low prices in the hope that parents would then purchase these specialist toys for home use. This proved less easy than had been anticipated. Firstly, parents of these children with special educational needs incurred many other expenses such as the additional costs of care. Furthermore because of the increased care which these children usually required, one of the parents often had to stay at home or could only take on part-time work. Consequently the parents' discretionary income was significantly less. In addition, whereas the company had hoped that the teachers would recommend its products to the parents, it became apparent that teachers were not doing so, being worried that the parents would not have the expertise to use some of the equipment properly. As a result the revenues from this market were not as large as had been anticipated, particularly as the products' placement in the schools were seen initially as loss-leaders. Nevertheless sales of Playwell's core products (the non-specialist toys) were still gradually increasing (8% a year), but the momentum of earlier years was now not being maintained. By the beginning of 20X5 Alexander decided that any future market expansion should be focused overseas, although he still intended to persevere with the 'special education' venture.

The company had acquired a good reputation within the United Kingdom and was operating in a growing niche market, in which Playwell was a significant participant. However, the company now decided that exports were to be the favoured means of growth. In an effort to avoid high risks Alexander decided to concentrate his activities in Western Europe. There were a number of advantages to this strategy – the purchasing processes of both parents and children were thought to be similar to that of the domestic market, transportation costs were likely to be lower than sales to America or Asia, and being part of the European Union there would be no trade barriers. However after an initial period of success Playwell discovered that sales were not as easily achieved as they had been in the UK. First the major European countries of France, Germany and Italy were at different stages in the business cycle to the UK. While the British economy was growing the continental ones were suffering from recession. Consequently the demand for products such as toys was not buoyant. Furthermore high interest rates within the UK resulted in a high level of the pound sterling against the Euro and other continental currencies, so making any exporting from the UK an expensive option. It appeared that price was now becoming a serious consideration in the customer's purchasing decision, particularly for a company with no strong overseas reputation. (Table 1 provides financial data for Playwell over the past few years.)

Alexander had now made two efforts to expand his business, neither of which could be judged as successful and he was now anxious to determine the future progress of the company.

Table 1

	20X2	20X3	20X4	20X5	20X6	20X7 (Forecast)
	$m	$m	$m	$m	$m	$m
Sales revenue to general toy retailers – UK	1.50	1.62	1.75	1.89	2.04	2.20
Cost of sales	0.53	0.57	0.62	0.67	0.72	0.78
UK Special needs toys sales revenue		0.30	0.30	0.25	0.25	0.15
Cost of sales		0.14	0.14	0.11	0.11	0.07
Overseas sales revenue				0.50	0.55	0.55
Cost of sales				0.30	0.33	0.33
Total sales revenue	1.50	1.92	2.05	2.64	2.84	2.90
Fixed costs	0.65	0.95	1.00	1.25	1.40	1.40

Required:

(a) Alexander Simmonds appears to be the only person who is determining the objectives and strategic direction of Playwell Ltd. Identify any other parties who could have an interest in the success of this company. How might their goals be different to those of Alexander and to what extent would these differences be relevant? (10 marks)

(b) You have been retained as a business consultant by Alexander to provide impartial advice as to the future strategy that the company should adopt. Given its relative failure in its last two ventures provide a briefing paper recommending a strategy that Playwell should pursue in the next two to three years. You should support your recommendation with appropriate financial analysis and the use of suitable analytical models. (20 marks)

(c) The exporting venture appears to have failed because of an inadequate knowledge of the market. Identify the main types of information concerning the company's business environment you would consider to be essential before committing the company to an export strategy, giving reasons to justify your selection. (10 marks)

(d) It has been argued that strategy can emerge rather than be the result of deliberate planning. Explain this statement and consider what factors might influence whether a strategy should be emergent or planned. (10 marks)

(Total: 50 marks)

66 AUTOFONE

Introduction

AutoFone was established almost twenty years ago at the beginning of the mobile telephone boom. It was formed by a dynamic Chief Executive Officer (CEO) who still remains a major shareholder of the company.

AutoFone brought two new concepts to the market. Firstly, it established retail shops where customers could go and handle the products and discuss mobile phone options with trained sales people. Before AutoFone, all mobile telephones were sold through the customer directly contacting the telephone network provider (like conventional home land line services) and were generally aimed at business rather than leisure users. Secondly, AutoFone sold products and services from all the four major network providers licensed by the government to provide telecommunications services in the country. Previously, customers could only choose products and services from within one network provider's range. AutoFone allowed customers to choose products and services across the range of the four providers and reflected this in the company's motto 'ethical advice: the customer's choice'.

In 1990, AutoFone signed a thirty-year supply contract with each provider. Although, in retrospect, these deals were on commercially favourable terms for AutoFone, the network providers were happy to agree these deals because none of them believed that mobile telephones could be successfully sold through retail shops. However, speaking in 20X3, the managing director of one of the networks suggested 'that AutoFone had got away with incredible profit margins' when they signed the deals in 1990. The four network providers themselves had re-signed twenty-five year licence deals with the government in 1995. Under the terms of these deals, licences will be restricted to the four current providers until their renewal date of 2020.

Retail shops Division

AutoFone currently has 415 shops around the country. To reduce costs most shops are on the edge of (but not in) the main shopping area of the town they serve. It is usual for AutoFone to sign a fifty-year shop lease in return for low initial annual rental and a rent-free period at the start of the lease while the company fits out the shop to reflect AutoFone's corporate image. In 1997, AutoFone floated on the country's stock market to assist the funding of further shops and so continue its organic growth. The national coverage of its shops, the publicity generated by its CEO and a successful television advertising campaign culminated, in 20X5, with it being rated by consumers as one of the top 20 brands in the country.

The CEO of AutoFone established the retail shops along, in his words, 'entrepreneurial lines'. He regards each shop as an independent business, having to achieve a profit target but without being closely monitored within these targets. He believes that the company is 'about providing opportunity to its employees, providing them with autonomy and responsibility to achieve their goals. It is not about monitoring them every hour of the day, stifling creativity and enthusiasm.' To support this approach, sales staff are given a relatively low basic salary with a substantial element of profit-related pay linked to the profit targets of the shop. Commission is also paid to sales staff who successfully sell mobile phone insurance to the customer. Each shop is relatively small, usually employing three or four people.

In recent years the CEO has been increasingly involved in television, sports promotion and charity work. At AutoFone he has established a strategic planning committee of senior headquarters managers to develop and implement the company's business strategy. This committee includes the two longest serving board directors. The strategy still continues to have at its heart the central business idea of giving independent and impartial advice to customers so that they can choose the best equipment and network for their needs.

Marketplace trends

Since AutoFone's arrival into the market, two significant trends have emerged:

(i)   The licensed network providers have opened their own retail stores, usually in city centres. AutoFone has reacted to the opening of these shops by stressing AutoFone's independence and impartiality. Only at AutoFone can impartial advice be received on all four competing networks and their supporting services. The CEO now refers to this as 'our central business idea' and, as well as being core to their strategy, it is heavily emphasised in all their promotional material.

(ii)   Mobile phones have become more sophisticated. Many now offer integrated cameras, mp3 players, web browsers and e-mail facilities. AutoFone offers these products in both its shops and through its Internet operation. Mobile phones are either purchased outright or provided on monthly contracts. The minimum contract period with the network provider is usually twelve months.

AutoFone has itself established its own Internet division, AFDirect, as a separate division within the group. It has also established an insurance division (AFInsure) offering insurance to cover loss or damage to mobile phones purchased from the company. Revenue earned from each division, analysed by the age of the customer, is shown in table 1.

Table 1: Analysis of AutoFone Sales: 20X7 (all figures in $m)

| Division | Age of customer | | | | | |
	Under 15	15–25	26–40	41–60	Over 60	Total
AutoFone retail shops	5	90	60	120	65	340
AFDirect	0	15	20	8	2	45
Total sales of mobile phones						385
AFInsure	0	1	3	7	3	14
Group total						399

Analysts agree that growth in the mobile phone business is slowing down and this is supported by the figures given in table 2 showing revenue from sales (both retail and Internet) for AutoFone and its competitors, the four licensed network providers, for the period 20X3–20X7.

Table 2: Market Analysis (all figures in $m) of sales of mobile phones

Company	20X7	20X6	20X5	20X4	20X3
AutoFone	385	377	367	340	*320*
NetAG	350	348	345	340	305
09Net	390	388	380	365	350
PhoneLine	315	315	315	305	300
NetConnex	295	295	294	290	285
Total	1,735	1,723	1,701	1,640	1,560

However, while the AFDirect and AFInsure divisions are prospering, there are increasing problems in the retail shops division. Profitability has been declining over the last few years (see table 3) and this has had a demoralising effect on shop employees. One shop manager commented, in his exit interview, that the profit targets were unattainable in the current market. 'They might have been appropriate in 1997, but they are not in 20X7.' Staff are particularly demoralised by spending time explaining a particular product to a customer who then leaves the shop and buys the product cheaper on the Internet. They have to wait for it to be delivered (usually two or three days) but they are prepared to do this to gain the lower prices offered by the direct Internet-based companies, including AFDirect. It is also increasingly common for customers who have bought from AFDirect to take their phones to AutoFone's retail shops for support and service. This activity is not recognised in the shop employee's reward package.

AutoFone's central city branch

Despite the overall decline in the profitability of the shops, one branch has continually met or exceeded its profitability targets and is held up by the CEO as an example of best practice – proof that the company's approach to mobile phone selling can still be profitably applied. This is the central city branch in one of the country's most prosperous cities.

The CEO arranged for three members of the strategic planning committee to visit the shop, posing as customers, to investigate the reasons for the shop's success. They found the staff very friendly and helpful. However, they also found that they were guided towards products and services which had higher profit margins. Further investigation showed this always to be the case and so customers were sold products which were profitable to the shop, rather than those best suited to the customer's needs. On receiving this information, AutoFone's board concluded that this was unethical as it compromised their central business idea which stressed impartial advice to guide the 'customer's choice'. The manager of the shop was reprimanded and asked to adhere to company policy. He resigned soon afterwards, followed by his two assistants. The shop is currently run by temporary staff and profitability has significantly dropped.

Future strategy

The two longest serving directors on the strategic planning committee are increasingly concerned about the company's decline in profitability (see table 3). They have written an internal paper suggesting that the retail division should be sold off and that AutoFone should re-position itself as an on-line retailer of phones. They believe that the retail shops business model is no longer appropriate. They argue that a company concentrating solely on Internet sales and insurance would be a 'smaller but more profitable and focused' business. The CEO is strongly opposed to this suggestion because it was the shop-based approach to selling mobile phones that formed the original business model of the company. He has a strong emotional attachment to the retail business. The two directors claim that this attachment is clouding his judgement and hence he is unable to see the logic of an 'economically justifiable exit from the retail business'.

Table 3: Extracted Financial Information for AutoFone (retail shops division only)

Extracted Financial Information (all figures in $m)

Extracted from the Statement of Financial Position (Balance Sheet)

	20X7	20X6	20X5	20X4	20X3
Total non-current assets	143	140	134	128	123
Current assets:					
Inventories	345	340	335	320	298
Trade receivables	1,386	1,258	1,216	1,174	1,120
Cash and cash equivalents	345	375	390	400	414
Total current assets	**2,076**	**1,973**	**1,941**	**1,894**	**1,832**

	20X7	20X6	20X5	20X4	20X3
Total assets	2,219	2,113	2,075	2,022	1,955
Total shareholder's equity	150	155	160	165	169
Non-current liabilities:					
Interest bearing long-term loans	55	50	45	40	35
Other provisions	16	15	13	13	10
Total non-current liabilities	71	65	58	53	45
Total current liabilities	1,998	1,893	1,857	1,804	1,741
Total equity and liabilities	2,219	2,113	2,075	2,022	1,955

Extracted from the Income Statement

	20X7	20X6	20X5	20X4	20X3
Revenue	340	337	332	320	305
Cost of Sales	250	252	230	220	205
Gross Profit	90	85	102	100	100
Wages & Salaries	39	38	37	35	33
Other expenses	40	38	35	30	30
Interest payable	4	4	3	3	3
Total	83	80	75	68	66
Net Profit before tax	7	5	27	32	34
Tax	2	3	5	4	4
Net Profit after tax	**5**	**2**	**22**	**28**	**30**

Extracted from annual reports

	20X7	20X6	20X5	20X4	20X3
Number of employees	1,400	1,375	1,325	1,300	1,275

Required:

(a) Using an appropriate model or models, analyse the competitive environment of AutoFone's retail shops division. Note: requirement (a) includes 2 professional marks. **(20 marks)**

(b) AutoFone's CEO is anxious to develop a rational and well argued case for retaining the retail shops division.

Write a briefing paper for the CEO to submit to the strategy planning committee explaining why the retail shops division should continue to form a key part of AutoFone's future strategy.

Note: Requirement (b) includes 3 professional marks. **(15 marks)**

(c) This requirement is no longer examinable. **(15 marks)**

(Total: 50 marks)

67 WET

Introduction

Arcadia is a country with great mineral wealth and a hard-working, well-educated population. It has recently enjoyed sustained economic growth generated by the expansion of its manufacturing industry. The population has grown as well and, as a result, agricultural output has increased to satisfy this population, with much previously marginal land converted to arable and pasture land. However, after 10 years of sustained economic growth the country, in 20X9, began to experience economic problems. Gross Domestic Product (GDP) has declined for three successive quarters and there is increasing unemployment. Surveys have shown that wages are stagnant and retail sales are falling. There are also increasing problems with servicing both personal and business debt leading to business bankruptcy and homelessness.

The climate of the country is also changing, becoming drier and windier. Last year, for the first time, the government had to ration water supply to domestic homes.

The formation of WET

In 20X2, the environmental campaigner Zohail Abbas published a book on the Wetlands of Arcadia. The Wetlands of Arcadia are areas of natural habitat made up of land that is saturated with moisture, such as a swamp, marsh or bog. Dr Abbas' book chronicled the systematic destruction of the wetlands due to population growth, increased economic development and climate change. Water had been progressively drained from the wetlands to provide land for farming and to provide water for the increasing population and industry of the country. Wetlands also provide an important habitat for wildlife. Dr Abbas showed that in the period from 1970 to 2000, there had been a dramatic decline in birds, mammals and fish dependent upon the wetland habitat. Some species had become extinct.

In 20X3, Dr Abbas formed the WEtland Trust (WET), with the aim of preserving, restoring and managing wetlands in Arcadia. Since its formation, the Trust has acquired the four remaining wetland sites left in the country. The Trust's work is funded through donations and membership fees. Donations are one-off contributions. Membership is through an annual subscription which gives members the right to visit the wetlands. Each wetland site is managed by volunteers who provide access and guidance to members. The wetlands are not currently open to the general public. Dr Abbas' work on the wetlands has brought him to the attention of the Arcadian public and he is now a popular television presenter. WET is also a strong brand, recognised by 85% of Arcadians in a recent green consumer survey.

GiftHelp

WET is a registered charity. Charities within Arcadia have to be registered with the Commission of Charities which regulates charities within the country. The number of charities has increased significantly in the last few years leading to widespread criticism from established charities, politicians and the public, who believe that many of these charities have been formed to exploit taxation advantages. Dr Abbas is a vociferous critic, particularly after the Commission of Charities gave permission for the establishment of a rival wetland charity (WWTFT) despite the fact that all wetlands in Arcadia are under WET's control. WWTFT promised to create new wetlands artificially in Arcadia. They have so far only raised $90,000 of the $151,000,000 required for a pilot site. Dr Abbas was part of a group that lobbied the government for the reform of the Commission of Charities, but the government has rejected their advice.

The government of Arcadia has recently changed the rules on charity taxation. Previously, once the charity's accounts had been audited, the government paid the charity a sum of 20% of the total value of donations and membership fees. This reflected the income tax the donor would have paid on the amount they had given to the charity. However, the government has now declared that this is unfair as not all donations or membership fees are from Arcadian taxpayers or from people in Arcadia who actually pay tax. Consequently, in the future, charities will have to prove that a donation or membership fee was from an Arcadian tax payer. Only donations or fees supported by this proof will receive the 20%, so called GiftHelp, refund. Research and evidence from other countries suggests that 30% of donors will not give the GiftHelp details required and so the charity will not be able to reclaim tax from these donors. An analysis of WET's income for 20X8 is given in Figure 1 and an analysis of income for all charities is given in Figure 2. Research has also shown that 55% of members and 85% of donors also give money to other charities.

Figure 1 – WET's income sources; year 20X8

	Members	Donors
Arcadian Taxpayers	$650,000	$100,000
Arcadian Non-taxpayers	$100,000	$50,000
Non-Arcadian	$50,000	$50,000
Total	$800,000	$200,000

Figure 2 – Income for all Arcadian charities; year 20X8 (in $millions)

	Amount donated to charity
Health charities	775.0
Social Care charities	275.5
International charities	149.8
Environmental charities (including WET)	45.6

WET 20X3–20X9

WET was originally a vehicle for promoting the vision and ideology of Dr Abbas. Volunteers were recruited to manage and administer the wetland sites and the number of members gradually increased (see Figure 3). Many of these volunteers have become acknowledged experts in wetlands and their knowledge and experience is valued by members. However, as the charity expanded a number of issues emerged.

1   Administrative costs rose at a faster rate than subscriptions and donations. Administrative staff are all full-time paid employees of the charity. However, despite an increase in staff numbers, there is a substantial backlog of cleared applications in the Membership Department which have not yet been entered into the membership computer system. The membership computer system is one of the systems used to support administration. However, the functionality of this software is relatively restricted and cumbersome and there have been complaints about its accuracy. For example, members claim that renewal reminders are often sent out to people who have already paid and that members who should have received renewal invoices have never received them. As a result 'we seem to be wasting money and losing members'.

2   Members have become increasingly frustrated by their limited access to the wetlands and many wish to participate more in determining the policies of the organisation. They feel that the wetland sites should also have better facilities, such as toilets and concealed positions for bird watching. There were increasing criticisms of Dr Abbas' domineering style and cavalier disregard for the members. Membership is currently falling and very little money is spent on sales and marketing to arrest this fall.

3   Volunteers have also become disgruntled with Dr Abbas' management style. They feel patronised and undervalued. The number of volunteers is declining (see Figure 3) which in itself is reducing the access of members to the wetlands. A recent decision not to pay travelling expenses to volunteers led to further resignations.

Figure 3 – Membership and volunteer statistics WET 20X2–20X9

	20X2	20X3	20X4	20X5	20X6	20X7	20X8	20X9
Members	12,000	14,000	15,000	20,000	22,000	25,000	23,000	20,000
Volunteers	30	35	35	45	50	52	50	40

At the 20X9 Annual General Meeting (AGM) Dr Abbas stood down and announced the appointment of a new Chief Executive Officer (CEO). Dr Abbas admitted in an emotional resignation speech that he had not sufficiently taken into account the views of members, donors or volunteers. 'It is a matter of deep regret that I spent more time focusing on wetlands rather than people'. He was made honorary president of WET in recognition of his work in establishing and expanding the charity.

The new CEO, Sheila Jenkins, wishes to pursue a more inclusive strategy, and immediately set about consulting the membership and voluntary staff about what they expected from WET. The two clearest messages that came from this consultation exercise were that:

- Members wanted much better access to wetlands and they were more interested in the wildlife that used the wetlands (particularly the birds) than the wetlands sites themselves. This was not a view shared by Dr Abbas who wanted the wetlands preserved for their own sake.

- Volunteers wished to be much more involved in the running of the organisation and wanted to be treated by management in a way that recognised their voluntary commitment.

System review

Sheila Jenkins is particularly keen to improve the technology that supports WET. She has stated that the better acquisition and management of members, volunteers and donors is an important objective of WET. WET's current website is very rudimentary, but she sees 'e-mail and website technology as facilitating the acquisition, retention and satisfaction of our customers' needs. And by customers, I mean both prospective and existing members, volunteers and donors of WET.' She also wishes to gain increased revenue from each member and donor.

The current membership renewal process has come under instant review and it is shown in the swim lane diagram (flowchart) of Figure 4. A narrative to support this diagram is given below.

Membership renewal process

One month before the date of membership renewal, the computer system (Membership System) sends a renewal invoice to a current (not lapsed) member giving subscription details and asking for payment. A copy of this invoice is sent to the Membership Department who file it away. Approximately 80% of members decide to renew and send their payment (either by providing credit card details (60%) or as a cheque (40%)) to WET. The Membership Department matches the payment with the renewal invoice copy. The invoice copy (stamped paid) is sent to Sales and Marketing who use it to produce a membership card and send this card together with a Guide to Sites booklet, to the member. The Membership Department passes the payment to the Finance Department.

Finance now submits payments to the bank. It currently takes the Finance Department an average of five days from the receipt of renewal to notifying the Membership Department of the cleared payment. Once cleared, Finance notifies the Membership Department by e-mail and they update the Membership System to record that the payment has been made. As mentioned before, there is a backlog in entering these details into the computer system.

Some cheques do not clear, often because they are filled in incorrectly (for example, they are unsigned or wrongly dated). In these circumstances, Finance raises a payment request and sends it to the member. Once the member re-submits a replacement cheque, it again goes through the clearing process.

Credit card payments are cleared instantly, but again there may be problems with the details. For example, incorrect numbers and incorrect expiry dates will lead to the transaction not being authorised and so, in these circumstances, Finance again raises a payment request.

The members' response to payment requests is very low (about 5%). The finance manager has described this as scandalous and 'an unethical response from supposedly ethical people'.

Also, not shown on the diagram: One week before renewal, the Membership System produces a renewal reminder and sends it to the member. Some members pay as a result of this reminder. If payment is not received then the member details are recorded as 'lapsed'.

Figure 4 – Membership renewal process

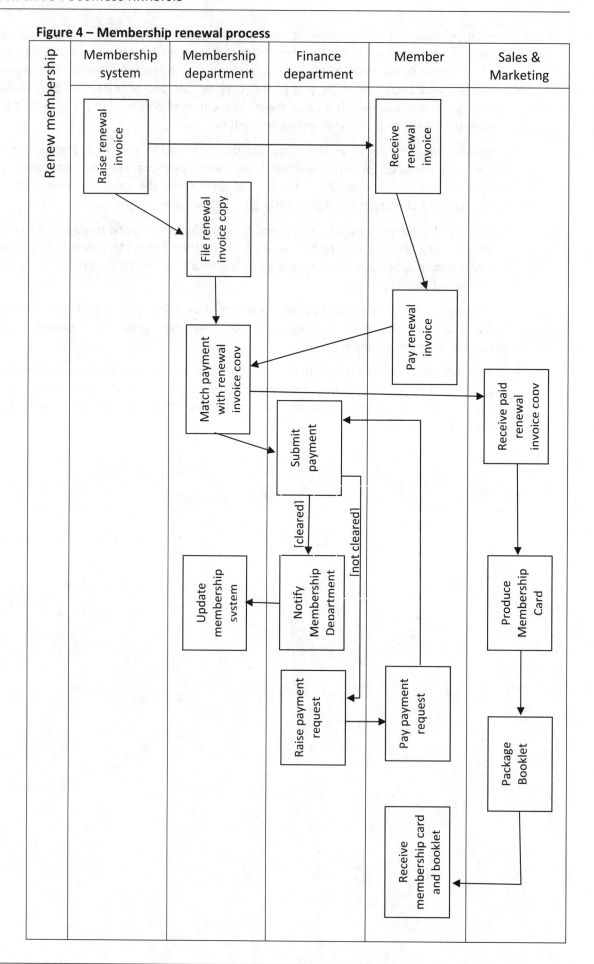

Required:

(a) The new CEO, Sheila Jenkins, recognises that she should understand the strategic position of WET before considering strategic options and changes. She wants a concise assessment of the strategic position; covering environment, strategic capability, stakeholder expectations and organisational mission.

Undertake the assessment, required by Sheila Jenkins, of the strategic position of WET. **(21 marks)**

Professional marks will be awarded in part (a) for the scope, structure and tone of the answer. **(4 marks)**

(b) Problems with the current membership renewal process include:

- the low response to payment requests
- the despatch of renewal reminders for people who have already paid
- the failure to send renewal invoices to some members.

Analyse faults in the current membership renewal process that cause the problems identified above. Suggest solutions that would remedy these faults. **(15 marks)**

(c) Sheila Jenkins sees customers as 'both prospective and existing members, volunteers and donors of WET'. She also wishes to gain increased revenue from each member and donor.

Evaluate how email and website technology might facilitate the acquisition and retention of WET's customers and support WET's aim to gain increased revenues from members and donors. **(10 marks)**

(Total: 50 marks)

68   LIONEL CARTWRIGHT

Lionel Cartwright considers himself to be an entrepreneur. He has been involved in many business ventures, each with minimal planning. He claims that this allows him to respond quickly to changing circumstances. His father had left him a small road haulage firm – three lorries – but he soon sold this to a larger operator when he recognised that operating margins were low and competition was severe. With the money received he bought a fast-food franchise, realising that this was where there was likely to be substantial growth. However, the franchisor required Lionel to limit both his ambitions and ideas for expansion to the development of this single franchise site. Lionel did not like this constraint and sold out and moved on. He then invested his money in an Internet firm, having identified the potential in this market. Unfortunately for Lionel his investment in the company was insufficiently large to permit him to have much say in the management of the company so he again sold out. He demonstrated his opportunism because he managed to sell his investment before the technology shares had fallen on the global stock exchanges. Lionel now has a cash sum of about $12 million seeking a suitable investment.

It is clear from Lionel's track record that he enjoys involvement in the management of businesses and he also prefers some element of control. He appears to have a skill in identifying potential growth markets and he also seems to have an intuitive knowledge of the market place. He is currently showing an interest again in the food/restaurant retailing market and he is looking at organic foods and juices (produce grown without the use of synthetic fertilisers or pesticides). He has noticed a growing trend in the USA for outlets selling fresh vegetable and fruit juices which are squeezed to the customer's demand, either to be consumed on premises or taken away for consumption, as is the case with many fast-food chains. This development is all part of the growing health-conscious climate. Lionel believes that the European market is ready for such a venture and this is his initial objective. He has already opened four outlets in Central London. To acquire the leases, fit out the premises, train labour and buy inventory plus some initial expenditure on marketing has already cost Lionel $3 million. He realises that to become profitable he must open several more outlets so as to gain both from the experience curve and from economies of scale. He estimates that about 30 outlets will provide him with the necessary critical mass. He believes that these outlets could be anywhere in Europe, given the right environment. He is confident that he has identified a transnational segment for a health focused nutritious juice – a segment of the market which is uniform, regardless of nationality. This is based upon the youth market which tends to have common tastes in both entertainment and leisure activities throughout Europe – France, Italy, Germany and the UK appear to be acceptable target areas.

However this segment is believed to be relatively sophisticated and affluent so outlets, therefore, will need to be in expensive city-centre areas or in other similar type areas which this target market group might regularly visit.

One of the problems facing Lionel's new venture and one of the pressures pushing him towards expansion is the need for regular access to suitable organic raw materials. These are in short supply. With large UK supermarkets generating increasing competitive demand for organic produce Lionel is finding it difficult to find reliable, quality suppliers. His current demand is too low and he needs to guarantee his suppliers a larger volume of orders so as to maintain their interest. He can only do this if he can rapidly expand the number of outlets he has or if he increases the volume sold through each outlet. The latter option is not really feasible. The area covered by each outlet is limited and to expand demand might mean either lowering the image which the outlet has developed and/or lowering the price of the products. Given the relative elasticities of demand, although the volumes of sales may rise, the profitability of each outlet may actually fall.

Another problem Lionel faces is obtaining suitable sites for his outlets. It is essential that these are in the appropriate locations. His current ones are in Central London where there is a young and affluent market and also where the tourist trade is high. Future sites need to be acquired if expansion is to be achieved. If he goes into the rest of Europe they will need to be in major city centres or in similar type sophisticated tourist areas. It is inevitable that the availability of these sites will be limited and the cost of acquisition will be expensive. In addition the juice enterprise needs to be marketed in a sympathetic way. The target clientele, being young, mobile and affluent will be easily deterred from buying the product if the marketing lacks subtlety. Consequently any rush towards expansion by using aggressive marketing techniques must be tempered with caution. It will be too easy to downgrade the enterprise's image, so damaging it in the eyes of its potential customers.

Lionel had made an effort to understand his core competences and he hoped that these would match the critical success factors needed for this industry. He believed that he had the necessary market knowledge, his operation was small enough to be flexible and responsive to sudden changes in market circumstances and he felt that he had the level of motivation required to be successful in such a fast-moving, consumer, non-durable industry.

After one year's operations the results from the four London outlets compared with a chain of similar outlets in the USA seem to demonstrate that Lionel's ambitions may be over-optimistic. Whilst recognising that the enterprise is still young (although there is the novelty attraction and also no near competition) the profits are nowhere near as attractive as those being obtained from a larger chain (20 outlets) in the USA. [See details in Table 1.]

If Lionel is to achieve his ambition of setting up a profitable chain of retail juice outlets he must seek expansion without alienating his customer-base. He can do this gradually and internally by funding any expansion through retained earnings. He could also attempt to acquire another retail/fast food chain and adapt it to this new format. Finally, he could seek some sort of alliance whereby he achieves expansion, using other people's efforts and resources, particularly financial ones. This could involve licensing or franchising agreements. Each of these modes of expansion has its own advantages, but there are also disadvantages associated with each.

Table 1: Details of performance of individual outlets in USA and in the United Kingdom ($000 where appropriate)

All figures refer to the previous calendar year

	UK outlet	USA outlet
Sales revenue	600	750
Cost of materials	200	200
Labour costs	125	125
Rental/lease costs	125	85
Inventories held	30	20
Wasted materials as a % of sales	22	9
Varieties of products available for juicing (actual numbers)	14	25
Marketing costs allocated per outlet	60	35
Administration costs allocated per outlet	20	10
Customers per week (actual numbers)	2,000	2,500
Size of store (square metres)	275	250
Numbers of staff	10	15
Number of hours open as a % of total hours available within any given week	40	65
Waiting time (from order to service) in minutes	15	8
Profit	70	295

Required:

(a)   It appears that Lionel is a follower of the emergent school of strategy formulation as distinct from the rational model (planning) approach. Discuss the benefits that such an opportunistic approach may bring Lionel and comment on any problems he may experience with such an approach to setting strategy.   **(10 marks)**

(b)   Assess the performance of the UK outlets compared with their US equivalents, as indicated in Table 1, and identify from your analysis any critical success factors which may be currently lacking in Lionel's enterprise.   **(15 marks)**

(c)   What external information would you recommend that Lionel should have obtained prior to his decision to enter this market? Consider appropriate academic models Lionel might have utilised to obtain this information.   **(10 marks)**

(d)   Discuss both the advantages and disadvantages of:

    (i)   internal growth

    (ii)   acquisition

    (iii)   franchising

as methods whereby Lionel can achieve the expansion which he believes is necessary for his fresh juice outlets.   **(15 marks)**

(Total: 50 marks)

69   MEMORIAL HOSPITAL

Assume that 'now' is June 20X7.

The Management Committee of the Bethesda Heights Memorial Hospital was meeting under crisis conditions. The Hospital had moved into a financial deficit and most of the key participants in the decision making process could not agree on the best way to resolve the crisis.

The Hospital was located in the less affluent part of a North American city. It was a large general purpose hospital which served a stable population. Its revenue came mainly from the central government in the form of a grant, based on the size of population served and the actual surgical and medical work carried out. Central government grants accounted for about 65% of total revenue, and the remainder was almost equally split between two other funding bodies. Firstly, the local city council provided about US$20 million of grants and secondly, private medical insurance companies paid a similar amount for treatment of their insurance holders. This gave a total annual revenue of some US$115 million, but costs had risen to US$125 million with all parts of the cost structure, including medicines, salaries and materials, seeing increases above the level of inflation. Unfortunately, the outlook did not look good for the Hospital. Revenue from central government was under pressure as the government sought to reduce public expenditure in order to fund significant tax cuts. Grants from the city council were linked to the level of the central government grant and consequently revenue from this source was not expected to increase. Even more depressing for the Hospital was its failure to attract private healthcare patients. They were choosing to go to a neighbouring hospital with a better reputation for patient care and more attractive facilities. Consequently income from medical insurance was likely to decline further.

(The current financial and comparative performance data for the two hospitals can be seen in Table 1.)

The Management Committee estimated that if the situation did not improve the Bethesda Heights Memorial Hospital would have a deficit of US$75 million within three years. Action needed to be taken urgently. The Management Committee was made up of a number of coalitions. One was led by Michael Gonzales, the Chief Executive of the Hospital. He was an administrator and an accountant by training. His concern was that Bethesda Heights should be run efficiently. To him, and his fellow administrators on the Management Committee, it was important that the Hospital should be financially viable. However efficiency and effectiveness are not always the same thing. In fact some of the actions taken may also lead to further ineffectiveness or inefficiencies elsewhere. An indication of this dilemma was the administrators' wish to reduce the length of time patients spent in hospital so as to reduce costs. However, sending patients home early could result in them requiring home visits from nursing staff for up to four or five extra days and in some circumstances this early release might require a re-admission to the Hospital. Consequently initial savings might be eroded by further unanticipated costs. Furthermore some medical staff suspected that these administrators were more concerned with short-term financial concerns than with medical ones. Certain medicines may be rationed or withheld to reduce costs and patients might be denied treatments such as physiotherapy or occupational therapy in a similar drive for cost savings.

Another group was represented by Stefan Kopechnik, a consultant surgeon. He was in favour of developing 'leading edge' micro-surgery. For Stefan and his fellow surgeons the Bethesda Heights Memorial Hospital was losing out to its rival hospital because it was seen as old-fashioned and out of touch with modern medicine and surgery. This was affecting its ability to attract the affluent private healthcare patient. Unfortunately the Hospital would require substantial capital investment to implement such a high-tech medical strategy.

A third group was influenced by the Mayor of the city, Elizabeth Fuller. This group was made up mainly of councillors (local politicians) who sat on various Hospital committees and were anxious to see the Hospital kept open and effectively serving the city's medical needs. Surprisingly, the city council had recently threatened to cut back its funding as a means of avoiding an increase in local taxes. The local news media had attempted to embarrass the local ruling party about this policy but the councillors involved, led by Mrs Fuller, were in no mood to give in to media pressure. There was a real fear that strategy might now be formulated in response to media headlines rather than rational argument.

Naturally the local population within the catchment area of the Hospital wanted it to continue its function as a viable concern and even invest in more modern facilities. Unfortunately this stakeholder group had little power or influence. The residents were socially disadvantaged and were unable to bring concerted pressure to bear on the Hospital's decision-makers.

There was one other important pressure group who were very vocal in their support of the Hospital. These were the employees, including the nurses and the general medical and support staff (not the high-ranking surgeons).Their interests were not political or financial, or even professional, unlike the surgeons who were looking to expand their power and influence. This employee grouping was primarily concerned with the maintenance of an efficient and effective hospital for the local population who could not afford private medical insurance and who relied mainly on government funded healthcare provision.

As one might have expected with these divisions, the Management Committee found it difficult to agree upon an acceptable strategy to solve the financial crisis. Eventually the one chosen reflected the power wielded by the surgeons. These senior medical staff (the surgeons) had threatened to resign if the Committee did not agree to a capital investment programme designed to enhance the Hospital's surgical reputation. The Hospital would effectively cease to function without its surgical teams. Unfortunately the trade-off for this investment was to reduce the number of beds within the Hospital.

It was argued that this reduced provision reflected the current utilisation patterns. Unfortunately this did not reflect the latent demand within the community. There were a significant number of patients who were not being given the treatment they needed as they did not have private healthcare insurance. Furthermore, waiting times for seeing the appropriate consultant surgeon or for being admitted to the Hospital were lengthening for this disadvantaged group of patients.

Table 1: Comparison of Statistical Data between Bethesda Heights Memorial Hospital and the Neighbouring Hospital for calendar year 20X6 (figures for 20X5 in brackets).

(Unless otherwise stated figures are in US$000).

	Bethesda Heights Hospital		Neighbouring Hospital	
Income from central government	76,000	(76,000)	85,000	(85,000)
Income from local government	20,000	(19,000)	22,000	(21,000)
Income from medical insurance	19,000	(23,000)	63,000	(60,000)
Total income	115,000	(118,000)	170,000	(166,000)
Labour costs	55,000	(53,000)	57,000	(55,000)
Medical equipment	20,000	(19,000)	28,000	(25,000)
Drugs	25,000	(22,000)	30,000	(28,000)
Other variable costs – catering, laundry	10,000	(9,000)	13,000	(12,000)
Fixed costs	15,000	(15,000)	17,000	(16,000)
Total costs	125,000	(118,000)	145,000	(136,000)
Surplus/deficit	−10,000	(0)	+25,000	(+30,000)
Further referrals required % (need for re-admittance)	17	(14)	9	(7)
Mortality % (% of patients dying in hospital)	0.05	(0.03)	0.007	(0.003)
Number of staff (actual)	1,000	(970)	1,100	(1,150)
Number of beds (actual)	350	(350)	450	(450)
	Bethesda Heights Hospital		Neighbouring Hospital	
Waiting time (days)*	95	(90)	35	(40)
Post-operation time in hospital (days)**	7	(8)	10	(10)
Day surgery operations*** (actual numbers)	1,500	(1,150)	7,000	(1,500)
Number of patients treated annually residentially	10,650	(10,900)	12,700	(12,500)
Ratio outpatients to those committed to hospital****	3:1	(3:1)	5:1	(4:1)

*   from seeing doctor to hospital admittance

**   number of days kept in hospital after an operation

***   minor operations which require no overnight stay

****   number of patients dealt with as external patients (excluding day surgery) compared with those committed to hospital for one night or longer

Required:

(a)   It is apparent that the goals and objectives of the senior medical staff have profoundly influenced the chosen strategy. Discuss the factors that have enabled this group to dominate the other stakeholders. What are the main arguments that the other groups might have used to promote their objectives?   **(15 marks)**

(b)   Using the quantitative data provided, identify the major problems facing the Bethesda Heights Memorial Hospital. Examine the extent to which the proposed high-tech strategy will address these problems.   **(15 marks)**

(c)   Assess the other strategic options open to the Management Committee. **(15 marks)**

(d) When dealing with issues concerning health care, financial outcomes are not the only criteria to be considered. Ethical factors must also be taken into account. Discuss the role that social responsibility might play in this context. **(5 marks)**

(Total: 50 marks)

70 WAMC

Assume that 'now' is December 20X7.

Kenneth Murphy is the Managing Director of the World-Wide Agricultural Machinery Company plc (WAMC). The company was founded almost 100 years ago and with its approaching centenary Murphy is worried that the company may be about to lose its independence. The company came into existence with the industrialisation of the United Kingdom agricultural sector. It manufactured tractors (power units) and an array of associated agricultural machinery such as rakes, balers, ploughs and grass cutting equipment. The company grew at a rapid rate in the early part of the twentieth century. The successful demand within the domestic market led the company into a false sense of security. It neglected both product and market development, despite its ambitious company name. It was unaware of the growth of competitors, mainly from mainland Europe and the USA. In recent years the company has attempted to improve its situation by exporting to the major countries within the European Union but again its marketing knowledge is poor. Agricultural policies in many European countries favour smaller farming units. Generally the size of these units is too small to necessitate the degree of mechanisation which WAMC caters for. Furthermore the lack of innovation within the company means that the products are old-fashioned, often costly to repair and lack the flexibility and adaptability of competitive machines. Furthermore as many farms are becoming more specialist in their output the need to purchase a wide range of equipment is less prevalent.

By the beginning of the 1990s the company had been experiencing a financial crisis. Profits had been low for a number of years but now small losses were occurring. Management consultants were brought in and suggested that the range of products should be drastically reduced so as to control a seemingly inexorable rise in costs. In 1998 Kenneth was appointed to oversee this strategy. He decided that one of the first areas to be axed should be the production of the power units – the tractors (referred to henceforth as tractor units). Research demonstrated that these products required the largest amount of investment. Unfortunately for the company total sales were insufficient to provide the economies of scale necessary for it to be successful in this area. In addition the large car producers, particularly the American ones, were now dominating this market. The strategy seemed a sensible one. Unfortunately it had disastrous results for WAMC. It became apparent that the remaining range of agricultural products (those towed behind a tractor unit) were seen as an ancillary to the tractors. Farmers, who now could no longer buy WAMC-produced tractor units, now decided not to buy WAMC's ploughs, rakes and balers etc. The farmers were looking for a single supplier for their mechanised equipment. This enabled them to have easier access to finance and it also gave the customer a more comprehensive and easily co-ordinated service facility. Sales by WAMC fell dramatically and by early 20X7 the company was making unacceptable losses. The company did attempt to impose some cost saving strategies. The number of factories, located throughout the country, was cut from seven to three, and redundancies reduced the work force to 700 from a total exceeding 2,500 in 1998, when Murphy had become MD. Most of the employees had been with the firm for all their working lives and were devastated by the savage cut-backs in employment. As a unionised organisation there had been some resistance to the redundancies, but after a costly strike the workers realised that there was no hope of keeping the organisation at the size it was and they reluctantly accepted the new structure.

The factories are now organised so that each of the three produce a narrow range of products, enabling specialisation to take place. This replaces the previously inefficient system whereby each of the seven factories produced the whole range of products, the theory being that they served local geographic markets, necessitating little transportation and enabling demand to be met quickly. The reality was that the costs of production were higher and inventory-holding was expensive even though regional demand was being more conveniently serviced.

Traditionally WAMC has owned and controlled its distribution outlets. There are 10 of these outlets spread regionally throughout the United Kingdom. Murphy is contemplating selling these off, to raise additional working capital. It is estimated that the sale could realise about $15 million, mainly because the company owned the freeholds of the land on which these outlets are built, and they could be profitably sold for development. Murphy is also contemplating re-entering the tractor-unit production business but in a less committed fashion. He is planning to sub-contract the manufacturing to an established tractor manufacturing company and having the WAMC brand placed on these products. This, he believes, will provide the company with the required flexibility but at minimum cost.

Murphy is also contemplating a strategy of product development to provide increased work for his factories. As the main business is now really in metal fabrication, not tractor units, he is looking to produce equipment for the road building and road repair industry, now expected to be more growth oriented given the central government's recent commitment to spend more on transport improvements. Such equipment could include portable traffic lights, metal signs and road barriers for improving motorway safety.

WAMC has also begun talks with a large financial institution with the intention of borrowing funds so that it (WAMC) can provide loans to farmers so that they can purchase the farm equipment at favourable terms of credit. Currently it is believed that WAMC is losing business because it is not able to offer potential customers sufficient financial support.

Whilst these negotiations are taking place the company has been approached by a rival producer from France. The French company, Agricole Mecanique (AM), is suggesting a defensive merger so as to better combat threats from competing US producers. The French company is slightly smaller than WAMC, with only 500 employees and two factories. However it is a relatively young company, only being established for ten years with a limited product range and a largely unknown brand name but it does have up-to-date manufacturing facilities, and it does produce its own tractor units. In the process of consolidation the French company is suggesting that much of the production should be transferred to the French factories and that most of the senior management positions in the new company should be French. Murphy has been offered a significant number of shares and a future management position in the newly merged company if he is able to successfully conclude such a 'merger', at a price acceptable to the French company. As the merger will be achieved by a share exchange between the two companies it is in the interests of Agricole Mecanique for the share price of WAMC to be low on the date of inception – a possibly illegal inducement to Murphy.

Murphy is fully aware of the precarious position of WAMC and he is not convinced of the wisdom of the so-called 'merger'. He feels that he is too involved in the situation to take a dispassionate view, so he has called in a management consultant, experienced in strategy formulation and in mergers and acquisitions, to advise him on the current situation.

Table 1: Financial Data for WAMC and Agricole Mecanique (AM) ($000)

	WAMC	WAMC	AM	AM
	20X5	20X6	20X5	20X6
Sales revenue	30,000	28,000	25,000	24,500
Cost of sales	18,000	18,200	13,000	12,900
Gross margin	12,000	9,800	12,000	11,600
Expenses	9,000	9,200	8,000	8,100
Marketing	4,000	4,000	1,500	2,000
R&D	3,000	3,000	4,500	4,100
Overheads	2,000	2,200	2,000	2,000
Operating profits	3,000	600	4,000	3,500
Interest paid	1,000	1,200	2,000	2,200
Profit/(loss) after interest	2,000	(600)	2,000	1,300
Non-current assets	24,000	24,000	19,000	19,500
Current assets	8,000	7,500	7,000	8,000
Current liabilities	6,500	6,300	5,000	6,000
Equity	27,000	27,000	14,000	14,500
Debt	12,000	14,000	12,000	15,000
Return on sales	10.0%	2.1%	16.0%	14.3%
P/E ratio	11	10	16	17
Gearing ratio	0.444	0.519	0.857	1.034

Required:

Acting in the role as management consultant:

(a) **Critically review the current position of the World-Wide Agricultural Machinery Company. Present your review in a report format and use academic models, wherever practical, to support your arguments. How does WAMC's performance compare with that of Agricole Mecanique?** **(20 marks)**

(b) **Evaluate the strategies being proposed by Kenneth Murphy. To what extent would they help to rectify the underlying problems?** **(15 marks)**

(c) **Identify the main factors which need to be considered if a merger is to be successful. (The answer must relate to the above case scenario.)** **(10 marks)**

(d) **What ethical problems might Murphy face in considering the incentive offered to him by Agricole Mecanique to facilitate the merger?** **(5 marks)**

(Total: 50 marks)

71 HAIR CARE LTD

Assume that 'now' is June 20X7.

Sam and Annabelle Burns own and manage the firm Hair Care Ltd, based in the United Kingdom. The firm was formed in 20X2 when Sam and his wife re-mortgaged their house and borrowed heavily from the bank to buy out the company from a conglomerate organisation who were disposing of non-core businesses. Sam had been a senior salesman with the hair-care subsidiary of the conglomerate. This subsidiary bought hair care products, mainly small value items and consumables – scissors, brushes, combs, hair nets, curlers and hair driers, from manufacturers and resold them to wholesalers and large retail chemist chains within the United Kingdom, mainly for use in hairdressing salons. The new business has continued in this direction.

	Main currency	20X7	19W7
Purchases from the Far East (mainly Hong Kong, China and Malaysia)	US $	66%	93%
Purchases from mainland Europe (mainly Italy and Germany)	Euro	29%	3%
Purchases from UK	GP £	5%	4%

The company has met with success very quickly and the initial loans have already been repaid ahead of schedule. The company now owns the freehold of a large warehouse/distribution centre, which is five times the size of the original depot, leased when the company first started trading five years ago. Sales revenue, now in excess of $5 million, has increased by more than 50% each year and shows little signs of slowing down. Despite this apparent rapid growth Hair Care Ltd only accounts for about half of the current market, leaving some potential for growth. The company is run cost effectively, with minimum staffing. Sam, as Managing Director is solely concerned with the marketing side of the business. He spends most of his time in the selling role and in customer care, which he rates as a major contributor to the company's success. The only other key manager is his wife who is responsible for managing the warehouse staff, arranging distribution, general administration and financial management. The company started with six employees, in addition to Sam and Annabelle, and now has 15. Staff rarely leave the company. The staff is almost entirely employed in the distribution and packaging function, although there are two other sales people apart from Sam, but they only deal with the smaller buyers. With the continued growth in sales revenue it is inevitable that the number of employees will have to increase. It is expected that there will have to be a total of about 30 staff, all non managerial, in two years if sales continue to increase at the current rate. The success of Hair Care Ltd can be accounted for by a number of factors. Sam is a very good salesman who is responsible for looking after all the major accounts. He is popular and much of the business is built on his personal relationship with the key clients. There is a considerable amount of customer loyalty which is mainly attributable to Sam, and both he and his wife are always accessible to customers and they go out of their way to provide a first class service. Even on vacation the two owners are in daily contact with the office. The company has been able to manage its purchases wisely. Most of the products, being purchased abroad, require payment in a foreign currency. Hair Care has been able to benefit from the relative weakness of the euro as against sterling for its European supplies. Likewise, the strength of US dollars has enabled Hair Care Ltd to negotiate lower purchasing prices with Far Eastern suppliers. However, it is questionable as to how long this situation concerning foreign exchange can be held. The situation may change should the United Kingdom join the euro in the near future or other factors weaken the strength of sterling.

Sam has also developed strong links with his suppliers and he has, until recently, attempted to trade with only a few so that his lines of communication and control are kept as simple as possible. Most of his current suppliers have been with him since the start of the company in 20X2. This has provided the company with reliable and good quality products. In fact Hair Care Ltd often has exclusive access to certain products. For example it has the sole rights to distribute an Italian hair-dryer which is generally recognised to be the best on the market. This product strength has enabled the company to build on the customer loyalty. However, it is inevitable that as demand has increased, existing suppliers have not been able to keep up with the necessary volumes and Sam has had to look for, and buy from new manufacturers.

The company has benefited from a period of relatively steady growth in the economy and even in the current economic downturn Sam has argued that demand for hair care products is usually recession-proof. Furthermore Hair Care Ltd has currently no near competitors. Many of the small competitors in the wholesale market place have chosen to concentrate on other areas of the hair care business – salon furnishings and the supply of cheap, low-value items such as towels, razors etc, leaving much of this basic business (sales of other relatively low-value and mainly disposable products) to Sam's company. Additionally quite a number of the small firms have even left the market. All this has helped to contribute to the overall growth rate of Hair Care Ltd. There are some major international companies who make shampoos, conditioners and other cosmetic type products who also buy-in consumer hairdressing products such as the ones sold by Hair Care Ltd. They then sell these mainly to the retail trade for domestic use by consumers and not directly to the hairdressing salons as does Hair Care Ltd. Furthermore these are large companies and Sam believes that they do not currently see his company as a major threat.

The company has registered a brand name for its main products, which it re-packages, rather than using the individual brands of the original manufacturers. This has enabled Hair Care Ltd to generate even greater loyalty from its customers and often to obtain a price premium from these products.

Sam believes that part of the company's success stems from the fact that he has an organisation with minimal administrative overheads. He outsources all of his products, adding value mainly through branding and the maintenance of customer care. He believes that strategy is not mainly about beating the competition but in serving the real needs of the customer. The company has also been able to develop a strong relationship with the country's leading retail chemist chain, providing it with good quality, low-cost disposable products such as hair nets and brushes to be sold under an own-brand label. Although the margins are inevitably small, the volumes involved more than compensate for this.

The company has had to incur increased investment as a result of the large growth in sales revenue. The building of the warehouse, the increased inventory-holding costs, capital expenditure on items such as computing systems, fork-lift trucks and automated inventory control and retrieval systems could not be financed out of current earnings, but the company's bank was only too ready to lend the company the necessary money considering that the original loan had been repaid ahead of schedule.

Table 1: Details of Performance of Hair Care Ltd: 20X4–20X7

	20X4	20X5	20X6	20X7 (Forecast)
	$000	$000	$000	$000
Sales revenue	2,300	3,500	5,010	7,500
Cost of sales	1,450	2,380	3,507	5,250
Marketing costs	200	250	290	350
Distribution costs	300	400	430	500
Administration	50	55	80	120
Interest payments	0	80	220	700
Operating profit	300	335	483	580
Loans	0	850	2,400	5,000
Number of suppliers (actual)	15	20	30	50
Range of products (actual)	35	85	110	130

Total staff including Sam and Annabelle	12	14	15	23
Inventories	230	400	700	1,400
Non-current assets	50	1,500	2,700	6,300

All the success which Hair Care Ltd has achieved has not diminished Sam's appetite for growth. He now seems to be driven more by seeking power and influence than acquiring wealth. He questions the ability of the company to continue its current growth in the prevailing environment and therefore he is looking for ideas which may facilitate corporate expansion. He has asked his accountant to provide some options for him to consider.

Required:

(a) **Prepare a report for Sam, evaluating the current position of Hair Care Ltd and highlighting any financial and strategic issues concerning future developments which you feel should be brought to his attention.** **(15 marks)**

(b) **As his accountant, prepare a short report for Sam, identifying and assessing the strategies, which he could consider in attempting to further the company's development.** **(15 marks)**

(c) **Sam seems pre-occupied with growth. Identify reasons for potential corporate decline and suggest ways that Sam could avoid them in the context of the case study scenario.** **(10 marks)**

(d) **Sam currently appears to have a successful formula for growth. Using the concept of the value chain, demonstrate how he has been able to achieve this success.**

(10 marks)

(Total: 50 marks)

72 ABC LEARNING

Introduction

ABC Learning plc (ABCL) is a large training company based in Arcadia. It specialises in professional certification training for accountants, lawyers, business analysts and business consultants. ABCL delivers training through face-to-face courses and e-learning, mainly using full-time lecturing staff. Thirty percent of its revenue is from e-learning solutions. It is constantly seeking new markets and acquisitions to improve shareholder value. It has become aware of the expanding business analysis certification training industry (BACTI) in the neighbouring country of Erewhon. ABCL has commissioned Xenon, a market intelligence company to undertake an analysis of the BACTI market in Erewhon with the aim of assessing its attractiveness and profitability before deciding whether or not to expand into Erewhon. ABCL is aware that an Arcadian competitor, Megatrain, has previously tried to establish itself in this market in Erewhon. Established providers in the BACTI industry in Erewhon responded by price cutting and strengthened promotional campaigns. This was supported by a campaign to discredit the CEO of Megatrain and to highlight its foreign ownership. Within six months Megatrain had withdrawn from the market in Erewhon.

Xenon interim report on the BACTI market in Erewhon – January 20X9

Introduction

The BACTI market in Erewhon is dominated by three suppliers; CATalyst, Batrain and Ecoba (collectively known as the 'big three'). CATalyst is a wholly owned subsidiary of the Tuition Group, a public limited company quoted on the Erewhon stock market. The last annual report of the Tuition Group identified CATalyst as core to their strategy and a source of significant growth. Batrain is a private limited company, with the shares equally divided between the eight founding directors. Four of these directors are under 40. Ecoba is also a private limited company with 95% of the shares owned by Gillian Vari. The other 5% are owned by her business partner Willy Senterit. Gillian is approaching retirement age.

Delivery model

Both CATalyst and Batrain have similar delivery models. They employ mainly full-time lecturing staff who are offered attractive salary packages, share options and generous benefits; such as ten weeks paid holiday. Even with these packages they find it hard to recruit. Teaching vacancies are advertised on both of their websites. CATalyst and Batrain both stress their 'brand' in their marketing material. On their websites there is no specific reference to the lecturers who will present each module. In contrast, Ecoba specifically identifies lecturers in both its advertisements (supported by photographs of the lecturers) and on their website, where the lecturer taking the module is specified. All the lecturers are 'high profile' names in the business analysis training community. None of these are directly employed by Ecoba. They are all on fixed-term contracts and are paid a premium daily rate for lecturing and assignment marking. Xenon interviewed Mike Wilson, a named management lecturer and asked him about the arrangement. He said that he felt relatively secure about it. 'Students are attracted to Ecoba because they know I will be teaching a particular module. I suppose I could be substituted by a cheaper lecturer but the students would soon complain that they had been misled.' Mike had also worked as a sub-contractor for CATalyst but no longer did so because he found that a booking could be cancelled at short notice if full-time staff became available. 'Gillian Vari (the MD of Ecoba) is much more transparent and straightforward in her treatment of sub-contract staff. The only problem is the time it takes to pay our invoices. We are always complaining about that.'

The 'big three' are recognised and established brands in the industry. Although the 'big three' are competitors there does appear to be a degree of mutual tolerance of each other. For example, they appear to have co-ordinated their response to the attempted entry of Megatrain into the industry. Three of the directors of Batrain used to work as lecturers for CATalyst and Gillian Vari (the MD of Ecoba) was a director of the company that spawned CATalyst. Mike Wilson has lectured for all of the 'big three' providers. However, there are also, approximately, twenty other providers in the industry in Erewhon (accounting for 20% of the total industry revenue).

Students and providers

The fees of 60% of students are paid for by their employers. There are around 15 major corporate clients who place significant contracts for certification training with providers. Most (but not all) of these are placed with the 'big three'. CATalyst is particularly strong in managing these contracts, setting up dedicated training sessions and a personalised website to support each contract. However, there is increasing evidence that providers are being played off against each other by the major corporate customers who are seeking to drive down costs. One of the large insurance companies recently moved all of its training to Ecoba after several years of using CATalyst as its sole provider. Another large customer has also recently moved their training contract to Ecoba because they were impressed by the 'named' lecturers that Ecoba used. Interestingly, in a new move for the industry, WAC, a major supplier of business analysis consultancy services, recently bought one of the smaller business analysis training providers and thus is now able to deliver all of its business analysis training in-house for its own staff.

Business Analysis certification in Erewhon is administered by the EIoBA (Erewhon Institute of Business Analysts) which sets the examination. There is no requirement for students to attend a certified training course. In fact 40% of students prepare themselves for the

[handwritten margin note: Threat of new substitutes ✓]

examinations using self-study. One of the smaller BACTI providers has gained some success by offering a blended learning solution that combines tutor support with e-learning modules. Interestingly, the 'big three' all appear to acknowledge the possibilities of e-learning but do not promote it. All three have invested money in specially designed training venues and so they seem committed, at least in the short term, to their classroom-based model. *[handwritten: B2E]*

EIoBA runs a certification scheme for providers of training. This operates at three levels; bronze, silver and gold. The 'big three' all have the highest level of certification (gold). Xenon recognises that gold certification offers a significant competitive advantage and that it will take any new entrant more than one year to achieve this level of certification.

[handwritten margin note: Barrier to new entrance ✓]

Ecoba Ltd: Background

[handwritten note: employees / suppliers (contractors)]

Ecoba is a private limited company. As well as being its managing director and majority shareholder, Gillian Vari is the only full-time lecturer. Mike Wilson told Xenon that Gillian is averse to employing full-time lecturing staff because 'they have to be paid if courses do not run and also during the long vacations'. Her policy appears to be to minimise overhead training and administrative costs. This may contribute to the slow payment of lecturers. Mike Wilson did comment that the 'full-time administrative staff seem to be under increasing pressure'. *[handwritten: ③ Government   ④ customers (corporate client, students)]*

[handwritten margin note: ① Bank]

Figure 1 provides comparative data for CATalyst and Batrain. Financial information for Ecoba is presented in Figure 2

Figure 1: Financial Analysis (all 20X8)

	CATalyst	Batrain
Revenue	$35,000,000	$25,000,000
Cost of sales as a percentage of revenue	65%	63%
Average payables settlement period	65 days	60 days
Average receivables settlement period	30 days	35 days
Sales revenue to capital employed	3.36	3.19
Gross profit margin	35%	37%
Net profit margin	6%	8%
Liquidity ratio	0.92	0.93
Gearing ratio	30%	25%
Interest cover ratio	3.25	4.75

Figure 2: Financial Analysis: Ecoba Ltd (All figures in $000)

Extract from the statement of financial position

	20X8	20X7
Assets		
Non-current assets		
Intangible assets	5,800	5,200
Property, plant, equipment	500	520
	6,300	5,720

Current assets		
Inventories	70	90
Trade receivables	4,300	3,000
Cash and cash equivalents	2,100	1,500
	6,470	4,590
Total assets	12,770	10,310
Current liabilities		
Trade payables	6,900	4,920
Current tax payable	20	15
	6,920	4,935
Non-current liabilities		
Long-term borrowings	200	225
	7,120	5,160
Equity		
Share capital	5,100	5,100
Retained earnings	550	50
Total equity and liabilities	12,770	10,310

Extract from the statement of comprehensive income

Revenue	22,000	17,000
Cost of sales	(17,500)	(13,750)
Gross profit	4,500	3,250
Overhead expenses	(3,500)	(2,500)
Profit before tax and finance costs	1,000	750
Finance costs	(20)	(20)
Profit before tax	980	730
Tax expense	(30)	(25)
Profit for the year	950	705

Required:

Xenon usually analyses an industry using Porter's five forces framework.

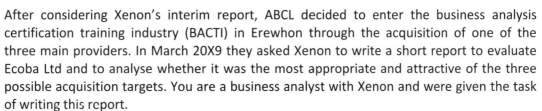

(a) **Using Porter's framework, analyse the business analysis certification industry (BACTI) in Erewhon and assess whether it is an attractive market for ABCL to enter.**
5 Forces **(20 marks)** 30 mins.

After considering Xenon's interim report, ABCL decided to enter the business analysis certification training industry (BACTI) in Erewhon through the acquisition of one of the three main providers. In March 20X9 they asked Xenon to write a short report to evaluate Ecoba Ltd and to analyse whether it was the most appropriate and attractive of the three possible acquisition targets. You are a business analyst with Xenon and were given the task of writing this report.

(b)   Write the requested short report evaluating Ecoba Ltd and analysing whether it was the most appropriate and attractive of the three possible acquisition targets for ABCL.   **(16 marks)**

Professional marks will be awarded in part (b) for clarity and format of your report   **(4 marks)**

In November 20X9 ABCL acquired Ecoba Ltd. Gillian Vari agreed to stay on for two years to assist the management of the ownership transition. However, her business partner became seriously ill and ABCL have agreed, on compassionate terms, for her to leave the company immediately. ABCL, from experience, know that they must manage stakeholders very carefully during this transition stage.

½ for each

(c)   Identify the stakeholders <u>in Ecoba Ltd</u> and analyse how ABCL could successfully manage them during the ownership transition.   **(10 marks)**

could use "Mendelow Matrix"   **(Total: 50 marks)**

certificate body. – key player

73   GREENTECH *Walk in the footsteps of a top tutor*

greenTech was established in 1990. The company began by specialising in the supply of low voltage, low emission, quiet, recyclable components to the electronic industry. Its components are used in the control systems of lifts, cars and kitchen appliances. Two medium-sized computer manufacturers use *greenTech* components in selected 'green' (that is, environmentally-friendly) models in their product range. Recent market research showed that 70% of the global electronics industry used *greenTech* components somewhere in its products.

In 1993 the company began a catalogue mail order service (now Internet-based) selling 'green' components to home users. Most of these customers were building their own computers and they required such components on either environmental grounds or because they wanted their computers to be extremely quiet and energy efficient. From 20X5, *greenTech* also offered fully assembled computer systems that could be ordered and configured over the Internet. All *greenTech*'s components are purchased from specialist suppliers. The company has no manufacturing capability, but it does have extensive hardware testing facilities and it has built up significant technical know-how in supplying appropriate components. The management team that formed the company in 1990 still runs the company.

Finance and revenue

The company has traded profitably since its foundation and has grown steadily in size and revenues. In 20X8, its revenues were $64 million, with a pre-tax profit of $10 million. The spread across the three revenue streams is shown in Figure 1:

All figures in $million	20X8	20X7	20X6
Component sales to electronics industry	40	36	34
Component sales to home users	20	18	16
Fully assembled green computers	4	3	2
Total	64	57	52

Figure 1: Turnover by revenue stream 20X6–20X8

The company has gradually accumulated a sizeable cash surplus. The board cannot agree on how this cash should be used. One beneficiary has been the marketing budget (see Figure 2), but the overall spend on marketing still remains relatively modest and, by April 20X8, the cash surplus stood at $17 million.

All figures in $	20X8	20X7	20X6
Internet development & marketing	100,000	70,000	60,000
Display advertising (manufacturers)	50,000	40,000	30,000
Display advertising (domestic customers)	20,000	15,000	15,000
Exhibitions & conferences	30,000	20,000	15,000
Marketing literature	10,000	5,000	5,000
Total	210,000	150,000	125,000

Figure 2: Marketing budget 20X6–20X8

Company Doctor

In 20X8 a television company wrote to *greenTech* to ask whether it would consider taking part in a television programme called 'Company Doctor'. In this programme three teams of consultants spend a week at a chosen company working on a solution to a problem identified by the company. At the end of the week all three teams present their proposal for dealing with the problem. A panel of experts, including representatives from the company, pick the winner and, in theory, implement the winning proposal. *greenTech* agreed to take part in the programme and selected their future strategic direction as the problem area to be analysed. Their cash surplus would then be used to fund the preferred option. The show was recorded in September 20X8 to be transmitted later in the year. A brief summary of the conclusions of each team of consultants is given below.

The accountants Lewis-Read suggested a strategic direction that planned to protect and build on greenTech's current strategic position. They believed that the company should invest in marketing the fully assembled 'green' computers to both commercial and home customers. They pointed out that the government had just agreed a preferential procurement policy for energy efficient computers with high recyclable content. 'This segment of the market is rapidly expanding and is completely under-exploited by greenTech at the moment', Lewis-Read concluded.

The corporate recovery specialists, Fenix, put forward a strategic direction that essentially offered more services to *greenTech*'s current customers in the electronics industry. They suggested that the company should expand its product range as well as being able to manufacture components to respond to special requirements. They also believed that potential supply problems could be avoided and supply costs could be cut if *greenTech* acquired its own manufacturing capability. 'You need to secure the supply chain, to protect your future position.' They felt that the surplus cash in the company should be used to acquire companies that already had these manufacturing capabilities.

The third team was led by Professor Ag Wan from MidShire University. Their main recommendation was that *greenTech* should not see itself as a supplier of components and computers but as a supplier of green technology. They suggested that the company should look at many other sectors (not just electronics) where quietness, low emissions and recyclable technology were important. 'The company needs to exploit its capabilities, not its products. It is looking too narrowly at the future. To compete in the future you need to develop your markets, not your products', concluded the professor.

Figure 3, which was shown on the television show, illustrates how each solution came from a different part of an amended Ansoff product/market matrix.

		Products	
		Existing	**New**
Markets	**Existing**	Protect/Build *Lewis-Read (option 1)*	Product development with new capabilities *Fenix (option 2)*
	New	Market development with new uses and capabilities *Professor Ag Wan (option 3)*	No team chose this option Diversification

Figure 3: Adapted Ansoff matrix showing the position of the three solutions

In the television programme, the panel chose option 3 (as suggested by Professor Ag Wan's team) as being the most appropriate strategic direction and, much to everyone's surprise, the company began to pursue this direction with much vigour. Objectives and goals were established and a set of processes was designed to facilitate business-tobusiness transactions with potential new customers. These processes allow customers, by using computer-aided design software, to view the specification of products available, to assemble them and to integrate their own components into the design. This means that they are able to construct virtual prototypes of machines and equipment. This process design, delivered through a web service, is still under development.

Tackling operational problems

In parallel, *greenTech* has decided to make tactical changes to current processes where the company has received poor customer feedback. One of these is the ordering of fully assembled green computers. The current Internet-based process for ordering and configuring these computers is described below. A swim-lane diagram (flowchart) showing the process is also included as Figure 4.

On-line customers use the *greenTech* web site to enter the specific computer configuration they require. These details are fed through to the sales department at *greenTech* which then e-mails Xsys – *greenTech*'s Korean manufacturer – to ask for a delivery date for the requested computer. Xsys e-mails the date back to *greenTech* which then e-mails the customer with delivery and cost details. The customer then decides whether they wish to proceed with their order. Currently, 40% of enquiries proceed no further, which is of concern to *greenTech* as it means that time and effort have been wasted.

For those enquiries that do proceed, customers are invited to enter their payment details (credit card only). These details are sent directly to Equicheck – a specialist credit checking agency. About 20% of orders are rejected at this point because the potential customer has a poor credit rating. For orders that pass the credit check, a payment confirmation is raised by *greenTech* and sent to the customer and *greenTech* place a confirmed order with Xsys for the computer.

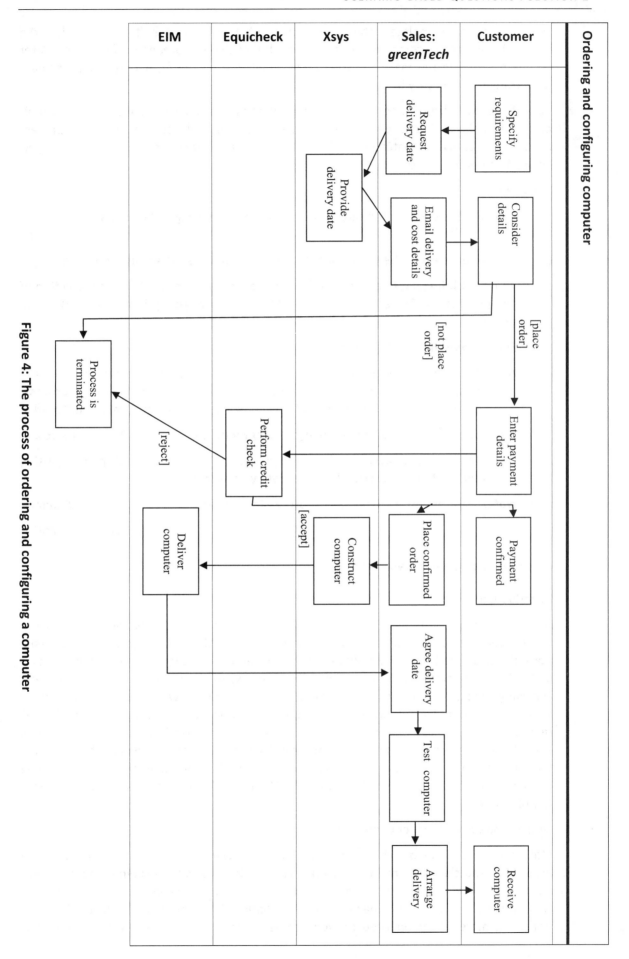

Figure 4: The process of ordering and configuring a computer

When Xsys has completed the construction of the computer it arranges for the international logistics company EIM to deliver the machine to *greenTech* for testing. After acceptance testing the machine, *greenTech* e-mails the customer, agrees a delivery date and arranges for delivery by courier.

Recent feedback from customers suggests that missing promised delivery dates is their biggest complaint. This is because the delivery date agreed early in the order process cannot necessarily be matched by Xsys when it actually receives the confirmed order. Figure 4 shows the process involved.

Required:

(a)   **Evaluate the current strategic position of greenTech using a SWOT analysis.**

(12 marks)

(b)   **The panel selected the proposal of Professor Ag Wan as the winning proposal.**

   Write a briefing paper evaluating the three proposals and justifying the selection of the proposal of Professor Ag Wan as the best strategic option for greenTech to pursue.

   Note: requirement (b) includes 2 professional marks.   (20 marks)

(c)   (i)   **Identify deficiencies in the current Internet-based process for ordering and configuring fully assembled green computers. Recommend a new process, together with its implications, for remedying these deficiencies.**   (10 marks)

   (ii)   **The board is determined to link strategy with current and future processes.**

      Analyse the relationship between process design and strategic planning using the context of greenTech to illustrate your analysis.

      Note: requirement (c)(ii) includes 2 professional marks.   (8 marks)

(Total: 50 marks)

74   UNIVERSAL ROOFING SYSTEMS

Introduction

Universal Roofing Systems is a family owned and managed business specialising in the design, assembly and installation of low maintenance PVC roofing products for domestic housing. These products include PVC fascia boards and rainwater drainage systems. Set up in 1997 by two brothers, Matthew and Simon Black, the firm has grown year on year, achieving almost $1 million sales revenue by the year 20X3. Universal's products, or rather services, are primarily for private house owners, though a significant amount of sales revenue is coming from commercial house owners, mainly local government authorities and housing associations, providing cheaper housing for rent. Universal has recently received central government recognition and an award for its contribution to providing employment in deprived inner city areas. In 20X4 and 20X5, it was the fastest growing inner city firm in the region.

Origins and competitive environment

Matthew and Simon's decision to go into business owed a considerable amount to the experience and skills they had gained working in their father's local cabinet and carpentry business. At their father's insistence, both were skilled cabinet-makers and shared his commitment to quality workmanship and installation. Their decision to start a business using PVC materials as opposed to wood came as an unwelcome shock to their father.

However, the opportunity to install PVC roofing boards on the house of a commercial contact provided the stimulus for them to go into business on their own account.

In the UK there are some 25 million houses, of which 17 million are privately owned and 8 million rented. New housing is now usually built with PVC doors and windows installed, so it is the replacement market of rotten wooden doors and windows in existing houses that the manufacturers and installers of PVC windows and doors focus on. PVC offers some significant advantages to the owner/occupier – it is virtually maintenance free and improves the appearance of the house. Consequently, there is a high demand for PVC replacement doors and windows, estimated at $1.5 billion in the year 20X2. This has attracted some large-scale manufacturers and installers. They compete aggressively for market share and use equally aggressive direct sales and promotion techniques to attract house owners to their product.

Although the market for PVC windows and doors is reasonably mature, there has been no significant movement of large companies into the installation of roofing products. Their complex design and location at the top of a house mean that these products are much more complex and difficult to install. Economies of scale are harder to achieve and, as a consequence, the installation of PVC roofing systems is largely in the hands of small businesses able to charge high prices and frequently giving a poor quality service to the house owner. In a market with potential sales revenue of $750 million a year, no firm accounts for more than 3%. It was against this fragmented, but significant market that Universal wanted to offer something distinctively different.

Operational processes

Matthew and Simon looked at the whole process of delivering a quality service in replacement PVC roofing systems. The experience of the PVC door and window installers showed the long-term rates of growth possible through actively promoting and selling the service. Supplies of PVC board and fittings were reasonably easy to obtain from the small number of large UK companies extruding PVC boards in large volumes. However, the unequal bargaining power meant that these suppliers dominated and were difficult to involve in any product development. Sales were generated by door-to-door canvassing, followed by a visit from a company sales representative who tried to complete the sale. Advertising in the press, radio and TV now supported this sales activity. In the early days the opportunity was taken to sell the service at Saturday markets and, being so small, Universal could often pleasantly surprise the house owner by offering virtually immediate installation. Matthew and Simon promoted, sold and installed the systems. One of their key early decisions was to use a new Mercedes van with Universal's name and logo prominently displayed, to carry the bulky PVC materials to their customers' houses. In one move they differentiated themselves from their low cost/low quality competitors and got the company's name recognised.

The skills and experience of the brothers meant that they were able to critically examine the installation process being used by their small competitors to deliver a poor standard of service. Their eventual design incorporated innovative roofing design and parts from Europe and a unique installation stand or frame that provided the installer with quick, easy and safe access to the roofs of the houses being worked on. This greatly improved the productivity of Universal's installation team over competitors using traditional methods. The brothers recognised that, without the ability to offer a service that could be packaged, given standard prices and procedures and made as 'installer friendly' as possible, they too would be limited to small scale operation and poor service. Being able to replicate a process time after time was the key to delivering an improved service and preventing each job being seen as a 'one-off'. In Matthew's words, 'Whenever the customer can have a predictable experience and you can say that this is what we are going to do, this is the way we are going to do it and this is how much it will cost, the product/service usually goes problem free'.

Ultimately, the installers of the roofing systems determined quality. The brothers quickly built up a team of installers, all of whom worked as sub-contractors and were not directly employed by the company. This gave the company the flexibility to vary the number of teams according to the level of customer demand. Installation took place throughout the year, though it could be affected by winter weather. The two-man teams were given comprehensive training in installation and customer care. Payment was by results and responsibility for correcting any installation faults rested with the team doing the particular installation.

Sales and marketing

Marketing and promotion were recognised as key to getting the company's name known and its reputation for a quality installation service established. Comprehensive sales support materials were created for use by the canvassers and sales representatives. Sales representative were able to offer significant discounts to house owners willing to make an immediate decision to buy a Universal roofing system. In addition Universal received a significant income stream from a finance house for roofing systems, sold on extended payment terms.

Universal offered a unique 10-year guarantee on its installations and proudly announced that over 30% of new customers were directly recommended from existing satisfied customers. The growth of the company had led to showrooms being set up in six large towns in the region and the business plans for 20X7 and 20X8 will see a further nine showrooms opening in the region, each of which costs $30k. Brand awareness was reinforced by the continued use of up-to-date Mercedes vans with the company's logo and contact details prominently shown.

Company structure and performance

By 20X7, the organisational structure of the company was in place, based on functional responsibilities. Matthew was now Managing Director, Simon was Operations Director with responsibility for the installation teams, and Matthew's wife, Fiona, was Company Secretary and responsible for the administration and scheduling side of the business. Two key appointments had facilitated Universal's rapid growth. In 20X4, Mick Hendry was appointed as Sales and Marketing Director. Mick had 20 years of experience with direct sales in a large installer of PVC windows and doors. Through his efforts, Universal achieved a step change in sales revenue growth, with sales revenue increasing from $1 million in 20X3 to $3.3 million in 20X4. However, the increased costs involved meant the company made a loss of some $250,000. 20X5 saw sales revenue increase to $5.4 million and a profit generated. 20X6 saw further sales revenue increase to $6.8 million and a net profit of about $400k. Matthew recognised the increasing pressure on his own time and an inability to control the financial side of the business. 20X5 saw Harry Potts appointed as Finance Director and put in much needed financial and management information systems.

Future growth and development

By 20X7 Universal had seen 10 years of significant growth and was facing some interesting decisions as to how that growth was to be sustained. First, there was the opportunity to move from a largely regional operation into being a national company. Indeed, the company's vision statement expressed the desire to become 'the most respected roofing company in Britain', based on a 'no surprises' philosophy that house owners all around the country could trust. Economic factors encouraging growth looked fairly promising with a growing economy, stable interest rates and house owners finding it fairly easy to raise additional funding necessary to pay for home improvements. Second, there was a real opportunity to develop their share of the commercial housing market. The government had committed itself to a significant improvement in the standard of housing provided to people renting from local authorities and housing associations. Despite the appointment of a Commercial Manager to concentrate on sales into this specialist market, Universal had real difficulty in committing sufficient resources into exploiting this opportunity. In 20X4 commercial sales revenue represented over 11% of total sales revenue, but currently commercial sales were around 5% of the total sales revenue. Such were the overall growth predictions, however, that to maintain this share of sales would need commercial sales revenue to more than double over the 20X7–9 period. Without the necessary commitment of resources, particularly people, this target was unlikely to be realised. Universal's products also need to be improved and this largely depended on its ability to get into partnerships with its large PVC suppliers. There were some encouraging signs in this direction, but Universal's reliance on PVC opened it to future challenges from installers using more environmentally friendly materials.

Above all, however, the rate of projected growth would place considerable pressures on the senior management team's ability to manage the process. The move towards becoming a national installer was already prompting thoughts about creating a regional level of management. Finally, such had been the firm's growth record that its inability to meet the budgeted sales revenue targets in the first quarter of 20X7 was causing real concern for Matthew and Simon.

Table 1: Information on Universal's current sales revenue and financial performance ($000) (where appropriate)

	20X3	20X4	20X5	20X6	20X7 Budget	20X8 Forecast	20X9 Forecast
Domestic sales revenue	854	2,914	5,073	6,451	9,600	15,000	20,500
Commercial sales revenue	36	362	269	324	450	750	1,100
Total sales revenue	890	3,276	5,342	6,775	10,050	15,750	21,600
Materials	169	589	766	925	1,339	2,105	2,890
Direct labour	329	1,105	1,941	2,290	3,333	5,125	7,019
Gross margin	392	1,582	2,635	3,560	5,378	8,520	11,691
Sales commission	20	369	627	781	1,171	1,845	2,501
Canvassers' commissions	74	563	764	962	1,420	2,190	2,993
Marketing	32	171	223	398	657	1,020	1,374
Total sales costs	126	1,103	1,614	2,141	3,248	5,055	6,868
Contribution before overhead	266	479	1,021	1,419	2,130	3,465	4,823
Total overheads	272	723	862	1,140	1,536	2,030	2,627
Trading profit before commission	−6	−244	159	279	594	1,435	2,196
Finance income	0	25	65	115	167	262	342
Net profit	−6	−219	224	394	761	1,697	2,538

Required:

(a) Using an appropriate model, analyse the ways in which Universal has provided a superior level of service to its customers. **(20 marks)**

(b) Using the information provided in the case scenario, strategically evaluate the performance of the company up to 20X6, indicating any areas of particular concern.

(15 marks)

Matthew Black is well aware that the achievement of the growth targets for the 20X7 to 20X9 period will depend on successful implementation of the strategy, affecting all parts of the company's activities.

Required:

(c) Explain the key issues affecting implementation and the changes necessary to achieve Universal's ambitious growth strategy. **(15 marks)**

(Total: 50 marks)

75 DATUM PAPER PRODUCTS (DPP)

Introduction and industry background

The current European market for Datum Paper Products (DPP) in 20X7 is not encouraging. The company designs and manufactures textile fabrics for use in the paper industry. Its main customers are large European and American paper making companies and while the UK market is fairly stable, over 80% of DPP's products are sold abroad. Its customers use highly expensive capital equipment, with a new paper mill costing $300 million or more. The paper makers supply paper to global newspaper and book publishers who themselves are under pressure to consolidate as a result of the growing competition from alternative information providers, such as TV and the Internet. The industry, therefore, carries many of the signs of a mature industry, the paper manufacturers have considerable overcapacity and are supplying customers who themselves are facing intense competition. Paper makers are looking to reduce the number of suppliers and for these suppliers to meet all their needs. The net result is heavy pressure on suppliers such as DPP to discount prices and improve international service levels, although there is little potential to increase sales volumes to achieve further economies of scale. DPP's response to this more competitive environment has been to attempt to secure higher volumes through increasing their market share and to search for cost reductions in spite of the need to improve customer service levels.

DPP is one of a number of operating companies in the paper and ancillary products division of Park Group Industries plc, a diversified company with other divisions in industrial materials, automotive products and speciality chemicals. The paper and ancillary products division itself is split into the North American Region and the European Region. There are some 30 companies in the division with plants in 13 countries. Within the paper and ancillary products division there is recognition that in order to survive let alone make a profit some industry restructuring is necessary. Currently, DP has some four UK plants manufacturing different parts of their product range. Any consolidation, including acquisition, is best done on a regional basis and Europe seems a logical place to start.

Strategic options – acquisition or a greenfield site?

Ken Drummond is Managing Director of DPP, and has spent a lifetime in the paper industry but has had little experience in acquiring other companies. The pressures faced by the European industry mean that there are, in reality, two strategic options to achieve the necessary restructuring. Firstly, there are opportunities to buy existing companies available in most European countries. The identification of suitable target companies, the carrying out of due diligence procedures before negotiating a deal and integration of the acquired company typically takes a year to complete. The second option is to move to one of the countries that have entered the European Union in 20X4 where operating costs are significantly lower. There are significant government and European Union incentives for firms that move to a new or greenfield site in one of the many economically depressed areas. The greenfield option would take up to three years to get a plant set up and operating.

The acquisition option

Ken is able to draw on the expertise of corporate headquarters that has had some experience with growth by both organic expansion and by acquisition. The initial search for possible acquisition candidates has revealed a French family owned and managed firm, 'Papier Presse', based in the southwest of France, some 800 kilometres from DPP's main plant in the UK. Papier Presse has three manufacturing plants in France, each heavily unionised and controlled by the owner Philippe Truffaud. Papier Presse's markets are exclusively with European paper makers and it has no significant international business outside of the EU. The technology used is more dated than DPP's and manning levels are significantly higher. Papier Presse's product range has some significant overlap with DPP's but there are also some distinctive products. Philippe's son, Francois, is Sales and Marketing Director and his son-in-law, Henri, is Operations Manager. Philippe himself is the third generation of Truffauds to run the firm. Ken recognises the considerable differences between DPP and its potential French partner – language being only the most obvious one. The sales, service and distribution systems of the two firms are totally distinct but their customers include the same European paper makers. Reconciling the two information systems would be difficult, with customers looking for much higher service levels. Historically, DPP, with its own research and development function, has a better record of product improvement and innovation. However, Papier Presse is better regarded by its customers for its flexibility in meeting their changing demands. In terms of strategic planning DPP contributes to the strategic plans drawn up at divisional level, while the family dominance at Papier Presse means that planning is much more opportunistic and largely focused on the year ahead. Each company has to operate within a climate of heightened environmental concern over toxic by-products of the manufacturing process. There are other similarities in that both companies have felt that product superiority is the route to success but whereas DPP's is through product innovation; Papier Presse's is through customer service. Clearly integrating the two companies will present some interesting challenges and the family ownership of Papier Presse means that a significant premium may have to be paid over the current book value of the company.

The greenfield option

Ken, however, also recognises that the apparent benefits of moving onto a new greenfield site in one of the countries recently admitted into the European Union will itself bring difficulties. One obvious difficulty is the lack of a modern support infrastructure in terms of suppliers, distributors and logistical support. There is also a strong tradition of government intervention in company growth and development. Although there are government agencies looking to attract new companies to set up in these countries, there are considerable bureaucratic and time consuming procedures to overcome. Above all there is continuing government financial support for small inefficient, formerly state-owned, companies making the products for the national paper makers, who themselves are small and inefficient compared to the customers being supplied by DPP and Papier Presse.

Table 1: Financial information on DPP and Papier Presse ($000,000) for 20X7

	Datum Paper Products	Papier Presse
Sales revenue	195.5	90.0
Cost of sales	122.2	67.5
Gross margin	73.3	22.5
Sales & administration	27.4	9.0
Marketing	9.5	1.4
R & D	4.5	0.5
Depreciation	10.0	1.0
Operating profit	21.9	10.6
Net assets	275.0	148.0
Debt	100.0	68.0
Equity	175.0	80.0
Earnings per share	12.5p	13.3p
Dividend per share	5.6p	10.0p
Return on sales revenue	11.2%	11.8%
Employees	1250	750
Absenteeism (days p.a.)	8	16
Patents – 20X6	5	0
Manufacturing facilities	4	3
Sales revenue from products less than 5 years old	20%	5%

	Datum Paper Products	Papier Presse
Share of major European markets:		
UK	45%	14%
France	10%	60%
Italy	8%	20%
Germany	15%	15%
Spain	10%	25%
Sales outside Europe	50%	5%
North America region	40%	3%
Rest of World	10%	2%

Required:

(a) Using the data provided and models where appropriate, assess the strategic fit between Datum Paper Products and Papier Presse, indicating areas where positive or negative synergies are likely to exist. **(20 marks)**

(b) Assuming that the acquisition proceeds, what steps will Datum Paper Products need to take to build a shared culture in the two companies? **(10 marks)**

(c) Assess the advantages and disadvantages to Datum Paper Products taking the greenfield option as opposed to the acquisition of Papier Presse. **(10 marks)**

(d) There is considerable evidence to suggest that as a result of implementation problems less than 50% of all acquisitions achieve their objectives and actually end up reducing shareholder value.

Required:

Provide Ken with a brief report on the most likely sources of integration problems and describe the key performance indicators he should use to measure progress towards acquisition objectives. **(10 marks)**

(Total: 50 marks)

76   CHURCHILL ICE CREAM

Churchill Ice Cream is a medium-sized family owned company, making and selling a range of premium ice cream products. Its origins were in the middle years of the twentieth century, when John Churchill saw an opportunity to supply a growing consumer demand for luxury products. John has been followed into the business by his two sons and the Churchill family has dominated the ownership and management of the company. In 20X2 there was recognition of the need to bring in outside management expertise and John reluctantly accepted the need to relinquish his position as chairman and chief executive of the company. Richard Smith, formerly a senior executive with one of the major supermarket chains, was appointed as chief executive. Within one year of Richard's appointment he had recruited Churchill's first sales and marketing director. Richard was consciously looking to reduce the dominance by the Churchill family and make the company a more marketing orientated business able to meet the increased competitive challenges of the 21st century.

Churchill's distinctive strategy

Churchill Ice Cream is in many ways an unusual company, choosing to both manufacture its premium ice cream and sell its products through its own stores. Specialist ice cream stores or parlours had started in the US and soon spread to the UK. Customers can both buy and eat ice cream in the store. John Churchill saw the growing demand for such specialist ice cream stores and created a unique store format, which quickly established the Churchill brand. Most of these stores are owned by the company, but there are also some smaller franchised outlets. By 20X6 it had 40 ice cream stores owned by the company and a further 18 owned by franchise holders. Franchise stores typically are in less attractive locations than their company-owned equivalents. All stores are located in and around the London area.

The logic for manufacturing its own ice cream is a strongly held belief that through sourcing its ingredients from local farmers and suppliers it gains a significant competitive advantage. Making its own ice cream also has enabled it to retain control over the unique recipes used in its premium ice cream product range. John Churchill summed up the policy saying 'We are no more expensive than the market leader but we are much better. We use real chocolate and it's real dairy ice cream. Half our expenditure goes on our ingredients and packaging. It's by far our highest cost.' Dairy ice cream, as opposed to cheaper ice cream, uses milk, butter and cream instead of vegetable oils to blend with sugar and flavourings. These ingredients are blended to produce a wide range of products. Churchill has also developed a product range with no artificial additives hoping to differentiate itself from the competition.

Product innovation is a key capability in the ice cream market and 40% of industry sales are made from products less than three years old. Churchill's products are made at a new purpose built factory and supplied quickly and directly to its own ice cream stores and other retail outlets. Unfortunately, detailed and timely information about product and store performance has suffered through a delay in introducing a management information system. Consequently its stores often faced product shortages during the peak summer months.

In 20X4 Churchill became the sponsor and sole supplier to a number of high profile summer sporting events held in London. Churchill also supplies eight million tubs of ice cream each year to London based cinemas and theatres. As a consequence, Churchill is now an established regional brand with 90% customer recognition in the London area. It also has major ambitions to become a national and eventually an international brand though facing significant competition from two global chains of US owned premium ice cream stores.

Their high profile moves into the UK market was backed with expensive advertising and succeeded in expanding the demand for all premium ice creams.

The UK retail ice cream market

Ice cream is bought in two main ways: either from retail outlets such as supermarkets for later consumption at home or on impulse for immediate consumption from a range of outlets, including ice cream stores such as Churchill's.

Impulse sales are much more dependent on the weather and in 20X4 sales of take home ice cream and impulse ice cream were roughly equal. Total sales revenue of ice cream in the UK reached $1.3 billion in 20X4. Premium ice cream in 20X6 accounted for 19% of the UK's take home market, up from 15% in 20X3.

Churchill itself does not use advertising. In John Churchill's words, 'There is no point in advertising your product if consumers are unable to buy the product.' Churchill has yet to achieve significant sales into the take home market. Two major barriers exist. Firstly, global manufacturers with significant global brands dominate the industry. Secondly, four major UK supermarket chains dominate the take home market. These supermarket chains account for over 80% of food spending in the UK and have the power to demand that suppliers manufacture their products under the supermarket's own label brand. Supermarkets currently account for 41% of the sales of ice cream in the UK.

However, it is proving difficult to get the Churchill product range into the ice cream cabinets of the supermarket chains. In John Churchill's opinion 'If you want to buy a tub of premium ice cream and you go to a supermarket you have a choice of two American brands or its own label. I think there should be a British brand in there. Our prices are competitive, at least $1 cheaper than our rivals and our aim is to get Churchill ice cream into every major supermarket.' Some limited success has been achieved with two of the smaller supermarket chains with premium ice cream supplied under their own label brands. However, margins are very slim on these sales.

Churchill's international strategy

Churchill, in seeking to increase its sales revenue, has had no success in moving into foreign markets. In the 1990s it tried both setting up its own ice cream stores abroad and acquiring specialist ice cream makers with their own ice cream outlets. Its attempted entry into the US market was by using the established Churchill ice cream store format. Two stores were opened in New York, but the hopes that the emphasis on classic English quality and style and the slogan 'tradition with taste', would prove successful did not materialise and the stores were closed with significant losses – each store took upwards of $100k to fit out.

Acquisition of two established ice cream makers, one in Germany and one in Italy also proved failures. Access to their retail outlets and to complementary product ranges did not overcome differences in taste and customer buying behaviour. Despite attempts to change some of the German and Italian outlets to the Churchill store format the results were less than impressive and the two companies were eventually sold at a combined loss of $5 million.

Table 1 Financial information on Churchill Ice Cream ($000)

	20X3	20X4	20X5	20X6	20X7 Forecast
Sales revenue	14,100	15,300	16,000	16,400	16,700
Cost of sales	12,790	14,250	14,990	15,360	15,760
Operating profit	1,310	1,050	1,010	1,040	940
Product development	340	530	560	310	500
Net profit	970	520	450	730	440

Non-current assets	10,910	10,400	9,670	8,880	8,320
Net assets	4,810	4,910	4,000	4,300	4,300
Gearing (%)	105	130	111	86	67
Number of UK outlets					
Own store	39	41	40	40	39
Franchised stores	11	13	16	18	20
Index of UK ice cream sales	106	109	107	104	109

Table 2 Typical product cost breakdown of a Churchill half-litre tub of premium ice cream

	$
Labour	0.63
Ingredients	1.00
Packaging	0.25
Overheads	0.28
Distribution	0.09
Total cost	2.25
Sales price	2.50
Net profit	0.25

Table 3 Sales revenue breakdown for Churchill's premium ice cream

Sales to own stores	60%
Sales to franchise stores	10%
Sales to leisure outlets	25%
Sales to supermarkets	5%
Sales to London region	90%
Sales outside London region	10%

Summary

Overall, Churchill has a distinctive strategy linking the manufacturing of premium ice cream with its distribution through the company's own ice cream stores. This has secured them a regional reputation for a quality product. It has had little success to date in penetrating the major supermarket chains with the Churchill brand and in moving its distinctive ice cream store format into foreign markets. Finally, to complicate both the manufacturing and retail sides of the Churchill business, seasonality is a real issue. Ice cream is still heavily dominated by sales in the summer months. In fact the peak demand in summer is typically five times the demand in the middle of winter. Equally serious is the impact of a cold summer on impulse ice cream sales. This has a number of consequences, which affect the costs of the product and capacity usage at both manufacturing and retail levels.

Despite this, Richard Smith has set three clear strategic goals to be achieved over the next five years. First, to become the leading premium ice cream brand in the UK, second, to increase sales revenue to $25 million and third, to penetrate the supermarket sector with the Churchill product range.

Required:

Richard Smith has set three clear strategic goals for Churchill's growth and development over the next five years.

(a) **Using models where appropriate, assess the advantages and disadvantages of the current strategy being pursued by Churchill Ice Cream and its impact on performance up to 20X6.** **(20 marks)**

(b) **Using relevant evaluation criteria, assess how achievable and compatible these three strategic goals are over the next five years.** **(15 marks)**

(c) **What changes to Churchill's existing marketing mix will be needed to achieve the three strategic goals?** **(10 marks)**

Churchill Ice Cream has to date made two unsuccessful attempts to become an international company.

(d) **What reasons would you suggest to explain this failure of Churchill Ice Cream to become an international company?** **(5 marks)**

(Total: 50 marks)

77 SHIRTMASTER GROUP

Introduction

Tony Masters, chairman and chief executive of the Shirtmaster Group, is worried. He has recently responded to his senior management team's concerns over the future of the Group by reluctantly agreeing to appoint an external management consultant. The consultant's brief is to fully analyse the performance of the privately owned company, identify key strategic and operational problems and recommend a future strategy for the company. Tony is concerned that the consultant's report will seriously question his role in the company and the growth strategy he is proposing.

Group origins and structure

Tony's father, Howard Masters, set up Shirtmaster in the 1950s. Howard was a skilled tailor and saw the potential for designing and manufacturing a distinctive range of men's shirts and ties marketed under the 'Shirtmaster' brand. Howard set up a shirt manufacturing company with good access to the employee skills needed to design and make shirts. Howard had recognised the opportunity to make distinctive shirts incorporating innovative design features including the latest man-made fibres. In the 1960s London was a global fashion centre exploiting the UK's leading position in popular music. Men became much more fashion conscious, and were willing to pay premium prices for clothes with style and flair. Shirtmaster by the 1960s had built up a UK network of more than 2,000 small independent clothing retailers. These retailers sold the full range of men's wear including made-to-measure suits, shirts and matching ties, shoes and other clothing accessories. Extensive and expensive TV and cinema advertising supported the Shirtmaster brand.

The Shirtmaster Group is made up of two divisions – the Shirtmaster division which concentrates on the retail shirt business and the Corporate Clothing division which supplies workwear to large industrial and commercial customers. Corporate Clothing has similar origins to Shirtmaster, also being a family owned and managed business and is located in the same town as Shirtmaster. It was set up to supply hardwearing jeans and workwear to the many factory workers in the region. The decline of UK manufacturing and allied industries led to profitability problems and in 1990 the Shirtmaster Group acquired it. Tony took over executive responsibility for the Group in 1996 and continues to act as managing director for the Shirtmaster Division.

Shirtmaster division – operations and market environment

By 20X7 the UK market for men's shirts was very different to that of the 1960s and 1970s when Shirtmaster had become one of the best known premium brands. In a mature market most of Shirtmaster's competitors have outsourced the making of their shirts to low cost manufacturers in Europe and the Far East. Shirtmaster is virtually alone in maintaining a UK manufacturing base. Once a year Tony and the buyer for the division go to Asia and the Far East, visiting cloth manufacturers and buying for inventory. This inventory, stored in the division's warehouse, gives the ability to create a wide range of shirt designs but creates real problems with excessive inventory holdings and outdated inventory. Shirtmaster prides itself on its ability to respond to the demands of its small retail customers and the long-term relationships built up with these retailers. Typically, these retailers order in small quantities and want quick delivery. Shirtmaster has to introduce new shirt designs throughout the year, contrasting with the spring and autumn ranges launched by its competitors. This creates real pressure on the small design team available.

The retail side of the shirt business has undergone even more fundamental change. Though the market for branded shirts continues to exist, such shirts are increasingly sold through large departmental stores. There is increasing competition between the shirt makers for the limited shelf space available in the departmental stores. Shopping centres and malls are increasingly dominated by nationwide chains of specialist clothing retailers. They sell to the premium segment of the market and are regarded as the trendsetters for the industry. These chains can develop quickly, often using franchising to achieve rapid growth, and are increasingly international in scope. All of them require their suppliers to make their clothes under the chain's own label brand. Some have moved successfully into selling via catalogues and the Internet. Finally, the UK supermarket chains have discovered the profitability of selling non-food goods. The shirts they sell are aimed at value for money rather than style, sourced wherever they can be made most cheaply and sold under the supermarket's own label. Small independent clothing retailers are declining both in number and market share.

The Shirtmaster division, with its continued over-reliance for its sales on these small independent retailers, is threatened by each of the retail driven changes, having neither the sales volume to compete on price nor the style to compete on fashion.

The Shirtmaster division's international strategy

Tony's answer to these changes is to make the Shirtmaster brand an international one. His initial strategy is to sell to European clothing retailers and once established, move the brand into the fast growing consumer markets in Asia and the Far East. He recognises that the division's current UK focus means that working with a European partner is a necessity. He has given the sales and marketing manager the job of finding major retailers, distributors or manufacturers with whom they can make a strategic alliance and so help get the Shirtmaster range onto the shelves of European clothing retailers.

Corporate Clothing division – operations and market environment

Corporate Clothing has in recent years implemented a major turnaround in its business as the market for corporate clothing began to grow significantly. Corporate Clothing designs, manufactures and distributes a comprehensive range of workwear for its corporate customers, sourcing much of its range from low cost foreign suppliers. It supplies the corporate clothing requirements of large customers in the private and public sectors. Major contracts have been gained with banks, airlines, airports and the police, fire and ambulance services.

The Corporate Clothing division supplies the whole range of workwear required and in the sizes needed for each individual employee. Its designers work closely with the buyers in its large customers and the division's sales revenue benefit from the regular introduction of new styles of uniforms and workwear. Corporate employers are increasingly aware of the external image they need to project and the clothes their employees wear are the key to this image.

Corporate Clothing has invested heavily in manufacturing and IT systems to ensure that it meets the needs of its demanding customers. It is particularly proud of its computer-aided design and manufacturing (CAD/CAM) systems, which can be linked to its customers and allows designs to be updated and manufacturing alterations to be introduced with its customers' approval. Much of its success can be attributed to the ability to offer a customer service package in which garments are stored by Corporate Clothing and distributed directly to the individual employee in personalised workwear sets as and when required. The UK market for corporate workwear was worth $500 million in 20X6. Evidence suggests that the demand for corporate workwear is likely to continue to grow.

The Corporate Clothing division also has ambitions to enter the markets for corporate clothing in Europe and recognises that might be most easily done through using a suitable strategic partner. There is friendly rivalry between the two divisions but each operates largely independently of the other. Over the past 10 years the fortunes of the two divisions have been completely reversed. Corporate Clothing now is a modest profit maker for the group – Shirtmaster is consistently losing money.

Shirtmaster Group – future strategy

Tony is determined to re-establish Shirtmaster as a leading shirt brand in the UK and successfully launch the brand in Europe. He sees a strategic alliance with a European partner as the key to achieving this ambition. Though he welcomes the success of the Corporate Clothing division and recognises its potential in Europe, he remains emotionally and strategically committed to restoring the fortunes of the Shirtmaster division. Unfortunately, his autocratic style of leadership tends to undermine the position of the senior management team at Shirtmaster. He continues to play an active role in both the operational and strategic sides of the business and is both well known and regarded by workers in the Shirtmaster division's factory.

The initial feedback meeting with the management consultant has confirmed the concern that he is not delegating sufficiently. The consultant commented that Tony's influence could be felt throughout the Shirtmaster division. Managers either try to anticipate the decisions they think he would make or, alternatively, not take the decisions until he has given his approval. The end result is a division not able to meet the challenges of an increasingly competitive retail marketplace, and losing both money and market share.

Table 1 – Financial Information on the Shirtmaster Group ($ million)

	20X4	20X5	20X6	20X7 Budget	20X8 Forecast	20X8 Forecast
Total sales revenue	25.0	23.8	21.4	23.5	24.4	26.7
UK sales revenue	24.5	23.2	21.0	22.7	23.4	24.7
Overseas sales revenue	0.5	0.6	0.4	0.8	1.0	2.0
Cost of sales	17.7	16.8	15.2	16.3	16.8	17.8
Gross profit	7.3	7.0	6.2	7.2	7.6	8.9

	20X4	20X5	20X6	20X7 Budget	20X8 Forecast	20X8 Forecast
Marketing	1.7	1.5	1.2	1.7	1.9	2.2
Distribution	1.6	1.4	1.2	1.4	1.5	1.9
Administration	1.8	1.8	1.7	1.9	1.9	2.1
	20X4	20X5	20X6	20X7 Budget	20X8 Forecast	20X8 Forecast
Net profit	2.2	2.3	1.2	3.2	2.3	2.7
Shirtmaster division						
Total sales revenue	14.8	12.6	10.3	11.7	12.0	13.5
UK sales revenue	14.3	12.0	9.9	10.9	11.0	11.5
Overseas sales revenue	0.5	0.6	0.4	0.8	1.0	2.0
Cost of sales	11.1	9.8	8.2	9.1	9.4	10.1
Gross profit	3.7	2.8	2.1	2.6	2.6	3.4
Marketing	1.5	1.3	1.0	1.5	1.7	2.0
Distribution	1.2	1.0	0.8	0.9	1.0	1.3
Administration	1.3	1.2	1.1	1.2	1.2	1.3
Net profit	(0.3)	(0.7)	(0.8)	(1.0)	(1.3)	(0.2)
Inventory	2.0	2.2	3.0	2.7	2.5	2.0
Employees	100	100	98	98	99	100

Required:

(a) Assess the strategic position and performance of the Shirtmaster Group and its divisions over the 20X4–20X6 period. Your analysis should make use of models where appropriate. **(20 marks)**

(b) Both divisions have recognised the need for a strategic alliance to help them achieve a successful entry into European markets.

Critically evaluate the advantages and disadvantages of the divisions using strategic alliances to develop their respective businesses in Europe. **(15 marks)**

(c) The Shirtmaster division and Corporate Clothing division, though being part of the same group, operate largely independently of one another.

Assess the costs and benefits of the two divisions continuing to operate independently of one another. **(8 marks)**

(d) Family owned and managed businesses often find delegation and succession difficult processes to get right.

What models would you recommend that Tony use in looking to change his leadership and management style to create a culture in the Shirtmaster Group better able to deal with the challenges it faces? **(7 marks)**

(Total: 50 marks)

78 NETWORK MANAGEMENT SYSTEMS

Introduction

Network Management Systems (NMS) is a privately owned high technology company established in 1997 by computer engineer, Ray Edwards. It is situated in the country of Elsidor, a prosperous developed nation with a stable well established political system. Successive governments in Elsidor have promoted technology by providing grants and tax incentives. Tax credits are also provided to offset company investment in research and development. The government, like many governments worldwide, have invested heavily in a national telecommunications infrastructure. However, in 2010 the country suffered an economic downturn that led many companies to postpone technological investment.

By 2010 NMS employed 75 full-time employees in a new, purpose-built factory and office unit. These employees were a mixture of technically qualified engineers, working in research and development (R&D), factory staff manufacturing and assembling products and a small sales and service support team.

Product areas

In 2010, NMS had three distinct product/service areas – data communication components, network management systems and, finally, technical support.

NMS sells data communication components to original equipment manufacturers (OEMs), who use these components in their hardware. Both the OEMs and their customers are predominantly large international companies. NMS has established a good reputation for the quality and performance of its components, which are competitively priced. However, NMS has less than 1% of the domestic marketplace and faces competition from over twenty significant suppliers, most of who also compete internationally. Furthermore, one of the company's OEM customers accounts for 40% of its sales in this area. The international market for data communication components had increased from $33billion in 2001 to $81billion in 2010. Forecasts for 2011 and beyond predict growth from increased sales to currently installed networks rather than from the installation of new networks. The maturity of the technology means that product lifecycles are becoming shorter. Success comes from producing high volumes of reliable components at relatively low prices. NMS produces components in a relatively prosperous country where there is significant legislation defining maximum work hours and minimum wage rates. All new components have to be approved by an appropriate government approval body in each country that NMS supplies. This approval process is both costly and time consuming.

The second product area is network management systems. NMS originally supplied fault detection systems to a small number of large end-users such as banks, public utility providers and global manufacturers. NMS recognised the unique requirements of each customer and so it customised its product to meet specific needs and requirements. They pioneered a modular design which allowed customers to adapt standard system modules to fit their exact networking requirements. The success of their product led to it being awarded a prestigious government technology award for "technological innovation in data communications". This further enhanced the company's reputation and enabled it to become a successful niche player in a relatively low volume market with gross margins in excess of 40%. They only have two or three competitors in this specialist market. Unlike component manufacture, there is no requirement to seek government approval for new network products.

Finally, the complexity of NMS products means that technical support is a third key business area. It has an excellent reputation for this support. However, it is increasingly difficult and costly to maintain the required level of support because the company does not have a geographically distributed network of support engineers. All technical support is provided from its headquarters. This contrasts with the national and international support services of their large competitors.

Current issues

NMS currently manufacture 40% of the components used in its products. The rest of the components, including semiconductors and microprocessors, are bought in from a few selected global suppliers. Serious production problems have resulted from periodic component shortages, creating significant delays in manufacturing, assembly and customer deliveries.

NMS is still a relatively immature organisation. There are small functional departments for sales and marketing, technical research and development, manufacturing and procurement. Ray still personally undertakes all staff recruitment and staff development. He is finding the recruitment of high calibre staff a problem, with NMS' small size and geographical location making it difficult to attract the key personnel necessary for future growth.

Financial situation

In response to poor internal investment decisions, Ray has introduced a more formal approach to quantifying costs and benefits in an attempt to prioritise projects that compete for his limited funds and time. His first formal cost-benefit analysis helped him select a new machine for producing certain components in his factory. The results of his analysis are shown in figure one. The cost of the machine was $90,000, with annual maintenance fees of $5,000. Ray has seen the machine working and he believes that he can save the cost of one technician straight away. These savings are shown as reduced staff costs. The manufacturer of the machine claims that the accuracy of the machine leads to reduced wastage of "up to 10%". NMS have detailed measures of the wastage of the current machine and Ray has used this to estimate wastage savings. The increased accuracy of the machine over time is reflected in his estimates. Finally, the manufacturer claims 'energy savings'. NMS currently know the energy costs of the whole factory – but not of individual machines. However, Ray thinks that his estimates for energy savings are realistic. He concludes that "over five years the machine breaks even, so this seems a reasonable business case to me". Overall summary financial data for NMS is presented in figure two.

Figure one: Business case for new machine

All figures in $000

Year	0	1	2	3	4
Cost of the machine	90				
Maintenance costs	5	5	5	5	5
Reduced staff costs	15	15	15	15	15
Reduced wastage	2	4	6	8	10
Energy savings	2	2	2	2	2

Figure two: Financial analysis NMS 2007–2010

Financial analysis – extracted from the statement of comprehensive income

All figures in $000	2010	2009	2008	2007
Revenue				
Domestic	6,235	6,930	6,300	4,500
International	520	650	500	300
Total	6,755	7,580	6,800	4,800
Cost of Sales	4,700	5,000	4,200	2,850
Gross profit	2,055	2,580	2,600	1,950
Overhead expenses	1,900	2,010	1,900	1,400
Profit before tax and finance costs	155	570	700	550
Finance costs	165	150	120	25
Tax expense	17	62	75	60
Profit for the year	-27	358	505	465

Extracted from internal statistical reports

Employees	75	75	60	45
% of orders late	6	10	7	5
Order book	2,500	3,750	4,150	3,505

Required:

(a)   Evaluate the macro-environment of NMS using a PESTEL analysis.

(15 marks)

(b)   Analyse the industry or marketplace environment that NMS is competing in.

(16 marks)

Professional marks will be awarded in part (b) for clarity, structure and an appropriate approach. (4 marks)

(c)   Figures one and two summarise two financial aspects of NMS

(i)   Analyse the financial position of NMS.   (9 marks)

(ii)   Evaluate the cost-benefit analysis used to justify the purchase of the new machine.   (6 marks)

(Total: 50 marks)

Section 3

ANSWERS TO PRACTICE QUESTIONS

STRATEGIC ANALYSIS

1 CTC TELECOMMUNICATION

Key answer tips

This is a standard question on objectives and strategic planning. The key is to apply as much as possible to the specific circumstances of CTC.

(a)   The objectives of CTC will have to change for the reasons discussed below.

Shareholder wealth

Before privatisation CTC's main stakeholder was the government of C with the main objective of providing the best service the nation could afford. Income was set by the government to cover resources, so CTC was not expected to do more than breakeven financially.

Now the key stakeholders are shareholders and CTC's primary focus should be to maximise shareholder wealth and be profitable. Objectives will need to be set to support this over-riding objective.

Competition

Before privatisation CTC had the luxury of being a monopolist with the government setting service and price levels. Now the market in C has been opened up to allow foreign competition.

This will force CTC into ensuring that it adopts a marketing orientation and offers a quality service with value for money, or customers will switch to the competition. Objectives will need to be set by reference to market conditions and the actions of competitors.

Customer preferences

Before privatisation CTC had to deliver the best service the country could afford. Now, service levels are determined by what customers are willing to pay for. Some may be prepared to pay higher amounts for additional services, so CTC will need to develop a range of new services and tariffs to meet demand and set corresponding objectives.

CTC's whole approach needs to become more market driven rather than doing the best it could with the allocated resources.

Efficiency

Many state monopolies are inefficient. Given imminent competition and more demanding customers CTC will need to become much more efficient. Firms which have already made such a transition have usually found that radical changes are needed to improve cost control and change the culture of the organisation. Objectives will need to be set regarding cost and efficiency levels.

Resources

Prior to privatisation the level of resources was determined by the government. After privatisation the directors need to attract investors and other financiers and will set resources levels. As a consequence the directors need to consider the key issues for such investors – e.g. risk, growth prospects and so on – and set corporate objectives accordingly.

(b) Suitable strategic objectives for CTC could include the following:

Tutorial note

These objectives should be SMART (Specific, Relevant, Measurable, Achievable, Timescale).

Market share

e.g. 'CTC aims to retain 60% of its domestic market over the next 5 years'.

This is a suitable objective, as market share must be defended from new entrants to ensure that CTC can benefit from economies of scale to be competitive.

Market development

e.g. 'CTC aims to develop other markets so 25% of its revenue is derived from outside C within five years'.

This is a suitable objective, as CTC must look to other markets to ensure future growth and to reduce its risk exposure. These are necessary to increase shareholder value in the long run.

(c) The directors should adopt the rational planning model as a basic framework for future strategic planning. This involves the following steps:

Tutorial note

You should frame your answer around Johnson, Scholes and Whittington's rational model.

1 Strategic analysis

Strategic analysis essentially involves three aspects:

- CTC should perform external analysis to identify opportunities and threats. In particular, it should assess the risk of new entrants into the industry and perform detailed competitor analysis on potential rivals.

- CTC should also perform internal analysis to determine its own strengths and weaknesses. Weaknesses will need to be rectified in order to be competitive and CTC will need to develop core competences upon which to build strategy.

- and assessing their expectations and power. This should allow CTC to formulate a mission statement and to set strategic objectives for potential strategies.

2   Strategic choice

Strategic choice also involves three aspects:

- How to compete – CTC will need to decide whether to compete against new rivals as a cost leader, relying on economies of scale, or as a differentiator offering a higher quality product. The latter seems less likely so a detailed strategy focusing on costs needs to be formulated.

- Where to compete – as well as its domestic market, CTC needs to consider expansion into new markets. This stage will involve identifying the most attractive markets and deciding whether they are worth investing in.

- Choosing the method of expansion – once suitable foreign markets have been identified CTC will need to decide whether to expand via organic growth, acquisition or via a joint arrangement.

3   Strategy implementation

Strategy implementation involves the following:

- Translating long-term strategic objectives into detailed tactical and operational targets.

- Setting of detailed budgets and performance appraisal to control the business.

- Ongoing assessment as to whether the plans are on track and, if not, what action needs to be taken to rectify the situation.

- With all of this, CTC should ensure that planning is not a formal once-a-year exercise but an ongoing process where there is the flexibility to allow strategies to emerge in response to a changing market. This effectively blurs the distinction between steps 2 and 3 above, as they happen simultaneously.

2   3C PHARMACEUTICALS

Key answer tips

Part (a) asks for application of the product life cycle to 3C (many students completed a BCG analysis, which was not required!). It is vital that you comment on each product in terms of the overall portfolio and not just in isolation.

In part (b) it is again vital that your comments concerning each option are put in the context of the impact on the portfolio as a whole.

In part (c) ensure that you discuss each option, explain why there is an ethical issue and conclude.

(a)   The product life cycle model classifies products into four main phases:

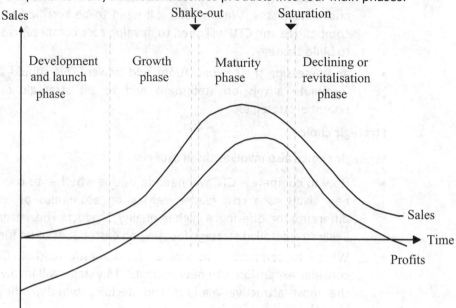

The model is normally used to assess the overall balance of the portfolio with respect to:

- Growth – e.g. new products replacing those at the end of the life cycle.

- Cash flow – e.g. positive cash flows from some products can help finance those that are currently cash negative.

- Other resource requirements.

- Risk – e.g. having some stable low risk products to compensate for other high risk ones.

The model can be applied to 3C as follows:

- The 240 drugs at various stages of development, either being tested or undergoing clinical trials, all of these fall into the 'development and launch' phase of the product life cycle. While being a significant drain on company resources, they are an essential part of the portfolio as they are needed to ensure the firm's future profitability by replacing older drugs that have come to the end of their life cycles.

- Epsilon is at the end of the 'growth' phase and is entering 'maturity', as high sales revenue growth has come to an end. As such it should be a net cash generator to help finance other products in the portfolio that are currently cash negative. However, it will not contribute to future growth.

- Beta is at the latter stages of the 'development and launch' phase as significant growth in sales revenue has yet to occur. As such it is unlikely to have reached breakeven sales revenue and is still a drain on the firm's resources.

- Alpha is coming to the end of the 'maturity' phase and will be entering 'decline' in 12 months' time when patent protection expires and generic copies flood the market. At present it is likely to be cash positive, helping to finance product development but will neither contribute to cash flow nor future growth beyond the next year.

Overall the portfolio is reasonably balanced in terms of future growth potential and cash flow. Beyond the next year it is vital that Beta becomes cash positive and further products move from development to launch.

(b)   The three options will affect the portfolio as follows:

Alpha2

Alpha2 has already completed clinical trials so is ready to launch. This would effectively allow the patent protection for Alpha to be extended a further five years, preventing Alpha from entering the decline phase and lengthening the maturity phase.

This should prevent the portfolio from becoming unbalanced with respect to cash flow as the revised Alpha2 will generate cash to finance other products in the portfolio. It will also reduce the risk of the portfolio as sales revenue for Alpha2 will be more certain than estimated returns for other products currently in development.

Beta

Investing in a marketing campaign for Beta would move it into the growth phase and improve the immediate growth prospects of the portfolio.

However, the presence of a close substitute in the market increases the risks attached to Beta and may result in lower growth than expected and even delay Beta breaking even as extra funds would be required to establish Beta ahead of its rival. In the short term Beta may place greater demands on the portfolio cash flow rather than helping it.

Gamma

If Gamma completes the final clinical trials successfully, then it will quickly move from development and launch into the growth stage. Even if prices are set at a high level, expected demand should result in very high growth, improving the overall growth balance of the portfolio. However, there is no guarantee that Gamma will be successful and, on balance, this is the most risky option presented.

The impact on overall portfolio cash flow will depend, to some extent, on the price set and the sales volumes generated. If Gamma truly is a breakthrough product then a high price and a high sales volume might both be available, though there is a risk that some resource-limited countries might produce generic copies of the drug before the patent ends.

Recommendation

On balance, investing in Alpha2 appears to offer the safest way to balance the portfolio in terms of cash flow whereas Gamma offers the highest growth and profit potential. The final decision will depend on the risk aversion of the directors.

(c)   Social responsibility is the idea that an organisation should behave responsibly in the interests of the society in which it operates.

The social responsibility implications of the three options given are as follows:

Alpha2

Extending the patent in the way described would delay competitors producing cheap generic copies. The ethical argument here is that, if 3C invests, then customers would not have access to cheaper pain killers so, in effect, 3C is increasing the pain of many sufferers.

However, there are many alternative pain killers on the market, including generic drugs, so the comparison is really between cheap pain relief and more expensive but better pain relief.

Beta

The ethical position with Beta is the other way round – one could argue that 3C has a moral duty to invest in Beta as this will increase the availability of drugs dealing with serious infection. However, if 3C does not invest in Beta, then there are equivalent drugs on the market for patients and hospitals are likely to prioritise such treatments anyway. What investment in Beta is likely to achieve is a fall in the price of such drugs due to extra competition. It could be argued that this should allow health trusts' funds to go further, thus treating more patients.

Gamma

The situation with Gamma is very different. Millions of people around the world are infected with HIV/AIDS and, although progress is being made with anti-retroviral drugs, Gamma would be a major step forward in treatment.

A separate ethical issue is the price that 3C should charge for Gamma. Selling Gamma at the lowest price possible would ensure greater access to sufferers, particularly in poorer countries in Africa where the situation is at its worst. A high price would effectively exclude such people from treatment.

There is thus a major ethical conflict between the higher profits that 3C could earn for its shareholders verses increased treatment for people in the developing world. While it could be argued that 'the business of business is business' and that it is up to governments to make funds available to pay for drugs, the ethical argument here is compelling.

Conclusion

On ethical grounds further investment should be put into Gamma. In fact, the key ethical argument against investing in Alpha2 or Beta is that they preclude investment in Gamma. The pricing issue is more complex.

3   EEE FLAVOURINGS

Key answer tips

This is a relatively straightforward question on stakeholder analysis. Mendelow's power-interest matrix is the obvious model to use for part (b) and has the advantage of generating action plans for part (c).

(a)   The advantages of EEE conducting a stakeholder analysis are as follows:

- EEE will be able to select investments that are more likely to satisfy the expectations of key stakeholders. For example, institutional shareholders will want to see shareholder value increased, so EEE should assess projects on the basis of their NPV.

- EEE will be able to incorporate the opinions of powerful stakeholders when designing projects.

- Identifying and winning over powerful stakeholders will make raising and using resources easier. For example, if the trade union agrees with the project, then staffing changes will be easier to implement.

- Anticipating stakeholder responses will allow proactive management and avoid conflicts. EEE will be able to identify potential objectors to investments and could then adjust how projects are done to reduce resistance. For example, by identifying the fact that some residents will complain about the smell, EEE could spend extra to reduce leakages.

- EEE will be able to identify the level of involvement each group requires. For example, which groups need to be included in detailed discussions and which simply need to be kept informed.

(b)   The principal stakeholders of EEE can be analysed using Mendelow's power-interest matrix as follows:

Trade union representative – high interest, high power

The trade union representative will have high interest as the decision could reduce the risk of job losses in the future. This person will also be very interested in their role as a local council member as the project will affect the local community in terms of jobs and also pollution.

They will also exercise considerable power as they could call for industrial action and council intervention if unhappy.

Overall one would expect that they will be for the project due to the job implications, although they may feel some conflict of interest as they will not want to see pollution in the community they represent.

Affluent local residents – high interest, low power

More affluent residents are more concerned with the leakages and associated smell than the local economy.

They probably have low power to influence the company's decisions, although their wealth may give them powerful friends.

Affluent residents will be against the investment because of the smell.

Other local residents – high interest, low power

Other local residents will be more interested in the future fortunes of the company because it is a major local employer.

These residents also have low power to influence the company's decisions.

Most of these residents will be in favour of the project because of its impact on the local economy. Some may object on environmental grounds.

Institutional shareholders – high interest, low power

Institutional investors will take high interest in all of their main investments, especially focusing on share price and future prospects.

With a collective shareholding of 20%, however, they have little power to influence decisions.

Overall they will be positive about the investment as it improves future prospects.

Customers – low interest, potentially high power

As long as supplies are of suitable quality at reasonable prices, then it is unlikely customers will take much interest in events. However, should adverse publicity arise over leakages, then they could take more interest as they would not want their images compromised.

Major customers will be able to exert some power by threatening to switch suppliers.

Customers will probably be pro the investment as it will increase supply and may reduce prices.

(c)   In the light of the above analysis, EEE should take the following action:

The trade union representative should be invited to participate in discussions and decision making to represent the views of both workers and local government. This could be facilitated by setting up a project team to manage the project and appointing the representative as a member of that team.

Local residents and institutional shareholders need to be kept informed. This should ensure that their interest does not result in them trying to gain power. For example, a report detailing the impact on future jobs and profitability should be communicated to shareholders and in local papers. A full environmental report should also be commissioned so edited highlights can be released to local residents reassuring them of their concerns.

Customers need to be kept satisfied. A brief communications stressing how the investment will lead to greater supply in the future should prevent them taking more interest in the project should they hear any adverse publicity concerning pollution.

4   SWIFT

Key answer tips

In part (a), when performing the analysis you should ensure that you include both financial measures *and* non-financial measures. Try to take a structured approach to your answer by using a strategic model – the answer uses the Johnson, Scholes and Whittington tests for evaluating a strategy, but other models such as the BCG matrix or Ashbridge portfolio display would also have been appropriate and scored marks.

In part (b) you need to have knowledge of Porter's diamond and be able to apply it to the scenario. This is not a commonly examined area, but this should reinforce the need for broad syllabus knowledge that is needed in order to pass this paper.

(a)   The acquisition of EVM can be analysed using the success criteria of *suitability, acceptability and feasibility*.

Suitability is concerned with whether a strategy addresses the issues identified when considering the strategic position of the company. In general terms the acquisition appears to make sense. The market is mature and competitive in Ambion, pushing down margins. These margins are further eroded by a government that is hostile to road transport resulting in high taxation on fuel, road taxes linked to carbon emission and restricted working practices. The acquisition of EVM provides an opportunity for Swift to exploit their core competencies in a different geographical market where demand is rising, the national government is investing in road infrastructure and competition is immature. The increased size of the group will further allow Swift to exploit economies of scale when purchasing trucks and other equipment.

Concerns around suitability surround the potential clash of cultures between Swift and EVM. Swift has no experience of acquiring or running foreign companies. It has no experience of trading in Ecuria. Furthermore, although EVM is now in private hands, it may be possible that the work practices and expectations of employees may still reflect the time when they were working for the central government. Although altering these practices may give scope for even greater profitability, it may lead to labour disputes that harm the service and reputation of the company. Swift wishes to acquire this company and adopt the practices, principles and technology of the Ambion operation. This may lead to conflict that they may find hard to resolve.

their own.

Acceptability is concerned with the expected performance of a strategy in terms of return, risk and stakeholder reactions.

Return: EVM delivers a very similar (18%) Return on Capital Employed (ROCE) to Swift Transport. This appears to be a strong performance for the sector, and should certainly be acceptable to the Swift shareholders. The gross profit margin (20%) is higher than Swift, but the net profit margin (7.5%) is lower. This may support some of the concerns discussed under suitability. The company may still be carrying high costs from its days as a nationalised company. Swift presumably believes that it can improve the net profit margin by implementing competences gained in the Ambion market.

Risk: Both the current liquidity ratio (1·14%) and the acid test ratio (1·05%) are lower than the Swift equivalents and Swift will need to look at this. The introduction of Swift's practices may help reduce trade payables. The gearing ratio (30%) for EVM is much lower than Swift and perhaps reflects a more conservative approach to long-term lending and a reflection of the fledgling capital markets in the country. However, the interest cover ratio (5) is half that of Swift, perhaps reflecting lower profitability and higher business taxation.

Stakeholders: Joe Swift and his family are the major stakeholders in what is still a family-run private limited company. It is unlikely that there will be any opposition to the acquisition from shareholders. However, stakeholders such as drivers might be wary of this strategy and also the government, outspokenly criticised by Joe, may also respond in some way. For example, by imposing taxation on foreign investment.

Feasibility is about whether an organisation has the resources and competencies to deliver the strategy. It appears that Swift does, as funds are in place and the competences are what are partly driving the acquisition.

(b)   In his book *The Competitive Advantage of Nations,* Michael Porter suggests that there are inherent reasons why some nations are more competitive than others, and also why some industries within nations are more competitive than others. He suggests that the national home base of the organisation plays an important role in creating international advantage, something that will be very important to Joe Swift. He identifies four main determinants of national advantage and arranges these as a diamond, with each of these determinants interacting with and reinforcing each other. Two further determinants, chance and government, are discussed outside of the diamond in terms of how they influence and interact with the determinants inside the diamond. This model answer uses Porter's diamond as its basis. However, credit will also be given to candidates who use an alternative appropriate framework or model.

The four main determinants are:

The nation's position in *factor conditions,* such as skilled labour or infrastructure, necessary for firms to compete in a given industry. The acknowledged work ethic of the people and the investment in transport infrastructure by the government are significant factor conditions in Ecuria.

The nature of the home *demand conditions* for the industry's product or service. Home demand influences economies of scale, but it also shapes the rate and character of improvement and innovation. In Ecuria, the move to a market economy has stimulated a rapid growth in the transport of goods. The Ecurian people are traditionally demanding in their standards. They have a passion for precision and promptness and this has shaped the operations of EVM.

The presence or absence of *related and supporting industries* that are internationally competitive. Competitive advantage in certain industries confers potential advantages on firms in other industries. Porter suggests that the 'Swiss success in pharmaceuticals was closely connected to previous international success in the dye industry'. There is no evidence in the case study that Ecuria has internationally competitive industries related to logistics. Hence, it is the absence of these that is significant when considering this determinant.

The final determinant is *firm* strategy, *structure and rivalry.* This concerns the conditions in the nation governing how companies are created, organised and managed. It also considers the nature of domestic rivalry. EVM was created by nationalising the state-run haulage system. For the first few years of operation it had few competitors. The nature of the capital markets makes it very difficult to raise finance in Ecuria. Consequently, most of EVM's competitors are small, family-run companies who offer a local service. Porter suggests that there is a strong relationship between vigorous domestic rivalry and the creation and persistence of competitive advantage in an industry. There is little evidence of this emerging in Ecuria.

Porter also recognises the influence of chance and government. Chance events are developments outside the control of firms and the nation's government. Wars, external political developments and a reduction in foreign demand are all examples of chance factors. Government, in effect, helps shape the diamond by enacting policies that influence each of the determinants. In Ecuria, the government's approach to infrastructure investment and policies towards capital markets has affected factor conditions and impacted on firm structure and rivalry.

ACCA marking scheme		
		Marks
(a)	1 mark for each relevant point up to a maximum of 15 marks.	15
(b)	1 mark for each relevant point up to a maximum of 10 marks.	10
Total		25

5 BOWLAND

Key answer tips

Part (a) of the question can be split into three parts – what are Bowland's existing competencies, what are the key success factors needed in retailing, and do these two things match up. So a good approach would be to split your time evenly between all three elements.

For part (b) an external analysis is normally a combination of both the PESTEL and 5 Forces models, but with only 15 marks available (and working on the basis of two marks per well explained point) you do not have to cover every element. So if, for example, you can't determine any relevant 'Technological' issues then just leave this factor out.

(a) An organisation's **distinctive competences** are those things which an organisation does particularly well. They include the organisation's unique resources and capabilities as well as its strengths and its ability to overcome weaknesses. These competences can include aspects such as budgetary control, a strong technology base, a culture conducive to change and marketing skills.

Key success factors are those requirements which it is essential to have if one is to survive and prosper in a chosen industry/environment. These can include areas such as good service networks, up-to-date marketing intelligence and tight cost controls where margins are small.

It is not guaranteed that the distinctive competences and the key success factors are always in alignment. A company moving into the retail sector may have an excellent product research and development capability, but this alone will not help if it has no concept of service or poorly sited retail outlets. It is critical to ensure that what the company excels at is what is needed to be successful in that particular area.

The **strengths of Bowland Carpets** include **strong brand names** which maintain integrity within the different market segments where the company operates. The company has a **balanced portfolio of customers** and the **range of products is equally balanced**, ensuring that any sectoral decline can be compensated for by growth in other markets. Other strengths which the company currently has include a **good relationship with distributors and strong support from a powerful parent company**. Some of its distinctive competences, such as a strong brand and a reasonable range of products, are critical in the proposed new environment, as will be the financial support of the parent company. However there are some aspects which are cause for concern in the proposed new business environment.

The strength in the contract and industrial carpet segment will not be affected by the proposed vertical integration – sales tend to be through direct sales force. The strong **relationship with distributors** will however be **jeopardised by the opening up of retail outlets**. Other retail chains will be unwilling to permit a rival to operate so freely, and therefore there will be a reluctance to stock Bowland Carpets. Unless Bowland Carpets can obtain wide retail market coverage to compensate for this potential problem, sales revenue will be adversely affected. The **cost of developing extensive market coverage** will be enormous and whether it is in High Street outlets or specialist out-of-town centres the investment may be greater than the parent company has budgeted for. The company also has **no expertise in site appraisal and selection**. Although the newly-structured value chain will generate greater control there is an associated **lack of flexibility** along with an **increase in the fixed cost base** of the business.

Another key success factor is the **need for expertise in retailing**. It may be that the UK company can import this from the USA but the culture of marketing household durables may not be transferable internationally. Bowland Carpets as the domestic company has no experience in this field.

A critical factor in successful retailing is the ability to provide a **comprehensive range of products**. Does Bowland Carpets have one? It is unlikely that the competitive carpet manufacturers will provide such a supply to one of their rivals.

It would, therefore, appear that there is no close conformity between the distinctive competences of Bowland Carpets and the key success factors required in the carpet retailing sector.

(b)   The **external environment** scan is an essential prerequisite prior to selecting a strategic option. It enables the company to identify and understand the key external and uncontrollable influences which will have an impact upon the company's strategy. The environment is increasingly turbulent and often hostile. Without this knowledge and appreciation the strategist will be operating in a mine-field. The acquisition of the external information is obtained by scanning the environment continuously and monitoring key indicators which should enable the company to position itself appropriately with respect to the external environment and the competition. The external scan should be structured around a SLEPT framework covering the following environments – social, legal, economic, political and technological. In addition it is also important to assess potential competitive reactions as part of the scanning process.

The environmental scan will influence the decision as to whether Bowland Carpets should concentrate on the UK or seek diversification elsewhere, either in products or markets. Possible factors are as follows:

- **Social issues**: Trends towards increasing car-centred shopping (superstores and out-of-town sites) or movements back to city centre shopping: trends in fashion and furnishing – will carpets become a fashion item and result in greater replacement sales? Other factors of importance to Bowland include the rate of growth or decline in populations and changes in the age distribution of the population. In the UK there will be an increasing proportion of the national population over retirement age. In developing countries there are very large numbers of young people. Rising standards of living lead to increased demand for certain types of goods. This is why developing countries are attractive to markets.

- **Legal issues**: Laws in the UK differ from the US. They come from common law, parliamentary legislation and government regulations derived from it, and obligations under EU membership and other treaties Legal factors that can influence decisions include aspects of employment law, e.g. minimum wage, laws to protect consumers and tax legislation. The monopoly/competition issues in this case are likely to be insignificant.

- **Economic issues**: An increased concentration for Bowland Carpets within the UK economy will depend upon future economic prospects, taxation policy (sales tax) and interest rates, income distribution and unemployment (influencing site location), trade barriers (cheap imports from Third World suppliers, or even low-cost tufted carpets from countries such as Belgium).

- **Political issues**: Government policy affects the whole economy and governments are responsible for enforcing and creating a stable framework in which business can be done. The quality of government policy is important in providing physical infrastructure, e.g. transport, social infrastructure, e.g. education and market infrastructure, e.g. planning and site development – town centre or out-of-town developments.

- **Technological issues**: is retailing technology evolutionary or revolutionary? Will it be costly or labour-saving? Will inventory control be facilitated so saving costs? Technology contributes to overall economic growth. It can increase total output with gains in productivity, reduced costs and new types of product. It influences the way in which markets are identified – database systems make it much easier to analyse the market place. Information technology encourages de-layering of organisational hierarchies and better communications.

- **Competitive issues**: It will be necessary to assess the likely responses of both carpet distributors and carpet manufacturers to the proposed incursion by Bowland Carpets. Will the reactions be benign or will they be aggressive?

6   MCGEORGE HOLDINGS PLC

Key answer tips

The question clearly states that you should use more than one model in part (a). Two of the most widely used models refer to the **product life cycle** and the **Boston Consulting Group (BCG) growth-share matrix**. It is on these two that this suggested answer will concentrate.

(a)   It is obvious that McGeorge Holdings plc has allowed its range of products to grow without too much regard to the overall efficiency and effectiveness of the product spread. It is required that a more rational approach should be taken so as to rationalise the product portfolio.

The **product life cycle** can be used to assess where each of the products is located. Some products, in their *introductory stage*, may not be contributing well to overall profits because of initial research and market development costs, but they may, in the future, provide a regular stream of income to the company. Those in the *growth stage* should already be profit providers. It is in the later stages of the life cycle that close attention needs to be paid to products. In the *maturity/saturation stages* it may be prudent to assess whether there is any long-term future in the products. Would investment in alternative products be more sensible? This question is more critical when one investigates products in the *decline stage*. One has to decide if withdrawing these products might be wise. Products can still be profitable in the decline stage, particularly if competitors are exiting the market faster than market demand is falling. It is also important to assess how these products contribute to the overall performance of the company. Maybe withdrawing from a given line might alienate key customers. The products may also provide a complementary range and withdrawal from one area may adversely affect other product sales. If one withdraws certain products are there others which consumers can turn to or must they seek products from key competitors? It is also important to assess how costs such as marketing, distribution and even manufacturing have been allocated. The withdrawal of certain products could result in others having to share and carry higher costs, so making them price uncompetitive. One must not rush into product rationalisation programmes without considering the consequences of such an action.

The **BCG growth-share matrix** examines the inter-relationships between market share and market growth of given products. It assesses resource generation alongside resource needs. The *'cash-cow'* is described as such because products in this category (low growth and high market share) are usually very profitable and generate surplus funds, and so are often used to finance other developments. Such products are not recommended for deletion.

The *'stars'* generate high revenues because the products have high market shares, but because the market is growing fast such products need to be invested in heavily to maintain their position. These are unlikely to be highly profitable as yet, but decisions to withdraw such products should be rejected. It is likely that such products will become more profitable as market growth stabilises. Today's stars will usually become tomorrow's cash cows.

The *'problem child'* or *'question mark'* product is probably currently losing money. A prognosis needs to be made of future movements. Can the product achieve a significant share of the market? If the answer is 'Yes' then the product may proceed to become a 'star' and later a 'cash cow'. However if there are considerable doubts then the product may have to be withdrawn. It is often assumed that *'dogs'* – those products with low market share and low growth potential should be withdrawn from the market place. However some 'dogs' are known as 'cash dogs'. They occupy a niche position and are still capable of returning a profit. If this is the case, then they can be persevered with until they have little to offer the company. However true 'dogs' need to be eradicated. They consume too much management time and money. These need to be focused on present and future winners.

Adrian Reed needs to be careful which products to remove from the portfolio. Some rationalisation will be needed but this should be carried out carefully and not rushed into.

(b)   'Benchmarking' the McGeorge organisation will enable Adrian Reed to assess in which areas the performance of his company falls short of that of his competitors and can help determine what action needs to be taken to correct any adverse findings.

There are several ways in which benchmarking can be carried out. **Internal benchmarking** can compare different units within McGeorge Holdings plc. Some centres may be more proficient than others and a transfer of knowledge and skills could be beneficial to the group as a whole. **Competitive benchmarking** attempts to compare products, processes and results and show where the company is failing with reference to those of competitors. The difficulty here is accessing confidential data of competitors. They are not going to make it easy for McGeorge by providing them with this information. **Customer benchmarking** attempts to compare corporate performance with the performance expected by customers. How far is there a gap between expected performance and actual? **Generic benchmarking** compares similar business functions between companies operating in different industries. For example how do financial results – gearing, liquidity, etc compare in differing industrial sectors? **Process or activity benchmarking** attempts to identify the current best practice within an organisation (regardless of sector) for activities such as manufacturing, engineering or human resource management. Then this best practice can be imported into the McGeorge organisation, assuming compatibility.

There are a number of limitations associated with benchmarking. Can relevant data be obtained to make any comparison meaningful? Some of the comparisons may be meaningless. Circumstances between firms, environments and products all differ so making a comparison appear like comparing 'apples with oranges'. The process can appear to be an historical exercise. The world moves on and what was acceptable yesterday may be out of date tomorrow. Furthermore there is an implicit assumption that there is an optimum solution. A process can be efficient but does it add value – is it effective? It is possible that distribution costs can be reduced to almost zero by distributing nothing. Is this solution useful? If benchmarking concentrates on efficiency, ignoring effectiveness, then it is missing its purpose.

Reed could use benchmarking to assess the performance of the company, but this needs to be implemented carefully and results must be analysed critically without snap judgements being made.

7   SALT AND SOAP

Key answer tips

There are a range of strategic models that could be used in art (a) of this question such as SWOT, 5 Forces, the value chain or the product life cycle. But none should be worth more than 4/5 marks and therefore you shouldn't spend lots of time on one model and perform a detailed analysis.

(a)   **To**: David Kirk   **From**: The Marketing Consultant

Sales and Marketing Director,   **Date**: June 20X7

Salt and Soap Ltd

Position analysis

Marketing strategy is concerned with making choices as to which products you supply and the markets into which you sell them. Your products are currently perceived as low priced necessities with the supermarkets able to take most of the value created. The emergence of new environmentally aware customers allows you to develop products satisfying new demands. You need to take immediate action to assess the size and significance of these new segments.

One model that is relevant to understand your position is Porter's five forces. Buyer power is intense, there is no real substitute for salt, there is little likelihood of new entrants into such a small market, there are few competitors, and Salt and Soap is a very small customer as far as your suppliers are concerned. All in all, the company remaining as a packager of salt and soap under the supermarkets' own brands would see marketing remain a largely unnecessary activity. Certainly the pressures on margins being exerted by their supermarket customers would support your desire to move into more attractive markets.

Staying with the Porter's models, the value chain would seem to offer more scope for developing marketing thinking and strategy. Currently, as essentially a packager of salt and soap, you are committed to fairly limited value adding activities. There is little or no contact with the final user of their products, i.e. the domestic customer. However, the identification of new uses and outlets for soap based products and the opportunity to extend the product range present some interesting opportunities to develop marketing activities. In terms of generic strategies Salt and Soap is very much a 'cost focuser', but the new opportunities mean you can move into more of a differentiation focuser role.

The move into new markets with product extensions also brings the Ansoff growth model into consideration, with associated consideration of product life cycles. Salt and soap are mature products, but evidence suggests that by scanning the environment for alternative uses, product extensions with significantly higher margins can be developed. This supports the argument that if managers regard their product as a mature commodity product they will ignore significant growth opportunities. Environmental analysis suggests new use segments, e.g. soda-based cleaning products which are environmentally friendly, are likely to become increasingly significant.

Signed:

Marketing Consultant

(b)   The scenario suggests that Salt and Soap has the ability to become a niche player in a number of markets. One advantage is that these 'new' products require little product development with the emphasis being on market development through accessing new distribution channels and appropriate branding and packaging. The marketing mix should clearly reflect the particular needs of these new markets. Becoming a niche player means Salt and Soap is choosing to specialise in meeting the needs of a defined customer segment with distinctive products. As the products are made from natural ingredients this will act as a significant barrier to entry by its global competitors.

The specialist nature of the markets and the wholesalers means that another barrier to entry is created.

The environmentally friendly products that appeal to gardeners are particularly attractive. Here the full range of marketing techniques can be used, from market analysis of the trend and its significance, through to the marketing mix by which the product is brought to the attention of both distributors and the final users. The product clearly has desirable attributes, which the environmentally aware customer will seek to use. It offers considerable opportunity to develop a pricing strategy that will produce margins far higher than currently obtainable from the supermarkets. Branding, using a name that is environmentally linked, now becomes a real possibility. Communication of the brand now becomes an issue – the use of specialist wholesalers and garden centres would suggest a more cost effective 'push' strategy could be put in place.

A pull strategy, using expensive advertising aimed at the final user seems unlikely to be feasible because of limited funding.

Certainly, the distribution side of the niche strategy will be important. The use of new wholesalers and distributors offers a real opportunity to grow the business and reduce dependency on the own label products.

All in all, Salt and Soap shows the relevance of marketing and marketing thinking to the small company. Without it the company is limited to selling what it makes, or rather packages, a product-led strategy. Using market research and appropriate market and product development, linked to the marketing mix, the company moves away from over reliance on one type of customer driven by cost and product range reduction.

8   INDEPENDENT LIVING

Key answer tips

In part (a) the key to success will be to combine knowledge with application. So there will be a mark firstly for explaining each element of the primary activities of the supply chain, and then another mark for explaining how it would apply to the scenario. Be careful to focus on primary activities and avoid the secondary/support activities. This will also be important in part (b). In this part there are 15 marks available spread over the 5 primary activities. So you should aim to make three suggestions for improvements in each of the five areas.

(a)   IL supplies both manufactured products (crutches, walking frames) and bought-in products (mobility scooters, bath lifts). The value chain for these two sets of products is different and this is reflected in the following analysis.

The primary activities of the value chain are:

Inbound Logistics

These are activities associated with receiving, storing and disseminating inputs to the product. Typical examples are materials handling, warehousing and inventory (stock) control.

For manufactured products this concerns collection of material from scrap merchants and the storage of that material prior to use. For bought-in products, inbound logistics is handled by the supplying manufacturers. Products are stored in the warehouse.

Operations

This is concerned with transforming inputs into the final product. This includes machining, assembly, testing and packaging. In the context of manufactured products this covers the production of crutches and walkers (and other simple aids), their testing and packaging. For bought-in products, operations is concerned with the careful opening of packaging, the addition of an IL transfer logo, the testing of the equipment and the re-packaging of the product into its original packaging.

Outbound logistics

These are activities associated with storing and then physically distributing the product to buyers. Finished goods warehousing, order processing and delivery is considered here.

At IL, both manufactured and bought-in products need to be stored prior to delivery. Distribution is undertaken by a national courier company. Orders are placed by telephone or through the website.

Marketing and Sales

These are activities by which customers can learn of the existence of and then purchase the products. It includes advertising, promotion, sales and pricing. At IL this covers leaflets in hospitals and surgeries, a website catalogue and order taking and the giving of advice.

Service

These are activities associated with providing a service to enhance or maintain the value of the product. It includes installation, repair, training, parts supply and product adjustment. The simple nature of the manufactured products means that service is inappropriate. For bought-in product, service is undertaken by the original manufacturer.

(b) The value chain is used as a basis for answering the question. Many of the potential re-structuring suggestions produce cost reductions. However, it must be acknowledged that the charity also has the objective of providing jobs for severely disabled people. Suggestions for change have to reflect this fact. It is also clear from the scenario that some customers are prepared to pay price premiums for the goods by making donations to the charity as part of their purchase of these goods.

Inbound logistics

For bought in products, IL could explore the possibility of reducing scrap metal storage costs by requesting dealers to store the metal until it is required. Furthermore, dealers may also be able to offer competitive delivery costs. This would remove the need for IL to maintain (and eventually replace) the lorry it uses for collection of this material. For bought in products, IL could explore the cost of using a specialist logistics company to carry out both its inbound and outbound logistics. This should produce economies of scale leading to reduced costs. Many of these logistics companies also offer storage facilities. However, IL already has storage at an airfield site and the employment of severely disabled labour is one of its objectives.

Operations

It seems vital that IL retains its manufacturing capability to help achieve its goal of providing work and income for severely disabled people. It could probably gain cost savings by outsourcing manufacture to cheaper countries (like its commercial competitors) but this would not meet its core objective. IL marketing could stress the location of the manufacture as an important differentiator. Customers might then perceive it as an ethical choice.

The operations part of the value chain for bought-in products is relatively labour intensive (see later notes) and could be simplified in two ways.

(1)   Asking manufacturers to affix the IL logo and label prior to despatch to IL. The testing of the products could also be delegated to the manufacturer as they provide post-delivery support.

(2)   Reducing inventory by arranging for bought in goods to be supplied to the customer directly by the manufacturer. Not only would this cut delivery costs but it would also reduce inventory costs, and eliminate the costly write-off of obsolete purchased inventory.

Employees in the warehouse could be reallocated to order processing and other administrative tasks.

Outbound logistics

The ordering of products through the website appears to be extremely effective. The site includes a product catalogue and a secure payment facility. However, although use of the website is growing, most orders are still placed by telephone. IL might consider ways of encouraging further use of the website, for example by offering discounts, cheaper prices and a wider range of products. It might also consider how it could make its website more available to potential consumers, perhaps by placing dedicated terminals in hospitals and surgeries.

The telephone ordering process is currently too complex because sales staff have to describe the products available and also provide purchasing advice and guidance. IL needs to consider ways of making details of their product range available to customers before they place the order (see below).

Marketing and Sales

Relatively little sales and marketing takes place at IL which is probably due its charitable status. Charities are usually very keen to minimise their overhead costs. Traditional marketing appears to be very limited, restricted to leaflets in hospitals and surgeries. IL could consider replacing its current leaflets (which just give a phone number and a website) with a leaflet that effectively doubles as a catalogue, showing the products on offer. This should help improve the efficiency of the telephone ordering service. Display advertising in magazines and newspapers with coupons to request a catalogue would also increase the profile of the brand.

Many charities use Customer Relationship Management (CRM) systems to manage their donors. IL should explore the potential of this. It already has records of purchasers and also those purchasers that have made extra donations.

All sales and marketing material needs to stress the charitable status of the organisation. This effectively differentiates it from commercial competitors. There is already evidence that some customers are willing to reflect this by increasing the price they pay for goods by including a donation to support the charity.

Service

Because of the nature of the product, little direct support is required. However, IL could expand its website to give general support and advice on mobility problems and independent living.

ACCA marking scheme		
		Marks
(a)	Up to 1 mark for identifying each primary activity (for example, inbound logistics) and up to 2 marks for discussing its application to IL in both contexts (metal scrap collection, supplier delivery) up to a maximum of 10 marks.	10
(b)	Up to 1 mark for each significant point (for example, arrange bought in products to be delivered directly to the customer from the manufacturer) up to a maximum of 15 marks.	15
Total		25

Examiner's comments

The first part of the question requested candidates to analyse the primary activities of the value chain for the product range at IL. Most candidates answered this fairly well, recognising that there were two value chains at IL, one concerned with manufactured goods and the other with "bought in" products. However, it was also clear that a significant number of candidates were not familiar with the terminology and structure of the value chain. The "Service" element of the value chain was also particularly misunderstood.

The second part of the question asked candidates to evaluate what changes IL might consider to the primary activities in the value chain to improve their competitiveness, whilst continuing to meet their charitable objectives. This part question was also answered fairly well although the inappropriateness of some solutions in the light of the charitable objectives was not sufficiently explored. Charities are an important part of the "not-for-profit" sector of the economy and their structure and objectives should be understood by candidates. Question scenarios will not always be drawn from the private or public sectors of the economy.

However, overall the question was answered relatively well.

9 ONE ENERGY PLC *Walk in the footsteps of a top tutor*

Tutor's top tips

(a) *Financial analysis (13 marks)*

Key to success:

Include a broad range of measures

Give opinions (not just calculations)

> *Give equal weighting to non-ratio information (such as overdraft level, level of non-TFA etc.)*
>
> *Give an overall opinion which is consistent with the requirement*
>
> ***Key dangers:***
>
> *Calculating too many ratios*
>
> *Too much detail in calculations*
>
> *Only doing ratios*
>
> *Lack of focus*
>
> (b) *Software package evaluation*
>
> ***Key to success:***
>
> *Solid knowledge*
>
> *Relate answers to the scenario*
>
> ***Key dangers:***
>
> *Lack of structure & knowledge*

(a) The judicious use of selected financial ratios should have indicated some cause for concern, leading to further investigation of the company and the industrial sector itself. It would have been very helpful to identify typical financial ratios in the sector that RiteSoftware is operating in. However, in the absence of such information, comparison between the two years will provide some evaluation and a basis for further investigation.

However, before calculating and commenting on the ratios, there are a number of things directly discernable from the financial figures provided by the company.

Firstly, goodwill is the most significant non-current asset. If the company is in the position that it needs further funding, then the extract suggests that there is little to secure this funding against. Most lenders prefer to lend against tangible assets, such as property. The value of goodwill has also increased substantially since 20X7, suggesting an acquisition. It would be useful to investigate this further.

Secondly, although trade receivables year on year have increased, in percentage terms, about the same as revenue, trade payables have increased significantly more. The efficiency ratios should cast more light on this; but it appears that the company may be using trade payables to finance cash flows. This hunch might be supported by the fact that the bank overdraft was actually reduced in 20X8.

Thirdly, although sales revenue increased by 10% in the period, cost of sales grew by a greater percentage, leading to a reduction in profit. It seems reasonable to assume that labour costs largely contributed to this cost of sales increase. The percentage increase in staff was almost 30%, a significant proportion for a small company to integrate and profitably utilise.

Finally, the extract from the accounts shows no retained profit, suggesting that this is being distributed to shareholders. This needs to be investigated.

Profitability

Two profitability ratios can be calculated from the extracted financial information. The ROCE (Return on Capital Employed) has almost halved. Although the actual profit remained the same, it was achieved with significantly higher borrowing.

The net profit margin has also almost halved. The absolute figures are also very low (less than 1% in 20X8) and this needs further investigation to see if such a figure is viable, or representative of the industry sector.

Efficiency

The general observation about trade payables made above appears to be borne out by the ratios. The average receivables settlement remains the same, suggesting good credit management in an expanding business. However, average payable days have increased significantly and are now beyond the 30 days normal for this business.

Sales revenue per employee has dropped from $33,500 in 20X7 to under $29,500 in 20X8.

Liquidity

Liquidity (measured through both the current and acid test ratios) has declined slightly during this period. Also, the values are rather low (approximately 0.76:1) and so this too would need investigation. Perhaps liquidity is traditionally low in this industry sector.

Financial gearing

The two gearing ratios discernible from the extracted information both give cause for concern. The gearing ratio itself has jumped from 25% to above 43%. The interest cover ratio has dropped to 2 from 7.5. Again, the sector needs investigation.

Conclusion

The financial figures of RiteSoftware do suggest that everything was not well and that further investigation was necessary. The figures suggest rising debt, cash flow problems, lowering efficiency and very poor profitability. Further investigation might have revealed that RiteSoftware was typical of the industry. However, it might have also identified the problems that led to the company's eventual demise.

(b)   The lack of a formal evaluation of the financial figures of RiteSoftware is the subject of the first part of the question. However, the financial position is just part of the analysis required of the potential supplier. The question requires FOUR further ways in which OneEnergy failed to follow a proper evaluation procedure. In this model answer, the four suggestions are:

1   A failure to investigate the supplier's organisational structure and ownership

2   A failure to evaluate functional requirements

3   A failure to evaluate non-functional requirements

4   A failure to set proper evaluation criteria and follow a selection process

However, other appropriate suggestions made by the candidate will be given credit.

Organisational structure and ownership

The evaluation should have included an investigation into the structure of RiteSoftware, its shareholders and directors. A simple inquiry at Companies House (for example) would have revealed that the managing director of RiteSoftware had the same surname as the HR director of OneEnergy. The HR director could then have been asked directly if he was related to the managing director of RiteSoftware. Of course, there may have been no impropriety intended, but the fact would have come to light and been considered in the evaluation. Many organisations will either not procure from companies where directors and senior managers have relatives or will ask for that information to be disclosed by the supplier in order that it can be weighted in the evaluation of alternative suppliers.

Functional requirements of the software

The evaluation process did not formally define the functional requirements of the required system. The scenario mentions that three months ago, another set of amendments was requested from RiteSoftware to allow one of the divisions in OneEnergy to pay bonuses to lorry drivers in a certain way. This functional requirement should have been defined in advance in the process and it would have then been compared with the functions offered by the package. The gap between requirement and package could then be evaluated in advance. This allows two things. Firstly, the match of functionality and package will form part of the evaluation. It is not expected that every function requirement will be completely fulfilled but the degree of compromise has to be assessed in some way. Secondly, an understanding of the gap allows the compromise to be managed in advance. For example, in the context of the pay for lorry drivers it might have been possible to change the pay structure in such a way that rewarded the drivers but avoided the expense of commissioning and maintaining software amendments.

Non-functional requirements of the software

Many software packages do actually offer most of the functionality that the users require. However, how they deliver that functionality is very important and usability can be a great differentiator between competing packages. In the scenario, it seems clear that non-functional requirements such as user-friendliness have not been considered properly in the evaluation. If they had been then it would be unlikely that users would have problems understanding some of the terminology and structure of the software. Problems leading to comments such as 'it just does not work like we do' should have been identified in advance. Understanding user competencies and expectations would allow the gap between users' ability and the requirements of the package to be properly assessed. This measure would be part of the evaluation. Again, if the package is selected, the gap can be planned for in advance so that the extra training costs, alluded to in the scenario, are budgeted for at the outset.

Evaluation criteria and process

Finally, the scenario suggests that the board decided to purchase the RitePay software package without evaluating alternative solutions. It was felt that payroll rules and processes were relatively standard and so there was no need to look further than a package recommended by the HR director. Certainly, the discovery that the HR director is related to the managing director of RiteSoftware now puts his impartiality in doubt. Furthermore, subsequent requested amendments to the functionality of the package suggest that OneEnergy's payroll rules were not as standard as expected. However, the real problem with choosing one solution without evaluating alternatives is that there is no auditable evidence about how the supplier and the product were selected. At best this looks amateurish; at worst it might cause concern to the non-executive member of the board and its internal auditors. OneEnergy is a plc. The scenario suggests that the company does have a policy on competitive procurement. Avoiding it raises the chance of impropriety, reduces the opportunity of negotiating a good deal, and should attract the attention of non-executive directors and other significant stakeholders.

ACCA marking scheme		
		Marks
(a)	Up to 1 mark for each non-ratio based observation up to a maximum of	5
	Up to 1 mark for each ratio based observation up to a maximum of	5
	Up to 3 marks for summary and integration of answer, giving a maximum of	13
(b)	Up to 1 mark for each relevant point up to a maximum of 3 marks for each failing. Four failings required, giving a maximum of	12

Examiner's comments

In part (a) consultants brought in to review the project had concluded that this information provided clear signs that RiteSoftware was in difficulty. Candidates were asked to confirm the consultant's conclusion. The data allowed candidates to calculate popular profitability, efficiency, liquidity and gearing ratios. There were also structural problems in the accounts concerning goodwill, retained profit and the financing of the company. It was clear that RiteSoftware was a company in trouble, run by directors that could see its imminent demise. Overall, candidates produced reasonable answers to this part question, many scoring pass marks on their analysis of a restricted set of ratios. However there was a wealth of information in the scenario that many candidates just did not use.

Part (b) asked the candidate to examine four ways in which the energy company failed to follow a proper evaluation procedure in the selection of the software package. The candidate was asked to include a discussion of the implication of each failing. This question should have resulted in answers that gave a relatively straightforward description of a rigorous evaluation process, comparing it to a company which had not used a process at all! The implication of each failing was signposted in the scenario. For example, the failure to define requirements in advance had led to the need to commission software amendments. Too many answers to this part question were disappointing and disorganised, failing to structure the answer in such a way to gain the marks on offer. In many instances this seemed to reflect unfamiliarity with this part of the syllabus.

10 4QX

Key answer tips

You must be prepared to discuss how an organisation can understand its marketing environment. Your answer can include a general discussion of factors that should be considered. However, PEST analysis is a useful technique for analysing the marketing environment. This technique ensures that all of the relevant points are covered and lends a natural structure to the answer. PESTEL analysis could also be used. This technique includes two additional factors, i.e. ecological and legal factors.

(a) Organisational performance will be dependent on the successful management of the opportunities, challenges and risks presented by changes in the external environment. No organisation exists in a vacuum, therefore it will be affected and will have an effect on its environment. By identifying and understanding the changes within the environment, 4QX will be able to adjust its operations to ensure long-term company profitability and survival.

There are a number of ways of classifying the different aspects of the environment. This analysis divides the business environment into four related but separate systems – political and legal, economic, social and technical (PEST).

The political and legal environment

Regulations governing business are widespread; they include those on health and safety, information disclosure, the dismissal of employees, vehicle emissions, use of pesticides and many more. Changes in the law can affect organisations in many ways. For example, a tightening of health and safety legislation may increase costs and premises failing to meet the higher standards could be closed down. Political factors can also have a direct impact on the way a business operates. Decisions made by government affect our everyday lives and can come in the form of policy or legislation.

In the case of the centre, a number of influences will be relevant. These include:

- the tax incentives to keep the population healthy – the centre may be able to take advantage of these but they may also encourage more competition

- any schemes set up to enable healthcare providers to pay the centre for exercise schemes for patients which could be a potential source of income

- changes in the legislation relating to children swimming unaccompanied – the existing legislation already has an impact on the services offered by the centre.

- the activities of the local council – if the decision were taken to upgrade the public facilities, this would have an impact on the demand for the use of the centre.

The economic environment

All businesses are affected by economical factors nationally and globally, such as interest rates. In addition, the economic climate dictates how consumers may behave within society. Whether an economy is in a boom, recession or recovery will affect consumer confidence and behaviour. When the economy is booming consumer confidence and spending is high. This will have a significant impact on the centre as membership of such facilities is often seen as a luxury and is likely to be one of the first items of expenditure which families cut back on when finances are under pressure.

Particular issues for the centre are:

- a healthy local economy which means that confidence and spending are high. Families and other local residents are more likely to sign up as members of the centre. This will also affect the price which they are prepared to pay for memberships and visits to the centre

- changes in the environment will affect the business at the centre – it will therefore be necessary for the management of the centre to pay close attention to the economic environment

- a booming economy may also attract new competitors.

The social environment

Forces within society such as family, friends and media can affect our attitude, interest and opinions. These forces shape who we are as people and the way we behave and what we ultimately purchase. Population changes also have a direct impact on all organisations – changes in the structure of a population will affect the supply and demand of goods and services within an economy. In addition, as society changes and as behaviours change, organisations must be able to offer products and services that aim to complement and benefit people's lifestyle and behaviour.

In the case of the centre:

- Attitudes are changing towards diet and health. As a result there is likely to be an increase in the number of people joining fitness clubs. There is also concern in many countries about the lack of exercise that young people are obtaining. This will have a significant impact on the demand for the centre's facilities.

- The attitude of the local population will also affect the kind of services which they are looking for and their expectations of service quality. The centre may be able to offer classes as well as memberships for example.

- The lifestyle of potential customers will also affect the means by which the centre markets itself. For example, if people are used to networking, then a significant amount of business may come by word of mouth, and the centre could perhaps offer incentives to members to introduce their friends.

The technological environment

Organisations need to be constantly aware of what is going on in the technological environment.

For the centre, technological change could influence the following:

- the type of equipment which the centre can install and the expectations of customers – if increasingly sophisticated equipment is available the centre may find that it has to invest in upgraded equipment to keep customers happy

- the cost of equipment

- new systems which could improve the efficiency of managing the centre

- different ways of marketing the centre and communicating with customers, such as the internet and email.

(b) Market segmentation is the division of a total market into distinct groups or sections. Buyers within each group should share common characteristics that will make them similar in their needs and preferences for products or services, or similar in the way in which they might react to a particular marketing initiative or marketing mix.

A challenge for the marketing management is to segment the market in a useful way. To be useful, a group of buyers or potential customers must respond differently from buyers in other market segments to the way a product is priced, or to the quality or features of the product, or to the way it is promoted, advertised or distributed.

If the centre is to segment the market, it needs to divide customers into subgroups which are:

- **measurable** – that is, the different characteristics can be measured

- **accessible** – customers in the segment can be easily reached

- **substantial** – big enough so that the cost of segmentation does not exceed the benefits.

Markets can be segmented on the basis of a variety of different characteristics, such as:

- demographics (age, socio-economic characteristics, and so on)

- lifestyle

- product usage and purchasing habits

- differing customer needs.

Products can then be designed, priced, promoted and made available in such a way that they will appeal to a targeted segment of the market.

The centre will need to carry out market research before identifying potential market segments. It will need to assess:

- the size of potential segments
- the competition
- the needs of different groups of customers
- the costs of marketing to the individual segments
- the impact on existing business of attracting particular customer groups.

It is likely that this exercise would result in the centre segmenting the market according to lifestyle and demographic characteristics, which are likely to be related.

Particular segmentation variables which they would want to consider would be:

- **age** – the age of customers and in particular the age of the children in any families targeted; for example, it may not be advantageous to market to parents of very young children if they are likely to want to swim in the late afternoon, as conference delegates swimming after a day's meetings may not be happy to share the pool with a large number of toddlers
- **the type of household** – which may be families or those without children
- **the disposable income of potential customers** – the centre will be looking to recruit members and customers with relatively high disposable income who are more likely to pay a high membership fee
- **social class** – potential customers are likely to come from higher socio-economic groups
- **occupation** – the centre may decide to target customers with a professional background as this is likely to be linked to the level of income.

(c) The income potential of the centre is the maximum level that can be reached under ideal conditions. This differs from the forecast of sales and income which is a prediction of the actual income that is expected in a future time period for a given level of marketing support.

Approach 1: A top-down approach, which can be taken by the company to estimate the income potential, is:

- analysing trends in the industry and economic forecasts, incorporating the impact of the environmental factors described in (a) above
- using this analysis to determine the overall market potential, that is the total potential demand for fitness club memberships or fitness facilities
- determining the local area market potential
- determining the centre's sales potential by considering its past performance, resources and future predicted market share, taking into account any decisions made about targeting particular groups.

Approach 2: An alternative approach would be to take a 'bottom-up' approach, as follows:

- generating estimates of future demand from customers or the company's salespeople
- combining the estimates to get a total forecast
- adjusting the forecast based on managerial insights into the industry, competition and general economic trends.

There are a number of techniques that can be used to forecast the market potential. These may be quantitative or qualitative. The choice of forecasting method depends on costs, type of product, characteristics of market, time span of the forecast, purpose of the forecast, stability of historical data, availability of required information and forecasters' expertise and experience. The most important criterion in the choice of a forecasting method is accuracy.

Quantitative forecasting methods

- Fitting a trend line assuming that sales influences fall into four categories:

  - trends (long-term changes)

  - cyclical changes

  - seasonal changes – this may be particularly relevant for the centre as it will include influences such New Year's resolutions leading to increased demand for memberships

  - irregular changes.

- Moving average: computes the average volume achieved in several periods and then uses it as a prediction for sales in the next period. With a strong trend in the series, the moving average lags behind. With more periods, the moving average forecast changes slowly.

- 'Simple' regression: trying to estimate the relationship between a single dependent variable (Y or sales) and a single independent variable (X) via a straight-line equation: $Y = a + bx$

Non-quantitative techniques for forecasting sales

- Sales force composite: a bottom-up method consisting of collecting estimates of sales for the future period from all salespeople. However this is not likely to be very useful to the centre as this is a new market which the centre has little or no experience of at the moment.

- Looking at the experience of other similar schemes in the same market.

- Jury of Executive Opinion – this opinions of a group of executives are pooled with data compiled by each executive or by marketing research. Individual forecasts may be combined by a specialist or by negotiation as a group. This method is valued as most important to marketing managers.

- Market testing by making the proposed product available to a selected number of customers and measuring their responses to the service and the price.

- Market research by asking local residents what facilities they would use and what price they would be prepared to pay.

Whatever method is used, estimating a forecast is costly in terms of time and money. It must be remembered that it is only an estimate and changes in fundamental conditions can cause the forecast to vary from actual results. There is no best technique for forecasting. Two forecasts undertaken with different approaches are better than one.

STRATEGIC CHOICE

11   DDD CHEMICALS

Key answer tips

This is a tricky question on identifying and responding to likely threats. The main problem lies in generating enough ideas to score well.

In part (a) Porter's five forces model has been used to provide at least some framework to help.

In part (b) when looking for strategic options, you could use the Ansoff matrix to generate ideas. Ansoff suggested internal efficiencies (long term contracts), market penetration (e.g. cut prices) and final new products and/or new markets (buy major threats).

Part (c) should be consistent with your analysis in part (b).

(a)   DDD is exposed to the following threats due to the imminent expiry of patents:

Increased competitive rivalry

Without patent protection to stop them, existing rivals will be able to produce cheaper copies of DDD chemicals. This will reduce the price DDD can charge for its products and reduce margins.

Tutorial note

Some pharmaceutical firms have seen drug prices fall by 90% once patent protection is removed.

Also, since the patents are attached to processes rather than specific chemicals, there is the threat that competitors will be able to use the processes to develop new chemicals before DDD.

Increased threat of entry

Existing patents also act as barriers deterring new entrants into DDD's markets. Without this barrier, there is a greater threat that new firms will enter the market, increasing competition and driving down prices and margins.

Increased power of customers

At present DDD exerts considerable power over customers as they have limited ability to switch suppliers. This is reflected by DDD's current high margins. Once patent protection is removed, competitors will be able to make similar chemicals giving customers more choice.

The pharmaceutical companies will thus be able to exert more influence over DDD in areas such as price (as discussed above) and also credit terms, delivery terms and so on.

Increased power of suppliers

Any fall in volume will reduce DDD's power over suppliers and bulk discounts may be lost.

Staffing issues

The expected fall in profits will affect the value of share options, which in turn will affect employee motivation. Also the likely fall in volumes could require DDD to consider redundancies.

(b) Possible courses of action include the following:

Try to establish new patents for existing processes

By changing various aspects of existing processes, it may be possible to establish new patents for them, eliminating the threats outlined above. This option should be pursued first by discussions with patent experts to assess the likelihood of success.

Develop new processes / products as part of product portfolio management

Presumably part of DDD's long-term planning process is such that it anticipates patent expiry as a normal part of its business and has already developed new patent-protected processes and chemicals to replace the ones concerned. If not, then resources need to be allocated to such portfolio development.

Cut prices to retain customers

DDD could seek to retain customers by cutting prices and relying on its existing good relationships with them. Low prices may also act as a deterrent to new entrants.

Volume economies of scale may still enable DDD to produce the chemicals concerned at a lower cost than competitors, allowing it to make a reasonable margin event with lower prices. However, if larger manufacturers enter the market, then this advantage would quickly become eroded.

Long-term contracts

An alternative way of retaining customers could be to offer them lower prices in exchange for signing long-term contracts. Particularly where patents are not due to expire immediately, customers could be tempted by lower prices now and the guarantee of no price rises in the future.

This would also be a way of responding to current pressure from customers to reduce prices.

Buy major threats

If DDD can identify specific threats from competitors, then one option would be to buy them. This is unfeasible given DDD's small size.

(c) Summary

It is recommended that the directors adopt the following course of action:

1. Try to establish new patents for existing processes to eliminate the threats.

2. If option 1 fails, DDD should try to get customers to sign up to long-term contracts in exchange for price cuts. This will create switching costs for customers and act as a barrier preventing new firms from entering the market.

Alongside this DDD should be developing new processes as part of its long-term portfolio management.

12   JURANIA

(a)   Competitive advantage

Key answer tips

This requirement looks at the link between competitive advantage and **location**. Porter's diamond is the main tool designed to explore such a link.

Michael Porter, in his book *The Competitive Advantage of Nations*, tried to isolate the national attributes that further competitive advantage in an industry. He argued that, for a country's industry to be successful, it needs to have the attributes and relationships shown in the diagram below.

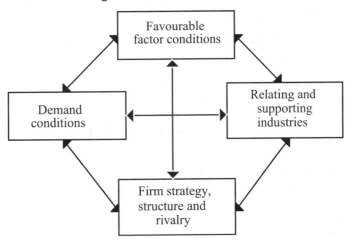

These can be applied to 222 as follows:

Favourable factor conditions

Industries can benefit from local factors such as physical resources, weather, capital, human resources, knowledge and infrastructure.

222 has clearly benefited from the local availability of suitably qualified staff, due partly to the excellent reputation of Jurania's university.

222 wishes to expand into other African countries so its factors need to be compared with those countries rather than globally. While it is doubtful whether the university at Jurania is producing better IT graduates than universities in the USA, for example, they will not demand such high wages either. There is more of a case, however, that 222 may have an advantage over firms from other African countries, with the possible exception of South Africa, provided 222 is not competing with any global foreign firms operating in those markets.

Overall, therefore, this should give 222 a competitive advantage in its chosen markets.

Demand conditions

There must be a strong home market demand for the product or service. This determines how industries perceive and respond to buyer needs and creates the pressure to innovate.

222 has benefited from the economic growth in Jurania and neighbouring countries in creating demand. Included within this demand are many top 100 companies who, presumably, put pressure on 222 to deliver better solutions than competitors. However, it is more doubtful that these firms will be as demanding as global customers encountered by global competitors.

As with factor conditions, it is likely that 222 has an advantage over indigenous local competitors but not against global players.

Relating and supporting industries

The success of an industry can be due to its suppliers and related industries.

222 has benefited from being close to several IT hardware and software companies and the country's largest ISP. However, there is little indication that any of these suppliers are world class and would have contributed to 222's competitive advantage.

Firm strategy, structure and rivalry

Porter found that domestic competition was vital as a spur to innovation and also enhanced global competitive advantage.

There is no indication that competition in Jurania has been intense so 222 will not have benefited in this way.

In conclusion, 222 has a basis for expansion into neighbouring countries but should be wary of becoming a global player.

(b) **Risks of proposed Internet strategy**

Tutorial note

Ensure you <u>evaluate</u> the risks as well as simply identifying them.

Using the services of a local specialist web designer

The main risks here are:

- The local specialist may not produce a site as well designed as that from a major firm with more experience and expertise.
- The local specialist may go bust and not be able to service future changes to the site.

As long as the local specialist can demonstrate a proven track record and evidence of financial stability, these risks should not deter 222. The advantages of having a local expert to deal with issues when they arise should outweigh the risks.

Having a sophisticated website with case studies

The risks here include:

- The site may be too complicated for users.
- The case studies may disclose secrets to competitors, thus eroding competitive advantage.
- Previous customers may refuse to allow their details to be posted, reducing the effectiveness of the idea.

The first risk is not significant as 222 sells to organisations that in most cases will have more sophisticated buyers with some knowledge of the technology involved. The others can be managed by careful disclosure on the website.

222 to host the website

The main risks of 222 hosting its own website and buying a powerful web server are:

- 222 might not have the specialist expertise that suppliers have, particularly to deal with problems. This could result in greater website downtime and lost business.
- There will also be the extra operating gearing risk due to investment in hardware, more expensive software licences, etc.
- There is also the risk of obsolescence regarding the server.

The first of these is the most significant risk, but all of them can be eliminated by using an external host. Competition to host websites is intense as firms could be based anywhere in the world and so the cost of external hosting is low.

Fibre-optic broadband

Fibre-optic broadband is growing in popularity around the world so would appear to be a low risk option. However, there are risks associated with the choice of supplier:

- The supplier is a new company so may not have the experience required to develop a problem-free network.
- The supplier may not have the financial strength to ensure its medium-term future, so may not be around to service any problems as they arise.

These risks are significant so it may be more prudent for 222 to use a more established firm.

13   ELITE FABRICS

Key answer tips

In part (a) you are specifically required to build up your answer around an accepted model. Choose an appropriate model on which to base your answer; the examiner uses Porter's value chain.

As the question suggests, part (b) should be tackled in two stages: first, the consequences of the proposed move; second, the change in competencies.

(a)   Elite Fabrics (EF) has chosen to use **vertical integration** to improve its profit and sales revenue performances. This has, until now, been a successful strategy. By ensuring its customer base, increasingly controlled through ownership, it has been able to guarantee sales and utilisation of its fabrics. The success has been brought about by the ability of the company to increase demand for its fabrics from its internal customers – the now integrated clothing manufacturer. In addition EF has been able to increase the profit margins on its sales revenue. Research has shown that the further a company moves 'downstream' in the manufacturing and distribution processes (that is, the nearer it is to the final consumer) the higher are the profit margins. This is because it becomes increasingly possible to differentiate and brand the product rather than operate in the commodity style environment as typified by normal fabric production – unless of course the fabric itself has a powerful brand identity, such as being Lycra-enhanced.

A number of models could be applied to this part of the question but probably Michael Porter's value chain is the most widely-known. It provides a structure to show the **benefits of vertical integration**. It evaluates each step of the operations where **value-added activities** are provided. 'These value-added activities are the physically and technologically distinctive activities which the firm performs' (*Porter*). The inbound logistics enable the dress manufacturing unit to have quality fabrics, delivered at the appropriate times, in the right quantity from within the group. Problems associated with inventory holding are minimised. Prices can be transferred between the relevant units so as to maximise their competitive position. By creating a larger demand for yarns the group is now able to counter-balance the power of the large yarn producers, ensuring supply and at competitive prices. So far the firm has no control over the sale of its finished garments – the outbound logistics. This could occur if the decision to integrate further forward is agreed upon.

It is important to understand that each part of the operation has an impact upon other activities. A failure in one area because of the lack of control or influence can damage the overall performance. The value chain illustrates how marketing and service functions are critical in supporting the manufacturing and distribution activities. It also is important to ensure that each component part of the organisation from purchasing, design, operations (including the technology used), and quality control are integrated and mutually supportive.

Although **vertical integration enables EF to exert increased control over its value chain**, there is a **danger in the loss of flexibility**. In particular, the garment manufacturing part of the group is obliged to buy from the fabric producing part. This could prevent the purchase of cheaper materials from foreign suppliers, or the use of more attractively designed fabrics. Both of these constraints could reduce the competitiveness of the company. The benefits of the inter-company transfer pricing could lead to inefficiencies within the system – dulled incentives. The fabric producing part of the organisation may become less competitive because it believes that it has a captive market with the garment producing unit obliged to buy from it. This complacency could be reduced by insisting upon 'arm's length' trading between the constituent parts of the organisation.

Diversification through vertical integration could harm EF's core competences. By not 'sticking to the knitting', the company could **reduce its competitive edge**. It needs to concentrate on what it does best, and not become side-tracked into non-core activities. Furthermore, as EF vertically expands, it may become **less responsive to environmental and technical change**. This lack of flexibility could result in the company being out-manoeuvred by smaller but more focused firms. In addition, by being totally self-contained the firm may be **deprived of technical and marketing insights** that might otherwise be available from outsiders.

The **increase in fixed costs** usually associated with vertical integration will mean a higher break-even point for sales revenue, and this will result in the company becoming more vulnerable to cyclical fluctuations in sales demand.

(b) The **benefits of further forward integration** by purchasing the chain of retail stores would include:

- guaranteed retail outlets for the dresses and associated products
- the ability to expand in key geographic areas and to control the margins
- the development and maintenance of a strong brand image
- improved quality control.

However there are some concerns about such a strategy. Firstly the **acquisition costs will be high** (equivalent to about four years post tax profits at current level).The financial burden of this could divert funds away from more critical needs, such as renewal of equipment or expenditure on marketing. The expansion into retail outlets could **antagonise other retail chains** and could jeopardise sales of EF products through these non-owned outlets. Nevertheless it would be essential to continue to distribute through independent outlets because the purchase price of $35 million would not be sufficient to guarantee the depth of retail coverage required. Furthermore, EF stores would probably require a wider range of products than could be provided by the integrated company itself. An essential prerequisite in this type of retailing is wide choice. However, other manufacturers are unlikely to be happy about using a rival manufacturer to distribute and market EF's product range.

Retailing requires competences other than those prevailing in manufacturing. **Managing multiple retail sites** and **delegating control to local staff** will be critical to the success of the endeavour. **Merchandising skills** such as shop displays and window dressing will also be an activity foreign to the company, but will be essential for success, as will be inventory control. **Financial controls** will need to be put in place, as margins in the retail trade can be volatile. Good and up-to-date **management information systems** will also be required. If the company is to expand in the future, **retail site assessment** will be required. Finally, **marketing and branding skills** will have to be further developed. The nearer the company is to the consumer, the more knowledge of the market is required. A company close to the consumer cannot rely on intermediaries and distributors to provide this marketing information.

14   GREENFIELD NURSERIES

Key answer tips

This is not a past exam question from the current examiner. The current examiner is more likely to make use of models such as Harmon's process-strategy matrix in his answers and you should aim to do the same.

(a)   There are a number of factors which should persuade Mark Roberts to focus his attention on retailing and 'buy in' the garden plants from outside independent suppliers, not least being that higher margins are usually obtained from the retailing side of the business. In addition by selecting from a number of suppliers it is possible to have access to a wider range of plants than could have been grown in the single nursery. Furthermore, by relying on specialist growers Roberts may be able to take advantage of the other growers' expertise. Also their production costs may be lower, resulting from production economies giving access to cheaper plants.

However, there are several reasons why companies may choose to 'make' rather than 'buy', but they are probably not all applicable in this scenario.

By being responsible for growing its own plants Greenfield Nursery does have control over the quality of the products and also has a guaranteed supply. There is always a possibility that reliance on others for key supplies involves high risks. If quality is sub-standard the consumer identifies the retailer as the source of the problem. It is rarely the ultimate supplier, who is usually unknown to the consumer, whose reputation is tarnished.

Companies may also 'grow' rather than 'buy' if they feel that the guarantee of supply is a critical issue. However, in these circumstances there are a number of alternative suppliers and it is unlikely that the nursery will be threatened by having to rely on one supplier. In such circumstances, with a large number of suppliers, few being dominant, buyer power should be quite large. Similarly companies often choose to 'make' rather than 'buy in' because of the specialist nature of the production and they wish to maintain a presence in that arena. This is not a critical issue here. The production technology and associated expertise is rather low, with relatively small capital costs (land excluded), and so barriers to entry will be low. Should the necessity arise Roberts and his Nursery could soon be able to re-enter this production area.

(b)   If one is going to rely on **outsourcing** as a means of obtaining supplies, there are a number of management issues which will need to be addressed.

Firstly, there is the issue of reporting and responsibility. This is where the line management concept breaks down. To whom are the employees responsible? If deliveries are late and/or are of poor quality then Mark Roberts has no direct link with the personnel responsible. He has to complain indirectly to his supplier at corporate level. While this is possible it can prove to be expensive and it would certainly be time-consuming.

This leads to the second significant management problem – there is a loss of direct control because the chain of command has effectively broken down. This can lead to a lack of discipline and little opportunity for remedial actions to be taken.

By allowing an independent entity to provide important, but non-core, functions there is the necessity for the 'buyer' to set up systems to manage and monitor the contract – contract compliance. There is also the potential for disputes which can now be less easily reconciled and may ultimately end up in court. Although many managers have seen outsourcing as a means of saving money and possibly accessing expertise, there is also now the prospect that operational flexibility might be curtailed.

15   ENVIRONMENT MANAGEMENT SOCIETY

Key answer tips

Try not to focus on simply regurgitating the pocket notes. Instead try to add as much relevance and specifics from the scenario as possible.

Context

The decline in the number of people taking the qualification appears to be a reflection of the maturity of the marketplace. The large pool of unqualified environmental managers and auditors that existed when the qualification was launched has now been exploited. There are now fewer candidates taking the examinations and fewer members joining the EMS. The organisation's response to this has been to look for international markets where it can promote the qualifications it currently offers. It hopes to find large pools of unqualified environmental managers and auditors in these markets.

The scenario suggests that EMS currently has relatively limited strategic ambitions. There is no evidence that EMS plans to develop new qualifications outside its current portfolio. Indeed, attempts to look at complementary qualifications (such as soil and water conservation) have been rejected by Council. Hence, expansion into new strategic business markets does not appear to be an option.

Strategy development

(a) **Internal development**

Internal development takes place when strategies are developed by building on or developing the organisation's own capabilities. It is often termed organic growth. This is how EMS has operated up to now. The original certificates were developed by the founders of the Society. Since then, additional certificates have been added and the Diploma programme developed at the instigation of members and officers of the Society.

In many ways this type of organic growth is particularly suited to the configuration of the organisation, one where there is a risk-averse and cautious culture. The organic approach spreads cost and risk over time and growth is much easier to control and manage. However, growth can be slow and indeed, as in the case of EMS, may have ceased altogether. Growth is also restricted by the breadth of the organisation's capabilities. For example, EMS has not been able to develop (or indeed even consider developing) any products outside of its fairly restricted product range. Furthermore, although internal development may be a reasonable strategy for developing a home market it maybe an inappropriate strategy for breaking into new market places and territories. This is particularly true when, as it appears in the case of the EMS, internal resources have no previous experience of developing products in overseas markets.

In summary, internal growth has been the method of strategy development at EMS up to now, based on a strategic direction of consolidation and market penetration. There is no evidence that EMS is considering developing new products to arrest the fall in qualification numbers. However, the Board has suggested developing new markets for the current qualification range and India, China and Russia have been identified as potential targets. It seems unlikely that internal development will be an appropriate method of pursuing this strategic direction.

(b) **Mergers and acquisitions**

A strategy of acquisition is one where one organisation (such as EMS) takes ownership of other existing organisations in the target countries. One of the most compelling reasons for acquisition is the speed it allows an organisation to enter a new product or market area. EMS might look to acquire organisations already offering certification in its target markets. These organisations would then become the mechanism for launching EMS qualifications into these markets. In addition, it is likely that these organisations will have qualifications that the EMS does not currently offer. These qualifications could then be offered, if appropriate, in EMS's home market. This arrangement would provide EMS with the opportunity to quickly offer its core competences into its target markets, as well as gaining new competencies which it could exploit at home.

However, acquisitions usually require considerable expenditure at some point in time and evidence suggests that there is a high risk that they will not deliver the returns that they promised. It is unlikely that the EMS will have enough money to fund such acquisitions and its status as a private limited entity means that it cannot currently access the markets to fund such growth. Any acquisitions will have to be funded from its cash reserves or from private equity investment groups. Furthermore, acquisitions also bring political and cultural issues which evidence suggests the organisation would have difficulty with. Under achievement in mergers and acquisitions often results from problems of cultural fit. This can be particularly problematic with international acquisitions, which is exactly the type of acquisition under consideration here. So, although acquisitions are a popular way of fuelling growth it is unlikely that EMS will have either the cash or the cultural will to pursue this method of strategy development. There is no evidence that EMS has any expertise in acquiring organisations in its home market and so such acquisitions overseas would be extremely risky.

(c)   **Strategic alliances**

A strategic alliance takes place when two or more organisations share resources and activities to pursue a particular strategy. This approach has become increasingly popular for a number of reasons. In the context of EMS it would allow the organisation to enter into a marketplace without the large financial outlay of acquiring a local organisation. Furthermore, it would avoid the cultural dislocation of either acquiring or merging with another organisation. The motive for the alliance would be cospecialisation with each partner concentrating on the activities that best match their capabilities. Johnson, Scholes and Whittington suggest that co-specialisation alliances 'are used to enter new geographic markets where an organisation needs local knowledge and expertise'. This fits the EMS requirement exactly.

The exact nature of the alliance would require much thought and indeed different types of alliance might be forged in the three markets targeted by EMS. A joint venture is where a new organisation is set up jointly owned by the parents. This is a formal alliance and will obviously take some time to establish.EMS will have to contribute cost and resources to the newly established company, but such costs and resources should be much less than those incurred in an acquisition. However, joint ventures take time to establish and it may be not be an option if EMS wants to quickly move into a target marketplace to speedily arrest its falling numbers. A licence agreement could be an alternative where EMS licenses the use of its qualification in the target market. This could be organised in a number of ways. For example, a local organisation could market the EMS qualification as its own and pay EMS a fee for each issued certificate and diploma. Alternatively, the qualification may be marketed by the local organisation as an EMS qualification and EMS pays this organisation a licence fee for every certificate and diploma it issues in that country. This requires less commitment from EMS but it is likely to bring in less financial returns, with less control over how the qualification is marketed. Furthermore, if the qualification is successful, there is the risk that the local organisation will develop its own alternative so that it gains all the income from the transaction, not just a percentage of the transaction fee.

At first sight, the strategic alliance appears very appropriate to EMS's current situation. The licensing approach is particularly attractive because it seems to offer very quick access to new markets without any great financial commitment and without any cultural upheaval within EMS itself. However, the uptake of the qualification is unpredictable and the marketing and promotion of the qualification is outside the control of EMS. EMS may find this difficult to accept. Furthermore, the EMS will only be receiving a fraction of the income and so it must ensure that this fraction is sufficient to fuel growth expectations and service the newly qualified members in other countries. Finally, there is often a paradox in organisations where internal development has been the strategic method adopted so far. An organisation used to internal development and control often finds it difficult to trust partners in an alliance. Yet trust and cooperation is probably the most important ingredient of making such strategic alliances work.

ACCA marking scheme	
	Marks
1 mark for each relevant point up to a maximum of 8 marks for internal development. There is a maximum of 4 marks for points relating to principles.	8
1 mark for each relevant point up to a maximum of 8 marks for acquisitions. There is a maximum of 4 marks for points relating to principles.	8
1 mark for each relevant point up to a maximum of 9 marks for strategic alliances. There is a maximum of 5 marks for points relating to principles.	9
Total marks available	**25**

16 MMI *Walk in the footsteps of a top tutor*

Tutor's top tips

This was a strategic question that mixed financial analysis and acquisition assessment. This is the second time that the examiner has had strategic elements in the option questions and we can expect to see more of this in the future. It was the first time that financial analysis has featured in the option questions and this may have taken some students by surprise. But the same technique points apply as would have applied if this was part of the compulsory question.

Part (a)

This part of the question asked students to explain why two acquisitions had taken place and assess their post-acquisition performance.

Key to success:

Use a recognised model to assess why the acquisitions had taken place. The best one would be the Ashbridge matrix (used by the examiner) and well prepared students should be reasonably comfortable with this approach. But models such as Porter's acquisition tests could be used equally as well. The examiner even brings in the BCG matrix.

As is usual with financial analysis the key to getting the arks will be to explain why a ratio has changed and what the implications of such a change might be. There wasn't a lot of financial information provided so it is likely to be important to use as much of it as possible.

> **Dangers:**
>
> Not using the financial analysis
>
> Not recognizing that the requirement had two elements (explain why the acquisitions had happened, and assessing their performance)
>
> **Part (b)**
>
> Having assessed two acquisitions that had already taken place, students were asked to assess a third proposed acquisition.
>
> **Key to success:**
>
> Apply the same techniques that were used in part (a). So use the same model and include financial analysis. Students could also have used the suitability, feasibility, and acceptability approach suggested by Johnson, Scholes and Whittington
>
> Make a recommendation as to whether the acquisition should proceed and justify it. It doesn't matter whether you think the acquisition should go ahead or not, as long as you have an opinion one way or the other and can back it up with sensible analysis.
>
> **Dangers:**
>
> The examiner complained that some students didn't include any financial analysis. This would have been a major error given the amount of financial information included in the question and the approach taken to part (a).

(a)   **First Leisure**

The initial motivation for the acquisition of First Leisure was the need to diversify out of a declining market place (falling 5% over the recorded period) into an expanding one (increasing over 25% in the recorded period). The cash generated by the quarrying company was used to purchase a profitable, well-run company in an expanding market. Diversification was a direct response to environmental changes. Increased costs and falling reserves meant that there was little chance of finding new sites in its core market. MMI initially played no managerial role in First Leisure, allowing the managers who had made it successful to continue running the company. However, buying a company concerned with leisure appeared to be an example of unrelated diversification and there were some negative comments about the financial wisdom of this acquisition.

After a period of consolidation, certain unexpected synergies emerged that had not been clear at the time of acquisition. These came from the conversion of disused or unprofitable quarry sites into leisure parks. This conversion was doubly advantageous. In the first instance it reduced the operating costs of MMI, allowing it to shed costs associated with running unprofitable mines and maintaining security and safety at disused sites. Secondly, it allowed First Leisure to acquire sites relatively easily and cheaply in an environment where it was becoming more expensive and harder, because of planning restrictions, to purchase new sites. Johnson, Scholes and Whittington discuss the principles of economies of scope where an organisation has underutilised resources that it cannot effectively use or dispose of. It makes sense to switch these if possible to a new activity, in this instance leisure parks.

The turnover of First Leisure has doubled in six years. The figures summarised in table 1 suggest an expanding company in an expanding market and its market share continues to grow (up from 13% to 21% in the recorded period). Furthermore, gross profit margins have remained fairly constant but recent increases in the net profit margin suggests that costs appear to be under control, despite the recent issues concerning the supply of boats from Boatland. In corporate management terms MMI probably perceived that it would initially be playing a 'portfolio management' role at First Leisure. However, the discovery of unexpected synergies has led to it adopting (and perhaps claiming in hindsight) a synergy manager role. In terms of the BCG matrix, First Leisure exhibits all the characteristics of a star business unit and so it should be retained in the portfolio. It has a high market share in a growing market and increasing margins means that even if it has spent heavily to gain this share (and there is no direct evidence of this in the scenario), costs are now beginning to fall.

Boatland

The synergies that emerged from acquiring First Leisure appear to have been unexpected. However, the acquisition of Boatland in 20X6 was largely justified on the grounds of synergy. Synergies were expected with First Leisure and with MMI itself. By this time the directors felt that they had built up significant managerial competencies that could be successfully applied to acquired companies. These managerial competencies could be used to drive extra value from underperforming companies and so deliver benefits to shareholders. In the case of Boatland the expected synergies with First Leisure were as follows:

- First Leisure had experienced difficulties in the supply and maintenance of boats for their leisure parks. Boatland seemed to offer a way out of this problem. First Leisure would become a preferred customer of Boatland, taking priority over other customers. MMI also perceived that cost savings could be found by bringing boat manufacture and maintenance into the Group. In this instance, MMI was pursuing a policy of backward integration, producing one of the inputs into First Leisure's current business activities.

- Secondly, Boatland itself appeared to be undervalued. The management team appeared to lack ambition, focusing on producing a limited number of craft to high specification. It was felt that the production of boats for First Leisure would help the company expand, allowing it to increase market share partly based on guaranteed orders from First Leisure.

In this instance MMI probably thought of itself as a synergy manager, helping Boatland develop strategic capabilities and exploiting synergies with both MMI and First Leisure. However, the acquisition has not brought the expected benefits. The boats provided for First Leisure have not been appropriately constructed for their purpose and, paradoxically, because of the way they are misused by holiday makers, maintenance costs and 'downtime' has increased. Furthermore, the status of First Leisure as a preferred customer has led to delays in boat manufacture and maintenance for established customers. Orders have fallen and so has the reputation of the company. This is reflected in the data provided in table 1. Revenue and market share has fallen in a static market place. More worrying is the significant fall in gross and net profit margins. The net profit margin has fallen from 13.04% in 2002 to just 4.29% in 20X8. Furthermore, difficulties also have been created for First Leisure, which are also disturbing its relationship with MMI. The problem at Boatland appears to be cultural and this is reflected not only on the results but in the loss of experienced boat building employees. When the company was bought it concentrated on building a small number of high quality boats to discerning customers who valued and cherished their boats. In contrast, First Leisure required a large number of simple, robust boats that could be used and abused by holiday makers. The products and markets are different and the perceived synergy was an illusion.

In BCG terms Boatland has a very small share of a static market. Although there is no evidence of it being a cash drain on MMI the conflict between the culture of Boatland and the cultures of MMI and First Leisure probably used up a disproportionate amount of company time and resources. In terms of the Ashridge Portfolio Display, Boatland appeared as a heartland business but it soon turned into a value trap business. It seems sensible to divest Boatland from the portfolio. However, the supply implications of this to First Leisure will have to be investigated and so divestment may have to wait until First Leisure has built up a relationship with an alternative supplier.

(b) **Introduction**

Since 2002 MMI have built up a small portfolio of businesses that reflect different strategic directions. It has consolidated in its own market by shedding unprofitable or closed quarries and purchasing smaller competitors. This is reflected in the data given in table 1. During a period when the marketplace has declined by 5%, MMI has increased its market share from 20% to 28%. Gross profitability has remained fairly steady during the period, but the net profit margin has increased significantly since 2004. The increase in market share is probably due to the acquisition, in 2004, of two smaller competitors. The increase in the net profit margin can largely be traced to the disposal of redundant and unprofitable quarries to First Leisure. MMI's attempts at diversification have had mixed success. First Leisure, acquired in 2002, turned out to be an inspired acquisition as unexpected synergies emerged which assisted MMI's profitability. However, the expected synergies from the Boatland purchase have not materialised and MMI appear to have destroyed rather than created value in this acquisition.

In 2004 MMI acquired two of its smaller competitors, bringing five further mines or quarries into the group. MMI introduced its own managers into these companies resulting in a spectacular rise in revenues and profits that caused the CEO of MMI to claim that corporate management capabilities were now an important asset of MMI. So there appears to be evidence that MMI management can successfully improve the performance of an acquisition. However, Boatland is in a significantly different industry to these earlier acquisitions. MMI managers are familiar with the management of mines and quarries and probably found that the employees of these companies shared the culture of an industry they were familiar with. In contrast, at Boatland the sought after synergy was with First Leisure, not MMI, and so the MMI managers entered an industry and an environment they were unfamiliar with. Evidence from the First Leisure and Boatland acquisitions suggests that MMI is more successful when it employs a 'hands-off' approach to managing acquisitions which are not directly related to its core mining and quarrying operations. The incumbent management team are left to get on with the job with minimal interference from MMI.

InfoTech

The current financial position of InfoTech suggests that its management team may not be able to deliver the turnaround required. Market share and gross and net profit margins have fallen over the recorded period. Revenues have decreased by 16% at InfoTech in a period where the size of the market has increased by almost 25%. If MMI acquires InfoTech then the preferred 'hands-off' approach will be very risky, particularly considering the financial investment the company requires. MMI appears to have two alternatives if it goes ahead with the acquisition. The first is to learn from its experience at Boatland and install managers who are more sensitive to the culture of the organisation and the industry as a whole. To do this, they will have to recognise that their perceived value adding managerial capabilities actually turned out to be value destroying at Boatland. MMI could recruit managers with established track records in the information technology industry. However, there is no evidence that MMI has successfully adopted this approach before.

The financial position alluded to above also needs to be considered. Boatland and First Leisure were both successful, profitable companies when they were acquired. In contrast, Infotech is making a loss and appears to require investment which it has failed to secure in its own right. This is a controversial reason for acquisition and in this context MMI is playing the role of a portfolio manager, one it has never played for a failing company. In terms of the BCG matrix, InfoTech is a business unit in a growing market but with a low market share. It would be defined as a question mark or problem child.

Suitability is one of the three success criteria Johnson, Scholes and Whittington use to judge strategic options. An approach which evaluates whether the acquisition addresses the situation in which MMI and InfoTech are operating would be a perfectly valid approach to answering this question.

ACCA marking scheme		Marks
(a)	**First Leisure**	
	Up to 2 marks for recognising that this unrelated diversification was driven by environmental change; supported by appropriate data.	
	Up to 2 marks for issues concerning economies of scope	
	Up to 3 marks for interpreting the financial and market data.	
	Up to 2 marks for recognising the likely parenting role and for locating First Leisure on an appropriate analysis matrix.	
	Boatland	
	Up to 2 marks for recognising the synergies expected from Boatland.	
	Up to 2 marks for interpreting the financial and market data.	
	Up to 3 marks for explaining the failure of the acquisition.	15
	Up to 2 marks for recognising the likely parenting role and for locating Boatland in an appropriate analysis matrix.	
(b)	Up to 3 marks for interpreting the financial performance of MMI and summarising its acquisition strategy.	
	Up to 2 marks for recognising that a 'hands-off' approach has been more successful when MMI has pursued unrelated diversification	
	Up to 2 marks for recognising the difficulty of pursuing this approach at InfoTech	
	Up to 2 marks for interpreting the financial and market data	
	Up to 2 marks for recognising the likely parenting role and for locating InfoTech in an appropriate analysis matrix	
		10
Total		**25**

17 RAMON SILVA

Key answer tips

In part (a) Porter's value chain is a useful model to discuss adding value. Marketing approaches to product definition could also have been used.

Part (b) is a more straightforward discussion of franchising. The key is to apply the issues to the scenario.

(a)   **Report**

To: Ramon Silva

From: Accountant

Value innovation in La Familia Amable hotel chain

In strategic terms, you are hoping to create a competitive advantage over existing hotels based on a cost focus strategy. The success of this niche marketing strategy will depend on your ability to attract customers from the existing providers, but there does seem a gap to exploit. In many ways you have an advantage in that you are not constrained by previous experience in the hotel industry and this has enabled you to look to deliver a significantly different value proposition to your customers and not simply look to improve marginally on what currently is on offer. One particular study on innovation drew attention to five dimensions of strategy where innovators can

significantly outperform existing companies. This is important, as the industry does not look particularly attractive with low growth and overcapacity – a recipe for low profitability. The five dimensions are:

Industry assumptions – here existing companies take the competitive conditions as given whereas innovators are looking to influence and change those conditions.

Strategic focus – simply benchmarking against the current hotel providers might not create any real advantage. Innovators are seeking to provide a step change in the experience given to the customer.

Customers – the route to success might not be through ever increasing segmentation and customisation, but by actually looking to focus on the shared attributes of the service that customers value – a good night's sleep for a low price being a prime example.

Assets and capabilities – rather than looking to leverage existing assets and capabilities, the innovator looks to ask what would we do if we were starting a new business.

Product and service offering – existing competitors may again be constrained in their thinking by the existing boundaries of the industry and the innovator by identifying new customers and services that take them outside this boundary may offer a 'total solution' that transforms the industry. The 'no frills', low cost budget airlines are a good example of such thinking.

In the hotel business 'location, location, location' is argued to be at the heart of a successful strategy. Clearly this will be your choice and is affected by the customer groups you are looking to attract. Establishing a brand name and reputation is an important marketing strategy and this will be facilitated by growing the chain rapidly and giving customers easy access to your hotels. In value chain terms, the company infrastructure looks lean, with a reliance on trained husband and wife teams to deliver the service. Franchising would also seem to be a route to grow the business that will place reduced strain on company headquarters. The creation of a chain should lend itself to significant buying and procurement advantages, right from the design of the hotels which will focus on the core value you are providing – namely quiet and cost. One French hotel chain was able to cut in half the average cost of building a room, its 'no frills' service cut staff costs from between 25% and 35% of sales revenue – the industry average – to between 20% and 23%.

Good design will therefore affect the quality of service that the operations side of the value chain delivers to the customer. This may be a simpler service to that provided by its competitors – simpler, more basic rooms, no expensive restaurants or lounge areas all impact on the cost of operations and consequently the price charged. Marketing, as previously referred to above, is much more effectively done through satisfied customers' recommendations than by expensive advertising. Many hotel chains have used technology to create customer loyalty schemes of questionable benefit to the customer. You will certainly have to seriously consider the value of such an after sales service. The established competitors often make assumptions as to what a customer wants and typically this is offering more and more services that are expensive to provide. Your entry into a 'mature' industry such as this, allows you to really challenge these assumptions and deliver a price/value combination that is hard to beat.

Yours,

A N Consultant

(b)   Franchising is typically seen as a quick and cost effective way of growing the business but Ramon should be aware of both the advantages and disadvantages of using it as the preferred method of growth. Franchised chains are argued to benefit from the sort of brand recognition and economies of scale not enjoyed by independent owner/managers. When combined with the high levels of motivation normally associated with owner/managed businesses, franchises can be argued to get the best of both worlds.

Franchising is defined as 'a contractual agreement between two legally independent companies whereby the franchisor grants the right to the franchisee to sell the franchisor's product or do business under its trademarks in a given location for a specified period of time. In return, the franchisee agrees to pay the franchisor a combination of fees, usually including an up-front franchise fee, royalties calculated as a percentage of unit revenues, and an advertising contribution that is also usually a percentage of unit sales.'

Ramon is considering a type of franchising called 'business-format franchising', where the franchisor sells a way of doing business to its franchisees. Business-format franchising is a model frequently found in the fast food and restaurant industry, hotels and motels, construction and maintenance, and non-food retailing. Often these franchises are labour intensive and relatively small-scale operations.

Franchising is seen as a safer alternative to growing the business organically. While this might be true of well established global franchises, failure rates among franchised small businesses were greater than those of independent businesses (in one US study a 34.7% failure rate for franchises as opposed to 28.0% for independents over a six or seven year period).Often it is the failure of the franchisor that brings down its franchisees. Failure stems from the franchisee not only having to rely on their own skills and enthusiasm but also the capacity of the franchisor and other franchisees to make the overall operation work.

The advantages to the franchisee are through gaining access to a well-regarded brand name that will generate a higher level of demand and use of a tried and tested business model that should reduce the franchisee's operating costs and risk. These benefits stem from being a member of a well-established franchised system. Yet La Familia Amable along with many other franchises will be new and small. These smaller franchises tend to be regional in scope, and fairly unknown outside their regional market. This has a significant effect on what the franchisees can expect to gain from their franchisors and their prospects of success. Both parties need to assess carefully the strengths and weaknesses of the system. Companies growing via franchises need to take the time to understand their business model thoroughly and determine how franchising fits with their long-term strategy. Care must be taken with the franchise agreement that creates a genuine partnership with the right balance between freedom and control over the franchisees.

18 CLYDE WILLIAMS

Key answer tips

The answer use the PESTEL model and stakeholder mapping. However, you could just as well have used Johnson, Scholes and Whittington's assessment technique for strategies and assessed feasibility, suitability and acceptability. You would have then generated a very similar answer.

(a)   The dilemma faced by Clyde shows the complex nature of strategic decisions, even within a small firm like Concrete Solutions. There is a need for Clyde to undertake a strategic appraisal, and identify the various stakeholders affected by his decision and their relative power and interest. The appraisal should involve both a PESTEL and stakeholder analysis to identify the key environmental factors affecting the opportunity – as shown in the table.

Factors		Stakeholders	
Political	Local council – opposition	Council	High interest and high power
	Rival council – support	Rival council	As above
Economic	Less disposable income		
Social	Less local employment	Employees	High int/low power
		Council	As above
Technological	Need to invest in CAM		
Environmental	Higher pollution	Council	As above
Legal	Limits on noxious emissions	Environmental agencies	High interest /moderate power

For Concrete Solutions, the move into the new product can be viewed as a related diversification – namely a new market and a new product with the attendant risk involved. Clyde will have to assess the resource implications of the move. A considered SWOT analysis, including his personal liability to manage the strategic change would be useful. There may be a significant investment in new technology and employee training to make the new blocks. In effect he will be forming a strategic alliance with the international company and making significant changes to both the value chain and value system. There will be no need to invest in sales and marketing as this will be the responsibility of its larger partner. As a major strategic option there is a need to address issues of its suitability, acceptability and feasibility. In terms of suitability the option seems to address many of the strategic problems attached to his current product range. It is a product that can be sold all year round and into a much wider geographical market area. It is in terms of acceptability that the dilemma reveals itself and the impact on the different stakeholders involved. Clyde may find stakeholder mapping and scenario building useful in coming to a decision. As the owner of the business he needs to assess the risk involved against the likely returns. Feasibility looks reasonably sound – new resources and skills will be needed but should be affordable and achievable with the support of the partner.

(b) Recent corporate scandals have increased the critical awareness of the need for businesses to operate ethically and in a socially responsible way. This is seen largely in the context of large firms and their governance but, as the Concrete Solutions scenario shows, small owner-managed firms are not immune from taking difficult decisions that have differing significant impacts on the firm's stakeholders and their expectations. Johnson, Scholes and Whittington see corporate social responsibility as 'concerned with the ways in which an organisation exceeds the minimum obligation to stakeholders specified through regulation and corporate governance'. They argue that it is useful to distinguish between contractual stakeholders – including customers, suppliers and employees – who have a legal relationship with an organisation, and community stakeholders – such as local communities – who do not have the same degree of legal protection as the first group. Clyde's local community and its representatives will face a dilemma – jobs v pollution – not an easy choice! Clearly there will be considerable negotiation between the key stakeholders and Clyde as the owner/manager should act ethically and with integrity in reaching a decision having profound effects for all parties concerned.

ORGANISATIONAL STRUCTURE

19   ALG TECHNOLOGY

Key answer tips

The scenario explicitly rejects a divisional structure so this would not score marks as a suggested structure in part (a).

(a)   ALG Technology is a company operating in a number of fields of complex technologies and in several dynamic markets. Its current organisational structure based upon a functional division of work is not providing the necessary integration of activities, nor is it responding sufficiently to market needs. It is likely that a **matrix structure** or one **based on project teams** might work better but there will also be disadvantages associated with such a structure. The basis of such a structure is a multi-functional project team. The team is often small, flexible and temporary. It is often set up when management do not wish to set up separate divisions but are looking for increased co-operation among all their staff. It generally has two reporting lines – one to functional departments and one devoted to specialist products or teams. In the case of ALG Technology there will be a team focused around each specialist product group and each team will have representations from the various functional areas.

The **advantages** of a matrix or project team structure are as follows:

- The teams do not lose sight of their long-term objectives. They can remain more focused.

- There is more integration between the differing functional specialists – they become inter-disciplinary, resulting in greater co-operation and understand opposing or alternative opinions.

- Such a team is more responsive and flexible to environmental and technical change, so important for a company such as ALG. Because the team is now less bureaucratic and more focused, outcomes are much quicker as the bureaucracy is now replaced by a direct interplay between specialists – the interested parties.

- No one single functional area is likely to dominate. In a company such as ALG there is a danger that the views of scientists and engineers may triumph at the expense of prudent financial advice and market needs may also be ignored. There is a danger of the company becoming too product-orientated.

- Because staff are more directly involved in planning, control and decision making they become more motivated and committed – a key benefit for any company.

- Junior staff experience a wider range of inputs from a broad spectrum of areas. They lose their specialised isolation and become more valuable and 'rounded' employees. This provides a good training platform for future general managers.

- Experiences from one project team can easily and quickly be transmitted to other teams.

There are also **disadvantages**:

- Because of the dual representation within the teams there is a potential for conflict between project managers and functional heads.

- The two reporting lines can lead to confusion for members of the team. Where does their long-term future lie and where is it being determined?

- Because of the above there is increased complexity in reporting, making such a structure costly to administer.

- Decision making can be slower and not be more responsive if every participant insists on full participation. This is a problem with all democratic and participatory organisations, as has been experienced by a number of Japanese companies.

- Because of least dual reporting, there is a problem of allocating responsibilities. Who is in charge?

- This proposed new structure may lead to a dilution of priorities, particularly in resource allocation.

As a guideline for organising innovative project teams it is essential that structures should be flexible so as to encourage experts to break through conventional boundaries into new areas. There should also be leadership within the team of staff with a good technical background (**expert power**) and the team should not be dominated by superiors armed only with authority (**position power**).

(b) Organisational design can be influenced by many factors which can generally be divided into two categories – internal and external influences.

The **internal influences** comprise:

- Poor performance in the past. If a company has had difficulties such as are currently being experienced by ALG Technology then it is not surprising that it is considering a change in its organisational structure.

- If a company is now heavily influenced by entrepreneurs and innovators, a more flexible structure would be welcome. A 'machine bureaucracy', which might be what ALG Technology has become, would not be sympathetic to this type of employee. An adhocracy or an entrepreneurial structure might be more appropriate. (*Mintzberg*)

- A change in organisational ownership would inevitably have given the new shareholders a greater say on matters such as organisational design. Design will be more influenced by their management philosophy.

- There may have been a change in organisational goals. If quality of delivery is now given greater priority than product performance, as in the case of ALG, a structure more oriented to marketing might now be encouraged.

- A change in strategy will also help to influence the design of the organisation. If the company intends to compete with low prices then costs will now become critical. It is likely that there will be a more mechanistic approach to the structure with less focus on the individual. However with a differentiation strategy there is a potential for more informality, with more decision making being devoted to junior managers. This will be reflected in a less bureaucratic organisational structure.

The **external factors** that might influence organisational design are as follows:

- A **change in knowledge available** to a company. An increase in the availability and application of information technology (IT) now enables organisations to have greater control and communication within an organisation while having a smaller infrastructure to accomplish these functions.

- **Economic opportunities** may change: the globalisation of markets will necessitate a change in organisational structure to reflect and respond to these changes. In certain parts of the world barter has been re-introduced because of shortages of liquidity within the banking system. Organisations must build into their structures recognition of this 'problem'. Certain companies have had to create whole departments to respond to this condition.

- **Socio-demographic changes**: as organisations now operate in different parts of the world, each with different demographic and social regimes then differences such as attitudes to older people working, women in management, educational abilities matching requirements and labour force availability can all influence the design of organisational structures, resulting in more flexible and responsive organisations suiting local needs and cultures.

- **Ecological considerations**: 'Green' issues are becoming more significant in importance. Decisions on purchasing and distribution will be influenced by this and these, in turn, may affect the organisational structure. 'Just-in-time' supply techniques may be affected here (although just-in-time may be driven more by economic rather than ecological consideration).

- The **prevailing ideological beliefs** may also influence organisational design. In some countries planning may still be more dominant than a market culture. This could affect the organisational infrastructure with a greater reliance on planning departments than on a marketing and customer service. There has been much discussion on the differences between Japanese and Western-based companies. Concepts popular in Japan in the 1970s and 1980s such as jobs for life, promotion by seniority, job rotation have all affected the way in which organisations are configured. However it is also true to say that with the recent increased tendency towards globalisation these ideological differences are being reduced.

As can be noted from the above discussion, a number of these factors can be used to justify ALG Technology's need to change its organisational structure. Probably the most pressing reason for the change is its current poor performance. Resulting from this, there will probably be changes in both objectives and strategies. Although the environmental factors may have limited relevance here, the fact that ALG is now operating in a dynamic and global market place means that it has to be more responsive to market needs. With improved IT, it can now control its enterprises from a distance without sacrificing responsiveness. It can do so with a relatively flat organisation without the need for an extensive supportive infrastructure.

20   RAMESES INTERNATIONAL

Key answer tips

There is a strategic model known as McKinsey's 7S's model which could be used to generate points for this answer. However this model is not mentioned explicitly in the syllabus and it would therefore not be necessary to use it in the examination in order to gain full marks in your answer.

(a)   **To**:   Members of the Board: Rameses International

From: Jeanette Singh, Strategic Policy Director

Date: xxxxxx

Reasons for Strategy Failure at Rameses International

Introduction

I believe that there are a number of reasons why our organisation has not been able to implement strategies successfully. These causes must be addressed if Rameses is to grow profitably in the future years. We need to provide a more professional and committed environment for any strategic changes.

Possible reasons for failure

–   A major cause for concern is the amount of strategic change which we have attempted to implement in a short period of time. We have sought to move into new product and market areas simultaneously as well as develop closer links with new suppliers. It would appear that there has been no clear priority. There has probably been a confusion in activities which has diverted the attention of both staff and suppliers and so led to inadequate strategic development.

–   This may have led to inadequate planning and resource utilisation. Many of our actions have been reactive and it is likely that our organisational structure is too traditional. For strategy implementation to be successful decisions often must cut across organisational lines. Without a flexible structure activities may be restricted and actions delayed.

–   Our information monitoring may be poor. In attempting to juggle with too many strategies it is possible that we have failed to obtain or even use valuable environmental information.

–   It would not be surprising if there was resistance to change. In attempting to implement so many changes it is probable that we have alienated or, at least, worried a number of our stakeholders, whether they be employees or associated suppliers. We must ensure that these stakeholders are committed to any changes which we propose. We need to explain the purpose of our changes to our suppliers, customers and employees so that they will be more committed to our strategic moves. Issues which need to be addressed will include: priorities for management, timescales, lessons learned from previous strategy implementation efforts, risk factors and any likely impact on either staff or organisational structure.

     –   We know that our competitors can make life difficult for us. It is almost certain that they will not ignore our strategic moves. A reason for our failure to develop appropriate strategies may be that we have failed to anticipate any competitive reactions to our strategic initiatives.

Conclusion

It is imperative that our strategic decisions should be implemented effectively. It is pointless investigating ways in which we can improve our long-term profitability if we fail to put in place mechanisms to ensure that our intentions are carried out.

(b)   Apart from ensuring that the above-mentioned problems do not occur – i.e. getting stakeholder commitment to strategies – there are a number of issues which must be addressed.

First, it is important that managers do not forget their existing business. They must not become obsessed with the new strategies and neglect core business. Shareholders will be unhappy if managers, by successfully implementing new strategies, let profits fall or customer service deteriorate.

The process of strategy implementation should be accompanied by relevant milestones and controls. The milestones measure what progress is being made towards final implementation. These intermediate measurements, whether financial or structural, can show whether remedial action needs to be taken. The controls are to ensure that financial, HR, and other guidelines – i.e. mission statement – are not breached during this implementation process – is it costing too much? Is the progress contrary to the organisation's objectives or mission?

Responsibilities and accountability must be clearly allocated so that every stakeholder knows what he/she must accomplish and can be held responsible for achieving what's necessary. Staff must be aware of the necessity for their participation in the strategy process.

Senior management must be committed to the strategic change. They must not remove themselves from the scene once it is time for a selected strategy to be implemented. Their role is not limited to strategy identification, evaluation and selection. They need to see the whole process through. In this way the rest of the organisation can see that the strategy implementation has a high priority.

It is also important that management should be prepared for the unexpected. There are always likely to be upsets. There must be a contingency plan in place with flair and innovation not being neglected.

21   ICC ORGANISATION

Key answer tips

Focus on the use of the matrix organisational form as a way to manage the complexity of organisations with multiple structural interdependencies. The question was not popular in the examination, but when answered it attracted good marks. Organisation structure and design is a fundamental aspect of strategy implementation and should not be seen as a peripheral topic.

Part (a) is relatively straightforward provided you avoid irrelevant generalisations and keep to the facts of the company in question.

Summarise the benefits of the proposed structure to answer part (b).

For part (c) firstly explain what is meant by the quotation – it implies a degree of instability and dynamism in the matrix structure – and then explain how this can be managed.

(a)   Complex organisations such as ICC contain multiple structural interdependencies such as geographic locations, product groups, market segments and functional specialisms (such as finance and R&D). Such organisations are unable to design a single structural form which adequately contains and optimises all the interdependencies. For example, a product-based structure focuses on product design and development but loses out on market responsiveness while a market or customer driven structure risks the failure to achieve product technical synergies.

Matrix structures have evolved from divisional structures as a response to this dilemma and as a means of meeting the structural needs of managing complex multinational organisations. Matrix structures are in themselves complex and require sophisticated management processes. A **matrix structure can be stable** (i.e. a permanent aspect of the structure, as is the case at ICC) **or transient**, i.e. a temporary multi-disciplinary team based structure as is frequently used to manage projects in high technology industries.

By choosing a matrix structure, the organisation does not choose one structure over another, but attempts to operate through two or more integrated structural forms by setting up dual or triple authority structures. In seeking to operate in this way, the organisation abandons the principle of unity of command in favour of the management of multiple interdependencies. ICC have adopted this principle for functional and geographic groupings. In other words functional managers based within a country report both to the country manager for local operational matters, but to their functional specialist at head office for technical direction.

(b)   Successfully adopted, designed, developed and operated, matrix forms can provide substantial advantages. A country-based matrix form combining S&M and SES would be based on two integrated dimensions – **product based and customer based**. The potential gains from the matrix form and how they could deal with the co-ordination problems can be summarised (**Johnson and Scholes**) under four main areas.

- **Improved decision-making** where there is potential conflict of interests such as 'product against market' or 'finance against sales'. The structure should assist in avoiding the danger of one element dominating the decision processes by combining interests at the point where the decision is made. The nature of the problem can be illustrated by reference to ICC, where SES and S&M operate as separate (non-matrix) divisions within each country. S&M are selling hardware that is not technically suitable and causing follow-on workload problems for the SES engineers.

- Within the matrix, **direct contact replaces the formalised reporting procedures** which may take place between independent divisions. Again we can see the consequences of a lack of co-ordination at ICC country level where SES staff are failing to pass on potential sales leads to the S&M staff.

- **Improved motivation**, due to closer involvement in the wider aspect of business strategy. For example, if ICC operated SES and S&M through a matrix, based on a customer account manager responsible for both product sales and customer support, then the motivation for achieving sales and selling the correct equipment would be achieved.

- **Improved management skills** with the ability to manage both customer/market and product decisions. The ensuing breadth of vision should create higher levels of flexibility and market responsiveness – a feature that ICC appear to have been missing at a customer level, where both product and market divisions were in part taken by surprise by the changes in the customers use of technology and changes in buying patterns.

(c) The matrix form demands a great deal of the manager who must have the capability to deal with the tension that can arise between apparent conflicting objectives. A balancing of tension can only be achieved through a process of reconciliation and negotiation, a difficult position for the manager at the centre and what has been described as 'no place for managers seeking security and stability' (*Mintzberg*). in practice, as could be expected, managers appear to need considerable time and support to evolve skills in managing in matrix organisational forms (*Kanter*).

There are a number of specific challenges which organisational design must confront and solve if the matrix form is to work effectively. These can be summarised under four main areas:

- **Management of conflict** resulting from the removal of typical departmental boundaries and the introduction of conflicting objectives and accountability. The essence is collaboration within the matrix rather than internal competition which exists in some organisations.

- **Management of stress** arising from role conflict and role ambiguity leading to the potential for role overload. For example, it is not always clear in the matrix form exactly who is responsible for what. Care should be taken to ensure an even balance of workloads across the matrix, appropriate management development training and the use of mentoring systems by which a manager is given a clear point of access generally within a functional line (e.g. finance, marketing, personnel) to seek advice and assistance.

- **Management of the balance of power** arising from differing lines of authority. If the balance is upset and one authority line dominates then in effect the matrix breaks down and the organisation reverts to a hierarchical form. Note that a balance of power without co-operative decision making also leads to inertia as conflict is passed up the chains of command until a point is reached in the structure where a decision can be made.

- The **cost of management** arising from more time spent in meetings, discussions, information exchange and administrative support and potentially more managers to operate the organisation.

BUSINESS PROCESS CHANGE

22 COUNTRY CAR CLUB

Key answer tips

Although the question does not explicitly ask for it, the process-strategy matrix suggested by Paul Harmon would provide an appropriate context for the answer to this question.

(a)

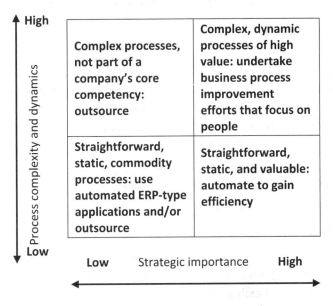

The process-strategy matrix

However, other appropriate models or frameworks could be used by candidates to answer this part of the question.

The process-strategy matrix has two axes. The vertical axis is concerned with process complexity and dynamics. At the base of the vertical axis are simple processes often with simple procedures while at the top are complex processes which may require negotiation, discussion and complicated design. On the horizontal axis is the strategic value of these processes. Their importance increases from left to right with low value processes concerned with things that must be done but which add little value to products or services. On the extreme right of this axis are high value processes which are very important to success and add significant value to goods and services. From these two axes, Harmon categorises four quadrants and makes suggestions about how processes should be tackled in each quadrant.

Low strategic importance, low process complexity and dynamics

This quadrant contains relatively straightforward stable processes which add little business value. They are processes that must be carried out by the company but add nothing to the company's value proposition. These processes need to be automated in the most efficient way possible. They are often called 'commodity processes' and are suitable for standard software package solutions or outsourcing to organisations that specialise in that area. Payroll is a good example of this. Many standard software packages are available in the market place. Alternatively, a computer bureau can be used to process the payroll on behalf of the organisation.

Low strategic importance, high process complexity and dynamics

This quadrant is for relatively complex processes that need to be done but do not add significant value to the company's products or services. They are not at the heart of the company's core competencies. Harmon suggests that these should be outsourced to organisations which have them as their core business.

High strategic importance, low process complexity and dynamics

These processes lie in the lower right quadrant of the model. They tend to be relatively straightforward processes which, nevertheless, have a significant role in the organisation's activities. They are central to what the business does. The aim is to automate these, if possible, to gain cost reduction and improve quality and efficiency.

High strategic importance, high process complexity and dynamics

Finally, in the top right hand quadrant are high value, complex processes which often include human judgement and expertise and are often very difficult to automate. Harmon suggests that these might be the focus of major process redesign initiatives focusing on business process improvement through the improved performance of the people undertaking those processes.

In the context of 3C, the following recommendations are suggested. Clearly these are value judgements and credit will be given for coherently argued answers which do not match the examiner's conclusions.

(i)   **Attendance at breakdowns**

This appears to be of high strategic importance and, although some breakdowns are bound to be simple to fix, it requires the repairer to be knowledgeable, flexible and diplomatic. Consequently, it appears to be a candidate for the upper right quadrant of the process-strategy matrix. Hence it is suggested that the service should remain in-house and attention should be paid to improving the competency of the 'service patrol engineers'. Information technology should be harnessed to seek improvements in response time to breakdowns by improving the organisation and distribution of these engineers. Systems might also be developed to technically support engineers and to help them diagnose and fix roadside problems.

(ii) **Membership renewal**

This should be a relatively straightforward process, so it sits in one of the two lower quadrants. It can be argued that it is a process that is core to the business and is not one (like payroll) which can be found across all businesses. It appears to be a candidate for the lower right quadrant. Hence it is a candidate for automation to gain efficiency. The organisation already has a bespoke system operated by in-house permanent employees. This seems an appropriate way of delivering this process. However, it might benefit from revisiting the way the bespoke system works. The scenario suggests that the current system sends out membership renewals on receipt of a confirmation from the member. The system might benefit from being built around a presumption of renewal, so that the member only contacts the organisation if he or she does not wish to renew.

(iii) **Vehicle insurance services**

These appear to be a relatively complex process which is of little strategic importance to 3C. It appears to inhabit the top left hand quadrant of the matrix. Insurance is not only technically complex, it carries large risks and substantial regulatory requirements. It is likely that these regulatory requirements will undergo frequent changes. It would appear attractive to 3C to outsource this service to a specialist provider who would then badge it under 3C's name. This is relatively common practice and 3C's venture into insurance must have been very expensive. Outsourcing provides it with opportunities for providing a wider service with reduced in-house costs.

(iv) **Membership queries**

Membership queries are of unpredictable complexity. They are also an important contact point between the company and their members. Failure to handle queries courteously and correctly could have important consequences for membership renewal. It is suggested that this is an upper right hand quadrant process – potentially complex and of high strategic importance to the company. Investment is required in people supported by innovative and speedy IT systems that allow the 3C staff to respond quickly and accurately to a wide range of questions. It is suggested that membership queries continue to remain in-house although the physical location of the call centre might reflect certain financial opportunities – such as low property rents and cheaper labour.

(v) **Vehicle history checks**

Vehicle history checks appear to be of relatively low strategic importance to 3C. Automation should make such checks relatively straightforward, although the combination of accident damage, stolen vehicles, finance agreements and time when the vehicle was voluntarily taken off the road may make determining this history more complex then it first appears. Furthermore, the consequences of providing inaccurate or incomplete information may be quite severe. Someone who has unsuspectingly purchased a car which has been damaged and repaired might claim for damages against 3C when this was revealed. These damages might be extensive if someone died in the vehicle as a result of a botched repair. Consequently it is suggested that this is predominantly an upper left hand quadrant process which should be outsourced to an organisation which is already in this field.

Table 2.1 summarises the advice to the BAC.

Table 2.1

Attendance at repairs	Remains in-house. Improve competency of repair staff. Support them with IT systems
Membership renewal	Remains in-house and revisit basis of automation
Vehicle insurance	Outsource
Membership queries	Remains in-house. Improve competency of call centre staff. Support them with IT systems
Vehicle history	Outsource

(b)   In the question scenario the decision to outsource the purchase and maintenance of 3C vehicles is justified by its low strategic importance and its low to medium complexity. However, this only makes it a *candidate* for outsourcing and so tangible and intangible benefits would have to be attached to this suggestion in a subsequent detailed analysis. This part of the question asks candidates to analyse the advantages of outsourcing the process of the purchase and maintenance of 3C vehicles. It is suggested that advantages would include:

Purchasing benefits from economies of scale

AutoDirect purchase thousands of cars and vans for their customers each year. They should be able to negotiate substantial discounts from manufacturers, some of which can be passed on to their customers.

Predictable costs

The vehicle lease payments with AutoDirect are monthly and they include full maintenance of the car, including tyres and exhausts. Hence 3C will have predictable costs for budgeting purposes. Previously, costs would have been variable and unpredictable, depending upon the reliability of the vehicles.

Reduced overhead costs – garage and purchasing

The overhead costs associated with the garage and the garage and purchasing employees have been lost (except for the one manager retained to manage the contract with AutoDirect). There may also be an opportunity for realising income from the sale of the garage site. It is described as being in a residential area with no room for expansion and severe parking congestion. It may be possible to sell the garage for residential development.

Higher vehicle availability

The central garage itself is a bottleneck. Vehicles have to be driven or transported to this garage from all parts of the country and left there while they are serviced or repaired. They then have to be driven back to their operational area. AutoDirect has repair and servicing centres throughout the country and so it will be possible for vehicles to be taken locally for services and repairs – thus reducing vehicle downtime.

Freeing cash to use for other investments – from purchase to lease

The policy of purchasing vehicles meant that a considerable amount of cash has been tied up in fast depreciating assets. Switching to leasing will release this cash for investment elsewhere in the company.

Access to expertise and legislation

It is likely that vehicles will become increasingly subject to legislation designed to reduce carbon emissions. This, together with the increasing technical complexity of vehicles, will mean that vehicles will become increasingly difficult to maintain without specialist monitoring and repair equipment. It is unlikely that 3C can maintain such a level of investment and so outsourcing to a specialist makes good sense. AutoDirect will have to monitor legislation, advise on its implications and implement its requirements for its large customer base.

Concentration on core business

Although this issue is not explicitly considered in the scenario it is something that impacts on all organisations. The management of the garage does not appear to be a core strategic requirement. It must consume some elements of senior management time. Outsourcing frees up that time so it can be used to focus on issues directly relevant to the customer and the business as a whole.

ACCA marking scheme			Marks
(a)	Up to 3 marks for the recommendation and its justification in each of the process areas required by the question		3
	Five process areas required giving a maximum of 15 marks		15
(b)	Up to 2 marks for each appropriate advantage identified by the candidate up to a maximum of 10 marks		10

Examiner's comments

The scenario for this question concerned a car club that was reviewing its processes. It had already decided to outsource the purchase and maintenance of its own vehicles. The advantage this outsourcing offered the car club was the subject of the second part of this question. This was answered relatively well, although some candidates confused the vehicles of 3C with the vehicles of the club's members. Other candidates failed to make their points relevant to the scenario, using Information Technology examples instead.

The first part of the question listed five major process areas and asked candidates to suggest and justify recommendations for outsourcing or improvement in each of those areas. Many candidates provided excellent answers, often using Paul Harmon's framework as a reference point. The suggested answers have specific recommendations; for example, outsourcing of vehicle insurance services. However, there is no absolutely correct answer and so candidates who provided coherent justification for retaining such services in-house were also awarded appropriate marks.

23 GGE

Key answer tips

This question is not of exam standard but it should serve as a useful revision tool of your knowledge in this syllabus areas. Other questions in this section will then allow you to apply this knowledge to exam standard scenarios.

(a) Business process re-engineering (BPR) is the analysis and design of work flows and processes within and between organisations. It involves the critical analysis and radical redesign of existing business processes to achieve breakthrough improvements in performance measures. For example, an enterprise that has decided to focus on customer service as its source of competitive advantage will redesign its business processes with customer service as its primary goals.

(b) Continuous improvement, or kaizen, is a management philosophy based on seeking gradual and small changes in all aspects of an entity's operations. Like TQM, it requires the commitment of all employees, and the development of a culture of quality and concern for the customer. Over time, the organisation will gradually change, adapt and improve its performance. BPR, in contrast, is based on dramatic change, involving the restructuring of an organisation, its systems, its use of IT, its management systems and its performance measurement systems. Dr Hammer described BPR as a fundamental rethinking and radical design of business processes, to achieve dramatic improvements in critical performance measures such as cost, quality, service and speed.

Whereas the ideas for improvement with kaizen come from employees themselves, the initial ideas for radical change in BPR might come from external specialist consultants. Employees will need to be persuaded of the need for change, and to be involved in the change process, but it is not necessary to develop a culture of believing in change and quality improvement.

Whereas continuous improvement considers changes in any aspect of the organisation and its operations, BPR might be more focused on specific processes rather than all the business processes within the organisation. BPR is probably more appropriate in circumstances where gradual improvements through kaizen might be too little and too late, or where the problems are fundamental such that small changes will not resolve them. Suitable circumstances might therefore exist when:

(i)   competitors are outperforming the company considerably

(ii)   there are conflicts within the organisation, particularly between functions and departments

(iii) a very large amount of management time is wasted in meetings

(iv)   there is an excessive use of unstructured communications such as e-mails and memos, and relatively little structured communication

(v)   there are serious weaknesses and inefficiencies in key processes.

(c)   Harmon's process strategy matrix is a matrix formed by:

1   An estimate of the strategic importance of a process (usually the horizontal axis) and

2   An estimate of the process complexity and/or dynamism (rate of change) on the other axis.

The purpose of the matrix is to suggest how processes should be developed, improved and how their output should be best provided.

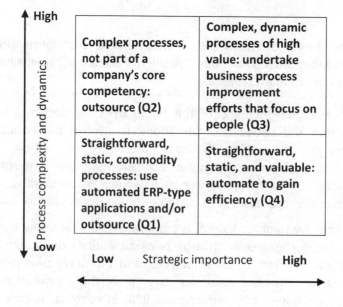

Examples of processes falling into each quadrant are:

Q1:   Maintaining the sales ledger. Simple, static, not strategically important (though administratively important)

Q2:   Running the company's IT department (if not strategically important).

Q3:   New product and service design; customer care.

Q4:   Assembly of a complex product.

24   PATTERSON'S ELECTRICAL SUPPLIERS

Key answer tips

In part (a) of this question, credit would be given for referring business planning and strategy back to the concepts covered in chapter 1 such as the Johnson, Scholes and Whittington approach and the strategy lenses.

(a)   For many companies there is a seamless join between developing a business strategy and developing an IT/IS strategy. No longer is the IT/IS function a purely supporting player in the business environment. It has become a major area for businesses to harness. Many business strategies are now based on the IT/IS feasibility to support them.

It is difficult if not impossible to manage a modern organisation without at least some knowledge of information systems and information technology, what IT/IS systems are, how they affect organisations and its employees, and how they can make businesses more competitive and efficient. Information systems have become essential for creating competitive firms, managing corporations, and providing useful products and services to customers.

Types of system

- *Operational level* – Information systems that monitor the elementary activities and transactions of the organisation.
- *Knowledge level* – Information systems that support knowledge and data workers of the organisation.
- *Management level* – Information systems that support the monitoring, controlling, decision-making, and administrative activities of middle managers.
- *Strategic level* – Information systems that support the long-range planning activities of senior management.

The kinds of systems built today are very important for the overall performance of the organisation. Information systems are driving both daily operations and organisational strategies. IT/IS have helped organisations become more flexible, eliminate layers of management, separate work from location and restructure work flows, giving new powers both to line workers and management.

(b)   **Automation**

This is using the computer to speed up the performance of existing tasks and processes. The most common form of IT-enabled organisational change is automation. In the early days of IT little attention was paid to analysing the tasks.

There was a general move just to assist the existing processes both in terms of input, process and output.

The early applications of information technology involved assisting employees perform their tasks more efficiently and effectively. This is a low risk strategy. Examples are: calculating pay-checks and payroll registers, giving bank tellers instant access to customer records, and developing a nationwide network of airline terminals. Automation is akin to putting a larger engine in an existing car.

Early automation in retail businesses such as Pattersons meant the introduction of electronic cash registers (keeping till receipts, balancing individual tills) leading on to basic Point of Sales (POS) systems.

Rationalisation

Businesses now begin to question the existing processes, taking a logical view of processes, and viewing the business in terms of what it does as opposed to how it does it.

Rationalisation creates a deeper form of organisational change, one that follows automation. The streamlining of standard operating procedures, eliminating obvious bottlenecks so that automation makes operating procedures more efficient. Automation frequently reveals new bottlenecks in production, and makes the existing arrangements of procedures and structures painfully cumbersome. Rationalisation of procedures is the streamlining of standard operating procedures, eliminating obvious bottlenecks so that automation can make operating procedures more efficient. Rationalisation often means integrating sections or departments by making changes to the infrastructure. Linking the order processing system with the inventory control system. Corporate databases, enabling all members of a company to share data. Provides support to the analysis and presentation of information for managerial decision-making. Rationalisation is a low/medium risk strategy.

In the case of Pattersons, such a strategy could mean linking many of the everyday business functions to an integrated inventory system: sales, inventory recording, purchasing and general order processing activities. Central warehouse replenishing the individual stores, suggesting one-stop ordering.

Re-engineering

Re-engineering involves the radical re-design of business processes, combining steps to cut waste and eliminating repetitive, paper-intensive tasks to improve cost, quality and service and to maximise the benefits of IT.

It is an example of how information technology is being used to restructure work by transforming business processes. A business process is any set of activities designed to produce a specified output for a customer or market. Hammer describes it as 'the fundamental rethinking and radical design of business processes to achieve dramatic improvements, such as cost, quality, service, and speed'. It focuses on the 'how' and the 'why' of a business process, so that major changes can be made in how work is accomplished.

Re-engineering often involves complete changes in a company's structure to enable this radical re-design to take place. It is a high-risk strategy, which goes much further than rationalisation of processes. It involves revolution, as opposed to evolution, of business strategy.

If Pattersons decides to develop Internet technology, this could be viewed as a fundamental change. It is a huge departure from its core business of cash and carry.

(c)   The principle causes of systems failure may be summarised as:

- Insufficient or improper user participation in the systems development process.
- Lack of management support.
- Poorly defined objectives.
- High levels of complexity and risk in the systems development process.
- Poor management of the implementation process.

Mismanagement of resources includes:

- Organisational/people failures, e.g. lack of commitment, co-ordination and communication.
- Financial failures, for example inadequate CBA (cost-benefit analysis) and risk analysis, overspent budgets, inadequate allocation of funds for implementation and training.
- Technological failures, such as poor IT selection of hardware, software and/or communication systems
- Information failures, such as vague or unclear objectives, plans and information.
- Lack of user involvement, with emphasis on technical objectives, and leading to user resistance.

Some key reasons for project failure:

- Unclear objectives, expectations not equalling intent, missed tasks, no change control, poor schedule management, no contingency planning (finance, time etc), over-commitment.
- Project management pitfalls.
- Poor or non-existent planning, lack of control, doing rather than managing, task rather than people skills, ineffective communications, poor control of time, bottlenecks, personal characteristics.

25   4D TEACHING HOSPITAL

Key answer tips

Part (a) is tricky because there are no universally accepted definitions of BPR and PI and some involve considerable overlap. In part (b) ensure that you explain and evaluate each benefit.

(a)   (i)   Business process re-engineering (BPR) is the fundamental re-thinking and rational re-design of existing business processes to achieve improvements in performance measures such as cost, quality, service and speed.

Process innovation (PI) is the invention of entirely new processes.

The main differences between BPR and PI are as follows:

- BPR focuses on existing processes whereas PI emphasises the invention of new processes.
- There is a much greater emphasis on human resource management in PI. BPR has often been criticised for neglecting HR issues.

- PI may involve rethinking the entire business and its mission rather than focusing on individual processes as is the case with BPR.

- With BPR the role of IT is generally as an implementation tool, for example to improve the speed of information processing. With PI, IT is often a change trigger allowing the development of new processes due to technological advances.

For example, improvements in the technology surrounding wireless LANS has allowed hospital consultants to refer to and update detailed patient records while doing ward rounds, completely changing the previous process of writing up notes later.

(ii) The new OTIS system could be viewed as an example of BPR on the grounds that:

- The new process is still one of linking students, lecturers and surgeons but on a larger scale. As such it is a development of an existing system.

However, it is more likely to be viewed as PI:

- The inclusion of remote students to participate in the system could be argued to be an entirely new process.

- Developments in web technology have triggered the change.

On balance the new system should be viewed as PI.

(b) The benefits of OTIS are as follows:

Key answer tips

Choose three benefits to 4D and two benefits to society from the following lists:

To 4D

- The new system will improve 4D's already good reputation. This could be significant as it might result in greater success in raising funds and reduce the chance of closure if local government decides that it has too many hospitals.

- The new system will considerably reduce the training cost per student, freeing up funds for other areas.

- The new system could also allow 4D to raise additional funds by charging remote students to participate. This could be a significant injection into the hospital finances, facilitating further expansion of the teaching side.

- The extra possibilities that the new system presents could allow 4D to attract and keep the very best professors, lecturers and consultants. Given the existing excellence, this is unlikely to be a major benefit.

To society

- The improved training should mean that the level of expertise among surgeons will be higher, improving the likelihood of a healthy recovery of patients undertaking surgery. In the local community the standard of clinical excellence was already very high so the improvement will not be significant. However, the possibility of receiving high level training and supervision for surgeons in more remote locations could give a dramatic improvement in patient prognoses.

- The new system should also mean that surgeons can be trained more cheaply and efficiently. Given that some finance is likely to come from public sources, this should free up funds for other services (e.g. social care) to be provided. This benefit will be less significant due to the sums involved.

- This should lead to improved worldwide care and consistency between countries. It should mean that when visiting foreign countries a similar level of care is possible as in a person's country of residence.

26   CADCO INC

Key answer tips

Part (a) of the question requires two things. Firstly, answers need to cover the key elements of BPR. Secondly, these need to be applied to the chain of supermarkets described in the mini-scenario. By applying BPR in this way it should be possible to illustrate the benefits that can arise from its adoption. Success in part (b) is heavily dependent on an understanding of what is meant by a virtual supply chain. Answers need to go beyond a definition of this concept to explore the activities and information systems that are needed to develop and support a virtual supply chain. Careful time control is needed in this section, as it is easy to overrun the time allocation.

(a)   **Business Process Re-engineering (BPR) definition**: BPR is the fundamental re-thinking and rational design of the business processes to achieve dramatic improvements in critical contemporary measures of performance such as cost, quality, service and speed.

The tendency in the past has been to simply automate processes that were traditionally performed manually; this led to the development of information systems that may be less than effective. Worse still, they may be hindering the competitive advantage they once gave the organisation. In order to regain competitive advantage, rather than improve the current information systems, it may be more effective to change the way that the organisation actually goes about its business and provide a system or systems to support this new approach.

A central notion of BPR is to ask radical questions about why things are done in a particular way and whether alternative methods could achieve better results. BPR is undertaken to achieve order-of-magnitude improvements over the 'old' form of the organisation. It is competitive restructuring that forms the current focus as distinct from competitive gain. At the heart of BPR is the notion of discontinuous thinking, of recognising and breaking out-of-date rules and assumptions that underlie current business operations.

A business strategy that involves the development of a virtual supply chain encompasses most of the ideas underpinning BPR. For many businesses it requires a radical rethink of the current methods employed in the supply chain. Theorists and practitioners alike state the importance of restructuring bad purchasing practices. They see BPR as the only viable way to ensure organisations can receive the savings of up to 90% they perceive as possible. Without these changes no real benefit can be gained, because essentially a new way of doing business is being sought whilst still using old methods. Organisations have to be prepared to fully embrace change, as with it will come the benefits so clearly and readily available. The majority of businesses have existing supply chains where radical re-design can apply. The various stages in the supply chain requiring communication and transfer of data/information make it appropriate to re-design using new technologies.

Often cited examples of the implementation of virtual supply chain systems include Tesco and Walmart, who are seen as revolutionising supermarket trading.

(b)   **Supply chain definition**: The physical entities required to supply goods or services to the customer. Those entities will include manufacturing places, distribution centres, retail outlets and couriers etc who handle the goods or knowledge en route to the final customer.

In *Porter's value chain model*, primary activities relate to the major components of the supply chain. Primary activities are those activities involved in the physical creation of the product and its sale and distribution to the buyer as well as after-sales service. These are the activities which add value to the product or service.

The supply chain is often viewed as the core component of E-business. Supply chain management is the coordination of all supply activities of an organisation from its suppliers and partners to its customers.

*   Basic models of supply chains identify three main components: Supplier – Organisation – Customer.

*   Realistic advanced models depict a rather more complex model: Supplier – Intermediaries – Organisation – Intermediaries – Customers.

    The additional intermediaries may well form several links in the chain. By applying information systems, companies can enhance or radically improve many activities in the supply chain.

There are four main characteristics of supply chain:

*   location
*   manufacturing
*   inventory management and
*   distribution.

Each of these is linked together in the supply chain. The virtual supply chain is a reworked model of the existing supply chain. Old supply chains are often defined as being composed of distinct and independent components, each operated in an insular fashion. Virtual supply chain combines interaction with integration, seeing all organisation components becoming an integrated part of the supply chain as a whole and each component interacting fully with other components. Essentially the underlying feature of the virtual supply chain is communication.

A virtual supply chain implies using advanced technologies to coordinate the activities within the supply chain. These technologies tend to be allied to the umbrella term web based technology. The use of the Internet, intranet, extranet, e-mail, web-based ordering, electronic order tracking systems etc have played a major role in facilitating new virtual models of the supply chain. By applying information systems, companies can enhance or radically improve many activities in the supply chain.

Advanced communication systems have permitted organisations to deal directly with some of the elements of the supply chain, in some cases eliminating subsidiary elements altogether. Benefits of deploying these technologies include:

- more efficient, lower-cost execution of processes
- reduced complexity of the supply chain (disintermediation)
- improved data integration between elements of the supply chain, enabling innovation and customer responsiveness.

Globalisation also requires a re-design of the supply chain. Globalisation in terms of a virtual supply chain gives the potential for business to be spread out over a wider geographical region than normal supply chains would have permitted. In the globalised world, where businesses are becoming more organised and streamlined so too does the supply chain. E-supply chain ensures supply chain efficiency on a global scale. Increased competition is characterised by the many new entrants into markets, creating the need for organisations to become 'cutting-edge' to withstand competition. This means enabling shorter product lifecycles to get products to market faster.

Specific examples include:

- **Electronic Data Interchange (EDI)**. Business to Business (B2B). Some companies use the Internet while others rely on electronic data interchange (EDI) via networks or extranets for direct computer to computer exchange of business transactions and documents with their business customers and suppliers. An example of the extended use of EDI is Walmart who as part of their business strategy (procurement) allow suppliers to have access to their inventory control system – when stocks fall to an agreed level the suppliers automatically replenish the stock items. The onus is now on the supplier to provide the goods, not on the customer to order the goods. This occurs without any formal human interaction. Orders, delivery notes and payments are handled in a similar fashion.
- **Electronic Funds Transfer (EFT).** Payment management can be made more efficient by using EFT to link all companies in the supply chain so that payments can be sent and received electronically.

INFORMATION TECHNOLOGY

27   PERFECT SHOPPER *Walk in the footsteps of a top tutor*

Tutor's top tips

Approach to the question

*If, as always, you start by reading **the first paragraph only** the following can be determined:*

- *the key competitors will be supermarkets*
- *it is a franchised network of local shops, with Perfect Shopper selling to the shops, who then in turn sell on to the public*
- *it is competing at the low end part of the market and aiming for economies of scale*
- *it uses large central warehouses*

- suppliers deliver directly to these warehouses

- there are no own-branded goods

Now look at the requirements **before** reading the rest of the question. This will ensure that you

- read the question in the correct manner,

- do not need to read the question more than once,

- save time and can begin planning.

Requirement

(a)   the primary activities of the value chain

This should be an easy start to the question that is a simple test of knowledge.

(b)   restructuring the upstream supply chain

They key here will be to focus on suppliers (and even the suppliers of suppliers). Set up a planning page that will record information on inbound logistics and procurement. A lot of the key points needed have already been read in the first paragraph of the question.

(c)   restructuring the downstream supply chain

The key here will be to focus on outbound logistics and to consider the relationship with both the neighbourhood shops as well as the end consumer.

Reading the question

Now **actively** read the question i.e. as you read it you should add all relevant points to your planning page(s).

- The key issues to pick out from the question as are as follows:

- Perfect Shopper (PS) use haulage contractors to deliver good to the franchisees

- franchisees purchasing costs are reduced by around 10% by using PS

- PS also manage their downstream chain by providing promotional material, signage and display units

- The next two paragraphs of the question give more details on the downstream supply chain and the problems should become evident at this point (e.g. sales representatives only have an input once every three months)

Answering the question

Part (a) Primary activities of the value chain

As the examiner's comments point out, the key issue to remember here is that there are only five marks available for describing the five primary activities. So you should only need one sentence on each activity – ideally related to the scenario.

Part (b) Upstream supply chain management

This may be the toughest part of the question as we are told very little about PS's upstream chain after the first paragraph in the question. What we are told is:

- PS use centralised warehousing

- PS buy in bulk in order to get price discounts

> - *Suppliers control the delivery of products to warehouses*
>
> - *PS only purchase pre-branded products*
>
> *In order to score marks in this question you could therefore examine how PS might change/ improve each of these four areas. The examiner suggests that there are 3 marks available for each valid point made.*
>
> **Part (c) Downstream supply chain management**
>
> *The question provides much more information on the relationship with franchisees such as:*
>
> - *PS provide some marketing material*
>
> - *franchisees are not exclusive*
>
> - *deliveries are made every two weeks*
>
> - *sales reps only meet every three months*
>
> - *prices need reviewing*
>
> - *there is low brand recognition*
>
> - *the ordering system is inflexible (and orders cannot be revised downwards)*
>
> - *order variations can only be made by phone*
>
> *So there are many areas to consider for improvement. You should choose three or four of these and create a paragraph which explains what you would change and how it would help the business.*

(a)   Inbound logistics: Handling and storing bulk orders delivered by suppliers and stored on large pallets in regional warehouses. All inbound logistics currently undertaken by the food suppliers or by contractors appointed by these suppliers.

Operations: Splitting bulk pallets into smaller packages, packing, sealing and storing these packages.

Outbound logistics: Delivery to neighbourhood shops using locally contracted distribution companies.

Marketing & Sales: Specially commissioned signs and personalised sales literature. Promotions and special offers.

Service: Specialist in-store display units for certain goods, three monthly meeting between franchisee and representative.

(b)   Perfect Shopper currently has a relatively short upstream supply chain. They are bulk purchasers from established suppliers of branded goods. Their main strength at the moment is to offer these branded goods at discounted prices to neighbourhood shops that would normally have to pay premium prices for these goods.

In the upstream supply chain, the issue of branding is a significant one. At present, Perfect Shopper only provides branded goods from established names to its customers. As far as the suppliers are concerned, Perfect Shopper is the customer and the company's regional warehouses are supplied as if they were the warehouses of conventional supermarkets. Perfect Shopper might look at the following restructuring opportunities within this context:

- Examining the arrangements for the delivery of products from suppliers to the regional warehouses. At present this is in the hands of the suppliers or contractors appointed by suppliers. It appears that when Perfect Shopper was established it decided not to contract its own distribution. This must now be open to review. It is likely that competitors have established contractual arrangements with logistics companies to collect products from suppliers. Perfect Shopper must examine this, accompanied by an investigation into downstream distribution. A significant distribution contract would probably include the branding of lorries and vans and this would provide an opportunity to increase brand visibility and so tackle this issue at the same time.

- Contracting the supply and distribution of goods also offers other opportunities. Many integrated logistics contractors also supply storage and warehousing solutions and it would be useful for Perfect Shopper to evaluate the costs of these. Essentially, distribution, warehousing and packaging could be outsourced to an integrated logistics company and Perfect Shopper could re-position itself as a primarily sales and marketing operation.

- Finally, Perfect Shopper must review how it communicates orders and ordering requirements with its suppliers. Their reliance on supplier deliveries suggests that the relationship is a relatively straightforward one. There may be opportunities for sharing information and allowing suppliers access to forecasted demand. There are many examples where organisations have allowed suppliers access to their information to reduce costs and to improve the efficiency of the supply chain as a whole.

The suggestions listed above assume that Perfect Shopper continues to only supply branded goods. Moving further upstream in the supply chain potentially moves the company into the manufacture and supply of goods. This will raise a number of significant issues about the franchise itself.

At present Perfect Shopper has, by necessity, concentrated on branded goods. It has not really had to understand how these goods sell in specific locations because it has not been able to offer alternatives. The content of the standing order reflects how the neighbourhood shop wishes to compete in its locality. However, if Perfect Shopper decides to commission its own brand then the breadth of products is increased. Neighbourhood shops would be able to offer 'own brand' products to compete with supermarkets who also focus on own brand products. It would also increase the visibility of the brand. However, Perfect Shopper must be sure that this approach is appropriate as a whole. It could easily produce an own brand that reduces the overall image of the company and hence devalues the franchise. Much more research is needed to assess the viability of producing 'own brand' goods.

(c) A number of opportunities appear to exist in the downstream supply chain.

As already mentioned above, Perfect Shopper can revisit its contract distribution arrangements. At present, distribution to neighbourhood shops is in the hands of locally appointed contract distributors. As already suggested, it may be possible to contract one integrated logistics company to carry out both inbound and outbound logistics, so gaining economies of scale and opportunities for branding.

One of the problems identified in the independent report was the inflexibility of the ordering and delivering system. The ordering system appears to be built around a fixed standard delivery made every two weeks, agreed in advance for a three month period. Variations can be made to this standard order, but only increases – not decreases. Presumably, this arrangement is required to allow Perfect Shopper to forecast demand over a three month period and to place bulk orders to reflect these commitments. However, this may cause at least two problems. The first is that participating shops place a relatively low standard order and rely on variations to fulfil demand. This causes problems for Perfect Shopper. Secondly, any unpredictable fall in demand during the three month period leads to the shop having storage problems and unsold stock. This potentially creates problems for the shop owner, who may also begin to question the value of the franchise. Hence Perfect Shopper might wish to consider a much more flexible system where orders can be made to match demand and deliveries can be made as required. This would also remove the requirement for a three monthly meeting between the franchisee and the sales representative from Perfect Shopper. Investments in IT systems will be required to support this, with participating shops placing orders over the Internet to reflect their requirements. This move towards a more flexible purchasing arrangement may also make the outsourcing of warehousing and distribution even more appealing.

Perfect Shopper may also wish to investigate whether they can also provide value added services to customers, which not only simplify the ordering system but also allow the shop managers to better understand their customers and fulfil their requirements. The supply chain may legitimately include the customer's customers, particularly for franchisers. This is already acknowledged because Perfect Shopper produces tailored marketing material aimed at the end-consumer. Point of Sales (PoS) devices feeding information back to Perfect Shopper would allow sales information to be analysed and fed back to the shopkeeper as well as allowing automatic replenishment based on purchasing trends. However, this may be culturally difficult for independent neighbourhood shopkeepers to accept. Furthermore, it would potentially include information outside the products offered by Perfect Shopper and the implications of this would have to be considered. However, a whole shop sales analysis might be a useful service to offer existing and potential franchisees.

Customers are increasingly willing to order products over the Internet. It seems unlikely that individual shopkeepers would be able to establish and maintain their own Internet-based service. It would be useful for Perfect Shopper to explore the potential of establishing a central website with customers placing orders from local shops. Again there are issues about scope, because Perfect Shopper does not offer a whole-shop service. However, Michael de Kare-Silver has identified groceries as a product area that has good potential for Internet purchase. In his electronic shopping potential test any product scoring over 20 has good potential. Groceries scored 27.

ACCA marking scheme		
		Marks
(a)	Up to 1 mark for each part of the value chain up	5
(b)	Up to 3 marks for each relevant point relating to the scenario	10
	Up to 3 marks for each relevant point relating to the scenario	10
Total		**25**

Examiner's comments

This question began by asking the candidate to identify the primary activities of the company's value chain. This was generally well answered by candidates. The next two parts of the question asked candidates to explain how the company might re-structure its upstream and downstream supply chain to address the problems identified in the case study scenario.

This question was the most popular of the optional questions and it was answered well by most candidates. In contrast to question two, most candidates explicitly referenced the case study scenario and some excellent answers were produced. The only criticism that could be made was that too many candidates wrote too much about the primary activities of the value chain. Some candidates wrote two or three pages on this, to gain the five marks on offer, when perhaps ten lines might have been sufficient. Such lengthy answers may have caused candidates time problems and meant that they did not complete the paper.

28   5E INTRANET UPGRADE

Key answer tips

Part (a) requires an in depth knowledge of IT/IS issues.

In part (b) ensure you use the stakeholders referred to in the scenario and, for each, explain their position in the matrix.

(a)   To upgrade the intranet as planned, 5E would need the following hardware and software:

Hardware

- A powerful intranet server to host the knowledgebase, manage traffic and facilitate access.

- A separate web server to host the website. Keeping this separate from the rest of 5E's activities is advised for security reasons.

- A high-speed broadband connection to allow many customers to access the intranet quickly. It would also be advisable to set up a virtual private network (VPN) for the firm's many offices.

- The system to ensure that only authorised users can access the data may involve the purchase of hardware such as challenge-response smart cards to generate passcodes.

Software

- ISP software to manage email traffic and host the website.

- Password software (e.g. encryption, public/private keys, digital signatures, etc) to ensure only authorised users can access data.

- Software to run the intranet – preferably the same as that used by X to ensure a straightforward handover.

- If web design is to be performed in-house, then a web design package, such as Macromedia Dreamweaver, will be required.

- It may be felt that the level of e-security will need to be upgraded so suitable software (e.g. anti-virus, adware, spyware, firewalls, etc) for data and system security will be required.

- If documents are to be sent / received, then the simplest way would be to use FTP (file transfer protocol) software.

- If it is planned to allow clients to interrogate and process data, then the processing should be server based (e.g. SQL) rather than PC-based (e.g. MSAccess) to allow greater speed and volume.

(b)   Mendelow designed his power-interest matrix to analyse stakeholder conflict:

Stakeholder Mapping: The Power Interest Matrix

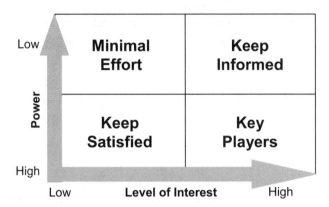

Within the context of the intranet upgrade the key stakeholders are as follows:

5E partners

- Partners have a high interest in the project. If it is successful, then it will allow 5E to offer clients a wider range of services, enhancing the firm's competitive advantage and reducing the likelihood of clients switching to competitors. Problems on the other hand (e.g. client confidentiality compromised) could result in a loss of goodwill.

- The partners also have high power as they ultimately control the firm and could terminate the project if they wished.

- Partners thus fall into the 'key players' quadrant.

X

- X has a high interest in the decision as it currently manages the intranet and will lose 5E's business and the fees involved, which may be significant.

- X cannot prevent 5E from switching to in-house provision, though it could make the transition very awkward and could even charge for helping data migration.

- Overall X will thus fall into the 'key players' quadrant.

Clients

- The interest of clients will vary and will be higher if they have approved cases for inclusion and if they make extensive use of the knowledgebase.

- Clients have the power to veto the use of cases involving them. Other clients can influence the firm by expressing their intention to move if such a system is not implemented, though the extent of this power will depend on whether or not they are considered to be major clients.

- Overall clients will thus fall into the 'keep informed' quadrant.

Ms Y

- Ms Y has a high interest in the project as she has proposed it and, presumably, will be held responsible for the ultimate success or failure of the project.

- Ms Y has medium power as she will exercise operational control over the project, subject to partner approval and intervention.

- Overall Ms Y will thus fall into the 'key players' quadrant.

Existing ISP

- The existing ISP has a low interest in the decision. While it will lose 5E's business, it is unlikely that fees are significant.
- The ISP has very low power to prevent 5E from switching to in-house provision.
- Overall the ISP will thus fall into the 'minimal effort' quadrant.

29 PROTECH-PUBLIC

Key answer tips

In this scenario, the organisation has yet to start trading on the Internet. However, the issue is not necessarily when to start trading using this medium, but whether or not to start trading. You will therefore need to review the scenario information to obtain information about OOB, and then think of the strategic issues involved with trading on the Internet. Many of the points that are relevant to the IT strategy of an organisation such as cost and support of core business will also be relevant in this situation. So, make a list of the strategic issues and provide relevant scenario information before writing out the answer in full. As a rough guide, you should have about six topics to discuss in order to achieve a good pass standard.

(a) The scenario suggests a number of reasons why outsourcing should be beneficial to the city authority.

Firstly, over the last decade there have been fluctuations in demand for IT staff. The authority has recruited to meet short-term demand but, because of the problems of shedding labour, the IT department has not proportionally contracted once that demand has passed. The implication is that, as a result, IT staff costs are higher than they should be. The outsourcing model provides a way of matching supply to demand. Employees are only brought in when there is a specific project for them to work on.

There has been a history of conflict between managers in the IT department and managers in the Finance Department. The Chief Executive Officer (CEO) has spent a significant amount of time trying to resolve this conflict. Employee surveys by the HR department have reported that morale is low in the IT department, despite above average pay and relatively secure employment. Outsourcing IT would appear to offer the following advantages to the authority.

The chief executive and his team would be able to focus on delivering services to the city, rather than spending time and energy on resolving internal problems. The chief executive has recently been criticised for failing to tackle the housing problems of the city. Outsourcing IT would give him more time to address external issues and services, which are the primary objectives and responsibilities of the authority.

Although the problems of low morale may be in part due to management problems, it must also be recognised that promotion opportunities and recognition will probably be lower in an organisation where IT is a relatively small support, rather than core activity. This is reflected in the ingratitude of users towards IT staff ('we are always being told that we are overhead, not core to the business of the authority'). It can be argued that IT staff might be better motivated in an organisation where IT is the core activity and where there should be greater scope for learning new skills and gaining promotion.

Finally, the dispute between IT managers and finance managers has still not been resolved. Outsourcing the IT department will, at best, eliminate the problem and, at worst, make this someone else's problem. In reality, the inability to resolve internal political problems is often given as an important reason for outsourcing.

The director of IT is keen to exploit the opportunities of web services and cloud computing but has not been able to recruit someone of sufficient calibre. As he says, 'there are probably other technologies that I have not even heard of that we should be exploring and exploiting'. An outsourced IT supplier should have a much greater range of knowledge and skills that it can then make available to its customers. It will be keen to be at the leading edge of technologies, because these technologies offer it possible competitive advantage, and so it will bear the cost of recruiting and retaining specialist employees.

Finally, the chief executive recognises that outsourcing IT is likely to be a model followed by other authorities. The formation of a separate company in which the city authority has a significant stake might provide an appropriate vehicle for gaining contracts with other authorities. They might be particularly attracted to working with a company which has significant public sector expertise and ownership. Profits made by the company may be distributed by dividend to the authority, bringing in income that can be used to reduce taxes or improve services.

(b)   In the past, business analysts have been employed within the IT department. It is proposed that these analysts will now move to a new BA department reporting directly to the chief executive. Their brief is 'to deliver solutions that demonstrably offer benefits to the organisation and to the people of the city, using information technology where appropriate'. They will be responsible for liaising between users and the new, outsourced IT company. The business analysts will have to establish credibility with the user departments, demonstrating the role and contribution of the business analyst role. The question focuses on new or enhanced competencies they will need, rather than generic skills such as 'good communication skills' and 'team working' which they would have needed when they were sited in the IT department.

Competencies they will require might include:

Strategy analysis They will have to develop an external business focus which, at the very least, looks for opportunities in the wider environment. The CEO expects them to be 'outward looking and unconstrained by current process and technology'. Techniques such as SWOT analysis might be useful here.

Business case development The absence of cross-charging suggests that business cases were relatively simple in the authority and it appears that business analysts were not involved in the process. In the new arrangement, agreeing the business case becomes their responsibility and so they will have to liaise with users to ensure that benefits are properly defined. If the solution requires an IT element then there are now very tangible costs which will be charged by an external supplier. This is particularly significant if software is involved. The supplier will need well specified requirements to estimate from. Costs and benefits will have to be compared using an appropriate approach. The business analyst will also have to participate in benefits realisation, assessing whether the promised benefits had actually been delivered at the cost envisaged in the original proposal.

Business process modelling The business analysts must be prepared to come up with solutions that do not include information technology. For example, they might suggest a small change to a clerical business process that delivers significant benefits. It is unlikely that they would have formulated such solutions when they were part of the IT department. Business process modelling and redesign skills will be needed to facilitate this.

Requirements definition Requirements definition would have been an important part of the business analysts' job when they were in the IT department. However, the scenario suggests a relatively flexible relationship with users, with changes to requirements being accommodated right up until software release. Although the outsourced IT supplier may take a similar approach, changes will be charged for. Hence in the outsourced arrangement there will be a need for business analysts to define requirements more completely and also to manage changes to those requirements. The detailed definition should also allow them to resolve issues where there is debate over whether the change is actually a change or is what was specified in the first place. The business analyst may also be involved in *testing* the solution received from the supplier.

Procurement The relationship between the city authority and the IT provider is now a supplier–customer relationship. The business analysts will have to gain supplier and contract management skills, allowing them to successfully manage this relationship.

ACCA marking scheme		
		Marks
(a)	1 mark for each relevant point up to a maximum of 12 marks.	12
(b)	1 mark for each relevant point up to a maximum of 7 marks.	7

Examiner's comments

The first part of the question asked candidates to evaluate the potential benefits of this outsourcing to the city authority and its IT employees. Most candidates answered this relatively well, although many did not recognise that the formation of a joint company might itself bring significant advantages to the city authority. The formation of a separate company in which the city authority has a significant stake might provide an appropriate vehicle for gaining contracts with other public authorities. They might be particularly attracted to working with a company which has significant public sector expertise and ownership. Profits made by the company may be distributed by dividend to the authority, bringing in income that can be used to reduce taxes or improve services.

The scenario acknowledged that business analysts within the city authority will need to gain new or enhanced competencies. The second part of the question asked candidates to analyse these competencies. Some of these were clearly signposted in the scenario; for example, strategy analysis and business case development. The need for a formal relationship between the authority and the outsource provider leads naturally to a discussion of requirements definition and procurement. Thus it should have been relatively easy to identify competencies around strategy, business cases, requirement definition and procurement. Two marks for each of these should have resulted in full marks for this part question. However, in practice, this was not the case. Many candidates failed to identify any relevant competencies (falling back on generalisations such as 'good communication skills') and hence did not score well in this part question.

30   GOOD SPORTS

Key answer tips

The key in this question is to split up your points between parts (a) and (b). Part (a) wants you to discuss fairly generic advantages and disadvantages of e-business (the 6M's model would be a useful one to use here. Part (b) then wants an application of these benefits and problems to Good Sports. A key issue to pick up on in part (b) will be the loss of competitive advantage that Good Sports gets from its personal contact with customers.

(a)   **To**:   Good Sports Limited

From: xxxxx

E – Business strategy

Clearly, the markets that Good Sports operates in are being affected by the development of e-business and its experiences to date are mixed to say the least. In many ways the advantages and disadvantages of e-business are best related to the benefit the customer gets from the activity.

- First, through integrating and accelerating business processes, e-business technologies enable response and delivery times to be speeded up.

- Second, there are new business opportunities for information-based products and services.

- Third, websites can be linked with customer databases and provide much greater insights into customer buying behaviour and needs.

- Fourth, there is far greater ability for interaction with the customer, which enables customisation and a dialogue to be developed.

- Finally, customers may themselves form communities able to contact one another.

There is considerable evidence to show how small operators like Good Sports are able to base their whole strategy on e-business and achieve high rates of growth. The key to Good Sport's survival is customer service – in strategic terms they are very much niche marketers supplying specialist service and advice to a small section of the local market. The nature of the business means that face-to-face contact is crucial in moving customers from awareness to action (AIDA – awareness, interest, desire and action). There are therefore limits to the ability of e-business to replace such contact.

Yours,

(b)   Good Sports has pursued a conscious niche or focus differentiation strategy, seeking to serve a local market in a way that isolates it from the competition of the large national sports good retailers competing on the basis of supplying famous brands at highly competitive prices. Does it make strategic sense for Good Sports to make the heavy investment necessary to supply goods online? Will this enhance its ability to supply their chosen market?

In terms of price, e-business is bringing much greater price transparency – the problem for companies like Good Sports is that customers may use their expertise to research into a particular type and brand of sports equipment and then simply search the Internet for the cheapest supply. Porter in an article examining the impact of the

Internet argues that rather than making strategy obsolete it has in fact made it more important. The Internet has tended to weaken industry profitability and made it more difficult to hold onto operational advantages. Choosing which customers you serve and how are even more critical decisions.

However the personal advice and performance side of the business could be linked to new ways of promoting the product and communicating with the customer. The development of customer communities referred to above could be a real way of increasing customer loyalty. The partners are anxious to avoid head-on competition with the national retailers. One way of increasing the size and strength of the niche they occupy is to use the Internet as a means of targeting their particular customers and providing insights into the use and performance of certain types of equipment by local clubs and users. There is considerable scope for innovation that enhances the service offered to their customers. As always there is a need to balance the costs and benefits of time spent. The Internet can provide a relatively cost effective way of providing greater service to their customers. There is little in the scenario to suggest they have reached saturation point in their chosen niche market. Overall there is a need for Good Sports to decide what and where its market is and how this can be improved by the use of e-business.

31   NEW SYSTEM

Key answer tips

This is not an exam standard question but it should be a useful revision tool in testing the knowledge you will have to apply in other questions in this area of the syllabus.

(a)   The main advantages of using package software are:

- Speed of delivery. The package is already developed.

- Cost. Likely to be much lower than having a system specially written because the cost of packages is spread over many users.

- Reliability. Unless the package has just been launched, most serious 'bugs' will have been found and corrected by earlier customers.

- Maintenance and support. Suppliers of packages have to provide some level of support for their many users. Selling updates is also very lucrative as the customer base is wide.

Apart from the reverse of the above points, the main disadvantage of buying off-the-shelf software is that the software is unlikely to provide all the features that an organisation might want, and that could be written into a bespoke system. Consequently, the benefits from an off-the-shelf system might be much less than the benefits from a bespoke system would be. This could have implications for the competitiveness of the organisation. (It might be possible to arrange for the software supplier to write an adapted version of its software for the organisation, but this would add to the cost of the software and delay its implementation, due to the need for writing amended programs and testing them.)

With off-the-shelf software, the user has no control over system amendments and new system versions. The content and timing of new software versions is decided by the software house.

(b)   A prototype is a working version or model, but not the finished item. When prototyping is used for system development, an initial working model is produced and sometimes implemented operationally. Experience with the prototype should enable the system user and system designers to identify both weaknesses in the system design and also additional or amended user requirements for the system. Through experience with the system, the user should be able to identify the system requirements more clearly. Even if not implemented, a prototype helps users better to understand their requirements.

After the first prototype, another is then developed, incorporating the improvements and amended requirements. There is an iterative process, with a succession of prototypes developed and introduced, until the final system version is produced.

Prototyping enables a system to be implemented more quickly, because it becomes operational with the first prototype, before the system development is completed.

Prototyping should also result in better systems, because the system requirements will have been refined and improved with the practical experience and lessons obtained from working with the prototypes.

(c)   Operations strategy is a vital element in the overall strategy of a firm. It concerns how the firm provides its products or services for delivery to the customer. The objective of a commercial firm might be stated as meeting customer needs with products or services, in order to increase the value of the firm over the long-term and the wealth of its shareholders. Meeting customer needs is critically important, particularly in competitive markets.

Harmon's process strategy matrix is a matrix formed by:

1   An estimate of the strategic importance of a process (usually the horizontal axis) and

2   An estimate of the process complexity and/or dynamism (rate of change) on the other axis.

The purpose of the matrix is to suggest how processes should be developed, improved and how their output should be best provided.

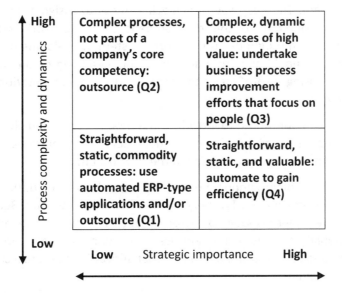

It is likely that the operations of this company fall into quadrant 4. The company supplies components, and it is assumed that there is no manufacturing process. The activities of the company are therefore likely to be non-complex and stable. We have been told, however, that the company is facing competition from other, more reliable suppliers. Implementing a system which improves their operations is therefore likely to be strategically important.

The company therefore needs to automate its order processing operations to generate efficiency and consistency. Aspects of operating performance include quality, speed, dependability and cost. The management of quality is important because with better quality, customer needs are met more effectively, and costs are reduced. Speed of throughput means that customer needs can be met more quickly. Lower costs mean that the company's objectives of increasing shareholder wealth should also be more achievable.

(d)   The marketing mix 'traditionally' consists of the 4Ps: product, place, price and promotion. 'Product' refers not only to the physical product itself, but also to the services that are provided in association with the physical product. 'Place' refers to the way in which a product is delivered to the customer, and the channel of distribution that is used.

The planned new customer order and delivery system can be used to provide a stronger marketing message to business buyers.

The new computer system could strengthen the 'product' or the 'place' depending on how the benefits of the new system are classified. If the new system is successful, customers will be offered a much more reliable delivery system, where the company can verify immediately whether items are in stock and provide a 'guaranteed' delivery date to the customer.

The company's customers are all business buyers, and reliability of supply appears to be a key requirement. The sales and marketing team should be able to promote this improvement and make the products appeal more strongly to potential buyers.

(e)   Staff training for a major new system should be organised in stages.

(i)   Initially, the company should ensure that some of its staff are familiar with the new system. The best way of achieving this is to assign a member or several members of staff to the development team, to work with the system developers throughout the entire system development phase. These individuals should acquire a sufficient understanding of the system, perhaps through using prototypes, to prepare user documentation and training materials.

(ii)   It might be appropriate to introduce the new system gradually, so that training in the new system can also be gradual. Selected operational staff should be given some 'class room' training in the new system.

(iii) Practical training cannot be carried out, however, until the system is sufficiently developed. Typically, this is after system testing. Before the system goes 'live', there should be user acceptability tests. The purpose of user acceptability tests is to provide user staff with experience in using the new system and also so that any operational difficulties that arise can be identified and resolved.

Training should therefore be a combination of formal training, practical training and user instructions (in documentation and/or as a help facility within the software). Operational staff working on the system for the first time should also be supervised carefully. The systems development team might also be used to check output from the system, identify any difficulties that individual members of staff are having with the system, and help to resolve them. This might be described as 'on-the-job' training.

MARKETING

32   AEC *Walk in the footsteps of a top tutor*

Tutor's top tips

Approach to the question

*If, as always, you start by reading the **first paragraph only** the following can be determined:*

the business runs accountancy courses

it is a worldwide business

it also targets the CPD market (though this is underperforming)

*Now look at the requirements **before** reading the rest of the question. This will ensure that you read the question in the correct manner, do not need to read the question more than once, save time and can begin planning.*

Requirement

(a)   The characteristics of electronic marketing

*The key to most requirements is to choose the most appropriate model – in this case the best model is McDonald and Wilson's 6I's model (as suggested in the official exam text). It is important to distinguish that in this section you are not being asked to create an e-marketing plan (that is required in part b) of the question), you are merely asked to **explain the differences that e-marketing** has to traditional marketing media. The 6I's model best achieves this .You could set up a planning page with the 6I's listed out and then add points to this plan as you read the question.*

(b)   Marketing mix

*In this part of the question you are asked **to use e-marketing**. You should be able to distinguish this clearly from part a) of the question and not mix your answers together – part a) wants you to explain e-marketing (this will focus on its differences and benefits), part b) then wants you to use it (this will focus on practical suggestions for AEC). The most appropriate model will be the 7P's model and you could approach this in the same way as part a) – set could set up a planning page with the 7P's listed out and then add points to this plan as you read the question.*

Reading the question

Now **actively** read the question i.e. as you read it you should add all relevant points to your planning page(s).

The key issues to pick out from the question as are as follows:

- AEC provide three products – training for professional examinations, material for these courses, and CPD courses. So part b) of your answer should explain how to market each of these courses/products.

- AEC have recently won a large, new customer. The impact on this customer should be considered in both parts of your answer.

- The company are planning to switch from traditional marketing to e-marketing but won't do both – there is only a 3% overall increase in marketing forecasted. Therefore you need to make clear in part a) that the e-marketing benefits will have to outweigh the loss of the traditional marketing channels.

Answering the question

Part (a) 6I's

As stated, if you have fully understood the impact of the final paragraph of the question, then there will be a mark or two for explaining that the e-marketing benefits will have to outweigh the loss of the traditional marketing channels. But there are plenty of other marks available if this point is missed.

There are 10 marks available and if you work to the normal rule of 2 marks per well explained point then you only have to cover 4 or 5 of the 6I's. The key issue will be to relate the model to the scenario (for example, by referencing the win of the new, large client).

For example, using independence of location, traditional marketing can be used to target customers in all parts of the world. But AEC could expand this through e-marketing by allowing these customers to also book courses online – something that isn't happening at the moment. So e-marketing should make it easier and therefore more attractive to customers to choose AEC as their training provider. It should also reduce administrative burdens for larger clients and might allow AEC to attract more multi-national customers.

Part (b) 7P's

As this is e-marketing it will probably be best to extend the traditional 4P's of the marketing mix to the 7P's i.e. we should include a discussion of processes, physical evidence and people. The key will be to make the points relevant to AEC (something that examiner suggested some students failed to do) and to perhaps explain the impact on all the company's products.

Using physical evidence for example, the website could stand out if it had useful links to other websites. For accountancy training courses these could be links to the relevant accounting bodies. For CPD courses, these could be links to relevant legislative bodies, standards, tax authorities etc. This might make the website more useful and encourage repeat visits.

(a)   A key characteristic of traditional marketing media such as advertising and direct mail is that it is predominantly a 'push' technology where the media is distributed to customers and potential customers. There is limited interaction with the customer and indeed, in the case of advertising and to a lesser degree direct mail, there is no certainty that the intended recipient actually received the message. In contrast, the new media, particularly the Internet, is predominantly a 'pull' technology – the customer having initiated the visit to the web site. This may lead to subsequent push activities, such as sending e-mails to people who have registered their interest on the site, but the initial communication is a pull event. The marketing manager must be careful that, by switching so much of her budget to pull technologies, she does not forego opportunities to find new customers – or reinforce her message – through established push technologies. She must ensure that the company's web site is established in such a way that sufficient people find it, and that when they do, they are prepared to record enough details to allow subsequent push activities.

Dave Chaffey examines the difference between traditional and new marketing media in the context of six 'I's; interactivity, intelligence, individualisation, integration, industry restructuring and independence of location. Four of these are used in this answer.

Interactivity is a significant feature of the new media, allowing a long-term dialogue to develop between the customer and the supplier. In the context of the web site, this is likely to be through e-mails, providing the customer with information and special offers for their areas of specific interest. To initiate this dialogue the web site must capture information such as e-mail address, name, age, gender and areas of interest. The AEC site only collects such information for people who wish to view downloadable study material. This is too restrictive and it will probably exclude all the potential CPD customers. AEC needs to consider ways of making it easier and worthwhile for visitors to the site to register their details. There is no evidence of AEC contemplating the potential use of interactive digital TV or mobile phones to establish long-term dialogues with their customers.

Intelligence has also been a key feature of the new media – allowing the relatively cheap collection of marketing research data about customers' requirements. This is routinely available from web logs and these logs need to be viewed and analysed using appropriate software. This type of analysis is rarely available in the traditional media. For example, AEC does not know how often their training course catalogue is accessed and which pages are looked at. It only knows which training courses are eventually bought. With the new media the company is able to see which services and products are accessed and also to measure how many of these are turned into actual sales. This conversion rate may be an important source of information – for example, why are certain web pages often visited but few sales result – is it a problem with the web page? – is it a problem with the product? An understanding of visit patterns allows the organisation to focus on particular products and services. This analysis should already be available to AEC but there is no evidence that it uses it or is even aware of it.

The new media also permit the marketing to be *individualised*, geared to a particular market segment, company or individual person. In the context of AEC this individualisation could be achieved in at least two ways to reflect clear market segmentation. AEC has recently won a contract to supply professional accountancy training to a global accounting company. All students working for this company will now be trained by AEC in one of its worldwide centres. At present this company and its students will be served through a generic web site. However, the flexibility of the new media means that a site could be developed specifically for this requirement. The whole site would be geared, and branded, towards the requirements of the global accounting company. Information that is irrelevant to that customer, such as CPD, would not appear on the site. This individualised approach should strengthen the relationship with the customer. Similarly, individuals may have their own access customised as a result of the profile that they have entered. So, for example, if they have already stated that they are currently sitting the professional stage of an examination scheme then only information relevant to that stage will be presented to them when they log in. This is an example of the principle of mass customisation that was only available in a limited form in the traditional media. AEC does not exploit this at present, but uses a generic web site that looks and feels the same, whoever the user is.

Finally, the new media provide *independence* of location allowing the company to move into geographical areas that would have been unreachable before. The Internet effectively provides a worldwide market that is open 24 hours per day, seven days per week. It is difficult to think of any traditional media which would have permitted this global reach so cheaply. Furthermore, the web site might also omit the actual physical location of the company because there is no requirement for information to be physically sent to an address. It should also be impossible for the potential customer to gauge the size of the supplying company. AEC has exploited this to some extent as it serves a world-wide market from no clear geographical centre. However, the absence of on-line course booking means that certain physical contact details have to be provided and these might undermine the global perspective.

(b) The marketing mix has traditionally consisted of four major components: product, place (distribution), promotion and price. More recently, three further elements have been added, particularly for the marketing of services – people, process and physical evidence. Some authors, however, contend that these new elements are really only sub-sets of the original four components.

In the context of this question, the Ps, whether there are 4 or 7, provide a good framework for the answer, although such a framework is not mandated. The model answer below actually uses '5Ps', relating them to both technology and the situation at AEC.

Product

The product is a fundamental element of the marketing mix. If the product is not 'right' it is unlikely that the marketers will be able to persuade customers to buy the product or, if they do buy it, to convince them to become repeat buyers. In the context of the new technology, an organisation may seek opportunities for developing the product or service. These opportunities emerge from re-considering the core product or identifying options for extending it.

In the context of AEC the consideration of the product is complicated by there being at least three products promoted on their web site; training courses and training manuals for students studying for professional qualifications and training courses for qualified accountants undertaking continuing professional development (CPD). The course training manual is a tangible physical product that can be handled before purchase. Potential customers can try before they buy because a sub-section of a manual is available for inspection. This is an admirable policy. Potential customers do not have to believe that the manuals are comprehensive and well-written; they can make their own judgement based on a sample. In contrast, the training courses are services, bought on the promise of satisfaction.

AEC might profitably consider delivering elements of both student and CPD training courses through web casts and pod casts. Such courses might be fully on-line or the new technologies might be integrated with older ones, such as workshops and offline assignments, to provide a blended approach to learning. This may be particularly appropriate for student tuition where competence is assessed by a formal examination, not by attendance at a course. AEC is already distributing course catalogues and course schedules through the Internet. However, there is no physical evidence to support the customer's evaluation of such courses. AEC might consider having sample videoed sessions available on the web so that prospective customers can assess the content and approach to training.

Although training documentation is currently available through the web site it could benefit from re-focusing. At present students pay a fixed fee which gives them access to the whole set of manuals. However, manuals for modules at the end of the scheme will only be relevant if the student passes the earlier modules. Lack of confidence may deter the student from committing to the whole manual set at the beginning of his or her studies. Similarly, candidates who become aware of AEC products only after they have passed the first few modules are unlikely to pay a fee for a manual set which includes manuals for modules that they have already passed or for which they are exempted. Consequently, it would appear more sensible to allow candidates to select the manuals they require and pay a fee per manual, with a discounted fee for buying the whole set.

AEC might also wish to consider *product bundling* where it offers further products and services to complement its core products. For example, travel booking, accommodation services and entertainment bookings might be offered to qualified accountants attending CPD courses. AEC is also in a market place where the product needs to be continually updated and developed to reflect changing or clarified requirements. For example, new training manuals may need releasing every year.

Price

The Internet has allowed pricing to be much more transparent to potential customers. They can easily visit the sites of competing companies and compare prices for similar products and services. Such accessibility may deter AEC from using the web site to offer *differential pricing*. The Internet makes products available worldwide but candidates in poorer countries are often unable to afford prices set in richer parts of the world. Consequently, AEC should consider the potential of differential pricing, making prices reflect local currencies and conditions. There is a risk of alienating people in richer countries but it may be a risk worth taking and it is possible that candidates in these richer countries may perceive differential pricing as ethical practice. Web sites produced in national languages using domain names registered in that country might not be discovered or accessed by candidates in the developed world and so differential pricing is never uncovered. However, there is still a risk that customers buying at a lower price will then sell to buyers in the segments that are charged a higher price – so AEC will have to monitor this.

The ability to continually update information on the Internet makes the dynamic pricing of products and services attractive. It is extensively used by airlines (booking early attracts large discounts) and hotels (auctioning off rooms they cannot fill that night). It appears that AEC should also consider differential pricing, particularly using early booking discounts to get the CPD courses up and running. It may also be possible to provide cheap 'late booking' offers to fill the last few places on a course. However, there is the possibility that this will alienate people who have already booked and paid the standard fee. Hence, this will also have to be given more detailed consideration.

AEC might also wish to consider an alternative pricing structure for the documentation. At present manuals are purchased and this might still be the case if it adopts the more modular approach suggested in the previous section. However, there may be large areas of the manual that the student is familiar with. An alternative approach is to charge the student only when they access the material. Hence, students pay for a web service on demand – rather than through purchased download. This 'on demand' payment for actual use is becoming an increasingly popular model of delivering products.

Finally, because off-line booking incurs administrative costs and overheads it is usual to offer on-line customers a significant discount. Hence the pricing structure must recognise this. People booking through an on-line channel now expect to get a discounted price.

Place

It has been argued that the Internet has the greatest implications for place in the marketing mix because, as a distribution channel, it has a global reach, available 24 hours per day, seven days per week. AEC is already exploiting this global reach, although it has to ensure that its products make sense in a global perspective. The training manuals are easy to exploit globally as they are downloaded products which can be printed off throughout the world. The dates and locations of training courses, in their current format, is also globally accessible but is only really relevant to people living in the geographical regions near to the eight training centres. This is particularly true of CPD courses which are only run in three centres worldwide. The global reach of the Internet can only be exploited in the context of the courses if they use the technology discussed in the *product* section of this answer, perhaps exploiting the *price* differentials discussed in the previous section.

Promotion

Although AEC has an established web site it has not actively promoted it. The promotion of the web site may involve both technology and established marketing media. From the technology perspective, AEC might consider the following to increase its web site visibility.

1   Search Engine registration. This remains the primary method of users finding products and services. Over 80% of web users state that they use search engines to find information. There are five main parameters on which search engines base the order of their ranking.

    – Title – keywords in the title of a web page

    – Meta tags

    – Frequency of keyword in the text

    – Hidden graphic text

    – Links from other sites

    AEC must ensure that their web site is constructed in such a way that it has a good chance of appearing on the first page of search engine listings.

2   Building links with other web sites should increase traffic to the site as well as improving search engine ranking. The current AEC site does not appear to link (or be linked) to any other sites.

3   Viral marketing is the term used when e-mail is used to transmit a promotional message to another potential customer. It enables a customer browsing the site to forward a page to a colleague. There is no evidence that the AEC site supports this.

4 On-line advertising includes *banner advertising*. As well as potentially driving customers to the site, the banner advert also builds brand awareness and reminds the customer about the company and its services. AEC must consider this.

Off-line marketing should also be concerned with promoting the web site in established media such as print, TV and radio. Key issues to communicate are the URL and the online value proposition. It may also be used for special sales promotions and offers to attract visitors to the site. 50% of the marketing manager's budget is being spent on off-line marketing media. She must consider how to integrate the web site into this part of the promotional mix.

Process

This concerns the processes used to support the customer's interaction with AEC. At present the training course part of the web site is predominantly an information site. It provides information about the product and the location and cost of the product. However, it is not used for either purchase or post-sales support. Hence if a student or a qualified accountant wishes to book on a course they have to physically contact a person who then takes booking and payment details. There is no evidence that post-sales support such as sending joining instructions, answering queries and receiving course feedback is supported by the web site. It would be useful for AEC to consider whether training purchase and post-sales processes could be integrated into its web site. After all, a payment process has already been set up for the training manual part of the site. The automation of routine processes and answers to common questions might help free up the company's administrative resources as well as providing a better service to customers and exploiting the Internet's *independence of location*.

	ACCA marking scheme	
		Marks
(a)	Up to 2 marks for recognising the distinction between push and pull technologies in the context of the scenario	2
	Up to 2 marks for issues concerned with interactivity	2
	Up to 2 marks for issues concerned with intelligence	2
	Up to 2 marks for issues concerned with individualisation	2
	Up to 2 marks for issues concerned with independence	2
	Credit will also be given for candidates who focus on Chaffey's other 'I's – industry restructuring and integration	
(b)	Up to 4 marks for issues concerned with product	4
	Up to 3 marks for issues concerned with price	3
	Up to 2 marks for issues concerned with place	2
	Up to 4 marks for issues concerned with promotion	4
	Up to 2 marks for issues concerned with process	2
	Credit will also be given for candidates who focus on other 'p's' – physical evidence and people	

Examiner's comments

Part (a) asked candidates how such e-media differed in characteristics from that of traditional marketing media such as advertising and direct mail. Many of the candidates used the McDonald and Wilson (quoted in Chaffey) '6Is' framework and this was a particularly effective approach because it allowed each I to be explored in the two contexts, supported by examples from the scenario. For example, electronic media allows communication to be tailored to the individual or defined group of individuals. In contrast, traditional media tends to deliver the same message to everyone. Within the context of the AEC case study, AEC could provide tailored service and support to the employees of the global accounting company whose training contract they have just won. The content, image and service could be adapted to focus on this particular group, rather than just serving them through a general web site. This part of the question was relatively well answered by candidates, many scoring seven marks or more out of the ten marks on offer.

Part (b) asked candidates to evaluate how the marketing manager might use electronic marketing to vary the marketing mix at AEC. The best answers adopted the marketing mix as the basis of the answer; using the Ps (price, place etc.) to structure points in the context of AEC. Unfortunately, many answers did not use the context of AEC at all, despite it being a context which all the candidates taking this examination should have been familiar with. Too many answers repeated points already made in the first part of the question, without referring to AEC and, in some cases, without reference to the marketing mix. This was a relatively straightforward question which, although answered quite well, should often have been answered better.

33   THE FANCY PACKAGING COMPANY

Key answer tips

In part (a) try to bring in external analysis tools   - especially Porter's Diamond which is designed specifically for overseas expansion. Part (b) is on the edge of the syllabus and is less likely to be examined under the current examiner.

(a)   **To:**   E Lomax, Marketing Director, The Fancy Packaging Company

       From: Accountant

       Date: XX/XX/XX

       Report on Proposed Overseas Sales Project

       Introduction

       It is important that you **research the market carefully** as any decision to sell into non-European markets, where your company has no experience, could prove to be expensive if it is not supported by reliable information. A wrong move could be financially damaging as well as being harmful to your corporate image and reputation. I have identified and analysed three key areas where information needs are critical:

       1   the customer profile

2   the external environment which could impinge upon this strategy

3   the competitive framework.

1   **The customer profile**

Here it is important to understand as much as possible about the companies to whom you sell. This information can be sub-divided into two areas – quantitative and qualitative data. **Quantitative data** is generally easier to obtain and there is less room for dispute or misunderstanding. Examples of quantitative data are the answers to questions such as: Who are the companies? Where they are located? What is their size and buying potential (quantities and frequency)? Who initiates the purchasing decision within the firm? All these questions could be useful in planning a market entry strategy.

However, the critical and more **qualitative information** (such as: Why do they prefer one supplier to another? What are the critical influences on the purchase decision – price, quality or availability?) generally answers to the question 'Why do they buy?', is more difficult to obtain but it usually provides more valuable and actionable information.

2   **The external environment**

This area is concerned with understanding the new environment in which you may have to operate. It will be advantageous to carry out a **SLEPT (or PESTEL) analysis**. I am providing a few pertinent examples, but these external influences are pervasive and need to be fully examined.

- Are there any socio-demographic factors that could influence the demand for the packaging products?

- Are 'green issues' sufficiently powerful to discourage this type of decorative packaging?

- Is the end-user profile favourably inclined to marketing and promotional expenditure?

- Are there legal issues that may influence your business? This could impinge on your relationships with agents, distributors and other contacts.

- There could be legal constraints on the amount of packaging material allowed.

- It is also critical to understand the economic environment as this can directly influence demand for your products. High interest rates, high unemployment and low economic growth are all factors which are likely to adversely affect demand for products which use decorative packaging. The economy may be too poor to warrant the use of decorative packaging.

- The political environment is also relevant. It is possible that the host government may be prejudiced against foreign companies and may favour indigenous suppliers. There may be threats of increased trade barriers (this could be considered as a political or an economic influence) which could be damaging to the proposed entry strategy.

- Changes in the technological environment need also to be monitored (for example, e-commerce). The technological infrastructure may be so limited that decorative packaging cannot be usefully employed. It is also possible that your machinery may soon become obsolete as a result of technological advances.

3   **The competitive framework**

This is an obvious area for research. Understanding who the competitors are – both current and hidden – and appreciating if there are any significant barriers to entry will be obviously important in planning a foreign market entry campaign. An application of **Porter's five force model** could be helpful here because it provides a wider assessment of the competitive framework. It not only considers existing competitors, either local or foreign, but it also looks at potential substitute products and even looks at customers from a competitive dimension – what power are they able to exert over suppliers. **Porter's Diamond** could also be of use, particularly with potential overseas expansion.

Conclusion

There is much information which needs to be gathered before beginning an overseas market entry strategy. I have highlighted just three areas but there are other areas that could be useful such as an analysis of the common marketing strategies used in this business. I trust that this information will be of help to you. Should you require any further information, please contact me again.

Signed:

(b)   **Market research**

Tutorial note

The key to success in market research questions is to suggest a mixture of both desk AND field research.

Given the wide range of information needed it is logical to use both primary (surveys) and secondary (desk research) data collection methods. It is sensible to collect secondary data first. This data is already published for some other purpose and hence it is cheaper to collect and is often readily available. Factual information on aspects such as the economy, size of markets, competition and legal and political constraints, can help determine whether a market is viable or not. This information can act as a filter, so avoiding unnecessary expense in obtaining qualitative data by more expensive and time-consuming survey methods when the desk research might itself show a market to be unattractive and lacking profit potential.

There are a **number of sources for this secondary information**.

- Government departments, embassies and consulates and commercial banks in particular are prime sources for obtaining this valuable information.
- Newspapers, trade journals, trade associations and the Internet are other valuable sources.

Having identified through desk research that a market has export potential it may require more detailed primary research to acquire the more specific qualitative data. Then one has to resort to **survey research**, involving **customer questionnaires**. These can either involve face-to-face interviews or postal or telephone interviewing can take place. As the sample population interviewed is often small, care has to be taken to avoid bias occurring. The agency being used to carry out the surveys can be local and will know the culture of the groups being interviewed. However, in some less-developed countries the agency may not have the necessary expertise. In this case an international agency may be used with the proviso that it may lack the necessary knowledge of the country, its industries and its culture.

Given the limited experience which The Fancy Packaging Company has in this foreign project it is important that any marketing research carried out is done by professionals in a logical and thorough manner. The exercise must not be rushed or done at the lowest cost.

34   RESTFUL HOTELS

Key answer tips

Easy marks are available here for the discussion of the key knowledge areas of pricing and market segmentation. However, it is more difficult to apply your knowledge to the scenario of a chain of hotels. However, good students will have practised a large number of scenario-based questions before the exam and will be prepared to apply their knowledge.

(a)   There are several ways in which pricing can be used as an element in marketing:

- Restful Hotels might be able to promote itself as a low cost hotel for the quality of service provided, but without putting the four star rating at risk. The company could then market its hotels as the cheapest in their area for the quality of services provided. To succeed with this pricing strategy, Restful Hotels would need to control costs.

- There are difficulties in generating revenue at new hotels. It might be appropriate to use promotion (for example, web site advertising) to boost the business at these hotels. However, if price is used as a marketing tool, it might be appropriate to charge low room rates until demand is more established, or offering special room prices for a short period of time. For example, it might be possible to have sales promotions offering cut-price rooms at any Restful Hotel in the world to customers who book before a specified date.

- The company should also consider charging different prices in different locations, such as higher prices in city centre hotels than at holiday resorts, because the type of customer is likely to differ between the different types of location.

- It might also be possible to have differential pricing, with room prices varying according to the day of the week or the season of the year.

- Another form of price differentiation to win more customers might be to offer special price deals for pensioners or even students.

- To improve the 'value for money' marketing message, it might be more appropriate to offer more services free of charge (within the room charge), rather than to lower prices. Examples of free add-on services might be a courtesy bus from airport to hotel at holiday resorts.

(b)   The hotel market is segmented in different ways. One method of segmentation is to classify hotels according to quality (number of 'stars') and price. However, a policy of moving from a portfolio of four-star hotels, say to a portfolio of five-star hotels or a mixed portfolio of four-star and three-star hotels, will take time to implement.

If market segmentation is to succeed within a fairly short space of time in boosting total sales revenue, marketing strategy should probably focus on creating a stronger appeal to a sector of the market that does not currently take accommodation at Restful Hotels.

Sectors of the market for hotel rooms might be analysed, for example, as business users, conference participants, and holiday makers. If the hotel group does not currently attract, say, conference business, it might consider a marketing initiative to promote this type of business. If room occupancy is low at weekends, it might be appropriate to promote 'bargain' weekend breaks.

There might also be opportunities for focussing on customers for other services of the hotel, other than rooms. For example, the company might consider developing its restaurant service and promoting these to the general public.

(c)   The company is aiming for the premium range of hotel accommodation. Cutting prices might attract some customers who were previously unwilling to pay market rates for a four star hotel, but might put off some of the company's existing customer base as staying at a Restful Hotels hotel will no longer have the same degree of exclusivity. It might also mean that existing customers are forced to share the hotel with a less select group of residents.

Reducing prices might create a loss of revenue and there is no guarantee that it will generate additional volume. The change in prices might have to be managed so that the reductions are offered in a discreet manner. For example, the 'rack rate' offered at the reception desk for any customer who contacts the hotel directly might remain unchanged, but the discount offered to travel agents could be increased so that the agents can enjoy a bigger commission from each sale. That might give them an incentive to send more customers to Restful Hotels.

The other big danger with cutting prices is that Restful Hotels might then trigger a price war with competing hotel chains. If competitors start to lose business they might cut their own prices, leaving Restful Hotels no more competitive than before but enjoying less profit from each and every sale.

35   REPLEX

Key answer tips

Given the marks available in part (a) it will be important to manage your time well and only cover a few of the key pricing strategies and apply them to the scenario. Do not try to cover every pricing method mentioned in the pocket notes.

(a)   Alternative pricing strategies that may be adopted when launching a new product are:

Price skimming

Initially, it may be possible to charge a very high price if the product is new, innovative and different. This is the case for the company's new product. Furthermore, as Replex expect demand to be inelastic, price skimming is particularly appropriate so that Replex can exploit those sections of the market which are insensitive to price.

Penetration pricing

Initially, Replex may want to sell at a very low price to discourage competition from entering the market. This would also encourage high volumes, and Replex may benefit from economies of scale. Low prices would help to gain rapid acceptance of the product, and, therefore, a significant market share.

Demand based pricing

With this method, the company could utilise some market research information to determine the selling price and level of demand to maximise company's profits. This relies heavily on the quality of market information and the estimate of the demand curve. Also, this method assumes that price is the only factor that influences the quantity demanded and ignores other factors such as quality, packaging, advertising and promotion.

Cost based pricing

Cost based pricing is the simplest pricing method. Replex would calculate the cost of producing the product and add on a percentage (profit) to give the selling price. This method although simple has two flaws; it takes no account of demand and there is no way of determining if potential customers will purchase the product at the calculated price.

(b) It is recommend that Replex adopt a price skimming strategy to benefit from the lack of competition in the first six months. In such a competitive market, it is unlikely that competitors would be deterred from entry by low prices, so a penetration strategy seems unsuitable.

Introduction stage

As the company's product is the first of its type, and incorporates the latest technology, Replex could initially set very high prices to take advantage of its novelty appeal during the introduction stage, as demand would be inelastic.

This method would help to recover the significant level of development costs quickly, and is recommended when the product life is short and competition is intense, as high initial returns and maximum profits can be gained before competitors enter the market.

Growth stage

During this stage of the product's lifecycle, the sales of the company's product in garages would be expected to grow rapidly. As the product starts to become accepted and established by the mass market, competition usually increases significantly. In order to maintain market share and dominance, Replex may find it necessary to lower the initial market skimming launch price, thereby reducing the company's profits margins.

Maturity stage

As product sales growth begins to slow down and level off, an established market price for the company's product will become apparent. An average price may be charged. The price will often reach its lowest point during this stage. However, if the company's company has a good reputation and is respected worldwide, Replex may be able to charge a premium price based on its reputation and a certain level of brand loyalty.

Replex may want to extend the maturity phase by launching upgrades, or by trying to sell in new markets. The product must achieve its lowest unit cost during this stage. Profits are likely to be highest in the maturity stage.

Decline

The decline stage is the final stage of the product's lifecycle. The initial new innovative technology would have, by now, been superseded by superior products. The company's own product may hold on to a small niche market, and the group of loyal garages still purchasing the company's product may be willing to pay a price that will ensure continued profitability.

PROJECT MANAGEMENT

36   ASW   *Walk in the footsteps of a top tutor*

Tutor's top tips

This question was unusual in that it had three parts to it (rather than the normal two). It covered project management, quality and systems development. The question included a diagram of a project plan.

Part (b)

Students were asked to suggest some options for solving project slippage that was occurring in the question.

Key to success:

Suggest a range of options rather than focusing on just one

Try to give as much specifics as possible to give an answer which is relevant to the scenario rather than simple regurgitation or bookwork

Dangers:

Determining which option was best was the final requirement and therefore shouldn't have been considered in this part of a student's answer

Simple regurgitation of the textbook is unlikely to get enough marks to pass the requirement

Part (c)

The final part of the requirement asked students to suggest which of the proposed options would be the best solution.

Key to success:

Justifying your suggestions

Avoid repetition of the points made in the previous part of the question

---

Dangers:

Not spotting the link to the previous part of the requirement. This part of the requirement clearly started with "As a result of your evaluation…." making it quite clear that your answer to part (c) must be based on what you argued in part (b)

(b)   The project manager could request an extension to the deadline The case study scenario suggests that early delays in the project were caused by the absence of key CaetInsure staff and changes in user requirements in the re-insurance module. These delays meant that the full system specification was signed off three weeks later than initially agreed. Unfortunately, the delivery date of the whole project was not re-negotiated at this point as it was suggested that 'time could be made up' during the programming stage. Furthermore, the marketing department of CaetInsure had already announced the launch of a new product to coincide with the implementation of the software and they did not want to change these dates. However, the project manager could now return to CaetInsure and inform them that it had not been possible to catch up with the proposed schedule and to remind them that the initial slippage had been caused by them. Although the deadline date is associated with a product launch it is unlikely that this is crucial. It is not a matter of life and death. It might be irksome to delay the launch by a few weeks, but it is unlikely that many people will notice or indeed care about it. There are many significant successful products which have been released long after their intended release date. In many ways it is an artificial deadline.

However, there are at least three problems associated with this suggestion. The first is that the delay is now longer than the three weeks incurred at the specification stage. Consequently, the project manager will have to explain that there have been further delays to the project. Secondly, the project manager will have to be very confident about his revised delivery date. The project plan does not explicitly contain any time for programmers fixing faults found in system and acceptance testing and it seems very likely that faults will be found in this testing. Finally, some negotiation will have to take place on the late delivery penalty clause charges the sales account manager agreed in the initial contract. If some (or all) of these clauses are enacted then the profitability of the project will be significantly affected.

The project manager could consider a functional reduction in the scope of the software solution.

The scenario suggests that the re-insurance functionality has been a problem throughout the project. There may also be unresolved issues in other parts of the software. However, it must be remembered that the ASW product is a proven software solution, bespoke development is only concerned with customising the basic product to fulfil certain customer requirements. Therefore it is likely that there are large areas of the software that can be successfully delivered to the customer. The key issue here is whether this reduced functionality will fulfil the requirements associated with the proposed new product which CaetInsure intends to launch. If it does then the delivery of a partial solution does not have a significant business impact and the product launch can go ahead as planned. The project manager needs to discuss this with the customer as quickly as possible. He has to be sure that the reduced scope does indeed fulfil these requirements and, if it does, to focus testing, migration and document production on these parts of the software. He will also have to estimate the delivery time of the second phase of the software that fulfils the complete user requirement.

There are three elements of this suggestion that the project manager should bear in mind. Firstly, the impact of reduced scope on the penalty clauses of the contract. It would appear harsh to deliver a part solution but to still be fully penalised for not delivering the total solution. Consequently some contract renegotiation is necessary. Secondly, there will be an unexpected overhead associated with delivering a second phase which contains the full product. This is the overhead of *regression testing*, making sure that changes made to the product in the second release do not unintentionally affect the software solution that has already been delivered. Finally, the specification of data migration programs will have to be reviewed to see if they need to be changed in the light of the reduced functionality. Any changes will affect data migration programs which are currently being written or tested.

The project manager could consider taking steps which might reduce the quality of the product

A number of options might be considered around the testing of the software. One option is to considerably reduce system testing and hand over the software to acceptance testing ahead of the proposed schedule. The point has already been made that the software is essentially a package that has to be tailored for specific functions. Consequently, large areas of the software have been tested before, much of it by actual users out in the businesses that are using this solution. Programs for the CaetInsure version will have been unit tested by programmers before they have been released to system testers and so no area of the system is *untested*, although there will be areas that have not been *independently tested*. Another option is to reduce the scope of system testing, focusing it on testing functionality rather than usability (which will be one focus of acceptance testing) and performance (which can be difficult to perform effectively in a software house environment where the user's actual hardware configuration cannot be easily mimicked). A further option is to execute system and acceptance testing in parallel.

There are a number of issues with this approach which the project manager needs to consider. The first is that the acceptance testers are likely to find significantly more faults than they would if full system testing had preceded acceptance testing. This can lead to a reduction in customer confidence which could jeopardise the whole project. Secondly, faults identified by both system and user acceptance testers have to be carefully managed. Configuration management becomes a very significant issue and appropriate version control of the software is an essential overhead. Confidence is undermined by the constant releases of new versions of the software, some of which, due to poor configuration management, contain faults which have already been reported and fixed in earlier versions of the software.

The project manager might consider requesting more resources

Finally the project manager may request further resources for the project. The current project plan is at a high level of detail. It does not show how many system testers are actually working on the system or how many technical authors are writing the documentation. It may be possible to add more resources and so reduce the elapsed time of the activity. Resources might also be asked to work smarter or work longer. For example, testing might be prioritised so that the most important areas of the software from the user's perspective are tested first. It may also be possible to automate certain areas of testing or to outsource it to specialist testing companies. Programmers might be asked to focus more on static testing (which is particularly effective at finding faults) and to work overtime to beat their deadlines.

However, the project manager must be aware that adding resources to a late running project often slows the project down as established members of the project team explain requirements, standards and procedures to any newcomers. A key factor here will be the precision of the requirements. If these are well specified then it should be possible to add testing staff reasonably effectively, or indeed to outsource testing to countries where it can be conducted relatively cheaply. It may also be possible to bring in technical authors and automated testing tools specialists who can speed up these activities. Programming is more of an issue. It will be very difficult to bring new programmers up to speed. However, it may be possible to transfer resources from other projects and to support the established programmers by providing appropriate hardware and software.

Finally, the addition of resources to the project will have an impact on project profitability. The project estimate will have assumed a certain commitment of resources. Adding resources will reduce the profit margin and indeed, in the extreme, may make the project itself unprofitable.

(c) There is no correct answer for this part of the question. However, it is suggested that a combination of the above strategies would be appropriate. The deadline is not crucial in the wider scheme of things and there is no statutory requirement to deliver on time. However the deadline is significant to the customer and a failure to meet this deadline may cause internal problems and a 'loss of face'. This is particularly significant in this context because ASW is an external supplier. It might have been easier to negotiate an extended deadline if the software were being supplied by an internal IT department. Hence, it might be suggested that, in these circumstances, the deadline should not be extended for an initial release. However, it may be possible to negotiate the scope of this release, making sure that the key functions are in place and tested when the software is delivered. The customer might accept this reduction in scope as recognition of the delays caused earlier in the project when, due to the absence of key personnel, the full system specification was signed off three weeks late.

It could be argued that the current tasks of ASW, system testing and writing the user manual, could be shortened by adding further resources to the project. Effective testing will depend upon the quality of the specifications but it may be possible to add more resources and back this up with reduced test coverage. The amount of testing performed is driven by risk. There has to be a balance between the cost and time of more testing and the consequences of failure. Although the insurance system appears to be mission-critical to CaetInsure, there is a robust current system that could be reverted to during the planned parallel running.

It would also appear that more resources could be added to writing the user manual. There is already slack between the scheduled completion of the user manual and its use in the training course.

ASW might also consider starting writing the data migration programs before week 22. It appears from the project plan that ASW are waiting for system testing to be complete before writing these programs. It may be possible to start beforehand, writing migration routines for the parts of the system that have already passed system testing.

The acceptance testing is outside the control of ASW. It is being performed by CaetInsure. However, again CaetInsure might consider reducing the time taken for acceptance testing by adding more resources to the task and by accepting a greater risk of failure during parallel running.

On balance, it might be suggested that further resources are quickly added to the project and that the test coverage is reduced. Hence the solution is largely concerned with adding resources and potentially reducing quality. If the customer is happy to slightly reduce the scope of the initial release to reflect past delays then this is a bonus. However, it is suggested that in this project the delivery date should remain fixed. Relaxing this is not an appropriate strategy in this instance.

ACCA marking scheme		
		Marks
(b)	Up to 1 mark for each relevant point up to a maximum of 3 marks for each strategy	10
(c)	Up to 2 marks for each relevant point up to a maximum of 6 marks for this part of the question.	6
Total		**16**

Examiner's comments

The project described in the scenario was slipping and, at present, it seems unlikely that it will meet its target delivery date. The part (b) of the question asked candidates to evaluate alternative strategies available to the project manager to address the project slippage problem. This was answered relatively well, with many candidates giving a range of options.

Finally, the last part of the question asked candidates to recommend and justify a preferred solution to the project slippage problem. There was often some overlap in answers between this and the previous part question. The distinction was that part b was really looking for the range of options available to the project manager, while part c required the candidate to select from that range, probably suggesting a mixed strategy. Many candidates did not adequately justify their answer in the context of the scenario.

37 QUARAX

Key answer tips

Part (a) is possibly more involved than a typical P3 question on this area may be. But it should serve as a good refresher on this topic. In part (b), make sure you focus upon the competitive and strategic level benefits and not operational level benefits such as time taken to process orders and the improvement to information organisation and presentation. Also ensure that you evaluate any benefits presented. Finally do not discuss the improved accounting software, as this is not what the question asked.

(a)   Financial Analysis of Project E

Net Present Value Calculation: (US$)

Time	0	0.5	1	2	3	4	5
Gross profit/cash inflow (W1)			33,333	36,667	40,333	44,367	48,803
Accounting Package	(14,000)						
Tailoring of above		(20,000)					
E-commerce package	(11,000)						
Tailoring of above		(8,000)					
Populating database		(5,000)					
Training			(10,000)				
Support (25 ÷ 5)			(5,000)	(5,000)	(5,000)	(5,000)	(5,000)
Hardware etc			(40,000)				
Broadband costs (20 ÷ 5)			(4,000)	(4,000)	(4,000)	(4,000)	(4,000)
Cash flow	(25,000)	(33,000)	(25,667)	27,667	31,333	35,367	39,803
Discount factor at 15% (W2)	1	0.933	0.870	0.756	0.658	0.572	0.497
PV	(25,000)	(30,789)	(22,330)	20,916	20,617	20,229	19,782

NPV   +**$3,425**

W1
Turnover in year 1   1,000,000
Increase from e-commerce (10%)   100,000
Profit (100 × 50/150)   **33,333**
This then grows at 10% p.a.

W2: DF for t=0.5
DF = $1/(1.15)^{0.5}$ =   0.933

The positive NPV of $3,425 suggests the project should be accepted.

However, this figure is rather small so sensitivity analysis is recommended to review key estimates. It should also be noted that this is a conservative estimate which ignores any benefits after 5 years of the systems being implemented. Furthermore the payback period is not until the 4th year. Financially therefore it is attractive but appears to be high risk.

(b)   The strategic and competitive benefits to Quarax of the proposed e-commerce system

The proposed e-commerce business will impact on every activity in Quarax. Using Porter's value chain, the benefits to each part of the organisation can be evaluated.

Primary Activities:

Inbound Logistics – Quarax builds components for old machinery. In order to establish which raw materials will be required for a part not made before, a qualified engineer either searches Quarax's archives for drawings or obtains them from the Original Equipment Manufacturer (OEM). This is only the beginning of the costing process carried out by the engineer who must then pull together an estimate to be approved by the customer. An e-commerce system would allow archives to be held on the system, possibly with links to OEM archives as well. The internet would be a key resource to see if components were being supplied by competitors and at what price. Quarax could therefore ensure a competitive quote or even access drawings from other sources.

If the parts required for each component were listed on the system, together with supplier details, it is possible that automatic orders for raw materials could be generated once a customer accepts a quotation. It would also be possible to give customers prices for components made previously by Quarax immediately; price lists could be available via email for example.

The work the qualified engineer carries out before the price is accepted by the customer needs to be kept to a minimum to maintain competitive advantage. By transferring purchasing information onto an e-commerce system and computerising archives with links to external information via the internet, as well as making electronic price lists and on line ordering available to customers, Quarax should be able to cut costs and so benefit strategically.

Operations – The production department is not able to schedule work until an accepted order is passed to them by a sales manager. If Quarax had an e-commerce system in place and orders were placed electronically, these orders could interface with the production schedule which could update automatically. This would be of particular strategic benefit if the system recorded standard labour hours for each 'known component'. The customer could be given an accurate completion date electronically, improving Quarax's core competence in customer care even further.

The small proportion of Quarax's business which comes from the large multinational OEM's may grow once these companies are able to deal with Quarax electronically. Since profits have been stagnant for the past 2 years, this would be hugely beneficial.

For items not made before, the estimate of the labour hours could also be built into the production schedule. One of the main strategic benefits to Quarax would be the ability to calculate instant variances using the e-commerce system. Since the production schedule will have standard or estimated hours built in to it, any overrun can be immediately flagged and investigated. Similarly, any estimate which is not correct can be altered to produce a realistic standard cost going forward.

Outbound Logistics- Quarax holds low levels of finished goods inventory already since goods are made to order. The main strategic benefit of an e-commerce system where outbound logistics is concerned will be the ability to give customers an accurate idea of when their components will be ready for delivery. In this way, Quarax can maintain their competitive advantage of minimal inventory holding costs.

At present, inventories of the most commonly ordered components are kept. With an e-commerce system, Quarax will have accurate, up to date management information as to which components should be included in this category. The system of holding such components as inventory could be replaced by a 'predictive' ordering system where Quarax assigns each component a realistic 'life expectancy' and a repeat order to a customer is automatically generated by Quarax's system at the end of that life. Quarax receives a significant amount of repeat business and regular customers are likely to see this as very beneficial.

Sales and Marketing – Quarax has not experienced growth for the last two years and this could be down to a lack of advertising and a reliance on 'word of mouth'. If Quarax invests in an e-commerce system and has its own website, growth is likely to result from potential customers searching the internet for suppliers. At present, with no internet presence, such potential buyers do not know that Quarax exists. A website would be advertising in itself and could be used to inform customers about Quarax's core values and mission statement as well as answer 'frequently asked questions'.

Service – If customers are given access to a website and an email address, they will be able to submit queries to Quarax. Dealing with customer enquiries on a timely basis will enable Quarax to maintain the personal service they pride themselves on. In addition, it will be possible to maintain customer mailing lists on line and to communicate on a regular basis with those businesses that have purchased components from Quarax.

Secondary Activities

Procurement-As previously mentioned Quarax will be able to save money with e-procurement, automatically searching the internet for the cheapest supplier of raw materials and therefore forcing suppliers to compete on price.

Information Technology- Quarax's accounting systems are not automated and transactions are recorded in manual ledgers. Investment in a computerised system means that Quarax can implement internal controls, reduce the risk of human error and become more competitive as a result. The quality of management information produced on an IT system will far outclass anything the company has at present.

HRM – In the future, Quarax is likely to need fewer employees since much of the manual work will be done automatically on the system. Currently, Quarax has 120 staff who, if they are retained may find they have more time to work on growing the business as their 'manual' workload decreases.

Infrastructure- The e-commerce system may bring beneficial changes to the culture and structure of Quarax, allowing it to be more flexible. Since far more information will be available on the system, it may be possible to alter working practices and gain competitive advantage. New roles could be created looking after overseas customers for example, who are now able to order via the internet. The strategic and competitive benefits of the new e-commerce system to Quarax can be seen throughout all of the businesses activities. In the long term, these benefits will enable costs to be cut and efficiencies to be exploited. Ultimately, Quarax will be able to provide a better service to more customers.

38 A CLOTHING COMPANY

Key answer tips

It is important that you recognise that each part of the question concerns different parts of this chapter – part (a) is on project initiation (and the PID in particular), whilst part (b) is on project management and how a manager can attribute to this. Don't mix the parts up and ensure that you put the right elements in the right part (your pocket notes should help here). After that you have to remember to apply your knowledge to the scenario.

Project .
Initiation .
Document .

(a) The production of initial documentation concerning the business case and initiation of the project would have addressed many of the issues that subsequently arose in the website re-design. This documentation would typically include:

- A summary of the business justification of the project. These are the business objectives that have been defined in the business case to justify the project.

- The scope of the project, defined in terms of project objectives and ultimate deliverables.

- Constraints and targets that apply to the project.

- Project roles and responsibilities, for example; the definition of the project sponsor and the project manager. It is useful if this part of the document specifies the level up to which named individuals (or roles) can authorise:

- The commitment of resources

- The sign-off of deliverables

- Changes to project objectives and deliverables

- Changes to constraints

- Resources committed to the project

- Risks and assumptions associated with the project. These are considered below in the context of the clothing company's website re-design project.

The business justification of the project

The MM does specify business objectives such as 'increase sales revenue' and 'improve market visibility' (see meeting 1) but these are poorly defined objectives in that they are not quantified. A formal cost-benefit analysis undertaken at the start of the project would have forced the MM to quantify how much sales would increase and by when. The MM would also have been required to document the assumptions behind these predictions and to demonstrate a causal link between the functionality of the website and sales volume. The other suggested objective, improve market visibility, also requires further specification and quantification. The MM provides no evidence of current market visibility (and what this actually means) and how its improvement will be measured. Some research is needed to quantify market visibility and to set realistic targets for its improvement. The statement of the project's business benefits is an important issue in contemporary project management. It is suggested that these benefits are kept constantly under review to ensure that the project has not strayed from its original justification. Furthermore, at the end of the project, the business benefits have to be reviewed to assess whether they have been realised. Because the MM has not specified measurable objectives in advance, the success of the project is impossible to assess. There is no benchmark to assess it against.

The scope of the project

On at least two occasions there appears to be confusion about the scope of the project. The TD originally produces a design that is too like the current site, 'We expected it to do much more' (meeting 2). However, the most significant misunderstanding about scope is between the board and the MM. It concerns the interpretation of the scope of the word 're-design'. The board appears to perceive that re-design does not include the development and implementation of the software, while the MM holds the opposite view. The scope of the re-design would have been clarified in a project initiation document.

Constraints that apply to the project

Constraints are often defined in terms of cost and time. The absence of a formal cost-benefit analysis for this project has already been recognised, so costs (and budget) were not formally agreed at the start of the project. There is also no evidence that a projected delivery time for the project was agreed at the start of the project. Indeed, it was the elapsed time, as well as the escalating cost, that first caused the board to be alarmed about the website re-design project. It also appears that the TD had technical constraints in mind which were also not articulated. These emerged in meeting 4 and caused delays documented in meetings 5 and 6. Again, technical constraints should have been documented in the project initiation document.

Project roles and responsibilities

Although it is not clearly stated, it appears that the sponsor of the project is the MM. However, at one critical point of the project the RP makes a decision to accept a design (meeting 4) which is subsequently overturned by the MM. This confusion of responsibility causes both cost and delay. If project roles and responsibilities had been properly defined, then it would have been recognised that the RP did not have sufficient authority to sign-off deliverables. Furthermore, the formal allocating of roles would have also meant that a project manager would have been nominated with the responsibility of delivering the project. In the scenario there is never any clear indication of who is playing the role of project manager and this is a major flaw.

Resources committed to the project

There is no evidence that the resources available to the project had been identified and documented at the start of the project. Problems only begin to emerge late in the project when the Board's decision to launch on 1 March prompts the TD to express concern that there are not enough developers to deliver the system on time.

Risks and assumptions associated with the project

Most project management methods suggest that risks should be formally documented and managed. Each risk is identified and its potential effect quantified. For each significant risk, avoidance actions are suggested which are steps that can be taken to prevent the risk from occurring. Mitigation actions are also defined for each risk. These are steps that can be taken to reduce the impact of the risks if they occur. Again there is no evidence to show that this has been done. As problems emerged in the project they were dealt with on an ad hoc basis. A consideration of risk at the outset of the project can lead to changes in how the project is conducted. For example, the risk of poor scoping of requirements could have prompted a more formal definition of requirements scope (an avoidance action).

Initial project structure and arrangements for management control

This is an initial project structure describing how the project will be broken down into stages with an associated list of project milestones. It is a very high-level plan which provides a context for the detailed plans that will follow. There is no evidence of such a structure in the website re-design project and so the absence of detailed planning (see below) goes unnoticed. The project initiation document might also include management control information concerning, for example, progress reporting and monitoring arrangements. If these had been defined in advance then their absence (see below) would have been clear in the actual project.

(b) Effective project management could have improved the conduct of the website re-design project in the following ways:

Detailed planning

During the delivery of the project the lack of a formal detailed plan means that there is no baseline for review and control. The absence of monitoring progress against that plan is also very evident. The meetings are events where, although progress appears to have been made, it is unclear how much progress has been made towards the delivery of the final re-designed website. Effective project management would have mandated the production of a detailed plan. There is no mention of a project plan, a critical path analysis, a Gantt chart or supporting project management software.

Effective monitoring and control

The board were not kept up to date about progress and were only alerted to potential issue when the finance director became concerned about spiralling costs. This is a failure of monitoring and control, aggravated by the fact that there is no project plan to monitor against. Effective project management would have required formal progress to the sponsor (in this case the board). Such monitoring should lead to project control, where suggested actions are considered and implemented to deal with project slippage. The planning, monitoring and controlling aspects of project management are completely absent from the scenario and so none of the usual project management monitoring and reporting structures were in place to alert the board.

Mandating of substitutes

Initial progress is hampered by the absence of key personnel at meetings 3 and 4 and the inappropriate sign-off by the RP (already discussed above) of the technical design. The requirement for the TD to produce a technical report also slows progress. These problems could have been addressed by ensuring that substitutes were available for these meetings who understood their role and the scope of their authority. Effective project management would have ensured that progress would not have been delayed by the absence of key personnel from the progress meetings.

Standards for cost-benefit analysis

The cost-benefit analysis provided by the MM is flawed in two ways. Firstly, the assumptions underpinning the benefits are not explained. There is no supporting documentation and it appears, at face value, that year four and five benefits have been greatly inflated to justify the project. Secondly, it would be usual to discount future costs and benefits using an agreed discount rate. This has not been done, so the time value of money has not been taken into account. Effective project management would have defined standards for the cost-benefit analysis based on accepted practice.

Estimating, risks and quality

The reaction of the board to the cost-benefit analysis also appears unrealistic. They appear to have suggested a budget and a timescale which does not take into account the complexity of the remaining work or the resources available to undertake it. The estimating part of the project management framework appears to be lacking. It is clear at the final meeting that the website will not be ready for launch. However, the MM decides to take the risk and achieve the imposed deadline and take a chance on the quality of the software. This decision is made against the advice of his TD and without any information about the quality of the software. Effective project management would have mandated a framework for considering the balance between risk and quality.

The MM does not inform the board of the TD's advice. The MM, like many project managers (because the MM now appears to have adopted this role) finds it politically more acceptable to deliver a poor quality product on time than a better quality product late. Unfortunately the product quality is so poor that the decision proves to be the wrong one and the removal of the software (and the resignation of the MM) ends the project scenario.

ACCA marking scheme		
		Marks
(a)	Up to 2 marks for each relevant point relating to the scenario	15
(b)	Up to 2 marks for each relevant point relating to the scenario	10
Total		**25**

Examiner's comments

This question was the least popular of the optional questions and it was also very poorly answered. Some candidates did appear to have a theoretical understanding of this part of the syllabus, but they failed to apply such knowledge to the circumstances described in the scenario. Most answers were general descriptions of the contents of a business case and a project initiation document. Such answers gained few marks, because this was not the focus of the question. The question concerned how such things would have helped prevent some of the problems documented in the scenario.

The second part of the question asked candidates to analyse how effective project management could have further improved both the process and outcomes of the web re-design project. This was an opportunity to discuss issues of the conduct and conclusion of a project. The scenario gave plenty of opportunity for the basis of a good answer, but most candidates again opted for a restricted, theoretical answer which did not use the context of the scenario. Some candidates also repeated some points from the first part of the question (concerning project initiation), failing to note that this part of the question specifically asked for further improvements.

39 M UNIVERSITY

Key answer tips

For part (a), 'Project management (PM) software' simply means using a computer system to do the job of a project manager, rather than the traditional pen and paper. Most of the advantages of using PM software to do a job would equally well apply to using any software to do any management-type job — so don't be afraid to use your imagination here! Take care to read the question carefully — it calls for a discussion of PM software, so don't go crazy listing its many functions — the marks are for advantages and disadvantages!

(a) **Project Management Software**

Many Project Management Software (PMS) applications have been written and released by software development houses to automate the handling of project management techniques. Typically PMS applications have graphical user interfaces (such as Windows) that allow easy manipulation of large volumes of data by the project manager. A very common example of PMS is Microsoft Project, part of Microsoft's Office suite.

PMS can perform a variety of different functions, such as calendars to handle time, construction of graphical models such as Gantt charts and network diagrams, resource planning functions such as production of resource histograms, and automatic production of slippage reports or progress reports, among many others.

How PMS might help the finance director and his team successfully carry out the project

Complexity

PMS is excellent for handling complex projects with large numbers of activities and resources. The M University project is a complex one, with many different facets, from constructing living accommodation, teaching accommodation, sports and recreation facilities, etc. It is doubtful that such a complex project could be adequately managed without PMS – a fact already acknowledged by the finance director (FD).

Accuracy

PMS automatically calculates project plans – thus removing human input from this part of plan generation. Assuming correct data is input into the PMS, accurate plans will necessarily be created for use in executing the project. This should help to reduce the risk posed to the project from inaccurate or inadequate planning.

Ease of use

Due to its graphical user interface, PMS such as MS Project is reasonably easy to use. It shares many consistent features with other MS Office applications, therefore the experience the FD will almost certainly possess in using MS Excel and Word will make learning MS Project relatively straightforward. This should reduce the time required for the FD to become adept at using the package, as well as his confidence in using it.

'What-if' analysis

'What-if' analysis involves changing individual variables in a project plan, and viewing the effect of this on overall project plans. The PMS can instantly recalculate the project plans in view of changes to variables, making it quick and easy for the FD to view the effect of alternative possible resource allocations on the overall project plan. This makes it quick and easy for the FD to generate alternative plans and contingency plans, and to evaluate different ways of using float identified in network charts.

Affordability

PMS is relatively cheap, costing perhaps $200 to $400. This is a relatively inconsequential sum of money compared to the likely overall total cost of the M University student village project – likely to be running into tens of millions of pounds. Compared to the benefits of having such software in the execution of the project, it is likely that the FD will consider the purchase and use of PMS to be eminently justifiable.

How PMS might hinder the finance director and his team in successfully carrying out the project

Even though it is apparent that the student village project is unlikely to be possible without PMS, it is important that the FD realises that PMS is simply a tool, and like any tool it can be used well or badly. Therefore it is useful to remind the FD that PMS can cause problems:

Use of estimates in creating plans

As indicated earlier, if the data input into PMS is accurate, then accurate plans will be raised by the PMS. Necessarily however, the majority of the data input into PMS will be based on estimates, and estimates can vary wildly with the experience levels or temperament of the estimator. The visually appealing and professional looking plans created from PMS can often mask the extent to which the plans are based on estimates, leading to false confidence in the plans, or a failure to recognise the subjective nature of the estimates.

Over-emphasis on maintaining plan at expense of managing the project

It is tempting for a project manager to become too focused on maintaining a plan in a large project, and therefore leave himself too little time to ensure the project itself is being managed adequately. The role of the project manager extends to more than simply creating plans – it also includes leading and motivating team members, viewing progress on the project, communicating with all stakeholders, etc. The student village project of M University is a large, complicated project, and the FD must consider carefully whether he should delegate the inputting of data into the PMS to a subordinate and use reports generated by the PMS to manage the project.

Consideration of skill levels

Project teams are made up of human beings – individuals with differing levels of skill, motivation, etc. It is possible for project managers to lose sight of this simple fact when immersing themselves into PMS, a tool that tends to manipulate resources and treat people as mere appendages to machines. When managing the M University project, the FD needs to be careful that throughout the planning of his project he keeps in mind that his team members are individuals. He should get to know these people so as to get the best use out of them, something that is beyond even the most advanced examples of PMS.

(b) **Why the finance director should consider the interests of the different stakeholders in the student village project**

Stakeholders are defined as being 'those persons and organisations that have an interest in the strategy of an organisation or of a project'. The student village project is a complex undertaking with a number of different stakeholders, and the initial reaction of two of the stakeholder groups of the student village project (namely the local residents and the affected university department staff) have been hostile to the student village project.

The FD must recognise that the stakeholders of the student village project can affect the successful outcome of the student village project, since they have power that they can exert over the project. If these stakeholders do not have their views taken into account in the student village project, conflict with M University might occur, and this might threaten the ability of the FD to successfully achieve the project objectives.

For example, it is within the power of local residents of the student village to influence the actions of the members of the local authority, either directly in meetings with their councillors, or indirectly through the power that they wield at local election time. The local authority members might, in turn, decide to withhold planning permission for the student village on the proposed site, or even decide not to sell the land to the University at all.

It is also likely that the staff of the two M University departments affected by the move would be unionised, and therefore industrial action might result from the staff (and also unionised staff of unaffected departments) that might threaten the ability of M University to deliver the new student village.

It is vital to the success of the student village project that the FD fully assesses the interest of both the local residents and the affected staff, as well as other stakeholders, so as to understand the reasons behind their initial opposition to the project. The FD can then draw up a detailed plan to try to win over the support of these interested groups to the project and so reduce the risk posed to the project's successful completion from these groups. The FD must do this in a way that continues to enjoy the support of other stakeholders in the project, such as the two local businesses involved in funding the venture.

40 ASHFELT

Key answer tips

In part (a) of this question it would be better to use Mendelow's power-interest matrix to assess the stakeholders of the company. Also remember in part (a) to answer all part of the requirement – it is necessary that stakeholders are not just assessed, but that you also explain how this can assist project management.

(a)   Stakeholders are the groups or individuals who have an interest in the project and its outcome. *Process stakeholders* have an interest in the process of the project work. The *outcome stakeholders* have an interest in the completed project. Some stakeholders might be both process and outcome stakeholders.

The process stakeholders include the shareholders of Ashfelt, who have an interest in the successful and profitable completion of the project. Similarly, the sub-contractors and their shareholders have a stakeholder interest for the same reason.

The senior management and directors of Ashfelt might have an interest in the project process, because successful completion of the project could affect their future prospects for career advancement and rewards (for example, bonus payments).

Individuals working on the project are process stakeholders. They are paid for their involvement in the project work, and could also be affected by the security aspects and the threat of action by demonstrators and protestors.

In view of the threats of demonstrations and disruption, the police force which has to maintain law and order, and the security firms involved in providing protection, have a stake in the project process. They will want to ensure that, as far as possible, order is maintained and individuals and assets are protected.

Central government, local governments and the protest groups are both process stakeholders and outcome stakeholders. Central government (the transport department) are sponsoring and financing the scheme, and so are concerned that the scheme should be completed on time and within budget. The central government will also have a concern that the completed scheme should meet its intended objectives for the improvement of road transport.

Local government, and presumably the protest groups, are also concerned with the process of the road-widening. Local governments will want to ensure that excessive environmental damage is not caused in their area. Protestors will be involved in demonstrating, and perhaps trying to disrupt, the project work. All of them also have a concern about the outcome from the project, which is likely to be a deterioration in the environment. The outcome will therefore affect the general public as a whole, not just the members of the protest groups.

The strength of the various stakeholder groups can be assessed with reference to their ability to ensure that their interests are protected or promoted. Clearly, two of the most influential stakeholders in this project are the central government, which is financing the work and can decide what should be done by the contract: if it is influenced by political pressure against the project, it also has the power to bring the project to an end. The management of Ashfelt are also major stakeholders, because they will decide how the work should be planned and implemented and they have control over day-to-day project operations.

However, the protest groups and the police authorities might also be significant stakeholders in this project. The strength of the protestors depends on their ability to arouse sympathetic publicity and political support, or to disrupt construction work. If a serious disturbance to the peace is threatened, the police force might use its power either to control the demonstrators or possibly to restrict the progress of the construction work.

The strength of the local governments is likely to be fairly limited, since local government is usually required to comply with the wishes of central government.

The strength of the protestors and the police cannot be properly assessed until the project work begins. However, the management of Ashfelt as well as central government will need to monitor the views and activities of these groups.

Trying to understand the concerns and interests of stakeholder groups – and the strength of each group – could be valuable for the management of Ashfelt. Instead of assuming that confrontation with protestors and demonstrators is inevitable, the management of Ashfelt might consider ways of restricting the impact of some of the work and consult with representatives of the protest groups. Similarly, Ashfelt management could consider the concerns of the police authorities, and take suitable measures to reduce the likelihood of police intervention to halt or slow down the construction work, in order to preserve public order.

Even if Ashfelt management cannot reach any meaningful agreement with the protestors, trying to understand their views, and what they might do to enforce their views, could be necessary simply in order to ensure the successful completion of the project work.

For central government, the issue is somewhat different. Central government should try to understand the concerns of the protest groups and the local government authorities, because losing the 'publicity war' with these groups could be damaging politically to the government.

(b)   Crucially, the feasibility study should consider how the work would be done, and whether all the conditions set by the customer (the central government) can be met, and whether the target completion date can be met. Ashfelt should not consider taking on the project if it does not have the necessary skills and resources to do the work successfully.

It might be necessary to carry out a technological feasibility study, if any aspect of the work might involve the use of complex or untried technology and construction methods.

The project must also be consistent with the overall business objectives of Ashfelt. In the case of this particular project, Ashfelt might have some concerns for the adverse publicity that the project might attract, and the possible damage to its reputation with the general public. On the other hand, if an important business objective of the company is winning contract work from central government, the feasibility study would consider the implications for future contract work of taking on this current project from the government.

Ashfelt is a profit-making business entity, and a feasibility study for the project should consider the financial aspect of the project. The project should be considered 'feasible' only if the expected return on the work is consistent with the company's financial objectives and targets. For example, if Ashfelt expects to make a return of at least 15% on a discounted basis on all its project work, the project should be evaluated and should not be undertaken if this financial target will not be achieved.

The feasibility study should also consider the social and ecological implications of the work that it will be doing. An ethical company should seek to avoid social and environmental damage where this is avoidable.

The feasibility study should also consider the risk implications of the project. The financial risk might be assessed through sensitivity analysis, and the operational risk might be considered by means of scenario testing, and considering 'worst possible' potential outcomes.

41   CFS

Key answer tips

In part (a) you must discuss project management skills, rather than writing everything you know about project management.

Part (b) is a more routine discussion of social responsibility and competitive advantage.

(a)   Simply defined, a project is 'activity that has a start, a middle and an end and consumes resources' – it is therefore a discrete activity aimed at achieving a specific objective or range of objectives. Graham is intent on using the 'environmentally aware' project to achieve a specific objective – the attainment of the international environmental standard. He is, however, aware that there are a number of internal stakeholders inside the company who question the significance of such a project.

Externally, he can point to significant stakeholders, including customers and government who are looking for CFS to become more environmentally aware. The project is likely to have strategic and not simply operational or administrative significance and the person appointed into the role of project manager, ideally, should have both the traditional skills associated with project management plus those of strategic management. Grundy and Brown list the traditional project management techniques as:

- defining the project(s)
- defining the project scope and interdependencies
- targeting the deliverables or results of the project
- identifying the key activities or sub-projects
- planning and managing timescales
- mobilising resources.

More strategic parts of the project management process will include:

- problem diagnosis
- option generation – not only what to do but how to do it. e.g. acquisitions
- managing stakeholders
- creating a strategic vision for the project
- identifying key implementation difficulties.

Clearly, the project manager must have the technical project management skills, being able to manage the project through its life cycle, which involves:

- defining the project in terms of project objectives and scope as defined by time, cost and quality
- planning the project in terms of breaking the overall project down into separate activities, estimating the resources required and linking activities to resources in terms of time and priorities
- implementing the plan, including reviewing the progress in meeting time and cost objectives and taking corrective action where and when necessary
- reviewing the outcomes of the project in terms of what was delivered to the customer and the extent to which client expectations were met.

The strategic nature of the project means that the project manager must have significant leadership skills, not only of the project team who are likely to come from different functions and parts of the company, but also influential stakeholders inside and outside the company. This implies they should have good 'political' and communication skills as the project is of strategic significance to the company. The ability to show how this particular project fits with the overall strategy of the firm is important. The project is an important part in the achievement of the company strategy and in CFS's case may help it differentiate itself from its competitors. However, the project manager must recognise that there will be resistance from existing managers who are reluctant to see resources committed to projects outside of the traditional value chain of the company. Certainly, the project manager for the 'environmentally aware' project will themselves need to be aware of the external environmental pressures prompting the firm to set itself specific environmental objectives and be able to link into supportive networks and alliances. Finally, Grundy and Brown argue that the project manager will be the key to reviewing and learning from the project, assessing whether defined objectives were achieved, the effectiveness or otherwise of the implementation process and how key stakeholders were managed. The danger is that projects are seen as 'one-off' rather than contributing to the knowledge and learning of the organisation. There may be a significant 'learning curve' that the firm has to go down and look to in order to continuously improve its project management process.

(b)   Increasingly, firms are becoming aware of their social responsibility and their need to develop strategies that are designed to meet this responsibility. Such responsibility can take many forms and is not a new phenomenon – many 19th century firms looked after the housing, education and health needs of the communities where they were located. Michael Porter and Claas van der Linde in their article 'Green and competitive' show how the traditional view that there is 'an inherent and fixed trade-off: ecology versus economy' is incorrect. This traditional view sees the benefits of government-imposed environmental standards, causing industry's private costs of prevention and clean up – 'costs that cause higher prices and reduced competitiveness'. Porter and Linde argue that, with properly designed and implemented environmental standards, firms will be encouraged to produce innovations that use a range of inputs more efficiently (e.g. energy, labour, raw materials) and in so doing increase resource productivity and in offsetting the costs of environmental improvement make industry more, not less, competitive. All too often in their opinion, companies resort to fighting environmental control through the courts rather than using innovation to increase resource productivity and meet environmental standards – 'environmental strategies must become an issue for general managers'.

CFS is, therefore, correct in seeing environmental standards as a positive step towards becoming more, not less, competitive. Key stakeholders in the form of both government and customers are looking to their suppliers to become 'greener'. These challenges are increasingly international and global. Building in positive environmental strategies can help CFS differentiate itself and through improved resource productivity become more competitive. Clearly, it will need the environmental scanning devices to become aware of environmental legislation and change. Awareness can then lead to analysis in the monitoring of macro-environmental challenges and the development of a SWOT analysis to match the company's strengths and weaknesses against the threats and opportunities created by environmental standards. Tools of strategic analysis such as PEST, five forces and value chain analysis lend themselves to understanding the significance of the environmental change and how it can stimulate innovation and, through innovation, competitive advantage.

42   JJG PLC

Key answer tips

There are some factors that affect the risk of all projects – the aim of this question is to apply those factors to three different projects. As you would expect, the risks are different with each project, so part of the question is to ensure that you can evaluate the risks sufficiently well.

The three risk categories that need to be discussed include the size of the project – there are two more to guess. Part (a) of the question simply asks for an explanation of these factors – but remember to show how the different factors fit together to provide an assessment of overall project risk.

Part (b) is the application part of this question. So, using the three factors outlined in part (a), you can now state how risky each project is. Remember to provide reasons for your assessment based on the scenario information.

(a) Systems differ considerably on key factors such as size, project structure and technology being used. These factors will combine to provide a risk assessment on how likely it is for a project to fail.

Project size

In general terms, the larger the size of the project in terms of:

- monetary expenditure
- project duration
- number of staff involved, and
- number of business units affected

the more likely it is to fail. Small projects, involving small amounts of money and affecting relatively few people therefore have a much higher chance of success than large projects, spending considerable sums of money, employing many staff and affecting all business units.

The main issue is that the larger the project, the more complex it is, and so the more things that can go wrong. Smaller projects are literally more controllable because the entire project can easily be monitored by relatively few people.

Project structure

Some projects have a very clear structure. That is, users know exactly what they want, and the system can be planned with outputs and processes clearly defined. A very clear project plan is therefore available and can be followed easily as the project progresses, and so the likelihood of reaching the end of project with a successful system implementation is high.

Projects that have unclear deliverables, or where users change their minds about what is required, are more likely to fail because it is difficult to complete a project where the final outcomes keep changing.

Experience with technology

IT technology is continually changing and developing, which leads to the need for continued training and development of IT staff. However, where training is lacking, or the technology being used is new and unfamiliar, then there is a higher risk of project failure. In these situations there is a higher risk of technical problems that cannot be solved, which will result in the failure of the project.

These three factors can be combined in a table to show the overall degree of risk associated with a project (based on Laudon and Laudon (1996)). Here are the two extremes of risk:

Project Size	Project Structure	Technology Level	Degree of Risk
Small	High	Low	Very Low
Large	Low	High	Very High

(b) **Comment on individual projects**

(i) Salary system

This project appears to be large – presumably all staff within the organisation need to be paid and it will affect all business units. However, the project does not appear to be complex, which will limit the amount of risk.

The project structure also appears to be clear; the Board is quite clear about what is required and there is a straightforward method of obtaining the software. The risk of errors in the software will be low as it is a third party system and will have been tested prior to implementation. Given that the package provides the necessary functionality, then it is unlikely to require any amendment, again decreasing the amount of risk.

No new technology is required to implement the system, so risk in this area is also low.

Risk assessment is low in all three categories, so overall implementation risk is low.

(ii) Inventory system

Although the overall project size is unclear, it may be large in terms of expenditure, as the whole system needs to be replaced. If all business units use the system then the change is pervasive to the whole organisation. The duration is limited, although this may not decrease the risk, as noted below.

Although the project has to be implemented relatively quickly, there does appear to be appropriate planning taking place; there are already plans in place, which indicate a high level of project structure.

There appears to be some risk with technology, as the system is moving from a DOS to a Windows system. File conversion will need to be checked in detail to ensure that no errors occur and that the new Windows system can provide the required reports.

Overall, the risk appears to be medium; Large project size, High project structure and high technology level.

(iii) Extranet

The Extranet project appears to be very speculative. The size of the project is unclear, although it may be relatively large given that it will involve linking internal databases with some form of Internet provision.

There is currently no defined project structure. The project manager has been appointed, but without any clear remit as to what to report or when. At present, there is no project plan or clear idea of deliverables.

The Extranet will mean using quite new technology, in a field that the organisation has very little experience in.

Overall risk is therefore high; medium to high project size, lack of structure and high use of new technology.

43 LDB

Key answer tips

The key to success in this question is to be as relevant and specific as possible. Do not simply regurgitate your notes. Instead only include areas of the project management syllabus area that are relevant to the question being asked, and add as much detail as possible to your suggestions.

(a)   The elements of good project management that helped make the branch rationalisation project successful might include:

    (1)   A sponsor (Len Peters) was appointed to own the project. A sponsor is required to make important and decisive decisions about project scope, conduct and approach. In the case study scenario, the precise terms of the voluntary redundancy arrangements were quickly specified. Without a sponsor projects tend to drift and to stall when important decisions have to be made.

    (2)   The objectives of the project were clearly defined. The target was to cut the number of branch banks by at least 20% and branch employment costs by at least 10%. Quantification makes these specific objectives measurable. It should be clear at the end of the project if the project has successfully met its objectives. Projects that have general objectives, such as 'improve management information' are less focused and more difficult to evaluate.

    (3)   Constraints were specified at the outset of the project. For example, a time constraint was defined (two years) and an operational constraint (no compulsory staff redundancies) agreed. This latter restriction meant that the project team was clear at the onset about the scope of the changes they could implement. If constraints are not defined in advance then project teams might suggest inappropriate solutions.

    (4)   An experienced full-time project manager was appointed. The project team was also made up of full-time staff seconded to the project. This meant that they could focus completely on the project and not be distracted by their usual jobs. Part-time secondments to projects rarely work because the team members still have to undertake elements of their day job and the urgency of these often takes precedence over project work.

    (5)   Potential slippage in the project and its cause was identified and dealt with relatively early in the project's life. This meant that early re-scheduling could be carried out and an extension to the deadline agreed. It helps the management of expectations and helps avoid unexpected last-minute changes in scope.

    (6)   The project team formally conducted benefits realisation, reporting on the actual performance of the project. This confirmed that the original objectives had been met. A formal post-project meeting was also held to review lessons learnt on the project. This led to a change in estimating assumptions which had lead to the original optimistic values. Lessons are learnt on many projects which are not fed back into the project management system. Consequently, another team commits the same mistake or operates under the same false assumption.

(b)   (i)   LDB could assess the priority of the three initiatives on the process-strategy matrix suggested by Paul Harmon. The matrix has two axes. The vertical axis is concerned with process complexity and dynamics. At the base of the vertical axis are simple procedures often with simple algorithms while at the top are complex processes which may require negotiation, discussion and complicated design. On the horizontal axis is the strategic value of these processes. Their importance increases from left to right with low value processes concerned with things that must be done but which add little value to products or services. On the extreme right of this axis are high value processes which are very important to success and add significant value to goods and services.

From these two axes, Harmon categorises four quadrants and makes suggestions about how processes should be tackled in each quadrant.

Low strategic importance, low process complexity and dynamics

This quadrant contains relatively straightforward stable processes which add little business value. They are processes that must be done in the company but add nothing to the company's value proposition. These processes need to be automated in the most efficient way possible. They are often called 'commodity processes' and are suitable for standard software package solutions and/or outsourcing to organisations that specialise in that area.

Low strategic importance, high process complexity and dynamics

This quadrant is for relatively complex processes that need to be done but do not add significant value to the company's products or services. They are not at the heart of the company's core competencies. Harmon suggests that these should be outsourced to organisations which have them as their core business.

High strategic importance, low process complexity and dynamics

These processes lie in the lower right quadrant of the model. They tend to be relatively straightforward processes which, nevertheless, have a significant role on the organisation's activities. They are central to what the business does. The aim is to automate these, if possible, to gain cost reduction and improve quality and efficiency.

High strategic importance, high process complexity and dynamics

Finally, in the top right hand quadrant are high value, complex processes which often include human judgement and expertise and are often very difficult to automate. Harmon suggests that these might be the focus of major process redesign initiatives focusing on business process improvement through the improved performance of the people undertaking those processes.

(ii) In the context of LDB, the following is suggested. Clearly these are value judgements and credit will be given for coherently argued answers which do not match the examiner's conclusions.

- *The integration of the two bespoke payroll systems currently operated by the two banks into one consolidated payroll system.* Payroll has to be produced but does not add significant value to the end-customer. It is unlikely that the recipients of the system (the bank staff) will notice any difference if a new system is implemented. The bank is considering re-developing this process because of the high cost of updating and maintaining two separate systems. This appears to be of low strategic importance. From the case study it is not clear how complex the payroll requirements are or how difficult it will be to transfer data from the current systems to a new solution. The most obvious approach is to suggest that a standardised software package is bought and data transferred to this solution. It appears sensible to undertake this work using the in-house IT departments who will be familiar with the current systems and so should be able to undertake accurate data mapping and successful data transfer to the new system. However, if this is difficult and time-consuming, there might be some benefit in outsourcing the solution and data transfer problems to a specialist software provider, allowing internal IT to concentrate on more strategic applications.

- *The updating of all personal computer hardware and software to reflect contemporary technologies and the subsequent maintenance of that hardware.* The bank is perhaps looking for efficiency savings through the standardisation of the desktop. Again, this does not appear to directly give value to the bank's customers. Consequently, this also appears to be of low strategic importance. However, it could be of relatively high complexity, particularly when considering the maintenance of hardware. There seems a clear case for outsourcing this process to a specialist technology company who can bring all hardware and software up to date and then maintain it at that level.

- *The development of processes, systems and software to support private banking.* This appears to be of high strategic importance and high complexity. It delivers services to end-customers who the bank has identified as a source of business growth. Elements of human judgement and interaction will be required when providing this service. The fulfilment of personal requirements for the wealthy customer will bring variety, risk and reward. The development of processes, systems and software to support private banking should have high priority and should be developed in-house. The success of such an operation should deliver handsome profits to LDB. This may mean that, given resources are finite, the development of the new payroll system should be outsourced to a specialist in that functional area.

ACCA marking scheme			
			Marks
(a)		Up to 1 mark for identifying an element of good project management (for example; the allocation of a sponsor). Up to 2 marks for describing the significance of each of these elements within the context of the scenario up to a total of 12 marks.	12.0
(b)	(i)	Up to 1 mark for each significant point (for example, describing the implications of a quadrant) up to a maximum of 4 marks.	4.0
	(ii)	Up to 1 mark for each recommendation and up to 2 marks for the justification of each recommendation up to a maximum of 3 marks for each process initiative. Three process initiatives gives a maximum of 9 marks.	9.0
Total			**25**

Examiner's comments

This first part question was poorly answered in two ways. Firstly, too many candidates developed answers that discussed project management in general and did not apply them to the scenario, although these links were relatively easy to make. Unsuccessful candidates are encouraged to read the model answer to see how this part question should have been structured.

Secondly, a significant number of candidates constructed theoretical answers around aspects of project management which were irrelevant or inappropriate to the case study scenario. Such answers seemed to be answering a different question – identify the principles of good project management – to the one set in the examination. Project management appears to be a significant area of weakness despite its relevance to accountants and real-world business.

Candidates need to understand the principles of project management and, more importantly, apply them to a case study scenario. The link between theory and application was very poor.

The second part of the question asked candidates to explain the principles of Paul Harmon's process-strategy matrix and then apply them to three process initiatives at the bank. This part of the question was answered slightly better, although the suggested solutions were often unjustified and many marks could not be given for very brief answers. There were three marks on offer for each solution. Answers such as "buy a software package" or "outsource to a specialist" are clearly insufficient to gain such marks. Answers need to be expanded and clearly justified.

Overall, answers were poor and insufficient for the marks on offer.

44   ELASH INCORPORATED

Key answer tips

(a)   This part also requires you to interpret the Gantt chart. You should aim to identify around 5 or 6 problems, explain them and suggest how they should have been avoided.

(b)   This should be straightforward, using the information given in the scenario and focusing on the relationship and communication issues.

(c)   Note that part (c) has a theoretical component (discuss the problems that may occur) and an application component (how they should have been handled by ZIPS).

(a)   **Problems with the original plan, and recommended changes**

Systems analysis and design – during the 22 weeks of analysis and design, concern was shown that the module teams had not met to co-ordinate and discuss the design considerations prior to integration of the individual modules. To reduce the costly and time consuming changes during integration, the systems analysis and design and module integration stages should have been combined, using an iterative approach to improve the chances of successful integration.

Module integration – the project is now in week 30 and most of the integration is still incomplete. There are problems with data controls within the financial reporting module and a lack of data security and compatibility between all modules.

If the systems analysis and design and module integration had run in parallel in the later weeks of the design activities, the integration problems would have been highlighted at an earlier stage of construction. During this time the inadequacy of controls and lack of security of data transmission between the modules should have been addressed. Some time for testing the integration of the modules and the controls should have also been incorporated into this period.

System testing – the five-week testing phase between module integration and file conversion is inadequate and poorly timed. A complex system such as this requires continual testing throughout the integration process and during the rest of the project implementation.

File conversion – the time allowed for file conversion suggests a radical file structure change, although there is no indication of whether the work is being carried out internally or externally by a bureau. If the database structure is similar to the existing structure, less time could be allowed for file conversion, taking into consideration the testing that should be performed to determine the accuracy and completeness of the converted data.

Changeover – although costs are minimised and less effort is required than for the alternatives, there are significant risks associated with direct changeovers. This method is chosen only when the system being replaced is not large or complicated, the phasing and parallel running approaches are not possible, only a brief changeover period is possible, and the users are in possession of the necessary specialist knowledge. This is not the case with the ZIPS project and a direct changeover could have disastrous consequences for Elash Incorporated if it went wrong. A phased conversion, changing one module at a time over a series of weeks, would give a greater degree of safety with less disruption at any time.

Training – the plan for two weeks' training during the testing phase just for senior managers seems bizarre. Because they are not critical users, they can be trained once the system is up and running.

Training for the users cannot wait until the system goes live. It should take place throughout the development process, as well as during the testing and file conversion phases, reducing the possibility of data entry errors caused by unfamiliarity when the system goes live.

Contingency – the planned contingency of two weeks is inadequate. It should have been extended to eight weeks because of the late arrival of the project manager. Although this would add extra time to the project development cycle, the problems that are likely to occur as a result of attempting direct changeover with inadequate user training will be avoided.

(b)   **Problems in the ZIPS project team relationships**

The main problem with the project team relationship stemmed from the choice of a project manager from Zurtoc. He was absent from the project during the early stages and was not able to perform the role and responsibilities of a project manager. Choosing someone from Elash Incorporated for the project manager could have reduced the team relationship problems. This would have ensured his or her continual presence, which in turn is likely to have improved motivation, communication and a sense of ownership of the project from within Elash Incorporated.

It is generally accepted that the project manager is the one person responsible for the project team's guidance, motivation, output, and control. Unfortunately, the leadership, communication and interpersonal skills of the project manager seemed to be weak. He or she delegated too much responsibility to the module leaders - all from Zurtoc, leading to the subsequent problems of poor module integration. The skills of the staff from Elash Incorporated were not utilised, despite them being in the best position to offer advice and expertise to the ZIPS project. If they had played a more active role within the module teams and been involved more at the analysis and design phase, rather than just the programming staff from Zurtoc, the result would have been a well-balanced and multi-disciplined project team.

Other responsibilities of a project manager are to co-ordinate resources, control the progress of project, set priorities, manage change and conflict and provide the formal process used to measure progress. Because the project manager was not available during the critical early stages of the project, adequate progress control was not maintained and the conflict that was building up between the analysts at Zurtoc and the internal staff of Elash Incorporated went unnoticed. A project manager from Elash Incorporated or a dedicated project manager from Zurtoc would have encouraged quicker decisions and responded to team members' concerns immediately.

(c)   **Communication and team meeting problems**

The progression of the project is dependent on the communication skills of the project manager. As well as the team members, he or she will communicate regularly with the key stakeholders.

Complex projects present some challenges:

- They often involve several parties with different interests, skills, expertise, work and social backgrounds, which may lead to conflict and a breakdown in communications. Some project team members may be dedicated staff committed to work only on the project, whereas some staff may participate in the project only occasionally. Co-ordination of teams and making sure that everyone participates in team meetings can be difficult

- The location of the team members may not be conducive to open communication.

- The delayed benefits of the project can cause a strain on the recipient who is faced with increasing expenditure for no immediate benefit.

Communications and team meetings for the ZIPS project should have proceeded as follows:

- key stakeholders identified

- a project manager with leadership and communication skills is chosen with more care

- channels of communication are established – formal (meetings) and informal (e-mail links and bulletin boards) – to ensure collaboration and interaction between team members and assist in the communication between the module development teams at different locations or the project manager when off-site

- early identification of the interface between the module teams with each team having a leader to communicate regularly with other module leaders, other related departments and the project manager

- team meetings on a structured and regular basis to ensure continuous progress towards the project milestones with the outcomes reported to other team members and the steering committee

- frequent briefing sessions by the project manager to retain interest and momentum in the project and keep the users and other members of Elash Incorporated informed and up-to-date on progress

- regular milestone meetings within all module teams and across module teams.

45 MICKEY'S KITS

Key answer tips

In part (a), don't just state what the problem might be. Try to explain it and, where possible, link it to the scenario. In part (b), it is a good idea to start your answer with a brief definition of what a matrix structure is before applying the pros/cons to the scenario.

(a) A project needs to be managed effectively throughout its lifecycle in order to avoid problems that could lead to project failure.

Without good planning the following problems could arise:

- Increased risk of failure – as part of the planning stage, feasibility studies should be undertaken, along with an assessment of the risks associated with the project. If these activities are skipped, the project manager will not be able to identify potential problems, determine appropriate responses to deal with them nor develop contingency plans.

- Stakeholder conflicts – the planning stage considers the impact of the project on different stakeholders and their likely responses. For example, failure to consider the impact on shareholders from the new project may lead to negative actions later in the project's life if problems develop.

- Scope creep – the planning stage involves determining the project scope. Failure to do this adequately makes the project more vulnerable to changing client specification and increases the chance of the project overrunning in terms of time and cost.

- Budgeting – a key part of the project planning process involves defining clear objectives and setting realistic estimates in terms of time and resources needed. Inadequate planning here would result in unrealistic timescales and possible budget overspend.

- Scheduling – within planning the different activities need to be sequenced in the most logical order and potential bottlenecks identified. Skipping this can result in a failure to make the most effective and efficient use of resources and delays in various stages of the project. Ultimately the project may fail to be completed on time.

- Control – it is at the planning stage that various control mechanisms, milestones and other targets for key deliverables are put in place. Without developing an appropriate control system there is the strong possibility of poor cost control and overspend.

- Teamwork – it is at the early stages within the project that roles and responsibilities are defined for the project team. Failure to do this could lead to duplication of activities or activities not being carried out at all. Furthermore, members of the project team may not work effectively together.

In summary, Donna is putting the smooth running of the project at risk by wanting to remove some elements of the planning stage.

(a)   Matrix structure

Introduction

A matrix structure is often used by firms to manage projects. The key feature of a matrix is that employees have two or more managers to report to. In the case of Mickey's Kits, employees will continue to have their current functional roles with a corresponding functional manager. The matrix suggested would create an additional identity where employees also see themselves as part of product development teams reporting to the head of those teams.

For example, an individual from the IT department could also belong to a team looking at developing a new tennis racquet. They would thus report to an IT manager and the NPD project team manager.

Advantages

The key advantage of a matrix structure is effective coordination of multi-disciplinary teams through the project teams. The lateral communication involved should cut across the barriers that the current functional structure creates. This should ensure that decisions will require less amendment when implemented as all perspectives have been incorporated from the beginning. This is particularly important for Mickey's Kits as speed to market is considered to be a critical success factor.

The structure should also provide for cross functional learning. It would mean, for example, that members from the marketing team would be working alongside the research and development team. This may reduce product failures if the marketing team can help the development team understand more clearly what the customer wants.

Matrix structures allow project teams to be created and changed relatively easily and quickly, giving Mickey's Kits extra flexibility to respond to market developments. This should also result in a quicker speed to market of new products.

Employees will also benefit from the matrix approach as they will learn new skills and have to adapt to solving a range of problems outside their functional specialisms.

Disadvantages

The main problem with matrix structures involves clarifying responsibilities and demands made on employees. Employees may feel stressed and confused when conflicting demands are made by functional and project managers. This is usually resolved by having frequent meetings between functional and project heads, taking up time that could used more effectively elsewhere. In some organisations functional heads have felt that their authority is diluted and project heads given priority.

Linked to the above, staff appraisal becomes more difficult with a matrix structure. There would also need to be more controls and monitoring and the HR department will have to provide more support to staff. All of this will add costs to the business – money that Donna Derry might feel would be better spent on product development.

FINANCING

46 PUBLICLY FUNDED DEPARTMENT

Key answer tips

The scenario of this question relates to a publicly funded service, which has reduced its activity levels to meet more demanding budget constraints. While this has been successfully achieved without making any staff cuts, the service is criticised for its inefficiency and lack of effectiveness. A consideration of the '3 Es' in discussing how the level of service can be improved would be appropriate.

The advisory service has been criticised with reference to last year for overspending its budget, being inefficient as regards its methods of delivery, and wastage of resources that had been allocated to it. Each of these constitutes a severe criticism of the manager of the health advisory service and therefore it is imperative that changes are implemented if the service is to continue.

It is essential that the whole method of operation is re-examined. This will, of necessity, entail a review of its economy, efficiency and effectiveness. In order to determine a revised strategy, the nature of the costs of the organisation must be analysed. Since approximately 80% of expenditure comprises staff costs, this aspect of the problem must be addressed as soon as possible. It seems obvious that the manager has 'protected the staffing levels' in order to avoid problems that might otherwise arise with the staff employed at the advisory service.

It is immediately apparent that major cost savings can only be achieved by tackling the area in which most of the resources are used. It appears that the manager is ineffective and not addressing the fundamental problems that arise as a direct consequence of the high staff costs borne by the organisation.

In order to address the problems being faced it is necessary to establish the overall aims and objectives of the advisory service. The expectations of the administrative authority as regards the publicly funded department need to be clearly understood by each party. It is vital that the aims and objectives of the managers of the advisory service are aligned with those of the authority. The managers need to ensure that the views of the stakeholders are understood and incorporated, insofar as is practicable, into the strategic planning process. Managers must also take steps to ensure that any performance indicators are appropriate to the advisory service. These will need to be reviewed periodically to ensure that they remain appropriate indicators of the performance of the advisory service.

Critical to the successful solution to the problems that have been experienced is the fundamental need for a strategic plan, which is focused and co-ordinated on the attainment of the goals of health advisory service and the local administrative authority. There is a clear need to review present levels of the '3 Es', i.e. economy, efficiency and effectiveness. In order to establish the overall goals and the alternative courses of action that could be implemented at varying levels of funding, a zero-based budgeting exercise could be undertaken.

It is important that the economy of the operation is determined, to ensure that costs are under control. This will entail an assessment as to whether the organisation is currently using the minimum resources necessary in order to provide the present level of services.

This will probably require comparisons to be made with costs of similar organisations in other regions. However, one must be careful to allow for regional variations which can, and will, inevitably exist. Another problem that can hamper comparisons is that output in service organisations is extremely difficult to measure. The provision of advice is common to organisations such as the health advisory service, but the time and resources needed per appointment can often vary considerably, and thus a performance measure such as the number of consultations may be inappropriate as the definitive measure of output.

The efficiency of the advisory service unit must also be measured and this will involve consideration as to whether the resources at the disposal of the advisory service are being used in an appropriate manner. The relationship between the inputs required to achieve the outputs of the advisory service unit will need to be reviewed and this too is a very subjective exercise, as the output of an advisory service cannot be measured in precise terms. In essence, it is attempting to assess the impact of the advice provided by the health advisory service and this will invariably prove to be a difficult task. However, notwithstanding the difficulties involved, it is essential that output is assessed in relation to input.

Lastly, the effectiveness of the organisation requires consideration. The review must establish that outcomes are satisfying the objectives of the organisation. Much will depend on the nature of the objectives that are identified at the beginning, and this will impact upon the extent to which the organisation is considered to be meeting its objectives. Again, this will prove to be a difficult task as the specification and quantification of objectives may well be problematic.

Only when these matters have been subject to detailed review and consideration will it be possible to review the alternative strategies that could be adopted. The potential effect of each alternate strategy will have to be assessed in terms of both the advisory service and the public who are the potential beneficiaries of the advice that is available from the advisory service.

It would be beneficial if managers were to undertake a benchmarking exercise to allow a comparison of the levels of costs and benefits with the inputs and outputs of providers of similar services to the public. This would enable the efficiency of the advisory service to be reviewed and necessary actions taken to meet the expectations of all stakeholders.

47 WOODS EDUCATIONAL INSTITUTION

Key answer tips

You are not given very much detail about the institution in the question, so it is important you make the most of what little information there is in order to make your answer as relevant as possible.

(a) •   In its current position, a financial objective is unlikely to be the major objective of the educational institution. However, as the institution develops its business of offering private sector courses and seminars, such that these account for perhaps 50% of total income, financial objectives will become a more significant element in strategic planning and control.

   •   The institution should first consider what its mission should be. The current mission is relevant to its research and academic programmes. It must decide whether private sector courses are intended simply to provide profits to finance research and academic programmes, or whether there is a new objective in the delivery of these courses. If there is, the mission statement would have to be amended.

- If the purpose of private sector courses is primarily to generate profits to help finance research and academic programmes, there should be financial objectives for sales income and profitability from these courses. The objective might be expressed in terms of achieving sufficient profits from private sector courses to finance a target percentage of research and academic courses. Alternatively, since profitability might be an arbitrary measurement (since many costs of academic programmes and private sector courses, particularly teaching staff costs, are common costs), the objective could be expressed in terms of achieving sales income targets. The aim of the Head of the institution that 50% of its income should come from private sector courses within five years could well be adopted as a strategic financial target.

- Income from the government will remain important. There are two financial objectives that could be relevant to the institution with regard to its cash limits. First, it should aim to remain within the cash limits it is set, plus the net cash income from its private sector training. Second, on the assumption that government policy on cash limits will remain consistent, targets could be set for maintaining or increasing the cash limits each year. This will only happen if the institution's staff produce sufficient research publications and achieve appropriate ratings for teaching quality. A target for cash limits would therefore be a supporting target, subsidiary to the more important objective of achieving the targeted standards of excellence in research and teaching.

- Although the institution is a not-for-profit organisation, it has to operate within its income. The institution appears to want to increase its income, or at least diversify its sources of income, in order to develop. Objectives relating to income and controlling spending within income limits therefore seem essential.

- It is unnecessary to make most of the financial objectives public. However, the institution needs to recognise that the nature of what it does will undergo significant changes. Private sector courses will become a major part of its activities, and this will affect the institution's staff. Teaching staff will presumably be expected to teach to both academic students and practising business executives, and the content of their teaching will have to be adapted for the different types of 'student'. Administrative staff will need to recognise that private sector clients will expect standards of service much higher than academic students would accept. In view of this major change in the character of the institution and its activities, it is important that all staff are fully aware of what is happening, so that they can more readily adapt to the 'new world'.

- It would therefore be sensible to make public a financial objective for increasing the percentage of total income of the institution from private sector training, to a target percentage within a stated period of time (e.g. to 50% of total income within five years).

(b)

Tutorial note

You are asked to choose two from each type of measure. The answer that follows discusses all the measures listed, in order to assist you with your studies.

The measures considered below could be applied primarily to the private sector training activities, and not so much to research or academic education.

Value added

- Value added is calculated as sales income less external purchase costs, such as the cost of materials and external services. Total value added can then be shared between the various stakeholder beneficiaries, which in the case of the institution would be staff salaries, non-current asset depreciation, new non-current asset purchases and so on. (For a company, beneficiaries of value added would also include payments of taxation to the government, payments of interest to lenders and payments of dividends to shareholders.)

- Private sector courses should generate extra value added, which can then be used to pay for more staff and equipment.

- The value added by research activities could be measured by looking at the number of articles that the institution's staff have had published in academic journals.

- Targets can be set for the value added to be achieved each year, and actual value added compared with the target.

Profitability

- The profitability of private sector courses can be measured. The usefulness of profit measures will depend on the extent to which costs can be directly attributed to private sector courses. If large amounts of cost are apportionments of shared costs, such as costs of administration and teaching staff and establishment running costs, then profit measures might be of limited value.

- The non-current assets of the institution may have been provided by the government many years ago, perhaps for free. It would assist the calculation of genuine profitability if fair values could be assigned to these assets for this purpose, for example to estimate a fair depreciation charge.

- It is important that private sector training does earn extra money for the institution, and measures of contribution earned from these activities and directly attributable profit would certainly be useful.

- As the institution develops its private sector training programmes, targets for profitability should rise year by year.

Return on investment

- Return on investment is commonly measured in accounting terms as profit divided by capital employed. The advantage of ROI as a performance measure, compared with profit, is that the amount of profit earned is related to the size of investment required to obtain the profit.

- Capital employed is measured as the book value of net assets, so again it would be useful if all the net assets could be revalued to fair value.

- In the context of the educational institution, it will be important to make sure that private sector training courses are not just profitable, but that they earn a sufficiently large profit to justify the effort and resources committed to them. Measuring ROI could be useful in this respect, although the measurement of profit and the assignment of assets employed to the private sector programmes is likely to be somewhat arbitrary.

- The current wording of the mission statement is entirely qualitative. It would be useful to introduce some quantitative measures such as ROI.

Customer satisfaction

- The purpose of measuring customer satisfaction is to test customer reaction to the organisation's services, which in this case would be the training courses and seminars. Low levels of satisfaction would indicate a need to improve course content or quality of delivery. High levels of satisfaction are necessary to sustain growth in the 'business'. It is widely accepted that setting targets for customer satisfaction (and monitoring actual performance against target) can help with the management of service quality, which in turn should help to achieve long-term growth.

- Unfortunately, the institution is unlikely to be able to afford expensive methods of measuring customer satisfaction, such as an externally-provided quality audit. It is likely to rely on the completion of course questionnaires by delegates at the end of their course. Responses in course questionnaires can be used to monitor the content and delivery of the course, the course materials, the venue, the catering arrangements, and so on – all factors that could influence decisions by customers to return again for more courses in the future.

- In the final analysis, customer satisfaction can be measured indirectly by the number of delegates returning to the institution. If they were unhappy with the course, they would not choose to come again for another course.

Competitive position

- Measurements of competitive position are generally qualitative rather than quantitative. They assess the position of the organisation in its market. In the case of the educational institution, competitive position could be measured in terms of being a high-price or low-price training provider, or a provider of general training programmes or specialist courses, or a provider of business courses or technical courses. The institution should decide what position it wants to establish in the training market, and what position it is currently in. It can then plan to move from its current position to its target position, and monitor progress towards the target over time.

- The major problem in assessing competitive position is to gain reliable information about competitors. You will know all the details about your own business, but you cannot identify your position in the market unless you can gather information about all the market participants.

Market share

- Market share is a measurement of the proportion of the total market that an organisation has captured. It is usually measured as a quantified percentage, such as a 25% market share. Targets can be set for the market share the institution would like to achieve, and actual market share monitored at regular intervals over time.

- However, the private sector training market is very fragmented, and there are no reliable measurements. Even within specific segments of the market, such as business studies training, or engineering training, it is difficult to measure the total market size.

- Targets for market share might therefore have to be qualitative rather than quantitative, such as a target of being the main provider of specific types of course to businesses in a specified geographical area.

- Market share is linked to customer satisfaction in the sense that, if customers are unhappy, they will leave and market share will fall. Therefore market share cannot be pursued as a target in isolation. Market share should be targeted together with a commitment to ensuring customer satisfaction.

48   POTATO-TO-GO INC

Key answer tips

For part (a) of the question, in the appendix, where you calculate the key ratios that you want to discuss in your financial analysis, there would be no need to calculate the ratios for every year. You should only need to compare this year's results to last year's results. In part (b) you might find it useful to bring in Porter's diamond (which is specifically designed to examine overseas expansion). In part (c), don't just list out possible sources of finance – make sure instead that you relate them to the scenario.

(a)   **Financial performance**

Recent performance indicators of the company are shown in the appendix. These show the following trends.

- Turnover has been falling for two years
- Profits have been falling for three years
- Net profit percentages have fallen from 34% in 2003 to 11% in 20X6
- There is now no significant growth in outlets
- Turnover per outlet has been falling for several years.
- In addition, dividend cover is currently very low. If profits continue to fall, then it will not be possible to maintain the current dividend, let alone supply future growth.

The relatively low P/E ratio may be the result of poor growth prospects and/or worries about the company's viability due to the $80m repayment of loan stock.

Appendix – Performance indicators

	20X2	20X3	20X4	20X5	20X6
% growth/(decline)	N/a	19%	2%	(7)%	(5)%
Net profit margin	32%	34%	24%	16%	11%
Turnover per outlet	0.54	0.59	0.58	0.53	0.50

(b)   **Overseas expansion**

Fast food companies such as McDonalds and Pizza Hut have been very successful on a global basis, enjoying marketing and purchasing economies of scale and developing brand strength. However, it is unclear whether the overseas operation that is planned will allow great economies of scale. To obtain those it may be necessary to expand rapidly once the operation has proved itself in the New England market.

North America shares the closest tastes in fast food to Europe, so the product should be well-received. On the other hand, existing types of fast food outlet (burger, pizza, taco, etc) are much more established so PTG will face intense competition.

Apart from the problem of raising finance (which is discussed below) particular problems and risks could arise from managing at a distance, misjudging the market and currency fluctuations.

Local professional advice will have to be sought on location, interior layout and decor, opening hours, prices, wage rates, types of employee and legal responsibilities.

Exit from the venture will be made easier if a separate operating subsidiary is set up with its own management. This would facilitate sale of the undertaking, and might insulate the parent company from some of the financing risks, although the parent company may be required to give guarantees.

(c)   **Financing the overseas expansion**

The lack of internally generated funds means that additional finance must first be raised to redeem the loan stock before considering how to finance the expansion. In total 80 + 130 = $210 million of new funds are required.

Equity

Equity does not appear to be a feasible solution:

- Rights issue: at the end of 20X6 the market capitalisation of PTG was

  $PAT \times P/E = 28 \times 9 = \$252$ million.

  It is highly unlikely that shareholders would be willing to invest a further $210 million via a rights issue. Furthermore, the Edwards family (51% stake) have indicated that they would be unwilling to take up rights, in which case their holding would be diluted.

- Public issue: the Edwards family own 51% of the shares, giving them control. Any significant public issue of shares would dilute their stake to below 50%, a situation they are unlikely to find acceptable.

- In any case the poor dividend cover and low P/E ratio mean that it is not a good time to issue equity.

Debt

Debt looks more attractive:

- If PTG can convince lenders that the decline in profits will not continue, then a replacement loan for the debentures might be available. The gearing level is not excessive and there appears to be plenty of security (non-current assets $180m, net current assets $60m) that could be provided by fixed or floating charges.

- Mortgages could be taken out to cover the bulk of the cost of acquiring overseas premises, though this still leaves fitting out the restaurants and working capital requirements.

Franchising

Global fast food firms often operate on a franchise system.

Franchising has two main advantages in this context:

- The franchisees themselves inject a substantial amount of capital, so helping to fund the enterprise.

- The franchisees have local expertise and experience, thus reducing cultural risks.

Joint ventures

To supply additional finance, PTG could consider a joint venture with a US company which could give further assistance in an unknown market and if it is with an organisation that already has suitable sites there could be considerable advantages.

- The joint venture approach was adopted when Burger King entered the Japanese market.

49   DAVID SILVESTER

Key answer tips

In part (b) of this question you may find it useful to split the critical success factors between those that come from the company's resources and those which come from its competencies (as is shown in the pocket notes).

(a)   **To:**   David Silvester

From:

Funding strategy for Gift Designs Ltd

Clearly, you have identified a real business opportunity and face both business and financial risks in turning the opportunity into reality. One possible model you can use is that of the product life cycle which as a one-product firm is effectively the life cycle for the company. Linking business risk to financial risk is important – in the early stages of the business the business risk is high and the high death rate among new start-ups is well publicised; consequently, there is a need to go for low financial risk. Funding the business is essentially deciding the balance between debt and equity finance, and equity offers the low risk that you should be looking for. As the firm grows and develops so the balance between debt and equity will change. A new business venture like this could, in Boston Consulting Group analysis terms, be seen as a problem child with a non-existent market share but high growth potential. The business risks are very high, and consequently the financial risks taken should be very low and so the financing method should avoid taking on large amounts of debt with a commitment to service the debt.

You need to take advantage of investors who are willing to accept the risks associated with a business start-up – venture capitalists and business angels accept the risks associated with putting equity capital in but may expect a significant share in the ownership of the business. This they will seek to realise once the business is successfully established. As the business moves into growth and then maturity so the business risks will reduce and access to debt finance becomes feasible and cost effective. In maturity the business should be able to generate significant retained earnings to finance further development. Dividend policy will also be affected by the stage in the life cycle that the business has reached.

Yours,

(b) David even at this early stage needs to identify the critical success factors and related performance indicators that will show that the concept is turning into a business reality. Many of the success factors will be linked to customer needs and expectations and therefore where David's business must excel in order to outperform the competition. As an innovator one of the critical success factors will be the time taken to develop and launch the new vase. Being first-to-market will be critical for success. His ability to generate sales revenue from demanding corporate customers will be a real indicator of that success.

David will need to ensure that he has adequate patent protection for the product and recognise that it will have a product life cycle.

There look to be a number of alternative markets and the ability to customise the product may be a CSF. Greiner indicates the different stages a growing business goes through and the different problems associated with each stage. One of David's key problems will be to decide what type of business he wants to be. From the scenario it looks as if he is aiming to carry out most of the functions himself and there is a need to decide what he does and what he gets others to do for him. Indeed the skills he has may be as an innovator rather than as someone who carries out manufacture, distribution, etc. Gift Designs may develop most quickly as a firm that creates new products and then licences them to larger firms with the skills to penetrate the many market opportunities that are present. It is important for David to recognise that turning the product concept into a viable and growing business may result in a business and a business model very different to what he anticipated. Gift Designs needs to have the flexibility and agility to take advantage of the opportunities that will emerge over time.

50   X PLC

Key answer tips

In part (a), the budget for the next four quarters is required. However, closing stock values are determined by the following quarter's sales demand and material usage, so the budget for Q5 will also need to be prepared.

(a)   *Tutorial note:*

Units	Q1	Q2	Q3	Q4	Q5
Sales demand	2,250	2,050	1,650	2,050	1,250
Add closing inventory (W1)	615	495	615	375	616
Less opening inventory (W2)	(675)	(615)	(495)	(615)	(375)
Production budget	2,190	1,930	1,770	1,810	1,490
Raw material usage (× 3kg)	6,570	5,790	5,310	5,430	4,470
Closing inventory (W3)	2,605.5	2,389.5	2,443.5	2,011.5	
Opening inventory (W4)	(2,956.5)	(2,605.5)	(2,389.5)	(2,443.5)	
Purchases budget for B in kgs	6,219	5,574	5,364	4,998	
Purchases budget for B in $	43,533	39,018	37,548	34,986	

Total purchases budget for material B for Quarters 1–4 = $155,085

Workings

(W1) Q1 0.3 × 2,050

(W2) The opening inventory for any quarter is the same as the closing inventory of the previous quarter. The opening inventory for Q1 is 0.3 × 2,250 = 675

(W3) Q1 0.45 × 5,790

(W4) The opening inventory for any quarter is the same as the closing inventory of the previous quarter. The opening inventory for Q1 is 0.45 × 6,570 = 2,956.5

(b) If Material A is in short supply then this becomes the principal budget factor. This will affect budget preparation because the first step in the budgetary process will be to determine the optimum mix of products according to their contribution per kg of Material A. The optimum production plan can then be determined and the sales budget can be derived from the production plan. It may be necessary to revise the policy for holding inventory whilst Material A is in short supply.

Once the production plan has been determined then Material B, labour and overhead budgets can be derived. The limit on the level of production may mean that there is spare capacity in the factory and the fixed overhead absorption rate will increase. This will increase the cost per unit of products and lower profitability. In addition lower production levels may mean that there are spare labour resources. This could mean that output of products which do not use Material A could be increased.

In the long term, if the supply of Material A continues to be limited, X plc may wish to seek alternative sources of supply, change product design or produce alternative products.

(c) Incremental budgeting is a method of budgeting that starts with the current year's budget and adjusts this for known changes. The main problems associated with it are that:

- it can lead to inaccurate allocation of resources;

- managers may build in slack to make achieving targets easier.

Zero-Based Budgeting is a method of budgeting that requires all costs to be specifically justified by the benefits expected. Costs are built up from a zero base and ranked against other activities competing for limited resources. This should eliminate slack and lead to an optimal allocation of resources.

(d) Linear regression analysis can be used to forecast sales when it can be assumed that there is a linear relationship between sales and time. Sales data can be plotted on a scattergraph and a line of best fit fitted by eye for forecasting purposes. Regression analysis is a statistical technique that calculates the line of best fit using formulae given for a and b in the straight line equation:

$y = a + bx$

where y = sales and x = time

Once the formula has been established, this can be used to forecast sales at any future time.

It can be seen that sales of Product W do not appear to have a linear trend over time. Linear regression analysis will therefore not be a suitable method for X plc to use for forecasting.

(e)   (i)   The net present value of a project is the sum of the present values of the future cash flows which have been discounted at a rate which takes account of the time value of money.

The expected net present value takes into account the uncertainty or risk associated with the campaigns by weighting each possible outcome by its probability and finding the sum of the results.

The expected value alone gives no indication of the range of possible outcomes. The standard deviation provides a measure of the spread of the possible outcomes; a higher standard deviation indicates a wide range of possible outcomes and therefore a higher level of risk.

(ii)   The company needs to assess the expected outcome of the different campaigns alongside the level of risk in order to decide which campaign to go ahead with. Campaigns J and L have the same expected outcome but L has a higher standard deviation, indicating a higher risk. Campaign J is therefore preferable to campaign L. Campaign K has the same level of risk as L but a higher expected value. K is therefore preferable to L. Campaign K has a higher expected value than J but also has a higher standard deviation and is therefore more risky. The choice between J and K will depend on the risk appetite of the company and how risk averse it is.

51   SATELLITE NAVIGATION SYSTEMS

Key answer tips

Common errors:

- Demonstrating an inability to link the variances reported to the possible causes, many of which were alluded to in the scenario.

- Not offering in the candidates' discussion many of their own ideas and not developing the report comprehensively.

Report

To   Operations Manager

From   Management Accountant

Date   May 2005

Subject Performance of S Limited for four months to 31 December

Production and sales

Production and sales were 1,100 units in September and October, 950 units in November and 900 units in December. There has thus been a marked decline over the four-month period. This good performance in the first two months and poor performance in the latter two months may be due to a seasonal variation. If this is the case, it would be good for the budget to reflect the expected seasonal variation, rather than just being a flat 1,000 units per month.

Tutorial note: The output was calculated by taking the standard cost of actual output and dividing by the standard cost per system, i.e. $1,276,000/$1,160 = 1,100 units, $1,102,000/$1,160 = 950 units and $1,044,000/$1,160 = 900 units.

Materials

The material price variance was favourable for the first two months, and then very adverse for November and December. This was possibly due to the exchange rate movement if the systems are imported. The effect of the exchange rate variations should be quantified. Any remaining adverse variances may be due to inefficient purchasing by the purchasing manager. It should be investigated as to whether there are alternative suppliers for the systems.

The material usage variance was adverse in every month, but was particularly bad in October and even worse in December. In October the variance was $7,200 A and as the material cost was $400 per unit, this meant that an extra $7,200/$400 = 18 units were used on a production of 1,100 units. In December, the variance was $16,000/$400 = 40 extra units on production of 900 units. This variance could possibly be due to the large batch of systems which did not have the correct adaptors. The variance needs careful investigation in order to find out where the excess units were used, which systems and which teams of fitters were involved.

Labour

The labour rate variance was adverse in September and October and substantially adverse in November and December. Expressing the variances as percentages, for September the standard labour cost was $320 × 1,100 units = $352,000 and thus the variance was $4,200 A/$352,000 = 1.1% A. In November the variance was $5,500 A/$352,000 = 1.6% A. These minor variances could be explained by more overtime than expected being worked, especially as production was high in the first two months. Then things were much worse in the latter two months, for November the variance was $23,100 A/($320 per unit × 950 units) = 7.6% A and in December the variance was $24,000 A/($320 per unit × 900 units) = 8.3%. These substantial variances are almost certainly due to higher wage rates being offered in order to retain the staff and lower the labour turnover. It would be very useful to have information on the number of staff leaving the business. Overtime is unlikely to be the cause for the variances in November and December as production was lower than budget.

The labour efficiency variance was $16,000 favourable in September ($16,000/$352,000 = 4.5% F), zero in October and $32,000 adverse in November and December ($32,000 A/$320 per unit × 950 units) = 10.5% A, and $32,000 A/$320 per unit × 900 units) = 11.1% A). It would be expected that some of this variance was due to the large batch of systems which did not have the correct adaptors. This problem was not apparent until fitting was attempted, thus involving the fitters in extra work. If this were the case then we would expect the labour efficiency variance to tie up with the material usage variance, but it does not. We are also told that there is a fluctuation of ± 25% in the fitting times, so even the substantial variances for November and December fall within this range and thus might not represent inefficiency, but simply the fitting of a higher proportion of more labour intensive systems. It would be useful to have information on the standard times for different systems and the numbers of the different systems, instead of treating all systems alike. The high labour turnover also means that experienced workers are leaving and that new workers are constantly having to be trained. The efficiency of the new workers would be poor to start off with.

Variable overheads

The variable overhead efficiency variance is based on labour hours and thus simply moves in line with the labour efficiency variance.

The expenditure variance was $7,000 A in September, improved to $2,000 A in October and then $2,000 F in November. It was zero in December. For this variance to have any meaning it must be sub-analysed into its different components in order to determine which ones are being overspent and which ones underspent.

Taking the variable overheads as a whole, the variance gets worse as production levels fall, perhaps indicating that the variable overheads are not entirely variable but may include a fixed element.

Fixed overheads

The fixed overhead volume variance simply reflects the better than expected production in the first two months and the worse than expected production in the latter two months. The fixed overhead volume variance has no significance as it does not represent a cash flow (if we make more or less units than expected then the fixed overheads do not change), but is simply a mathematical device to reconcile budgeted profit with actual profit in an absorption costing system.

The fixed overhead expenditure variance is $5,000 A, $10,000 A, $20,000 A and $20,000 A over the four months and thus shows a worsening pattern, but again in order to understand where things are going wrong we need to sub-analyse the fixed overhead into their different components. We have been told that rent, rates insurance and computing costs have risen in price noticeably; these costs may be regarded as uncontrollable. Managers' attention should be devoted to investigating the controllable costs and reducing any overspend.

Conclusion

Overall the actual cost was 4.4% worse than expected (($4,906,201 − $4,698,000)/ $4,698,000). Whilst this variance might not be regarded as significant, the individual variances in many cases are much bigger and should be investigated. There is a marked decline in performance in November and December. It is important that the individual variances are investigated and their causes understood so that future performance improves.

52   ARLAND BANK

Key answer tips

Calculating bank balances for all types of customers should have been feasible by most students, however the calculation of investment revenue foregone would only have been incorporated by the best prepared. Nevertheless, 2 marks would have been given for the calculation of transaction charges under each option, with one mark for interest revenue and a couple for opportunity costs – the savings income at 3%. (2 marks for the calculation of net balances under the existing option.)

(i) **Continuing with existing bank account**

	Workings	Profit £
Business Customers	1 million × (1-20%) = 800,000	
Routine Transactions per year	800m	
Transaction charges	800m × 0.60	480,000,000
Customers with positive bank balances	45% × 800,000 = 360,000	
Interest paid to 'positive' customers	£2,000 average balance × 0.1% × 360,000	(720,000)
Customers with negative bank balances	55% × 800,000 = 440,000	
Interest charged to overdrawn customers	£4,000 average balance × 20% × 440,000	352,000,000
Current profit		**£831,280,000**

Note: Current business customers net balances :

(360,000 × £2000 average balance) - (440,000 × £4000 average overdraft) = £(1,040,000,000)

(ii) **Assessment of each new option**

Account Option One

	Workings	Profit £
Business Customers	1 million × 1.05 = 1,050,000	
Charges	£10 × 12 months × 1,050,000 customers	126,000,000
Customers with positive bank balances	45% × 1,050,000 = 472,500	
Interest paid to 'positive' customers	£2,000 average balance × 0.5% × 472,500	(4,725,000)
Customers with negative bank balances	55% × 1,050,000 = 577,500	
Interest charged to overdrawn customers	£4,000 average balance × 20% × 577,500	462,000,000
Business Customers net balances	(472,500 × £2000 average balance) - (577,500 × £4000 average overdraft) = £(1,365,000,000)	
Opportunity cost	(£1,365,000,000 - £1,040,000,000) × 3%	(£9,750,000)
Option 1 annual profit		**£573,525,000**

Account Option Two

	Workings	Profit
		£
Business Customers	1 million × 1.10 = 1,100,000	
Customers with positive bank balances	45% × 1,100,000 = 495,000	
Interest paid to 'positive' customers	NIL	
Customers with negative bank balances	55% × 1,100,000 = 605,500	
Interest charged to overdrawn customers	£4,000 average balance × 20% × 605,500	484,000,000
Business Customers net balances	(495,000 × £2000 average balance) - (605,000 × £4000 average overdraft) = £(1,430,000,000)	
Opportunity cost	(£1,430,000,000 - £1,040,000,000) × 3%	(11,700,000)
Option 2 annual profit		**£472,300,000**

Conclusion

On the basis of the above calculations, the bank should keep its existing charging structure.

53 OFFMAT INC

Key answer tips

In part (a) it will be important that you don't simply explain the *type* of cost, but focus instead on how it is *behaving* in the scenario. This will mean that you will have to refer to the particular levels of outputs and may have to perform some calculations in order to define the exact relationship between the variables. To score full marks you will also have to discuss the possible *causes* of these relationships.

Part (b) is a much more straightforward variance question. In order to succeed in this requirement you have to begin by calculating the standard cost of materials, labour and overheads for one unit of production using the budgeted information. From that point onwards you then have to work through 6 variances in your usual approach.

(a) Cost behaviour

Average variable cost per unit

This cost appears to exhibiting features of both economies and diseconomies of scale. As the production increases there is a fall in the average cost which reflects economies of scale that could come from bulk discounts, learning curve effects etc. But when production reached 25,000 units, the average cost rises again and exhibits diseconomies of scale. These can be caused by factors such as the duplication of effort or inertia in the business.

Fixed costs

These costs appear to be stepped in nature. They are fixed at certain levels of production, but they appear to rise by $300,000 after each 10,000 units of production. This could be caused by the need for more space or more supervisors as production increases beyond certain levels.

Head office costs

This cost appears to be related directly at 6% of production. Therefore, as production increases this cost increases in a direct, variable nature.

(b) Operating statement

					$
Budgeted production cost	(3,200,000 x 76,000 / 80,000)				3,040,000

Variances:			Fav	Adv		
	Workings		$	$		
Materials price	(W1)		52,000			
Materials usage	(W1)			64,500		
Labour rate	(W2)			48,000		
Labour efficiency	(W2)			58,800		
Overhead expenditure	(W3)		50,000			
Overhead volume	(W3)			32,000		
			102,000	203,300	101,300	A
Actual production cost					3,141,300	

(W1) Material variances

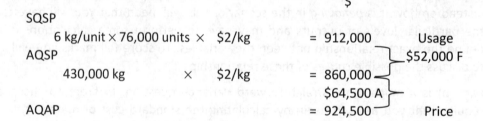

```
                                              $
SQSP
      6 kg/unit × 76,000 units ×   $2/kg    = 912,000         Usage
AQSP                                                         $52,000 F
            430,000 kg        ×    $2/kg    = 860,000
                                             $64,500 A
AQAP                                        = 924,500         Price
```

(W2) **Labour variances – surgical team fees**

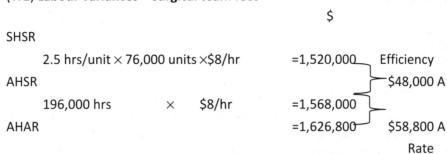

$

SHSR

    2.5 hrs/unit × 76,000 units ×$8/hr   =1,520,000   Efficiency

AHSR $48,000 A

    196,000 hrs   × $8/hr   =1,568,000

AHAR   =1,626,800 $58,800 A

                                                               Rate

(W3) **Fixed overhead expenditure variance**

	$
Budgeted Cost	640,000
Actual Cost	590,000
	50,000 F

Fixed overhead volume variance

	Units
Budgeted output	80,000
Actual output	76,000
	4,000 A
× Std fixed overhead cost per unit	× $8
	$32,000 A

The variances can also be calculated in a more traditional manner as follows:

(W1) **Material:**

Rate variance	=	($2/kg x 430,000hrs) – 924,500
	=	$64,500 (A)
Usage variance	=	(6 kgs × 76,000 × $2) - ($2 x 430,000kgs)
	=	$52,000 (F)

(W2) **Labour:**

Rate variance	=	($8/hr x 196,000hrs) – 1,626,800
	=	$58,800 (A)
Efficiency variance	=	(2.5 hrs × 76,000 × $8) - ($8 x 196,000hrs)
	=	$48,000 (A)

(W3) **Fixed overhead:**

Expenditure variance	=	$640,000 – 590,000
	=	$50,000 (F)
Volume variance	=	(80,000 – 76,000) × ($640,000 / 80,000)
	=	$32,000 (A)

54   COOLFREEZE

Key answer tips

These are new areas to the syllabus but not to the qualification. These are areas that have been covered at lower level papers. However, notice that at this level the emphasis is on the analysis of the numbers in terms of what they tell us and what their limitations might be, rather than on performing lots of detailed calculations.

(a)   **Spreadsheet analysis**

I have had the opportunity to analyse the spreadsheet that you provided. My analysis suggests that the forecasting team used moving averages to help them analyse past sales and forecast the future. This is a well-established technique of analysing a time series and you are incorrect in your assumption that it is "not based on a well-accepted approach".

Explanation of the spreadsheet construction

The technique is based on averaging figures in the time series. For example, column D is calculated by adding up the first four figures (56,70,74,60) and then adding this total to the total moved on by one quarter (70, 74,60,60). This value is than divided by 8 (the number of values in the total calculation) to give the average value in column E. This represents the trend of the time series.

The figures in column F are the variation of the trend from the actual sales figures. These variations are analysed in part 2 where a seasonal variation is calculated.

This seasonal variation is then subtracted from the total variation of each quarter to determine the random or residual variation (column H)

The author of the spreadsheet has checked that the total of the trend plus seasonal plus random variation comes to the original sales figure (column I).

It is difficult to identify where the forecast figures come from. They are roughly in line with the observed trends and represent a very modest increase on the previous year (less than 1% growth). The forecasting group probably thought they were being very realistic.

Analysis

Time series analysis is based on past data. It cannot be used to predict sudden changes in the marketplace. The sales manager had expressed reservations when the forecasts were agreed. His sales staff had already reported that customers were less optimistic about the future because of a weakening economy and the availability of cheap foreign imports. In retrospect, a greater consideration of the external environment should have been included in the overall forecasting approach. Perhaps a number of scenarios should have been considered that took into account changes in the external marketplace.

However, even without such consideration it is clear from the trend figures that growth had been weakening. The growth from 2006 to 2007 (based on the quarter 3 trend figure) was about 11%. In contrast the growth from quarter 2 of 2008 to quarter 2 of 2009 (again based on the trend values) was less than 1%. The final two actual sales figures for 2009 were, in total, exactly the same as the previous year (150 units). This weakening was reflected in the cautious forecasts put forward by the forecasting team. However, there appears very little in the statistical data that suggests that the rapid decline in sales experienced in quarter 2 of 2010 could have been anticipated from the data alone.

The forecasting team might have given further consideration to the sudden increase in random variations in the last three analysed quarters. These might have suggested that the external environment was changing and that other factors were beginning to influence the marketplace. The absolute random variation reported in the last three quarters is greater than that reported in total in the preceding six quarters.

One of the weaknesses of the approach used by the forecasting team is that data from four years ago is given as much weight as much more recent data. This could have been addressed by using exponential smoothing that uses a smoothing constant to reduce the influence of early data considered in the time series. This method uses a series of weights with higher weights given to the most recent data.

(b) **Performance analysis**

The budgeted sales volume for the second quarter of 2010 was 83 units. Except for warnings from the sales manager, there was no evidence that this would not be achieved. The actual sales for the previous three quarters had been in-line with the forecast and so there was no clear case for the budgeting committee to change its sales forecast.

Flexing the budget allows us to look at the consequences if the planned level of output had been 50 (actual sales) rather than 83 (planned sales).

This flexed budget is presented below.

Output (sales)	50 units
Sales revenue	$45,000
Raw materials	($17,500)
Labour	($16,250)
Fixed overheads	($18,000)
Operating profit (loss)	($6,750)

The table below compares budget, actual and the flexed budget.

	Budget	Actual	Flexed Budget
Units	83	50	50
Price	$1,000.00	$900.00	$900.00
Revenue	$83,000.00	$45,000.00	$45,000.00
Raw materials	($29,050.00)	($15,000.00)	($17,500.00)
Labour	($26,975.00)	($15,750.00)	($16,250.00)
Fixed overheads	($18,000.00)	($18,000.00)	($18,000.00)
Operating profit	$8,975.00	($3,750.00)	($6,750.00)

A number of conclusions can be drawn.

Sales volume

The sales volume variance for quarter 1 is an adverse variance. The sales manager should be held accountable for this.

However, in fairness to him, he had warned of weakening demand at the meeting of the planning committee that set the targets for the four quarters. The reasons appear to be associated with changes in the external environment. Customers are reluctant to invest in new machines or replace old machinery in times of difficult trading conditions. Cheaper foreign imports have also been identified.

Sales price variance

The sales price variance for quarter 1 is also an adverse variance. This is due to lower prices being charged. The sales manager is again accountable for this. He has probably discounted prices to compete with cheaper foreign imports. He warned in the scenario of cheaper foreign imports undercutting prices by about 10%. It appears that the sales manager has had to match these prices, as the sales unit price fell to $900 in this quarter.

Materials variance

The materials variance is a favourable variance because actual costs ($15,000) are less than the flexed budget $17,500.

There may be at least two reasons for this. On the one hand the production manager may have been able to reduce the amount of raw material used in the manufacture of the equipment. This may be possible, although with such a well-established product this seems unlikely. It is more likely that the procurement manger has been able to negotiate lower prices for raw materials.

CoolFreeze has had to reduce its prices (reflected in the sales price variance) but this has been partly offset by obtaining lower prices from suppliers.

Labour variance

The labour variance is again favourable because actual labour costs were less than the flexed budget. The variance is relatively small; $500. There may, again, be two possible reasons for this. Firstly, that labour costs have been reduced by paying lower rates. This would be the responsibility of the personnel department. This may be possible; perhaps some employees have left and have been replaced by cheaper employees. Alternatively, perhaps the number of hours required to produce each unit has been reduced. This would be the responsibility of the production manager. Further information is needed to come to a firm conclusion.

Overhead costs

Fixed overheads have remained as per the original budget.

Summary

Your assertion that "we have all made mistakes" seems rather sweeping. The main problems to be addressed appear to be in sales volume and sales price. These are the responsibility of the sales manager. In contrast, raw materials and labour costs have been well controlled with positive variances achieved by the production and procurement managers. Similarly, overheads have been maintained at their budgeted value.

STRATEGY AND PEOPLE

55   JOB DESIGN

Key answer tips

This is in no way an exam standard or exam style question. However it should provide useful coverage of a topic that may become more important in future exams. You may want to simply read the answer to this question rather than sitting the question under exam style conditions.

(a)   **Consequences of routine, repetitive jobs**

Aside from the everyday experience of millions of employees, systematic research suggests that repetitive, routine work results in subjective feelings of monotony and boredom and that this in turn leads to less than optimum performance by the workforce.

Studies of workers in car assembly factories in various parts of the world have confirmed that a large proportion of the workforce dislikes the repetitive nature of assembly line work, and that it is strongly associated with above average levels of absenteeism, labour turnover and industrial action. These problems are most apparent in times of full employment, but their lack of visibility in times of high unemployment and job insecurity does not mean they disappear but that workers are less ready to risk their jobs by taking any form of industrial action.

All the problems which characterise low discretion, routine work, as highlighted by Harriet, inflict costs in terms of poor quality work, lower levels of production, costs of cover for absent employees, loss of output and damage to trust and co- operation between management and employees.

The kind of behaviour exhibited by employees required to carry out tedious work operations is often explained as arising from a lack of need fulfilment. Psychologists such as A Maslow and F Herzberg, for instance, argue that routine, repetitive work does not meet the higher level social and self-actualising needs of people. Employees frustrated by the lack of self fulfilment in their work seek to avoid it by frequent absence from the organisation on the grounds of sickness or by seeking more interesting and challenging work elsewhere. Their readiness to take industrial action is explained in terms of yet another means of venting their frustration by striking for some socially acceptable reasons such as higher pay and/or better working conditions.

(b)   **Job enrichment and job enlargement**

Job design can be defined as a method of redesigning jobs by taking into account the needs of individual workers as well as the objectives of the organisation. For the individual this can lead to greater job satisfaction and greater control over his work environment. It may also be a vehicle for increasing the participation of employees in the immediate work area.

In an effort to improve the variety of work for employees, additional tasks are often added to those contained in the current job description.

Job enrichment (sometimes called *vertical* increase) – provides the employee with extra tasks that demand use of authority, skills, behaviour and decision-making at a higher level than that required in his or her normal job.

This gives the manager:

- more time to concentrate on higher level tasks
- an opportunity to assess the potential of the employee
- an opportunity to develop communication.

Employees have motivation factors provided, e.g. recognition, achievement, growth. They also have a chance to prove their potential and gain rewards and an opportunity to work with less supervision.

Examples include:

(i) A senior could be taken 'on site' by a manager/partner to gain experience and eventually be given an area of client visits that he/she alone would organise.

(ii) A clerk could be given training on computer terminals and word processors so that he/she could carry out secretarial and machine room operations as well as the normal tasks.

Disadvantages of job enrichment include

(i) The new jobs have to come from somewhere or someone, so there may be organisational problems. There can also be friction between colleagues when one of them is 'specially chosen'. Less capable employees may be worried about the additional skills required.

(ii) There is the risk in certain areas that control by segregation of duties might be lost.

(iii) The cashier who opens the mail and writes up the books might be vulnerable to corruption if inadequately supervised.

Job enlargement (sometimes called *horizontal* increase) occurs when additional tasks are given to the employee essentially at a similar or lower level than his present job, giving the job a longer cycle time. This reduces the amount of repetition and may require the exercise of a wider range of skills.

Unfortunately, it is unlikely to be a positive motivator, but it does provide recognition and job variety.

This technique gives the manager the benefits of a busier workforce capable of carrying out a variety of tasks with the ability to assess potential or training needs.

The employee has job variety and can develop new skills and can show potential and develop positive attitudes

Examples of job enlargement include the following.

(i) A salesperson, even if only a booking clerk or building society cashier could advise customers on more services/bargains available.

(ii) Retail salespeople could become more involved in inventory control, and ultimately ordering/buying.

(c) **Benefits of job design**

If jobs are designed to match the tasks with available resources the following benefits should be achieved:

(a) higher overall efficiency

(b) less fatiguing work

(c) fewer errors

(d) higher morale

(e) more even flow of work

(f) balanced work loading

(g) highly motivated staff

(h) good company reputation

(i) development of autonomous work groups.

(d) **Difficulty in changing the design of jobs**

Four problems that may make it difficult for Harriet to change the design of such jobs are as follows:

(i) **Staff**

Problems may occur if a few of the current workforce are unable to meet the demands required from the implementation of some of these changes. For example, some of the workers in an autonomous work group may feel pressurised if they prove to be less efficient than others in the group, and friction may arise if more able members feel held back by their less able colleagues.

(ii) **Delay**

It may be necessary to implement some form of staff training that might affect production output over a period of time. Even on-the-job training in undemanding jobs (e.g. through job rotation) would probably result in a small decrease in output until employees become familiar with new tasks. In this situation a reduction in output, even in the short term, may be unacceptable to management and they may decide not to go ahead.

(iii) **Costs**

The cost of implementing many of the changes may be prohibitive. For example, it may be relatively cheap to train operators on the job, but it may prove expensive to train managers in the techniques needed to monitor the impact of these changes (appraisal techniques, setting of objectives, etc.). The introduction of flexitime would necessitate the purchase of some form of clocking-in and clocking-out system.

(iv) **Organisation culture**

Before making any changes, management should consider that the values, attitudes and beliefs that make up an organisation's culture are shared and accepted throughout the company. Thus, it is important to make sure that changes made in one department are not wrongly perceived by another department. For example, staff in a management accounts department may construe the introduction of job enlargement into the financial accounts department as a way of promoting staff previously on the same level as themselves.

56   GRUMIT

Key answer tips

The structure of part (a) is dictated by the question, and this is helpful in structuring your answer. Begin by dealing with the general HRM approach, then move on to the three detailed areas in order.

In part (b) you need to produce a fairly general discussion of change in organisations, but with specific reference to the situation facing Grumit.

(a)   The approach to be taken must address the specific issues facing Grumit, but should also fit in with the overall human resource management (HRM) philosophy. An agreed approach to people issues acts as a frame of reference against which the organisation takes specific decisions. It is not clear to what extent Grumit has an agreed HRM philosophy. If not, now is a good time to open up the debate on what it should be. Grumit is about to be transformed from a manufacturing organisation to a downsized service-led organisation. In a service-led organisation employees are the key resource and the HRM approach must be based on the need to:

(i)   ensure positive commitment from employees

(ii)   encourage flexibility to meet and respond to change

(iii)   create a climate of quality and customer care.

The extent of the change at Grumit will require extremely careful management if employee motivation and commitment is to be preserved. Given the apparently unexpected closure decision imposed on Grumit by its parent company, the HRM function can do no more than adopt a reactive role. Since this is a major change situation, there is a need for a participative approach to dealing with problems – involvement should be sought and encouraged at all levels in the organisation in so far as sensitivities allow.

Of immediate concern is how employee relations are to be handled – particularly communications and the role ascribed to the unions, both recognised and unrecognised. In the medium term a restructured and downsized organisation may well wish to consider the position of single union-harmonisation. If these longer term issues can be clarified, they can be reflected in the handling of the current situation.

Taking each of the three questions separately:

(i)   **Communications 'letting people know'.** Given the extent of the changes, there is a need to consider communication in the short term (to deal with redundancy situation) and the long term (to fit the culture of the new organisation). Does the organisation have current policies and practices and are these suitable as to method (channel and media) and message? For the immediate redundancy situation, Grumit must decide the respective roles of top management, line management, the personnel function and unions and the appropriate communications media – mass meetings, group briefings, line managers. For the longer term, Grumit could add to this list: suggestion box schemes, quality circles, joint consultation committees, in-house magazine and notice boards. The key, however, is management style (for example, management by walking about) which should shift the communication focus from 'telling' to 'exchanging'.

(ii)   **Redundancy**. Closure of the manufacturing facility has been set as a priority therefore there is a need to have both policy and procedure for managing the redundancy process. These may not be in existence or may be inappropriate. Policies and procedure must deal with:

- communication of the reasons for the redundancies
- categories to be made redundant (numbers and job types)
- policy on selection of employees
- procedures to be followed – payment levels and terms, whether out placement is to be used, retraining needs and possibilities, the exact time scale of each stage in the procedure, consultative and negotiating procedures
- the need to deal with unions in a manner which is in line with current agreements and sets the tone for future policy.

Note: In the UK, there are specified legal requirements for days' notice of redundancy, notification to recognised trade unions and compensation payments based on age and length of service.

(iii)   **Training, retraining and staff development**. There is a need to develop a positive attitude towards developing staff. (It is not clear whether Grumit have specialist training and development staff). Specifically for the current situation, a training plan for sales and service staff covering technical aspects and product awareness. The plan must cover costs, schedules and timescales. On a longer term basis Grumit must adopt an overall training and development policy which reflects short and long term needs:

- the possibility of creating a 'learning organisation'
- the development of training plans linked to strategy
- management development programmes, career progression, succession planning
- appraisal systems, clearly linked to the development of employees.

(b)   Change strategies have been studied extensively by management writers, and while the process can vary considerably from situation to situation there are valuable lessons to be learned from successful change management. These lessons include:

(i)   The need to understand why people resist change and how to overcome such resistance. Areas to consider include:

- uncertainty and fear (job loss, security, loss of status)
- lack of understanding (poor communication)
- lack of trust (past history and culture of the organisation)
- self-interest, individual attitudes and personality.

(ii)   The influence of the background reasons for the changes. Some change factors can make change easier to gain acceptance than others. For example, the threat of closure due to competition may enable management to implement radical changes which in normal circumstances unions might find unacceptable.

(iii)   The influence of organisational culture, climate, politics and group cohesiveness on the change process. For example, does the culture support change?

(iv) The change process to be adopted. Johnson and Scholes identify four styles, each of which may be appropriate in certain circumstances. Where incremental change over long time horizons are possible then change models using education and communication and participation are appropriate. Where change must be rapid and is in response to a crisis, then coercion and edict methods may be appropriate. For intermediate situations an interventionist approach may be taken.

A number of change process models can be considered. No one is necessarily better than the others, and each needs to be adapted to the specific circumstances:

- A typical approach is to consider the need to unfreeze the situation first then change it and refreeze it. **Lewin's force field model** is helpful in identifying the forces supporting and those resisting change.

- A **four phase integrated model** (explore, plan, action, integration) to change situations.

- An **action learning approach**, involving the organisation (senior managers), subjects (those affected by the change) and a change agent or change leader (such as an internal or external consultant).

- **Participative models**, which draw on the human relations school and the work of Peters, Kanter and others.

57 ROCK BOTTOM *Walk in the footsteps of a top tutor*

Tutor's top tips

Part (a) Life cycle and management style

Key to success:

Allocate time equally between 3 phases. There are 3 phases x 2 elements = 6 parts to the question. So with 18 marks available in total that gives you around 3 marks per part. So you cannot spend too much time on any element of any phase of the requirement (in fact, you have time to make a maximum of two issues per element).

Answer both elements i.e. the reasons for success and failure, and the contribution of Rick Hein's leadership style.

Understand the scenario. The examiner suggested some students misunderstood that whilst franchising was considered, other opportunities were pursued

You could use a model to generate ideas. Even something as simple as a SWOT - reasons for success could come from strengths and opportunities, whilst the reasons for failure could come from the weaknesses and threats. The answer uses PLC to distinguish stages and you might also have found this useful.

Recognising that each stage was very different – stage 1: mainly successful, stage 2: some success and some failures, stage 3: mainly failures.

> *Key dangers:*
>
> *Lack of structure*
>
> *Mixing stages together*
>
> *Too much time spent on one stage*
>
> *Simply regurgitating the scenario (not adding value). For example, regurgitation would state that at stage 2 the company listed on stock exchange. But to gain marks in the exam you would have to develop this further, for example, by explaining that this would mean that the company would need to be more transparent and have strong corporate governance.*
>
> *In part (b)it is important that you have the correct focus on the answer requirements rather than simply explaining franchising. This means explaining that in 1988 franchising was feasible (because the business would have been to attractive to franchisees), but that by 20X7 it was unattractive to franchisees and franchising would not have been feasible. So we focus on the feasibility of franchising rather than its advantages and disadvantages.*

(a)   The product life cycle model suggests that a product passes through six stages: introduction, development, growth, shakeout, maturity and decline. The first Rock Bottom phase appears to coincide with the introduction, development and growth periods of the products offered by the company. These highly specified, high quality products were new to the country and were quickly adopted by a certain consumer segment (see below). The life cycle concept also applies to services, and the innovative way in which Rock Bottom sold and marketed the products distinguished the company from potential competitors. Not only were these competitors still selling inferior and older products but their retail methods looked outdated compared with Rock

Bottom's bright, specialist shops. Rock Bottom's entry into the market-place also exploited two important changes in the external environment. The first was the technological advance of the Japanese consumer electronics industry. The second was the growing economic power of young people, who wished to spend their increasing disposable income on products that allowed them to enjoy popular music. Early entrants into an industry gain experience of that industry sooner than others. This may not only be translated into cost advantages but also into customer loyalty that helps them through subsequent stages of the product's life cycle. Rock Bottom enjoyed the advantages of a first mover in this industry.

Hein's leadership style appears to have been consistent with contemporary society and more than acceptable to his young target market. As an entrepreneur, his charismatic leadership was concerned with building a vision for the organisation and then energising people to achieve it. The latter he achieved through appointing branch managers who reflected, to some degree, his own style and approach. His willingness to delegate considerable responsibility to these leaders, and to reward them well, was also relatively innovative. The shops were also staffed by young people who understood the capabilities of the products they were selling. It was an early recognition that intangible resources of skills and knowledge were important to the organisation.

In summary, in the first phase Rock Bottom's organisation and Hein's leadership style appear to have been aligned with contemporary society, the customer base, employees and Rock Bottom's position in the product/service life cycle.

The second phase of the Rock Bottom story appears to reflect the shakeout and maturity phases of the product life cycle. The entry of competitors into the market is a feature of the growth stage. However, it is in the shakeout stage that the market becomes saturated with competitors. The Rock Bottom product and service approach is easily imitated. Hein initially reacted to these new challenges by a growing maturity, recognising that outrageous behaviour might deter the banks from lending to him. However, the need to raise money to fund expansion and a latent need to realise (and enjoy) his investment led to the company being floated on the country's stock exchange. This, eventually, created two problems.

The first was the need for the company to provide acceptable returns to shareholders. This would have been a new challenge for Hein. He would have to not only maintain dividends to external shareholders, but he would also have to monitor and improve the publicly quoted share price. In an attempt to establish an organisation that could deliver such value, changes were made in the organisational structure and style. Most of the phase 1 entrepreneur-style managers left. This may have been inevitable anyway as Rock Bottom would have had problems continuing with such high individual reward packages in a maturing market. However, the new public limited organisation also demanded managers who were more transactional leaders, focusing on designing systems and controlling performance. This style of management was alien to Rick's approach. The second problem was the need for the organisation to become more transparent. The publishing of Hein's financial details was embarrassing, particularly as his income fuelled a life-style that was becoming less acceptable to society. What had once appeared innovative and amusing now looked like an indulgence. The challenge now was for Hein to change his leadership style to suit the new situation. However, he ultimately failed to do this. Like many leaders who have risen to their position through entrepreneurial ability and a dominant spirit, the concept of serving stakeholders rather than ordering them around proved too difficult to grasp. The sensible thing would have been to leave Rock Bottom and start afresh. However, like many entrepreneurs he was emotionally attached to the company and so he persuaded a group of private equity financiers to help him buy it back. Combining the roles of Chairman and Chief Executive Officer (CEO) is also controversial and likely to attract criticism concerning corporate governance.

In summary, in the second phase of Hein's leadership he failed to change his approach to reflect changing social values, a maturing product/service market-place and the need to serve new and important stakeholders in the organisation. He clearly saw the public limited company as a 'shackle' on his ambition and its obligations an infringement of his personal privacy.

It can be argued that Hein took Rock Bottom back into private ownership just as the product life cycle moved into its decline stage. The product life cycle is a timely reminder that any product or service has a finite life. Forty years earlier, as a young man, Hein was in touch with the technological and social changes that created a demand for his product and service. However, he had now lost touch with the forces shaping the external environment. Products have now moved on. Music is increasingly delivered through downloaded files that are then played through computers (for home use) or MP3s (for portable use). Even where consumers use traditional electronic equipment, the reliability of this equipment means that it is seldom replaced. The delivery method, through specialised shops, which once seemed so innovative is now widely imitated and increasingly, due to the Internet, less cost-effective. Consumers of these products are knowledgeable buyers and are only willing to purchase, after careful cost and delivery comparisons, through the Internet. Hence, Hein is in a situation where he faces more competition to supply products which are used and replaced less frequently, using a sales channel that is increasingly uncompetitive. Consequently, Hein's attempt to re-vitalise the shops by using the approach he adopted in phase 1 of the company was always doomed to failure. This failure was also guaranteed by the continued presence of the managers appointed in phase 2 of the company. These were managers used to tight controls and targets set by centralised management. To suddenly be let loose was not what they wanted and Hein appears to have reacted to their inability to act entrepreneurially with anger and abuse. Hein's final acts of reinvention concerned the return to a hedonistic, conspicuous life style that he had enjoyed in the early days of the company. He probably felt that this was possible now that he did not have the reporting requirements of the public limited company. However, he had failed to recognise significant changes in society. He celebrated the freeing of 'Rock Bottom from its shackles' by throwing a large celebration party. Celebrities were flown in from all over the world to attend. It seems inevitable that the cost and carbon footprint of such an event would now attract criticism.

Finally, in summary, Hein's approach and leadership style in phase 3 became increasingly out of step with society's expectations, customers' requirements and employees' expectations. However, unlike phase 2, Hein was now free of the responsibilities and controls of professional management in a public limited company. This led him to conspicuous activities that further devalued the brand, meaning that its demise was inevitable.

(b)   At the end of the first phase Hein still had managers who were entrepreneurial in their outlook. It might have been attractive for them to become franchisees, particularly as this might be a way of protecting their income through the more challenging stages of the product and service life cycle that lay ahead. However, by the time Hein came to look at franchising again (phase 3), the managers were unlikely to be of the type that would take up the challenge of running a franchise. These were managers used to meeting targets within the context of centrally determined policies and budgets within a public limited company. Hein would have to make these employees redundant (at significant cost) and with no certainty that he could find franchisees to replace them.

At the end of phase 1, Rock Bottom was a strong brand, associated with youth and innovation. First movers often retain customer loyalty even when their products and approach have been imitated by new aggressive entrants to the market. A strong brand is essential for a successful franchise as it is a significant part of what the franchisee is buying. However, by the time Hein came to look at franchising again in phase 3, the brand was devalued by his behaviour and incongruent with customer expectations and sales channels. For example, it had no Internet sales channel. If Hein had developed Rock Bottom as a franchise it would have given him the opportunity to focus on building the brand, rather than financing the expansion of the business through the issue of shares.

At the end of phase 1, Rock Bottom was still a financially successful company. If it had been franchised at this point, then Hein could have realised some of his investment (through franchise fees) and used some of this to reward himself, and the rest of the money could have been used to consolidate the brand. Much of the future financial risk would have been passed to the franchisees. There would have been no need to take Rock Bottom public and so suffer the scrutiny associated with a public limited company. However, by the time Hein came to look at franchising again in phase 3, most of the shops were trading at a loss. He saw franchising as a way of disposing of the company in what he hoped was a sufficiently well-structured way. In effect, it was to minimise losses. It seems highly unlikely that franchisees would have been attracted by investing in something that was actually making a loss. Even if they were, it is unlikely that the franchise fees (and hence the money immediately realised) would be very high.

ACCA marking scheme		
		Marks
(a)	Up to 1 mark for each relevant point up to a maximum of 6 marks for each phase.	
	Three phases required, giving a maximum of	18
(b)	Up to 1 mark for each relevant point up to a maximum of	7
Total		**25**

Examiner's comments

Most candidates provided a good analysis of phase one (1965 – 1988), but their analyses of the subsequent phases was less comprehensive. There was also some confusion arising from the second part of the question. Many candidates assumed that he did franchise the shops at the start of phase two, but actually he did not. The scenario states that he considered it, but "instead, he floated the company on the country's stock exchange". Consequently, on some scripts, some parts of the analysis were irrelevant. There was plenty of material for comprehensive analyses of phases two and three (see the published questions and answers) but many candidates just did not use it.

The second part of question two asked candidates to explain the key factors that would have made franchising Rock Bottom feasible in 1988 but unlikely to be successful in 20X7. Most candidates were able to identify sufficient key points to achieve a pass in this part question.

Overall, question two was a popular and (overall) well-answered question. Candidates entered into the spirit of the scenario, often referring to well-known business figures who display more than a passing resemblance to Rick Hein!

58   NATIONAL COLLEGE

Key answer tips

You will need knowledge on competency frameworks. Without this knowledge it will be difficult to score a high mark. The ACCA qualification is built on a competency framework and you should use that as a foundation for your knowledge.

(b)   Competencies define what is expected from an individual in an organisation, both in terms of content and levels of performance. They should provide a map of the behaviours that will be valued, recognised and, in some organisations, rewarded. Employees have a set of objectives to work towards and are clear about how they are expected to perform their jobs. This would have been very useful at National College because the inappropriateness of some of the performance measures would have become clearer at a much earlier stage.

Originally, many competency frameworks concentrated on behavioural elements, for example, developing softer skills such as problem-solving. However, competency frameworks are increasingly becoming more ambitious and including technical competencies that in many ways are more specific and easier to assess than behaviours. Many examination syllabuses are cross-referenced to national competency frameworks and the Institute of Managerial Finance might consider this for their examinations. Competencies are normally expressed at a number of levels; reflecting increasing demands in those competences. For example, in the Skills Framework for the Information Age (SFIA), which has four levels (3–7), level 3 is apply, level 4 is enable, level 5 advise and level 6 initiate or influence.

The competency framework usually defines competencies for each *role* within the organisation. There are typically ten or less competencies for each role. The detail for each competence has to be carefully balanced. If it is too general then employees are unsure of what is required and managers will have a problem in assessing staff against the defined competency. On the other hand, if the definition of each competence is too detailed, it can be excessively time-consuming to develop, administer and maintain. In reality, defining the appropriate level of detail is one of the key challenges of defining an effective competency framework. Performance against current competencies and the development of desired competencies becomes one of the focuses of the appraisal. Adopting an appropriate competency framework should lead to a fairer appraisal system at the National College. It should also improve the fairness of the recruitment process.

Competency frameworks may be developed internally, usually using HR consultants. KPMG developed theirs in partnership with Saville & Holdsworth Ltd (ACCA Case Study). Alternatively, the organisation can use a framework published by an external organisation – usually a trade association or a government body. The best solution is often a compromise between the two, using externally proven frameworks but tuning them so that they are relevant to the organisation. This has the added promise of providing a link between organisational and personal objectives. SFIA is published in two variants; SFIA, which is intended as a basis for tailoring to an organisation's needs, and SFIAplus which should be treated as a standard and should not be customised.

Competency frameworks were originally focused on performance management and development. However, contemporary advocates now see competency frameworks as a significant contributor to organisational performance through focusing and reviewing an individual's capability and potential. The competency framework might also be an important element in change management. The CIPD Change Agenda Focus on the Learner concluded that 'competencies have been a feature of progressive human resources development for more than a decade. What is new is their central importance as a means of providing a framework for the learner to take responsibility for their own learning'. Gold (referencing Holbeche, 1999) suggests that advocates of competencies perceive them as a mechanism for aligning organisational objectives with 'the various HR activities of recruitment, selection, appraisal, training and reward'.

ACCA marking scheme		
		Marks
(b)	1 mark for each relevant point up to a maximum of 10 marks	10

59 GLOBAL IMAGING

Key answer tips

(a) It is vital that you link a discussion of the different aspects of a HR plan to the growth objective. Just discussing a typical HR plan will score poorly.

(b) Rather than comments on outsourcing the whole of HR, it is easier to approach part (b) by discussing specific HR functions – e.g. payroll. Better answers will link the decision to outsource to strategic issues such as competitive advantage and the growth objective.

(a) **To:** Paul Simpson – HR Manager

From:

Human Resource Planning and Global Imaging's future growth

I will use this report to highlight the main phases in HR (human resource) planning and then deal with the specific HR activities, which will be needed to support the achievement of the growth strategy.

There are four major stages in creating a human resource plan:

- First, auditing the current HR resources in Global Imaging, as a relatively young company one could anticipate it having a relatively young labour force many of whom will be professionally qualified.

- Second, the planned growth will require a forecast of both the number and type of people who will be needed to implement the strategy.

- Third, planning will be needed on how to meet the needs identified in the forecast – how do we fill the gap in between the human resources we currently have and those needed to fulfil the plan?

- Finally, there will be the need to control those resources in terms of measuring performance against the goals set.

The key activities to achieve the growth goals will be:

- Recruitment, selection and staffing – here the key issues will be to recruit the necessary additional staff and mix of suitably qualified workers. The growth of the company will create management succession issues including the two managing directors, who are looking to exit the business in the foreseeable future. The rate of growth will also make it necessary to manage significant internal transfers of people in the company as new positions and promotion opportunities are created.

- Compensation and benefits – the start up phase of a company's life is often a stage where a formal reward structure has not been created. It also may be necessary to meet or exceed the labour market rates in order to attract the necessary talent. As the firm grows there will be a need to ensure that the firm is competitive in terms of the rewards offered, but there is an increasing need to ensure equity between newcomers and staff already employed in the firm. These pressures will normally lead to the creation of a formal compensation structure.

- Employee training and development – here there is a need to create an effective management team through management development and organisational development.

- Labour employee relations – here there is a need to establish harmonious labour relations and employee motivation and morale.

Overall, the HR implications of the proposed growth strategy are profound and there is a significant danger that failure to link strategy and the consequent HR needs will act as a major constraint on achieving the strategy.

Yours,

(b)   It is important to note that there is nothing in the nature of the activities carried out by HR staff and departments that prevents outsourcing being looked at as a serious option. Indeed, among larger companies the outsourcing of some parts of the HR function is already well under way, with one source estimating that HR outsourcing is growing by 27% each year. Paul, therefore, needs to look at the HR activities identified above and assess the advantages and disadvantages of outsourcing a particular HR activity. Outsourcing certain parts of the recruitment process has long been accepted, with professional recruitment agencies and 'head-hunters' being heavily involved in the advertising and short listing of candidates for senior management positions. Some HR specialists argue that outsourcing much of the routine personnel work, including maintaining employees' records, frees the HR specialist to make a real contribution to the strategic planning process. One study argues that 'HR should become a partner with senior and line managers in strategy execution'.

If Paul is able to outsource the routine HR activities this will free him to contribute to the development of the growth strategy and the critical people needs that strategy will require. In many ways the HR specialist is in a unique position to assess current skills and capabilities of existing staff and the extent to which these can be 'leveraged' to achieve the desired strategy. In Hamel and Prahalad's terms this strategy is likely to 'stretch' the people resources of the company and require the recruitment of additional staff with the relevant capabilities. Paul needs to show how long it will take to develop the necessary staff resources as this will significantly influence the time needed to achieve the growth strategy.

Outsourcing passes on to the provider the heavy investment needed if the company sets up its own internal HR services with much of this investment now going into web-based systems. The benefits are reduced costs and improved service quality. The downside is a perceived loss of control and a reduced ability to differentiate the HR function from that of competitors. Issues of employee confidentiality are also relevant in the decision to outsource.

MANAGING STRATEGIC CHANGE

60 TC COMPANY

Key answer tips

Notice that lots of the parts of this question are asking you to do more than one thing. For example, in part (a) you have to identify the change triggers *and* discuss the barriers to change. It is therefore important that you answer all elements of each requirement.

(a) Triggers for change

Organisational change can be driven by both external developments and/or internal organisational factors. The key triggers for change in TC Company are as follows:

External triggers	Internal triggers
• Government decisions to deregulate the telecommunications industry	• Senior management decisions to enter broadband Internet services
• Technological developments in broadband and wireless technology	• Managers' decision to sack workers
• Development of VOIP	• Workers' decision to take industrial action to preserve jobs
• Shift in consumer tastes away from fixed line telephones to mobile phones.	• Trade union's decision to support the actions of TC Company employees.
• New mobile phone/VOIP technology	

The key difficulties that the TC Company is likely to face in making all the necessary changes are as follows.

Existing culture

The inherited culture is described as still being a bureaucratic, role culture where the rules and procedures are likely to act as a barrier to change.

Employees' resistance to change

Employees will resist change due to:

• fear of being unable to cope with the new technology
• unwillingness to throw away existing skills and learn new ones
• fear of job losses
• fear that new jobs will be more specialised and more boring.

Action of trade unions

The threat of action by the trade union will make change even more difficult.

(b)   The change process

Success to date

TC Company has had a mixed record of success in the management of change to date.

The main success is that it has managed to change from being a provider of only fixed line telephone services to one that now also provides mobile and broadband Internet services. This is despite the old bureaucratic culture and structure.

The main failures have been as follows:

- Attempts to downsize the workforce resulted in industrial action that cost TC Company many millions.

- The current implementation of broadband services and public wireless access points is also meeting with resistance. Engineers have threatened industrial action in support of a large pay rise.

Managing future change

Tutorial note

In any question that involves managing change Lewin's is a good model to use in order to structure an answer.

There is no universal plan for the successful management of change as each situation is different. At best, there are useful models and principles to help in the design of the change process. One such model was developed by Lewin.

Lewin argued that some (usually external) forces are outside management's control and so management should concentrate on the internal forces driving change and those resisting change. Lewin suggested a three-step process to then manage the change as follows:

- 'Unfreezing' – which involves reducing forces that resist change. This involves providing people with an understanding of why change needs to occur so that they can more easily accept it.

- 'Changing behaviour' – in such a way that new attitudes, values and behaviour become part of employees' new ways of thinking.

- 'Refreezing' – introducing mechanisms, such as reward systems and structures, to ensure that the new behaviour pattern is maintained.

In the case of TC Company, many of the forces for change are outside the control of the senior management. Management needs to accept the changes in the market place and adopt strategies to deal with the threats and opportunities the changes present.

Unfreezing

Management can use the threat of competition to persuade employees and the trade union that, unless changes are made, the very survival of the company and, therefore, the jobs of employees, are at risk. This should create dissatisfaction with existing methods.

Changing behaviour

Changing behaviour is difficult and will require a range of methods:

- effective communication of what needs to be changed and why
- regular meetings involving all employees
- negotiation with unions to ensure their participation in the change process.

The directors may be tempted to force changes through regardless of the reasons for resistance. The danger of this approach is that employees often return to the old ways of working once the pressure is removed.

Refreezing

- To consolidate changes made appropriate incentives and penalties must be put in place.
- Rather than sitting still there should be an emphasis on constant improvement to raise levels of productivity even further.

(c) The most obvious mechanism is the control and manipulation of organisational resources. Senior management can allocate resources in such a way that managers and departments are encouraged to embrace the new culture. This might be combined with the development of revised internal reporting systems so that resistance to change is highlighted and penalised in terms of performance measures.

Management might publicise its desire to change the culture within the company. Amongst other things, this could be raised as an issue by board members who are participating in interviews for promoted posts. Middle management might, therefore, be encouraged to align itself with the interests of this elite.

The company's systems need to be consistent with the whole process of change. If reporting and decision-making systems are based on the outmoded culture then it will persist and will, indeed, be viewed as the board's preferred approach.

The board might even resort to symbolic devices. Creating positive messages in support of those who embrace the changes and adapt to it will speed implementation more quickly.

61 PSI

Key answer tips

(a) The first part of the question asked candidates to analyse the nature, scope and type of strategic change at PSI. This should have been straightforward if students were aware of the different categories in the text – evolution v revolution, adaptation v reconstruction.

(b) The second part of the question asked candidates to identify and analyse the internal contextual features that could influence the success or failure of the chief executive's proposed strategic change at PSI. The terms used pointed to the Balogun and Hope Hailey model. However, even if students were not aware of this model, there were many easy points that could have been made form issues identified in the question.

(a) The proposal to develop and sell a software package for the general retail industry represents a major strategic decision for PSI. Up till now it has been relatively successful in identifying and servicing the software needs of a specialist niche market – the retail pharmacy market. In Michael Porter's terms it is currently a focused differentiator. Its proposed entry into the general retail market represents both a new product and a new market and so, using the perspective of Ansoff's growth matrix, it is a diversification strategy with high levels of risk. The proposal would lead to significant strategic change and, perhaps not surprisingly, is meeting resistance from the software development director who is responsible for a key activity in this change.

Johnson, Scholes and Whittington (JSW) argue that there is a danger in believing that there is 'only one way, or one best way, to change organisational strategies'. They believe that most strategies are profoundly influenced by earlier strategies and their success or failure. Consequently, strategies are often incremental in nature, adding to or adapting, previous or existing strategy. Rarely is the proposed change so fundamental that it challenges the existing business model and the processes and activities that support it.

JSW make use of a model developed by Balogun and Hope Hailey, which identifies four types of change which have very different degrees of impact. It is suggested that there are two key measures of change. Firstly, the *nature of change* – how big is it? *Incremental* or 'step-by-step' change does not challenge the existing way of doing things and may indeed reinforce the organisation's processes and culture. It is therefore likely to meet less resistance than *Big Bang* or quantum change, which represents significant change to most or all the organisation. Often this *Big Bang* change is necessary to respond to a crisis facing the firm, such as a major fall in profitability, and/or the appointment of a new chief executive.

Secondly, the *scope* of change process is important – how much of the firm's activities are to be changed? If the change does not alter the basic business model (or 'paradigm' in JSW's terms) then it is regarded as 'a *realignment of strategy* rather than a fundamental change in strategic direction' (JSW). However, if the proposed change is a radical challenge to the existing business model or paradigm then it is regarded as a *transformational* change.

The consideration of the two key measures of change enables the identification of four types of change. These four types are used in this answer but other models and approaches would be acceptable.

	Scope of change	
Nature of Change	Realignment	Transformation
Incremental	**Adaptation**	**Evolution**
Big Bang	**Reconstruction**	**Revolution**

–   *Adaptation* is a change that can be made within the current business model (realignment) and it occurs incrementally. JSW argue this is the most common form of change in organisations.

–   *Reconstruction* represents significant change in the organisation, often prompted by a crisis, such as an unwelcome takeover bid, but it does not require a fundamental change to the business model. Turnaround strategies where the aim is to rapidly reduce costs or increase revenues to ensure business survival may affect the whole organisation, but not change the basic business model.

- *Evolution* is a change in strategy, which requires the business model to be significantly changed over a period of time. The perceived need for 'transformation' may be as result of careful business analysis leading to a planned evolutionary change. Alternatively, change may take place through an emergent process where the scope of change only becomes apparent once it is completed.

- *Revolution* affects the whole of the organisation and the scope of change requires a fundamental shift in the business model – the way the firm chooses to compete.

Viewed dispassionately, it appears that PSI's proposed move into the general retail market represents an evolutionary change. It is incremental because it will build on the skills, routines and beliefs of those in the organisation. However, it is transformational because the proposed move away from the current market niche to a market which requires a generic solution is a fundamental change in strategic direction. It is likely that internal processes and activities will need to significantly change for the company to successfully develop and sell the new packages. In PSI's case, the evolution is driven top-down, by the chief executive's desire to create a company which is an attractive acquisition, at which point he can realise some or all of his investment in the company.

Interestingly, the three directors may not all perceive the change as evolutionary. The entrepreneurial chief executive and the sales and marketing director may see the proposal as adaptive change, realigning the company to take advantage of a business opportunity which will lead to realising their personal goals. Indeed they may see the current product as just the specific implementation of a generic retail software solution. In contrast, the software development director is more likely to agree with our assessment of the change as evolutionary.

(b) JSW argue that successfully managing change depends on context. This context is made up of a number of factors or contingencies peculiar to the organisation under consideration. How change is managed in a relatively small privately owned firm like PSI is very different to how it might be managed in a large international firm of accountants with hundreds of partners.

Tutorial note

Balogun and Hope Hailey's contextual features are a key model in the management of strategic change.

JSW again use the work of Balogun and Hope Hailey to consider the contextual features that need to be taken into account in deciding how a strategic change programme should be managed. These features are shown in the diagram below and are used in the model answer. However candidates could adopt other models and approaches.

Contextual features and their influence on strategic change programmes

Source: Johnson, Scholes and Whittington

In the context of PSI, the following observations could be made.

– *Time* – the company is not facing any immediate financial or business problems and so there is no apparent need for rapid change. Figure 1 suggests a company that is slowly consolidating in its market place. There is no evidence of a crisis that requires urgent remedial action. It is likely that it will take a relatively long time to develop the new generic software package, particularly when the current pressures on the software development team are taken into account. They are already having problems meeting deadlines for the current product. The only urgency is that injected by the impatience of the chief executive who may want to quickly introduce change to achieve the objectives of realising his investment in the company. The natural inclination of the software team and their director will be to use any available time to consolidate the current product and to improve its quality. In contrast, the chief executive will want to use available time to produce the new generic product. This will almost certainly lead to conflict, both within the organisation and with customers pressurising the software team for fault rectification and new requirements. The increased concentration of pharmacies into nationwide chains may also increase the power of certain customers.

– *Scope* – the degree of change should not be underestimated in a relatively small firm like PSI. Supplying a clearly defined segment supported by a vertical marketing strategy is very different to the horizontal marketing strategy required for the proposed move into the general retail market. The company has built up expertise in a niche market. It is unlikely that it will have comparable expertise in the generic retail market as well as in the other niche retail markets that it intends to target with its configurable software package.

– *Preservation* – clearly software development skills are a crucial resource and capability and must be preserved to enable the proposed strategic change. The retention of the software team's expertise and motivation is essential. If they are upset by the proposed change and disturbed by the further pressures it is likely to create then it is unlikely that they will support it. The agreement of the software development director to the change is also vital and some way of securing this must be explored. Although the proposed change is largely based on the competency of current personnel, it is likely that they will be disturbed by the increased pressure imposed on them and so there is a high probability that key employees will leave the company.

–   *Diversity* – Change may be helped if there is a diversity of experience. However, change may be hampered if the organisation has followed a particular strategy for a number of years. The relative stability of the last three years and the company's stated objective to be a 'highly skilled professional company providing quality software services to the retail pharmacy industry' seem at odds with the chief executive's vision of expansion. There is also evidence to suggest that the goals of the sales force and those of the software developers are already conflicting and there seems even more opportunity for this to occur in the context of a generic retail software package. Change will be hampered by the current conflict between sales and development.

–   *Capability* – The chief executive and sales and marketing director are entrepreneurial in outlook and want change to fuel growth and their personal aspirations. The software development director is much less enthusiastic as he can clearly see the implications of the proposed change in strategic direction. Furthermore, over the last three years the workforce has been relatively settled and has not been subject to much significant change. In some ways the small size of the business may make change easy to facilitate (see power), but there may also be significant barriers to change. The software development director and his staff control and implement the key activity of the new strategy. It may be difficult to overcome their lack of enthusiasm for the proposed change.

–   *Capacity* is concerned with resources such as people, finance and information. More detailed analysis will be necessary to see if PSI has the necessary resources to implement the proposed change. However, evidence from the scenario is not encouraging. For example, the company has recently been criticised at a user group conference for failing to meet its proposed release deadlines. The acquisition of necessary resources will take both time and money. There is no evidence that the company has the finances to support the acquisition of new resources. It is a private company and so it will not be able to raise money through the stock market. It will rely on further investments from the current shareholders (and the software development director may be reluctant to participate in this) or on bank finance. Furthermore, it usually takes a long time to integrate software developers into a business. There is a long learning curve during which they have to learn not only how the product works, but how it is designed. Hence they are unlikely to be productive until several months after appointment and this lack of progress might again clash with the impatience of the chief executive.

–   *Readiness* – There is no evidence that the organisation is ready for the type of change proposed by the chief executive. In fact the current pressure on the software development team suggests that they may not welcome the proposed new strategy. What they might be ready for is a strategy that leads to a consolidation of the pharmaceutical product so that faults are fixed and new requirements released on time.

– *Power* – the chief executive has the ultimate power in this organisation, reinforced by (through combining with the sales and marketing director) ownership of the majority of the shares. However he must secure the co-operation of the software development director to make progress. The fact that he has power may lead to him forcing through a strategy which is essentially wrong for the organisation.

Overall, an analysis of the context for change at PSI should provide warning signs to the chief executive. Although the chief executive has the power to impose change, there are concerns about the scope and capacity for change which may make it very difficult for the company to preserve its current resources and competencies. There is a real concern that these will actually be destroyed by the proposed change and this will lead to major difficulties in their current market. There is already evidence of this from the scenario. The company has been criticised at a user group conference for quality failures and there are doubts about whether planned new features will be released on time. The product is fundamental to the efficient purchasing and stock control required in contemporary pharmacies. Customers may switch to a competitor if they feel that their emerging requirements are not met with sufficient promptness and quality.

The workforce is neither ready for change nor diverse enough to welcome change. There are current conflicts between sales and development which are likely to be escalated by the proposed strategic change. Finally, there are also grave doubts about the capacity of the company to deliver the proposed change within the likely time scale required by the chief executive.

There is a concern that the chief executive will rely on managing change through coercion, which 'is the imposition of change or the issuing of edicts about change'. This is not unusual in small firms where the chief executive also has a large ownership stake in the business. It is most appropriate in crisis situations where time is of the essence and clear direction is imperative. However, PSI does not appear to be in a crisis situation. Unfortunately, however, it looks like the chief executive is about to create one!

ACCA marking scheme		
		Marks
(a)	Up to 2 marks for recognising that PSI is pursuing a diversification strategy	2
	Up to 2 marks for explaining the nature of change	2
	Up to 2 marks for explaining the scope of change	2
	Up to 4 marks for exploring the types of change with particular reference to the situation at PSI	4
(b)	Up to 3 marks for an analysis of each feature that could influence the success or failure of the proposed strategic change at	3
	PSI up to a maximum of 15 marks	15
	Eight possible features are described in detail in the model answer	
	A possible mark allocation (1 mark per point up to a maximum of 3 marks) for one of these features (time) is given below.	3
	– Explanation of possible effect of time	
	– Recognition that time is not an issue at PSI – there is no evidence of a crisis that requires remedial action	
	– Relatively long time to develop a new product given current time pressures	
	– Impatience of the chief executive imposes arbitrary urgency	
	– Conflict between chief executive and software development director over time allocation.	

Examiner's comments

This question concerned strategic change. It was the least popular of the optional questions. Candidates who attempted this question seldom scored more than half marks. The question relates to section C2 of the syllabus and it was clear that candidates, by and large, were unfamiliar with this area of the syllabus. The suggested answer is based around two models. The first part of the question asked candidates to analyse the nature, scope and type of strategic change at PSI (the company considered in the scenario). The suggested answer uses the Balogun and Hope Hailey model which specifically addresses these issues and uses these terms. Some candidates were familiar with this model and scored well as a result. The second part of the question asked candidates to identify and analyse the internal contextual features that could influence the success or failure of the chief executive's proposed strategic change at PSI. The suggested answer again uses a model attributable to Balogun and Hope Hailey. The cultural web would also have been an appropriate basis for answering this question.

However, notwithstanding a lack of familiarity with this part of the syllabus, there were plenty of clues in the case study scenario that could have provided the basis of an answer. For example:

Issues concerned with moving from supplying a specialist niche market (retail pharmacies) to a general retail market. This is quite a substantial change for a company of this size operating in a marketplace which they are currently struggling to service

Issues concerned with the clash between the chief executive and sales director on one hand and the software development director on the other. The software development director (and his staff) are key to the success of the new strategy but are unenthusiastic about proposed changes.

Issues concerned with leadership style of the chief executive, particularly in the context of a relatively small private limited company. The chief executive has significant power and can impose change, even though this change may be wrong for the organisation. As a private company it is unclear how the organisation will finance the software product development.

Issues concerned with the problems currently experienced with the software product and the demands of existing retail pharmacy customers for new features and facilities. The company is failing to satisfy customers even in its established niche market.

Issues concerning the conflicting goals between the sales force and the software developers. There is increased pressure on the software development team which is bound to intensify if the generic software package is developed and delivered.

Issues around the need for change. The company is not facing any immediate financial or business problems and there is no evidence of a crisis requiring immediate remedial action. The exit strategy of the chief executive appears to be driving the strategy.

Even if the candidate was unfamiliar with this syllabus area, an answer to this question (particularly part b) could probably have been crafted out of the general points listed above, without resorting to any specific published model.

62 STRATEGIES

Key answer tips

Marks would be available in this question for bringing in the Johnson, Scholes and Whittington approach to strategic planning.

(a)   Strategy formulation is a continuous process of refinement based on past trends, current conditions and estimates of the future, resulting in a clear expression of strategic direction, the implementation of which is also planned in terms of resource allocation and structure. The strategy then comes about or is realised in actuality. This process is shown in the diagram below as the planned intended strategy (also known as the deliberate strategy). In Honda's case the plan was to compete with the larger European and American bikes of 250ccs and over. However, the actual strategy pursued by a company over a three- to five-year period may diverge from the deliberate strategy for many reasons, as outlined below:

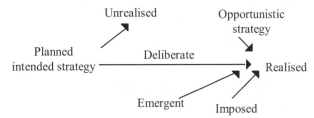

The obvious reason is that an intended strategy is not implemented because its underlying assumptions turn out to be invalid or because the pace of developments overtakes it. Factors affecting the strategy realisation will include changes in the organisation's external environment e.g. changes in the market for the goods and services that the firm produces and in the nature of the competition facing the company, and also its internal environment. Honda had problems with their large machines and resorted to selling the small 50cc bikes just to raise money.

Mintzberg argues that strategies can emerge, perhaps as a result of the processes of negotiation, bargaining and compromise, rather than be due to a deliberate planning process. This emergent strategy would be one that arises from an external stimulus not envisaged in the planned strategy. For example, if a supplier, pursuing modern ideas on supplier/customer relationships, encouraged a partnership approach to sourcing.

It is easy to imagine that buyers in the customer organisation might see benefits in this, and could pursue the idea to the point where sourcing strategy took on an aspect, not at all contemplated when planned strategic developments were laid down.

Sometimes changes from the intended strategy come about in opportunistic or entrepreneurial ways, e.g. an enterprise can find a new process or resource that enables dramatic cost reductions.Finally, strategy may be imposed. For example, recession and threat of a takeover may force a strategy of cost cutting and retrenchment. Technological developments may cause an organisation to develop new products to replace the ones that have become obsolescent.

(b) **Strategic Planning**

A rational process is considered to be one 'based on reasoning'; one that is not subjective but objective; one that is logical and sensible. Using rational behaviour, policy is formed by defining the end objectives first, and then selecting the means to achieve them by rational analysis. Empirical analysis is valued while qualitative information may be devalued. Economic and financial factors are used as the platform for planning. Strong systems are established and substantial effort is spent in understanding the reasons for deviations from planned results. The rational model of strategy management, i.e. the management of deliberate strategies has three elements: strategic analysis; strategic choice and strategic implementation – planning how the chosen strategy will be implemented.

Strategic analysis is concerned with understanding the strategic position of the organisation. It deals with the following:

- the environmental and competitive factors surrounding the organisation, which offer both opportunities and threats. The environmental factors include the political, economic, social and technological issues that affect the organisation
- the resources of the organisation, i.e. its strengths and weaknesses
- the stakeholders' expectations.

Strategic choice is based on strategic analysis. Briefly, it involves the following:

- strategic options generation – a variety of alternatives are considered
- strategic options evaluation – each option is then examined on its merits
- strategy selection.

This planning process is based on rational behaviour, whereby planners, management and organisations are expected to behave logically. People acting or deciding rationally are attempting to reach some goal that cannot be attained without action. They must have a clear understanding of alternative courses of action by which a goal can be reached under existing circumstances and limitations. They must also have the information and the ability to analyse and evaluate alternatives in the light of the goal sought. Finally, they must have a desire to come to the best solution by selecting the alternative that most effectively satisfies goal achievement.

Herbert Simon was aware that this ideal model could not readily be realised in practice. In practice, people seldom achieve complete rationality, especially in managing. In the first place, decisions must operate in the future and this almost certainly involves uncertainties. Secondly, it is difficult to recognise all the alternatives that might be followed to reach a goal. This is particularly true when decision-making involves opportunities to do something that has not been done before. Also, in most instances, it is difficult to analyse all the alternatives, even with the newest analytical techniques and computers.

A limiting factor is something that stands in the way of accomplishing a desired objective. Recognising the limiting factors in a given situation makes it possible to narrow the search for alternatives to those that will overcome them.

A manager must settle for limited or 'bounded' rationality. Limitations of information, time and certainty limit rationality even though a manager tries to be completely rational. Because managers find it difficult to be completely rational in practice, they sometimes allow their dislike of risk to interfere with their desire to reach the best solution under the circumstances.

Simon evolved a 'best practicable model', which would fit the problems of real life. In this model the manager does not optimise (i.e. get the best possible solution). Instead the manager satisfices. In other words, the manager carries on searching until he or she finds an option, which appears tolerably satisfactory, and adopts it, even though it may be less than perfect. This approach Simon characterised as bounded rationality.

Section 4

ANSWERS TO SCENARIO-BASED QUESTIONS

Tutorial note

These model answers are considerably longer and more detailed than would be expected from any candidate in the examination. They should be used as a guide to the form, style and technical standard (but not in length) of answer that candidates should aim to achieve. However, these answers may not include all valid points mentioned by a candidate – credit will be given to candidates mentioning such points.

63   OCEANIA NATIONAL AIRLINES (ONA) *Walk in the footsteps of a top tutor*

Tutor's top tips

Approach to the question

*Always start the large, compulsory question by reading the **first paragraph only** so that information on the company, it's market etc. can be determined.*

From the first paragraph in this question you can discover:

- *there are 2 distinct markets – tourists and business users*

- *the company runs an airline business*

- *they aim to exploit the growth in business and leisure travel*

*Now look at the requirements **before** reading the rest of the question. This will ensure that you read the question in the correct manner, do not need to read the question more than once, save time and can begin planning.*

Requirement

(a)   *Evaluation of strengths and weaknesses*

The key to most requirements is to choose the most appropriate model. The examiner suggests that more than one model can score marks, but that does not mean that you have to use a lot of models. The key will be to choose the most appropriate model, build an answer around that model, and then, if you have time, to briefly show how other models could have been useful.

The examiner clearly states that opportunities and threats are not required, so the SWOT model would be inappropriate. However, the first part of the model (SW) could have been used – this is what the official answer does. An assessment of strengths and weaknesses is an internal assessment and therefore an internal tool such as the resource audit or the value chain would have been most appropriate.

It is important to choose the model with which you are most comfortable. For the purpose of this walkthrough the resource audit (sometimes called the 'M's model') is chosen. A brief plan of the resource audit should be set up on a blank page with space for each of the key areas (i.e. manpower, machinery, markets, money etc.). This can be used to record key information in the question as you read it, and also it should ensure that you do not miss anything important from your answer.

(b)   *Strategy evaluation*

The question asks for an explanation and evaluation of a 'no frills' strategy. The official text for the syllabus suggests that strategies are best evaluated using three criteria: feasibility, suitability and acceptability. So again, these headings can be recorded on a planning page and you can add points to them as you read the question.

(c)   *Strategic choice*

The key again will be to determine which model will be most appropriate. There are 3 choices: Porter's generics, the strategic clock or Ansoff. The first two models will be important if ONA want to improve their position, the second would be most appropriate if ONA are looking for new ways to grow. It is not entirely clear which goal is most relevant at this stage, so part of the task when reading the question should be to determine which model is most relevant.

Reading the question

Now **actively** read the question i.e. as you read it you should add all relevant points to your planning page(s).

The key issues to pick out from the question as are as follows:

*   *ONA serve two markets – the regional and international sectors. Therefore, when choosing strategies in part c), you should choose a strategy for each sector.*

*   *The company's strengths seem to be laid out clearly in the section on image, service and employment. Weaknesses are less apparent and it is therefore very likely that they will arise from numerical analysis of the three sets of data that have been provided.*

*   *The market is very competitive and there have been lots of new entrants (especially at the 'no frills' part of the market).*

*   *Sales channels appear to be a critical success factor and it will be important that answers discuss the issues between using website sales and travel agent sales.*

- *In the section on future strategy it appears that ONA want to solve their existing problems rather than try new markets or diversify, so for part c) of the question Porter's generics or the strategic clock may be more important than the Ansoff matrix.*

Answering the question

Part (a) Strengths and weaknesses

This is the analysis part of the question and therefore one of the most important things to remember will be to include an analysis of the numbers that have been provided in the question. There are no marks for illustrating, explaining or calculating ratios so don't get bogged down on these. Also, you should only need to calculate the ratios for 20X4 and 20X6 rather than doing the calculations for all three years which would add little to your answer. Instead, allocate around half of the total marks for quantitative analysis (therefore 10 marks) and work on the basis of around 2 marks for each well explained point. This means that you should choose 5 or 6 key ratios and explain why they might have changed and whether they create a strength or weakness for the company.

For example, there has been a 2.5% fall in net profit margin which could be down to poor control of overheads (e.g. wages and salaries) and this indicates a weakness of the business.

For other strengths and weaknesses, go through as many of the 'M's' in the resource audit as possible. Remember for each one that you should explain why it is a strength or weakness. If we take 'manpower' as an example; the service provided and motivation of staff can be seen as a strength of ONA. But on the other hand, the fact that salaries are above industry average and have attached expensive benefits will create a weakness for the company.

This is just one part of the resource audit, but all of the elements can be considered in the same manner in order to create a complete answer to this part of the question when combined with the quantitative analysis.

Part (b) Strategy evaluation

The examiner explains that the first part of this section on the features of a 'no frills' approach was well answered.

For the second part it is very important to reach the same conclusion as the company – that this is an inappropriate strategy for ONA. The 3 professional marks available are likely to be available for justifying this position.

If you use the feasibility, suitability and acceptability model suggested by Johnson, Scholes and Whittington you should achieve a good, well balanced answer. Some of the key issues might be as follows:

(i) *Feasibility*

This examines whether a strategy is possible based on a company's current resources and position. Therefore it will be important to link it back to some of the issues discovered in part a).

The key issues to discuss might be:

- *ONA have higher wage rates than rivals*

- *because ONA have older aircraft their maintenance costs are likely to be higher*

- *it would be easier to achieve if the sales channels were changed so that more sales were made via a website than through the travel agents*

- *ONA may need to seek out alternative airports with lower landing fees and baggage handling costs etc.*

- *it should be possible to copy the ideas of successful 'no frills' airlines and avoid their past mistakes*

(ii)   Suitability

This examines whether the strategy is appropriate for the company's environment and whether it will solve the businesses problems.

The key issues to discuss might be:

- *there is already significant competition in this part of the market who will have lower cost bases and more experience at offering a no frill service*

- *these rivals may also react aggressively to any attempt by ONA to enter the market*

- *in order for ONA to achieve this strategy greater economies of scale would be necessary. This would mean an investment in more aircraft, more destinations etc. but it is likely that ONA would still be behind the scale of rivals*

(iii)   Acceptability

This area examines whether the strategy will be acceptable to the key stakeholders of the business.

The key issues to discuss might be:

- *this is likely to require a reduction in customer service – something that ONA prides itself on. This may be unacceptable to both customers and shareholders*

- *moving to alternative/cheaper destinations may not be acceptable to business users*

- *a change of selling channels may not be acceptable to the citizens of Oceania who have a culture of using travel agents to make their bookings.*

Overall, there are 13 marks available (excluding the professional marks) which allows for about 4 marks for each of the three evaluation criteria. So you should aim to cover 2 issues under each of the headings above and finish with an overall conclusion that this is an inappropriate strategy.

Part (c) Strategic choice

As already stated it will probably be more relevant in this section to use a competitive strategy model, such as Porter's generics or the strategic clock, than to use the Ansoff matrix. Also, as there are 2 market segments (regional and international) then the answer can choose strategies for each segment. There are around 4/5 marks available for each segment so you should only have to make 2 points for each one. The key will be to make the points relevant to the company in the question and to avoid suggesting a no frills approach that has already been discarded in part b).

Overall

The key points to take away from this question and apply to other compulsory, strategic questions are:

- *find the requirements before reading the full question*

- *for each part of the question, choose one key model and apply it to the scenario*

- *include quantitative analysis in all analysis answers*

- *allocate your time appropriately between all sections of the requirement*

(a) **Strengths**

(1) Strong brand identity particularly with the citizens of Oceania. A quoted recent survey suggested that 90% of people preferred to travel ONA for regional flights and 70% preferred to travel ONA for international flights. 85% of respondents were proud of their airline and felt that it projected a positive image of Oceania.

(2) ONA have an exemplary safety record. There have been no fatal accidents since its formation in 1997.

(3) Excellent customer service recognised by the Regional Airline of the Year award and the Golden Bowl as provider of the best airline food in the world.

(4) High business class load factors, particularly in the regional sector. This appears to suggest that ONA are particularly strong in the business market.

(5) Relatively strong cargo performance. In the period 20X4–20X6 when passenger air travel revenue had increased by 12% (and air travel to Oceania by 15%) and cargo revenue by 10%, ONA increased cargo revenue by 11%, just above the industry average.

(6) Financially, although the net profit margin has fallen (see weaknesses), the gross profit margin remains relatively stable. Hence the cost of sales (excluding wages, salaries and financing) has moved roughly in line with revenue. The gross profit margin for 20X4 is 37.04% and for 20X6 it is 36.98%, very little change.

(7) The settlement of debt is an important issue for an organisation. The average settlement period for receivables is concerned with how long it takes for customers to pay the amounts owing. This is low at ONA (29 days) and reducing, suggesting effective credit control and an industry where many customers pay before they are able to use the service. It is likely that much of the debt is tied-up with commission sales and cargo services.

(8) The gearing ratio measures the contribution of long-term lenders to the long-term capital structure of the business. Gearing for ONA remained relatively stable during the period 20X4–20X6. It stood at 71.13% in 20X6, a marginal increase on the 20X4 figure of 71.05%.

(9) Conveniently scheduled flights to business travel for the regional sector. Allows business to be conducted in one day, with a flight out in the morning and a flight back in the evening. Most cities in this sector also receive an extra flight in the middle of the day.

(10) Highly motivated, courteous employees.

Weaknesses

(1) High cost base. The most tangible evidence of this is the average pilot salary given in Table 1. Pilot salary costs appear to be over 10% higher than their competitors. The scenario also suggests that ONA pay above industry average salaries, offer excellent benefits (such as free health care) and have a generous non-contributory pension scheme. Other hints of high costs (insourced non-core activities such as catering, highly unionised) are also mentioned in the scenario. High costs are also hinted at in Tables 1 and 2, with ONA having relatively older aircraft, presumably requiring more maintenance, and lower utilisation hours than their competitors. The average wage of an employee rose by about 7% during the period under consideration.

(2)   Poor growth rate. The scenario makes the point that in the period 20X4–20X6, passenger air travel revenue has increased world-wide by 12% (and revenue from air travel to Oceania by 15%). However, ONA only recorded a 4.6% increase in passenger revenue in this period.

(3)   Low frequency of flights in the international sector, where there is on average only one flight per day to each destination. This makes it very difficult for the airline to gain any operational economies of scale in this sector.

(4)   The mixed airliner fleet is largely a result of the merger of the two airlines that formed ONA. The airframes for the bulk of the fleet are from two competing manufacturers (Boeing and Airbus). The information given in Table 1 suggests that the two aircraft types (Boeing 737 and A320) are very similar. The need to service and maintain two aircraft types creates an unnecessary cost.

(5)   Although the airline offers on-line booking, it does not currently offer on-line check-in. Hence overheads still remain in the embarkation process. Business travellers particularly favour on-line check-in as it means they can leave their homes and meetings later. In 20X6 the New Straits Times reported a recent global survey that showed that air travellers spend an average of four days in a year in queues at airline check-in counters.

(6)   Table 2 shows below average load factors in standard class seating. This is particularly significant on international sector flights.

(7)   Return on capital employed (ROCE) and return on ordinary shareholders' funds (ROSF) are important measures of profitability. Both of these ratios show a significant fall in 20X6. The fall can be largely attributed to a decline in net profit due to increases in costs outstripping increases in revenue.

(8)   The reduction in profitability is also revealed by the net profit margin which has reduced from 12.10% in 20X4 to 9.66% in 20X6. However, the gross profit percentage remains relatively stable and so it appears that it is the increased cost of wages, salaries and borrowing that has caused ONA profitability problems.

(9)   Efficiency ratios are used to examine how well the resources of the business are managed. The sales revenue per employee has reduced during the period, perhaps suggesting a reduction in productivity that needs to be investigated. In contrast, the average settlement period for payables shows a marginal rise.

       Trade payables provide a free source of finance, but extending the average settlement period too far can lead to loss of goodwill with suppliers. ONA already have a high settlement period for payables, although this may be typical in this industry.

(10)   Liquidity (both current and acid test ratios) fell significantly in 20X6. This may affect the ability of the company to meet its short-term obligations.

(11)   Finally, the interest cover ratio has declined considerably during the period covered in Table 1. In 20X4, it was 5.44, but by 20X6 it had declined to 3.73. The lower the level of profit coverage, the greater the risk to lenders that interest payments will not be met.

Credit will also be given to points which are discernible from the scenario but have not been covered above. The extent of unionisation and the percentage of sales made through commission sales might be thought of as strengths or weaknesses depending upon perspective.

(b)   (i)   A 'no frills' strategy combines low price with low perceived benefits of the product or service. It is primarily associated with commodity goods and services where customers do not discern or value differences in the products or services offered by competing suppliers. In some circumstances the customer cannot afford the better quality product or service of a particular supplier. 'No frills' strategies are particularly attractive in price-sensitive markets. Within the airline sector, the term 'no frills' is associated with a low cost pricing strategy. In Europe, at the time of writing, easyJet and Ryanair are the two dominant 'no frills' low-cost budget airlines. In Asia, AirAsia and Tiger Airways are examples of 'no frills' low-cost budget carriers. 'No frills' strategies usually exist in markets where buyers have high power coupled with low switching costs and so there is little brand loyalty. It is also prevalent in markets where there are few providers with similar market shares. As a result of this the cost structure of each provider is similar and new product and service initiatives are quickly copied. Finally a 'no frills' strategy might be pursued by a company entering the market, using this as a strategy to gain market share before progressing to alternative strategies.

(ii)   'No frills' low-cost budget airlines are usually associated with the following characteristics. Each of these characteristics is considered in the context of Oceania National Airlines (ONA).

- Operational economies of scale

   Increased flight frequency brings operational economies and is attractive to both business and leisure travellers. In the international sector where ONA is currently experiencing competition from established 'no frills' low-cost budget airlines ONA has, on average, one flight per day to each city. It would have to greatly extend its flight network, flight frequency and the size of its aircraft fleet if it planned to become a 'no frills' carrier in this sector. This fleet expansion appears counter to the culture of an organisation that has expanded very gradually since its formation. Table 1 shows only three aircraft added to the fleet in the period 20X4–20X6. It is likely that the fleet size would have to double for ONA to become a serious 'no frills' operator in the international sector. In the regional sector, the flight density, an average of three flights per day, is more characteristic of a 'no frills' airline. However, ONA would have to address the relatively low utilisation of its aircraft (see Tables 1 and 2) and the cost of maintenance associated with a relatively old fleet of aircraft.

- Reduced costs through direct sales

   On-line booking is primarily aimed at eliminating commission sales (usually made through travel agents). 'No frills' low-cost budget airlines typically achieve over 80% of their sales on-line. The comparative figure for ONA (see Table 2) is 40% for regional sales and 60% for international sales, compared with an average of 84% for their competitors. Clearly a major change in selling channels would have to take place for ONA to become a 'no frills' low-cost budget airline. It is difficult to know whether this is possible. The low percentage of regional on-line sales seems to suggest that the citizens of Oceania may be more comfortable buying through third parties such as travel agents.

- Reduced customer service

  'No frills' low-cost budget airlines usually do not offer customer services such as free meals, free drinks and the allocation of passengers to specific seats. ONA prides itself on its in-flight customer service and this was one of the major factors that led to its accolade as Regional Airline of the Year. To move to a 'no frills' strategy, ONA would have to abandon a long held tradition of excellent customer service. This would require a major cultural change within the organisation. It would also probably lead to disbanding the award winning (Golden Bowl) catering department and the redundancies of catering staff could prove difficult to implement in a heavily unionised organisation.

Johnson, Scholes and Whittington have suggested that if an organisation is to 'achieve competitive advantage through a low price strategy then it has two basic choices. The first is to try and identify a market segment which is unattractive (or inaccessible) to competitors and in this way avoid competitive pressures to erode price.' It is not possible for ONA to pursue this policy in the international sector because of significant competition from established continental 'no frills' low-cost budget airlines. It may be a candidate strategy for the regional sector, but the emergence of small 'no frills' low-cost budget airlines in these countries threaten this. Many of these airlines enter the market with very low overheads and use the 'no frills' approach as a strategy to gain market share before progressing to alternative strategies.

Secondly, a 'no frills' strategy depends for its success on margin. Johnson, Scholes and Whittington suggest that 'in the long run, a low price strategy cannot be pursued without a low-cost base'. Evidence from the scenario suggests that ONA does not have a low cost base. It continues to maintain overheads (such as a catering department) that its competitors have either disbanded or outsourced. More fundamentally (from Table 2), its flight crew enjoy above average wages and the whole company is heavily unionised. The scenario acknowledges that the company pays above industry salaries and offers excellent benefits such as a generous non-contributory pension. Aircraft utilisation and aircraft age also suggest a relatively high cost base. The aircraft are older than their competitors and presumably incur greater maintenance costs. ONA's utilisation of its aircraft is also lower than its competitors. It seems highly unlikely that ONA can achieve the changes required in culture, cost base and operations required for it to become a 'no frills' low-cost budget airline. Other factors serve to reinforce this. For example:

- Many 'no frills' low-cost budget airlines fly into airports that offer cheaper taking off and landing fees. Many of these airports are relatively remote from the cities they serve. This may be acceptable to leisure travellers, but not to business travellers – ONA's primary market in the regional sector.

- Most 'no frills' low-cost budget airlines have a standardised fleet leading to commonality and familiarity in maintenance. Although ONA has a relatively small fleet it is split between three aircraft types. This is due to historical reasons. The Boeing 737s and Airbus A320s appear to be very similar aircraft. However, the Boeings were inherited from OceaniaAir and the Airbuses from Transport Oceania.

In conclusion, the CEO's decision to reject a 'no frills' strategy for ONA appears to be justifiable. It would require major changes in structure, cost and culture that would be difficult to justify given ONA's current position. Revolution is the term used by Balogun and Hope to describe a major rapid strategic change. It is associated with a sudden transformation required to react to extreme pressures on the organisation. Such an approach is often required when the company is facing a crisis and needs to quickly change direction. There is no evidence to support the need for a radical transformation. This is why the CEO brands the change to a 'no frills' low-cost budget airline as 'unnecessary'. The financial situation (Table 3) is still relatively healthy and there is no evidence of corporate predators. It can be argued that a more incremental approach to change would be beneficial, building on the strengths of the organisation and the competencies of its employees. Moving ONA to a 'no frills' model would require seismic changes in cost and culture. If ONA really wanted to move into this sector then they would be better advised to start afresh with a separate brand and airline and to concentrate on the regional sector where it has a head start over many of its competitors.

(c)   Within the strategy clock, ONA might consider both differentiation and focus. A differentiation strategy seeks to provide products or services that offer different benefits from those offered by competitors. These benefits are valued by customers and so can lead to increased market share and, in the context of ONA, higher seat utilisation. Differentiation is particularly attractive when it provides the opportunity of providing a price premium. In other words, margins are enhanced through differentiation. Air travellers may be willing to pay more to travel with an airline that offers seat allocation and free in-flight food and drinks.

However, such a broad-based differentiation strategy may be inappropriate for ONA because of the need to service both business and leisure travellers. Consequently, the potential strategy also has to be considered in the context of the two sectors that the company perceives that it services. In the regional sector a focused differentiation strategy looks particularly attractive. Here, the strategy focuses on a selected niche or market segment. The most obvious focus is on business travel and building the company's strengths in this sector. This focus on the business traveller might be achieved through:

- Ensuring that flight times are appropriate for the business working day. This is already a perceived strength of the company. This needs to be built on.

- Providing more space in the aircraft by changing the seating configuration – and the balance between business and standard class. ONA currently has a low seat occupancy rate and a reduction in seat capacity could be borne.

- Fewer passengers in the aircraft may also lead to improved throughput times. Loading and unloading aircraft is quicker, minimising the delays encountered by the traveller.

- Providing supporting business services – lounges with fax and internet facilities.

- Speeding the process of booking and embarkation (through electronic check-in), so making the process of booking and embarkation easier and faster.

- Providing loyalty schemes that are aimed at the business traveller.

Although this focused differentiation is aimed at the business customer it is also likely that particular aspects of it will be valued by certain leisure travellers. Given the strong regional brand (people from Oceania are likely to travel ONA) and the nature of the leisure travel in this sector (families visiting relatives) it seems unlikely that there will be a significant fall off in leisure travel in the regional sector.

In the international sector, the strategic customer is less clear. This sector is serving both the leisure and business market and is also competing with strong 'no frills' competitors. The nature of customer and competition is different. A strategy of differentiation could still be pursued, although perhaps general differentiation (without a price premium) may be more effective with the aim of increasing seat occupancy rate. This sector would also benefit from most of the suggested improvements of the regional sector – providing more space in aircraft, faster passenger throughput, electronic check-in etc. However, these small changes will not address the relatively low flight frequency in this sector. This could be addressed through seeking alliances with established airlines in the continental countries that it services. Simple code share agreements could double ONA's frequencies overnight. Obviously, ONA would be seeking a good cultural fit – the 'no frills' low-cost budget airlines would not be candidates for code shares.

ONA's perception of market segmentation, reflected in splitting regional from international travel and distinguishing leisure from business appears to be a sensible understanding of the marketplace. However, it might also be useful for them to consider on-line customers and commission customers (travel agents) as different segments. Perceiving travel agents as the strategic customer would lead to a different strategic focus, one in which the amount and structure of commission played an important part.

Finally, whichever strategy ONA adopts, it must continue to review its operational efficiency. An important strategic capability in any organisation is to ensure that attention is paid to cost-efficiency. It can be argued that a continual reduction in costs is necessary for any organisation in a competitive market. Management of costs is a threshold competence for survival. ONA needs to address some of the weaknesses identified earlier in the question. Specific points, not covered elsewhere, include:

- Improved employee productivity to address the downward decline in efficiency ratios.

- Progressive standardisation of the fleet to produce economies of scale in maintenance and training. This should reduce the cost base.

- Careful monitoring of expenditure, particularly on wages and salaries, to ensure that these do not exceed revenue increases.

Candidates may address this question in a number of ways. In the model answer given above, the strategy clock is used – as it uses the term 'no frills' in its definition and so it seems appropriate to look at other options within this structure. However, answers that use other frameworks (such as Ansoff's product/market matrix) are perfectly acceptable. Furthermore, answers which focus on the suitability, acceptability and feasibility of certain options are also acceptable.

	ACCA marking scheme		
			Marks
(a)		Up to 2 marks for each identified strength up to a maximum of 10 marks for strengths	
		Up to 2 marks for each identified weakness up to a maximum of 10 marks for weaknesses	20
(b)	(i)	Up to 1 mark for each relevant point up to a maximum of 4 marks	
	(ii)	Up to 2 marks for each relevant point concerning the inappropriateness of a no-frills solution, up to a maximum of 13 marks	
		Professional presentation of coherent argument: up to 3 marks	20
(c)		Explanation of alternative strategies: Up to 2 marks for each significant point up to a maximum of 8 marks.	
		2 marks also available for professional presentation and coherence of the complete answer.	10
Total			**50**

Examiner's comments

The first part of this question asked candidates to evaluate the strengths and weaknesses of ONA and to explore how these impacted on the company's performance. Many of these strengths and weaknesses were signposted in the text and others were readily discernable from the tabular and financial data. Most candidates answered this part of the question reasonably well. However, three points need to be made;

1   Not enough use was made of the financial data. Relatively easy marks were available for calculating and interpreting standard financial ratios. One marker commented that the 'analysis of the financial information was often weak. Use of this information often went no further than extracting superficial data that was immediately obvious from the tables, for example that net profit after tax had fallen'.

2   Some candidates adopted over-elaborate frameworks and models to answer the question. On one hand this was good to see, but on the other it did mean that many of the answers were very long. Valuable time was taken up in explaining the model, rather than the strengths and weaknesses of ONA. This was a particular problem when inappropriate models were used (such as PESTEL), leading candidates to discuss opportunities and threats which were explicitly excluded from the question.

3   One marker commented that 'candidates frequently started this question with a paragraph describing SWOT analysis and then noting that only strengths and weaknesses were required for the answer. This was a complete waste of time'.

The second part of the compulsory question asked candidates to explain the key features of a 'no-frills' low-cost strategy. Credit was given for both generic answers and for answers which specifically referenced the airline industry. This was answered relatively well.

The question then asked candidates to explain why moving to a 'no-frills' low-cost strategy would be inappropriate for ONA. This part of the question was not answered particularly well. The question asked candidates to adopt and support a particular position. Overall, candidates did not give sufficient ideas to get the marks on offer. The better answers actually adopted the suitability, acceptability and feasibility success criteria suggested by Johnson, Scholes and Whittingham.

Not only did this give plenty of scope for a good answer, it also allowed candidates to score well on the professional marks available for this question. Professional marks were given to answers that strongly supported the specified position – the inappropriateness of a move to a 'no-frills' low cost airline. Too many answers were neutral in tone and did not carry sufficient conviction. Answers were diluted by offering alternatives (the focus of the next part of the question) or by suggestions about how a 'no-frills' approach might be made to work. Although some of these ideas were interesting, they were not the intended focus of the question.

Finally, candidates were asked to evaluate other strategic options ONA could consider to address the airline's current financial and operational weaknesses. There are two key parts of this requirement. The word 'other', meaning other than 'no frills' and so marks could not be awarded for an option which had been specifically rejected by the organisation. Secondly, the question was particularly looking for strategic options, encouraging candidates to explore the strategy clock or any other appropriate framework. Indeed the better answers adopted the strategy clock, Ansoff's matrix or further applied the suitability, acceptability and feasibility success criteria. Answers that used these approaches tended to score well and gained the professional marks on offer. Unfortunately, some candidates did not pitch their answers at a strategic level, focusing more on piecemeal operational improvements. Credit was given for such suggestions, but such answers tended to be quite limited and were not awarded the professional marks, as they did not address strategic options in an appropriate framework.

Three further aspects also need stressing;

1   Financial and quantitative information is provided in scenarios for a reason. Please use it appropriately. Many candidates ignored this information completely.

2   The information in the scenario is very important. Many answers were too general and lacked appropriate context. Candidates must also make sure that they answer the question set, not the question they would like to have been set.

3   Do not use theories inappropriately in a scatter-gun approach. Trying to reference too many theories led to some answers becoming too complicated, too long and too irrelevant. Candidates must make sure that answers are focussed and contain enough relevant points to get the marks on offer.

64   THE NATIONAL MUSEUM   *Walk in the footsteps of a top tutor*

Tutor's top tips

Part (a)

This part of the requirement explicitly asked for a PESTEL analysis. This should have given students the correct focus and avoided doubt about which model should be used in answers.

Key to success:

Apply the model to the scenario.

Try to cover all areas of the PESTEL (the examiner complained that some students failed to cover the "legal" issues.

Dangers:

Using alternative models. When the examiner is explicit in which model should be used then no other models are deemed necessary.

Straying into internal issues (e.g. strengths and weaknesses of the museum). A PESTEL model is an examination of the external influences on an organisation (the examiner highlights this by referring to it in the question as a "macro-environmental" analysis).

Poor time management. The examiner suggested that the majority of students found this to be a straightforward section of the exam but that weaker students often spent too long on it at the expense of other parts of the exam. Certainly spending more than five minutes per section of the PESTEL would not be time efficient.

Part (b)

This part of the requirement wanted students to assess the organisational cultural issues that caused the failure of the museums strategy.

Key to success:

Use an appropriate model. There are a range of cultural models that can be used (Handy, Peters & Waterman, the cultural web) and generally the examiner expects students to choose one model and apply it to the scenario. The cultural web plays a big part in the syllabus and is covered in two different chapters of the textbook so it should be seen as the most easily assessable and familiar model for students. The examiner used this model in his answer.

Apply the model to the scenario. Don't simply explain what the model is. Instead use examples from the case of stories, structure, symbols etc. to explain why the problems arose. Show a link between the parts of the cultural web (e.g. there are clear status symbols for some staff in the museum) and the failure of the strategy (the Director General proposed removing these).

Dangers:

Not focusing on culture. Some students strayed into change management (perhaps because this had featured in the June 20X8 exam?). The examiner's opinion was that there was not enough material given in the case to 20 marks worth of material on change management. The requirement also clearly stated it wanted the focus to be on cultural issues.

Part (c)

Key to success:

Note the two parts of this requirement – there will be marks available for explaining the lenses and then applying the lenses to the scenario. So start with the explanation of what they are (but recognise that this is only likely to be worth a couple of marks and should be done briefly/quickly).

Show how each lense would apply to the museum and why/how the one that was used caused the problems that occurred.

Dangers:

The examiner specifically highlighted this area as one of the parts of the paper that a significant minority of students exhibited a lack of knowledge. It is important for the exam that you cover all the main areas of the syllabus – and Johnson, Scholes and Whittington are seen by the examiner as being key to the design of the whole syllabus

(a)   The PESTEL framework may be used to explore the macro-environmental influences that might affect an organisation. There are six main influences in the framework: political, economic, social, technological, environmental and legal. However, these influences are inter-linked and so, for example, political developments and environmental requirements are often implemented through enacting legislation. Candidates will be given credit for identifying the main macro-environmental influences that affect the NM, whether or not they are classified under the same influences as the examiner's model answer.

Political

Monitoring, understanding and adapting to the political environment is absolutely essential for the National Museum. It is currently very reliant on government funding and so is significantly affected by the recently elected government's decision to gradually reduce that funding. The implications of this were recognised by the Board of Trustees and led to the appointment of a new Director General. Unfortunately, senior staff at the museum did not share this perception of the significance of the funding changes. Their opposition to change, which culminated in the Director General's resignation, has led to further political ramifications. The government is now threatening heavier funding cuts and further political trustee appointments. Furthermore, it does appear that the political context has changed for the foreseeable future. The government has only just been elected and the opposition also agrees that the reliance of museums on government funding has to be reduced.

The political appointment of two (and possibly more) trustees is also important to the National Museum. It was significant that it was the two trustees appointed by the government who supported the Director General and his proposed changes. Finally, the continued funding of the government will now largely depend on performance measures – such as accessibility – which have been determined by a political agenda. The museum must strive to meet these objectives even if they are not shared by senior staff. The old ways – built around an assessment of Heritage Collections – appear to have gone forever and senior staff members need to recognise this.

Economic

Up to now the National Museum has been largely sheltered from the economic environment. It has been funded by the government, not the marketplace, and that funding has been largely determined by stable internal factors, such as artefacts in the Heritage Collection. Evidence from the scenario and Figure 1, suggests that this funding is stable, increasing on an annual basis to reflect inflation. However, the progressive reduction of government funding will mean that the museum will be exposed to economic realities. It will have to set realistic admission charges. Resources will also have to be used effectively and new opportunities identified and exploited for increasing income. The Director General included a number of these ideas in his proposals. However, it will be difficult to set a charge that will attract sufficient customers to cover the museum's costs, particularly as visitors have been used to paying only a nominal entry charge.

Social

The social environment is important to the museum from at least two different perspectives. The first is that social inclusion is an important part of the government's targets. The government is committed to increasing museum attendance by both lower social classes and by younger people who they feel need to be made more aware of their heritage. The visitor information shown in Figure 3 suggests that not only are visitor numbers declining in total, but the average age of these visitors is increasing. The percentage of visitors aged 22 and under visiting the NM has decreased from 19% of the total visitors (in 20X4) to just over 12% in 20X7. The museum needs to identify what it needs to do to attract such groups to the museum. The Director General had suggested free admission. This could be combined with popular exhibitions (perhaps tied in with television programmes or films) and 'hands-on' opportunities. It appears that the immediate neighbourhood of the museum now houses many of the people the government would like as visitors and so, from this angle, the location of the museum is an advantage. However, the comment of the Director of Art and Architecture about popularity and historical significance hardly bodes well for the future.

The decay of the neighbourhood and the increased crime rate may also deter fee-paying visitors. The museum is becoming increasingly isolated in its environment, with many of its traditional middle-class customers moving away from the area and reluctant to visit. The extensive reporting of a recent assault on a visitor is also likely to deter visitors. The museum needs to react to these issues by ensuring that good and safe transport links are maintained to the museum and by improving security both in the museum and in its immediate vicinity. Visitors need to feel safe and secure. If the museum believes this to be unachievable, then it might consider moving to a new site.

Technological

It is estimated that only 10% of the museum's collection is on view to visitors. Technology provides opportunities for displaying and viewing artefacts on-line. It provides an opportunity for the museum to become a virtual museum – allowing visitors from all over the world access to images and information about its collections. Indeed, such an approach should also help the museum achieve some of its technology and accessibility targets set by the government. Technology can also be used to increase marketing activity, providing on-line access to products and allowing these products to be bought through a secure payment facility. The appropriate use of technology frees the museum from its physical space constraints and also overcomes issues associated with its physical location.

Environmental

It can be argued that all contemporary organisations have to be aware of environmental issues and the impact their activities have on the environment. These are likely to be exacerbated by the museum being located in an old building which itself requires regular maintenance and upgrading to reflect government requirements. It is also very unlikely that such an old building will be energy efficient and so heating costs are likely to be high and to continue to increase. The museum needs to adopt appropriate policies on recycling and energy conservation, but it may be difficult to achieve these targets in the context of an old building. Consequently, environmental issues may combine with social issues to encourage the consideration of the possible relocation of the museum to a modern building in a more appropriate location. However, the museum building is also of architectural importance, and so some acceptable alternative use for the building might also have to be suggested.

Legal

Legal issues affect the museum in at least two ways. Firstly, there is already evidence that the museum has had to adapt to legal requirements for disability access and to reflect health and safety requirements. Some of these requirements appear to have required changes in the building which have been met with disapproval. It is likely that modifications will be expensive and relatively awkward, leading again to unsightly and aesthetically unpleasing modifications to the building. Further tightening of legislation might be expected from a government with a mandate for social inclusion. For example, it might specify that all documentation should be available in Braille or in different languages. Legislation concerning fire safety, heating, cooking and food preparation might also exist or be expected.

Secondly, the museum is run by a Board of Trustees. There are legal requirements about the behaviour of such trustees. The museum must be aware of these and ensure that their work is properly scoped and monitored. Trustees have, and must accept, ultimate responsibility for directing the affairs of the museum, ensuring that it is solvent, well-run, and meeting the needs for which it has been set up. The museum is a charity and it is the responsibility of the trustees to ensure that its operation complies with the charity law of the country.

(b)   The underlying cultural issues that would explain the failure of the Director General's strategy at the National Museum can be explored using the cultural web. It can be used to understand the behaviours of an organisation – the day-to-day way in which the organisation operates – and the taken-for-granted assumptions that lie at the core of an organisation's culture. The question suggests that it was a lack of understanding of the National Museum's culture that lay at the heart of the Director General's failure. In this suggested answer the cultural web is used as a way of exploring the failure of the Director General's strategy from a cultural perspective. However, other appropriate models and frameworks that explore the cultural perspective will also be given credit.

A cultural web for the National Museum is suggested in Figure 1. The cultural web is made up of a set of factors that overlap and reinforce each other. The symbols explore the logos, offices, titles and terminology of the organisation. The large offices, the special dining room and the dedicated personal assistants are clear symbols of hierarchy and power in the museum. Furthermore, the language used by directors in their stories (see below) suggests a certain amount of disdain for both customers and managers. The status of professor conferred on section heads with Heritage Collections also provides relative status within the heads of collection sections themselves. The proposal of the Director General to close the heads' dining room and to remove their dedicated personal assistants would take away two important symbols of status and is likely to be an unpopular suggestion.

The *power* structures of the organisation are significant. Power can be seen as the ability of certain groups to persuade or coerce others to follow a certain course of action. At present, power is vested in the heads of collection sections, reflected by their dominance on the Board of Directors. Three of the five directors represent collection sections. Similarly the Board of Trustees is dominated by people who are well-known and respected in academic fields relevant to the museum's collections. The power of external stakeholders (such as the government) has, until the election of the new government, been relatively weak. They have merely handed over funding for the trustees to distribute. The Director General of the museum has been a part-time post. The appointment of an external, full-time Director General with private sector experience threatens this power base and his suggestion for the new organisation structure takes away the dominance of the collection heads. On his proposed board, only one of six directors represents the collection sections.

The *organisational* structure is likely to reflect and reinforce the power structure. This appears to be the case at the museum. However, it is interesting to note that the collections themselves are not evenly represented. Both the Director of Industrial Art and the Director of Media and Contemporary Art represent five collection sections.

However, only two collection areas are represented by the Director of Art and Architecture. This imbalance, reinforced by different symbols (professorships) and reflected in stories (see later) might suggest a certain amount of disharmony between the collection heads, which the Director General might have been able to exploit. Management at the museum are largely seen as administrators facilitating the museum's activities. This is reinforced by the title of the director concerned; Director of Administration.

The *controls* of the organisation relate to the measurements and reward systems which emphasise what is important to the organisation. At the National Museum the relative budget of each section has been heavily influenced by the Heritage Collections. These collections help determine how much the museum receives as a whole and it appears (from the budget figures) that the Board of Trustees also use this as a guide when allocating the finance internally. Certainly, the sections with the Heritage Collections appear to receive the largest budgets. Once this division has been established the principle of allocating increases based on last year's allocation, plus a percentage, perpetuates the division and indeed accentuates it in real financial terms. Hence, smaller sections remain small and their chance of obtaining artefacts for them to be defined a Heritage Collection becomes slimmer every year. Again, this may suggest a potential conflict between the larger and smaller collection sections of the museum. Finally, up until the election of the new government, there appears to have been no required measures of outputs (visitor numbers, accessibility etc). The museum was given a budget to maintain the collections, not to attract visitors. The proposal of the Director General to allocate budgets on visitor popularity disturbs the well-established way of distributing budgets in a way that reinforced the current power base.

The *routines and rituals* are the way members of the organisation go about their daily work and the special events or particular activities that reinforce the 'way we do things around here'. It is clear from the scenario that it is not thought unacceptable for directors to directly lobby the Board of Trustees and to write letters to the press and appear on television programmes to promote their views. In many organisations issues within the boardroom remain confidential and are resolved there. However, this is clearly not now the case at the National Museum. The scenario suggests that there are certain *rites of challenge* (exemplified by the new Director General's proposals) but equally there are strong *rites of counter-challenge*, resistance to the new ways of doing things. Often such rites are limited to grumbling or working-to-rule, but at the National Museum they extend to lobbying powerful external forces in the hope that these forces can be combined to resist the suggested changes.

Stories are used by members of the organisation to tell people what is important in the organisation. The quotes included in the scenario are illuminating both in content and language. The Director of Art and Architecture believes that Heritage Collections have a value that transcends popularity with the 'undiscerning public'. He also alludes to the relative importance of collections. He suggests that fashion may not be a suitable subject for a collection, unlike art and architecture. Similarly, the anonymous quote about lack of consultation, that includes a reference to the new Director General as 'an ex-grocer', attempts to belittle both management and commerce.

In the centre of the cultural web is the paradigm of the National Museum. This is the set of assumptions that are largely held in common and are taken for granted in the organisation. These might be:

–   The museum exists for the good of the nation

–   It is a guardian of the continuity of the nation's heritage and culture

–   What constitutes heritage and culture is determined by experts

–   The government funds the purchase and maintenance of artefacts that represent this heritage and culture

There are two important elements of the Director General's proposals that are missing from this paradigm; visitors and customers. Changing the current paradigm may take considerable time and effort.

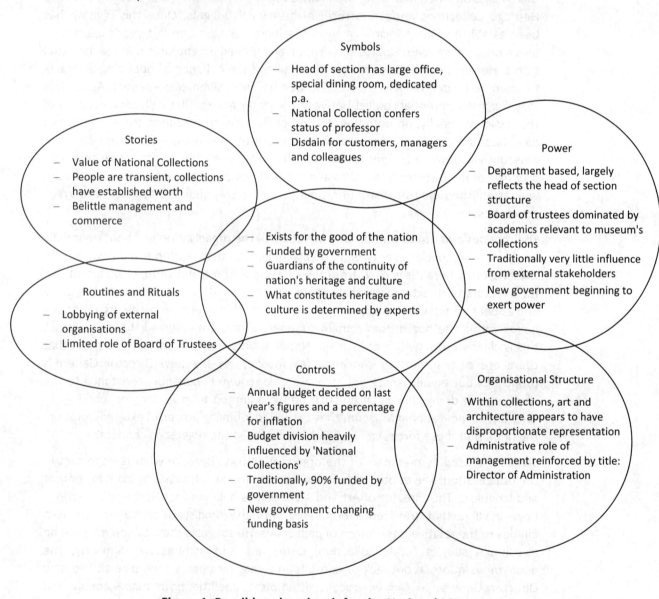

Figure 1: Possible cultural web for the National Museum

Candidate answers which considered the cultural web from a perspective of how it might have helped the Director General develop and implement proposals are also acceptable. For example:

- He may have considered deferring one or both of the proposals to remove the head of collection sections' dining room and their dedicated personal assistants. These are important symbols of their status and the financial gains from removing them seem unlikely to outweigh the consequences of their removal.

- He might have considered simply adding directors to the organisational structure, rather than inviting conflict by removing two of the collection directors. For example, replacing the current Director of Administration with the four new directors of his proposed structure (Finance, Visitor Services, Resources, Information Systems) might then have been more acceptable. The actual number of collection related directors remains the same (three), but their relative power in the board would have been decreased.

- An analysis of the cultural web identifies a possible conflict between the collection section heads that could have been exploited. A significant number of sections are not designated as Heritage Collections and so are not headed by professors. These sections are also less well represented on the board and they receive less money, which is allocated in a way that accentuates and perpetuates the relative wealth of the powerful sections. Published stories and deriding fashion, reinforces this division. The Director General could have identified proposals that could have brought the heads of certain sections 'on side' and so destroy the apparently harmonious position of the collection heads.

- He also needed to recognise the structure of the Board of Trustees. Their current composition meant that there was little chance that they would support his proposals.

- Finally, he would have benefited from understanding the paradigm of the National Museum and how at odds this paradigm is with his own vision and with the vision of the incoming government. In this context the cultural web has important implications for the heads of collection sections. Both the *power and controls* elements of the cultural web are undergoing significant change. The new government is exploiting its position as a major stakeholder and insisting on new controls and measures that reflect their paradigm. Although the heads of collection sections have successfully lobbied for the removal of the Director General, they are very unlikely to change the government's policy. Indeed the sacking of the Director General has strengthened the government's action and resolve. The sacking of the Director General may have been a *pyrrhic victory* and a much worse defeat now awaits the heads of collection sections.

(c) The *design* lens views strategy as the deliberate positioning of an organisation as the result of some 'rational, analytical, structured and directive process'. Through the design lens it is the responsibility of top management to plan the destiny of the organisation. Lower levels of management carry out the operational actions required by the strategy. The design lens is associated with objective setting and a plan for moving the organisation towards these objectives. In the context of the scenario, the government is now significantly involved in objective setting and tying funding to those objectives. The Director General has responsibility for defining and delivering a strategy within these objectives. There is evidence that he has gone about this in a 'top-down' way and not sought advice from current employees. On the television programme, employees were particularly critical of a lack of consultation; 'these proposals have been produced with no input from museum staff. They have been handed down from on-high'. In many ways, the approach taken at the National Museum under the new Director General represents the design lens view of strategy. Such an approach is not unusual in public sector organisations, where elements of strategy are dictated by government manifestos.

Strategy as *experience* provides a more adaptive approach to strategy, building on and changing the existing strategy. Changes are incremental as the organisation adapts to new opportunities and threats in the environment. The experience lens views strategy development as the combination of individual and collective experience together with the taken-for-granted assumptions of cultural influences. However, it has to be recognised that the assumptions and practices of the organisation may become so ingrained that it is difficult for people to question or change them. This certainly appears to be true for the heads of collection sections at the National Museum. The museum is now facing a fundamental change in the way it will be funded and the increased influence of the government suggests a change in the paradigm of the organisation. It seems unlikely that people with a vested interest in the current arrangement and perpetuating that current arrangement will come up with the change in strategy that is now required. The 'taken-for-granted' behaviour of people in organisations is one of the major barriers to developing innovative strategies. Strategy as experience seems innately conservative. It could work well when a small incremental change is required within a stable environment. However, this does not appear to be the situation at the National Museum and so developing strategy as experience may not seem a possible way forward and perhaps this is why the Director General explicitly rejected this approach.

Strategy as *ideas* has a central role for innovation and new ideas. It sees strategy as emerging from the variety and diversity in an organisation. It is as likely to come from the bottom of the organisation as from the top. Consequently, the organisation should foster conditions that allow ideas to emerge and to be considered for inclusion in a 'mainstream strategy'. Certain conditions, such as a changing and unpredictable environment foster ideas and innovation. It could be argued that the macro-environmental conditions for adopting this lens are present at the National Museum. Political, social and environmental influences might lead to new ideas – for example, the relocation of the museum and the exploitation of on-line access to resources creating a virtual museum. The museum is undergoing a fundamental change in priorities and funding and the consequences of these changes is unpredictable. On the other hand, the museum is a long-established conservative organisation with many symbols of hierarchy and deference. There is no evidence in the scenario of a group of people generating conflicting ideas and encouraged to compete with each other in an open and supportive environment. The National Museum seems to be dominated by powerful individuals protecting their own interests. Finally, a key factor in the selection of ideas is the marketplace. The National Museum is currently operating in a protected economic environment, although this is set to change.

There is plenty of evidence to suggest that it is difficult to change strategies in a hierarchical or deferential structure. At the National Museum the Director General decided to pursue a designed strategy. In many ways this appeared to be the natural lens to adopt given the objectives set by the newly elected government that was beginning to exert its power. This strategy may have worked if he had been more sensitive to the cultural web and, also, if he had not asked for the backing of the Board of Trustees. This was always unlikely to be forthcoming given its composition. The paradigm change means that it is unlikely that the experience lens would have proved fruitful. However, it may have been possible to exploit strategy as ideas if the Director General had carefully selected heads of collection sections who were relative losers under the current system.

ACCA marking scheme		
		Marks
(a)	Up to 2 marks for identifying appropriate macro-environmental influences in each of the six PESTEL areas – even if it is justifying the lack of influence. A further 8 marks are available for giving credit to candidates who have extended their argument in selected areas of the framework. It must be accepted that each area of the PESTEL will have a differential effect.	20
(b)	Up to 2 marks for each significant cultural factor identified by the candidate up to a maximum of 8 marks.	
	Up to 2 marks for an explanation of how each factor contributed to the rejection of the Director General's proposals, up to a maximum of 10 marks. This includes any ethical issues raised within the cultural analysis.	20
	Up to 2 professional marks are available for the overall clarity and coherence of the analysis	
(c)	Up to 8 marks for the insights offered by the lenses into the case study scenario.	
	Up to 2 professional marks are available for the overall clarity and coherence of the analysis.	10
Total		**50**

Examiner's comments

The first part of this question asked candidates to analyse the macro-environment of the National Museum. This was a straight forward question and, by specifically asking for a PESTEL analysis, it mimicked the same question part of the pilot paper. There were plenty of clues in the case study, most of which featured in candidate's answers. The only area that did not get much coverage was the legal responsibilities of the Board of Trustees.

PESTEL is concerned with the external environment and so points made about internal budget allocations could not be given marks. Overall, straying on to internal issues (such as strengths and weaknesses) was the only mistake made by candidates answering this part question. In general, it was answered very well.

The second part of this question asked candidates to assess the underlying organisational cultural issues that would explain the failure of the Director General's proposed strategy at the National Museum. Unlike the previous part of the question, no specific model or framework was suggested for this part of the question. A quote from one of the trustees was given to help candidates understand what was meant by organisational culture. This guidance appeared to be successful as the vast majority of answers did focus on organisational culture and not cultural forces concerned with nationality, history, arts or religion.

The model answer to this question uses the cultural web as a way of exploring cultural influences at the National Museum and considering how they would be affected by the Director General's proposed strategy. The case study scenario is rich with material to support this approach. For example, there are clear symbols of status which the Director General proposes to withdraw. There are important stories in the case study scenario which demonstrate how certain staff members view the public and management. There are well established financial controls which will be disturbed by the proposed new budgetary allocation method. There are important clues in the current and proposed organisation structure about how the Director General wished to redistribute power in the organisation.

Candidates could also have used the cultural web to reflect upon the acceptability of staff lobbying external organisations (television and press) and publically criticising the Director General. By failing to consider these factors (and indeed in some instances, failing to exploit divisions that a cultural web analysis would have exposed) the Director General's proposed strategy was doomed to failure. It is clear that the organisation's current culture is not compatible with the strategy that the Director General wishes to develop. Candidates who used the cultural web, if only in part, in their answers generally scored reasonably well in this part question. However, despite the explicit reference to cultural issues, many candidates focussed their answers on the scope and nature of change, accusing the Director General of proposing big bang change when incremental change would be more appropriate and pursuing revolution to evolution. These answers did gain marks, but only significant marks if they were related to the focus of the question; *the underlying organisational cultural issues.* Without such references such answers were light on detail, because the case study did not have enough information to support such an approach to the analysis. Consequently, answers tended to focus solely on blaming the Director General for not consulting staff when formulating his proposed strategy. This may be a legitimate point, but was insufficient to gain the twenty marks on offer for this part question. The final part of this question asked candidates to explain the three strategy lenses; design, experience and ideas and explain how each of these lenses could help our understanding of the process of strategy development at the National Museum. Understanding these lenses is not only a defined objective in the study guide, but also underpins the whole of the Business Analysis syllabus. Some candidates were very well prepared for this part question, showed great understanding and gained full marks. Others showed very little knowledge and so only scored two or three marks.

65   PLAYWELL LTD

Key answer tips

The first part of this question focuses on the goals and objectives of Alexander Simmonds and requires you to identify the stakeholders who could have an interest in the success of this company and how their goals might differ from his. The stakeholders introduced in the scenario are employees, the supplier, customers (in particular the special educational schools, and the retailer), and the bank.   You need to identify possible objectives, which would not always be identical to Alexander's, although there might be some overlap.

Part (b) – in the form of a briefing paper from a business consultant should highlight the key mistakes which Playwell made in its earlier expansion ventures and then to recommend action for the future.

In part (c) the main types of information concerning the company's business environment will come from the internal and external environmental audits and the competitor analysis.

Part (d) is straightforward bookwork, using the theories put forward by Quinn (logical incrementalism) and Mintzberg (emergent strategies).

(a)   Alexander Simmonds appears to be the principal stakeholder, determining both objectives and strategy for Playwell. He appears to follow the **'single sovereign' model** where the right and power to govern the organisation is vested in the single and ultimate authority – the Managing Director.

He appears not to be influenced by the goals or views of other stakeholders – although there is evidence that he does take a caring attitude towards his workers – *' – any future increase in sales revenue ought to generate improved profit margins. This was important if the company was to prosper and grow and provide security for the workers in an area where employment opportunities were limited.'*

His main objective has been to increase sales revenue with a hope that an improvement in capacity utilisation would improve profits and hence security for the firm. His strategy had been a **mix of market penetration and market development**. A constant theme has been the UK sales of the traditional toys through the major retailer and via direct mail. The two later strategies – toys for the special educational needs market and the European venture – have not proved successful.

There are a number of **other stakeholders** – employees, the supplier, customers (in particular the special educational schools, and the retailer) and the bank. Unsurprisingly, each of these had objectives that would not always be identical to Alexander's, although there might be some overlap. The employees, living in an area where potential for re-employment is low, are mainly concerned with job-security. Growth in sales revenue and profits would improve their chances of remaining in employment. They are unlikely to be knowledgeable or critical of the attempts of the company to seek new markets. Nevertheless they probably would not welcome ventures that detracted from the profitable core business. Stability, security and a concentration on core business are likely to be their watchwords.

The **supplier** has been generous to the company. Reliable sources of materials, with cheap credit provided until Playwell received final payment, provided Alexander with a good start to his entrepreneurial career. It is natural that this stakeholder would also welcome a growth in business. There is no indication as to how important Playwell is as a customer. However, looking at cost of sales figures, and recognising that labour will be a significant cost factor, it is unlikely that the supplier is heavily dependent on Playwell as a customer. Consequently the concern would be more about security and regularity of payment rather than continued growth. Any strategy that compromises that position would be unwelcome. Although the supplier could not influence a growth strategy, a change in the terms of supply could adversely affect the cash flow situation of Playwell.

Playwell is in a stronger position with regard to its **customers**. The **special schools** have enjoyed receiving products from Playwell at low cost in the expectation that further orders would be generated via the parents of the children. The schools would like to see a continuation of this practice. However, with the poor performance in this market, Alexander might want to withdraw from it or at least have sales which contributed some profit to the company. The schools have little or no leverage with Playwell, so it is highly unlikely that their objectives will bear much weight in this situation. The **multiple retailer** has more influence. Currently 40% of Playwell's profitable business is through this channel, and the retailer also depends on Playwell for a significant amount of its supplies. This mutual dependence should engender a compatibility of interests. Playwell wants guaranteed and profitable sales, whereas the retailer is looking for a continuity in supply of high quality but reasonably priced toys. Although Alexander will not formally take into consideration the goals of his key customer he will nevertheless pursue goals that will not damage this mutually-beneficial relationship.

The **bank** is also a stakeholder of Playwell. It has, in the past, provided the company with credit to fund its expansion plans. The company is still relatively small, although profitable, and therefore the bank is unlikely to be interested in the corporate objectives of Playwell, its main concern being that the company should be able to repay its debts.

There appear to be no other significant stakeholders. There is no evidence of other shareholders, and the company is insufficiently large or important for the local community or the government to have much interest in the corporate objectives of Playwell. Most of the drive and initiative has stemmed from Alexander. He is the driving force, and he is unlikely to take into account other people's views where they differ from his. Most will be happy with the objectives of corporate growth and profitability, as these will be supportive of their own primary goals. However, none of these other stakeholders would be able to exert sufficient power over Alexander to persuade him to adapt his objectives or change his direction.

(b)   **To**:   Alexander Simmonds

From: A N Other

Date: XX/XX/XX

Proposals for strategy development over the next 2–3 years

Introduction

The purpose of this briefing paper is firstly to highlight the key mistakes which Playwell made in its earlier expansion ventures and then to recommend action for the future. An analysis of the past will help to provide a framework for change so as to ensure a more disciplined future.

Past experiences

Although Playwell is continuing to make profits, it is obvious that the two most recent ventures into expansion have not been totally successful. The first venture has been into developing toys for the special education needs market. An inadequate assumption that sales into the special schools will generate many private sales demonstrates inadequate environmental research. The willingness to subsidise such sales is only justifiable if more full-priced sales could be achieved from selling to the parents of the children with special educational needs. This has not proved to be the case. In fact sales into this segment of the market are falling.

The second venture into overseas markets also illustrates poor research into the overseas environment. These overseas sales are stable but they are not generating the same level of profits achieved in the domestic market.

In examining the financial data it is obvious that the two recent developments have been relatively unsuccessful. Whereas sales in these areas have not grown as anticipated, there has been a deterioration in overall costs. Fixed costs have more than doubled over the past five years, outpacing the sales revenue. This unusual phenomenon is probably the result of requiring new expenditure to fund the new ventures. Unless the sales in these areas can be increased, these fixed costs will impose an increasing burden on the rest of the enterprise.

Looking at the cost of sales figures, whereas non-special UK sales show costs as about 35% of sales revenue, they are nearly 50% for the specialist market and 60% for the overseas market. It is obvious that the economies of scale being achieved in the UK toy market are not being achieved elsewhere. This can probably be explained by the following facts:

- The two specialist markets (overseas and special educational needs) have shorter production runs.
- The quality and safety of the products for the special needs schools needs to be higher.
- The margins here are deliberately set much lower in this sector.
- The costs of breaking into foreign markets are higher than expected.

It would appear that in the pursuit of growth, the **core business**, while profitable, has been neglected. Sales in this core business have risen by almost 50% over the previous five years whereas fixed costs have more than doubled. UK sales to these non-specialist outlets account for 75% of total sales revenue but only 66% of the direct costs. There is a strong likelihood that these market development strategies are gradually eroding Playwell's profitability.

Future development

If the company is still requiring growth, it might be advisable to withdraw from those areas discussed above, where growth is proving to be elusive but where costs appear to be higher than expected. Attention can then be focused on the UK market for toys. This market is still growing by 8% a year, without much effort. However, Playwell is still mainly using direct mail and one multiple retailer with 15 shops. This one group takes 40% of Playwell's sales in this sector. Using **Ansoff's product/market growth model** it seems advisable for Playwell to concentrate on the **'penetration' option** and to withdraw from the two specialist areas of special educational needs products and overseas markets. **Richardson and Richardson** developed these ideas and listed options as follows:

- **'Vegetate'** is a do-nothing strategy. This is not advisable here, as it would simply encourage Playwell to drift. This would be dangerous in a changing and difficult environment. The situation would deteriorate and the future option might be to liquidate all its activities.
- It is probably sensible to **'liquidate'** its current position in the two specialist areas — special needs and overseas. However, even this option has some alternative approaches. A quick divestment is unattractive. Capital has been invested here and it would be a waste to write it off immediately. Additionally a sudden withdrawal from the special needs market could attract unwelcome publicity.

- A better approach would be to **'harvest'** these less profitable parts of the company. This could be done gradually so as to improve cash flows. Prices could be increased and wherever possible costs and investment could be reduced. A further part of this strategy may involve **'attenuation'**, which involves cutting back or shrinking the business. This could include cost reduction strategies, improved marketing and possible asset reduction. This may be preferable if it provides a firmer base for future **'consolidation'**, where growth can be achieved by further penetration of the domestic toy market.

In this case the company can protect, maintain and even improve its market position by **enhancing the company's marketing mix** – improving the range, design and quality of its products, adjusting its prices, developing its distribution systems and redesigning its promotional campaigns. It might be possible for Playwell to buy up some of the competition or buy the order books of liquidating competitors. However, it would be important to ensure that the price was right and that there was no detrimental impact on the good name of Playwell. According to Richardson and Richardson a consolidation strategy would match Playwell's characteristics. It is operating in a relatively low growth market where it has a medium-sized market share. The company's position is strong and it is relatively open to change. This all suggests that the company should concentrate on what it does best and not take risks by diversifying too much into alternative markets or products.

Conclusion

It is my recommendation that Playwell should gradually dispense with the two latest ventures. Neither have demonstrated much growth potential, but nevertheless costs of maintaining a presence in these markets have risen. By concentrating on core business – 'sticking to the knitting' – the company should be able to generate sufficient growth to compensate for its other withdrawals.

Signed

(c)   It is essential to carry out a comprehensive audit before finalising a decision to enter an overseas market. There are three main areas to focus attention on:

1   the internal environmental audit

2   the external environmental audit

3   competitor analysis.

Internal audit

For a small company like Playwell, it is important to know whether the company has the skills and resources to successfully develop such a strategy. If it has no expertise in exporting, can it acquire it easily or can it cooperate with other small companies? Does it have the financial resources to be able to fund a potentially slow cash recovery programme? Is its culture flexible and responsive to adapt to different business practices? This assessment requires an honest analysis. A company, hoping to move into exporting, should not attempt to mask these problems. If it feels competent to deal with an overseas environment, it should go on to analyse this area in detail.

External audit

This could be summarised under a **PESTEL** (or SLEPT) **analysis**.

The **social factors** would examine demographic, cultural and purchasing variations within the selected markets. For Playwell this would focus on attitudes towards toy purchasing, the importance on quality, tradition, style, usage and price. It would also look at the main channels of distribution and assess whether these would be open to Playwell.

The **legal and political variables** need also to be assessed. These are often inter-dependent and can be looked at together. Restrictions on imports (trade barriers), quality standards, promotional and distribution regulations can all require adjustment to the way a company does or can trade internationally. It was apparent in the case scenario that the company was not well known and therefore its ability to command a premium price was limited. If Playwell does not wish to get into a price-cutting situation overseas it has to generate an attractive brand image. This will require a significant promotional spend and will also take more time to achieve than Playwell comfortably has.

The **technological variable** is unlikely to be critical. The company's products are not high-tech and do not appeal to that type of consumer. It is also unlikely that the mode of production will change. Much of the beauty and attraction of the product is because of its high quality, labour intensive method of manufacture.

Economics is possibly the most important environmental variable here. It is essential to monitor movements in areas such as the growth in national income, inflation, unemployment and currency levels. In a product such as toys that tend to have an elastic demand any adverse changes in the above variable will damage export potential.

Competitor analysis

It is important to evaluate competition in such a situation. **Michael Porter's five forces model** could be a useful analytical tool here. Locally-based competition is always going to be a threat for a company attempting to enter foreign market. It is necessary to assess how powerful the competitor is. Is it dominant within the market place, does it have strong distributor links? To what extent is the sector targeted by the exporter critical to the indigenous producer? If it is critical, the resistance towards imports will be high. It is not only existing competitors that need monitoring, but also potential new entrants. Are there significant barriers to entry? It is also important to consider whether product substitution is likely.

Without such knowledge of the overseas market and an assessment of the company's own corporate capabilities, it is probable that a company's venture into an overseas market will face many difficulties.

(d) **Strategic Planning**

Tutorial note

The current examiner is likely to include a discussion on Johnson, Scholes and Whittington in his answer to this question.

Quinn argued that many strategies are not the result of a fundamental re-think of an organisation's position with an associated transformational switch in direction. **Strategy shifts are evolutionary, and not revolutionary.** This has been termed **'logical incrementalism'.** There is a strong central and stable core of activity but there are changes on the periphery.

Mintzberg develops this concept by suggesting that **many incremental changes are 'emergent'** rather than deliberately planned. Ideas can be generated from anywhere within the organisation – a salesman responding to a customer's enquiries or an R & D scientist identifying a new use for a product or a process. Strategies do not have to be formulated by means of a thorough and fundamental review of the environments – internal and external – although such a process would be desirable if the strategy switch was to be substantial in response to a large change in environmental conditions. These emergent strategies reflect a flexible and reactive style of management which is well suited to a small firm operating in changing environment – Playwell.

There are a number of factors that will influence whether an emergent strategy is appropriate or not.

- In a small company, the managing director is usually in close touch with operational activities and so can initiate marginal changes as well as transformational changes should the situation require it. However, in a large company emergent strategies are better developed from the bottom where speed of response and detailed knowledge are more critical. **The success of emergent strategies here will depend on the culture of the company, the managerial style and the ability of the staff.** If the company does not delegate, tolerate failure or train its staff then it is unlikely that the climate will be ripe for encouraging emergent strategies. Staff will be unable to generate emergent strategies, or they will fear the consequences of being unsuccessful. If a company is in a critical position and swift and fundamental change is required, it is usually appropriate for the strategic decisions to be taken by the senior management. They are likely to be more effective. They have the knowledge of the organisation as a whole and not just part of it, they can usually command the most resources and they can push the whole organisation through change more forcefully.

- The **technology of the industry** is also an important factor. In a highly complex environment it is unlikely that the senior management can initiate the strategy if they do not fully understand it. This would encourage initiative from more junior managers and strategy will be emergent-oriented. However, if the investment costs of strategy change are substantial because of the complexity of the technology then strategy may have to be more deliberate. Similarly the existence of a dynamic environment can have divergent effects.

With a changing environment, it may seem desirable to encourage strategy development from throughout the organisation. This would result in speed of strategy adoption that is critical in fast moving times. However, if the environmental change is so dynamic, it may require a much larger strategy switch and this could not be accommodated by a more marginally effective emergent strategy. Such a fundamental change in strategy would need to be deliberate in style. It appears that emergent strategies are probably best-suited to complex technologies in a reasonably dynamic environment. However when technology initiatives involve high investment costs, or where the environmental change requires a fundamental change in strategy, then a more deliberate approach is advisable.

66 AUTOFONE

Key answer tips

There can be confusion for some students in part (a), when asked for a competitive analysis, as to which model to use. The examiner will be looking for Porter's Five Forces analysis. But the examiner has stated that, in future, where he believes such confusion might arise, he will be more explicit as to which model to use.

(a) One possible approach to answering this part of the question is provided by using Michael Porter's five forces framework. The framework is designed to analyse 'the structure of an industry and its competitors' (Porter, 20X4). There are five inter-connecting forces in the framework; potential entrants (the threat of entry), the bargaining power of suppliers, the bargaining power of buyers, the threat of substitutes and the competitive rivalry that exists amongst existing organisations in the industry. Each of these is now considered in turn in the context of AutoFone, focusing on those factors that have a significant effect on their industry. It must be recognised that other models might have been used in framing this answer and credit will be given for using appropriate models in the context of the AutoFone retail shops division.

Potential entrants (the threat of entry)

New entrants into an industry bring new capacity and resources with which they aim to gain market share. Their entry may lead to price reductions, increased costs and reduced profitability for organisations already in that market. Potential entrants may be deterred by high barriers to entry and by the threat of aggressive retaliation from existing competitors in the industry.

In the context of AutoFone's retail sales business, the following barriers appear to be the most significant:

Access to supply channels

The retail outlets of AutoFone were established before the network providers developed their own retail outlets. At the time, the network providers were sceptical that mobile phones could be sold through shops. Consequently, AutoFone was able to negotiate favourable long-term supply deals. It now seems unlikely that the network providers would sign such deals (because the new entrant will be a competitor of their own retail business) and, if they did, any deals would be at less favourable terms. As the managing director of one of the networks suggested, 'AutoFone had got away with incredible profit margins' when they signed the original deals in 1990. Improved supply terms would be attractive to the network provider and phone manufacturers (who would increase their profitability on each unit sold) but it would also cause profitability problems for the new entrant. Furthermore, the provision of networks is currently highly regulated, with licences still having thirteen years to run. It seems unlikely that public policy restricting the number of network providers allowed to provide services will change in the foreseeable future and so access to supply channels will remain a very significant barrier to entry.

Economies of scale deter entry by forcing the new entrant to come in at such a large scale that they risk strong reaction from existing firms in the marketplace. In the context of AutoFone, these economies of scale are associated with purchasing, service and distribution of products through a large scale retail network of 415 shops. Any new entrant would have to enter at a scale that would incur relatively significant capital investment. Furthermore, evidence suggests that the AutoFone brand is well known in the market place, with consumers identifying it, in 20X5, as one of the 'top 20' brands in the country. New entrants would not only have to fund a large number of retail outlets, they would also have to support their entry by investing heavily in 'un-recoverable up-front advertising' (Porter, 20X4). Capital will also be required for establishing significant inventories in the large number of retail shops required to achieve the required economies of scale.

Bargaining power of suppliers

Suppliers exert bargaining power over participants in an industry by raising prices or reducing the quality of their goods and services. Suppliers tend to be powerful when the industry is dominated by a few companies. This is the case with the mobile phone industry where the supply of networks is dominated by relatively few suppliers. The potential role of suppliers restricting the supply channel has already been recognised as a barrier to entry. However, when supplier power is high, there is a possibility that the suppliers themselves will seek forward integration, with 'suppliers competing directly with their buyers if they do not obtain the prices, and hence the margins that they seek' (Johnson, Scholes and Whittington, 20X5). This is exactly the situation affecting AutoFone, with network suppliers now running their own retail outlets.

There are two further elements of the retail phone market which encourage the supplier group to exert significant power. These are:

–   The supplier group does not have to contend with other substitute products for sale to the industry. There are few direct substitutes for the mobile phone (see below).

–   The supplier's product is an important input to the buyer's business. In AutoFone's situation it is a vital input into the business.

Hence the bargaining power of suppliers is extremely high in AutoFone's retail industry, although this is reduced by AutoFone's long-term supply contracts.

Tutorial note

Notice how the answer finishes with a conclusion on each force before proceeding.

Bargaining power of buyers

Buyers attempt to obtain lower prices or seek to get increased or better quality services or products. They do this by playing competitors off against each other. Under certain conditions a buyer group can have considerable influence. Many of these conditions only arise when the buyer itself is an organisation, not an individual consumer. For example, Porter suggests that buyer power is high when there is a credible threat of the buyer integrating backwards into the market place and so becoming a competitor. Such conditions do not appear to apply to the retail phone industry which is largely aimed at individual consumers.

However, some of the circumstances of significant buyer bargaining power do appear to exist in the industry. For example: *the products buyers purchase are standard or undifferentiated*. Buyers are always sure that they can find an alternative supplier and so they can play one supplier off against another. This is the case for sale of mobile phones as a whole, not just the retail sector. Furthermore, *buyers face few switching costs*. The only real lock-in is the term of the contract, currently twelve months long, after which buyers can switch to a competitor without penalty.

Threat of substitutes

Substitute products are usually products that can perform the same *function* as the product of the industry under consideration. The threat to the mobile phone industry is largely from other products that support mobile communication, such as Personal Digital Assistants (PDAs). However, the trend has been to integrate this technology into the offerings of the industry. The products offered by AutoFone include phones that are also mp3 players, radios, cameras and allow email and web access. Hence the industry appears to be relatively free of potential substitutes.

Competitive rivalry in the industry

Rivalry normally always takes place within an industry. Rivals jockey for position by reducing prices, launching advertising campaigns and improving customer service or product warranty. In the context of the retail mobile phone industry, the intensity of the rivalry is fuelled by:

Equally balanced competitors. The information in Table 2 suggests that the retail sales market is relatively equally divided between the five main suppliers. Evidence suggests this creates instability in the market because the companies are 'prone to fight each other and have the resources for sustained and vigorous retaliation'. (Porter, 20X4)

Lack of differentiation or switching costs. Mobile phones are largely perceived by customers as commodities. In such circumstances buyer choice is based on price and service, and this results in intense pressure for price and service competition.

Slowing industry growth. Evidence from Table 2 also suggests that industry growth is slowing considerably. There was less than 1% growth in 20X7. This means that competitors will increasingly pursue growth by increasing market share. This will intensify the rivalry between the competitors.

(b)   The two longest serving directors of AutoFone have suggested that the retail business should be divested and that AutoFone should re-position itself as an on-line retailer of phones. They argue that an organisation concentrating solely on Internet sales and insurance would be a 'smaller but more profitable' organisation. The CEO is vehemently opposed to such a strategy because it was the shop-based approach to selling mobile phones that formed the original basis of the company. He has strong emotional attachment to the retail business. The two directors claim that this attachment is clouding his judgement and hence he is unable to see the logic of an 'economically justifiable exit from the retail business'.

This question asks the candidate to draft a supporting case for the CEO's position, so that his response is not just seen to be based upon emotional attachment. The briefing paper should challenge the suggestion of the two directors and provide a reasoned case for opposing the divestment of the retail sales business. Of course, divestment might be the best option. The four network providers might pay a handsome price to remove AutoFone from the market. However, this is not the focus of the question!

Briefing paper

Introduction

This paper begins by looking at the basis of the directors' suggestion and claims that they have not interpreted the business situation correctly. It then goes on to examine the exit barriers that AutoFone must consider if they are to seriously consider moving out of the retail sales market.

Product and industry life cycles

It has to be recognised that industries and products move through life-cycles. The slowdown in market growth documented in table 2 suggests that, in the context of the product life-cycle model, the mobile phone market appears to be in either the shake-out or maturity stage. This means that buyers will be increasingly selective and that for many buyers the purchase will be a repeat event affected by previous experience. Companies in the market will have to fight to gain market share and the emphasis will increasingly be on efficiency and low cost. Similarly, industries pass from rapid growth into the more modest growth associated with industry maturity. Like most infant industries the mobile phone industry experienced rapid growth as it developed. However, evidence from table 2 and table 3 suggests that both growth and profits are now reducing as the industry matures. Slowing growth in the industry means that there is more competition for market share as companies seek to maintain their own growth at the expense of others. The transition to maturity usually means that the old 'way of life' of the company has to change. It is significant that the idea for divestment has come from the two longest serving directors. They can recall the excitement associated with rapid growth and, in the case of AutoFone, the pioneering of a business idea. In many ways the current expansion of AFDirect recalls the early period of AutoFone and so operating in the growing Internet market appeals to them.

Financial analysis

An analysis of Table 3 shows how profitability has fallen. The ROCE has steadily declined from over 18% in 20X3 to just over 5% in 20X7. Net profit margin has fallen from just over 12% in 20X3 to just over 3% in 20X7. Gross profit margins have not fallen quite as much as this. However, liquidity has remained almost constant during this period and so the ability of the company to meet its short term financial obligations has not been impaired by the fall in profitability. Gearing has risen during the period, from just over 21% to just over 32% and this reflects increased dependence on borrowed money. However, the absolute level of gearing should probably not be a cause for concern.

Porter suggests that one of the issues of the transition to a mature market is that directors have to scale down their expectations of financial performance. 'If managers try to meet the old standards, they may take actions that are extremely dysfunctional for the long-term health of the company.' The concern is that the two directors are pursuing such a policy, giving up too quickly and sacrificing a market and market share in favour of a course of action that they believe will deliver short-term profits. Divestment means that they are avoiding the challenges of taking a business like AutoFone into its mature stage.

Industry structure

Evidence from the analysis of AutoFone's competitive position (part a) suggests that AutoFone is in a retail industry dominated by powerful suppliers. Customer bargaining power is also relatively strong and reduced growth in the industry has led to relatively fierce competition. However, there is little threat from substitutes or new entrants because of the high entry barriers. Consequently, AutoFone is in a unique position based on its early entry into the market before the network providers became aware of the potential of retail sales. Furthermore, the company's uniqueness is enhanced by the fact that it is the only retail outlet to offer genuinely independent advice. The two directors appear to wish to carry on in the old way rather than changing strategy and expectations to reflect the maturing of the product and the industry. The real challenge for the board is to exploit AutoFone's unique market position in this changing landscape.

Exit barriers

Exit barriers are economic, strategic and emotional factors that keep companies competing in industries in which they are earning low or even negative returns. These are the barriers concerned with preventing the company from leaving the industry. In the context of AutoFone there are at least two potential non-emotional exit barriers which need to be considered.

Costs associated with leaving the industry

- The high cost of terminating shop leases. AutoFone achieved low start up costs by taking on very long leases. These leases are often in areas just outside the main shopping areas and so may be difficult to re-let.

- The high cost of staff redundancies and the liquidation of stock. There are currently 1,400 employees in the retail shops division.

Loss of strategic interrelationship with other parts of the company

The divestment of the retail shops business is likely to have an important effect on the two remaining divisions (AFDirect and AFInsure) in at least two ways

Reduced brand perception. Research has shown that AutoFone is a well recognised brand. However, most of this brand awareness was built by the retail shops division. The brand is also being constantly reinforced by consumers seeing and visiting these shops. Removing these will lose this reinforcement. Indeed if shops lie empty (because of the difficulty of reletting shops with long leases) it could harm the brand. Customers may perceive that AutoFone is a company in trouble (or indeed has ceased trading altogether) and so the Internet and insurance arms suffer as a result.

Reduced sell-on into related businesses. Evidence (from table 2) suggests that most insurance sales are in the age bands which predominantly purchase from the retail shops. Hence it seems likely that most insurance sales result from the sales of mobile phones in the retail sales operation. There are probably two reasons for this. Firstly, retail sales are mainly to customers in a certain age group. These customers are less confident in their purchase (which is why they are visiting the shop) and as a result can be guided in the purchase of insurance. Secondly, sales assistants giving this advice are given commission incentives to sell insurance. Consequently, the closing of the shops may have a major effect on the income of the insurance business.

There is also the issue of the cross-selling benefits between the retail sales and Internet sales business. There is evidence to suggest that some customers visit a retail branch to physically see the phones and to get advice before ordering on the Internet. This is currently an issue for staff in the shops who spend time explaining the features of a particular phone only to see the potential customer leave and order the same item on the Internet. Of course not all of these Internet orders are made through AFDirect because customers may take advantage of better offers from rival suppliers. However, a percentage of those sales must be as a result of a shop visit and the company potentially loses the benefit of these goodwill sales as a result of closing their shops. There is also evidence that Internet customers value the option of visiting a shop to get after-sales service for a product bought from AFDirect over the Internet. Although sales staff currently dislike offering this service, removing it may again hit Internet sales.

Conclusion

The company needs to recognise that the mobile phone market has matured and this has implications for both growth and profits. However, AutoFone remains in good shape to exploit the opportunities, such as repeat buying, of a maturing market place. Although profitability has declined, liquidity has remained constant. Gearing has increased but it has not risen to a figure which would cause concern. There are significant exit barriers to leaving the market place. The most significant of these is the loss of a strategic interrelationship with other parts of the company. The Internet division could suffer significantly if AutoFone closed its retail shops division.

	ACCA marking scheme	Marks
(a)	Up to 5 marks are available for recognising issues concerned with the difficulties facing potential new entrants into this industry.	5
	Up to 4 marks for recognising the very powerful bargaining position of suppliers in this industry.	4
	Up to 3 marks for identifying the bargaining power of customers.	3
	Up to 2 marks for identifying the threat of substitutes to the products offered in the industry.	2
	Up to 4 marks for identifying how competitors in the industry compete with each other.	4
	Up to 2 professional marks for the logical structure and clarity of information in the context of the case study scenario.	2
(b)	Up to 3 marks for recognising the brand recognition implications of moving out of retail sales.	3
	Up to 3 marks for recognising the likely impact on AFDirect and AFInsure	3
	Up to 2 marks for recognising cost implications of exit on leases, staff, stock	2
	Up to 2 marks for recognising that the financial position is not as poor as suggested by the two directors	2
	Up to 2 marks for interpreting the structural changes in the industry	2
	Up to 3 professional marks for using an appropriate style for the report and for the strength of argument and for appropriately utilising evidence from within the context of the case study	3

Examiner's comments

The only general point I wish to make concerns the use of case study scenarios. Many candidates had a problem applying the theoretical knowledge they had learned to the context of the scenario. At this level, there are relatively few marks available for describing a model such as Porter's five competitive forces. The vast majority of the marks are for recognising the presence and effect of these forces in the context of the case study scenario. Many of the answers seemed to suggest that candidates had very little practice in the application of models. If this is the case, candidates should integrate such practice into their preparation for the examination.

It is important that the fifteen minute reading time at the start of the examination is used effectively. One of the ways of making it more effective is to read the questions before reading the case study! This allows the candidate to put the case study into the context of the questions.

As in other papers, there is no irrelevant information in the case study scenarios. Candidates must concentrate on linking the scenario information to questions and (where applicable) to appropriate models. For example, the case study for section A stressed the value of the brand. This was relevant to part a (as an entry barrier to potential suppliers) and part b (as a reason for not leaving the retail market).

This question was based on a scenario of a mobile telephone company – AutoFone. There were three parts to this question. The first part asked candidates to analyse the competitive environment of AutoFone's retail sales division. This was worth twenty marks which included two professional marks. Two of the directors of AutoFone had suggested that this division should be sold off and that AutoFone should reposition itself as an on-line retailer of phones. The second part of the question asked candidates to write a briefing paper to the CEO to support the strategy of retaining the retail shops division. This was worth fifteen marks including three professional marks.

The first part of the question asked candidates to use an appropriate model or models to analyse the competitive environment. As expected, most candidates chose to use Porter's five competitive forces as a framework for answering this question. The scenario itself was constructed to encourage this approach. For example, there are very clear barriers to entry signposted in the scenario and the data summarised in table 2 provided information about industry competitors. Some candidates chose to use PESTEL and SWOT. PESTEL is concerned primarily with the macro environment and SWOT considers internal factors as well as external ones. However, candidates who used these two models could gain marks as they do identify relevant issues in the scenario. For example, the political perspective of PESTEL helps identify the issue of the government control of network licences and the long-term implications of this. Unfortunately many candidates penalised themselves by actually describing and using all three models (five forces, PESTEL and SWOT), leading to long answers with significant repetition. There is little to be gained by using different models to make the same points. It was also apparent that this repetition led to some candidates having time problems later on in the examination. This part of the question was only worth 20 marks and time should have been allocated accordingly. In general, this part of the question was answered relatively well with many candidates making appropriate use of the model they had selected.

The second part of the question asked candidates to draft a briefing paper to support a particular strategy. The CEO is strongly opposed to the suggestion of the two directors to sell off the retail shops division and to reposition the company as an on-line retailer of phones. The three professional marks associated with this part of the question reflect the fact that candidates are given extra credit for a well-argued, coherent case for retaining the retail shops division. Candidates needed to extract the information in the scenario that could be marshalled to support the case for retention. This part of the question was not answered well by many candidates. Consequently, I thought it would be useful to look at this part of the question in some depth and to identify how marks might have been gained by using information from the scenario.

The scenario explicitly defines two financial exit barriers. The first is the long shop leases that AutoFone have agreed in order to secure low initial rentals. It seems unlikely that these will all be immediately reassigned, particularly given their location on the edge of main shopping areas. The second is the cost of making the employees of the retail shops redundant. The scenario also makes it clear that brand image is a significant strength of AutoFone. Indeed it is has been 'rated by consumers as one of the top 20 brands in the country'. Closing retail branches sends the wrong message. The visibility of the brand is reduced as consumers no longer see the retail shops that serve to reinforce the brand image.

Furthermore, if the shops are closed down and perhaps some lie empty for a while, the brand can be tarnished and AutoFone would be seen as a company in difficulties or, perhaps, as one that has ceased trading altogether. Many candidates recognised that the closure of the branches removed the possibility of cross-selling that exists at the moment. It can be argued that internet sales will be affected by removing the pre-sales discussion and post-sales service and support provided by the shops. A further significant point is that table 1 shows that insurance is sold primarily to the age groups that purchase from the retail shops. 54% of retail shop sales are to people aged 41 and over. 71% of insurance sales are made to this age category. This compares with 22% of internet sales (AFDirect) made to people aged 41 and over. The inference is that AFInsure will suffer from closing the retail shops division. Many candidates also stated that people aged 41 and over had more disposable income than younger people and so were a more attractive market. This fact was not explicitly stated in the scenario, but it seems a reasonable assumption and credit was given for this observation.

The financial information that supported this case study primarily showed that the retail shops division is still in reasonably good shape. Nothing in the figures suggests that a radical change in strategic direction is necessary. The company is still profitable and indeed profit margins have improved in 20X7, compared to 20X6. Liquidity has remained fairly constant since 20X3, and although gearing has increased it is not significantly geared given the type of retail operation it is running. Some candidates did recognise this, suggesting that the two directors were panicking to think of closing a division that produced 85% of the company's revenue. They suggested that the two directors should just recognise that the product/market has reached a mature stage (table 2 and the financial figures support this) and so should scale down their expectations and adjust to new circumstances.

So, here in point form, are the main issues raised above. Each point (in suitably expanded form) would be worth one or two marks. It is not an exhaustive list, but it shows how marks can be gained by using the information in the scenario. There is a maximum of twelve marks for this question (remember the three other marks are for style, format and approach). However, more significantly, a candidate had to only make some of the following points to guarantee a pass mark on this question. Unfortunately many failed to do so.

- Cost of continuing leases, re-assignment costs
- Cost of making staff redundant
- Visibility of the brand
- Damage to the brand (closure, empty shops)
- Effect on internet sales of removal of pre-sales and post-sales support
- Effect on insurance sales and that division
- Age group analysis of retail and insurance sales (wealthy consumers)
- Financial figures do not support case for radical change
- Profitability has improved in 20X7 compared with 20X6 (corner turned?)
- Liquidity constant since 20X3
- Gearing slightly increased but not significant
- Retail division generates 85% of the revenue
- Recognition of mature stage of product/market (table 2 supports this)
- Directors over-reacting, need to recognise change and manage accordingly

67   WET

Key answer tips

In part (a) it is best to use the guidance given in the requirement as sub-headings. So there are 4 areas to cover and you should have four sub-headings. The best model to use overall is probably a SWOT analysis (this is the best/easiest model on 'strategic position' analysis), but lots of other models could have been used as long as you stick to the principle of keeping them relevant.

In part (b) there are three things to do: identify problems in the process (aim to find 4 or 5), discuss why they are a problem, and then attempt to solve them (try to find one solution for each problem). This should keep your answer relevant and specific and avoid the temptation to discuss unnecessary theoretical aspects of process redesign.

In part (c) it was important that you recognise that you are being asked about Customer Relationship Management from the terminology used in the requirement – namely 'acquisition' and 'retention'. Therefore it was important not to discuss e-business in general or get to involved in models such as the 7P's or 6I's.

(a)   This first part of the question asks the candidate to analyse the strategic position at WET. Johnson, Scholes and Whittington describe the strategic position in terms of three aspects; the environment, strategic capability and expectations and purpose. All three aspects are appropriate in the analysis of the strategic position of WET and this classification forms the basis of the model answer. However, candidates could have adopted a number of approaches to this question, perhaps choosing to focus on certain models (such as the value chain) or exploring the organisation through an analysis of the cultural web. All such answers will be given credit as long as they are within the context of WET and consider the external environment, internal resources and capabilities, and the expectations of various stakeholders. In the context of the ACCA *Business Analysis* syllabus, the strategic position is defined within section A of the detailed syllabus.

The environment

The PESTEL framework can be used to analyse the macro-environment. A number of influences are discernable from the case study scenario.

90% of WET's income is from members and donors (see Figure 1) who live in Arcadia, a country which has had ten years of sustained economic growth but which is now experiencing economic problems. The scenario reports a decline in Gross Domestic Product (GDP) for three successive quarters, increasing unemployment, stagnant wages and a fall in retail sales. There are also increasing problems with servicing both personal and business debt leading to business bankruptcy and homelessness. These are classic symptoms of a recession and this will have an effect on both individual and business donations and also on membership renewal. WET is 20% funded by donations (see Figure 1). In general, people give more when they earn more and lower earnings will almost inevitably mean lower donations. Furthermore, it could reasonably be expected that a recession places greater demand on certain charities, such as those dealing with social care (for example, homelessness). WET is not one of those charities (and so should not experience an increase in demand), so there must also be a concern that donors will switch donations to social care charities in times of recession. Similarly, current members may not renew their membership for financial reasons.

The pressures in the economy also appear to have stimulated the government to change the rules on charity taxation in an effort to raise government revenues. Previously, charities received an income from the government of 20% of the total value of donations and membership fees to reflect the income tax the donor would have paid on the amount paid to the charity. However, the government has declared that this is unfair as not all donations or membership fees are from Arcadian taxpayers or from people in Arcadia who actually pay tax. Consequently, in the future, charities will have to prove that the donation or membership fee was from an Arcadian tax payer. Collecting the donor's details will place an increased administrative strain on the charity, incurring more costs. The changes are also likely to lead to a fall in income. There are two reasons for this. Firstly, some of the donations were actually from non-Arcadian taxpayers (see Figure 1) and also research and evidence from elsewhere suggests that 30% of donors will not give the GiftHelp details required and so the charity will not be able to reclaim tax.

Although the recession in Arcadia has brought economic and political issues to the fore, the wider environment remains very significant to WET. The wetlands that they depend upon are likely to be drying out in a country where rainfall has dropped significantly. This will lead to the loss of the habitat that the charity wishes to protect. The charity must continue to monitor the situation and to support initiatives that should reduce climate change and perhaps increase rainfall.

The five forces framework proposed by Porter is usually applied to private profit-making organisations. However, the framework could also be useful in a not-for-profit organisation, considering the services provided by a sector (however that sector is defined). In such sectors, competitiveness may be about gaining advantage through demonstrable excellence. From WET's perspective, it needs to consider two overlapping sectors. Figure 1 suggests that 55% of members and 85% of donors give money (through donations or membership) to other charities. In such circumstances, WET is competing for the 'charity dollar'. However, 45% of members and 15% of donors gave no money to other charities, suggesting that these people are focused on the wetlands cause.

If charities as a whole are considered as a sector, then there appears to be a constant threat to WET of new entrants into this sector. The *barriers to entry* appear to be quite low. The ease with which a charity can be established has been widely criticised, but suggested reforms to the Commission of Charities have been rejected by the Government. However, if wetland preservation is perceived as a sector then the barriers to entry are quite considerable. WET already owns all of the significant wetland sites in Arcadia and, because of climate change, new sites would have to be artificially created at great expense. The scenario mentions a charity that has been formed to raise money to create a new wetland. The amount of money pledged so far ($90,000) is not only well below their target but also represents money that may have been donated to WET if this new charity had not been permitted.

The threat of substitutes is ever-present. WET competes for disposable income and so is exposed to *generic substitution* where donors and members decide to 'do without' or to spend their money elsewhere, including other charitable causes such as social care, particularly in a recession. If donors are giving to increase their own well-being and to feel good about themselves ('warm glow') then perhaps any charity will do, as *switching costs* are very low. The point has already been made that certain charities will experience higher demand during a recession and so WET will be vulnerable to such competition. However, if donors are committed to the wetland cause then supplier power is high because WET is the only significant wetland charity in Arcadia. The competitive rivalry again depends upon the perception of the sector WET is competing in. In the charity sector as a whole, WET is a small player. Figure 2 illustrates that most money is given to health charities, followed by social care and international causes. However, in the wetland sector, WET is the dominant charity, led by a recognised and charismatic public figure.

Strategic capability

The strategic capability of an organisation is made up of resources and competences. Considering this capability leads to a consideration of *strengths and weaknesses,* with the aim of forming a view of the internal influences on future strategic choices.

WET have significant tangible resources in terms of the wetlands that they own. They also have experienced and knowledgeable human resources, many of whom give their services for free. They also have a strong brand, associated with a well-known public figure. However, although these resources are significant and represent important strengths, the way they have been deployed needs examination. This analysis concerns the competences of the organisation; the activities and processes through which an organisation deploys its resources. The wetlands are uninviting to members, with poor access and poor facilities. The volunteers are disillusioned by poor management and feel that they are not valued. These significant weaknesses appear to be contributing to the organisation's inability to maintain the *threshold capabilities* required to retain members.

However, it also has to be recognised that WET does have unique resources (the wetlands) that competitors would find it almost impossible to obtain. It also has, in Zohail Abbas, a well recognised public figure that potential competitors in the wetlands sector would find hard to imitate. However, these *unique resources,* do need to be better exploited.

A cursory examination of the value chain reinforces some of the weaknesses identified above and identifies others. Within the primary activities, service is weak and this is contributing to a decline in membership. Marketing and sales is also an acknowledged weakness of the organisation. Within the support activities, human resource management (particularly of volunteers) has already been identified as a problem. Technology development (in terms of IT technology) is also a problem with restricted and cumbersome systems causing problems in the primary activities.

Summary of Strengths and Weaknesses

Strengths	Weaknesses
Ownership of wetlands	Management of volunteers
Experienced volunteer work force	Wetland access and facilities
Strong brand	Marketing and sales
High profile leader	Information systems

Expectations and purposes

The two previous sections have considered the influence of the environment and the resources available to the organisation. This section looks at what people expect from the organisation. This is particularly significant in WET because it has undergone a significant change in what Johnson, Scholes and Whittington term 'its ethical stance'. Under Zohail Abbas, the organisation was shaped by ideology and was 'mission-driven', demonstrating a single-minded zeal that charities usually require to achieve their aims. However, charities still have to be financially and operationally viable and WET relies on two important stakeholders; members and volunteers. In his speech at the 20X9 AGM Dr Abbas admitted that he had failed to sufficiently take into account the needs of members (leading to a decline in membership) and of volunteers (leading to a large turnover and scarcity of volunteers). WET now needs to recognise that 'stakeholder interests and expectations should be more explicitly incorporated in the organisation's purposes and strategies' (Johnson, Scholes and Whittington). Any strategy devised by the CEO needs to recognise this shift in ethical stance.

Understanding stakeholder perspectives and expectations is an important part of analysing the organisation's strategic position. Members require better access to wetland sites and more feedback on the activities of the organisation. Volunteers wish to be valued more, treated professionally and be given the chance to participate in decision-making. Having sufficient, knowledgeable volunteers appears to be necessary if some of the members' expectations are to be fulfilled. The contribution of volunteers becomes even more significant in a recession, when an organisation might have to reduce paid staff. WET also have to be aware of the potential effects of the recession on individual volunteers. For example, it appears that the failure to pay travelling expenses may have caused unnecessary hardship and led to the loss of volunteers. The CEO must also be aware that the consultation exercise with both members and volunteers will have fostered the expectations of a more open and democratic leadership culture, contrasting with Dr Abbas's autocratic style.

The original mission statement of WET was to preserve, restore and manage wetlands in Arcadia. It might be an appropriate time to revisit this mission statement, to explicitly recognise stakeholder concerns. For example, many members and volunteers are concerned with observing and saving wildlife, not wetlands. This could be explicitly recognised in the mission statement 'to save wetlands and their wildlife' or perhaps to 'preserve, restore and manage wetlands for wildlife and those who wish to observe them'. This would be a mission statement to which most of the stakeholders in WET could subscribe.

(b)   A number of problems have been explicitly identified in the scenario. However, the swim lane flowchart helps identify two further problems, which may themselves explain some of the other documented difficulties.

1   Firstly, the flowchart clearly shows that sales and marketing receive renewal confirmations before payment is cleared. This means that membership cards and booklets are being sent to members whose payments have not yet cleared. The receipt of this documentation probably suggests to these members that payment has cleared, so response to the payment request is not necessary. They probably see it as an administrative mistake and ignore the reminder. This would help explain the very low rates of people who pay when they receive their payment request. It is not, as the finance manager said 'an unethical response from supposedly ethical people', but a problem caused by their own system. Perhaps those that do subsequently pay have taken the trouble of checking whether money has been debited to WET from their bank or credit card account. The consequence of this faulty process is that a significant number of members unwittingly receive a free year's membership. It may also help explain why a number of members do not receive a renewal invoice at the end of their membership year. These renewal invoices are only sent to members who have been updated on the system after their payments

have cleared. If the payment never cleared, then the membership will have lapsed on the system and a renewal invoice will not be raised the following year.

2   Secondly, the receipt of a cleared renewal payment is only recorded when the membership details are updated on the Membership computer system by the Membership Department. Consequently, renewal reminders will be sent out to members whose payment is still awaiting clearance. It currently takes the Finance Department an average of five days from the receipt of the renewal to notifying the Membership Department of the cleared payment. There is also a backlog of cleared notifications in this department, awaiting entry into the computer system. These members may also receive unwanted renewal reminders. Finally, members who have received a membership card and booklet through the process described in the previous paragraph will also receive a renewal reminder letter. Presumably most members ignore this letter (after all, they have received the new card and booklet) and believe that the charity is inefficient and is wasting money on producing renewal reminders for those who have already renewed their membership. Charities have to be careful about spending money on wasteful administrative processes. It might be these renewal reminders that led to the accusations about the charity wasting money.

A number of options can be considered for redesigning the membership renewal process. Some are given below. They range from simple changes, remedying the faults identified in the previous answer, to significant changes in the way WET will accept payment. Credit will be given for answers that suggest feasible amendments and also specify the likely consequences of the change to WET as an organisation, to employees in affected departments and to the systems they use.

- Remedy the fault identified in the previous part of the question 1(b) by only notifying sales and marketing of membership renewal once payment has been cleared, not just received. The consequence of this is that a membership card and booklet will only be sent to members who have paid their subscriptions. This should lead to an increase in subscription income because a percentage of members whose payment did not clear first time will now make sure that their payment clears. No changes are required to the membership computer system or departmental responsibilities.

- Remedy the second fault identified above, so that renewal reminders are only sent to members who have not responded to the renewal invoice, not to members who have responded but whose payment is still awaiting clearance. This could be achieved by initially updating the membership system when a payment is received. The consequence of this is that renewal reminder letters will not be sent to members who have renewed, but not yet had their payment cleared. This will reduce waste and improve member's perception of the efficiency of the organisation. However, it will require a change to the computer system and will also lead to more work for the Membership Department and another handoff between the Finance and Membership Departments. This handoff will introduce the chance of error and delay. The Membership Department already has a backlog in entering the details of members' renewals where payments have successfully cleared.

- A suggested generic process improvement is to reduce the number of handoffs between parts of the organisation by reducing the number of swim lanes. It is perceived that handoffs have the potential for introducing delay, cost and error. A number of options are possible, but perhaps the most obvious is to merge (for the purpose of this process) the functions of the Finance and the Membership Departments. This is because at one point (and perhaps two, if the previous suggestion is adopted) Finance are simply notifying the Membership Department of an event (payment cleared and, potentially, payment received), which the Membership Department has to then enter into the computer system. The case study scenario suggests that there is a backlog of membership details to enter. This probably results in renewal reminders being sent to members who have already renewed and whose payment has cleared. Merging the swim lanes will require all staff to have access to the computer system, sufficient competency in using it and sufficient numbers to clear the backlog. The likely consequence of the change is that renewal reminder letters will not be sent to members who have already renewed and paid. This will reduce waste and improve members' perception of the efficiency of the organisation. Another likely consequence is that staff may need re-training, their jobs redefined and any political problems caused by merging two departments will have to be identified and addressed.

- Another generic process improvement approach is to make sure that validation takes place as soon as possible. It should be part of the primary activity, not a separate activity as it is at the moment. This approach is particularly appropriate in the checking of payment details in the renew membership process. The early validation of payment could be achieved by giving the member the option of renewing by credit card over the Internet. 60% of the payments are made through credit cards. About 5% of these payments are completed incorrectly and the Finance Department have to raise a finance request to ask for the correct details. If a member was able to make a credit card payment over the internet then all errors should be eliminated, as the validation of details will be made straight away by the credit card provider. WET should receive the money sooner (improving the cash flow position) and there should be a reduction in finance requests. This should reduce costs and perhaps allow a reduction in head count in the Finance Department. However, the internet site would have to be extended to include an e-commerce solution and this will cost money. As well as the initial cost, the provider of the financial solution will also charge a fee for each transaction.

- The final option presented here is a more radical solution that is currently used by many subscription organisations. The principle is that renewal will happen automatically unless the member specifically asks for it not to. They have to 'opt out', rather than 'opt in' as under the present solution. Automatic renewals could initially charge the credit card used for the previous year's membership. Renewals that required a positive response would only be sent out to those who paid by cheque. Renewals to credit card customers would remind them that the card would be debited on a certain date, but that no action was necessary to secure another year's membership. This should help address the retained membership issue discussed in the scenario, based on the fact that opting out is much harder than opting in. WET might also consider offering payment by direct debit, using similar process logic to that used for credit cards. In a bid to reduce members who pay by cheque, discounts may be offered for paying by direct debit or automatically triggered credit card transactions. As well as increasing subscription income from higher member retention, the solution should lead to improved cash flow and reduced administrative costs. Changes to the membership computer system will have to be specified, implemented and tested.

(c) The incoming CEO of WET has identified the better acquisition and management of members, volunteers and donors as an important objective. She has identified them all as important *customers of WET* and she sees e-mail and website technology as facilitating the acquisition, retention and exploitation of these customers. In discussing customer relationship management, Dave Chaffey (see syllabus Reading List) considers customer acquisition, customer retention and what he terms customer extension. This classification is used in this model answer. However answers that still make the same points, but do not use this classification, are perfectly acceptable.

Customer acquisition

Customer acquisition is concerned with two things. The first is using the website to acquire new customers (donors, members and volunteers). The second is to convert customers acquired through conventional means into on-line customers.

When people visit the WET website they may already be committed to becoming a member, a volunteer or giving a donation. For these people, the process of enrolment or donation must be completely clear and complete. There must be no break in the process which might allow doubt or hesitation and lead the participant to withdrawing. The final two options suggested in the answer to question 1(b), would provide such a complete solution. Customers enrolling or donating on the website might also be given inducements, such as a reduced membership rate or a free book.

People who visit the website and are still uncertain about joining or donating might be induced to take part in an offer, which requires them to enter basic details (such as name and e-mail address) in return for some service or product. For example, free tickets for an open day or discounted prices on selected books. These e-mail details are essentially sales leads and become the basis of selected future e-mails encouraging recipients to join or donate. They might also be used (if a phone number is requested) for telephone sales calls.

Incentives may also be required to convert current customers to the web site. A typical approach is to define a members' area where members have access to various resources and offers. For example, a webcam showing live action from selected wetlands. Existing members would also be encouraged to renew membership on-line, as discussed in the previous part question.

Customer retention

Customer profiling is a key area of both acquisition and retention. WET needs to understand the needs and interests of individuals and target them accordingly. At the broader level, customers can be differentiated into segments, such as prospects, members, volunteers and donors. These segments will be communicated to in different ways and this can be reflected in the website, for example, by establishing different areas for volunteers and members. However, profiling can also take place at the individual level, reflected in personalised e-mails to individuals that reference known interests and so encourage continued participation in WET.

On-line communities are a key feature of e-business and may be created to reflect purpose, position, interest or profession. Two of these communities are particularly relevant to WET. The primary one is of *interest,* creating a community for people who share the same interest or passion for wetlands and the wildlife they support. This could be created as an extension of the current WET website or as an independent site, where criticisms of WET itself could be posted. WET should either sponsor or co-brand such a site. Communities provide an opportunity for members and volunteers to actively contribute to WET and build up loyalty, making continued membership more likely. They also provide WET with important feedback and ideas for improving their service to both members and volunteers. WET themselves might also wish to get involved in communities of *purpose* where people are going through the same process or trying to achieve a particular objective. For example, there are websites dedicated to providing a one-stop-shop for those wishing to make donation to charity.

Customer extension

This has the aim of increasing the lifetime value of the customer by encouraging cross-sales. This may be within the scope of WET itself, for example, by selling WET branded goods. However, it is also likely to include links and advertising on the WET site for associated products. WET will receive income from direct advertising fees or from a commission in the sales generated from the site. For example, book purchases may be handled through a specialist book site (leading to commission payments) or binoculars purchased from a manufacturer (payment for advertising space). Direct e-mail is also an effective way of telling customers about the products of other companies and can also be used to publicise promotions and new features and so encourage visits to the website.

ACCA marking scheme
(a)   1 mark for each relevant point up to a maximum of 25 marks. This includes a professional mark for appropriate tone, a professional mark for appropriate structure and two professional marks for the scope of the answer (4 marks in total).
(b)   1 mark for each relevant point up to a maximum of 15 marks.
(c)   1 mark for each relevant point up to a maximum of 10 marks.

Examiner's comments

In general, the first part question was answered well by candidates, using a wide range of appropriate models and frameworks. PESTEL analysis was widely used, and although this was appropriate, there was insufficient information in the case study scenario to completely answer the question using this framework. For example, there was little about technology and socio-cultural issues. Consequently, many candidates discussed the restricted web site technology of WET under this heading, which is strictly an internal weakness. In this instance, we were prepared to give credit, as this weakness was part of the wider understanding of the strategic position. However, candidates must be careful in the future to stick to external issues if a PESTEL analysis is specified in the question.

Relatively few candidates used the five forces framework, although valuable points could have been made using this approach. For example, the low barriers to entry were a particular issue raised by the Commission of Charities reluctance to tighten up on charity registration. Similarly, the threat of substitutes is ever present, with WET competing for the 'charity dollar' in an environment where 'doing without' is also likely. A discussion of low switching costs would also have brought credit.

Finally, some candidates did not restrict themselves to assessing the strategic position. They began to suggest strategic solutions and options which were not required by the question and so no credit was no given. This reinforces the need for the candidate to carefully read the question and to answer within its scope.

However, overall this part question was answered well, if a little narrowly, with many answers well-written and well-structured, so gaining most of the professional marks on offer.

The case study scenario included a description of the process for membership renewal. This textual description was supported by a swim lane flowchart. Candidates were asked to analyse faults in the renewal process and to suggest solutions. This part of the question was worth 15 marks. It required an analysis of the business situation and the formulation of appropriate solutions. It did not require long theoretical descriptions of process redesign patterns, although these could have been usefully applied to the scenario.

This was a practical analysis question and it is disappointing that many candidates were unable to answer it effectively. Too many answers simply suggested that the computer system was at fault and should be fixed. Candidates failed to spot glaring errors in the process (sales and marketing received renewal confirmations before payment was cleared, delayed acknowledgement of payments led to renewal notifications being sent to members who had paid) and so many answers were too general and did not gain the marks on offer. Good answers needed to identify the fault, describe its consequences and suggest solutions, which could have been quite simple, and did not require any cross-reference to theoretical concepts.

Effective customer relationship management is essential to charities. Sheila Jenkins wishes to use email and website technology to facilitate the acquisition and retention of WET's customers and support WET's aim to gain increased revenues from members and donors. This part question was about effective customer relationship management; acquiring, retaining and exploiting customers. It was not a general question about the principles and benefits of web site and email technology. Too many answers were not in the context of the question. For example, independence of location (place) may be an attribute of the new media, but how can this be harnessed (if it can) in the context of customer relationship management? Many candidates probably thought they had answered this question relatively well (talking about 7Ps and 6Is) but in reality many answers did not score well and overall, this part question was disappointedly answered. In many cases, candidates provided good answers to a very different question.

68   LIONEL CARTWRIGHT

Key answer tips

As you read the scenario you should discover the following key issues:

A problem faced by the business is a shortage of supply of organic produce. Lionel does not have enough purchasing power and he needs to open more outlets.

Finding suitable outlets for new sites is also a problem.

It is suggested that Lionel believes that his core competences match the critical success factors for the industry. His core competences appear to be: market knowledge, a flexible operation and motivation. But what are the CSFs? The business compares badly with similar outlets in the US.

With any case study question, you will probably be required to extract information from a table of data. Here, the comparison is between a UK and comparable US outlet. In making a comparison, it would seem clear that higher sales revenue/gross profit margin and lower lease costs are significant differences.   Why are costs better controlled in the US? Compare expenses as well as materials costs. Why are sales per outlet higher in the US? The data points to longer opening hours, a larger range of products, and more customers. A higher number of staff per outlet might also affect sales revenue, as well as speed of service to customers.

(a)   The main focus of this part of the question is on the benefits of **emergent or opportunistic strategy formulation as opposed to the more rational or deliberate approach**.

There are some advantages in Lionel favouring the non-planned approach. The size of Lionel's enterprise and resource commitments is sufficiently small that a disciplined integration of activities is not essential. Furthermore, whereas a deliberate strategy often tends to ignore the human dimension, an emergent strategy is likely to fit into Lionel's philosophical outlook. Lionel has demonstrated that he needs to respond quickly to environmental changes if he is to take advantage of the opportunities available to him. If he had to rely on a formal planned set of procedures this would be an impediment to his 'flexibility'. There is a likelihood of 'paralysis by analysis'. There is also a risk that entrepreneurs such as Lionel may be given a false sense of security by the planning process. It may encourage them to ignore initiative and intuition, believing in the superiority of the planning process. Lionel is known to have a 'feel' for the market and the associated environmental factors. It would be a shame if these skills were to be sacrificed because of an over-confidence in the planning process. It is essential that Lionel should adopt a process that allows him to have the flexibility to respond to changes in the fast moving markets in which he has chosen to do business. One must also recognise that it is not always possible for a small company to finance, or have the skills to acquire the requisite knowledge necessary for, a deliberately planned strategy. Furthermore, as Mintzberg has written, an emergent strategy allows for learning to take place. Ideas develop until 'patterns emerge'. A deliberate strategy would discourage such organisational learning.

However, there are some problems which Lionel might experience as a result of relying on an unplanned approach. It appears that Lionel has **no real sense of direction**. He has moved from road haulage to fast foods, from information technology to health foods. There is no common theme, apart from responding to entrepreneurial instincts. There is **unlikely to be any accumulated learning** from these previous ventures to benefit Lionel in his latest enterprise. Because Lionel only has an intuitive feel for the market, he has **not much expert knowledge of the industry or the relevant environmental factors**. Consequently he will find it difficult to choose between competing alternatives with respect to strategic options. He may also not fully appreciate the resource implications of his decisions, nor may he be able to fully integrate the required activities for strategic implementation. Lionel's track record does not suggest that he has a long-term set of ambitions.

A more **planned approach** might encourage him to be more consistent in his actions and allow the strategies to be more completely fulfilled. Although he seems to have enough financial liquidity at the moment, his past performance might discourage banks or other financial institutions from considering him to be a good risk. In some industries where there are long time frames for decision-making, decisions must be agreed upon and adhered to, otherwise there will be confusion. As *Lynch* has stated, experimentation may be appropriate in the early years but later strategy needs to be more fixed for lengthy projects. It is also easier to control activities if there is a planned scenario. The danger with Lionel's mode of strategy formulation is that it is difficult to assess whether anything is going wrong, because there are no prescribed targets. The rational approach should not be spurned simply because it does not fit in with the entrepreneur's way of working. Evidence and logic can be helpful in formulating a coherent and reliable strategy. Finally if the strategic direction is not clearly specified then it will be difficult for employees to understand their roles and functions within the enterprise. Confusion will reign and there will be a lack of integration of activities.

(b)   It is obvious from the financial data that Lionel's stores are not as profitable as those in the USA. He has chosen to operate in a high profile market, focusing on the affluent, trans-national youth segment. This market needs aggressive promotion but Lionel does not have the volume of stores necessary to provide the revenue to fund the necessary level of advertising. Furthermore, although Lionel claims to understand the market, he has no expertise in this line of business. His recent ventures have shown no continuity, so it is unlikely that he will be able to bring much insider knowledge into this operation. Motivation and entrepreneurial activity are no substitutes for operating knowledge.

A number of key pointers can be derived from the table. The two most critical factors differentiating the UK stores from those in the USA are, firstly, the UK stores sell less than those in the USA, despite being larger in shop space, and the rental costs in the USA are much lower. Labour costs in the two areas are about the same but the US shops are open longer and have more staff, possibly an indication of a higher level of service. This might also account for the longer waiting time within UK stores – a point not likely to endear itself to the rather selective clientele who would be seeking improved service. If one takes into account the level of sales in the UK it is apparent that the cost of materials is somewhat higher than in the USA. It would also appear that operating efficiency within the UK is lower. A UK store requires a higher level of inventories and has greater wastage despite offering less choice than its US counterpart.

As one might expect the UK administrative and marketing costs are higher but with a larger number of outlets to spread these charges over these would fall substantially. In fact one might argue that marketing expenditure should be increased – a necessity if the image and demand is to be enhanced. These indicators illustrate the poor performance of Lionel's stores compared with those in the USA.

It would appear that Lionel's company does not possess the **critical success factors** required for this type of enterprise. He has over-exaggerated the existence of his core competences. This embryonic company needs a number of competences if it is to survive and prosper in this high profile and competitive market. Firstly it needs a strong reputation to attract the affluent youth market, which can be exceptionally fickle and possesses limited brand loyalty. The company has no real reputation in this field. Its expenditure on advertising is relatively low and it owns only a few centrally-located sites that are needed to attract the required market. In fact these sites are not only few in number but they are exceptionally expensive to acquire.

They need to be in expensive city centres and Lionel is unlikely to have the finance to expand his empire rapidly. It is also critical that the company should have access to cheap and guaranteed high quality produce. It appears from the case scenario that these supplies are becoming increasingly difficult to obtain with increased competition from larger and wealthier buyers. Any disruption in, and reduction in the quality of, the supplies will adversely affect the reputation of the juice outlets, so damaging the valuable and critical image of Lionel's outlets. Another important critical success factor, which does not appear to be a core competence of Lionel's young company, is the issue of operating efficiency. Compared with US stores (seen as competitors/role models in a global market place) the UK stores are performing poorly. There appears to be less choice of juices, the waiting time (a reflection of customer service) and opening hours are inferior to what is expected within the USA. Unless Lionel can achieve an improvement in these areas, his outlets are unlikely to achieve the profit levels experienced in America.

(c)   **External Analysis**

Key answer tips

The key here is to use a couple of key models – the PESTEL, SWOT and 5 Forces are likely to be best. You shouldn't have to cover more than two or three models in order to get all the marks available. The answer shows how other models could have been used but there would be no need to do this under exam conditions.

It is critical that Lionel should obtain as much **external data** concerning the juice market as possible. The methodology basically can be summarised under a number of headings – a study of the **competitive framework** and an understanding as to how the **SLEPT factors** (social, legal, economic, political and technological) can influence demand. **Michael Porter's five forces model** would be a suitable approach for assessing the **competitive environment**. Not only would it assess direct competition, but it would also look at latent competition as well as threats from unanticipated substitutes – other fashion areas which could compete for the spending power of the affluent, sophisticated youth market. This model also would consider the position of the suppliers and examine how they might adversely affect the success of Lionel's enterprise. The model might also help Lionel reflect on his relationships with his prime customers. The benefit of the Porter model is that it provides a comprehensive view over the competitive environment. However, the downside is that it can be too indiscriminate in its approach.

Strategic group analysis may be a more focused tool. This gives more detail as to the positioning of the company with relationship to strategies of the most direct competitors – in this case similar companies in the fashionable café markets in Europe and in the USA. In order to make the boundaries of the market clearly 'strategic group analysis' attempts to identify closely defined groups with similar strategic characteristics. In Lionel's case these similar characteristics could include – the extent of product or service diversity, the type of market segment covered, the level of quality and the distribution methods used. This should enable Lionel to know more about his competitive position.

Another model which could have helped Lionel to make a rational decision as to whether he should enter this new market is the **General Electric matrix (multifactor portfolio model)**. This enables a manager to 'harmonise' his corporate business strengths with the attractive features of the proposed industry. It is more frequently applied to strategic business units so as to assess where future investment should take place. However it could equally well be applied here. Lionel could then assess what the attractive features in the market place are and whether they will be helpful to him.

What is the annual rate of growth? Is the market stable or volatile? Is it a seasonal demand or regular throughout the year? Is the competition fragmented or dominated by a major player? Are customers brand loyal or not? Is demand price sensitive or not? These, with many other features, could help provide Lionel with a picture of the market place and give him an indication as to whether the venture is likely to be successful or not.

Another obvious model is **SWOT analysis**. By examining the external opportunities and threats much of this information should be uncovered and be made available to Lionel.

The **SLEPT environmental model** should enable a scanning and monitoring approach to be used to help Lionel to design an appropriate strategic plan to best attack and capture the target market. Lionel should have been advised to carry out some marketing research to try to uncover the main determinants of demand for the juice drinks – was it health, fashion or convenience that mainly influenced the potential customers? Is the market price-sensitive? Uncovering all of this would be helpful in devising a promotional policy, involving both advertising and sales promotion. It would also be important to have information about 'traffic patterns' so as to know the optimum areas for locating the stores. This would enable Lionel to investigate the availability of potentially suitable outlets. There would also need to be an awareness about food labelling regulations, particularly with reference to promotional activity. It also might be helpful if Lionel and his employees knew about the latest technology and operational techniques. This should help to provide an improved level of service, better inventory control, quicker service, wider choice of products, the need for fewer staff, etc. It would also be useful to know the socio-demographic structure of the population so as to be able to estimate the size of the potential market. An understanding of economic conditions might help Lionel to appreciate whether the economy was buoyant or not. Products such as organic juices are likely to sell better when incomes are growing and the population feels better off, i.e. higher discretionary income and lower income taxes. Equally an understanding of the legal regulations such as employment law and sales taxes would be useful.

If Lionel could have a greater understanding as to how the environment might impact upon his operations then he might be able to take remedial action to improve the situation.

(d) (i) Lionel would gain a few advantages from **internal growth** but these would be offset by substantial disadvantages. A main advantage of pursuing internal growth is that the company can gain and maintain knowledge of both markets and products. However as this is not a high-tech innovative industry the need to obtain and safeguard proprietary knowledge is not critical. Another benefit of this strategy is that Lionel will not be dependent upon others and he will be able to **maintain control** with no clash in management styles. This will be particularly attractive to Lionel who has already demonstrated that he likes to have control (his IT venture) and that he did not enjoy his experience as a franchisee. There is also a benefit with the internal or organic approach – there would be **minimal disruption to the existing business** as might occur with a strategy of acquisition. However, given the size of Lionel's current enterprise, this is not a critical issue. A major benefit of internal growth is that it is often **cheaper**. While this is certainly true compared with a strategy of acquisitions, the use of strategic alliances involving franchise agreements can be cheaper as partners usually provide much of the finance. The problems of such an approach are, however, important. Lionel desperately needs to expand the number of outlets. This would give him wider exposure and permit him to achieve both operational and purchasing economies of scale.

To attempt this on one's own would be slow, providing **less impetus for growth**. By associating with others, Lionel might overcome barriers to entry by building up networks so getting access to sites and supplies.

(ii) While **acquisitions** provide a rapid means of expansion and could provide Lionel's enterprise with the necessary critical mass, there are some disadvantages that need to be understood. First this mode of development can be extremely **expensive**, beyond the means of a smallish entrepreneur such as Lionel. Furthermore there are often **difficulties in integrating** another company or group of companies with the original company. There may be a **lack of cultural fit**. This is very likely with a person like Lionel who appears to have an individualistic, even idiosyncratic, approach to business. Nevertheless the **quick means of expansion** is an attractive proposition in this scenario. Furthermore an acquisition can often provide a company with **access to product and market knowledge**, often otherwise denied to the acquiring business. **Synergies** can often be obtained, whereby scarce resources can be integrated with other more abundant factors. In this situation Lionel may provide the management and know-how whereas the acquired company could bring to the deal retail sites, finance and even retail skills. It has been suggested that a reason for an acquisition is to buy out a latent competitor. Given the small size of this specialist market segment this does not seem to be a realistic argument in this case.

If both internal/organic development and an acquisition seem to be unattractive modes of corporate growth, another option is a strategic alliance or, as in this case, a franchise operation as the preferred means of development.

(iii)   The advantage to Lionel of a **franchise operation** is that it can be a quick method of achieving market expansion. One can use the **capital and local market knowledge of the franchisees**. This could be particularly beneficial in developing outlets overseas where expenditure would be high and Lionel possesses no expertise. An additional advantage is that **franchisees are often highly motivated**, having a stake in the enterprise and a share of the profits. This increased commitment from the partners, coupled with the **lower risk and financial exposure** for Lionel might encourage him to consider this form of development. However Lionel, having been a dissatisfied franchisee earlier in his career might not be so enthusiastic. He will recognise the **potential for a conflict of interests**. He may also suspect the **competence of franchise partners**. Will they have access to the necessary prime retail sites and will they understand this new and fashionable business? Another benefit of a franchise operation is that invisible assets (goodwill and brand development) are often at less risk. These assets are often isolated for the purpose of management and with trade-mark/brand protection there should be a reduced threat to Lionel of any asset expropriation.

There is not an easy option for Lionel to choose for market development. Each of the options has fundamental flaws, Lionel must select the one which permits him to have rapid expansion, while maintaining an up-market image. He must protect his existing **investments** and, at the same time, not over-commit himself financially. Other factors should also be taken into consideration but Lionel should not allow personal prejudices to overcome a rational decision. For once this decision needs to be well thought out and argued. It ought not to be intuitively taken.

ACCA marking scheme		Marks
(a)	Distinction between rational and emergent strategies. Reasons for emergent strategy.	2
	– Size of Lionel's company	2
	– Lionel's philosophical approach	2
	– Need to be flexible	2
	– Danger of being over-confident in planning process	2
	Problems with emergent strategy	
	– No sense of corporate direction	2
	– No consistency in action	2
	– Less support from financial institutions	2
	– Reduced opportunity for control	2
	– Fails to give employees sense of purpose	2
	Maximum marks for part (a):	10
(b)	Current situation and analysis of data	8
	Critical success factors	
	– Need for good promotion/strong reputation	3
	– Access to prime sites	3
	– Access to raw materials	2
	– Acquisition of operational efficiencies	2
	Maximum marks for part (b):	15
(c)	SLEPT factors and marketing research: customer knowledge, traffic patterns, food labelling legislation, economic conditions, technical/operational techniques	3
	SWOT analysis	3
	Competitive framework: Porter's five force model and/or Strategic Group Analysis	4
	Maximum marks for part (c):	10

(d)	Advantages of internal growth: gain and safeguard knowledge, maintain control, less dependent upon others, no problems of confused management style: but (problems) slower to achieve results, no guarantees, can be expensive if trying to cover all areas.	6
	Advantages of acquisition: rapid growth, access to markets and products (retail sites), pre-emptive strike on competition: but (problems) expensive, risk of poor cultural fit.	6
	Advantages of franchise operations: quick, use other people's resources, increased motivation from franchises: but (problems) conflict of interests, poor competence of franchisees.	5
	Maximum marks for part (d):	15
Total marks available		**50**

69 MEMORIAL HOSPITAL

Key answer tips

In part (a) of the question you are asked to analyse stakeholders. The best model to use would be Mendelow's Power-Interest Matrix. To evaluate a strategy in part (b) you should use Johnson and Scholes' tests of feasibility, suitability and acceptability. For part (c) you could use either the Ansoff matrix or Porter's generics in order to suggest possible strategic options.

(a) In examining the factors which enabled the surgeons to impose their will on the other stakeholders, it might be beneficial to refer to the Mendelow matrix. This links the power of stakeholders with the willingness of these stakeholders to involve themselves in determining the objectives and strategies of an organisation. It is clear from the case scenario that this stakeholder group has both power and the intention and willingness to use it. According to the matrix this makes them 'key players'.

The **power of these surgeons** is correlated to their **scarcity** and also to their **status**. With reference to their status, surgeons and senior consultants have traditionally been held in high repute and other staff have often deferred to their wishes. They have often been seen to operate in an altruistic fashion, putting medical issues above financial and political concerns. They appear to operate with an ethical concern that supposedly places them above self-seeking concerns. However, their current threat to withdraw their labour questions this belief and clearly suggests that they now have vested interests to pursue. Ethical considerations appear to have been ignored.

The real source of their power is less their status and reputation and is more due to the fact that they can resort to the traditional threats of withdrawing their labour. They are one of the few stakeholder groups where the supply of labour is relatively inelastic. There are few people with their training and expertise. If they do not work it is difficult to find replacements. Other staff are less critical. Administrators and finance specialists can be recruited from other non-medical sectors. Staff in less specialist fields – catering, laundry – are not so scarce and although any threat by them to withdraw their labour would be inconvenient, it would not have a long-term damaging effect on the Hospital. Replacements would be found. The nursing sector might pose some problem but the supply of nurses is substantially greater than that of surgeons and it is unlikely that this group would be able to hold the Hospital to ransom. The smaller the supply of any commodity (in this case the surgeons) the easier it is to use the threat of withdrawing it to win concessions – usually a price or wages rise, but in this case the agreement to their strategy.

Few of the other stakeholder groups have such power or have such unanimous commitment to a given set of objectives as the surgeons. The **patients**, as a group, have minimal power. There might possess some limited political influence, but it is apparent that the poor, in general, have little political leverage. It is usually the more affluent and educated middle class who can exert political pressure and these are the people who will have private medical insurance and do not use Bethesda Heights significantly. The **local politicians** have a conflict of interests. On the one hand they claim that they want to retain the facilities of the Hospital; nevertheless they are unwilling to fund the activities. This lack of clarity in their objectives makes them vulnerable in attempting to impose their objectives on others. They are not sure what their objectives are – lower taxation or a better-funded hospital. The general medical support staff and the administrators do not appear to be as cohesive a unit as the surgeons and are unlikely to impose their will on others. The **general medical support staff** seem to be more altruistic and would be unwilling to jeopardise the well-being of patients, whereas the **administrators** will always suffer from appearing to consider money ahead of medical welfare. Consequently, these other stakeholder groups seem unable to challenge the potential self-seeking objectives of the surgeons. Nevertheless they could have used stronger arguments to attempt to defeat the financially damaging strategy currently being proposed – higher capital investment but a smaller medical base, incurring likely redundancies. The surgeons claim that the new investment will improve the potential and image of the Hospital but it could involve high human costs – less medical care for the poorer community and redundancies for other stakeholders.

The general medical staff could emphasise the ethical issues – the focus of the Hospital should be on those who are unable to care for themselves. There are already facilities for those with private insurance. Where will the poor now be able to go to if Bethesda Heights Memorial Hospital turns its back on them?

Similarly the local politicians have an electorate to consider. They should publicise the dangers of this proposed strategy – curtailing opportunities for treatment for the disadvantaged – but they will have to abandon their strategy of reducing funding to the Hospital. This group cannot logically hold both positions. It is likely that such a strategy (of maintaining at least the level of existing funding) would be electorally popular and should be pursued with vigour by the politicians. The financial administrators need to highlight the dangers of pursuing the surgeons' approach. The Hospital could have a forecasted deficit of US $75 million within three years. This increased capital investment plus the likely down-sizing of the Hospital, so lowering the government funding available does not seem to be a viable strategy for long-term survival. This needs to be emphasised.

The other stakeholder groups seem to have surrendered to the bullying tactics of the surgeons, despite having supportable positions themselves. With the limited information available it is difficult to be confident in any outcome. What is certain is that the surgeons have harnessed and utilised their power and influence to impose their decisions on others. Alternative viewpoints have not really been presented and it is difficult to assess whether this is the optimum outcome for Bethesda Heights Memorial Hospital.

(b) The current strategy, proposed by the Management Committee, is to invest in improved surgical facilities in order to improve the image and reputation of the Hospital as a provider of surgical services and facilities. This decision has been taken, despite the proposed deficit for the Hospital over the next few years. The objective is to win over patients with private medical insurance. There is a likelihood that the Hospital will have to reduce its bed capacity to fund this development. This strategy ignores some fundamental issues. A significant proportion of its revenue comes from both central and local government based upon work carried out. The proposed down-sizing of the revenue will threaten some of this income. It is unlikely that the private medical insurance will compensate for this fall. Even the neighbouring local hospital only receives about 30% of its revenue from private insurance. It will take time before private patients are convinced by the new facilities to switch their patronage. Furthermore, there is no assumption that the neighbouring hospital will not compete to keep its wealthier market segment. The strategy fails to address the **one key issue – a shortage of income**.

There are a number of other problems highlighted by Table 1 in the question, and it is unlikely that the proposed strategy will correct these issues. Costs in both hospitals are rising by a comparable percentage – about 6% over the year, so it is unlikely that Bethesda can change this too much. Costs of labour, equipment and drugs are probably standard throughout the country. However, if one considers the **cost per bed** then it is obvious that Bethesda is uncompetitive. Its costs are more than 10% higher than its rival's. It is difficult to make accurate calculations because of the lack of knowledge of the private business done by the two hospitals, but assuming that the governments –both local and central – calculate their grants in an equitable fashion, then the rival hospital is still carrying out more medical work for non-private patients than is Bethesda, despite the impression given within the case scenario.

An obvious problem for Bethesda is the **low revenue from medical insurance**. Only about 30% of the rival's income comes from this source. The situation is being aggravated by the fact that whereas income from medical insurance for Bethesda is falling that for its competitor hospital is actually rising.

It is possible that the proposed strategy of seeking surgical excellence might increase income from this private sector, but if it results in fewer hospital beds, as threatened, then it is likely to reduce income from governmental sources.

It can be seen from other quantitative data that Bethesda is **not operating as efficiently** as its rival. The proposed new strategy is unlikely to alter the hospital's performance greatly. The numbers of residential patients treated annually by both hospitals has been rising but if one attempts to calculate capacity usage in each facility Bethesda's performance is inferior to that of its rival (the calculation involves the number of beds multiplied by days in the year divided by the average length of stay in hospital – in the calculation for Bethesda this is $350 \times 365/10$ (including days prior to and including the operation).

Full capacity would be about 12,750 operations whereas in reality only 10,650 were carried out. This **failure to fully utilise existing capacity** is made all the worse because waiting times, being three times as long as in the rival facility, have actually lengthened over the last year whereas in the other hospital delays are now shorter. Whilst recognising that 100% capacity utilisation may be unrealistic, the hospital should be able to improve on this under-utilisation.

It would also appear that Bethesda's **quality is not always up to an acceptable standard**. Re-admission rates are almost double those of its rival. This of course could be function of the shorter period spent in hospital – a premature release and it could also be the result of dealing with more complex medical conditions, although there is no evidence of this. On the evidence available, Bethesda should try to improve on its performance here. It is hardly a good promotional message for the hospital in attempting to attract more privately-insured patients. Similarly the mortality rate is rather high. As inferred earlier, this type of outcome could be explained by the hospital treating more complex medical conditions, but there is no evidence to suggest this.

A critical statistic involves the **staff numbers employed** by the two hospitals. Bethesda employs more staff per bed available than does its rival. Furthermore, whereas the rival hospital is cutting back on its numbers, Bethesda is actually increasing the staff it employs without a corresponding increase in hospital capacity. As labour in this service industry is a significant cost the hospital should be focusing more on this unfavourable trend and attempting to correct it.

The **trend towards day surgery for minor operations**, involving no overnight stay in hospital, appears to have been actively pursued by the neighbouring hospital. This appears to be a cheaper and more efficient method of utilising scarce resources. The number of day operations carried out there has increased by nearly 500% whereas at Bethesda the increase has been much more modest. Such a move towards day surgery needs to be encouraged. It is an attractive option for the medical insurance companies who will be actively seeking to minimise their expenditure for hospital payments. If Bethesda falls significantly behind in this area it will be much less competitive in attracting new business. Furthermore Bethesda Hospital has failed to improve on its ratio of out-patients to those committed to hospital. These patients may require only consultations, as distinct from expensive surgery. This facility is nevertheless a valuable adjunct to the array of services and facilities offered by the hospital. It is invariably a cheaper alternative to surgery. Whereas its competitor seems to be enhancing its position in this regard, Bethesda, whilst not neglecting this potential, is not expanding its facilities rapidly enough.

Whilst the strategy proposed by the surgeons will have little direct impact on many of these areas it is possible that the resultant reduction in hospital beds availability might encourage Bethesda to operate in a more efficient manner. It is possible that capacity utilisation might improve, and labour may be reduced to reflect improve productivity. However it is also possible that the new strategy might see a shift in resources towards more day surgery but it is unlikely that there will be improved out-patient services.

(c)   There are a number of alternative strategies that the Management Committee could have selected. It could have placed pressure on the local government to increase its funding to the Hospital. Adverse publicity could be damaging to the local government and so political as well as moral pressure could have been exerted on that stakeholder group.

As mentioned earlier, there are a number of glaring inefficiencies in the way the Hospital currently operates. Using the Ansoff market/product matrix, the Hospital could concentrate on improving internal efficiencies. Cost reductions and increased productivity could enable the Hospital to reduce its deficits. This might involve staff reductions and increased bed utilisation. An improvement in the Hospital's reputation/image might make Bethesda more attractive to private patients and hence to the medical insurance companies. Furthermore, **product development strategies**, the Hospital focusing more on day surgery or out-patient services might attract increased funding from either local or central government.

It is possible to introduce **Porter's generic strategies** within this context. Cost leadership itself may not be a suitable strategy to pursue. For this to be effective, Bethesda should be able to obtain economies of scale. From the evidence provided, the Hospital is smaller than its direct competitor and therefore the opportunities for such an approach are limited. Furthermore, price is an unlikely competitive tool within this environment. Nevertheless, the other generic strategies might be more appropriately employed. **Focus strategies** could be used to advantage. By concentrating on specific areas – care for the elderly, the young children, mental health or even transplant surgery – it is possible that Bethesda could build up a strong reputation in the medical world and consequently widen its catchment area. Such a strategy might enable the Hospital to concentrate its scarce resources more effectively, operate more efficiently and increase its income base. A **differentiation strategy** is also a possibility. Bethesda could offer distinctive services such as improved after-care and home support facilities. However, as with so many of these options an initial investment will be required which may be difficult for this hospital to afford.

It is possible that **collaborative strategies** could also be employed. Medical costs, including the cost of pharmaceutical drugs, are demonstrating an inexorable rise throughout the world. It may make sense for Bethesda to seek an alliance with the neighbouring hospital. In an ethical industry such as medical care, it is unattractive to have expensive competition between rivals. There is no shortage of demand for their services and so competition is not a matter of survival here, although it might of course engender increased performance within the different institutions. By working more closely together, the two hospitals may avoid a costly and wasteful duplication of resources. The hospitals, both faced with the threat of reduced government support, could choose to be mutually supportive. They could share certain facilities such as Accident and Emergency wards and Intensive Care Units. They may even be able to benefit by having common purchasing programmes. This may help to reduce the increasing costs of drugs and medical equipment. Such co-operation may enable both hospitals to concentrate on specialist medical areas (another way of achieving a focus strategy). Perhaps one hospital may choose to concentrate on cancer treatment, whereas the other may target heart disease. This would not prevent both hospitals providing a comprehensive range of the most common and demanded medical and surgical services. However it would discourage the hospitals from pursuing expensive expansion in areas where demand may be limited. Maybe micro-surgery is one of those areas.

It is impossible with the limited information available to select one particular option. However the decision should be taken in a less-threatened and more rational climate. The one taken in favour of the surgeons' strategy does not seem to have been well thought out. In evaluating any proposed strategy it is important that certain criteria should be met (*Johnson and Scholes*).

- Is the strategy acceptable?
- Does it meet the requirements of all stakeholders? Clearly the strategy chosen does not satisfy this criterion.
- Is the strategy suitable?
- Does it satisfy organisational objectives? Bethesda's immediate objective is to avoid the forecasted financial deficits. It is probable that the proposed strategy will cause the situation to deteriorate in the short term.
- Is the strategy feasible?

- Will it match organisational capabilities and the market requirements? This is less easy to answer. There is no strong data within the case scenario to help to make a decision. Nevertheless in the absence of strong supportive evidence, it does seem that the selected strategy is highly risky.

(d) **Ethics/social responsibility** can be considered to be very relevant in this context. No government is likely to leave medical care entirely to the market economy where only those with the means to pay for treatment can be given care. Many governments may apply tools derived from the market economy but these are primarily used to instil efficiency and not to ration care. Many theorists have recognised that organisations need a 'moral' position if the organisation's objectives are to be adhered to and supported by the workforce. Campbell and Yeung show how values and behaviour standards need to be included in a mission statement (the **Ashridge Mission Model**) as well as focusing on more tangible issues such as purpose and strategy. Peters and Waterman, in developing the **7S model** for their publication *In Search of Excellence*, developed the concept of 'superordinate goals', demonstrating the supremacy of some type of vision, ethical or otherwise, over the other more finite concepts of style and systems, etc. Mintzberg has developed the concept of a **missionary organisation** whereby the various parts of the organisation unite around a dogma or belief. This should reduce the opportunity for competition or organisational conflict. If Bethesda had been inculcated with such ethical concerns it is unlikely that the Management Committee would have been held to ransom by the surgeon stakeholder group.

In many organisations, there are stakeholders who are there not just for self-gain. The relatively low financial rewards of many ancillary medical staff – nurses, junior doctors and support staff – is evidence of this. This ignores one major stakeholder group – the patients. In such an environment where ethics and social responsibility appear to be so important the short term interests of certain stakeholder groups should not be pursued at the expense of those stakeholders who are without power and who need protecting. The objectives should not be just about short-term gain but, as Johnson and Scholes comment, they should help to 'shape society'. Charities, including hospitals, may be viewed in this light, but this does not mean that decisions and objectives should be devoid of commercial sense. Organisations have to survive if they are to fulfil their purpose – they must remain financially viable. Therefore occasionally decisions may have to be taken which appear to conflict with an ethical stance – redundancies, closure, etc. These decisions have to be taken to ensure a long-term survival.

If Bethesda Heights Memorial Hospital can **generate a stronger ethical culture**, it may be easier for the differing stakeholder groups to unify around a set of objectives and strategies (the missionary organisation introduced above) and unilateral and possibly selfish actions may be avoided. It may be that the surgeons have strong non-selfish arguments in favour of their option. Unfortunately these have not been clearly stated and their proposal appears both divisive and self-centred. They need to be more open in their reasoning. They should place best practice, commercial integrity, altruism and a concern for others at the top of the agenda. There must be some accommodation between business ethics and enlightened self-interest.

ACCA marking scheme		
		Marks
(a) Factors giving surgeons a powerful negotiating position		
– Scarcity of labour		2
– Status		2
– Single-mindedness and unity of purpose		2
– Power and influence		2
Maximum marks available for this section		7
Arguments from other stakeholder groups		
– patients		3
– local government		3
– general medical and other staff		3
– local community		3
Maximum marks available for this section		8
(b) Problems being experienced by Bethesda		
– reduced income		3
– increased costs		3
– low income from medical insurance		3
– poor operational efficiencies:		
Lower bed capacity usage		2
Higher mortality rates		2
Staff numbers higher		2
Re-admission rates higher		2
Less use of day surgery		2
Poorer ratio of out-patients to residential care		2
Maximum marks available for this section		10
Unlikely to solve the problems of Bethesda		
– fewer beds		3
– increased costs of investment (scarce resource)		3
– does not address the real problems – failing revenue etc		3
Maximum marks available for this section		5
(c) Other strategies including evaluation		
– Improve internal efficiencies		5
– Collaborative strategies		5
– Use of generic strategies – focus, differentiation etc		7
Maximum marks available for this section		15
(d) Definition of social responsibility and its application to a hospital environment		2
Use of social responsibility in academic models		3
Stakeholders' objectives linked with social responsibility		3
Maximum marks available for this section		5
Total		**50**

70 WAMC

Key answer tips

You may have chosen to use a SWOT analysis or the 6M model and some may apply the value chain, demonstrating that the company has not successfully integrated all its activities clearly. Some candidates may even focus on the need to market more comprehensively using the marketing mix model. Even life cycle analysis could be employed, demonstrating the urgent need for new product development. The answer could contain all these models (and even more) and marks will be awarded where appropriate. There is no one precise and correct methodology in answering this section.

(a) **Position Analysis**

To: Kenneth Murphy, Managing Director World-Wide Agricultural Machinery Company

From:

Date:

A Review of the Position of the World-Wide Agricultural Machinery Company (WAMC)

Introduction

I have chosen to evaluate WAMC by assessing its current internal capabilities and by considering the external environment and trying to identify where the company is failing to match its capabilities with the requirements of the environment. I will also, where feasible, attempt to identify any critical differences in performance between the two companies. This will not be as a special sub-section but will be integrated into the main body of the text.

Internal capabilities

Manufacturing

WAMC has a reasonable range of products but specifically lacks a tractor unit which is critical as this is a lead product which influences customers in buying additional ancillary equipment. The company has traditionally neglected product development and has little history of innovation. Although the company has had a number of regional factories these have recently been reduced in number. While manufacturing flexibility might have been reduced there has supposedly been a saving in the cost base as fragmentation in production has been eliminated and more economic manufacturing routines have been put in place. The French company, however, appears to be a leaner manufacturing organisation. They have only two factories with modern plant, even though the product range is restricted. Although the cost saving measures undertaken by WAMC seem to be working, the value of output per employee is still low compared with AM – in 20X6 it was $40,000 compared with $49,000 for AM. The French company also spends significantly more on R & D than WAMC although recently Agricole Mecanique has reduced its expenditure in this area by about 10%.

Marketing

Neither company has a strong reputation in this field. WAMC has traditionally neglected market development and even when it moved into overseas markets – Europe – it did not gather sufficient market intelligence about its customers or even its competitors. Nevertheless it has its own distribution network which should give it more control and easier access to customers and it spends significantly more on marketing than AM, although the costs of this distribution network are likely to be included in this total. It appears that AM has a weak brand name in comparison to that of WAMC. In summary it would appear that whereas the French company has a strong technical reputation it is rather weak in marketing. The UK firm spends more on marketing and appears to have a stronger marketing infrastructure but much of this effort seems to be unfocused.

Human resources

There is little data here. The firms are not too dissimilar in terms of numbers employed. However, the UK firm has savagely reduced numbers of a loyal and long established workforce which appears to have resulted in an alienated group, possibly reluctant to accept further changes. They have already seen specialisation imposed on a seemingly craft-based manufacturing process in pursuit of cost savings. How much more will they be prepared to accept? However the French company is young, having only been established 10 years, and it is likely that the workforce may be more flexible. It has also not had the trauma of large-scale redundancies.

Finance

A major problem of WAMC, possibly accounting for the current losses is the cost of sales. For WAMC this accounts for 65% of total revenue whereas for the French company it is just over 52%. The spending on marketing is higher in the UK company (as previously stated this may be accounted for by the larger costs of the wholly owned distribution outlets) whereas the French spend more on R & D. This could be an argument for synergy to be obtained from merging the two companies' operations. The French administrative costs are relatively higher but unlike those in WAMC they appear to be stable. A major area of concern for the French company might be its level of debt and its inferior gearing ratio as compared with that of WAMC. This could account for the improved price/earnings ratio of Agricole Mecanique as the French company has correspondingly less equity capital. However, one must recognise that this improved ratio may be offset by the reduced flexibility of a company with a much heavier debt burden. These factors need to be considered when contemplating a merger or acquisition.

External environment

Two seemingly obvious models to use for such an external evaluation are (a) a SLEPT analysis and (b) the Porter five forces model. Unfortunately the amount of data provided does not permit a comprehensive review and so I will summarise what the limited material suggests under the following headings.

Buyer requirements

Varied agricultural policies require different products and possibly differing marketing techniques when attempting to enter foreign markets, particularly in Continental Europe. Demand tends to be more limited as farmers now require more specialist equipment. It is increasingly unlikely that one buyer will buy a whole range of products. Nevertheless they do seem to want to buy their specialist equipment from the company which supplies the tractor unit. Buyers are also looking for innovative products which are less costly to repair and which are more flexible. It is uncertain as to whether WAMC can meet these requirements. Buyers also are looking for better and more comprehensive service facilities as well as to financial credit when purchasing these capital items. There is evidence that WAMC does not have the capacity to provide this level of support.

Competition

There is little data on competition but it would be surprising if each European nation with an agricultural sector did not have its own traditional equipment producer. It is probable that many, similar to WAMC, will not have reacted to changes effectively, but there are likely to be a number of new companies such as Agricole Mecanique which will be now threatening the established producers. The farming sector has traditionally been seen as conservative in its buying habits and there could be some residual loyalty to the older suppliers, but one must never forget that farming has been seeing margins squeezed and so it is to be expected that price will be a pertinent factor. The only established fact about the competition is that the large automobile manufacturers, particularly the US ones, are now strong in the tractor unit production sector. This must act as a deterrent to existing agricultural equipment producers. The US companies have the volume, income and reputation to defeat any local-based rivals. They can afford the investment for innovation and new product development. They have the funds to maintain the required infrastructure service and credit facilities – which customers desire.

Conclusion

The evidence suggests that WAMC, in its current form, is ill-equipped to satisfy market needs, while maintaining its position as a major supplier within the UK market. It has attempted to improve its productivity but this may prove to be inadequate in the long term. It needs to focus more precisely on market needs, and match these to its capabilities. It will be unwise to aim to return to its traditional position. The world has moved on. Small fragmented producers are unlikely to be able to survive other than as niche market players. There will probably need to be consolidation in the market place.

I hope that this brief overview will be of use to you.

Signed:

(b)   Kenneth Murphy is currently proposing four strategies to improve the situation of the World-Wide Agricultural Machinery Company. Each of these strategies has merits but there are associated disadvantages which may worsen WAMC's overall position.

Selling off the distribution network

It is estimated that this would result in a cash injection for WAMC of $15 million. Given its current financial position this would provide the company with both funds and a breathing space to initiate both product and market development. This suggestion should be evaluated. However it will also be necessary to investigate how much of the company's current business is dependent upon having a wholly owned and controlled distributor network. One must remember that withdrawing from tractor manufacturing did not have the beneficial effect that was expected. A cost-benefit analysis should be carried out. Furthermore in the light of the proposed merger between the two companies the strength of WAMC's marketing infrastructure may supply a necessary synergy to complement the R & D expertise of Agricole Mecanique.

Buying in tractors

Recognising the importance of the tractor unit in selling ancillary agricultural equipment, WAMC is belatedly seeking to rectify the situation. Understandably setting up a new production facility would be financially expensive for the company, although a merger with AM would achieve this objective for little financial outlay (control being a different matter). There are dangers of relying on sub-contractors for the supply of critical products. Firstly will the quality be up to WAMC's requirements? It will be foolish to jeopardise one's reputation by using products manufactured outside one's own control but carrying the all-important brand. Secondly will the supplier be prepared to change production schedules when and if demand requires it to do so? Furthermore if the products prove to be popular for WAMC it will certainly affect the sub-contractor's other markets. How will this sub-contractor react? Refuse to supply or will there be an incursion into WAMC's domain? This strategy appears to have more disadvantages than merits.

Making loans to customers

This would appear to be a dangerous exercise. Admittedly customers would like access to financial credit, but does WAMC have to provide the service itself? Many producers of capital equipment and consumer durables have a relationship with a financial institution – bank or credit provision agency – referring a proposed buyer to such an institution on the proviso that given a good credit rating the prospective purchaser will be given a loan. They (the producers of capital goods) do not carry the financial risk (non payment and irrecoverable debts) themselves. WAMC has no expertise in this field. By borrowing from a bank and re-lending they are unlikely to be as competitive as other lenders. As price is probably critical in many equipment sales this structure will disadvantage WAMC. It should stick to its core competences and liaise with an independent financial institution to provide the service required by customers.

New product development

This strategy of diversification (Ansoff product/market vector analysis) could lead WAMC into new and profitable growth areas. However, it is a high risk venture. The technology, although not complex, is new to the company and the market – the public sector – is certainly unknown to them. There is no data about competition and with a market this size any competitors are likely to be large and well established. The market itself could be volatile, given the nature of public investment programmes. Furthermore the low-tech nature of the product implies that barriers to entry will be low. Is this the type of industry which will provide the stability which WAMC is looking for or will it divert its attention away from the core business and impede it from putting necessary improvements in place? This strategy does not seem to have much commercial logic to it and requires far more research before it should be considered in depth.

Conclusion

These four strategies appear to be reactive. The decision to re-enter into tractor production (albeit indirectly) and to provide financial facilities both are responses to consumer demand. It must be remembered that the satisfaction of consumer demand should only be undertaken where this can be done effectively and profitably, otherwise losses will be incurred. Whilst both the objectives are reasonable there are other ways of providing the financial services and supplying tractor units and these should be explored. The diversification strategy offers both risk and profit. However, given the current precarious situation of WAMC it seems advisable that the company should pursue a more conservative strategy, operating in technologies or markets where it has some expertise or experience. The proposed sale of the distribution outlets could provide the company with some well-needed finance, but the company could also be losing a distinctive competence and a bargaining counter in its likely negotiations with AM. Also the value of the distributor network appears to be mainly based on the development value of the land. This is likely to appreciate in value and a delay now could result in higher returns later.

(c) For the proposed merger to be considered successful a number of conditions must be complied with.

Firstly it **must be shown that the merger adds value** to the performance of the two companies. Outcomes must be better than those achieved by the two companies individually. It would be a mistake to merge if the main driving force was the ego of senior management. Furthermore one must not be influenced by potential volume increases if these could be at the expense of profit. The key criterion here should be to achieve long term profitable growth.

Another issue to be taken into consideration is **the attitude of the customers** – the farmers. If the merger reduces choice and appears to be leading to market dominance (unlikely here) this could lead to a build up of buyer resistance and possibly a referral to governmental anti-monopoly agencies. Mergers must also be seen to be in the interests of the customer. The costs of the merger must be taken into consideration. The costs of incorporation may offset any of the perceived benefits of the merger. This is particularly true if the merger is pursued in an irrational manner with little reference to economic logic. Both of these agricultural equipment producing companies may see the merger as providing them with the strengths they currently lack and, as a result, they may choose to ignore unpalatable facts such as the costs that may be incurred.

It is important to ask **whether the two firms are operationally and culturally compatible**. In this particular case the companies appear to have certain functional synergies – WAMC being proficient at marketing and AM at R & D and manufacturing. However, the cultural fit may be more problematical. The French company is younger and has historically been smaller. The UK company is older-established with a unionised workforce which has seen draconian cut-backs. With the proposal to move a substantial part of the manufacturing to France there is every likelihood of resistance within the UK. The chance of a smooth incorporation of the merger, with both workforces being involved harmoniously, is not high.

The **financial structure of the two companies** is dissimilar. One (WAMC) is mainly financed through an equity stake whereas the other is more dependent upon debt finance. WAMC shareholders must ensure that the merger does not leave them vulnerable to heavy interest payments and unacceptable payback clauses.

It may be possible to adapt Porter's tests for assessing the effectiveness of a diversification strategy to this merger situation.

1   The **attractiveness test**: Is the industry in which this merger takes place attractive or capable of being made attractive?

2   The **cost-of-entry test**: the cost of the merger must not damage future profits.

3   The **better-off test**: the two companies must gain competitive advantage from their association with the merger.

(d)   Kenneth Murphy needs to be very careful when negotiating the merger terms. It would not only be unethical for him to seek personal financial advantage by arranging for the WAMC share price to be low, it would also be illegal. It is hardly the action of a reputable and honest senior manager to negotiate away the independence of a company while, at the same time, ensuring his own personal survival.

Murphy must recognise that in his position he must not prioritise his own interests but he has to **safeguard the interests of all stakeholders**. By artificially lowering the share value of WAMC for the benefit of AM and himself he is effectively stealing from the company's shareholders, hardly an ethical action. Furthermore by agreeing to relocate significant amounts of manufacturing to France he is not protecting the interests of the workforce, many of whom will become unemployed, and any associated stakeholders – suppliers to WAMC and any other companies within the local communities which will be adversely affected – the local community, shops, etc.

Customers will also be affected, particularly if products are now not so readily available. Although the company is small there will, nevertheless, be some impact on tax receipts and the earning of foreign exchange by WAMC.

At all times Murphy must act with utmost propriety. He is in a position of trust, to represent the best interests of WAMC and all its stakeholders. The proposal put to him requires him to act selfishly and in doing so place other stakeholders at a disadvantage. He has access to inside information but he must beware of acting in a unilateral manner. He seems to have questioned the commercial wisdom of the merger and there is also some evidence that he has questioned the morality of the method by which the merger could be accomplished. He feels he is too personally involved in the situation. He recognizes that personal gain can influence his decision making and wisely he has asked for a dispassionate and unbiased view from a consultant. Murphy may be correct to pursue a policy which results in a large reduction of the work force. It is better to safeguard the position of some of the workers rather than see the whole firm collapse. However, he must be careful not to be seen to be protecting his own position at the expense of the rest of the company.

	ACCA marking scheme	
		Marks
(a)	Internal review	8
	External review including competition	4
	Comparison between two companies	8
(b)	Advantages and disadvantages of each strategy	5
	Selling distribution network	5
	Buying in tractors	5
	Setting up financial facility	5
	Product development	5
(c)	Aspects to cover	
	Added-value	3
	Costs	3
	Cultural fit	3
	Operational fit	3
	Financial acceptability	3
(d)	Discussion on Murphy's position	2
	Needs of stakeholders: for each stakeholder mentioned	2
Total		**50**

71   HAIR CARE LTD

Key answer tips

You may find it better to do part (d) of the question before part (a) in order to avoid repetition between the two sections (as a lot of the business' strengths will be covered in the value chain. For part (b) of the question, when asked for strategic options, the Ansoff matrix will almost certainly be the best model to use.

(a) **To**:   Sam Burns, Managing Director, Hair Care Ltd

From: The Accountant

Date:

Assessment of Current Corporate Position of Hair Care Ltd

Introduction

I have assessed the current financial position of your company and I have also taken the liberty of drawing your attention to some difficulties which may arise in the future. Whilst your financial position is currently sound, there are some worrying trends which need to be addressed. Furthermore you need to be careful not to be over-optimistic and assume that current favourable conditions will continue. You need to put in place some contingency plans.

Conclusions drawn from the quantitative data obtained from Table 1

You have prided yourself in running a lean organisation. However the data suggests that this is becoming less so. The **cost of sales has risen** from just over 63% in the year 20X1 to 70% in the forecasts for the coming year. This could be the result of higher costs by buying from less efficient suppliers or a squeezing of margins in a more competitive environment. It is unlikely to be the result of currency exchange deterioration as there has been little noticeable change over the past few years. You have been fortunate because this worsening in the cost of sales figure has been compensated for by favourable cost movements elsewhere. Costs of distribution and marketing, whilst increasing, are doing so at a slower rate than the increase in sales revenue. This is to be expected to a certain extent as economies of scale are now being achieved. **Administrative costs are rising** more swiftly, possibly as a result of the increased number of employees within the firm.

The one key statistic is the **level of loans taken out**. In the next forecasted year this is expected to be about 67% of turnover. It is recognized that you need to have access to increased storage capacity, especially with the forecasted increase in turnover. However, other methods of achieving this might have been explored – rental, leasing. I appreciate that owning the freehold might give you more flexibility and that you will benefit from any appreciation in the land values. However, in the short term it is a burden on the company despite the relative low rates of interest (although your rates have risen as your level of debt has soared). This is a prime factor in the worsening of your return on sales revenue position, forecast to be about 7.7%, almost half the level achieved three years ago.

Another worrying trend is the **increase in the number of products** which your company deals in. The range has almost quadrupled in the past three years. While recognizing that customers are looking for greater choice, this accelerated increase must have an adverse effect on the efficiency of your company's operations. It also probably accounts for a significant part of the **increase in the level of inventories** being held, the cost of which is affecting your profits. Maybe some rationalisation of this position needs to be considered.

Although this is not a financial issue I feel that I should draw to your attention the fact that the **proposed increase in employee levels** may put a strain on your management systems. Goal congruence may be eroded. Currently the running of the company is centred on you and your wife. I appreciate that you founded the company and incurred all the financial risk and that you wish to maintain your control over the company. Notwithstanding this, the company is vulnerable if anything should happen to either of you even for a short period of time. You need to ensure that operations can continue in your absence. Maybe you should **consider implementing a staff development programme**. Too many of your staff are currently concerned with low level

operations. You need to appoint one or two (maybe newcomers) who could, in an emergency, take over the management of the company. So far you have been able to maintain direct control over all your staff. However, as the number of employees grows, the span of control is likely to be too large to be effective. You will tend to become over-burdened by operational issues when you should be spending more time on strategic concerns.

Issues for your future consideration

It is apparent that you have taken advantage of some **favourable foreign exchange rates** in your product purchases. The likelihood of the United Kingdom joining the euro-system will have a mixed effect upon your position. It is possible that sterling will have to depreciate against the euro to prevent problems from entry at too high a level as occurred with the previous ill-fated exchange rate mechanism (ERM). This will mean that your imports from Europe will be more expensive.

(**Tutorial note**: when this question was set, sterling was considered over-valued against the euro.)

However there are also signs that the dollar, currently claiming to be over-valued as a result of high levels of foreign investment into the USA, may seek a lower level to make its current adverse balance of trade more acceptable. If this is the case then your purchases from the Far East, denominated in dollars, could be cheaper in sterling terms. It is important that you continue to watch the movements in foreign exchange rates and do not get dangerously caught out by any adverse movements.

You have implied that you are too small to attract attention from **the major UK hair care companies** who deal directly with the retail market. This is a myopic perspective. If you continue to grow at about 50% per annum you will soon impinge on their markets, or make the competitors aware of the potential in your arena. They will surely react in an aggressive manner at some point. Furthermore your assertion that the market is recession-proof is optimistic. You have been fortunate in that your company has only existed in a period of relative prosperity. While it may be true that the demand for hair care products may be relatively constant there is a danger that your consumers may move down market. You are currently selling premium-priced products to hairdressing salons. It is a possibility that they may seek out cheaper products if the market becomes more competitive.

You have argued that a significant contribution to your success is the **relationship developed with your suppliers**. Will you be able to continue to develop this relationship with the increased number of suppliers you are now dealing with? Will these suppliers also be able to maintain the quality you have come to expect and will the reliability of delivery be continued?

Conclusion

Although your company is still profitable and showing strong signs of growth, the level of profitability is falling. Your level of debt needs to be addressed and you need to consider your organisational structure as well as range of products and your relationship with suppliers. There are also a number of environmental factors which can impinge on Hair Care Ltd – exchange rate movements, competitive reactions and economic conditions. These all need to be monitored to assess their likely impact on your company. It is better to anticipate change rather than react to it.

If you need any further advice or information please contact me whenever you wish.

Accountant to Hair Care Ltd

Signed:

(b) **To**:   Sam Burns, Managing Director, Hair Care Ltd

From: The Accountant

Date:

Strategies for achieving growth

1   **Introduction**

There are a number of options which will enable Hair Care Ltd to achieve continued growth in the future. These can be usefully summarized, using Ansoff's product-market matrix. Apart from considering different directions of growth it is useful to assess whether a strategy involving an acquisition or a strategic alliance might prove to be beneficial.

2   **Strategic options**

Market penetration

You have stated that you think that in the current environment there is little opportunity for continued growth in the present direction. Any further penetration in the current market is likely to bring you up against larger and more powerful competitors. This could be disastrous for your business and should be avoided. There are other areas for expansion where the opportunities may be greater and the risks smaller.

Product development

You may consider focusing on selling a range of different products into the same market. However, as noted in my earlier report, your decision to already widen your range of products appears to be adversely affecting the efficiency of your organisation. The products would inevitably have to be focused on hair- dressing businesses. Products such as hair-dressing hardware and furniture – wash basins, and chairs are high-value items and not the type of products in which you have experience. Furthermore these products may require an installation service which you are currently unable to provide. You may consider selling fast-moving consumables such as shampoos and conditioners. However, these items are usually well-known brands and such a move will bring you into direct competition with some of the powerful toiletries and chemical producers. I do not believe that you can effectively compete at this level.

Market development

This can be examined from two perspectives. You can attempt to sell to similar sectors internationally, maybe in continental Europe. There will need to be considerable marketing research carried out to assess the similarities and differences in market conditions. And given favourable findings, this could be a realistic strategy, but you would need to develop stronger links with the key buyers (that being one of your key strengths) and assess the strength of the existing competition. Secondly you may wish to focus on a different segment within the UK. An obvious one is the retail market – selling to the general household market. This has large potential but it is doubtful whether you have sufficient resources to effectively operate within this segment. Additionally this will bring you into competition with the major players in this market – an unattractive proposition.

Diversification

The concept of you moving into new markets with new products is unappealing. It is a high risk strategy (despite the potential of high rewards) and will use none of your strengths. There are also options of related diversification by means of vertical integration. Moving downstream into buying some of the outlets will be very expensive, and given your current levels of debt, it is not an attractive proposition. Furthermore the concept of moving upstream into manufacturing is not really an option. Your success is built on your ability to outsource many of your activities, buying from the best and most competitive suppliers. You have no expertise in the manufacturing field and such a move risks more than it promises to deliver.

Focus

You could decide to shrink the organisation slightly and focus more on profitability and not simply on turnover. You will need to concentrate both on your most profitable lines and your key customers. A reduction in the products offered could minimize problems with dealing with increasing numbers of suppliers and by focusing on key clients, this could reduce your workload and enable you to direct more of your energies towards planning for the future and any critical strategic issues not currently being attended to.

Acquisition

You could achieve growth by means of an acquisition, maybe accessing an international market in this way. However, again, this may prove to be expensive and the new acquisition may not fit smoothly into your way of doing business. I suspect that any domestic acquisition will be irrelevant. The acquired company is either going to operate in an area which is of no direct interest to you or if it is in your area of influence then you could possibly grow organically at its expense without incurring the costs of acquisition.

Strategic alliance

Although this strategic approach may enable you to grow much faster, using another company's technical or marketing knowledge, I am not sure that you would be sympathetic to such an approach. You are an entrepreneur by nature and you personally like to have the levers of control in your possession. Sharing power does not come easily to you. I do not think that you would be happy in such a situation.

3   **Conclusion**

You appear intent on growing faster as a company. You may wish to consider consolidating your current position and reducing your debt but if you are seeking a growth strategy the one which may provide expansion within your areas of expertise may be market development internationally. However this is not without risk and any venture into this area should not be contemplated without carrying out the necessary marketing research.

Signed:

Accountant to Hair Care Ltd

(c)   It is important that Sam is aware of some major causes of corporate failure so that he does not make the same mistakes. Two of them – **falling levels of profitability** and **increased debt** – have already been brought to his attention. He must also be aware of the **danger of falling sales revenue**. The company has geared itself up to a continuing increase in sales with the new warehouse and increased inventory-holding. If sales should not materialise as expected then the company will be incurring high fixed costs on a lower level of sales revenue, resulting in higher average costs, making the company less competitive. Many companies have problems as a result of a **lack of planning and strategic direction**. Sam's approach shows no sign of formalised planning. Much of what is done appears to be intuitive, driven by Sam's knowledge of the market and his enthusiasm. This is acceptable whilst the company is a small niche player. However as the company becomes larger a more formalised approach could be beneficial. There is an **absence of key management-type staff** that can provide an input into the strategy process. But it is important that the innovative spirit, currently driving the firm, is not extinguished by bureaucratic structures and systems. A balance must be struck.

Complacency is also often a cause of decline. Given Sam's temperament this does not seem to be a danger. However, **inadequate management systems and structures** might limit Hair Care Ltd's capability to grow successfully. *Argenti* has argued that an autocratic chief executive and overtrading (expanding faster than cash funding) are often precursors of company failure. There is no direct evidence of these features being prevalent at the moment but Sam should be made aware of the dangers associated here.

Other factors which can contribute to failure can include a **rise in inventory levels** which are costly to finance and could easily become obsolete, an **over-reliance on principal suppliers or customers**, or the **influence of a competitor** who can dominate the market.

Sam needs to monitor all these factors so that he may not be taken by surprise and avoid being led into an attitude of complacency, conditioned by his past success.

(d)   Sam's company has been successful because he has concentrated on those things he does well and has integrated the separate elements effectively. He has built up a profitable and, until relatively recently, a cost-effective organisation. By using **Michael Porter's model of the value chain** it is possible to demonstrate how this success has been achieved. If one examines the five primary value activities, the **inbound and outbound logistics** can be assessed together. Sam has taken a personal interest in these two areas, dealing directly with both suppliers and key customers. He believes that his success depends upon buying wisely and in keeping his customers satisfied. He has invested in up-to-date warehousing and inventory control facilities and order processing and distribution is given high priority. This is complemented by efficient and, until recently, relatively cost-effective **operations**. As noted in the case scenario these operations have been kept to a minimum by most of the business being outsourced.

The other two primary activities appear to have been given considerable attention. Sam sees **service** as one of his critical success factors to the extent that he almost seems obsessive about it – he feels unable to delegate here. Additionally the **branding decision** demonstrates that Hair Care Ltd is aware of the benefits that can accrue from such an approach. The company has been able to generate a premium pricing strategy by doing this. This not only generates more revenue, it removes the company from the danger of predatory commodity pricing.

The **support or secondary value activities** have been used to support and develop the primary activities. The firm's infrastructure is simple to operate and understand. Overheads have generally been kept under control. This area may show signs of deteriorating as the number of employees grow and as the debt levels rise, almost an inevitability given the current growth rates but Sam needs to be aware of the dangers that can arise from such a rapid expansion.

Human resource management needs addressing. Negligible staff turnover is often a sound indicator of reasonable morale and sound management. However there is a marked absence of managerial training and succession planning within the organisation. Everything depends upon Sam and Annabelle, understandable in a small and entrepreneurial company. But as the company grows there should be more rigorous structures and systems set in place.

Technology development appears to be satisfactory. There has been a large investment in warehousing, computing and in inventory control and retrieval systems. Sam realises that an efficient distribution facility is critical to the company's success and he is prepared to invest to ensure that this area does not fail him. Similarly **procurement** is central to the company's operations. The interface between suppliers and the company is seen as being of critical importance and, as such, is given high priority.

There are no obvious, critical weaknesses. Overall the operations are geared towards accessing good value products as competitively as possible. The company operates with minimal overheads and aims to distribute products as efficiently as possible. Customer and supplier care are considered to be important, as is the image of the own-brand products. It appears that **Hair Care Ltd is using the value chain effectively**.

ACCA marking scheme		
		Marks
(a)	Analysis of quantitative data	
	– trend in costs	3
	– level of debt	4
	– range of products	3
	– inventory levels	3
	– non-current assets	2
	Maximum marks available for this section	10
	Future developments	
	– exchange rates	2
	– management succession	2
	– relationship with competitors	2
	– supplier rapport	2
	– relationship with customers/branding	2
	Maximum marks available for this section	5
(b)	Market penetration	2
	Market development	3
	Product development	3
	Diversification	3
	Focus	3
	Acquisition	3
	Strategic alliance	3
	Maximum marks available for this section	15

(c)	Profit decline	3
	Debt levels	3
	Complacency	3
	Operational inefficiencies, i.e. inventory levels	3
	Maximum marks available for this section	10
(d)	Primary activities: up to 1.5 marks each	7.5
	Support activities: up to 1 mark each	4.5
	Maximum marks available for this section	10
	Total marks available	50

72 ABC LEARNING

Key answer tips

It is clear in the scenario and the requirement that the company uses Porter's Five Forces to analyse its environment. Therefore it is important to focus on this model in part (a) and there is no need to use any other model in order to score full marks. In part (b) the company has made a decision to enter a new market. Therefore do not discuss the validity of this decision. Instead focus on what the requirement wants – is the particular target company they are considering the right one to buy? The key to any question on stakeholders – as was required in part (c) – is to use Mendelow's matrix. Applying this model to the scenario would help you score high marks in this part of the question.

(a) This question asks candidates to analyse the business analysis certification training industry (BACTI) in Erewhon using Porter's five forces framework. This is the preferred approach of Xenon, the company commissioned to undertake the study. In this context it seems a reasonable model to use. The forces ultimately determine the profit potential of the industry and ABCL will be keen to invest in an industry where there is long-term return on its investment. The framework also helps identify how a potential new entrant (such as ABCL) might position itself in the industry. The five forces driving industry competition are the threat of entrants, the threat of substitute products or services, the bargaining power of suppliers, the bargaining power of buyers and the competitive rivalry between existing firms in the industry. Looking at each of these in turn:

The threat of entry / Barrier to new entrants

New entrants to an industry bring new capacity. Existing suppliers stand to lose market share and have their profitability eroded. In the context of ABCL, the threat of entry is a particularly significant issue because they are, themselves, threatening to enter the industry. Consequently they need to understand the barriers to entry to see if they are sufficient to deter or delay their potential entrance. Furthermore, an understanding of these barriers will give them an understanding of how likely it is that other companies will consider entering the industry. If barriers are high then the threat of entry is low.

In the context of the scenario, the main barriers appear to be:

- Access to supply channels. The industry is dominated by three established providers who know the industry very well and have established relationships with key suppliers of expertise; the lecturing staff. In two instances, CATalyst and Batrain, lecturers are full-time employees with attractive salary packages, share options and generous benefits. In the case of Ecoba Ltd, the company promotes the images and expertise of the high-profile presenters that it uses. Although these presenters are on sub-contract, they feel secure about the arrangement. As one of them commented 'students are attracted to the company because they know I will be teaching a certain module. I suppose I could be substituted by a cheaper resource, but the students would soon complain that they had been misled.'

- The fees of 60% of all students are paid for by their employer. The three established suppliers have good relationships with the major corporate customers and, in some cases, have set up infrastructure (dedicated training sessions, personalised websites) to support these contracts. Although corporate customers do switch provider (see later), it might be difficult, in the short term, for ABCL to gain corporate clients.

- Expected retaliation is an accepted barrier to entry. The industry in Erewhon has a history of vigorous retaliation to entrants. The scenario mentions that ABCL has commissioned the study from Xenon because of the well documented experience of another Arcadian company, Megatrain. Megatrain's proposed entry into this market place was met by price-cutting and promotional campaigns from the established suppliers. This was supported by a campaign to discredit the CEO of Megatrain and to highlight its foreign ownership. Porter makes the point that there is a strong likelihood of retaliation where there are established firms with great commitment to the industry and who are relatively illiquid. This is supported by evidence from Ecoba's balance sheet where goodwill and property are both significant assets.

- The cost and time taken to achieve gold level certification may also deter ABCL from entering the industry. All three main providers currently have EIoBA's gold standard. To be a creditable alternative, ABCL has to achieve this level of certification. Evidence from the case study suggests that it takes at least one year to achieve this certification. In the meantime ABCL will be trading at a disadvantage.

- The three providers dominating the industry have well-established brands, supported by extensive marketing. ABCL will have to invest heavily to overcome existing customer loyalties and to build up a brand that appears to be a credible player in the industry. This will require time, and investment in building a brand name is particularly risky since, as nPorter explicitly recognised 'it has no salvage value if entry fails'. However, there are only 15 major corporate customers. ABCL could target these to gain market share. It is possible that ABCL already works with these customers in Arcadia, and they may also be attracted by ABCL's e-learning expertise.

Threat of substitutes

The threat of substitutes is again important to ABCL because it would not want to invest in an industry where the product or service is under threat. Substitution reduces demand and might, in extreme cases, lead to the product or service becoming obsolete.

The threat of substitutes appears to be constant in this industry. There is no legislative or certification requirement to study for the examinations with an accredited provider. Evidence from the case study suggests that a large proportion of students do not attend formal classes but prefer to study on their own.

The case study also mentions that one of the smaller providers has gained some success by providing 'blended' learning solutions where tutors provide some support, but students are expected to complete e-learning modules. In effect, these students are substituting face-to-face tuition with e-learning. The case study scenario mentions that the three established providers, whilst acknowledging the possibilities of e-learning, are retaining their classroom-based model. Not only is it profitable, but it allows the companies to employ their investments in specially-designed classrooms, buildings and staff.

ABCL might consider the threat of substitutes as a business opportunity. They do have expertise in providing e-learning materials and it might be a way of entering the market place with products that are significantly differentiated from their competitors.

Bargaining power of buyers

The power of buyers concerns the ability of buyers to force down prices, bargaining for higher quality or more services by playing providers off against each other. In the scenario it appears that:

(1) The power of the corporate buyers is relatively high. The scenario mentions that 60% of all students are paid for by their employer. There is a history of these corporate buyers regularly changing providers to gain better prices. For example, the scenario states that a large insurance company had recently placed all its training with Ecoba after several years of using CATalyst as its sole provider.

(2) The cost of switching providers is relatively low. This applies to both corporate buyers and individual students.

(3) In general, the products purchased are standard and undifferentiated. The three main providers all deliver training through face-to-face classroom training. Buyers are always sure that they can find alternative providers.

(4) There is some threat of the supplier (provider) being bought by a buyer (customer). The case study scenario provides an example where WAC, a major supplier of business analysis consultancy services, has itself bought one of the smaller providers and now delivers all of its business analysis training in-house. Hence there is a credible threat of backward integration.

All of the above suggest that the bargaining power of buyers is high in this industry.

Bargaining power of suppliers

Suppliers exert bargaining powers by threatening to raise prices or reduce the quality of their services. The conditions that make suppliers powerful tend to mirror those that make a buyer powerful. Very few of the conditions that would lead to high supplier (provider) power appear to exist in the case study scenario. The only circumstances that might apply are:

- The supplier (provider) industry is dominated by a few companies and is certainly more concentrated than the industries it sells to. Suppliers selling to more fragmented buyers will normally be able to influence prices, acceptable quality and supply terms.

- Porter also recognises that labour is a supplier. The case study scenario suggests that it is difficult to find competent, committed lecturing staff. This, of course, poses another problem for the providers. Lecturers on flexible contracts can threaten to either move to work with competitors or set up their own business to compete in the market.

Competitive rivalry between existing firms

The rivalry amongst existing firms needs to be understood. Are rivals bitter and aggressive or do they appear to exhibit a large degree of mutual tolerance? In the case study scenario the three companies that dominate the industry seem to co-exist on relatively good terms and indeed appeared to co-operate to provide a co-ordinated response to Megatrain's potential entry into the industry. They also appear to tolerate the existence of a relatively large number of smaller providers. Industry growth is still strong and this means that firms can expand and improve their performance by just keeping up with industry growth.

However, the products are relatively undifferentiated, particularly once gold level certification has been achieved. They are all providing training services for certification examinations using classroom-based tuition. As already recognised there is little to stop customers switching between competitors, and this will increase competitive rivalry.

The preoccupation of the three main providers seems to be the protection of their marketplace from large new entrants. Hence ABCL can expect a vigorous response to their proposed entry into the industry.

(b)   **Report Title:** An evaluation of the attractiveness of Ecoba Ltd as an acquisition target for ABCL

Author: A business analyst, Xenon Ltd

Date: March 20X9

Executive Summary

In January 20X9, Xenon Ltd (referred to from this point as we or us) produced an interim report analysing the business analysis certification training industry (BACTI) in Erewhon. As a result of this report, ABCL asked us to evaluate the attractiveness of Ecoba Ltd as an acquisition target. This report examines the ownership, business model and performance of the three main suppliers in the industry. Ecoba Ltd has a dominant shareholder who is approaching retirement and so is likely to be amenable to realising her investment in the company. In contrast, the other two main suppliers have relatively complex ownership structures which, in our experience, lead to immediate rebuttal or protracted negotiation. Ecoba's business model currently minimises training and administrative overheads and could be retained or, in the longer term, remodelled to reflect the operating preferences of the acquiring company. Ecoba's financial performance is acceptable. It is not as profitable as its competitors, but it is very lightly geared, while other ratios are roughly in line with industry competitors. Our conclusion is that Ecoba Ltd is a viable and attractive acquisition proposition for ABCL.

Introduction

In January 20X9, Xenon Ltd (referred to from this point as we) produced an interim report analysing the business analysis certification training industry (BACTI) in Erewhon. As a result of this report, ABCL asked us to evaluate the attractiveness of Ecoba Ltd as an acquisition target. This report examines the ownership, business model and performance of the three main suppliers in the industry. This short report analyses the current operational and financial position of Ecoba. It also explains why we believe that Ecoba is, between the three main suppliers in the industry, the most appropriate target for acquisition.

Analysis

Ecoba is a private limited company, almost wholly owned by its founder Gillian Vari. It is the smallest of the three providers that dominate the BACTI marketplace. CATalyst is a wholly owned subsidiary of the Tuition Group, a training and education provider quoted on the Erewhon stock market. In their latest annual report, Tuition Group identified CATalyst as core to their strategy and a source of significant growth. We do not believe that they would be interested in selling CATalyst, except at a premium price. Batrain is a private limited company, with shares equally divided between the eight founding directors. Given this share distribution, and the age profile of the directors, we feel that it is likely that any proposed acquisition of Batrain would either be immediately rebuffed or it would lead to a complex and drawn out negotiation given the number of stakeholders involved. In contrast, Gillian Vari is approaching retirement. She holds 95% of Ecoba's shares and we feel that she might be amenable to realising her investment in Ecoba.

Ecoba itself does not employ any full-time teaching staff (except Gillian herself). Their strategy is to employ well-known industry 'names' on sub-contract and to publicise these names in their advertisements, website and other publicity. They also publish the name of the lecturer on their class timetables. Gillian is averse to employing full-time lecturing staff because 'they have to be paid if courses do not run and during the long vacations'. It is perhaps this reliance on sub-contract staff that leads to the cost of sales running at about 80% of revenue. This figure is significantly higher than their two main competitors (65% and 63%) and this needs further investigation. We suspect that the competitors classify full-time staff as overheads (rather than cost of sales) but we need to investigate this.

Overall, sub-contract lecturers appear quite happy with this arrangement as they believe that there is little chance of being replaced by lesser 'names' or, as happens at the other two companies, by full-time staff at too short notice to arrange alternative work bookings. However, they do complain about how long it takes Ecoba to pay their invoices. This is supported by the financial data. The average payables settlement period is 144 days in 20X8, up from 130 days in 20X7. Comparing these with the two rivals suggests that this is not the industry norm. It will be important, in the short-term at least, to retain these lecturers. Any concerns they might have about working for new management might be partly offset by the goodwill generated by paying their invoices much more quickly.

The inefficiency that leads to a high number of settlement days for payables is also reflected in the average receivables settlement days. In 20X8 this was up to 71 days, compared to 64 days the previous year. Again, comparisons suggest that this is not the norm for the industry. Gillian has always been careful to keep administrative overheads relatively low. However, this suggests that they are finding it increasingly difficult to manage the payment of suppliers and the chasing of customer payments. Increased efficiencies in this area appear to be on offer to any company that acquires Ecoba. The sales revenue to capital employed (another efficiency or activity ratio) has increased from 3.16 to 3.76 in the past year. This improvement now means that it outperforms its rivals (3.36 and 3.19).

Before considering any further financial ratios, the extracted financial information suggests the following:

- Significant increases in trade payables (40%) and trade receivables (43%)

- Significant rise in revenue (almost 30% from 20X7 to 20X8)

- Significant rise in cash and cash equivalents (40%)

- Increase in retained earnings

- Increase in valuation of intangible assets. This would need investigation

Ecoba is not as profitable as its two main rivals. Gross profit is much lower (at about 20%, compared with 35% and 37%) although this probably reflects the large scale employment of sub-contract staff. Net profit is also lower, but not substantially so (at 4.55%, compared with 6% and 8%). However, all profitability ratios at Ecoba (ROCE, gross profit margin and net profit margin) showed slight improvements in 20X8 compared with 20X7.

Liquidity at Ecoba appears to be relatively stable. Inventories are relatively low in this industry and so the current and the acid test ratios are almost exactly the same. Although the absolute value of these ratios is relatively low (0.91 – 0.93), similar figures are returned by their competitors and so there does not seem to be any particular cause for concern.

Ecoba is very lightly geared, with gearing ratios much lower than their competitors. In 20X7 the gearing ratio was 4.2% with an interest cover ratio of 37.5 times. This had reduced in 20X8 to 3.8% and the interest cover ratio had increased to 50.

Conclusion

The picture that emerges is of a company that is relatively risk averse. This is reflected in their employment of sub-contract lecturing staff rather than full-time staff (allowing Gillian to balance supply with demand) and the minimisation of overhead administrative staffing costs. This latter appears to have been a false economy as it has led to poor credit control and complaints from suppliers about late payment. Financial gearing is very low and any buyer of the company has the opportunity to use the company's unused borrowing capacity. Gillian has also been prepared to live with lower profitability figures than her rivals and this may be a reflection of the fact that she has fewer shareholders to consider.

Any company that acquires Ecoba gets a company where changes can be quickly made to improve efficiency. We suggest that Gillian's business model should be retained in the short term, but in the long term it would be possible to change the model to potentially improve profitability. In conclusion, we believe that acquiring Ecoba will provide ABCL with a cost-effective entry into the BACTI market in Erewhon.

(c)   Transfer in ownership of a company creates anxieties amongst customers, suppliers and employees. ABCL are right to consider stakeholder management during this transition, particularly now that Gillian Vari has left the company. However, there is insufficient time to manage everyone to the same degree. Also, it is not necessary. There may be stakeholders who are indifferent to the change and involving them may be difficult to achieve, unsettling and time-consuming.

Stakeholder analysis usually involves some mapping of power against interest. This can be used to determine how they should be managed. The following represent the most likely stakeholders that the management of ABCL will need to manage. The suggested categorisation is arguable, so students do not have to agree completely with this analysis to gain the marks on offer.

Corporate customers: the scenario mentions that two corporate customers have recently switched their training contracts to Ecoba. They may be unsettled by the change, particularly as the person who negotiated those contracts (Gillian Vari) has now left the company. One of the customers specifically changed provider because they were impressed by the 'named' lecturers that Ecoba could provide. They would need to be reassured that these lecturers will remain under new ownership. In stakeholder mapping terms it could be argued that corporate customers have high power (because they can move their contracts elsewhere) and high interest. It is advisable for ABCL to actively manage these key players during the transition period, perhaps by appointing account managers with specific responsibility for each corporate customer.

Lecturers: these are the named 'suppliers' on contract to Ecoba. It is likely that these stakeholders will be anxious about the acquisition as they know that the two main competitors employ full-time lecturers. ABCL also employ full-time tutors in its operations in Arcadia. Lecturers will be worried that the business model of Ecoba will be changed by the new management. On the other hand, Ecoba will, at least in the short term, wish to retain these names to allow business continuity and to fulfil the expectations of at least one corporate client. This group of stakeholders might be classified as having high power (because they can work for established competitors) and some interest. A reasonable stakeholder strategy might be to keep these lecturers satisfied. An early move to prompt invoice payment may help keep them onside.

Full-time administrative staff employed by Ecoba. There is evidence in the case study scenario that administration is under pressure and this will have to be investigated. Failure to pay suppliers on time or chase up debts might be due to time pressure or incompetence. In stakeholder management terms this group can probably be defined as having high interest but very little power. They are best managed by keeping them informed about proposed changes. At most, they should be kept onside.

Individual students. This is a large, diverse group. As customers they are focused on passing examinations. Individually, they have relatively low power, and, in the context of the transition, they probably have very little interest. The size and diversity of the group make it difficult to agree a stakeholder management strategy. There could be an argument for ignoring this group completely. As long as lecturers and, to some extent, administrative staff, are properly managed then this group should see little tangible change. Minimal effort should be put into managing individual students.

EIoBA. The EIoBA run the certification scheme. They will wish to be assured that ABCL will maintain the standards achieved by Ecoba. The EIoBA is a powerful stakeholder as it could potentially withdraw accreditation. Hence it has high power. It is difficult to gauge its interest as the scenario gives little information about it. However, at worst it should be kept satisfied throughout the transition process, so that it does not become excessively interested and hence a key player in the success of the transition.

ACCA marking scheme		
		Marks
(a)	1 mark for each significant point (for example, access to supply channels) up to a maximum of 20 marks.	20
(b)	1 mark for each significant point (for example, issue of poor credit control) and up to 1 mark for each supporting calculation (for example, accounts receivable – 71 days and rising) up to a maximum of 16 marks	
	Up to 4 additional professional marks for structure, persuasiveness and a coherent conclusion supporting the acquisition of Ecoba.	
		16
(c)	1 mark for each significant point (e.g. classification of stakeholders) up to a maximum of 10 marks.	10
Total		**46**

Examiner's comments

This compulsory question was answered relatively well, with good use of the case study material.

The first part of the question asked candidates to use Porter's framework to analyse the business analysis certification industry (BACTI) in Erewhon and to assess whether it was an attractive market for ABCL to enter. Most candidates answered this question relatively well, showing an understanding of Porter's framework and an ability to apply it to the case study scenario. The scenario explicitly stated that Xenon analyses an industry by using Porter's five forces framework. It was expected that candidates would use this in their analysis. However, some candidates elected to use his "diamond" analysis instead. The two frameworks overlap to some extent and so candidates using this approach were able to gain some marks, although there was probably insufficient information in the case study scenario to get a pass mark using this approach.

The second part of the compulsory question assumed that Xenon had decided to enter the BACTI market by acquiring one of the three big companies currently dominating the marketplace. Ecoba Ltd had been identified as the most appropriate target and candidates were required to write a short report evaluating Ecoba Ltd, analysing whether it was the most appropriate and attractive of the three possible acquisition targets of ABCL. Overall, candidates answered this part question relatively well, calculating and using financial information that had been signposted in the scenario. Some candidates took the suitability, feasibility, acceptability approach which sometimes led to answers with little reference to the case study scenario. A straightforward financial evaluation would have been more appropriate. Furthermore, some candidates questioned the attractiveness of the marketplace as a whole. This was not the point of this part question, it had already been considered in the first part of the question. ABCL have already decided to enter this marketplace, it is now just a question of which company to acquire.

The final part of the compulsory question asked candidates to identify and analyse the stakeholders in Ecoba Ltd and analyse how ABCL could successfully manage them during the ownership transition. Markers were instructed to interpret stakeholders quite widely and to include some that are not identified in the model answer. Most candidates answered this part question relatively well, with appropriate use of the Mendelow matrix often leading to high marks for this part question.

73   GREENTECH *Walk in the footsteps of a top tutor*

Tutor's top tips

Approach to the question

(a)   SWOT Analysis

The examiner seen this as a way of giving students some easy marks to start off

Key to success:

Stick to this model – the examiner plans to be more explicit in terms of which models to use in these sorts of exam scenarios. There will be no need for other models and use of other models will achieve nothing except wasting your time.

Manage your time well – a common mistake is to read the requirement and then allow yourself 1.8 minutes/ mark. But this ignores the fact that it will have taken you around 25/30 minutes to read the requirement leaving you with only around 60 minutes for 50 marks. So you need to allocate 1.2 minutes per mark which means that you can spend no longer than 15 minutes on this part of the requirement.

Cover all 4 areas – in 15 minutes you only have enough time to cover around two factors in each area of the SWOT. Any more than this will waste time and gain you few extra marks.

Key dangers:

Using other models

Spending too long on this section

Not using full sentences. For example, when discussing strengths a weaker student might simply write that 'The company is in a good financial position'. But the better student will write a more specific answer such as 'The company has a good financial position and has built up $17m of surplus cash.

(b)   Strategy evaluation

Key to success:

Recognise the technique to use: "evaluate.....the strategy options" is a very common exam requirement. The examiner normally uses the Johnson, Scholes and Whittington criteria of suitability, feasibility and acceptability to assess strategies and answer these requirements.

Evaluate all three proposals

Link back to part (a)

Answer the question: justify the selection. Don't take other views and don't suggest alternatives. You will only get the 2 professional marks if you take the correct 'slant'. That is, all 3 likely to be feasible, but Ang's is MOST suitable, and only one that's likely to be acceptable.

Use P3 terminology – such as "product development", "market development" etc.

Expand points by answering "so what?"

Good time management. There are 3 strategies and we need to assess 3 criteria for each (9 things to do), and then provide a justification for the strategy that was followed. So overall there are 10 things to do for 20 marks. This means that each 'element' is only worth 2 marks each so you can't afford to spend too long on any single element.

Key dangers:

Spending too much time on one strategy

Incorrect focus

No/incorrect model

(c) (i) Process redesign

Key to success:

Be prepared for the topic – process redesign is seen as a key topic by the current examiner and it forms a link to many other areas within the syllabus.

Be comfortable with interpreting diagrams – again, the new examiner likes to provide diagrams for you to interpret. You will never have to draw them, but you need to be able to look at one and spot the problems.

Link problems and solutions. For example we discover a problem: 20% of orders are rejected late in the process; therefore we need to develop a solution to this problem: move credit checks to earlier in the process.

Key dangers:

Drawing diagrams

Explaining "process", "redesign" etc. The examiner is not testing your knowledge here. This is a test of how you can apply this knowledge to a scenario.

(ii) Strategic planning

Key to success:

Try to use a recognised model. For example, the answer uses the strategy lenses, but you could just as easily have used JSW's approach, Harmon's process strategy matrix (both words are used in the requirement) or compared the rational approach (strategy leads process redesign) to the incremental/ emergent approach (process redesigns lead strategy)..

Key dangers:

Lack of focus

Answers which are too general

(a)   The current strategic position of *greenTech* could be summarised in a brief SWOT analysis. Credit will also be given to candidates who have used appropriate alternative models or frameworks.

Strengths

The company has a good financial position, with, by April 20X8, a cash surplus of $17 million.

The company has explicitly positioned itself as a focused differentiator in a very competitive market place.

The company has a stable, successful management team that has been in place since 1990.

The company has important core competencies in the production of green technology. It was the development of these competencies that formed the basis of Professor Ag Wan's suggestion.

Weaknesses

Despite recent increases, marketing as a whole is under-funded. It currently stands at about 0.3% of turnover.

None of the marketing budget is specifically aimed at the sale of fully assembled green computers. This was recognized by Lewis-Read, who believed that the company should invest in marketing these computers to both home and corporate customers.

The current process for ordering and configuring computers has a number of efficiency problems. This leads to low conversion of enquiries into accepted orders.

Opportunities

The Lewis-Read proposal points out that the government has just agreed a preferential procurement policy for energy efficient computers with high recyclable content.

The general public is increasingly conscious of the need to conserve the environment. 'Green consumers' are increasing both in numbers and visibility.

Other industrial sectors are looking for opportunities to provide products that are quiet, recyclable and have low emissions.

Web-based technology now exists that allows customers to construct virtual prototypes of machines and equipment.

Threats

Although sales are increasing, the company is still relatively small in global terms and so it is unlikely to be able to compete with the established global suppliers of fully assembled computers. There are significant barriers to entry to this market.

Lack of manufacturing capability is a threat as it makes the company vulnerable to problems in the supply chain. The acquisition of a manufacturing company to address this is part of Fenix's proposal.

(b)   The team from the accountants Lewis-Read has suggested a strategy that protects and builds on the company's current position. Johnson, Scholes and Whittington identify two broad options within this approach. The first concerns *consolidation* which may include downsizing or withdrawal from certain activities. The second is *market penetration* where an organisation gains market share, usually by increasing marketing activity. This seems to be what Lewis-Read has in mind.

However, their proposal appears to envisage market penetration in only one of the three specific sectors served by *greenTech*, the provision of fully assembled green computers. This focus is probably based on a perception of high potential demand coupled with low current marketing investment in this area. Trends suggest that the overall market for this type of computer should be growing rapidly. Domestic customers and companies are increasingly aware of their carbon footprint and wish to reduce consumption both on ethical and economic grounds. The scenario also states that the government is promoting energy efficient computers with high recyclable content in their procurement policy. Consequently, demand should be growing. On the other hand, *greenTech*'s marketing spend suggests that not only is the overall budget relatively small, but that none of it appears to be specifically aimed at the green consumer. In contrast, over half of the budget is currently specifically targeted at the electronics industry or home buyers of components. This lack of marketing investment may explain the relatively small growth in sales in the fully assembled green computer's revenue stream. Thus it appears that the company is failing to address a growing market because its marketing spend is too small, with none of it specifically focused on that sector.

It is possible that *greenTech*'s reluctance to market their computers directly to domestic and commercial companies is due to their perception that they will be seen to be competing with two of their commercial customers. This will require careful consideration. However, withdrawal from some activities is a legitimate tactic within a 'protect and build' strategy. Perhaps the loss of some commercial customers will be more than compensated for by direct computer sales to customers.

The second proposal, from the team representing the corporate recovery specialists, Fenix, is to develop products to offer a more comprehensive service to the electronics industry. This is a strategic direction of *product development,* where organisations deliver modified or new products to existing markets. Fenix's suggestion is primarily focused on adding new products (expanded product range) and services (special requirements) beyond current capabilities. The scenario suggests that 70% of the electronics industry currently use *greenTech* components somewhere in their products. However, there may be scope for supplying more products and services to these established customers as well as supplying to those who do not currently use *greenTech's* products.

Fenix also makes the point that buying a manufacturing capability will protect the supply chain. greenTech currently has no manufacturing capability of their own and so they are at the mercy of their suppliers. These suppliers might raise prices, supply competitors, fail to meet demand or go out of business. A manufacturing facility could avoid all of these as well as perhaps providing an opportunity to cut supply costs. Furthermore, it could be argued that supplying a more comprehensive range of products to established customers may help protect current business with these customers.

However, Fenix recognise that manufacturing is beyond *greenTech's* current capabilities. Consequently, there is the issue of how these capabilities will be acquired. Their proposal is for the company to spend its cash surplus acquiring companies that already have these capabilities. It would be costly, risky and time-consuming to develop these capabilities organically. So, although *greenTech* has no experience of making acquisitions and making them work, Fenix's suggestion of acquisition seems very sensible.

The final proposal from Professor Ag Wan from MidShire University is for *greenTech* to look for opportunities where the company could use its core competencies with green technology within other industries and products. This is the strategic direction of *finding new* uses *for existing products and knowledge.* Johnson, Scholes and Whittington provide an example: 'manufacturers of stainless steel have progressively found new applications for existing products, which were originally used for cutlery and tableware. Nowadays the uses include aerospace, automobile exhausts, beer barrels and many applications in the chemical manufacturing industry.' For the company itself, this is probably quite a radical way of looking at itself. Instead of being seen as essentially a components supplier it becomes a supplier of ideas and technology. Professor Ag Wan's suggestion makes *greenTech* re-consider what industry they are in and this reflection should allow them to see a potentially much bigger market (green technology) in which they have already demonstrated capabilities in one sector (electronics).

Contemporary social trends also support Professor Ag Wan's suggestion. All industries will have to find greener ways of working if they are to satisfy three important forces. The first is the 'green consumers' who wish to purchase from companies with demonstrable sustainability policies. The second is governments who are increasingly likely to pass laws on emissions and responsibility for waste disposal. The third force is the increasing cost of disposal as the number of potential disposal sites decreases. Thus the market *for greenTech's* products, know-how and testing should be large and increasing.

The problem facing *greenTech* is how they will find these markets and exploit them. Professor Ag Wan's suggestion is that the surplus cash should be spent on finding these markets using market research.

The scenario states that *greenTech* opted for the third option (from Professor Ag Wan) and put it into operation. This briefing paper suggests why this option was selected by the company. Although all three of the suggestions are feasible it argues that Ag Wan's proposal is a more suitable fit.

The first suggestion, from Lewis-Read, appears to address the imbalance between a large potential market (green computers) and an under-promoted and under-sold product (fully assembled green computers). However, the supply of computers is a very competitive market and the money that greenTech has to spend on marketing is probably insufficient for it to make a serious impact. There are already global brands supplying computers at highly competitive prices. It must be recognised that *greenTech's* products could be sold initially at a premium price to reflect its niche position. However, if the market-place demands it, the major suppliers will have little difficulty in producing machines that directly compete with *greenTech*. The product can easily be imitated. Indeed the scenario reveals that *greenTech* already supplies two medium-sized computer manufacturers with components for green products in their range. These manufacturers might feel uneasy about greenTech becoming a significant competitor and consequently withdraw their business, so weakening this revenue stream. greenTech may be better advised to position their fully assembled computers as a complete kit, just as kit car manufacturers are prepared to provide assembled cars to customers without the time or expertise to assemble them.

Overall, Lewis-Read's proposal does not appear to be a particularly *feasible* strategy. Johnson, Scholes and Whittington suggest that an assessment has to be made about the extent to which the organisation's current capabilities (resources and competences) have to change to reach the *threshold* requirements for a strategy. In the case of *greenTech,* major investment would be required to overcome entry barriers and maintain market share. It is unlikely that the cash available would be sufficient to cope with the global players who already supply fully assembled computers.

The second suggestion, from Fenix, has many good points. *greenTech* is currently reliant on its suppliers because it lacks a manufacturing capability. It appears to make sense to move upstream in the supply chain to secure supply. Flexibility in the products supplied and reduced costs are also attractive bonuses. However, the company has grown organically and it is still run by the management team that formed it in 1990. It has no experience in acquiring companies, integrating them and running them successfully. All evidence suggests that many acquisitions do not deliver the benefits that had been claimed for them, even when they are acquired by experienced managers. Furthermore, it is likely for cost reasons that the acquired company would be in another country, perhaps creating both language and cultural difficulties. Overall, greenTech appears to be a relatively conservative, risk-averse company and so it is the unfamiliarity and risk associated with this proposal that means it should be rejected. In the terms of Johnson, Scholes and Whittington, the Fenix proposal is not a particularly *acceptable* strategy to the existing management because of the risk involved with acquisition.

Professor Ag Wan's suggestion may have won by default; after all the television show has to have a winner! However, it also has two significant strengths. The first, central to his proposal, is that it allows the company to see itself in a new and exciting way. The recognition of these core green technology and know-how competencies and their significance in an important and expanding market should be very motivating to *greenTech's* management and employees. Secondly, it has to be recognised that most of *greenTech's* current business activities are with fellow electronics companies or enthusiasts. Professor Ag Wan's proposal continues that tradition. Transactions will be business-to-business, often at quite a technical level. *greenTech* is comfortable with and experienced in such transactions. Professor Ag Wan's suggestion appears to be suitable, in that the strategy addresses the situation in which the company is operating. It is acceptable because it is in line with the expectations and values of the shareholders. Finally, it appears to be feasible as it does not require excessive funding and most of this funding is focused in one specific area: market research. The proposal is an excellent cultural fit and so was justifiably selected as the winner in the programme.

(c)   (i)   A number of issues can be identified in this process.

First of all, 40% of enquiries do not proceed after the delivery and payment details have been sent to the customer. The scenario suggests that this is of concern to *greenTech* because it wastes time and effort. However, it also impacts upon Xsys and for both of these companies this wastage means the loss of significant selling opportunities. The reason for this high wastage rate is not specified. Three possibilities include:

The cost of the computer was more than expected. In this case it would be useful to supply the cost as soon as delivery details have been completed. This means making sure that the web site has access to Xsys pricing details.

The delivery date was later than required. Although it would be tempting to automatically show the delivery date on the screen alongside cost details, this might not be commercially sensible. It would be better to direct effort at reducing the delivery time so that it was no longer an issue.

Finally, the delay gives the customer time to reflect and change their mind. It would be preferable to get customer commitment much earlier in the ordering process.

The credit check is performed too late in the ordering cycle. 20% of orders are rejected at this point. Hence greenTech and Xsys have wasted time and money communicating with the customer. The suggestion again is to bring payment and credit checking forward to the start of the ordering process. This would remove two processes from the greenTech swim lane: 'request delivery date' and 'e-mail delivery and cost details'.

Bringing ordering, payment and payment checking to the start of the process eradicates the need for Xsys to provide two delivery dates, one on initial ordering and a second on confirmation.

The problem of delivery time could be addressed by using EIM (or a similar courier company) to deliver directly to the end customer. This would remove two further processes from the *greenTech* swim lane – 'agree delivery date' and 'arrange delivery to customer'.

Making the changes proposed above now only leaves 'place confirmed order' and 'test computer' in the *greenTech* swim lane. 'Place confirmed order' can be automatically triggered near the start of the ordering process. If responsibility for testing was given to Xsys (and there are good reasons why it should be), then there would be nothing left in the *greenTech* swim lane. greenTech becomes a virtual supplier and the sales department can get on with making sales rather than processing orders.

(ii) The design of processes can be viewed as an implementation of strategic planning. This is normally associated with what Johnson, Scholes and Whittington term the design lens. It views strategy development as the deliberate positioning of an organisation through some analytical, directive process. It is often associated with 'top-down' design in that the objectives and goals are determined first and then processes are designed to realise them. In the context of the scenario, the new strategic direction now being followed will required a set of processes designed to facilitate business-to-business transactions with potential new customers. Process is following strategy. As a result process design and associated measures should align with business goals and objectives.

Alternatively, the investigation and potential re-design of the way processes take place within an organisation supports the lenses that Johnson, Scholes and Whittington termed, respectively, experience and ideas. An investigation of current processes might suggest that process goals and measures may not be aligned with strategy. This may be because the processes have diverged from their original specification or it may be because the strategy is not operationally feasible and the people undertaking the processes to implement it know this. Consequently, processes are often modified by employees and managers to make them workable and eventually, strategy is modified to accept this.

The re-design of processes may lead to incremental changes or it may lead to a significant strategic shift. Opportunities discovered while focusing on specific processes may have very significant repercussions. In the case study, the potential role of greenTech as a virtual supplier may be very interesting to the board. It would eradicate delay, reduce operational costs, reduce delivery costs and perhaps provide better (but certainly quicker) customer service. However, this is quite a significant strategic move and the decision to follow the chosen strategy would have to be re-evaluated if the company changed its strategic position.

		ACCA marking scheme	
			Marks
(a)		Up to 1 mark for each significant point up to a maximum of	12
(b)		Up to 1 mark for each significant point in the evaluation of each proposal up to a maximum of 4 marks for each proposal. There are three proposals, giving a maximum of 12 marks.	12
		Up to 1 mark for each significant point in the justification of the winning proposal up to a maximum of	6
		2 professional marks for appropriate tone, recognition of context of scenario, conviction of answer	
(c)	(i)	Up to 1 mark for each identified deficiency, suggestion or implication up to a maximum of	10
	(ii)	Up to 1 mark for each significant point up to a maximum of	6
		Up to 2 professional marks for clarity of the analysis	

Examiner's comments

Part (a) was designed as a gentle introduction to the paper, giving candidates an early opportunity to confidently gain relatively easy marks. It should have also helped candidates prepare themselves for the subsequent evaluation of strategic options (part b of this question). The P3 examination panel decided to restrict candidates to a SWOT analysis so that answers did not use too many alternative models, consuming a disproportionate amount of examination time. Candidates generally answered this question very well with many answers gaining ten marks or more of the twelve on offer. However, despite restricting the question to a SWOT analysis, there was evidence that some candidates spent too long on this part question, writing too much and causing themselves time problems later in the examination.

Part (b) asked candidates to evaluate the three proposals suggested in the scenario and to justify the selection of the proposal from Professor Ag Wan as the best strategic option for greenTech to pursue. This was a significant part question (worth twenty marks). Although it was answered quite well, many candidates did not apply sufficient analysis and evaluation. For example, in considering Fenix's suggestion to buy manufacturing capability, many candidates made the legitimate point that this would secure the supply chain and potentially reduce supply costs. However, fewer candidates recognised that greenTech had grown organically to this point and had no demonstrable capability in acquiring companies and managing these acquisitions. Even fewer candidates pointed out that evidence suggests that few acquisitions (even when made by experienced acquirers) deliver the anticipated benefits. The justification of the Ag Wan selection was also relatively weak. Some candidates felt that it was not the best option and explained why in their answer. Although this analysis might be legitimate it is not answering the question. The question requires the candidate to take a position and to justify this position whether they believe it or not.

The final part of the compulsory question was split into two parts. The first part asked candidates to identify deficiencies in the current Internet-based process for ordering and configuring fully assembled green computers and to recommend a new process for remedying these deficiencies. This type of question has not been asked as a compulsory question before. Despite this, most candidates provided good answers, showing good business analysis skills within the constraint of a time-constrained examination.

The second part of this question asked candidates to reflect on the relationship between strategic planning and process design. This was poorly answered, with many candidates providing only cursory answers. Some candidates did answer this question using the framework of the Harmon process-strategy grid. Although this is not recognised in the suggested model answer, credit was given for using this approach and relating it to the case study.

74 UNIVERSAL ROOFING SYSTEMS

Key answer tips

Part (a) asks for an analysis of universal's level of service. The main problem faced by students is the choice of 'an appropriate model'. The value chain is generally a safe model to use when discussing any aspect of competitive advantage. However, it is vital that you do not limit yourself just to one model. Note how the examiner also uses Porter's five forces and the typical characteristics of services (intangibility, etc).

Part (b) is a standard performance evaluation exercise. As always, you must use both the narrative and the numbers given and ensure that you draw conclusions from any ratios calculated.

Part (c) looks at strategy implementation and is made easier by adopting a standard model such as McKinsey's 7S framework.

Part (d) asks for an assessment of 'excellence' – easy if you remembered the aspects described by Peters and Waterman!

(a) Matthew sees the business as providing a predictable experience for the customer, one that meets, if not exceeds, their expectations. Using Porter's five forces clearly the individual house owner buying Universal's roofing products has little power, but Matthew rightly recognises the power of 'word of mouth' recommendation in a service-orientated business. With 30% of new business coming from existing customer recommendation, customers can exert significant power on the future growth of the company. Competitors to date have mainly been from 'small' businesses offering inferior levels of service at inflated prices. Much of Universal's growth to date and in the future depends on getting all parts of the value chain right so as to deliver high levels of customer service. As yet the major PVC windows and doors installers have largely ignored this specialist niche market with its need for different competences and skills. Whether they continue to do so depends on their core market for replacement doors and windows. Clearly, there are barriers to entry into the roofing market, but these are not insurmountable. The only real substitutes for the PVC roofing products come from using other materials, though there is evidence of board made from recycled materials beginning to be used. Suppliers who are much larger than Universal are beginning to recognise the significant growth of the firm and its demand for PVC materials and fittings. As a consequence, they may be willing to work with Universal in necessary improvements to the product and the way it is installed.

Matthew regards Universal as being in the service business though clearly, when one comes to analyse its value chain, there is a significant product element. Many authors have tried to identify the differences between the supply of goods and services. As Levitt commented, 'There is no such thing as service industries. There are only industries whose service components are greater or less than those of other industries. Everybody is in service.'

Clearly, a value chain analysis is important in showing where the company adds value and, equally importantly, the linkages between the different parts of the value chain.

Tutorial Note

The following notes on the differences of services are mainly for tuition purposes and you would not be expected to produce them in the exam. Full marks are available for focusing on the value chain analysis only.

Firstly, an understanding of where services differ from products is helpful in understanding the nature of the service being provided by Universal.

1   **Intangibility** – many of the elements of good service (e.g. in Universal's case the way the service is sold to the customer and the care taken over installation) are experienced by the customer, but there is no tangible evidence apart from a satisfied customer. This does not, however, prevent service standards being set and appropriate training given to the company staff delivering that part of the service. Where there is heavy reliance on sub-contractors or self-employed staff being paid by commission, there is an even greater need to ensure that these 'front line' or customer interface staff deliver the service levels expected of them. The customer 'experience' is Universal's main source of competitive advantage and one that is distinguishing it from its competition.

2   **Inseparability** – in certain services the person selling the service and performing the service are one and the same – hairdressers are an obvious example. In Universal, different people do sales and installation, but both are vital in delivering the service. Again the need for careful selection and training is paramount.

3   **Heterogeneity** – the heavy reliance on people means that it is difficult to standardise the service output – our varying experience in the same restaurant shows how difficult standardisation is. Matthew has placed a correct emphasis on making all elements of the service as predictable as possible and this is achieved by breaking the service down into its component parts and ensuring staff are familiar with the processes being used and can consistently deliver a quality service. Even when processes and systems are standardised, the customer experience varies according to the particular team of installers but, through training, each team will be aware of the key elements of service they have to deliver.

4   **Perishability** – for some services, storage is not possible, e.g. a table unused at a restaurant. Here time is a key dimension. If the service is consumed as soon as it is provided, then it is impossible to store it in some stockroom. This may have profound significance on the costs of operating a service. In an airline, for

instance, the seat utilisation rate is key to profitability. If the airline can increase its seat utilisation from, say 80% to 90% of seat capacity the revenue and profit impact is considerable. Universal has similar capacity utilisation issues; though it can increase or decrease the number of installation teams, increasingly many of its costs are fixed, making the continued growth of the business very important.

5   **Ownership** – here the customer buys a service but does not 'own' it in the sense of having it to keep. Most entertainment services – cinemas, theatres and bowling alleys – provide the service, but do not give ownership to the customer. House owners, however, because of the tangible elements in the service provided enjoy long-term benefits in the shape of their houses looking better and being maintenance free.

Universal's value chain and system – primary activities

Unbound logistics – here the development of correctly located depots where the PVC parts and board can be stored are an important decision and cost. The nature of Universal's product/service means that transport costs are likely to be a significant cost. Relationships with suppliers are key to meeting demand and developing new products.

Operations – from the cutting up of PVC board to match the customer's requirements and associated fixtures and fittings, through to delivery, using the company's vans and installation using an advanced roof access system, Universal has seen operations as a real source of added value. It is here that the standardisation of processes means that installation teams can be less skilled but can provide a superior service. Installation in a product-based firm is usually seen as a service coming after the product has been sold; in Universal's business installation lies at the heart of the operations activity – this is what the customer experiences and determines customer satisfaction. Universal has placed considerable emphasis on using installation as a means of differentiating itself from its competition.

Marketing and sales – once again, an area of significant value added. The sales model has been adapted from the large-scale PVC doors and window installers. Canvassers are used to develop 'warm' leads, which are then followed up by sales representatives. Universal has developed excellent sales support materials, including demonstration units and easy-to-follow steps for the potential customer. There is use of liberal discounts to encourage the customer to commit to purchase and installation dates, which are convenient to both customer and company – a real 'win-win' situation. Efficient 'back-office' systems are needed to confirm the sale and schedule the installation. Here the value added in efficiently linking sales and installation can be seen. Most of us can recount experiences where the promised delivery date fails to be met. Service quality is confirmed by a follow-up visit and the customer signing to say they are satisfied. The company has seen marketing as key to understanding its customers and making them aware of Universal's service. A full range of promotional techniques is being used.

Service – here the provision of a superior warranty and regular checks after installation are important in maintaining the company's reputation. The firm provides incentives for customers to recommend the company to friends and neighbours.

Support activities

Support activities are key to the delivery of a predictable service. These may be neglected activities in the early growth of the firm but become increasingly important if that growth is to be sustained. Matthew and Simon 'walk-the talk' and have shared their view of what constitutes a quality service with company staff coming into contact with the customer. The head office or infrastructure co-ordinates the scheduling of procurement which ensures the timely receipt of PVC materials but also the heavy investment in showrooms and depots. Without the growth of both showrooms and depots, the selling and installation activities would cease to be as efficient and affect the quality of service delivered. Technology clearly has been used to good effect –helping shape the design and installation of Universal's PVC roofing products. Technology is also linked with a heavy commitment to training and development in the delivery of a 'no surprises' policy. Human resource management is rightly seen as a key way of adding value to the service given to the customer through the training and development of staff interfacing with the customer. Support staff are equally well developed.

(b) Essentially, Universal is a one product or service company selling its services into two main customer segments in the housing market. From the performance information provided in Table 1, the company has achieved impressive rates of growth over the 20X3–6 period and this growth has come almost exclusively from private house owners. Universal is in the replacement market. Its customers are looking to replace existing roofing systems with low maintenance/high attractiveness Universal systems. To date growth has been exclusively within one region and has been achieved by growing the area served through investment in showrooms and depots.

Universal has chosen to grow its business through a differentiation focus strategy. It has identified a niche not served by the major PVC doors and windows installers and poorly served by small independent installers. The value chain analysis discussed above has shown the ways in which Universal has successfully distinguished itself from its competitors. Growth has been through increasing its market penetration of one particular region. Such is the size of the private house owner market and the lack of effective competition that the company has achieved a significant share of the market in its particular region. However, in national terms, with 1% of the available market, Universal is a small operator. What is clear from the sales revenue figures is that as the firm grows bigger the relative rate of growth inevitably slows down, so that by 20X6 it has an annual growth of 27% – still impressive by most companies' standards. The move into supplying the commercial housing market has been successful, but the share of total sales revenue seems to have stabilised at around 5%. Universal clearly is finding it difficult to commit sufficient new resources to this sector while coping with the growth from the domestic housing sector. Direct labour and other direct costs seem to be a reasonable proportion of sales revenue and predictably grow with the number of installation teams. Overall, the gross margin, which sustains sales, marketing and overhead expenses, is moving in the right direction with a gross margin of 52.6% achieved in 20X6.

Labour, not surprisingly in a service business, consumes a considerable amount of costs. If one combines the direct labour with the commission costs of sales canvassers and representatives together with salaries to staff in head office, one is in a business where well over 50% of costs are attributable to people. Equally important is the fact that over 80% of the staff employed by Universal are paid by results. This has significant consequences for the structure of reward systems and the training and development of staff looking to maximise their incomes through either their individual or team performance. Clearly, Universal sees no incompatibility between a reward system dominated by payments by results and the delivery of a quality service differentiating it from its competitors.

Marketing has grown considerably over the period and reflects the recruitment of Mick Hendry as Sales and Marketing Director in 20X4. The marketing and sales model is very much influenced by the one used by large PVC installers of doors and windows. Here there is a heavy emphasis on direct selling techniques supported by increasing levels of advertising. Universal sells to its customers directly and therefore avoids the costs and channel complications of using third parties to provide its services. In many ways the direct selling techniques used are a very well established way of reaching the customer. Elements of the marketing mix may be influenced by changes in communication technology, but the nature of the service requires effective face-to-face contact with the customer. Sales to private house owners using credit generates significant finance commission and is an important source of extra margin to Universal. Often in businesses depending on significant amounts of credit sales the sales representative receives significant reward for selling a finance arrangement to the customer.

In terms of net profit achieved, 20X3 and 20X4 represents a significant change and, as argued in the scenario, this reflects the recruitment of the Sales and Marketing Director. The achievement of this 'step change' in sales revenue required commensurate increases in most costs, but it is the significant increase in sales costs that explains the losses experienced in 20X4. Sales costs as a proportion of total sales revenue rose from 14% in 20X1 to almost 34% in 20X4.

Particularly significant is the increase in sales commissions paid. The detailed changes in the way commission is paid are not given in the case scenario, but it seems likely to reflect the previous experience of the Sales and Marketing Director in a closely related industry. Similar levels of sales costs are incurred in 20X5 and 20X6 but the increase in sales revenue, improvement in gross margin and slower rate of growth in commissions paid explain the improved return on sales revenue from –6.7% in 20X4 to 4.2% in 20X5 and 5.8% in 20X6.

Equally significant is the growth in showrooms and depots to support the growth in sales revenue. Each additional facility costs in the order of $30k with significant additions to costs in terms of staff and inventory. Overall the performance of Universal over the 20X3–20X6 period is of a company achieving high rates of growth, incurring significant costs in so doing and moving into modest levels of profit over the period. Its cost structure reflects the service it provides and the staff and reward systems enabling the service to be provided.

(c) Matthew has set ambitious growth goals for the 20X7–9 period in his quest to become 'unquestioned leader' in their region and to roll out the model nationally. Clearly there are choices to be made in terms of implementing the strategy and much of the success of the strategy will depend on the extent to which appropriate resources, structure and systems are in place to facilitate growth. Many alternative models consider how strategy is implemented, but one of the most popular is the McKinsey 7S model in which the 7Ss are strategy, structure, systems (the so called 'hard' or tangible variables) and staff, style, skills and shared values (the 'soft' or less tangible variables). The 7S model has a number of key assumptions built into it. Normally we tend to think of strategy being the first variable in the strategic management process, with all other variables dependent on the chosen strategy. However, Peters and Waterman argue that the assertion, for instance, that a firm's structure follows from its strategy ignores the fact that a particular structure may equally influence the strategy chosen. If we have a simple functional structure, this may severely limit the ability of the firm to move or diversify into other areas of business. Equally important is to understand the linkages between the variables, just as with the value chain, recognising that if you change one of the variables then you have to see the consequences for each of the other variables.

Our earlier analysis will have provided us with an understanding of the strategy being pursued by Universal. It is now looking to offer its service to other parts of the country and become a national provider. In strategy terms, this is a process of growth by way of market development, with the same service in different regions or markets. Universal's experience is dominated by operating in one region and the consequences of moving into new regions should not be underestimated. There are interesting examples of companies having conspicuous success in their home territory but finding competition and customer relationships very different outside their home market, even in the same country.

Matthew has already recognised the need to create a new structure to handle the growth strategy. This is 'growth by geographic expansion' and, while it may be the most simple growth strategy to control and co-ordinate, the creation of regional centres managing the sales and installations in the region will add an additional level of administration and complexity.

This structural change will have significant implications for the systems employed by the company. Development of a national operation will necessitate new methods of communication and reporting. Customer service levels depend on the management information systems available. There is an opportunity for the new regions to benchmark themselves against the home region. Efficient systems lie at the heart of Universal's ability to offer a higher value added service to the customer. Standardised processes have allowed a 'no surprises' policy to be successfully implemented. The extent to which the same business models can be simply repeated in region after region will have to be tested. There is little mention of IT systems, but the pace of expansion should be closely linked to the system's ability to cope with increased demands.

Staff – reference has been made earlier to Universal being a people business, able to deliver a better quality of service to the customer. The heavy reliance on self-employed staff means that a very active recruitment and training process will have to be in place as Universal moves into different regions. New layers and levels of management will have implications for the recruitment and development of both managers and staff reporting to them. The degrees of autonomy given to each of the regions will materially affect the way they operate. Reward systems clearly link both staff and systems dimensions and there is a need to ensure that the right number and calibre of staff are recruited to expand the market coverage. Does Universal have a staffing model that is easily 'rolled' out into other regions?

Equally important are any changes to the skill set needed by staff to operate nationally. Matthew feels that the model is relatively lowly skilled with staff controlled through standardised systems. However, change is inevitable and the recruitment and retention of staff in a labour-intensive service will be key to success.

Universal is very much a family business dominated by the two founding brothers. Even with expansion being entirely within their local region, the rate of growth to a $6 million turnover business predicted to treble in size over the next three years, will necessitate changes in the style of management. Time management issues among the owner-managers have already begun to emerge and a move from involvement with day-to-day management to a more strategic role is needed. Certainly growth to date has been more emergent than planned, but vision and planning will be equally necessary as the firm operates nationally. There are tensions for Matthew in making sure that his change in role and responsibilities does not result in him becoming remote from his management and staff. Communication of the core values of the company will become even more necessary and communication is key to managing the growth process.

The 7Ss is not the only model that will be useful in understanding the problems of implementing the growth strategy. Johnson and Scholes now refer to strategic implementation as 'strategy in action' made up of three key activities, structuring an organisation to support successful performance. Universal's move from a regional to a national company will call for different structures and relationships. Enabling links the particular strengths and competences, built round separate resource areas, to be combined to support the strategy – which in turn recognises and builds on identified strengths. Finally, growth strategies will involve change and the management of the change process. They argue that change will involve the need to change day-to-day routines and cultural aspects of the firm, together with overcoming resistance to change.

All too often, a company grows at a rate that exceeds the capacity to implement the necessary change. This can expose the firm to high levels of risk. Growth pressures can stimulate positive change and innovation but, in companies such as Universal where considerable stress is placed on performance, targets and quality may be a casualty. Equally concerning is if the rate of growth exceeds the capacity to invest in more people and technology. Growing the people and the systems is almost a prerequisite to growing the business.

ACCA marking scheme		
		Marks
(a)	Value chain analysis:	
	Primary activities	Up to 5 marks
	Support activities	Up to 5 marks
	Linking activities	Up to 5 marks
	Value system	Up to 5 marks
	Features that distinguish services	Up to 5 marks
		Maximum 20 marks
(b)	Performance analysis:	
	Rate of sales revenue growth	Up to 3 marks
	Cost behaviour	Up to 3 marks
	Profit margins	Up to 3 marks
	Staff	Up to 3 marks
	Owner/managers	Up to 3 marks
	Other measures	Up to 3 marks
		Maximum 15 marks
(c)	Implementation:	
	Strategy	Up to 2 marks
	Structure	Up to 2 marks
	Systems	Up to 2 marks
	Skills	Up to 2 marks
	Staff	Up to 2 marks
	Style	Up to 2 marks
	Shared values	Up to 2 marks
	Other implementation issues	Up to 4 marks
		Maximum 15 marks
		Total: 50 marks

75 DATUM PAPER PRODUCTS (DPP)

Key answer tips

A detailed question on a proposed acquisition.

In part (a) a systematic approach is needed to cover the wide range of possible issues – breadth over depth is the safest way to success here. The question asks for models where appropriate – Porter's three tests of an acquisition is the most obvious framework to choose but your answer could also have incorporated more explicit references to Porter's generic strategies for competitive advantage, Porter's value chain analysis, McKinsey's 7S model to compare resources, etc. As always with such questions, it is vital that you use the figures provided to support your analysis.

Part (b) looks at building a shared culture. Since the requirement asks for 'steps', Lewin's model is perhaps the most obvious to incorporate, but some analysis of the existing cultures (e.g. using Mintzberg) would also be useful.

The comparison of organic (greenfield) growth and acquisition in part (c) should generate a standard list of issues in students' minds. The key here is to apply such issues to the scenario and argue your points. For example, as well as comparing timescales you could also discuss why timescales are important.

In part (d) you should aim to identify acquisition objectives and try to describe a range of KPIs for each.

(a)   In order to maximise the chances of a successful merger, clear objectives for the acquisition need to be set. As one source expresses it, 'In today's sophisticated financial markets there is only one good justification for doing a deal. This is the unique ability of the acquirer to obtain higher economic value from the assets of the potential target.' In other words, bringing the two firms together creates a combined entity where the positive synergies outweigh the negative ones. This, of course, is profoundly affected by the attractiveness or otherwise of the target company. If it is performing well then this will be reflected in the price to acquire it. This premium will then require a longer period before it is paid off and enhanced value emerges.

There is considerable evidence that suggests it is the shareholders of the firm being acquired who enjoy the benefits of the premium paid.

Strategic fit when applied to an acquisition suggests that the combined firm is better suited to the demands of its competitive environment. The tests of suitability, acceptability and feasibility can all be applied to this proposed acquisition and its ability to create value for the stakeholders concerned. One of Porter's tests of diversification, 'the better off' test, is also a useful indication of the strategic fit between the two companies. If Papier Presse is not 'better off' as a result of joining the Park Industries Group then the acquisition will fail. It is often an interesting question who is adding value to whom? Hence the need for clear acquisition objectives. DPP is clearly looking to the acquisition to improve its competitive position in the industry. As described in the scenario, the industry does not look overly attractive and Porter's 5 forces may help in showing the reason why. Essentially, it is a low growth, mature industry with significant buyer power. DPP and Papier Presse's products are dependent on the demand for newsprint, which in turn is being affected by the emergence of substitute technologies such as the TV and

Internet. Clearly, barriers to entry into the industry exist, but entry is likely from existing international companies looking to capture market share and reduce industry capacity.

Any assessment of the synergies between the two companies needs to draw on their respective value chains and the benefits of integrating the two operations. DPP is unlikely to buy Papier Presse to simply eliminate a competitor and reduce industry capacity. It therefore has to look to positive strategic, operational and administrative synergies (as shown in the table below) to make the acquisition worthwhile. There would seem to be some useful market coverage advantages to be gained – DPP is relatively strong in North America, Papier Presse's focus is very much European. DPP has capabilities in R & D, Papier Presse in customer service. In many ways the success or otherwise of the acquisition will depend on the way the systems are integrated – evidence suggests this will be a key issue. Ultimately, it is likely to be culture and people issues that will determine successful integration of the two companies – merging the two management systems and retaining key personnel will be critical.

Activity	DPP	Papier Presse	Synergy
Ownership/Management	Professionally managed	Owner manager	Potential
R & D	Proficient	Minimal	Shared know-how
HR	Professionally managed	Paternalistic	Key integration
IT systems	Separate	Separate	Key integration
Inbound logistics	Separate	Separate	Some integration
Operations	Separate	Separate	Rationalisation
Outbound logistics	Separate	Separate	Some integration
Marketing & sales	Separate	Separate	Key integration
Service	Separate	Separate	Integration

Analysis of the performance data also is revealing. Papier Presse sales revenue are some 46% of DPP's, so this is a significant acquisition, with a consequent need to get things right. Cost of sales are significantly higher at Papier Presse (75% compared with 63%) and this is likely to reflect higher staffing levels. Indeed, sales revenue per employee – a key productivity measure – are $120k at Papier Presse compared with $156k at DPP. Clearly, there are significant differences in marketing and R & D spend and clear consequences as a result. Very different levels of depreciation may reflect a lack of investment at Papier Presse. One intriguing figure is that of dividend payout – on the face of it the Truffaud family are paying themselves significant dividends but largely as a result of low levels of capital expenditure. In many ways their higher return on sales revenue figure does not reflect superior performance.

One study of cross-border acquisitions found that the acquisition of smaller owner-managed companies operating in core related technologies and markets offer the best chance for a strategic fit. As a consequence, such companies offered the greatest chance of success and the lowest risk – 87% of the companies studied had acquisitions that were related horizontally to existing products and markets. The ability to build up the operational knowledge base of the source of cross-border problems allows the learning curve to be a positive one. In Porter's terms, once the one-off benefits of restructuring the acquired firm have occurred, the long-term synergies that will lead to competitive advantage come from the sharing of resources, competences and the transfer of knowledge.

(b) Developing a shared culture will be one of the key determinants of whether the anticipated benefits of the acquisition actually materialise. Due diligence procedures before the merger should have established the key people issues. This will include reviewing the two management styles and cultures. Clearly these are very different, looking at internal communication pre and post acquisition, understanding the nature of reward systems in the firm to be acquired, assessing the nature of training programmes in the firm both before and after the acquisition and attempting to gauge existing employee attitudes towards Papier Presse and the likely reaction to the acquisition. Reviewing areas where there have been significant staff problems and consequent negotiations will also be an important clue as to employee attitudes and morale. 'Hard' people issues including pensions, management rewards, health insurance and redundancy terms will need to be realistically assessed and the implications for both the price paid for the company and subsequent integration fully understood. All too often the compelling strategic vision for the enlarged company ignores the people costs involved and the time needed to develop shared HR systems.

Many models on culture and culture management could help to achieve a successful transition. Mintzberg's cultural or organisational configuration model, which would facilitate an understanding of the difference in structures and systems, could be a useful starting point. DPP comes from a divisionalised company where the middle line managers are given considerable autonomy in achieving agreed levels of performance. Papier Presse, with its dominance by family ownership and management, could be argued to be entrepreneurial in character, where the owner/managers at the strategic apex of the company operate a 'hands-on' approach and direct control of subordinates. Reconciling these different cultures and structures will not be an easy task.

Lewin's 3-step model of change can be used in helping a positive culture emerge from the combining of the two companies. There is a need to unfreeze the current situation in which employees of both organisations are likely to be reluctant or resistant to change. There needs to be a clear understanding of who does what in the new organisation – leadership and the role of the French owners will be a critical factor in successfully changing the culture. Robbins emphasises the need for positive top management role models in promoting and communicating the need for a change in culture. Policies to affect change on both the hard and soft factors referred to above need to be in place to move the integration forward. A clear timescale and vision for change will be a key part of the change process. Finally the systems will need to be in place to re-freeze or rather reinforce the attitudes and behaviours necessary to achieve success in the merged organisation. Operating across national borders creates real culture issues to be solved as shown in studies by Hofstede and Bartlett and Ghoshal.

(c) From the information given in the scenario, DPP will face significant problems if it chooses to develop a greenfield site. The bureaucratic planning procedures adopted by the host government can add considerable time to get an efficient plant up and running. In some ways, such governments are in a dilemma, anxious to secure foreign direct investment, but at the same time protect inefficient domestic manufacturers. Certainly, DPP in its own risk assessment would need to take political risk into account. In assessing the risks of a greenfield site, Ken could use Porter's 'diamond' to good effect. Factor conditions might be seen as quite favourable, with an educated, trained, albeit low productivity, labour force. However, the lack of demanding tough global customers, a weak and inefficient domestic industry to supply the new venture and competitors who have been highly protected mean that DPP will have to battle to create a supportive and sustaining environment. Financial exposure may be increased through currency risk.

Clearly, the fresh start will allow integrated information systems to be developed and the latest technology to be used. However, the new capacity will have a significant impact on DPP's existing plants. The extent to which expatriate management is used is clearly an issue. The host government is likely to require some commitment to the training of local management and the degree of autonomy given to the new plant may well be an issue. Cultural issues and sensitivities will be significant – often shop floor workers and managers will be used to high levels of absenteeism being tolerated in government owned and controlled firms. Also the issue of involvement and participation could be an issue – there may be a marked reluctance on the shop floor to contribute ideas towards raising productivity and quality. DPP is part of a group that has experience of operating abroad and there is a real need to access information on key problems in greenfield operations.

In many ways the move to a greenfield site links the macro environmental analysis generated by a SLEPT or PEST to five forces industry analysis with its focus on customers, competitors and suppliers. Certainly, creating an integrated value chain with DPP's existing business will be a real challenge to the management. It also adds capacity to a European industry where there is already a problem. Choosing between the two options to achieve the strategic goal of a lower cost base can be done using the tests of suitability, acceptability and feasibility. The decision will not be an easy one.

(d)   **Report**

To: Ken Drummond

From:

Integration Problems

Many academic studies, together with actual managerial experience, point to the post-acquisition integration phase as being the key to an acquirer achieving their acquisition objectives. In particular, the creation (or destruction) of shareholder value rests most heavily on the success of the integration phase, which in turn helps determine whether the acquirer has chosen the 'right' target company and paid the right price for it. One source strongly argues that the capability to manage the integration of the two organisational structures, in particular the conversion of information systems and retention and motivation of key employees, determines how much value can be extracted from the combined entities. The ability to manage the integration process will therefore affect the success of the prior phases of the acquisition process – the search for and screening of potential candidates, the effective carrying out of due diligence, financial evaluation and successful negotiation of the deal.

Unfortunately, the failure to develop the necessary integration skills dooms many firms to continued failure with their acquisitions, though some firms are conspicuously successful in developing such a capability and they gain significant competitive advantage over their less successful competitors and create value for the stakeholders. One explanation for this conspicuous inability to learn from past acquisition experience, compared with other activities in the value chain, lies with their infrequency and variety. 'No acquisition is like another.' Much of the difficulty however lies in the complex interrelationship and interdependency between the activities being integrated and a consequent difficulty of knowing what is causing performance problems. Thus, it is no good communicating all the positives to the customer if there is a failure to retain and motivate the sales force. To this complexity of integrating different processes is added the problem of developing appropriate measures of and accurate monitoring of the integration processes. In one study of US bank acquirers, only 40% had developed specific performance measures for the systems conversion process, despite the critical importance of systems integration to efficient operation of the combined banks. Key performance indicators need to be set in the areas previously identified as offering major opportunities for synergies. These synergies will affect both the cost and revenue side of the business. Real cost reductions are clearly a major reason for the proposed acquisition in view of the competitive environment faced. Equally relevant are appropriate measures of customer service. Each area will need appropriate key performance indicators showing priorities and relevant timescales for achievement.

Therefore, there is a critical need to learn from previous experience and the relationship between decisions made, actions taken and performance outcomes. This knowledge and experience needs to be effectively recorded and shared. It can then influence the earlier phases of the acquisition referred to above, thus leading to a virtuous circle of better integration and acquisitions that actually enhance value. In so doing, acquisitions can lead to faster growth and better performance.

Suitable KPIs could include the following:

Integration Objective	KPIs
Conversion of information systems	• Downtime
Retention and motivation of staff	• Staff turnover
	• Days lost due to strikes
	• Productivity per employee
Cost synergy	• Cost per unit
	• Number of staff 'rationalised' and salaries saved
Revenue synergy	• Growth in revenue, market share
	• Cross selling targets for revenue
Customer service	• Customer satisfaction surveys
	• Repeat business
	• Number of customers lost

ACCA marking scheme		Marks
(a)	Areas of strategic fit: customers, value chains, technology, systems, style etc.	
	Areas of positive synergy and areas of negative synergy	Up to 3 per point
		Up to 2 per point
		Maximum 20 marks
(b)	Shared values and mission, clear objectives, top management commitment, communication, cross organisational and functional teams etc.	Up to 2 per point
		Maximum 10 marks
(c)	Advantages and disadvantages of Greenfield option	Up to 2 per point
	Advantages and disadvantages of acquisition	Up to 2 per point
		Maximum 10 marks
(d)	Identification of integration problems	Up to 2 per point
	Selection of key performance indicators	Up to 2 per point
		Maximum 10 marks
		Total: 50 marks

76   CHURCHILL ICE CREAM

Key answer tips

(a)   This requirement has two aspects – first an assessment of the current strategy and second its impact on performance. These can be combined or kept separate. To discuss the strategy you need to first identify it – this is done in the summary section of the question 'Churchill has a distinctive strategy linking the manufacturing of premium ice-cream with its distribution through the company's own ice cream parlours'. Your answer should thus address both aspects, along with franchising and geographical targeting. Suitable models include Ansoff's matrix and Porter's generic strategies.

(b)   The easiest approach is to use the 'suitability, feasibility, acceptability' framework of Johnson and Scholes but other approaches would also gain credit.

(c)   This should be relatively straightforward with three goals and 4Ps to work with.

(d)   It is more difficult to identify a suitable model to use here but your answer should focus on differences in culture, taste and competitive forces.

(a)   The case scenario gives a five-year insight into the growth and development of Churchill Ice Cream. Throughout its history it has followed a strategy of in-house manufacture, retailing largely through the company's own shops and, to a lesser extent, through franchising. This vertically integrated strategy gives more control, which is particularly important given its use of fresh ingredients and emphasis on premium product quality. But it exposes Churchill to the twin problems of both manufacturing and retailing a product which is highly seasonal in demand and equally vulnerable to the vagaries of the British summer. In fact, there is a close correlation between the average summer temperature and the volume of ice cream consumed. The case, therefore, provides us with an opportunity to develop an understanding of the implications of a company's pattern of vertical integration for competitive advantage and the strategic development of the company. Clearly, if key activities and capabilities are kept inside the company, this makes imitation far more costly and complex. The question is whether Churchill Ice Cream has developed a unique format that delivers competitive advantage and superior performance. John Churchill would almost certainly argue that through its retail operation it gains a unique insight into its customers' needs and desires. With premium ice cream we are dealing with a luxury product increasingly bought by consumers looking to indulge themselves. One of the problems of being both a manufacturer and retailer is where you decide to place the emphasis – commitment of resources to one area almost inevitably leads to resources being constrained in the other. There is evidence in the case to suggest that Churchill Ice Cream with its newly-built factory is tending to favour the manufacturing side of the business. But with ice cream stores costing $100K to fit out and needing constant refurbishment this places a heavy investment load on the company.

A company's make or buy decisions therefore profoundly affect the shape and scope of the company and the types of competitive advantage. In Porter's generic strategy terms, Churchill Ice Cream is looking to be a focused differentiator able to earn (though there is less evidence of its strategy working) above average returns through its focus. This belief in and commitment to a vertically integrated strategy almost certainly reflects the beliefs and values of the Churchill family. In terms of Porter's five forces, the ownership of its own shops has in the past given it some protection from the need to sell through the large supermarket chains and the consequent impact on the company's profit margins. As indicated above, this should provide the company with some unique insights into customer buying behaviour, but unfortunately the delay in introducing a new management information system prevents full advantage being taken of this information. Churchill also maintains control over its distinctive ice cream recipes and this helps forestall integration strategies by either suppliers or retailers. There is no evidence in the scenario to suggest any significant supplier power although their reliance on the company owned shops might mean commercial property owners may be able to exert some power. In terms of new entrants, the company's heavy reliance on the London region makes them vulnerable to similar retail formats being opened in other parts of the UK. The presence of two major US manufacturers with their own ice cream stores may offer a real threat. Certainly ice cream is very much a global product and foreign manufacturers may find the UK a very attractive market to enter.

The company is facing significant competitive rivalry and its competitive strategy based upon differentiation comes from its product ingredients and manufacturing expertise, the development of a regional brand name, control of the point of sale and, more recently, product innovation with a market very responsive to it increasing the product range. Churchill, through its vertical integration, presents a different product experience to the customer and this helps to shelter it from the major manufacturers and powerful supermarkets.

However, there are some downsides – the seasonal pattern of demand implies an under use of manufacturing and retailing capacity for a significant part of the year. Churchill has done little to reduce the impact of a highly seasonal demand. Overall, therefore, the company has adopted a distinctive vertically integrated strategy which has supported its desire to be different and has major implications for the capabilities needed in the business and the type of resources required.

There are some conflicting performance indicators – both financial and non-financial – which require an explanation. Churchill Ice Cream seems to have a quality product and a good reputation, albeit only a regional one. Their sponsorship of major sporting events is a high profile achievement, but there is little point achieving such exposure if customers can only buy the product once a year! As a family business they have shown an ability to survive, but have a miniscule share of a major market. There is some growth of sales revenue, unfortunately at a declining rate, but the return on sales revenue is consistently poor. Comment has already been made on their regional presence, but the progress with opening new stores is modest to say the least and not moving them into becoming a national brand.

Perhaps more disquieting is their failure to move the retail format abroad. Their international strategy is commented on below but they have had two costly failures to date and yet seem committed to proving they can operate abroad. It would be interesting to know what has been learned from these two international ventures. In terms of the efficiency of business processes there is the comment that they have a new purpose built factory and that their products are 'supplied quickly and directly'. This performance is not currently having any significant impact on costs and profits.

From the information given in the retail sales index the performance of the ice cream industry is not very exciting. However, Churchill Ice Cream is clearly located in the premium segment of the market and the growth of sales revenue of US-owned competitors supported by huge advertising budgets has led to significant growth of the premium sector. Therefore, Churchill Ice Cream sales revenue growth looks less impressive seen against an overall growth for the premium sector market. Equally worrying is their relative failure to get their product and brand accepted by the supermarkets. The supermarkets are dominant and squeezing sales through the more traditional outlets. Again, Churchill Ice Cream's lack of a national brand presence may be limiting their ability to get into the supermarkets' ice cream cabinets.

Finally, the firm is in an interesting transition phase from being family owned and managed through to being professionally managed. There is little evidence to date of this transition having any significant impact on performance.

(b)   The three strategic goals are to become the leading premium ice cream brand in the UK; to increase sales revenue to $25 million; and to achieve a significant entry into the supermarket sector. On the basis of performance to date these goals will certainly be stretching. All three strategies will involve significant growth in the company. Johnson and Scholes list three success criteria against which the strategies can be assessed, namely suitability, acceptability and feasibility. Suitability is a test of whether a strategy addresses the situation in which a company is operating. In Johnson and Scholes' terms it is the firm's 'strategic position', an understanding of which comes from the analysis done in the answer to the question above. Acceptability is concerned with the likely performance outcomes of the strategy and in particular whether the return and risk are in line with the expectations of the stakeholders. Feasibility is the extent to which the strategy can be made to work and is determined by the strategic capability of the company reflecting the resources available to implement the strategy. It is interesting to see that the three growth related goals are compatible in that becoming the leading premium brand will involve increased market penetration, product development and market development. If achieved it will increase sales revenue and necessitate a successful entry into the supermarket sector. Time will be an important influence on the success or otherwise of these growth goals – five years seems to be a reasonable length of time to achieve these ambitious targets.

Suitability – Churchill is currently a small but significant player at the premium end of the market. This segment is becoming more significant and is attractive because of the high prices and high margins attainable. This is leading to more intense competition with global companies. One immediate question that springs to mind is what precisely does 'leading brand' mean? The most obvious test is that of market share and unless Churchill achieve the access to the supermarkets looked for in the third strategic goal, seems difficult to achieve. If 'leading brand' implies brand recognition this again looks very ambitious. On the positive side this segment of the ice cream market is showing significant growth and Churchill's success in gaining sponsorship rights to major sporting events is a step in the right direction. The combination of high price and high quality should position the company where it wants to be. Achieving sales revenue of $25 million represents a quantum shift in performance in a company that has to date only achieved modest levels of sales revenue growth.

Acceptability – as a family owned business the balance between risk and return is an important one. The family to date has been 'happy' with a modest rate of growth and modest return in terms of profits. The other significant stakeholder group is the professional managers headed up by Richard Smith. They seem much more growth orientated and may be happier with the risks that the growth strategy entails. The family members seem more interested in the manufacturing side than the retailing side of the business and their bad previous experiences with growing the business through international market development may mean they are risk averse and less willing to invest the necessary resources.

Feasibility – again this is linked to how 'leading brand' is defined. If as seems likely the brand becomes more widely known through increasing the number of company owned ice cream stores then a significant investment in retail outlets will be necessary. Increasing the number of franchised outlets will reduce the financial resources required but may be at the expense of the brand's reputation. Certainly there would seem to be a need for increased levels of advertising and promotion – particularly to gain access to the ice cream cabinets in the supermarket chains. This is likely to mean an increase in the number of sales and marketing staff. Equally important will be the ability to develop and launch new products in a luxury market shaped by impulse buying and customers looking to indulge themselves.

Overall, becoming the leading brand of premium ice cream may well be the key to achieving the desired presence in the supermarket ice cream cabinets, which in turn is a pre-requisite for increasing company sales revenue to $25 million. So the three strategic goals may be regarded as consistent and compatible with one another. However each strategic goal will have to be broken down into its key elements. For example in achieving sales revenue of $25 million what proportion of sales revenue will come from its own ice cream stores and what proportion from other outlets including the supermarkets? Sales to date of Churchill ice cream are dominated by impulse purchases but in achieving sales revenue of $25 million penetrating the take home market will be essential. Finally, what proportion of these take home sales will be under the supermarkets' own label brands? Over reliance on own label sales will seriously weaken Churchill's desire to become the leading national brand of premium ice cream. It looks to be an ambitious but attainable strategy but will require a significant planning effort to develop the necessary resources and capabilities vital to successful implementation of the strategy.

(c) Each of the strategic goals will have a profound impact on the marketing mix as it currently exists. As each goal affects the market position of Churchill developing an appropriate marketing mix will be the key to successful implementation of the overall growth strategy. The product, the brand and the reputation it creates are at the heart of the company's marketing strategy. Their focus on the premium segment of the market seems a sensible one and one which allows a small family-owned business to survive and grow slowly. Evidence suggests this is a luxury indulgence market reflecting changing consumer tastes and lifestyles. Managing the product range will be a major marketing activity. While the core products may develop an almost timeless quality there will be a need to respond to the product innovations introduced by its much larger competitors. The company's emphasis on the quality of its products resulting from the quality of its ingredients is at the heart of its competitive advantage. Growing the product range will also bring the danger of underperforming products and a consequent need to divest such products. Packaging is likely to be a key part of the products' appeal and will be an area where constant innovation is important.

Pricing raises a number of issues. Why is Churchill's core product priced at $1 less than its immediate competition? What is the basis on which Churchill prices this product? Each of the methods of pricing has its advantages and disadvantages. Using cost plus may create an illusion of security in that all costs are covered, but at the same time raises issues as to whether relevant costs have been included and allocated. Should the company price in anticipation of cost reductions as volume increases? Should the basis for pricing be what your competitors are charging? As a luxury product one would assume that its demand is relatively price inelastic: a significant increase in price e.g. $1 would lead to only a small reduction in quantity demanded. Certainly, profit margins would be enhanced to help provide the financial resources the company needs if it is to grow. One interesting issue on pricing is the extent to which it is pursuing a price skimming or price penetration policy – evidence from the scenario suggests more of a price skimming policy in line with the luxury nature of the product.

Place is an equally important issue – the vertical integration strategy of the company has led to company-owned shops being the main way customers can buy the product. At the same time, this distribution strategy has led to Churchill's sales being largely confined to one region in the UK – although it is the most populous. If Churchill has a desire to grow, does it do this through expanding the number of company owned and franchised outlets or look for other channels of distribution in particular the increasingly dominant supermarket chains? Each distribution strategy will have significant implications for other elements in the marketing mix and for the resources and capabilities required in the company.

Finally, **promotion** is an interesting issue for the company. The relatively recent appointment of a sales and marketing director perhaps reflects a need to balance the previous dominance of the manufacturing side of the business. Certainly there is evidence to suggest that John Churchill is not convinced of the need to advertise. There are some real concerns about how the brand is developed and promoted. Certainly sponsorship is now seen as a key part of the firm's promotional strategy. The company has a good reputation but customer access to the product is fairly limited. Overall there is scope for the company to critically review its marketing mix and implement a very different mix if it wants to grow.

The four Ps above are very much the 'hard' elements in the marketing mix and Churchill in its desire to grow will need to ensure that the 'softer' elements of people, physical evidence and processes are aligned to its ambitious strategy.

(d) The two international strategies pursued to date are through organic growth (the stores in North America) and acquisition (the companies in Germany and Italy). Neither seems to have worked. Here there seem to be some contradictions while global tastes and lifestyles are argued to have developed – convergence of consumer tastes lies at the heart of this – but this does not seem to have benefited Churchill. One questions the learning that these two unfortunate experiences have created. Of the three core methods of achieving growth, namely organic, acquisition and joint venture, only joint venture remains to be tried.

The reasons for the international failures are clearly complex but one could argue that the strategy has been curiously naïve. Certainly, it has pursued a high-risk strategy. Exporting, perhaps through identifying a suitable partner, might create the learning to lead to a more significant market entry. There is a need to understand local tastes; indeed the whole of the marketing mix in the chosen market(s), and decide on appropriate strategy. A strategy based upon the acquisition of companies and their consequent development represents a large investment of capital and requires considerable managerial attention and expertise. Equally, the attempt to use the Churchill domestic format of opening its own stores creates both a major financial commitment and the need to manage a radically different operation. One must seriously question whether Churchill has these capabilities within a family-owned business. Clearly there are differences between the ice cream markets in various countries, though the emergence of global brands suggests some convergence of tastes. Such differences reflect differing cultures, tastes and competitive behaviour in each country. The lesson from Churchill's international initiatives is that national differences need to be carefully understood. There is little evidence that Churchill has understood these differences or indeed learnt from them.

ACCA marking scheme		
		Marks
(a)	Advantages of current strategy including:	Up to 2 per point
	Control obtained through vertical integration	
	Value chain linkages	
	Closer to the final customer	
	Strategy difficult to imitate	
	New product innovation easier	
	Reduced buyer power	
	Flexibility in meeting varying demand levels	
	Disadvantages of current strategy including:	Up to 2 per point
	Increased level of resource/capabilities needed	
	Internal competition between manufacturing and retail	
	sides of business	
	Increased operational/organisational complexity	
	Growth function of number of ice cream stores	
	Cost implication of varying levels of demand	
	Performance analysis	Up to 6
	Use of models where appropriate including:	Up to 5
	Value chain/system, Five forces analysis, Ansoff's growth matrix	
		Maximum 20 marks
(b)	Suitability:	Up to 6
	SWOT Analysis	
	Gap and 'fit' analysis	
	Resource/capability analysis	
	Acceptability:	Up to 5
	Risk and return analysis	
	Screening process	
	Stakeholder analysis – owners v managers	
	Feasibility:	Up to 5
	Funds availability	
	Resources/ capabilities availability	
	Compatibility of three strategic goals	Up to 4
		Maximum 15 marks
(c)	Identification of current marketing mix	Up to 2 per element
	Changes to the mix for each goal including:	Up to 3 per goal
	Becoming leading national brand – product innovation, premium pricing strategy, national availability and national promotion	
	Sales revenue of $25 million – higher take home sales, increased product range, national availability, increased advertising	
	Penetration of supermarkets – own label brands, lower prices, national distribution, promotion support	
		Maximum 10 marks
(d)	Analysis and explanation for failure of the international strategy including:	Up to 2 per point
	Ethnocentric approach	
	Differences in customer buying behaviour	
	Cultural differences	
	Failure to understand risk	
	Resources overstretched	
Total		Maximum 5 marks
		50

77   SHIRTMASTER GROUP

Key answer tips

In part (a), ensure you assess all three elements of the business – its overall performance and the separate performance of each division. Also ensure that you include an analysis of the financial information provided in the question. In terms of models, there are lots that you could use (such as SWOT and value chains) but it is important that you simply use these as a framework for your analysis rather than spending time explaining them or developing them.

In parts (b) and (c) you should attempt to apply points to the company and use information from the scenario, rather than simply regurgitate knowledge from your pocket notes.

In part (d), the answer is a little out of date and the current examiner is more likely to refer to more modern theories. So in change management you could refer to Lewin and the cultural web, and in leadership styles you could bring in Kotter and Schlesinger, and Balogun and Hope Hailey.

(a)   The Shirtmaster Group is performing poorly by any standards and this reflects the poor strategic position of a major part of the group – namely the Shirtmaster division. Using a 5-forces and value chain analysis we can see that the chosen strategy of being an integrated shirt manufacturer carrying out all the activities needed to design, manufacture and distribute its shirts is now seriously open to question. Most of its UK competitors have recognised the need to source shirts from low cost manufacturing countries. Shirtmaster, in the shape of Tony Masters, seems to be alone in thinking that by maintaining a UK manufacturing capability this will give it some competitive advantage. The economics of the industry have changed dramatically with foreign shirt makers able to supply both the quality of shirt required in the premium shirt market and at prices that would enable Shirtmaster to radically improve its profit margins. The division seems to be in the classic 'stuck in the middle' position having neither the volumes to achieve cost leadership or the skills to differentiate itself in the market as it has in the past. Its strategic choice has been to concentrate on the premium end of the shirt market but this focus strategy is now under considerable challenge.

The two key forces at work seem to be the intensity of rivalry between the shirt makers and the increased buying power of their customers – the retail outlets for their shirts. The Shirtmaster division has remained heavily dependent on its small independent retailers, who themselves are under threat from the specialist clothing retailers and the supermarkets. There is a pressing need to analyse the changes taking place in the value chain underlying the shirt business. There is no evidence to suggest that Shirtmaster is willing to make shirts under the own label brands of the dominant retailers.

The Shirtmaster division's reliance on small independent clothing retailers is having significant cost effects on its value chain. In terms of in-bound logistics Tony's expensive trips to buy cloth from foreign suppliers is resulting in large inventories of expensive cloth. Meeting the individual demands of its many small customers must have a real impact on its manufacturing and distribution costs. Marketing expenses supporting the Shirtmaster brand are both significant and yielding decreasing returns.

In terms of the support activities, questions need to be asked at the infrastructure and HR levels in terms of Tony's influence over strategy and operations, at the technology level in terms of their apparent lack of investment in CAD/CAM systems compared with the Corporate Clothing division and the procurement strategy has already been questioned.

The net result of these problems is revealed in a comparison of financial performance:

	Shirtmaster division	Corporate clothing division
Sales revenue growth	Declining	Increasing
Manufacturing efficiency/gross margin	Low and falling	Higher and sustained
Labour productivity/sales per employee	Modest	Improving
Marketing expenditure	Relatively high	Relatively low
Inventory holding	Relatively high	Modest
Net margins	Low/negative	Modest/positive
Market share	Minimal	Small but growing
Innovation – product	Stalled	Customer driven
Innovation – processes	Little evidence	Significant
Divisional co-operation and learning	Minimal	Minimal
Customer segment	Declining	Growing

The measures above reflect a balanced scorecard approach to overall performance and clearly the Corporate Clothing division's results bring the problems of the Shirtmaster division into even more focus – comparisons are odious! Corporate Clothing is operating in a more attractive market and through close attention to its customers' demands is enjoying modest growth and profitability. Looking after a small number of large industrial customers and integrating its value chain with theirs has had positive results. All parts of its value chain/system seem to be involved in providing a superior service to its customers. One could point in particular to the link between its technology and its manufacturing operations as a critical area for success, and its willingness to hold inventory the customer wants and has paid for, shapes its outbound logistics with workwear supplied to the individual employee.

Overall the performance of the Shirtmaster Group is a composite of two very different performances achieved by the separate divisions. These divisions are operating in very different markets with very different strategies. At present there is little or no synergy between the two divisions and they add very little value to one another.

(b) Johnson, Scholes and Whittington define a strategic alliance as 'where two or more organisations share resources and activities to pursue a strategy'. There are a number of types of alliance ranging from a formal joint venture through to networks where there is collaboration but no formal agreement. The type of strategic alliance will be affected by how quickly market conditions are changing – swift rates of change may require flexible less formal types of alliance and determine whether specific dedicated resources are required or whether the partners can use existing resources. Johnson, Scholes and Whittington argue that for an alliance to be successful there needs to be a clear strategic purpose and senior management support; compatibility between the partners at all levels – this may be complicated if it is a cross-border alliance; time spent defining and meeting performance expectations including clear goals, governance and organisational arrangements; and finally trust both in terms of respective competences and trustworthiness.

The advantages that may be gained by a successful strategic alliance include creating a joint operation that has a 'critical mass' that may lead to lower costs or an improved offer to the customer. It may also allow each partner to specialise in areas where they have a particular advantage or competence. Interestingly, alliances are often entered into where a company is seeking to enter new geographical markets, as is the case with both divisions. The partner brings local knowledge and expertise in distribution, marketing and customer support. A good strategic alliance will also enable the partners to learn from one another and develop competences that may be used in other markets. Often firms looking to develop an e-business will use an alliance with a partner with experience in website development. Once its e-business is up and running a firm may eventually decide to bring the website design skills in-house and acquire the partner.

Disadvantages of alliances range from over-dependence on the partner, not developing own core competences and a tendency for them not to have a defined end date. Clearly there is a real danger of the partner eventually becoming a competitor.

In assessing the suitability for each division in using a strategic alliance to enter European markets one clearly has to analyse the very different positions of the divisions in terms of what they can offer a potential partner. The earlier analysis suggests that the Shirtmaster division may have the greater difficulty in attracting a partner. One may seriously question the feasibility of using the Shirtmaster brand in Europe and the competences the division has in terms of manufacturing and selling to large numbers of small independent UK clothing retailers would seem inappropriate to potential European partners. Ironically, if the management consultant recommends that the Shirtmaster division sources some or all of its shirts from low cost manufacturers in Europe this may provide a reason for setting up an alliance with such a manufacturer.

The prospects of developing a strategic alliance in the Corporate Clothing division are much more favourable. The division has developed a value added service for its corporate customers, indeed its relationship with its customers can be seen as a relatively informal network or alliance and there seems every chance this could be replicated with large corporate customers in Europe. Equally, there may be European workwear companies looking to grow and develop who would welcome sharing the Corporate Clothing division's expertise.

(c)   The Shirtmaster Group has decided to structure itself using two divisions who are dealing with very different markets, customers and buying behaviours. In so doing the intention is to provide more value to the customer through a better understanding of their needs. The existence of the two divisions also reflects the origins of the two family businesses. Mintzberg in his work on organisation design and structure sees divisional configurations as being appropriate in relatively simple and static environments where significant strategic power is delegated from the 'strategic apex' to the 'middle line' general managers with responsibility for the performance of the division. Indeed one of the benefits cited for divisionalised companies is their ability to provide a good training ground in strategic decision making for general managers who can then progress to senior positions at company headquarters. Tony Masters' reluctance to delegate real strategic decision making power to the senior managers in the Shirtmaster division may be preventing those managers developing key managerial skills.

Using the BCG model one could classify the Shirtmaster division as a 'dog' with low market share in a market exhibiting change but little growth. The Corporate Clothing division, by contrast, can be regarded as a 'problem child' having a small share but of a growing market. Porter's 'better-off test' needs to be met – are the two divisions better off being in the same Group? As it stands there seems little synergy between the two divisions – there seems to be little evidence of the two divisions sharing resources or transferring skills or learning between the two divisions. Their two value chains and systems are both separate and different though on the face of it there are many activities that are similar. Operating independently may encourage healthy competition between the two divisions and consequently better performance through better motivated staff. Specialised competences such as Corporate Clothing division's on-line response to customer orders and design changes are more easily developed within a divisionalised structure. Performance can be clearly identified and controlled and resources channelled to those areas showing potential. However, this may be at the expense of costly duplication of resources and an inability to get the necessary scale to compete in either of their separate markets. Certainly, the lack of co-operation between the divisions in areas such as information systems may lead to higher costs and poorer performance.

(d) Much has been written on the links between leadership and culture and in particular the influence of the founder on the culture of the organisation. Schein actually argues that leadership and culture are two sides of the same coin. Tony's father had a particular vision of the type of company he wanted and importance of product innovation to the success of the business. Tony is clearly influenced by that cultural legacy and has maintained a dominant role in the business though there is little evidence of continuing innovation. Using the McKinsey 7-S model the founder or leader is the main influence on the development of the shared values in the firm that shapes the culture. However, it is clear from the scenario that Tony through his 'hands-on' style of leadership is affecting the other elements in the model – strategy, structure and systems – the 'hard' factors and the senior staff and their skills – the 'soft' factors – in making strategic decisions.

Delegation has been highlighted as one of the problems Tony has to face and it is a familiar one in family firms. Certainly there could be need for him to give his senior management team the responsibility for the functional areas they nominally control. Tony's style is very much a 'hands-on' style but this may be inappropriate for handling the problems that the company faces. Equally, he seems too responsible for the strategic decisions the company is taking and not effectively involving his team in the strategy process. Style is seen as a key factor in influencing the culture of an organisation and getting the right balance between being seen as a paternalistic owner-manager and a chairman and chief executive looking to develop his senior management team is difficult. Leadership is increasingly being seen as encouraging and enabling others to handle change and challenge and questioning the assumptions that have influenced Shirtmaster's strategic thinking and development to date. The positive side of Tony's style of leadership is that he is both known and well regarded by the staff on the factory floor. Unfortunately, if the decision is taken to source shirts from abroad this may mean that the manufacturing capability disappears.

Tony should be aware that changing the culture of an organisation is not an easy task and that as well as his leadership style influencing, his leadership can also be constrained by the existing culture that exists in the Shirtmaster Group. Other models that could be useful include Johnson, Scholes and Whittington's cultural web and Lewin's three-stage model of change and forcefield analysis. Finally, Peters and Waterman in their classic study 'In search of excellence' provides insights into the close relationship between leadership and creating a winning culture.

	ACCA marking scheme	
		Marks
(a)	Shirtmaster Group position and performance:	Up to 3 marks
	Static sales revenue	
	Low margins	
	Little synergy in Group	
	Shirtmaster division:	Up to 10 marks
	'Stuck in the middle' – brand performance	
	Sourcing strategy	
	Customers segment served declining	
	High inventories and distribution costs	
	Value system declining in importance	
	Corporate clothing division:	Up to 10 marks
	Differentiated product	
	Growing market	
	Positive market	
	Positive profit margins	
	Value chain integrated with customers' value chains	
	Use of models	Up to 3 marks
		Maximum 20
(b)	Advantages of successful strategic alliances:	Up to 2 per point
	Economies of scale and scope	
	Co-specialisation and synergies	
	Attaining 'critical mass'	
	Learning from partners and developing competences	
	Disadvantages of strategic alliances:	Up to 2 per point
	Over dependency on partner	
	Failure to develop own core competences	
	No end date to partnership	
	Creation of a competitor	
		Maximum 15
(c)	Costs of divisions operating independently:	Up to 2 per point
	Duplicated costs	
	No sharing of resources/transfer of skills	
	No shared learning	
	Competition for resources	
	Benefits of divisions operating independently:	Up to 2 per point
	Development of necessary competences	
	Ability to serve distinctive market needs	
	Motivation and accountability	
	Risk reduction	
	Allows measurement of divisional performance	
		Maximum 8
(d)	Models linking leadership and culture:	Up to 3 per model
	McKinsey 7-S model	
	Cultural web	
	Lewin's change model	
	'Excellence' model	Maximum 7
		Total: 50

78   NETWORK MANAGEMENT SYSTEMS

Key answer tips

In part (a), it is clear which model should be used – the PESTEL. Do not use any other models. In answering the question you should ensure that you are not simply highlighting issues, but that you are also consider how they impact on NMS and its growth prospects. There are no marks for describing/explaining the model, so don't waste time on this.

In parts (b), there is less guidance as to which model to use. But there is a hint that it is one of the external tools in that it wants an 'industry' or 'environment' analysis. It also mentions the word 'competing'. When you put these factors together you should come to the conclusion that Porter's 5 forces is required. Follow the same technique points as used in part (a).

In part (c), focus as much on what the numbers tell us as you do in performing calculations. In part (ii) consider using some of the Ward and Daniel analysis on project appraisal.

(a)   **PESTEL Analysis**

The PESTEL framework may be used to explore the macro-environmental influences that might affect an organisation. There are six main influences in the framework: political, economic, socio-cultural, technological, environmental and legal. However, these influences are inter-linked. For example, political developments and environmental requirements are often implemented through legislation. Candidates will be given credit for defining the main macro-economic influences that affect NMS, rather than the strict classification of these in the PESTEL framework.

Political

The political environment in which organisations operate is very significant. Political parties may encourage or discourage economic activity through taxation policies and legislative programmes.

NMS is based in a stable, prosperous country, where successive governments have valued and encouraged technology. Tax incentives and grants are given to companies that invest in technology and in research and development. Tax credits are also provided to companies that invest in research and development. These incentives are open to NMS, its domestic competitors and its domestic customers. The government has also promoted the use of technology through a well-publicised awards scheme. NMS is a recent beneficiary of such an award – for "technological innovation in data communications".

The scenario suggests that the government itself is a major investor in communications technology. This technology has to be delivered through equipment that meets certain standards of reliability and compatibility. The government has put an approval process in place to ensure such standards. Such a process should ensure that technically inferior goods do not make it into the market place.

The current political environment wishes to protect its citizens who are employees, by enacting legislation concerning employment hours, conditions and reward.

Economic

The stage or phase of the economic or business cycle clearly affects customer buying decisions. The case study suggests that 2010 saw a downturn in the domestic economy which resulted in a reduction of customer commitment to long-term investment. Customers may postpone their buying decisions, although if innovative products bring cost and communication advantages then they will eventually have to invest in them.

Despite worsening economic conditions, labour costs remain high in Elsidor and the company may have to re-consider their commitment to manufacturing in the country.

Socio-cultural

It appears that electronic communication and information exchange will continue to increase with implications for companies supplying products and systems to meet these growing needs. All evidence suggests that the social use of services on such networks will increase. Hence, although demand appears to be currently dropping off, new social uses for telecommunication networks might spark off a new wave of investment.

Technological

Technology is a significant factor in shaping the life cycles of existing products and the introduction of new ones. The technology sector is extremely innovative, with new and improved technologies constantly emerging. NMS must scan the external environment for such technologies and identify how they might affect the future of their current products. NMS must also consider how such emergent technologies might be used in their own products. The forecast that increased sales will come from currently installed networks rather than from the installation of new networks is also relevant here.

Environmental issues

Green issues have an increasing impact on organisations, particularly in prosperous developed countries. The reduction of emissions and improvement of re-cycling are likely to be reflected in socio-cultural trends and enshrined in legislation.

The cost of waste disposal is also increasing. All these issues combine to increase the costs of manufacture and affect the competitiveness of the company in its market place.

Legal

NMS operates in a country where there are laws defining employer responsibilities and employee rights. It is likely that such regulation will continue and NMS, like all companies working in Elsidor, have to evaluate the benefits and costs of working within such constraints. Some organisations seek to gain competitive advantage by moving to countries where regulation is more lax and hence avoid the compliance costs incurred by their competitors. The case study scenario suggests that NMS has significant international competitors. It is likely that some of these will be based in countries where employment and other legislation are less onerous.

Summary

In the context of the case study scenario, it is political, legal and economic factors that significantly affect NMS. However, as a technology company with significant investment in research and development, NMS must continue to scan the technological environment to identify trends that could undermine, enhance or replace their products.

(b) Michael Porter provides, through his five forces framework, a useful way of analysing the competitive environment of NMS. Analysis suggests that the following key factors are shaping this environment. Other appropriate models and frameworks could be used and appropriate credit would be given.

Bargaining power of buyers

NMS is competing in two discrete market places. In the data communications component market it where it has less than 1% of the market share it is, at best, a supplier of marginal significance. The customers are OEMs, large industrial buyers who are likely to demand a testing combination of low prices, high quality and reliability. They are unlikely to tolerate the late delivery of orders. It appears that alternative sources of supply are readily available and that switching costs are relatively low. This combination of circumstances suggests that OEMs have significant bargaining power in this market place. This is particularly true for the OEM who currently accounts for 40% of NMS' current sales.

In the second market place, where network management systems are supplied to large end users, the buyers appear to have less bargaining power. NMS is catering for each customer's specific needs and so each solution is, to some degree, a bespoke solution. This makes it much harder for buyers to compare products and prices of potential suppliers, unlike in the commodity-like data communication component market. Alternative sources of supply are much more difficult to find as there only two or three companies in this specialist marketplace. Furthermore, the product purchase is likely to represent a relatively small part of the buyer's overall investment in information and communication systems. Reduced bargaining power makes this product less price sensitive and so provides an opportunity to generate good margins. Large international customers are likely to be cautious about moving to new suppliers.

The bargaining power of suppliers

It seems unlikely that NMS will be able to exert much influence on it suppliers. They are purchasing semiconductors and microprocessors from major global companies, who probably have well-known and powerful brands. NMS, as a small company, will not have the power to exert buyer pressure on its suppliers, either in terms of price or delivery. Current problems associated with the delivery of components are having a significant impact on the company's ability to meet customer deadlines and expectations. Clearly an audit needs to be made of supplier performance and the opportunity, or otherwise, for NMS to concentrate on suppliers able to deliver on time. However, for a small company like NMS, the supplier appears to be in an excellent bargaining position.

If labour is seen as a supplier, then evidence again suggests that NMS is in a relatively weak position. The scenario notes the difficulty of finding high calibre staff with NMS's "small size and location making it difficult to attract the key personnel necessary for future growth".

Threats from new entrants

NMS is operating in an industry where the costs of entry are significant because it is capital and knowledge intensive. NMS has shown that there is a place for smaller innovative companies able to identify and exploit specialist market niches. Economies of scale compel new entrants to enter at significant output levels or suffer a cost disadvantage. The products are complex and there is likely to be a significant learning curve with costs only falling as volume builds up over time.

The need for government approval of new data communications components creates an approval process that is both lengthy and expensive and so creates a significant barrier to new entrants. New entrants may be discouraged by the uncertainty surrounding the industry, in terms of technology, user acceptance and the R&D investment necessary to create components and systems compatible with OEM's equipment and end user systems. Furthermore, the need to offer comprehensive after sales support, although a problem for NMS, does also create a significant barrier to new entrants.

Finally, the exit costs and barriers to exit in the shape of industry-specific knowledge, skills and assets reduce the attractiveness of the marketplace to new entrants.

Threats from substitutes

High technology industries are, by their very nature, prone to new technologies emerging that threaten and then eventually replace the established technology. Hence it is very important that companies in such industries constantly scan the external environment to identify and anticipate such threats. There is evidence that large, successful, high technology companies are particularly vulnerable to ignoring the challenge from disruptive new technologies. However, the small size of the NMS may give it a competitive advantage in its ability to respond quickly and flexibly to change.

Rivalry amongst competitors

Very different levels of competition are being experienced in the two market places NMS is operating in. Unfortunately the financial data given does not separate out the revenue and costs for each market place. However, it is clear that the high-volume, low-margin component business offers intense competition with buyers who are able to use their size to extract favourable prices. NMS has less than 1% of the home market and there are over twenty competing suppliers, some of whom have significant international presence, with a dedicated, geographically distributed support team. The ability of NMs to generate better market share and volumes through product innovation in this market seems highly unlikely. Competitive rivalry is high when there are many competing firms and the costs of leaving the industry are high.

The intensity of rivalry in the network management systems market is significantly less because there are only two or three competitors in this specialist market. NMS is dealing with a small number of large end users, designing products specific to their needs. In Porter's terms, NMS are adopting a focused differentiation strategy. In these low-volume, high-margin markers the emphasis has to be on increasing the volume side of the business, but at the same time making sure that they have the resources to handle new customers.

(c)   (i)   The financial data shows revenue climbing to a peak in 2009, before falling away (by about 10%) in 2010. During this period the percentage of sales from international contracts remained fairly constant. NMS is still overwhelmingly dependent on the domestic market, accounting for about 92% of revenue.

                Although 2009 was a record year for revenues, increased cost of sales meant that gross profit declined slightly. Indeed the gross profit margin has declined every year in the period under consideration, and the reasons for this need to be investigated.

	2010	2009	2008	2007
Gross profit margin (gross profit/revenue)	30.42%	34.04%	38.24%	40.63%

Unfortunately the financial data does not distinguish revenues and cost of sales between the three distinct product/service areas. However, the scenario suggests that gross profit margins of 40% are being achieved in the network management systems area. If this is so, then the gross profit margin on data communication components is clearly significantly lower.

In 2010, overhead costs were reduced, but at a slower rate than the fall in revenue. This led to a dramatic fall in the net profit margin. Again, analysis shows that the net profit margin has also declined every year in the period under consideration. In general, this fall has mirrored the decline in the gross profit margin. However, the rapid fall in 2010 suggests that operating costs have not been brought under control to reflect the sudden sales decline.

	2010	2009	2008	2007
Net profit margin (net profit before interest and tax/revenue)	2.29%	7.52%	10.29%	11.46%

The number of staff employed in 2010 was exactly the same as the previous year. This has meant a rapid fall in the sales revenue per employee.

	2010	2009	2008	2007
Sales revenue per employee	90	101	113	107

Finally, the companies order forward order book has also reduced over the period. In 2007 it stood at 73% of sales revenue. This has declined to 37% by 2010.

The overall financial picture is of a company that failed to control costs as it sought increases in revenue. This appeared to work relatively well whilst revenues were increasing (the company was profitable in 2007, 2008 and 2009) but it was a problem as soon as revenues dropped. Costs were not cut at the same rate as revenue decline, leading to a trading loss in 2010.

(ii) Ray Edwards has effectively undertaken an informal time to payback calculation. His assertion that the machine will pay for itself after five years is correct. A more formal representation of the approach is given below.

All figures in $000s

Year	0	1	2	3	4
Brought forward	76	60	42	22	
Cost of the machine	90				
Maintenance costs	5	5	5	5	5
Reduced staff costs	15	15	15	15	15
Reduced wastage	2	4	6	8	10
Energy savings	2	2	2	2	2
Carried forward	76	60	42	22	0

There are two issues that need further consideration. The first concerns the approach to investment appraisal. Time to payback is a legitimate approach, but Ray has to be sure that it is a reasonable way of evaluating project investment in the context of NMS. It does not take into account the time value of money and so future cash flows are not discounted, unlike the Net Present Value (NPV) approach. This is significant here, because most of the cash outflows of the project are almost immediate (half of the costs are incurred in year zero), whilst significant benefits do not accrue until years three and four. If time to payback is acceptable, then Ray has to consider whether the payback time (five years) is acceptable and, more importantly, whether there other investments within the company which might pay back sooner, given that projects will be competing for limited resources.

Secondly, the costs of buying the new machine are very tangible. However, Ray's classification of benefits requires further consideration. Although all three categories of benefit have been given a financial value, these values are not of the same degree of reliability. Ray has already calculated that less labour is needed to use this machine and has estimated a reduction of $15,000 per annum based on observed performance. This appears to be a relatively tangible financial benefit. In Ward and Daniel's term this is a quantifiable benefit, because sufficient evidence exists to forecast how much benefit should result from the change. Wastage is currently being measured in NMS, but there is a risk of transferring the manufacturer's claims of savings of 'up to 10%' directly to the NMS environment. It is impossible to predict how much will be saved in advance in the specific context of NMS. It will be possible to measure reduced wastage once the machine has entered into service, but it is difficult to predict accurately in advance. In Ward and Daniel's terms this is a measurable benefit for which a reliable measure currently exists and the improvement can be measured once the machine is working.

ACCA marking scheme		
		Marks
(a)	Up to three marks for each element of the PESTEL analysis.	15 marks
(b)	Customer analysis	Up to 3 marks
	Supplier analysis	Up to 2 marks
	Substitute analysis	Up to 2 marks
	New entrant analysis	Up to 3 marks
	Competitor analysis	Up to 3 marks
	Recognising and defining the three market places that NMS compete in.	Up to 3 marks
	Professional marks are awarded as follows – up to one mark for clarity, up to one mark for structure and up to two marks for justifying and explaining an appropriate framework for the analysis	Up to 4 marks
		20 marks

(c)	(i)	Up to two marks for the calculation and interpretation of each of the following ratios –	
		– gross profit margin	Up to 2 marks
		– net profit margin	Up to 2 marks
		– revenue per employee.	Up to 2 marks
		Up to one mark for further appropriate points	Up to 3 marks
			Maximum 9 marks
	(ii)	payback issues	Up to 2 marks
		identifying drawbacks and suggesting alternatives	Up to 2 marks
		identifying issues about benefit identification and quantification	Up to 4 marks
			Maximum 6 marks
			Total: 50 marks